WORLD WAR II

DAY BY DAY

WORLD WAR II
DAY BY DAY

DONALD SOMMERVILLE

MAGNA BOOKS

Published by Magna Books
Magna Road
Wigston
Leicester LE8 2ZH

Produced by Bison Books Ltd.
Kimbolton House
117A Fulham Road
London SW3 6RL

ISBN 1-85422-081-0

Printed in Hong Kong

Page 1: US Airborne troops prepare to take-off to secure vital Rhine crossing points, 24 March 1945.
Page 2-3: The wreck of a Japanese heavy cruiser after the Battle of Midway, June 1945.
This page: Hawker Hurricane fighters of the RAF take-off to intercept German aircraft during the Battle of Britain, 16 August 1940.

CONTENTS

THE APPROACH TO WAR

June 1919

The Treaty of Versailles is concluded. This treaty, and the similar Treaty of St Germain between Austria-Hungary and the Allies together help to foster some of the grievances and weaknesses which will form the causes of World War II. Germany is to be largely disarmed and the Rhineland is to be occupied by Allied forces. Considerable reparations are to be paid but the amount of the burden is not yet fixed. The map of Europe is substantially redrawn. From the wreck of the former Austro-Hungarian Empire a whole group of new states is created. Each of these states has grievances against the others and none has a wholly homogeneous population. Poland too has been created and will fight successfully in 1920 to retain its independence against the Soviet Union. Japan (still allied with Britain) gains a mandate over islands in the Pacific, including the Marshalls, Marianas and Carolines. The Charter of the League of Nations is part of the Versailles agreement but its scope is left substantially weakened by the refusal of the United States Congress to ratify it.

September 1919

A young German army political-instruction officer named Adolf Hitler is ordered to investigate a small right-wing political party, the German Workers' Party (DAP), in Munich. He joins it, becomes an important public speaker and by July 1921 is its leader. Hitler changes the title to the National Socialist German Workers' Party (NSDAP). He obtains money from army political funds to purchase a newspaper, the *Völkischer Beobachter* (this title can be translated as Racist Observer). Hitler leaves the army in April 1920 but retains some of his former contacts, especially with a Major Roehm. His program, with its radical tone and its combination of anti-Communism and nationalist opposition to Versailles, is designed to have wide appeal. His technique and the reforms advocated are backed unashamedly with violence.

Previous page: Adolf Hitler (left) and Ernst Roehm.
Below: Japanese troops enter the Chinese city of Nanking.

November 1921-February 1922

The leading naval powers meet in Washington to discuss limitation of their forces. The conference was originally planned as a general disarmament meeting but the French refused to discuss army reductions because the guarantees of their security which had formed part of the Versailles agreement have not come into force through the United States' refusal to ratify. The battleship-building race which had been about to begin is halted. The British and Americans accept parity in their main forces. The Japanese are to have about two-thirds of this strength and the French and Italians about one-half of the Japanese force. Although none of the signatories, with the possible exception of the United States, is particularly happy with the terms they all conform, largely due to economic pressure. The effects for the Japanese are particularly important. They feel that in a sense they have been denied an equal position in the world by the Western Powers and begin to look more toward Asian affairs. More- or less-overtly racist immigration measures taken by the Western countries during the next few years contribute to this hurt attitude. The almost total dependence of the Japanese on outside sources for their raw materials can only increase this tendency to look for foreign gains and be wary of restrictions.

October 1922

Mussolini's Fascists stage a 'March on Rome' to demand power. They succeed and the party blackshirts begin operations to eliminate opposition.

January 1923

France and Belgium occupy the Ruhr in an attempt to enforce the payment of reparations in which Germany has fallen behind. In 1921 a provisional figure of 132,000,000,000 marks has been set (equivalent to $33,000,000,000 or £6,850,000,000). One of the reasons for Germany's failure to keep up with payments is the decline in the value of the mark. In 1918 it stood at four marks to the dollar, in the summer of 1921 at 75, in 1922 at 400, it is now over 7000 and by July it will be 160,000. The peak is not reached until November 1923 when the rate will be 130,000,000,000 marks to the dollar.

November 1923

The financial weakness in Germany contributes to political unrest, to the benefit of the more-radical parties. One such is Hitler's NSDAP in Munich. In conjunction with the wartime leader General Ludendorff he attempts a *putsch* to seize power in Bavaria. It fails, partly because it is ill planned and led, but mainly because the army is not included in the scheme. Hitler is tried early in 1924 and is sentenced to serve two years. He stays in prison for nine months and spends his time writing *Mein Kampf*. This rambling diatribe explains his political ideas, notably his anti-Communism, his violent anti-Semitism and his intention to look for *Lebensraum* for Germany in Eastern Europe. His connection with Ludendorff brings him some prominence. From the failure of the *putsch* he learns the importance of maintaining an appearance of legality which he will try to keep up until the war begins. The appearance of legality does not prevent the party thugs from intimidating opponents.

January 1924

The first national congress of the Kuomintang is held. This party represents the growing forces of Chinese nationalism. Its leader at this stage is Sun Yat-sen but General Chiang Kai-shek has an increasing influence. It is only loosely a party in the Western sense, with little formal structure. It draws support from a variety of groups in Chinese society, generally among the more affluent. Its army is the main basis of its power. The Chinese Communist Party was founded in 1922 and it also has a growing appeal. The Communists and the Kuomintang are not yet confirmed enemies.

April 1924

The Dawes Plan provides new arrangements for the payment of German reparations and forms the background to the stabilization of the German currency. About $250,000,000 is to be paid each year and much of the money to finance this is to be borrowed from abroad.

April 1925

Field Marshal von Hindenburg, war hero of the 1914-18 conflict, becomes president of Germany.

October 1925

The Locarno treaties are concluded. By these agreements Britain and Italy promise to guarantee the Franco-German frontier against violation by either side. No similar promise is made for Germany's eastern borders. This is a blow to the French because their policy has been to try to keep Germany contained by the threat of attack from the west and by having allies in the Little Entente (Czechoslovakia, Yugoslavia and Rumania) in the east. Britain prefers to be friendly toward Germany and wants to avoid being entangled in Balkan problems. In this way armaments can be kept low and there will be no need to call for help from the British Empire.

September 1926

Germany joins the League of Nations. This step illustrates the progress being made by the Weimar regime during this comparatively untroubled period. Although the radical parties of the left and right have a considerable following, they are not yet a major force in German affairs.

April 1927

Shanghai falls to the Kuomintang. Chiang Kai-shek chooses to have the support of the rich merchants of the port rather than the Communists and eliminates many of their officials there.

August 1928

The Kellogg-Briand Pact is signed. By its terms the United States, Great Britain, France, Germany, Italy and Japan agree to renounce aggressive war.

June 1929

A committee of experts under the chairmanship of the American banker Owen Young presents the Young Plan for the final settlement of the German reparations bill. It fixes the amount which is owed and gives a date by which payments are to be completed. Although the terms are less harsh than those previously fixed they are not as good as the German authorities hoped. They are, however, accepted by the German government although Hitler joins with the Nationalist Party, led by the industrialist Hugenberg, in opposing the settlement. This campaign brings new financial backing for the Nazis and makes Hitler a national figure.

23 October 1929

The New York Stock Exchange collapses. A worldwide economic depression begins. There has been a worldwide tendency for agricultural overproduction which combined with a decline in international trade has led to protectionist measures. The economic system has been unbalanced by the reparations and other war debts. The debts have been largely covered by loans from the United States but, because of protection, other countries have been unable to sell in the United States and therefore have had to borrow still more. This borrowing will now come to an end.

April 1930

The London Naval Treaty is agreed. By its terms no new battleships are to be built before 1937. Limitations are also agreed to cover submarines, cruisers and destroyers.

May 1930

The Japanese Prime Minister Inukai is assassinated by a group of young officers because of his support for the London Treaty. The militants had hoped for parity with Britain and the United States. The fixing of the number of cruisers allowed to Japan as an arbitrary fraction of that of Britain and the United States is seen as particularly obnoxious. This murder is only one token of a growing anarchy within the Japanese ruling class. Various pressure groups and 'patriotic' societies are developing in which junior officers are becoming deeply involved. They are prepared to take the law into their own hands and act without regard for the more cautious policies which some Japanese statesmen and many of the Japanese people prefer.

September 1930

In the German elections the Nazis become the second-largest party. They receive 20 percent of the vote. The Communists also do well. The Nazis are still a long way from being in a dominant position but they have taken over from Hugenberg's National Party as the leading party of the right.

May 1931

The principal Austrian bank, the Credit-Anstalt, fails. This is a result of French-led financial pressure because of the Austro-German negotiations for a customs union, which the French think is a prelude to German unification. In July a German bank, the Darmstadter-National, also fails. These failures only increase the economic problems in Germany, which are acute anyway because of the depression. The plan for the customs union has to be abandoned. This is a real humiliation for the government and a bonus for the nationalist parties. Although reparation payments are suspended for a year and then abandoned altogether, this is of little consequence for the German unemployed.

September 1931

Following an incident at Mukden on the South Manchurian Railroad (the railroad line was sabotaged), the Japanese army sends forces to occupy south and central Manchuria. Chinese resistance is comparatively weak and by early in 1932 the conquest is complete. From the speed of the army reaction it seems likely that the incident at Mukden has been deliberately engineered by the Japanese army. The Japanese government is not consulted by the army and can do little except follow on. The Japanese constitution provides that any government must have serving officers as navy and army ministers and this means that if either service is set on a course of action it can bring down a government which tries to oppose it.

China appeals to the League of Nations soon after the attack begins, the League calls on Japan to withdraw and appoints a Commission to investigate the rights and wrongs of the situation. This is the first time the League has been asked to intervene in a case where a great power is involved and the eventual failure of the intervention illustrates only too clear the weakness of the League.

January 1932

In Shanghai a boycott of Japanese goods by the Chinese leads to riots and then fighting, with Japanese troops protecting the Japanese enclave in the Treaty port. Early in February the Japanese bring their forces up to four divisions and by March control the port and the area around it.

February 1932

Japan declares the independence of the former Manchuria as the puppet state Manchukuo. The puppet government is headed by a descendant of the Manchu emperors. The Japanese make little attempt either to make themselves popular or to give the Manchukuo government even the appearance of authority. There is much direct, open economic exploitation in which the power of the Japanese-owned railroad company is extended considerably. The opium trade is also encouraged.

Below: Japanese cavalry move at speed across a river in northern China, acting as a spearhead for the Japanese invasion forces.

March-April 1932

There are presidential elections in Germany in which Hitler stands unsuccessfully against Hindenburg. During April the Nazi SA is banned after plans for a coup are discovered. Hitler denies knowledge of these plans and insists that the Party continues to work within the electoral system.

May 1932

The conservative leader Franz von Papen becomes chancellor. The leading member of his Cabinet is General Schleicher.

June 1932

The ban on the SA is lifted after the Nazis have promised to give some support to the government. Later, in July, the Nazis become the largest party in the Reichstag after elections in which the thugs of the SA have done much to intimidate opponents. The Nazis now hold 230 out of 608 seats but this is not a majority. Papen remains chancellor but in September his government is defeated by a combination of the Nazis and Communists.

November 1932

After the new elections the Nazis are still the largest party in the Reichstag, but their share of the vote has declined from 37 percent to 33 percent. The Communist vote increases. General Schleicher is worred by this and by Papen's failure to put together a solid parliamentary majority. Papen resigns believing that he will be recalled once coalition negotiations with the Nazis fail.

December 1932

President Hindenburg is ready to recall Papen when Schleicher declares that the army has no confidence in him. Instead Schleicher himself becomes chancellor.

January 1933

Adolf Hitler becomes chancellor of Germany. In the political maneuverings during the month it becomes clear that Schleicher cannot construct a coalition government and that Hitler, Papen and the other right-wing parties probably can. The president refuses to give Schleicher powers to rule without the Reichstag and he is forced to resign. Papen becomes vice-chancellor in the new Hitler government and his supporters hold many of the key posts. The coalition talks with the Center Party fail, as the Nazis hope, and Hitler is able to call for elections for March.

February 1933

On the night of the 27th the Reichstag is set on fire. Four Communists are tried and executed for this crime but it seems likely that the Nazis have had a hand in it. Whoever is responsible it works to the Nazis' advantage. The intimidation campaign against their opponents is stepped up, backed by the Prussian police who are now controlled by Goering and packed with Nazi nominees. A special presidential decree, granted after the fire, increases their powers.

March 1933

In the elections the Nazis poll 43 percent of the vote but even with the support of the Nationalists they only have a bare majority. Most of the Communist deputies are arrested along with some of the Social Democrats. When the Reichstag assembles the Nazis have succeeded, with support from the Vatican, in winning the votes of the mainly Catholic Center Party for a special constitutional law. This Enabling Act is passed on the 23rd and with it Hitler becomes independent of the presidential power. A token of the ability the Nazis now have to eliminate all opposition is that in this month the first concentration camp, Dachau, is established near Munich.

Japan announces that it intends to leave the League of Nations. This follows the report of the investigating commission on Manchuria. Although it concedes that Japan had important interests to protect and may have been provoked, it also makes no bones about accusing Japan of aggression. Japan's exit from the League only makes the position of the more militant sections of opinion stronger. Money is granted for army modernization plans.

October 1933

Hitler leaves the League of Nations and ends German participation in the disarmament conferences, ostensibly because other countries have refused to reduce their military to the German level.

January 1934

Germany and Poland conclude a nonaggression pact. This is a setback for France's system of Eastern European alliances.

March 1934

Mussolini makes agreements with Hungary and Austria. German and Italian policy on Austria is entirely different. Mussolini does not want to see any form of union between the German-speaking nations and, therefore, supports Chancellor Dollfuss in opposition both to socialism and Nazism.

June 1934

On the Night of the Long Knives Hitler destroys his enemies, particularly within the SA. Ernst Roehm, the leader of the SA, Gregor Strasser, who leads the working-class left of the Nazi party, and General Schleicher are the most prominent of the victims. The SA is subjected to tighter party control and Himmler's SS becomes more important. The purge takes place on the night of the 30th.

July 1934

The Austrian Nazis stage a coup and assassinate Chancellor Dollfus. Mussolini sends troops to the Italian border and Hitler does not intervene. The Austrian authorities recover and Schuschnigg is the new chancellor.

August 1934

President Hindenburg dies. Hitler proclaims himself Fuehrer and chancellor. The Armed Forces are prevailed upon to swear personal allegiance to the new head of state.

September 1934

The Soviet Union joins the League of Nations. Stalin is obviously disturbed by the possibility of a threat from the new Germany.

October 1934

King Alexander of Yugoslavia and Foreign Minister Barthou of France are assassinated by a Croat terrorist group. The assassins have Italian backing and the aim is to disrupt the Franco-Yugoslav alliance. The Yugoslav regency which follows is indeed weak and open to German and Italian pressure. Barthou has been distinguished also by his opposition to Hitler.

October 1934-November 1935

The Chinese Communist move their main forces from Kiangsi to Shensi province in the Long March. Some groups travel as much as 6000 miles. There are many casualties on the way but the regime established in Shensi is better placed to fight off the Kuomintang and to draw recruits. The Communists are strongly in favor of war with the Japanese.

December 1934

The Japanese abrogate the Washington Naval Treaty.

There is a clash between Italian and Abyssinian troops in a disputed area of the border between Italian Somaliland and Abyssinia.

January 1935

In a referendum the people of the Saar region vote overwhelmingly for union with Germany. This is an important success for the Nazis.

March 1935

Hitler introduces compulsory military service and announces the existence of a German air force. This is in direct contravention of the Versailles Treaty. The so-called Nuremberg decrees are issued, which greatly increase the persecution of the Jews in Germany.

April 1935

At Stresa, Britain, France and Italy join in condemning breaches of the Versailles Treaty. There is little substance to this agreement. The Anglo-German naval talks which soon follow and the growing Italian involvement in Africa will end this brief anti-German unity.

The Neutrality Act is passed in the United States. This prevents financial assistance being given to any country involved in war and states that no protection can be offered to US citizens who enter a war zone. The War Policy Act of May 1937 modifies these provisions a little, giving the president some discretion in their application.

Far left: Adolf Hitler (left) and President Hindenburg, 1933. *Above:* Italian Fascist leader Benito Mussolini (left) greets the German Chancellor Adolf Hitler. *Left:* Japanese infantry man a camouflaged anti-aircraft machine gun.

May 1935

France and the USSR conclude a mutual assistance pact. Later in the year a similar pact is made between Czechoslovakia and the Soviets. The Franco-Soviet agreement is not ratified for nine months. The British are still reluctant to think of the Soviets as friends against Germany and although Foreign Secretary Eden visits Moscow later in the year, no agreement is made.

June 1935

The Anglo-German Naval Agreement is signed. Germany is to be allowed to build a fleet of up to 35 percent of the British fleet. U-Boats are permitted.

This contravenes both the Versailles Treaty and the Stresa agreement. France is not told of the talks until a late stage and the subsequent protests are ignored.

A more general naval conference is also held in London later in the year and proposals to continue the limitations on size and numbers of ships are produced, but these are never finally agreed.

October 1935

Italy moves against Abyssinia in force. Britain and France lead the League of Nations into imposing sanctions against Italy in November, but these are halfhearted. Oil supplies are left unhindered and nothing is done to close the Suez Canal to Italian troopships. Mussolini is none-

Above: Nationalist troops, loyal to General Franco, take up position in a battered village in Spain.

theless driven to look toward Germany for support. In turn Germany receives a free demonstration of the ineffectiveness of the League and some indication of what can be achieved by determination and brute force.

December 1935

There is an important series of anti-Japanese riots by Chinese students in Peking. These reflect the popular Chinese feeling. The Kuomintang has been growing stronger and its army better trained in the recent months but Chiang Kai-shek has been using his forces principally to fight the Communists and not the Japanese.

February 1936

A far-reaching plot by a group of younger officers to seize power in Japan only just fails. They have planned a program of assassinations, to be followed by the imposition of a new Cabinet on the emperor. Not all the killings are carried out and after a few days' confusion senior politicians regain control. Although trials and executions follow the dangerous scope for independent action at junior levels is made only too clear.

March 1936

In Hitler's first foreign-policy triumph the Rhineland, demilitarized by the provisions of Versailles and the Locarno agreement, is reoccupied by German troops. The French and British governments do little more than briefly protest. To take the step, Hitler has had to overcome opposition from his generals and by being proved right his supremacy over them and his self-esteem are confirmed. Implicitly this act suggests that Germany and not France is now the leading power on the continent of Europe and that France lacks the will to protect its allies to the east.

May 1936

The war in Abyssinia comes to an end with the occupation of Addis Ababa and the flight of Haile Selassie. The Italians formally annex the country.

July 1936

Sanctions against Italy come to an end.

The Spanish Civil War begins. This is important to wider issues of international relations for several reasons. It sharpens the ideas of a Fascist-Communist conflict and brings Italy and Germany closer together. It weakens the ties between France and the USSR because France refuses to help the Republicans. The British reputation for hypocrisy is confirmed with Britain once again content to take only ineffective steps to prevent foreign interference in the war. It also provides several shattering demonstrations of the power of the new Luftwaffe.

November 1936

The Anti-Comintern Pact is concluded by Germany and Japan. Italy joins later. Secret clauses of the pact make it clear that the main aim is to threaten the USSR from both west and east. It is not, however, a formal alliance since the Japanese do not want to be drawn in to a future European war. They hope that by strengthening Germany against the Soviets that Britain will be distracted from Asian affairs.

December 1936

Chiang Kai-shek is arrested by one of his generals, Chang Hseuh-liang, while visiting some troops employed in blockading the Communist Shensi province. After complicated negotiations involving the Communist Chou En-lai Chiang is eventually released but he has been compelled to agree to take a more definitely anti-Japanese line. A recent defeat for a Japanese-backed warlord in Suiyuan province has shown that the Japanese can be beaten.

January 1937

Hitler formally abrogates all of the provisions of the Versailles Treaty in a Reichstag speech, claiming that it is impossible for a great power to accept restrictions of this nature.

May 1937

Neville Chamberlain becomes prime minister of Britain.

June 1937

The purges of the Soviet Communist Party are extended to take in the army. About 35,000 officers will be arrested and executed or will simply disappear during the coming months. Three of the five marshals of the Soviet Union, 13 out of 15 army commanders, all the military district commanders and well over half of all officers of general rank will be included. The most prominent casualty is Marshal Tukhachevsky who has been working to convert the army to run on the most modern lines with the emphasis on independent tank forces. These ideas are abandoned after his fall.

July 1937

There is an outbreak of fighting near Peking at the Marco Polo bridge. During the next few weeks the fighting spreads throughout north China. Peking and Tientsin are controlled by the Japanese before the end of the month. Throughout this time negotiations are continuing and not ungenerous offers of settlement are made by the Japanese, but by early August Chiang Kai-shek has decided to fight.

August-November 1937

There is heavy fighting around Shanghai in which the Japanese, for some time seriously outnumbered, are very hard pressed. During September the Communist forces in Shansi score an important, morale-boosting victory over the Japanese 5th Infantry Division. By early November the Japnese forces in Shanghai have been increased and, aided by landings nearby to threaten the Chinese rear, they drive the Chinese back. They begin to advance toward Nanking.

During October and November there are further Japanese proposals for a settlement but these come to nothing. Equally abortive is a conference of Far East powers held in Brussels in November. The Japanese do not attend because they see it as an attempt by the West to deny them the profits of their strength. Although Chiang has hoped for at least economic help, he gets little satisfaction from the conference. The United States maintains its isolation policy and the Europeans are not prepared to act unless the United States does.

November 1937

Hitler holds an important conference in which he explains his intentions for Germany during the next few years. A record of the conference is kept by Colonel Hossbach and is known as the Hossbach Memorandum. Hitler explains his aim to look for *Lebensraum* in Eastern Europe and specifically accepts that it will probably be necessary to use force to attain this. In the short term he is considering action againt Austria and Czechoslovakia. He is not certain of the timing of these moves, preferring to wait on opportunity, but he intends that the whole process be over by between 1943 and 1945 because by that time he will be past his peak and other nations will be catching Germany's lead in arms.

Private discussions between Britain and France decide that nothing should be done about any German move against Austria. France maintains that its treaty obligations will compel it to fight for Czechoslovakia. Britain would not be able to keep out of such a war for fear of a French defeat. The British policy is, therefore, to try to obtain an agreement between Germany and Czechoslovakia and the only way to achieve this is to put pressure on the Czechs to make concessions. This pressure now begins.

December 1937

The Japanese forces advancing from Shanghai reach and capture Nanking. The Japanese now offer new, rigorous terms to Chiang Kai-shek but these are not accepted. Many Japanese are prepared to look for peace and consider less harsh terms. The fighting is a growing economic burden and the heavy involvement is an unwelcome commitment to the Army General Staff who would prefer to prepare to fight the USSR. The army is, however, not easy to control. The incident on 12 December when the American gunboat *Panay* is sunk, the air attack in August on the British ambassador's car and, worst of all, the several days rampage of murder and rape which follow the capture of Nanking, all provide evidence of the army's lack of restraint.

February 1938

British Foreign Secretary Eden resigns. He resigns over a quarrel concerning policy toward Italy but this is only part of his disagreement with Chamberlain over how to combat Hitler.

Early in the month Hitler also reorganizes his administration. In January War Minister Blomberg was dismissed for marrying a former prostitute and the Army Commander in Chief Fritsch was sacked on trumped-up charges that he is homosexual. At the start of February Hitler announces the abolition of the War Ministry and its replacement by a new organization, Armed Forces High Command (OKW). Keitel is appointed to head it. This is a serious demotion for the army. Instead of having a Ministry of their own they are now only a department (OKH) within a larger organization. More seriously for the future, the army expertise in strategic planning and in policy advice is put at a distance from Hitler, further confirming his supremacy and isolation. Foreign Minister Neurath and Papen, who is ambassador in Vienna, are also dismissed to be replaced by reliable Nazis. Brauchitsch becomes Commander in Chief of the army. The army does succeed in obtaining a court of inquiry on the Fritsch case in which he is cleared of the charges against him but this is not held until after the *Anschluss* when Hitler's position is impregnable.

Also this month Austrian Chancellor Schuschnigg visits Hitler and is browbeaten into giving greater recognition to the Austrian Nazis. The Nazi Seyss-Inquart is to become interior minister.

March 1938

The Germans annex Austria in the *Anschluss.* Hitler acts because early in the month Chancellor Schuschnigg has tried to organize a plebiscite to strengthen his hand against the Austrian Nazis. At the last minute Schuschnigg is prepared to cancel the plebiscite and resigns. The Nazis demand that Seyss-Inquart be made Chancellor, they take to the streets to seize control of government offices and President Miklas gives in. Even so, on the morning of 12 March German troops cross the border. Mussolini, once so opposed to German penetration of Austria, does nothing. On 13 March Austria is proclaimed a province of the German Reich (contravening Versailles). The arrests begin – more than 70,000 in Vienna alone. In a plebiscite held later under Nazi auspices 99.75 percent of the 'vote' is in favor of the new situation. Hitler is even able to claim that his action is in line with the principles of self-determination advocated by President Wilson and enshrined in the Versailles terms.

April 1938

In a series of battles in Shantung province the Japanese North China Army loses heavily to the Chinese Nationalist forces.

May 1938

A partial Czech mobilization is announced because of reports of German military preparations. Britain and France back the Czechs with a warning to Germany. Although supporting the Czechs in public, the British and French are annoyed at having to risk war on the basis of some tenuous rumors. They fail to realize that the German attitude is more concilliatory for a while, although Hitler is furious at having thus to climb down.

June-July 1938

The Japanese attack west from Kaifeng but their advance is halted near Chengchow by massive flooding cause by the Chinese breaching the dikes along the Yellow River. The Japanese lose a considerable number of casualties in this flood but it is also estimated that as many as 1,000,000 Chinese peasants have died. Many more are made homeless.

In July there is an important Soviet-Japanese clash on the border of Manchukuo near Lake Hassan. This has been provoked by the Japanese. Both sides reinforce and in the fierce fighting which follows the Japanese lose heavily.

September 1938

The Munich Crisis. The Czechoslovakian state created by Versailles has in 1938 a population of about 14,000,000 of whom 3,000,000 are German speaking. These Germans live principally in the area known as the Sudetenland. Agitation for union of this area with Germany is led by Konrad Henlein's Sudeten German Party with strong Nazi support. There has been trouble in the past and more occurs following an inflammatory speech by Hitler on 12 September. By 15 September the Czechs have control of the situation and Henlein has fled to Germany. Chamberlain flies to Germany, despite Hitler's hand in the trouble, in an attempt to find a solution. He has a plan which he has only discussed with a few advisers and not with the French for ceding to Germany areas where more than half of the population supports this. This is acceptable to Hitler. The French have up to this stage been resigned to fighting for Czechoslovakia but under British pressure they join in making President Beneš agree to this plan. Hitler now says that this is not enough. Chamberlain returns to Germany on the 22nd and after talks he again wishes to give in to Hitler but he is opposed by the British Cabinet on his return. On the 23rd the Czechs mobilize. On the 27th the British Fleet is sent to its war stations. Negotiations have been going on behind the scenes and an appeal has been sent to Mussolini to mediate, convincing Hitler of Anglo-French weakness. Chamberlain and Daladier go to Munich on the 29th and accept proposals put forward by Mussolini but drafted by the German Foreign Office which amount virtually to Hitler's last demands. Just before leaving, Chamberlain has Hitler sign a vague friendship agreement and with this he proclaims on his return home that he has secured 'peace for our time.'

Below: British Prime Minister Neville Chamberlain (hand raised) announces his agreement with Hitler after the Munich meeting, 1938.

Chamberlain's policy has dominated the Anglo-French side of the negotiations. He seems to have believed that fundamentally Hitler is a normal, reasonable and responsible statesman who will keep his word. He is, therefore, able to regard the Czech problem as a small central-European issue and the French guarantee as a way of dragging Britain into war for comparatively minor reasons. France is presented with a choice of staying aligned with Britain or fighting for the Czechs. The Czechs are, therefore, abandoned. Some historians argue that to have gone to war at this time would have been foolish because Britain and France were most unprepared. This argument is not convincing. At this time Czechoslovakia is perhaps the only country in Europe which is ready for war. The Czech army has almost as many trained troops as the German army and is as well, if not better, equipped. The Czech frontier defenses are stronger than the French Maginot Line and are far more comprehensive. At the height of the crisis the Germans can only allocate five divisions to the Western Front to meet the whole of the French army. Certainly Britain and France are weak in the air, but the necessity for a long campaign against the Czechs would almost certainly have prevented heavy attacks from the Luftwaffe. The argument that time is gained for rearmament is also weak. German production continues to be greater and their lead is extended by September 1939.

Below: A group of German political prisoners line up for roll-call at Dachau concentration camp, June 1938.

October 1938

President Beneš of Czechoslovakia resigns as the Germans move in to the Sudeten land. President Hacha takes over. Czechoslovakia is now split into three fairly autonomous provinces: Bohemia-Moravia, Slovakia and Ruthenia. Poland joins in the dismemberment, taking the long-disputed Teschen area from the Czechs.

The Japanese Central China Army completes its advance up the Yangtze to Hankow and captures the city. The battles of this campaign are the fiercest of the whole war between China and Japan. Chiang Kai-shek and the Nationalist government move to Chungking. In a separate campaign the Japanese forces make landings near Hong Kong and advance inland to take Canton. The Japanese now control all China's major ports, cutting the Nationalists off from most of their support from the outside world. Some supplies can still come in through French Indochina or over the Burma Road but the main route is now through the USSR.

November 1938

The Japanese announce the establishment of the New Order for East Asia. Effectively this means that Japan is to be the dominant economic power, with the Western countries perhaps allowed access to what is left over. Britain and the United States, who have already been worried by Japanese conduct in China, now become more definitely opposed to the Japanese expansion.

The partition of Czechoslovakia continues, with Hungary now getting a share. This is achieved by the German-sponsored Vienna Award which the Czechs are unable to resist. A large area of Ruthenia and 1,000,000 people are given to Hungary.

In Germany itself the persecution of the Jews is stepped up. On the night of 9/10 November, following the murder of a German diplomat in Paris by a young Jew, Jewish homes and businesses throughout Germany are attacked by Nazi thugs in what becomes known as the *Kristallnacht* – so called from the window breaking of many Jewish shops and business premises. There is worldwide condemnation.

December 1938

France and Germany reach a friendship agreement similar to Chamberlain's Munich paper. Germany disavows interest in Alsace-Lorraine and during the coming months Hitler will quote this as proof of his peaceful intentions.

February 1939

Japanese troops occupy Hainan Island. In Britain this is seen as a threat to communications between Hong Kong and Singapore.

March 1939

Germany completes the destruction of Czechoslovakia. Following internal political troubles early in the month President Hacha dismisses the Ruthenian and Slovak governments. This is an unexpected opportunity for Hitler. Hacha is summoned to Berlin and forced to capitulate while at the same time the Slovak parliament is pressured into accepting an independence proclamation. German troops begin to move in, and on 15 March Hitler proclaims the establishment of the Protectorate of Bohemia and Moravia. Hungary also takes the opportunity to take some land in the Carpatho-Ukraine. Britain and France do nothing, saying that the guarantees they gave at Munich were to the whole of Czechoslovakia and that these are rendered invalid by the secession of Slovakia.

Germany's gains continue with an ultimatum presented to Lithuania that the district around Memel be ceded. This is done on 22 March. On 23 March an economic agreement is concluded with Rumania which gives Germany considerable access to oil at privileged terms.

The only Allied response is the granting to Prime Minister Daladier of special powers by the French Parliament and at the end of the month the issue of a British and French guarantee to Poland. Although by the terms of this offer Poland is to decide when it should be put into action, from the British and French point of view it is seen more as a device for putting pressure on Poland to reach a reasonable compromise with Hitler. Unfortunately, this agreement can only make contact with the USSR more difficult without putting anything very strong in its place.

April 1939

Britain and France issue guarantees to Greece and Rumania against both Germany and Italy. The Italian attack on Albania begins early in the month. On 18 April Litvinov approaches the Western powers with proposals for talks. Toward the end of the month Hitler rejects a mediation attempt by President Roosevelt. He revokes the 1934 Nonaggression Pact with Poland, the 1935 Anglo-German Naval Agreement and in a typically violent speech demands that Danzig be returned to Germany and that Poland give Germany ground for a road through the Polish Corridor linking with Danzig and the German province of East Prussia.

May 1939

Britain introduces conscription.

Germany and Italy announce the agreement of a formal alliance, 'The Pact of Steel.' This is signed in Berlin on the 22nd.

Although Foreign Minister Litvinov is replaced by Molotov early in the month talks between the USSR and Britain and France begin later. Litvinov has been regarded as more in favor of collective security policies and contact with the West.

There are British proposals to limit Jewish entry to Palestine and to work to establish a joint Jewish and Arab government. These are resisted chiefly by the Zionist movement.

May-August 1939

There is more fighting between the USSR and Japan. The incident this time is on the border between Manchukuo and Outer Mongolia near the Khalka River. The Japanese are the first to reinforce and they gain the upper hand for a while. The Soviets then increase their strength and, led by General Zhukov, they win a major victory by 20 August. This defeat and the simultaneous political developments in Europe seriously worry the Japanese and they come to terms. This indication of the efficiency of the Red Army is little noticed in Europe.

June-July 1939

Formal talks start in Moscow between the Soviets and British and French representatives. Britain and France are trying to arrange help for Poland and Rumania. Stalin's attitude is rather different. In essence he seems to be prepared to fight Hitler now only if he is granted a free hand in the future in Eastern Europe. He wants Poland, for example, to allow Soviet troops on her territory. The British and French feel that they are being asked to blackmail Poland and the talks do not make much progress for the moment.

Late in July there is an important meeting in Warsaw between a British and a Polish representative at which the British are given two Polish Enigma coding machines. These are based on the German versions of the machine and give a valuable start to the code-breaking effort which will be a vital tool for Allied commanders in the future.

At the end of the month a further step is taken toward war in the Far East when the United States announces its intention to withdraw from the 1911 commercial treaty with Japan.

12 August 1939

An Anglo-French military mission begins talks in Moscow. They continue until 19 August but no agreement is reached because of the dispute about Soviet troops being allowed into Poland.

15 August 1939

British forces in Egypt are reinforced by the arrival of Indian troops at Suez.

19 August 1939

The German navy sends 14 U-Boats to patrol positions in the North Atlantic because of the tense international situation. The pocket battleships *Graf Spee* and *Deutschland* are sent off on 21 and 24 August. Supply ships are also sent out to cooperate with these units.

20 August 1939

German-Soviet negotiations have been proceeding for some time at growing speed and Hitler now sends a personal message to Stalin asking if he will receive Foreign Minister Ribbentrop. An economic agreement has already been prepared.

21 August 1939

The Soviet-German economic agreement is signed and Stalin announces that he will see Ribbentrop for further talks.

23-24 August 1939

The Soviet-German Nonaggression Pact is concluded and signed in Moscow. Secret terms of the agreement define the countries' spheres of interest. Poland is to be divided approximately in half, Germany is to be allowed to control Lithuania and the USSR is allotted Finland, Estonia and Latvia. Later this will be revised to place Lithuania in the Soviet sphere and to give more of Poland to Germany.

There is an exchange of messages between Chamberlain and Hitler in which Chamberlain warns that Britain is prepared to help Poland with force and Hitler says that he can never renounce his interest in Danzig and the Corridor. Forster, the Nazi leader in Danzig, is proclaimed head of state by the Danzig Senate.

25 August 1939

Hitler orders the German attack on Poland to begin on 26 August but he cancels it at the last moment on hearing that Britain and Poland have signed a formal alliance and that Mussolini refuses to join a war at this stage. Britain and France are trying independently to talk to Hitler through Mussolini. They only succeed in exposing their disunity since France is notably more intransigent that Britain.

26-30 August 1939

There is intense diplomatic activity in the major European capitals. The Swede Dahlerus is used as an emissary by the Germans and shuttles to and fro from London with various proposals. Hitler offers to negotiate if the Poles immediately send a representative with full powers to Berlin. The Poles are prepared to negotiate but realize only too well the pressure that will be put on any diplomat negotiating in Berlin.

31 August 1939

Hitler decides to invade Poland on 1 September. Mussolini proposes a European conference and the Polish Ambassador in Berlin makes another futile offer to negotiate. Hitler signs the order at noon and the German troops move up to the frontier. At 2000 hours the German radio station at Gliewitz is 'attacked.' The attackers are members of the SS in Polish uniforms and they leave behind some bodies (of concentration-camp inmates) in Polish uniforms to convince the world that Poland is the aggressor.

Below: Josef Stalin (sixth from left) watches as his Foreign Minister Molotov signs the Non-Aggression Pact with Germany, 1939.

1939

1 September 1939

Poland At 0445 hours the German forces invade Poland without a declaration of war. The operation is code named *Fall Weiss* (Plan White). The Germans put 53 divisions into the attack, including their six armored and all their motorized units. Of the divisions left on the Western Front only about 10 are regarded by the Germans as being fit for any kind of action. General Brauchitsch, the Commander in Chief, will be left in full charge of the campaign and, indeed, will only meet Hitler on a few occasions in the course of the battles. Bock leads Army Group North and Rundstedt leads Army Group South. Bock's army commanders are Küchler (Third Army) and Kluge (Fourth Army). Rundstedt's men are Blaskowitz (Eighth Army), Reichenau (Tenth Army) and List (Fourteenth Army). Guderian and Kleist lead Panzer Corps. Air support comes from Kesselring's and Löhr's Air Fleets which have around 1600 aircraft. Rundstedt's troops, advancing from Silesia, are to provide the main German attacks. Blaskowitz on the left is to move toward Poznan, List on the right toward Krakow and the Carpathian flank, while the principal thrust is to be delivered by Reichenau who is to advance in the center to the Vistula between Warsaw and Sandomierz. Küchler from East Prussia is to move south toward Warsaw and the line of the Bug to the east. Kluge is to cross the Polish Corridor and join Küchler in moving south.

The Poles have 23 regular infantry divisions prepared with seven more assembling, one weak armored division and an inadequate quantity of artillery. They also have a considerable force of cavalry. (Although it is commonly believed, it is not true that cavalry will be used later in the campaign to charge German tanks.) The reserve units were only called up on 30 August and are not, therefore, mobilized as yet. In the air almost all the 500 Polish planes are obsolete and will be able to do very little to blunt the impact of the German attack. During this period the Germans also strike at Warsaw, Lodz and Krakow by air.

Previous page: A German propaganda unit records an interview with Soviet soldiers.
Below: German artillery in Poland, 1939.

The Polish Commander in Chief, Marshal Rydz-Smigly, has deployed the stronger parts of his army in the northwestern half of the country, including large forces in the Poznan area and in the Polish Corridor. Although there are few natural barriers favoring defense in the western half of the country (the dry summer weather confirms this), he hopes to hold the Germans to only gradual gains. By thus stationing his forces well forward and by the attack tactics adopted, Rydz-Smigly has risked a serious defeat. Many units will be overrun before their reinforcements from the reserve mobilization can arrive.

All along the front the superior training, equipment and strength of the Germans quickly brings them the advantage in the first battles. At sea, as in the air, the story of Polish inferiority and crushing early attacks is much the same. Three of the four Polish destroyers manage to leave for Britain before hostilities begin and later one submarine also escapes. On the first day the old pre-Dreadnought battleship *Schleswig-Holstein* bombards the Polish naval base at Westerplatte.

Above: British schoolchildren gather at a London railway station for evacuation, September 1939.

Diplomatic Relations Britain and France immediately demand a German withdrawal from Poland. The British army is mobilized. Italy announces that she will not take any military initiative.

Britain, Home Front Because of the fear of air attacks the evacuation of young children from London and other supposedly vulnerable areas is begun.

2 September 1939

Poland Rundstedt's troops are already over the River Warta in many places after rapid but expensive victories in the frontier battles. Krakow is now near the front line. In the north Kluge's Fourth Army make contact with the Third Army from East Prussia. The Luftwaffe is spreading chaos in the Polish rear. The Polish regular troops have been stationed too far forward so the German advance is soon in their rear areas, preventing the movement of reserves and completely dislocating any communications left unscathed by the Luftwaffe's repeated attacks in support of the ground forces.

Diplomatic Relations Throughout the day there are frantic talks in London and Paris attempting to decide how to oppose Germany. Mussolini again declares Italian neutrality and calls for a peace conference. Germany announces that Norwegian neutrality will be respected.

The British Parliament is openly opposed to the passive line that Chamberlain's government is taking and in the evening the Cabinet decides to present an ultimatum to Germany. A French ultimatum is also to be sent.

3 September 1939

Diplomatic Relations The British ultimatum to Germany expires at 1100 hours and at 1115 hours Chamberlain broadcasts to announce that war has begun. Australia and New Zealand also declare war immediately. Chamberlain forms a War Cabinet which includes Churchill as First Lord of the Admiralty (Navy Minister) and Eden as Secretary for the Dominions. Churchill and Eden have been the most prominent opponents of an appeasement policy. At 1135 hours, as if to confirm the state of war, there is an air-raid warning in London but it is a false alarm.

In the afternoon, at 1700 hours, the French follow suit and declare war in fact before their ultimatum expires.

Poland The Polish Lodz Army is now in retreat after being beaten in the frontier battles with Army Group South. General Reichenau's forces have crossed the Warta in some areas while List's troops are converging on Krakow.

Battle of the Atlantic The liner SS *Athenia* is torpedoed off the northwest coast of Ireland by *U.30* as the *Athenia* is believed to be an auxiliary cruiser. There are 112 dead including 28 American citizens. Britain believes that this is the start of unrestricted submarine warfare but in fact after this the German naval authorities impose even stricter controls. The controls are gradually removed after about the middle of October.

At this stage 39 of the German fleet of 58 U-Boats are at sea. Doenitz, the submarine chief, had hoped for a fleet of 300 before contemplating war with Britain. Two U-Boats are sunk this month. Allied shipping losses are 53 ships, of which 41 of 153,800 tons are sunk by German submarines.

4 September 1939

Europe, Air Operations The first attacks by RAF Bomber Command go in against German warships in the Heligoland Bight. The *Admiral Scheer* is hit three times but the bombs do not explode. Of the 24 attacking aircraft six are lost. There is no question at this stage of attacking targets in Germany. For the next few months only leaflets are dropped and when the question is raised in Parliament in October the government reply is that there can be no thought of bombing industry in the Ruhr because it is private property!

Poland In the north the Polish Modlin Army begins to retreat after putting up a stubborn defense around Mlawa. In the south General Reichenau's forces have already advanced more than 50 miles.

5 September 1939

United States, Politics The United States proclaims its neutrality. On 12 September naval patrols to protect this status are begun.

South Africa, Politics After a dispute in the existing Cabinet over whether to join the war, Smuts forms a new ministry and on 6 September South Africa declares war on Germany.

6 September 1939

Poland Reichenau's Tenth Army continues to lead the German advance, having already penetrated to the east of Lodz. Krakow is taken by troops of List's Fourteenth Army. The Polish government and supreme command leave Warsaw. They issue orders for their forces to retire to the line of the Rivers Narew, Vistula and San.

7 September 1939

Western Front French patrols cross the frontier into Germany near Saarbrucken. The French mobilization is too slow and their tactical system too inflexible to permit any grander offensive operation. These gentle probings continue until 17 September when a larger advance is meant to be made but is in fact cancelled because the Polish collapse makes it pointless.

Poland The Polish naval base at Westerplatte surrenders after renewed German bombardment. The Polish command decides that it will be impossible to hold the line of the Narew although the order to do so has only been in force for one day. The forces in the Narew area are to retire to the Bug.

Battle of the Atlantic The first British Atlantic convoys set out. The convoy system has already been reintroduced on the east coast. Although escorts can only be provided as far as 12.5 degrees West they do provide effective protection against U-Boats. Many of the faster ships and some particularly slow ones do not sail in convoy at this stage or later in the war. During 1939 almost all the U-Boat successes are from such 'independents.'

8 September 1939

Poland Advance units of a part of Reichenau's force reach the southeastern suburbs of Warsaw late in the day. Other sections of Tenth Army are heavily engaged around Radom. List's Fourteenth Army reaches the San north and south of Přzemyśl. In the north Guderian's Panzer Corps is attacking along the line of the Bug east of Warsaw.

9 September 1939

Poland The German 4th Panzer Division mounts an attack in the southeast suburbs of Warsaw but is beaten off. The German command believes that almost all the Polish forces have retired east of the Vistula but in fact fresh units from the Poznan Army and part of the Pomorze Group have joined together around Kutno. About 10 Polish divisions are assembled in this area under the command of General Kutrzeba. They now begin a counter-attack over the Bzura against the German Eighth Army. The battles which follow will be the hardest fought of the campaign. For the first two or three days the Poles gain some success.

10 September 1939

Diplomatic Relations Canada declares war on Germany.

Western Front The first major units of the BEF begin to land in France. Field Marshal Lord Gort is in command. Small advance parties have been arriving since 4 September. In the first month 160,000 men, 24,000 vehicles and 140,000 tons of supplies are sent to France.

11 September 1939

Poland The German forces cross the River San north and south of Přzemyśl. The battle on the Bzura continues but the leaders of the German Army Group South, Rundstedt and his Chief of Staff, Manstein, are beginning to assemble reinforcements for Eighth Army.

Allied Planning The first meeting of the Anglo-French Supreme War Council takes place.

12 September 1939

Poland Some of List's troops are fighting near Lvov while others are moving north from their bridgeheads over the San.

Below: Hitler (center), surrounded by Army and SS officers, watches the advance into Poland, September 1939.

13 September 1939

Poland A small German force begins to cross the Vistula just south of Warsaw. The Bzura battles are now going badly for the Polish forces. The heaviest fighting will be over by 15 September but some engagements will continue until the 19th. Although the Germans will take their largest single haul of 150,000 prisoners in this battle, by 19 September units of two Polish brigades and elements of others will manage to escape to Warsaw.

France, Politics Prime Minister Daladier forms a War Cabinet in which he is responsible for foreign affairs as well as his normal duties.

14 September 1939

Poland German troops enter Gdynia. Guderian's XIX Panzer Corps reaches Brest Litovsk.

16 September 1939

Poland Warsaw is now surrounded but a surrender demand is refused. Part of List's army is still fighting west of Lvov while other units are advancing north to link with Guderian's forces who are maintaining their attack along the Bug.

17 September 1939

Poland Soviet troops enter Poland. Naturally because of the German attack there is almost no defense in the east. The Soviets employ two Army Groups or Fronts. The Poles have only 18 battalions in the east of their country.

Battle of the Atlantic The British aircraft carrier *Courageous* is sunk by *U.29* while on anti-submarine patrol off the southwest of Ireland. The carrier *Ark Royal* had a lucky escape on 14 September from a submarine attack while similarly misemployed. After these incidents the carriers are withdrawn from such work.

18 September 1939

Poland, Politics The Polish president, Moscicki and the Commander in Chief Rydz-Smigly enter Rumania and are interned. They leave behind messages telling their troops to fight on.

19 September 1939

Poland The Soviet advance reaches the Hungarian frontier. In the north Vilna is taken. The Soviets link up with the Germans at Brest Litovsk which is given up to the Soviets according to the provisions of the secret agreement of 23 August.

20 September 1939

Poland Hitler makes a triumphant entry into the city of Danzig, enthusiastically welcomed by its mainly German population.

21 September 1939

Rumania The Rumanian prime minister, Calinescu, is murdered by the Iron Guard, a Fascist organization.

22 September 1939

Poland The rapidly advancing Soviet troops take Lvov.

23 September 1939

Japan, Politics Admiral Nomura becomes foreign minister in General Abe's recently appointed government. Between now and their fall in January 1940 some conciliatory moves are made toward the United States. These are not reciprocated and this strengthens the beliefs and standing of the more militant Japanese politicians.

25 September 1939

Poland The Germans step up their bombardment of Warsaw and add heavy air attacks to it. Hitler wishes to complete the conquest as soon as possible and since the garrison is fairly strong it is necessary to force them to submit by terrorizing the civilian population. The bombing continues until the surrender.

Germany, Home Front Food rationing is introduced.

26 September 1939

Battle of the Atlantic After a near miss in an air attack German propaganda machine claims that the *Ark Royal* has been sunk. This is the first of several such false claims made during the coming months.

27 September 1939

Poland Warsaw surrenders after two days of vicious bombardment. There are 150,000 prisoners.

Germany, Planning Hitler tells his service chiefs that he plans to attack in the west as soon as possible. He has reached this decision entirely on his own. The army's opposition is very strong.

Britain, Home Front Chancellor of the Exchequer Sir John Simon presents his first War Budget. Income tax is raised from 5/6d (25½p) to 7/6d (37½p) in the pound.

28 September 1939

Poland The fortress of Modlin surrenders to the Germans and elsewhere the Polish resistance is nearly over.

29 September 1939

Diplomatic Relations A Soviet-German Treaty of Friendship is announced. By its terms Poland is partitioned. The Soviet Union gets slightly more land but the Germans now control the majority of the population and the industrial and mining centers.

The Soviets begin to put real pressure on the Baltic states. A Soviet-Estonian Mutual Assistance Pact is signed, giving the USSR the use of bases in Estonia. A similar agreement is concluded with Latvia on 5 October and with Lithuania on 10 October. Vilna is ceded to Lithuania. These pacts are designed to ensure Soviet control of the Baltic, particularly in the event of future German aggression.

30 September 1939

Poland, Politics A new Polish government is formed in Paris. Raczkiewicz is the new president and General Sikorski the Commander in Chief of the Armed Forces.

October 1939

Atomic Research President Roosevelt, after receiving advice from Einstein, sets up the Advisory Committee on Uranium. The research at this stage is still fairly slow paced.

1 October 1939

German Raiders The first news of the German pocket-battleships *Graf Spee* and *Deutsch-*

Below: Map showing the German advance into Poland, September 1939.

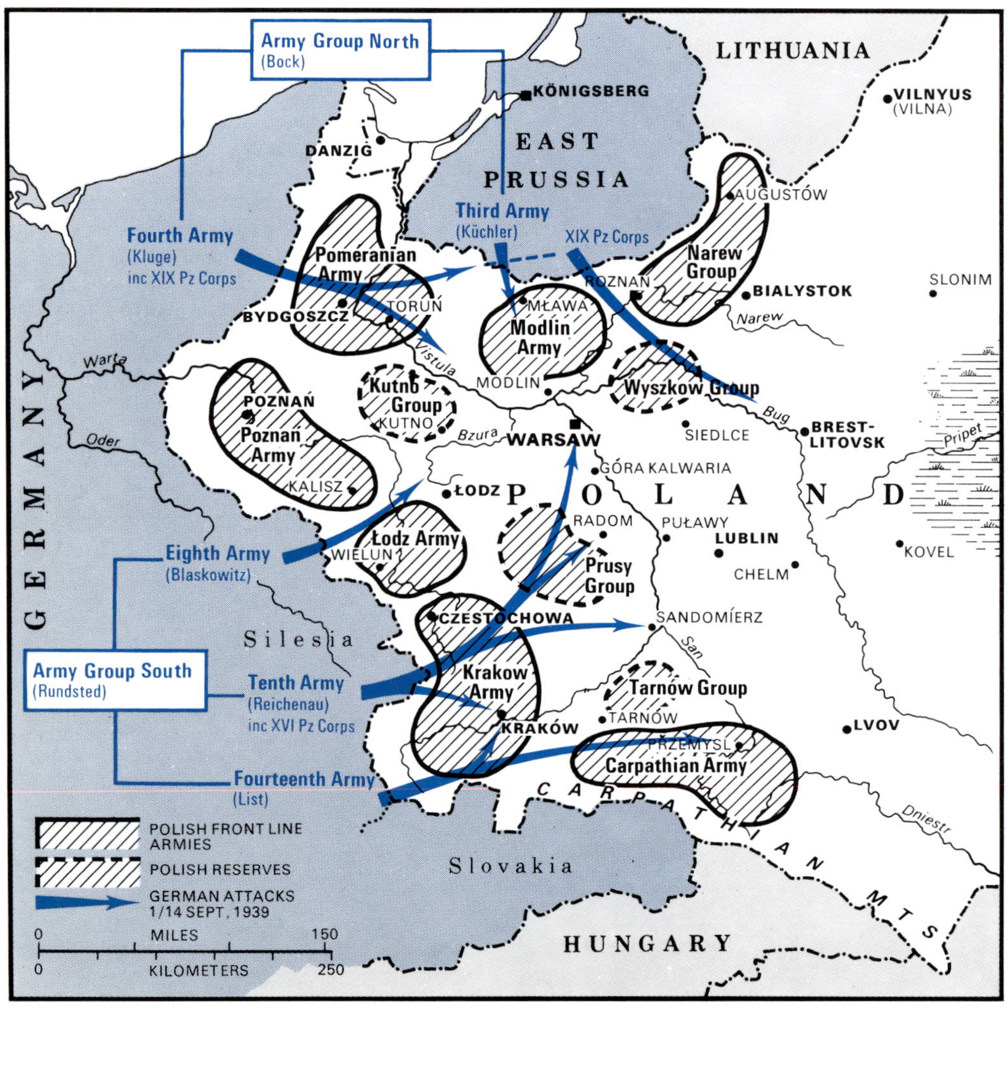

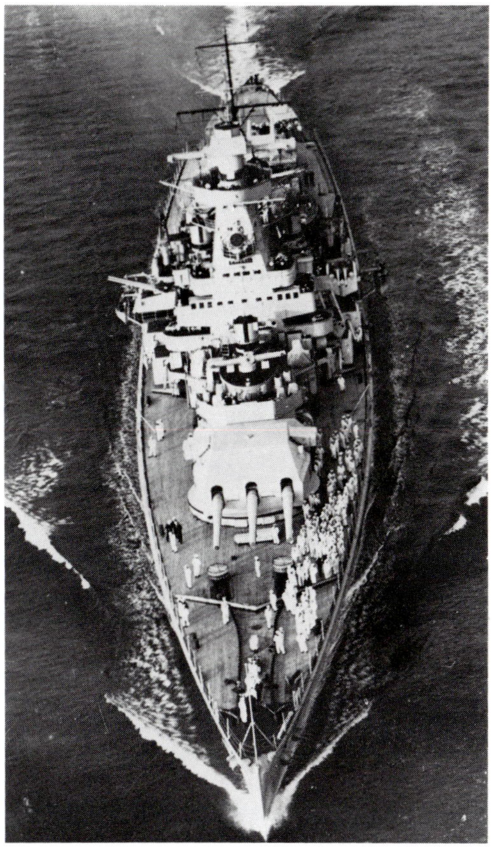

Above: The German pocket battleship *Graf Spee* at sea, 1939. *Below:* Map showing German and Soviet advances into central Poland – yet another 'partition' of Poland.

Above: Polish troops surrender to a German officer, Lemburg, September 1939. By 3 October the campaign was effectively over.

land reaches the Admiralty. On 30 September the *Graf Spee* sank its first merchant ship. Before the battle of December *Graf Spee* will sink nine ships of 50,000 tons altogether, a totally inadequate return for such a valuable unit.

In October Allied shipping losses are 196,000 tons. Five U-Boats are sunk.

Poland Admiral Unrug's Polish garrison on the Hela Peninsula surrenders after a gallant fight. As well as land attacks they have endured a considerable naval bombardment.

2 October 1939

World Affairs The Pan-American Conference, with 21 countries participating, establishes a 300-mile security zone off the American coast in which any act of war is to be interpreted as a hostile act against the nearby American country. The belligerents will, of course, ignore this.

3 October 1939

France The I Corps of the BEF takes over responsibility for an appropriate section of the Franco-Belgian frontier.

Poland The last significant units of the Polish army surrender near Luck. The Germans have taken 700,000 prisoners and the Soviets 200,000. Polish casualties have been severe. The Germans have lost 10,000 dead and 30,000 wounded. Many Poles have escaped and will gradually find their way to the West.

Although tanks units have played a notable part in the campaign, it is interesting to note that the contemporary German official appreciations lay more stress on the traditional-style infantry battles. The tank forces are seen at this stage, except by enthusiasts like Guderian, as little more than useful auxiliaries who can help the infantry do the real work. The first plans for the attack in the west will reflect this official attitude.

5 October 1939

German Raiders Eight British and French hunting groups are formed to hunt for the *Graf Spee*. At this stage the British and the French can afford to divert considerable forces to such a task.

5-23 October 1939

Diplomatic Relations The Soviets continue their moves to strengthen their position in the Baltic by asking the Finnish government for new talks on altering their boundaries. The Soviets want the cession of some territory near Leningrad, control of the islands in the Gulf of Finland, use of the port of Hanko and other rearrangements of the border in the far north near Murmansk. In return they offer rather more land than they demand in the Suomussalmi area. The Finns only feel able to offer a much smaller range of concessions. There are talks on 12-14 and 23 October but there is little change in the terms offered by either side. The Soviet demands are probably based on genuine worries

Above: The merchant ship *Ashlea* is torpedoed by the German pocket battleship *Graf Spee* in the South Atlantic, 7 October 1939. The cruise of the *Graf Spee* would not last long, however.

about the security of Leningrad and Murmansk but, understandably, the Finns believe that to give in would only invite more extreme claims. On 6 October the Finns mobilize their standing military forces. On 10 October they call up their reserves and begin the evacuation of some frontier districts.

6 October 1939

Diplomatic Relations In a major speech to the Reichstag Hitler speaks of his desire for peace with Britain and France. Hitler says that up to now he has done nothing more than correct the unjust Versailles Treaty and that he has no war aims against France or Britain. He blames warmongers like Churchill for the present state of affairs and calls for a European conference to meet to resolve the few remaining differences. On 10 and 12 October Daladier and Chamberlain respectively reject the offer. Chamberlain says that to consider such terms would be to forgive Germany for all aggression.

8 October 1939

Baltic States In accordance with the Soviet-German agreement, 'Reich Germans' are evacuated from the Baltic States to what the Nazis believe is their racial home in Germany.

9 October 1939

Germany, Planning Hitler issues Directive No 6. Its message is simple: 'Should it become evident in the near future that England, and, under her influence, France also, are not disposed to bring the war to an end, I have decided, without further loss of time to go over to the offensive.'

The offensive is to be directed across the Low Countries and is intended to defeat strong sections of the French and British armies when these arrive to help the Dutch and Belgians. The ground taken is to provide protection for the Ruhr and to give bases for the air war against Britain. The aims of the plan are, therefore, limited when compared with the Schlieffen Plan of 1914 or with the scheme which is actually adopted in May 1940. There is no mention of completely defeating France.

This order is a further blow to the autonomy of the German army. Their view is that, although it lies within Hitler's authority as head of state and Commander in Chief of the Wehrmacht to order an attack to be prepared as soon as possible, the army should be asked where and how this attack should take place. Even the normally subservient Keitel argues against Hitler on this issue.

10 October 1939

Germany, Planning Admiral Raeder mentions to Hitler for the first time the possibility of invading Norway to secure naval and especially submarine bases (*see* 8 December 1939 *and* 27 January 1940). Churchill is, at this time, arguing in the British Cabinet that Norwegian coastal waters should be mined to interfere with German iron-ore traffic.

14 October 1939

War at Sea The old British battleship *Royal Oak* is sunk at anchor in the main fleet base at Scapa Flow by *U.47* commanded by Kapitänleutnant Prien. This is a blow to British prestige as well as an indication of a very serious weakness in the defenses at Scapa Flow, which is promptly rectified.

19 October 1939

Germany, Planning OKH issues *Fall Gelb* (Plan Yellow) in response to Hitler's Directive of 9 October. It provides for a holding action on the French border with the main attack being sent through central Belgium and some attention being devoted to the Dutch. It is reissued in a slightly modified form on 29 October with the main thrust shifted slightly south and less strength being sent against Holland. It is clear that neither Hitler nor any of the senior commanders is particularly happy with it and there is much debate as to how it should be modified. This continues until mid-February 1940 when those voices calling for a radical change manage to have their way. General Manstein will lead this movement.

Poland Hitler officially incorporates western Poland into the German Reich. The first Jewish ghetto is established in Lublin.

31 October-9 November 1939

Diplomatic Relations There are three further sets of discussions between the Soviets and the Finns over the recent Soviet demands. No agreement is reached. The Finnish negotiators wish to accept some concessions but their government sees the Soviet attempts to bargain as a sign of weakness. Marshal Mannerheim opposes this view. In fact, because Molotov has explained the nature of the talks in a public speech, the Soviets are probably even more firmly committed with prestige at stake. Although it is not apparent to the Finns, there will be no more serious talks.

November 1939

Allied Intelligence Polish and French cryptanalysts working in France begin occasionally to read the Luftwaffe Enigma transmissions. This is the first such breakthrough of which later developments will give the British invaluable intelligence. The Luftwaffe is the least security conscious of the German services.

Battle of the Atlantic The German submarine campaign is less effective this month, sinking only 21 ships of 51,600 tons. More than twice this tonnage is sunk by mines.

4 November 1939

United States, Politics A modification of the Neutrality Acts passes into law in the United States. Although by its terms the ban on American ships and citizens in clearly defined war zones is confirmed, it does provide for supply of arms to belligerents on a 'Cash and Carry' basis. Such arms must be ordered from private companies, paid for on the nail and transported to the war zone in the buyer's own ships. British naval strength means that, as is intended, only the Allies will benefit from this. Within a few days both the British and the French establish Purchasing Missions in Washington.

5 November 1939

Germany, Planning Brauchitsch meets Hitler to discuss the plans for the attack in the west. He

Below: U-Boat captain Gunther Prien poses for the camera soon after sinking the *Royal Oak*.

Above: Finnish troops prepare an ambush position in the snow, during the Russo-Finnish 'Winter War', December 1939.

argues very strongly that it should not take place as scheduled on 12 November because of weaknesses in the army. Hitler shouts him down.

General Halder, Brauchitsch's Chief of Staff, leads a group which has planned to overthrow Hitler if he is not persuaded to abandon the plan and timing for the attack. Although fairly detailed plans have been made for an army takeover, Halder has received few firm promises of support from the senior officers he has sounded out. The more junior officers tend to follow the Nazi line more closely and, from their positions, can see little wrong with Hitler's leadership. Halder, in any case, is unwilling as a senior serving officer to murder the head of state in wartime. This, combined with the poor prospects of success and a chance remark of Hitler's that suggests that he knows of a plot, persuades Halder to cancel the preparations.

It is important to note that the army opposition to Hitler is at this time not really based on moral principle but rather on resentment of his usurpation of their function as strategic planners and advisers.

7 November 1939

Germany, Planning The German attack in the west is postponed because of bad weather. This postponement will be repeated another 14 times until 16 January 1940.

Diplomatic Relations Queen Wilhelmina of the Netherlands and King Leopold of Belgium issue an appeal for peace. King George VI and President Lebrun reply on 12 November.

8 November 1939

Germany, Home Front A bomb explodes in the Burgerbraukeller in Munich shortly after Hitler has left after speaking there. It has in fact been planted by the Nazis themselves as an excuse for measures against what remains of the German Left and as anti-British propaganda.

Germany, Intelligence Two officers of the British Secret Intelligence Service (MI6), Major Stevens and Captain Best, are kidnapped at Venlo on the German-Dutch border. They have been lured there by a German agent who has promised that they will meet a disaffected German general. Unfortunately, one is carrying a list of British agents with him and from this, other indiscretions and from their interrogation, the Germans are able to arrest many British agents in Czechoslovakia and other occupied territory. The Venlo Incident is a serious setback for British Intelligence.

Poland Hans Frank is appointed Governor General of Poland by the Germans. He quickly encourages the persecution of the Jews.

16 November 1939

Czechoslovakia, Resistance After some recent unrest, martial law is declared in Prague. There are many shootings and deportations.

17 November 1939

Czechoslovakia, Politics A Czechoslovak National Committee is established in Paris. It is recognized by Britain and France in mid-December.

Allied Planning The Supreme Allied Council meeting in Paris endorses General Gamelin's Plan D (*see* 10 May 1940).

21 November 1939

War at Sea The brand-new British cruiser *Belfast* is seriously damaged by a mine in the Firth of Forth.

23 November 1939

War at Sea One of the first batch of magnetic mines to be dropped by air by the Germans lands on the mud flats at Shoeburyness. A British expert succeeds in defusing it and it can therefore be examined to devise countermeasures. These mines have been in use since 16 October and already they have been responsible for the loss of 50,000 tons of shipping.

German Raiders Between Iceland and the Faroes the British armed merchant cruiser *Rawalpindi*, armed with only four 6-inch guns, meets the German battlecruiser *Scharnhorst* and is blown out of the water. *Scharnhorst* has been sailing in the company of *Gneisenau* and because of this meeting they turn back from their raiding mission. They evade searches by many British ships during the next few days and return to base safely. Their escape is made easier by the German ability to read British naval codes.

26-29 November 1939

Diplomatic Relations Relations between the Soviet Union and Finland continue to deteriorate. On the 26th there are attacks on Finland in the Soviet press and an official complaint concerning a spurious border incident. The Finnish reply to this is to suggest that both sides should pull their forces back from the border. The Soviets denounce this as ridiculous, saying that they would have to retreat to the suburbs of Leningrad to comply. On the 28th the Soviets renounce their nonaggression pact with Finland. Orders are issued to the Red Army to invade on the 30th. On the 29th the Soviets break off diplomatic relations while the Finns at last offer new discussions.

The approach of war can only be described as a failure for the Finnish government. They have no outside help, they are not well armed and the Soviets have no other worries for the moment. It should have been obvious that the Soviets meant business and that the correct interpretation of their willingness to negotiate was a desire to avoid war and not a sign of weakness.

30 November 1939

Finland The Russo-Finnish War begins. The Soviets invade Filand. Helsinki is bombed. The Finnish army can only muster about 150,000 men in nine divisions, with a tenth being formed. There are also a number of smaller independent units but their reserves of manpower are small. They have little heavy equipment and virtually no tanks. They are handicapped here in having relied on their limited domestic arms production since late 1938 in an attempt to confirm their neutrality. Ammunition is an especially pressing problem and even toward the end of the war shell production will be only about 10 rounds per day for each gun in the army. The air force has about 100 planes which are not very modern. These weaknesses are partly offset by the training and morale of the Finnish troops. They are especially adept in rapid cross-country movement in winter conditions. Such conditions do, however, partly devalue the normal defensive strength of much of the terrain in the Karelian Isthmus, interspersed as it is with river lines and marshy ground. There are also some fairly strong fortifications in this area but the system is by no means comprehensive.

The Soviet forces present a very different picture. Their divisions are larger, with artillery components three times as strong as their Finnish equivalents and each is accompanied by more tanks than the entire Finnish army possesses. Independent tank and artillery units add even more weight. At the start the Soviets employ 26 divisions (not all at full strength), mustered in four armies. Seventh Army, the strongest with 12 divisions, attacks the five Finnish divisions on the Karelian Isthmus. Eighth Army advances in the area immediately to the north of Lake Ladoga, Ninth Army attacks from Soviet Karelia in the direction of the head of the Gulf of Bothnia and Fourteenth Army moves out from Murmansk in the far north. Despite this lavish deployment in greater strength than the Finns expect, the Soviets are not well prepared for the winter conditions and the coordination between their infantry and other arms is not at all good. Their preparations have been rushed.

The Soviets announce that their action is in support of the Finnish People's Government whose existence is now announced. This puppet organization is led by Otto Kuusinen, an exile who has long been a member of the Soviet-sponsored Comintern.

December 1939

Battle of the Atlantic Allied shipping losses are 73 ships of 189,900 tons. U-Boats sink 25 of these ships at a cost of one of their number.

1 December 1939

Finland The legitimate Finnish government is reorganized. Dr Ryti becomes prime minister.

2 December 1939

Finland Finland appeals to the League of Nations to mediate in their quarrel with the Soviets. The League meets between 9-11 December and agrees to intervene. The Soviets refuse to recognize this offer and are expelled on 14 December. This is one of the few times that the League has attempted to take a decisive stand. Of course it is now quite useless.

In the fighting there are Soviet landings with naval support near Petsamo and other units of Fourteenth Army are attacking overland nearby. Elsewhere the slow advance of the Soviet forces continues. The Finnish defenses have not yet been reached in most areas.

3 December 1939

Finland The Soviet Eighth Army achieves a small success near Suojärvi. The Finns pull back a little in this sector. They also send a small reinforcement to the forces opposing the advance of the Soviet 54th Division of Ninth Army near Kuhmo.

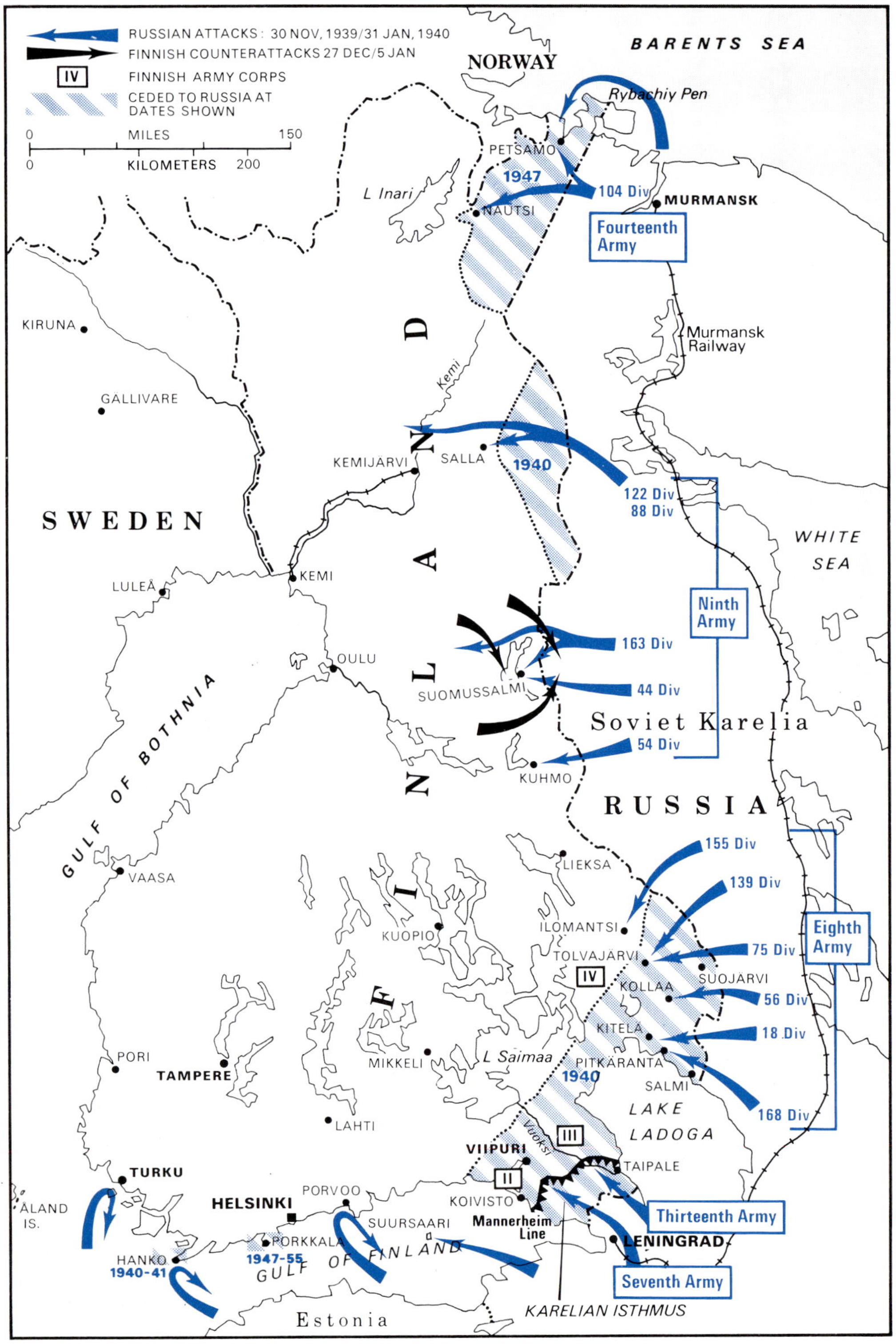

4 December 1939

War at Sea The British battleship *Nelson* is damaged by a magnetic mine off Loch Ewe. This is the last major success for this weapon. The Germans have been employing this and other types of mine to good effect. By the end of the year the Allied shipping lost to mines will amount to 79 ships of 262,700 tons.

5 December 1939

Finland Forward units of the Soviet Seventh Army reach the main Finnish defenses, the Mannerheim Line, on the Karelian Isthmus. Mannerheim is the Finnish Commander in Chief. Already the Finns are learning to exploit the poor management of the Soviet advance. They are developing tactics to master the Soviet tanks by separating them from their supporting infantry and emerging from concealed positions during the night to destroy them.

7 December 1939

Finland In the area north of Lake Ladoga the Finnish positions at Kollaa are attacked. Farther north Soviet troops enter Suomussalmi on the east side of Lake Kianta after it has been evacuated by the Finns.

8 December 1939

Germany, Planning Raeder again talks to Hitler of invading Norway. Rosenberg, the Nazi Party's political and racial 'expert' also introduces the head of the tiny Norwegian National Unity Party to Hitler. His name is Vidkun Quisling (*see* 27 January 1940).

8-9 December 1939

Finland The Finns bring the attacks of the Soviet Ninth Army in the Kuhmo sector to a halt on 8 December. Near Suomussalmi they have a similar success on the 9th. A brilliant night attack is also mounted on Eighth Army units near Kollaa.

11 December 1939

Finland The Soviet 163rd Division is cut off in Suomussalmi by the attack of the Finnish 9th Brigade.

12-15 December 1939

Finland The Finns send in a series of attacks against the Soviet Eighth Army. The 139th Division at Tolvajärvi is virtually destroyed and the 75th Division is also hard hit. The Finns capture much valuable equipment. Finnish attacks near Kollaa meet with less success.

13 December 1939

Battle of the River Plate The British Commodore Harwood has brought his squadron to the River Plate estuary hoping that the *Graf Spee* will come hunting there. Harwood has the heavy cruiser *Exeter* and the light cruisers *Ajax* and *Achilles*. When Langsdorff does appear in *Graf Spee* there is a fierce two-hour battle. *Exeter* is very badly damaged, *Ajax* also heavily hit and *Achilles* less so. *Graf Spee* has received some damage as well and Langsdorff decides to break off the action. He heads for Montevideo to make quick repairs and have his wounded treated. *Ajax* and *Achilles* take station off the port.

War at Sea In the North Sea the British submarine *Salmon* torpedoes the German cruisers *Leipzig* and *Nürnberg*. *Leipzig* will only return to service in 1941 and solely as a training ship. *Nürnberg* will be out of action until May 1940.

Far left: Map showing Soviet attacks on Finland, 1939-40. *Above:* Soviet troops dismantle anti-tank obstacles.

16 December 1939

Finland The main forces of Seventh Army have now advanced to the Mannerheim Line and a major Soviet attack, therefore, begins. The first efforts are subsidiary moves against the north-east end of the Line. They continue for two days without success.

17 December 1939

Battle of the River Plate Since 13 December the British Admiralty has been sending ships speeding to Montevideo. Only the heavy cruiser *Cumberland* has arrived so far. Local British diplomats try to have the *Graf Spee* held for a few more days until stronger forces arrive and at the same time contrive to give the impression that heavy units, including the battlecruiser *Renown*, are already in position. Langsdorff, an extremely humane man, therefore decides to scuttle his ship rather than fight a hopeless battle. *Graf Spee* is sunk outside the port with an audience of thousands lining the waterfront. On 20 December Langsdorff kills himself.

17-22 December 1939

Finland The main Soviet attacks go in against the Mannerheim Line around Summa. The same pattern is repeated for the first three days. The advancing tanks penetrate into the Finnish positions during each day. The infantry are held off and the tanks mostly destroyed during the nights by the Finnish troops who then emerge from their defenses. The attacks on 20-22 December are less forceful.

On 20 December the Soviet 122nd Division is cut off by Finnish attacks while advancing toward Salla from positions near the White Sea.

23 December 1939

Finland A Finnish counterattack on the Karelian Isthmus is sharply rebuffed.

Allied Preparations The first Canadian troops arrive in the United Kingdom. A heavily protected convoy has brought over 7500 men of the 1st Canadian Division.

World Affairs The Pan-American Conference protests about the fighting inside the 'security zone' during the River Plate Battle.

25-27 December 1939

Finland The Soviets repeat their earlier attacks on the north end of the Mannerheim Line with little success.

27 December 1939

Western Front The first Indian army troops arrive to join the BEF in France.

27 December 1939-6 January 1940

Finland The Finns inflict a series of defeats on the Soviet Eighth and Ninth Armies. On 27-28 December the 163rd Division, which has been holding a tenuous position around Suomussalmi, is attacked and largely broken up. Help was expected to arrive from the 44th Division but this unit has been unable to move forward. It is in turn cut off on 2 January and by 6 January has been broken into small groups.

The Soviet Eighth Army suffers equally heavily. The Finnish offensive against these units also begins on 27 December and continues to achieve success until about 5 January. By this time the Soviet 18th and 168th Divisions have been cut off but they have not been destroyed. Instead they have formed themselves into 'hedgehog' defensive positions which the Finns cannot break without heavy weapons. The Soviet forces receive some supplies by air.

The Finnish tactic in all these operations is to isolate the individual Soviet columns as they move along the forest tracks by moving around them with small units. Each column can then be harassed and wiped out in turn. The Soviets are not able to counter these tactics because their troops are not as well trained or equipped for cross-country skiing.

28 December 1939

Britain, Home Front Meat rationing begins.

War at Sea The British battleship *Barham* is hit by a torpedo from *U.30* while cruising off northwest Scotland. Repairs will take three months to complete.

Below: The *Graf Spee*, scuttled by her captain off the River Plate, settles in the water, 17 December 1939.

1940

January 1940

Battle of the Atlantic At this time Doenitz has only 32 operational U-Boats which means that only six or eight can be on patrol on any one occasion. The rest will either be in transit or in port. Of course, a larger force can be concentrated after a lull in operations.

During January the U-Boats sink 40 ships of 111,200 tons. The total Allied losses are 73 ships of 214,500 tons. The main U-Boat successes are in the North Sea and particularly in the Moray Firth area.

4 January 1940

Germany, Home Front Goering is given overall control of German war industry.

5 January 1940

Britain, Politics There is a ministerial reshuffle. Oliver Stanley replaces Leslie Hore-Belisha at the War Office (that is, the Army Ministry), Lord Reith becomes Minister for Information and Sir Andrew Duncan comes to the Board of Trade.

7 January 1940

Finland General Timoshenko takes command of all the Soviet forces. His troops on the Karelian Isthmus are now organized in two armies, Seventh and Thirteenth. The Finns are in the process of a reorganization also. During January they will be able to form, but only partially equip, two new divisions. Additional defenses are being constructed behind the Mannerheim Line.

Timoshenko immediately institutes a program of training for his forces, emphasizing cooperation between all arms. New equipment is also arriving for the Soviet forces. Their already dominant artillery is being strengthened and among the new tanks are some of the latest KV types. Intensive patrolling to investigate the Finnish lines is also begun.

Previous page: St Paul's Cathedral under a Luftwaffe attack, December 1940. *Below:* A Finnish officer calls up artillery support.

In the fighting north of Lake Ladoga the Finnish pressure on the Soviet 18th and 168th Divisions continues but their defensive positions known as *mottis* to the Finns, are strong. The Finns will have to keep forces committed against these *mottis* until the end of the war.

8 January 1940

Britain, Home Front Bacon, butter and sugar are all put on the ration list and will only be available in small quantities.

10 January 1940

Western Front Two German officers carrying copies of the plan for the attack in the west are forced down when their plane strays off course over Belgium. They land at Mechelen. They are unable to destroy their documents and the Belgian authorities pass on details to the British and French. At this stage Hitler plans to attack on 17 January, but this will be postponed.

11 January 1940

France, Home Front The government announces that Friday will be a 'meatless day' and that no beef, veal or mutton will be sold on Mondays or Tuesdays.

14 January 1940

Japan, Politics Prime Minister Abe and all his Cabinet resign and Admiral Mitsumasa Yonai is chosen to form a new government.

15 January 1940

Western Front The Mechelen incident (*see* 10 January) has been followed by much diplomatic activity. For a time the British and French have believed that they will be invited to move troops into Belgium even before a German attack but this possibility is now firmly ruled out by the Belgian government.

Finland The Soviet forces begin to bombard the Finnish lines around Summa. This softening-up process continues until the end of the month, giving the defending Finnish troops little rest and doing considerable damage to their vital defenses.

16 January 1940

Germany, Planning Hitler decides to cancel the German attack in the west until the spring. The loss of the plans at Mechelen and the continuing bad weather are the principal reasons for this decision.

19 January 1940

Finland There is an unsuccessful Finnish attack against the positions of the Soviet 122nd Division at Salla.

25 January 1940

Canada, Politics Parliament is dissolved for an election of 28 March because of recent controversy over the alleged weakness of war preparations.

27 January 1940

South Africa, Politics A peace resolution introduced into the South African Parliament by the opposition leader General Hertzog is defeated by 81 votes to 59.

Germany, Planning The German plans for invading Norway are put on a more formal basis with the allocation of the code name *Weserübung* (*see* 21 February).

28 January 1940

Finland The Finnish 9th Division attacks the Soviet 54th Division near Kuhmo and succeeds in splitting the Soviet force into three separate groups. The Finns are not able to press their attacks home. They are further distracted by relief attempts by the Soviet 23rd Division. These are held off, as is an advance by Soviet ski troops between 10-13 February. This force is wiped out.

29 January 1940

Finland In diplomatic exchanges made via Sweden it emerges that the Soviets are prepared to negotiate with the legitimate Finnish government and, implicitly, to abandon support for the puppet communist regime.

February 1940

Battle of the Atlantic Allied shipping losses amount to 226,900 tons, of which submarines sink 45 ships of 169,500 tons. Again, about half of the U-Boat successes are in the North Sea.

1 February 1940

Japan, Politics A record budget is presented to the Japanese Diet. Almost half is to be devoted to military expenditure. Clearly, this is a portent of things to come.

1-8 February 1940

Finland There are new Soviet attacks against the Mannerheim Line, especially in the Summa sector. There is an extensive preliminary bombardment to add to the artillery efforts of the past two weeks. The Soviet Seventh and Thirteenth Armies have 14 divisions and six tank brigades in the advance, with strong reserves. The Finnish 3rd Division, holding the Summa sector, takes much of the weight. During these days there is no attempt at a breakthrough but almost continuous heavy pressure is maintained. By the 8th the Finns are very tired and their artillery is running short of ammunition. Throughout this period the diplomatic exchanges via Sweden continue, but achieve nothing in the face of Soviet refusals to modify their terms. The Soviet negotiators sense final victory.

Above: Hitler surrounded by some of his more important staff officers – Keitel to his right, Jodl and Bormann to his immediate left.

5 February 1940

Allied Planning In their Supreme War Council the British and French decide to intervene in Norway and send help to Finland. They plan to begin with landings at Narvik and three other towns on or about 20 March. They rely on the Norwegians and Swedes acquiescing and doing nothing to maintain their neutrality. Allied preparations are, however, vague, irresolute and amateurish. The pretext of going to help Finland is most unconvincing and it is the obvious intention to devote more effort to stopping the Swedish iron ore reaching Germany.

9 February 1940

Germany, Planning General Manstein is appointed to command the German XXXIII Army Corps. Although this promotion is well deserved it seems that the German High Command hopes to shift Manstein to a less influential post than his present appointment as Chief of Staff to Rundstedt at Army Group A. He has had considerable influence in policy making and has been the leading figure arguing for a radical change in the plans for the attack on the west (*see* 17 February 1940).

11 February 1940

Diplomatic Relations The Germans and Soviets sign a further trade and economics agreement. The Soviets will supply raw materials, especially oil and food, in return for manufactured products of all kinds, including arms.
Finland The Soviet 123rd Division succeeds in breaking into the Finnish defenses on the Mannerheim Line near Summa.

12 February 1940

Finland A counterattack late in the day by the Finnish 5th Division fails to expel the Soviet forces from their hold on the Summa position.

In the diplomatic negotiations the Soviets raise their terms a little further to match their growing military success.

14 February 1940

Finland The British government announces that it will allow volunteers to go and help the Finns. This is, of course, far too late.
War at Sea The British government announces that all British merchant ships in the North Sea will be armed. On 15 February the Germans reply that all such ships will be treated as warships.

15 February 1940

Finland The Soviets take Summa. The Finnish forces are ordered to retire from the Mannerheim Line to their intermediate position.

16 February 1940

Norway Acting on instructions from Churchill, the British destroyer *Cossack* (Captain Vian) enters Norwegian territorial waters and removes 299 British prisoners from the German transport *Altmark. Altmark* has entered Norwegian waters on 14 February and, according to International Law the prisoners should have been released. The *Altmark*'s captain has denied that he is carrying prisoners. The Norwegians have made no real attempt to search and in fact have provided a torpedo boat as escort. The British action is of course also contrary to international law and although very popular at home, it serves to convince the Germans that the British are contemplating sterner measures against Norway. This gives further impetus to the German plans for an invasion.

17 February 1940

Germany, Planning General Manstein visits Hitler and discusses with him the plan for the armored attack through the Ardennes which Manstein has devised. Hitler has been thinking along these lines himself and is very impressed with Manstein's work.
Finland The Soviet advance has completely cleared the Mannerheim Line. All the Finnish defenders are now established in their second line of defense. The Finnish 23rd Division, brought forward from the reserve, has been slow to arrive because of air attacks.

19 February 1940

Finland The Finnish intermediate defense line is broken in some places by Soviet tank attacks.

21 February 1940

Germany, Planning The preparations for an attack on Norway move forward another stage with the appointment of General Falkenhorst to command. He had been selected by the OKW staff without consulting the Army High Command (*see* 1 March).
Occupied Europe Work begins on the construction of the concentration camp at Auschwitz.

22 February 1940

Finland The Soviets begin to occupy the islands in the Gulf of Finland. The Finns evacuate Koivisto after blowing up the coast-defense guns there.

24 February 1940

Germany, Planning Revised orders for the attack in the west are issued. OKH has been conducting exercises throughout the winter and especially in the early days of this month because of dissatisfaction with the attack plan. Following Manstein's conversation with Hitler on the 17th and an OKH presentation to him on the 18th it has been decided to revise the plans to emphasize the role of Army Group A and an attack through the Ardennes. As far as technique goes the plans are fairly traditional. The emphasis is still not yet fully on the possibilities of the Panzer advance. Rundstedt and Bock, who will be the principal commanders are, despite their considerable abilities, wedded to the conventional infantry-based ideas. Although the direction of the attack is certainly bold, the old school see early problems when it becomes necessary to cross the Meuse. The tank enthusiasts, like Guderian, are more concerned about exploiting the advance after the crossing.

26 February 1940

Finland After the failure of counterattacks against the Soviet penetrations, the Finnish command orders their forces to retreat to their third, final line of defense.

29 February 1940

Finland The Finns decide that they must give in to the Soviet demands but their note to that effect is not sent immediately because of British and French reactions to the news. The French government has become deeply committed to a policy of supporting Finland and persuades the British to join in making rash promises that cannot possibly be kept. Franco-British foreign policy towards Finland is to be characterized by muddle and incompetence.

March 1940

Battle of the Atlantic The German U-Boat campaign is less effective this month because many of them are withdrawn to prepare for the Norwegian campaign. The Allies lose 45 ships altogether, 23 to submarine attack. Three U-Boats are sunk.

1 March 1940

Germany, Planning The final directive for the invasion of Norway and Denmark is issued. On 3 March the date for the attack is set as 17 March but this will be altered to early April.

2 March 1940

Finland The Soviet forces begin major attacks on the new Finnish defense line. Pressure is exerted against all points but is strongest at the north and south ends. Vuosalmi in the north is attacked by Thirteenth Army forces while the reserve corps of Seventh Army is advancing over the sea ice toward the west side of Viipuri Gulf.

3 March 1940

Finland The Soviets begin attacks on Viipuri, Finland's second city.

5-7 March 1940

Finland The Finns correctly deduce on 5 March that the British and French promises are valueless and, therefore, tell the Soviets that they agree to meet their terms. A Finnish delegation is sent to Moscow, led by Ryti and Paasikivi, and arrives on 7 March.

8 March 1940

Finland The Soviets capture part of Viipuri. Their pressure on the Finnish defenses northeast of the city is beginning to wear down the Finnish resistance.

11 March 1940

Finland The final terms of the armistice between the USSR and Finland are concluded. Finland is to give up the whole of the Karelian Isthmus, including Viipuri, territory in the 'waist' of the country near Salla, and the Rybachiy Peninsula near Murmansk and is to grant a lease on the port of Hanko to the Soviets. Petsamo is returned to the Finns. When the recent Soviet military successes are taken into account these terms can be described as fairly moderate.

In a final bid to prevent the Finns agreeing to an armistice Chamberlain and Daladier announce that Britain and France will send help to Finland. The plan to do so is shelved when the Finns conclude their agreement with the Soviets and with it is abandoned the scheme to block the supply of Swedish iron ore to Germany.

13 March 1940

Finland After the Finnish delegation have received formal permission from their government, the treaty with the Soviets is signed in Moscow in the early hours of the morning.

The Finns have never had more than 200,000 men in the fight and have lost 25,000 dead and 45,000 wounded. Altogether the war has absorbed, on the Soviet side, 1,200,000 men, 1500 tanks and 3000 planes. Official sources put their losses at 48,000 dead and 158,000 wounded but this may well be a considerable understatement. This disparity in losses suggests to Allied and Axis observers that the effects of Stalin's officer purges have still not been overcome. This impression of inefficiency contributes to Hitler's decision to invade the USSR and makes the British and Americans a little reluctant to send supplies to the Soviets when the Germans do invade because they expect that the Germans will win quickly.

14 March 1940

Australia, Politics Prime Minister Menzies forms a new coalition Cabinet to improve the direction of the war effort.

16 March 1940

War at Sea There is a German air raid on the British fleet base at Scapa Flow. One cruiser is slightly damaged. The raid is more notable for causing the first civilian casualties in Britain.

18 March 1940

Axis Diplomacy Hitler and Mussolini meet at the Brenner Pass. Mussolini says that he is ready to join Germany and its allies in the war against France and Britain.

Below: Sailors on board a German merchant raider watch as one of their victims slides beneath the waves.

Above: Cheerful British Tommies maintain their morale in a trench 'somewhere in France' during the Phoney War period, early 1940.

20 March 1940

France, Politics Daladier, the French prime minister, is forced to resign. On 21 March Paul Reynaud forms the new government. Daladier has been criticized for failing to bring effective help to Finland. In France this has been seen as a way for the Allies to seize the initiative in the war and take the fighting away from French soil and, by association, avoid all the horrors of World War I.

28 March 1940

Allied Planning In their Supreme War Council the British and French decide to make a formal agreement that neither will make a separate peace.

In the same meeting it is also decided to mine Norwegian coastal waters and, if the Germans seem ready to interfere, to send a military expedition to Norway. The contingency plan prpared for such an eventuality has had to be abandoned, however, because the excuse for landings in Norway was to have been a clause in the constitution of the League of Nations allowing transit for troops if they were going to the aid of a victim of aggression. This is now invalid, of course, because of the Finnish surrender. The operation is timed to start on 5 April but is later deferred to 8 April – a vital difference in view of the timing the Germans fix for their own landings (*see* 1 April).
Canada, Politics Mackenzie King's Liberal Party is returned to power in the Canadian elections.

30 March 1940

China A Japanese-sponsored puppet government is established in Nanking. The Japanese have been able to persuade Wang Ching-wei, formerly a respected Nationalist politician, to lead this body.

31 March 1940

German Raiders The first German armed merchant cruiser, *Atlantis,* sails for operations against Allied shipping. Up to seven vessels will be in service later in 1940 and 1941. Generally these ships are better armed than their British equivalents and must therefore be hunted down by real cruisers. They cause considerable disruption. Their total successes in their period of operation are 87 ships of more than 600,000 tons, which is approximately one-fifth of British losses in this time.

The *Atlantis* will be the most successful raider. In a cruise lasting until 22 November 1941 she will sink 22 ships of 145,700 tons.

April 1940

Atomic Research Following a memorandum presented by Professor Rudolf Peierls and Dr Otto Frisch the British government establishes the Maud committee to supervise further nuclear work (*see* June 1941).
Battle of the Atlantic This month U-Boats only sink seven ships at a cost of five of their number. This poor return is because they are heavily involved in the Norwegian campaign. Allied shipping losses are still considerable, however. Fifty-eight ships of 158,200 tons are sunk.

1 April 1940

Germany, Planning Hitler approves the plans for the invasion of Norway. On the 2nd he fixes the date for the operation as 9 April.

3 April 1940

Britain, Politics Lord Chatfield resigns his post as Minister for the Co-ordination of Defence. Although he has had a distinguished naval career, he has not been a success in this job. Churchill is appointed to chair the Ministerial Defence Committee – a significant increase in his responsibilities. The decision-making machinery is still clumsy, however, and there is need for an even stronger directing hand and for more provision for interservice cooperation.

One of Churchill's first acts in his new post is to obtain final consent for the mining of the Norwegian Leads.

In the same Cabinet reshuffle Lord Woolton becomes Minister of Food. Perhaps his most famous initiative in this office is the invention of the 'Woolton Pie' – intended to be a nourishing and appetizing use of ration materials. It will not be widely liked.

5 April 1940

Diplomatic Relations Britain and France send a note to Norway announcing that they reserve the right to act to deprive Germany of Norwegian resources.
Britain, Politics In a major public speech Chamberlain proclaims that Hitler has 'missed the bus' – a most unfortunately timed remark.

7 April 1940

Norway The German warships begin to leave their home ports for the invasion of Norway. The British have detected the concentration of shipping in Kiel but because they have no previous information to compare this with they fail to appreciate the significance. Some of the German units are sighted and attacked by British aircraft, however. Independently British units are preparing to sail for their own mining operations. In the evening the main forces of the Home Fleet sail. The whole of the German surface fleet is committed to this operation, sailing at different times in six groups. They plan to land at Narvik, Trondheim, Bergen, Kristiansand, Oslo and a small detachment at Egersund. The battlecruisers *Scharnhorst* and *Gneisenau* sail with the Narvik group but are to go on to operate against shipping in the Arctic. A large part of the U-Boat fleet is also involved in the campaign but they achieve very little, partly because they use torpedoes with magnetic exploders which do not function properly in high latitudes. This error is discovered during the campaign and is later rectified.

The ships carry units of three divisions for the assault. Three more are earmarked for a second wave. Only one, 3rd Mountain Division, is regarded by the Germans as being of best quality. They have air support from 500 transport planes, over 300 bombers and 100 fighters. For this air support to be effective it will be necessary quickly to take airfields in north Denmark and Norway itself. This difficult task will be achieved.

8 April 1940

Norway Early in the morning the British destroyer *Glowworm* meets part of the German force bound for Narvik off Trondheim Fiord. After ramming the heavy cruiser *Hipper, Glowworm* is sunk. About midday the German transport *Rio de Janeiro* is sunk by a British submarine in the Skaggerak and many German soldiers are rescued by Norwegian fishing boats. Despite these and other indications the Norwegian authorities only alert the coastal forces in the evening. The British naval forces at sea are of course alerted, but are not kept up to date with all the information available to London and are, therefore, deployed too far out to sea to hope for interceptions of a landing force. Instead they guard against a raid out toward the Atlantic. The troops embarking at Rosyth for the Anglo-French expedition to Narvik are sent back

Above: Lt Commander Gerard Roope, RN, captain of the destroyer HMS *Glowworm.* *Right:* Map showing the German assault on Denmark and Norway, April-May 1940.

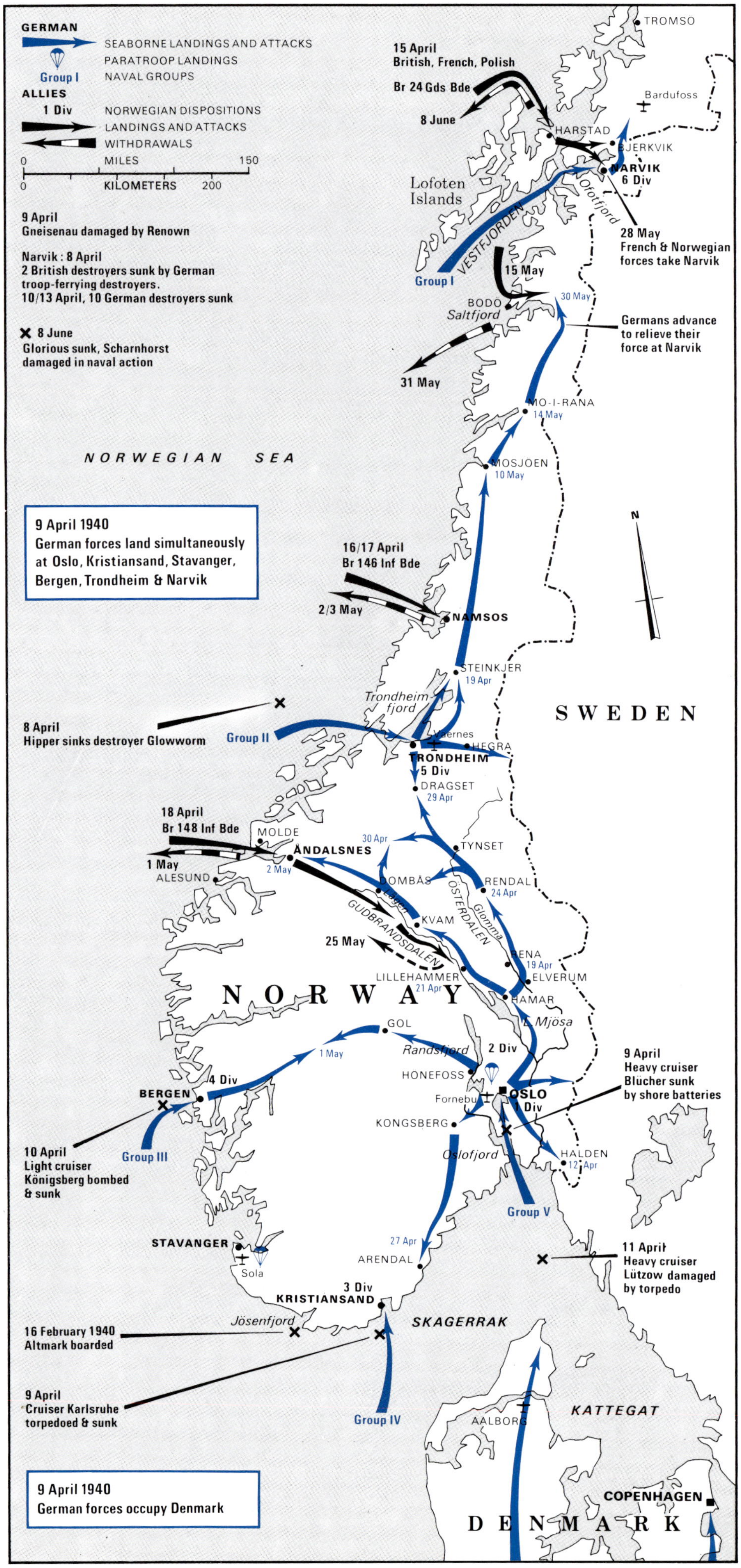

onshore and their cruiser transports sail. In fact these troops could easily have reached their objectives before the German landings, or at least have been on hand for an attempt on Narvik early in the campaign when this would have been most worthwhile.

9 April 1940

Denmark Two German divisions under the command of General Kaupitsch invade Denmark. Copenhagen is taken within 12 hours.

Norway The German landings begin. The group of ships intended for Oslo meet increasing resistance as they sail up the Oslo Fiord. At the Oscarsborg Narrows the brand-new heavy cruiser *Blücher* is sunk. The troops are compelled to land below this point but are, however, soon in the town. Airborne units take some casualties in a simultaneous landing at Oslo airport. Fog disrupts the German landings at Kristiansand but eventually the troops get ashore. At Stavanger the vital airfield is quickly taken by airborne attack but much of the airborne force's equipment is sunk offshore by a Norwegian destroyer.

At Bergen surprise is also achieved but the cruiser *Königsberg* is damaged by a coastal battery. To the north, Trondheim is taken practically without a shot. The most questionable part of the German plan is the move on Narvik. By a combination of luck and bad weather they pass the British patrols en route and once up the fiord quickly sink the two old coast-defense ships. Offshore there is an engagement between the battlecruiser *Renown* and *Scharnhorst* and *Gneisenau* in which, despite the disparity of force, *Gneisenau* is damaged before the German ships break off the action. A British destroyer force is on the way to Narvik. Off Kristiansand the cruiser *Karlsruhe* is sunk by a British submarine. Overall the Germans have succeeded brilliantly in getting their forces ashore and their hold on Stavanger airport will prove crucial later in the campaign. Their airpower is already restricting British operations, having sunk one destroyer and damaged the battleship *Rodney*.

10 April 1940

Norway First Battle of Narvik. Captain Warburton-Lee leads five destroyers in a surprise attack up Narvik Fiord. There are 10 German destroyers in various inlets off the main fiord but in a series of quick, confused actions both sides lose two ships. The British have one more seriously damaged while the Germans have four vessels hit – two very badly.

The German pocket battleship *Lützow* is badly damaged by submarine attack while homeward bound. Other German merchant ships from a convoy for Oslo are also sunk.

The Germans cruiser *Königsberg* is dive bombed by land-based British naval aircraft while in Bergen harbor and sinks. This is the first major warship to be sunk by this method of attack. This is very much an isolated success for the British air forces in this campaign since only one carrier is with the Home Fleet at this stage, the others being in the Mediterranean.

The Norwegian government and Royal Family have left Oslo and Quisling has been installed to lead a puppet government. With their seizure of so many of the country's large towns the Germans have taken most of the stocks of arms at the Norwegian mobilization centers. The Norwegians, therefore, have even less chance for resistance than might have been expected.

11 April 1940

Norway A new Commander in Chief, General Ruge, is appointed for the Norwegian Army. He replaces General Laake, who has resigned.

12 April 1940

Norway *Gneisenau, Scharnhorst* and *Admiral Hipper* are located by air reconnaissance southwest of Stavanger on their way home. Attacks by British land-based and carrier aircraft fail. Despite this escape the German navy has lost heavily in the campaign so far and will lose more ships at Narvik on 13 April.

On land the German forces are pushing out from Oslo in all directions. They take Kongsberg to the southwest of the capital.

13 April 1940

Norway Second Battle of Narvik. All eight German destroyers remaining in the fiord are sunk by a British force which includes the battleship *Warspite* as well as nine destroyers. A U-Boat is also sunk by the *Warspite*'s scout plane. The German commander, Captain Bey, has missed several opportunities to get at least some of his ships away during the previous few days. Now, as later in his career when in command of the *Scharnhorst*, he is not decisive enough. Hitler is very worried by the situation in Norway and is only just prevented by his staff from issuing a series of very rash orders, particularly to the troops in Narvik.

14 April 1940

Norway The Norwegian forces are fighting a series of delaying actions in the Glomma Valley and around Lake Mjösa against the German forces advancing north from Oslo. There are small British landings at Namsos and Harstad. The British and French are considering a number of possible strategies with the object of freeing Trondheim and Narvik. During the next few days, however, direct assaults on these places will be ruled out. Instead the chosen plan for the Trondheim area will involve a buildup at Namsos and Andalsnes and for Narvik preparations at Harstad.

Above: Wrecked German shipping litters Narvik Bay in northern Norway after the first attack by British warships, 10 April 1940.

15 April 1940

Norway Quisling resigns and is replaced for the moment by Ingolf Christensen as the head of the German-sponsored puppet government.

The main body of the 24th British Guards Brigade arrives at Harstad.

16 April 1940

Norway The British 146th Brigade lands at Namsos during the night and is immediately moved inland to Steinkjer.

17 April 1940

Norway The British heavy cruiser *Suffolk* carries out a fairly effective bombardment of the German-held Stavanger airfield but is severely damaged by air attacks while retiring. Late in the day the first British forces land at Andalsnes.

18-19 April 1940

Norway The British 148th Brigade lands at Andalsnes during 18 April. General Paget is in command. During the night part of the 5th *Demi-brigade Chasseurs Alpins* lands at Namsos. There has, however, been a mistake made with the equipment for this force and they lack some of the bindings necessary for their skis. This sort of elementary error is typical of the muddled way the whole Norwegian campaign has been conducted and will go on being conducted on the Allied side.

The units of the British 146th Brigade which have advanced from Namsos to Steinkjer are forced to retreat on the 19th by German troops who have support from the warships in Trondheim Fiord.

20 April 1940

Norway Namsos is heavily bombed by the Germans and the harbor installations, such as they are, are severely damaged. There is no natural cover from air attacks and, of course, the Germans have complete air superiority. The German forces advancing from Oslo reach the Norwegian positions at Lillehammer and Rena.

21 April 1940

Norway The Norwegian forces are pushed out of Lillehammer by German attacks on both sides of Lake Mjösa.

22-24 April 1940

Norway The British 148th Brigade is attacked north of Lillehammer by the superior German force advancing up the Gudbrandsdal. On each day the British troops are forced to retreat. On the night of 23 April the British 15th Brigade lands at Molde and Andalsnes and is soon moving forward to relieve the 148th Brigade. On 24 April the German forces in the Osterdal reach Rendal. In the north Narvik is bombarded in an attempt to bring about the surrender of the German garrison. If this looks likely a landing is to be made. The battleship *Warspite,* a heavy cruiser and three light cruisers are used but despite this concentration of force the commanding general decides that the naval guns will not have sufficiently disrupted the German positions because of their unsuitable, flat trajectory of fire. The naval commander is Admiral of the Fleet Lord Cork. This officer has been brought back to active service at Churchill's request and his position is somewhat anomalous. He is senior in the service to even the commander of the Home Fleet but is using ships from that fleet for his mission. His seniority poses problems in his relations with the military commanders who are at times reluctant to insist on measures which their military knowledge makes them believe essential. Churchill and his political colleagues have done little to clarify this situation.

25-27 April 1940

Norway The fighting in the Gudbrandsdal continues. The British 15th Brigade and the Norwegian units put up a fierce resistance but are repeatedly forced back. The Germans advance even more rapidly in the Osterdal. In the north the Norwegian forces begin attacks toward Narvik.

On 27 April the British decide to evacuate their forces from Namsos and Andalsnes, giving up any attempt to reach Trondheim. Andalsnes is heavily attacked from the air.

28 April 1940

Norway A further detachment of French mountain troops arrives at Harstad.

29-30 April 1940

Norway King Hakkon and his government are evacuated from Molde on the British cruiser *Glasgow* and taken to Tromso where they arrive on 1 May. The Norwegian gold reserves go with them. During 29 April the German units which have moved up the Osterdal link with their Trondheim force at Dragset. The British and French forces in the Gudbrandsdal are fighting south of Dombas when the order to retire reaches them. The Norwegian troops in this area will be forced to surrender when their Allies leave.

30-31 April 1940

Norway During the night the British begin to evacuate their troops from Andalsnes.

May 1940

Battle of the Atlantic The U-Boat effort this month is again fairly small. Only 13 ships of 55,500 tons are sunk this way. The start of the German campaign in western Europe is, however, marked by an increase in air and mining activity. The total Allied losses are 101 ships of 288,400 tons. New corvette-type escort vessels are beginning to come into service with the British forces. These ships are slower than is ideal and very uncomfortable for their crews in rough Atlantic weather but they are, nonetheless, of vital importance because they have good range and can be built quickly.

On 16 May the British Admiralty decide to close the Mediterranean to normal British merchant shipping. This adds more than 20,000 miles to the round trip from Britain to Suez and since many of the convoys on this route will carry important troop and arms convoys they must be escorted strongly. After the French surrender, Freetown will be the only port available on the west coast of Africa but the facilities there

Below: German mountain troops lay down supporting fire from an MG34 machine gun in the snows of northern Norway, May 1940.

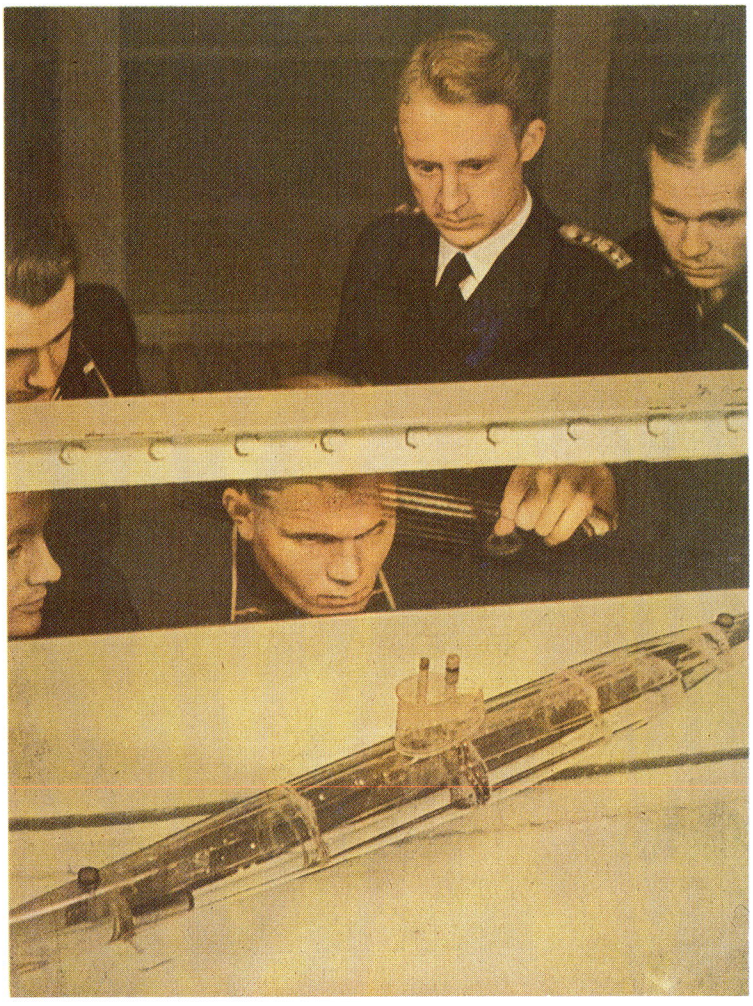

Below: German U-Boat crew members under training familiarize themselves with the finer points of their chosen weapon.

will be inadequate to cope with all the traffic. There will be considerable strain on British resources.

1 May 1940

Norway The evacuation of Andalsnes is completed. Altogether 4400 men have been taken off but much equipment has been lost.

2 May 1940

Norway The Germans reach Andalsnes. The Allies begin to leave Namsos. Before dawn 5400 French and British troops have been evacuated. Small French and British forces are landed at Mosjoen to try to help block the road north to Narvik.

5 May 1940

Norway The German forces continue to advance north from Trondheim. More Allied troops arrive in the north at Tromso and Harstad. This contingent is from the French Foreign Legion and the exiled Polish forces.

7-8 May 1940

Britain, Politics There is a major debate in the House of Commons on the conduct of the war and especially of the Norwegian campaign. At the vote Chamberlain's government has a majority of 281-200 but when compared to former support this is not sufficient to allow the government to continue to claim to be representative. Chamberlain resigns. In fact the errors of the Norwegian campaign have been at least as much Churchill's as any others. However, in a wider sense the responsibility is Chamberlain's for failing to establish a coherent decision-making structure to see that plans were properly coordinated and that subordinates worked sensibly and efficiently.

Above: British and French troops meet in Namsos in Norway, 20 April 1940. *Left:* German mountain troops negotiate a snow-covered route, similar to those experienced in Norway, April 1940. The German invasion of Norway was a text-book operation of the highest order.

For a while on 8 May it seems that Lord Halifax will be the next prime minister. Most of the Conservative majority in Parliament would prefer to have Halifax, and the Labour minority are also ready to support him. The problem is that as a peer he sits in the House of Lords and this is not ideal for a national leader. At the meeting of senior Conservatives Halifax's own worries about this leave Churchill as the only alternative. He visits the King and officially takes office on 10 May.

Even when he is established as the choice for prime minister he still has to win the confidence of his own party. The civil service and the military leaders are also suspicious of him. By a combination of his oratory, his forceful energy, far surpassing Chamberlain's, in all his work and the soundness of his administrative decisions, he quickly attains an unrivalled position. He will not always be easy to work with and often produces wild, impractical ideas but in the major issues, his handling is usually sound. Part of his success is owed to the way he delegates responsibility for home affairs to others, for he is less able in this capacity.

8 May 1940

Soviet Union, Command Timoshenko replaces Voroshilov as commissar for defense.

Training programs are soon introduced to correct some of the defects which have appeared during the Finnish war.

9 May 1940

France, Politics Reynaud has been growing more and more unhappy with the leadership of Gamelin, the Supreme Commander. He has been unable to dismiss him because he is supported in Cabinet by Daladier, who remains influential although he is no longer prime minister. These quarrels now come to a head but no announcement is made pending the formation of a new government. The German attack on 10 May will cause the changes to be deferred.

Western Front The Belgian army is placed on alert because of recent tension and signs of German troop movements. The Luftwaffe has been successful in keeping Allied reconnaissance flights away from the German preparations.

10 May 1940

Western Front The Germans begin their attack in the west. Their plans are for Leeb's Army Group C to hold the frontier opposite the Maginot Line while Rundstedt's Army Group A makes the main attack, with most of the armor, through the Ardennes and Bock's Army Group B sends a secondary advance through Belgium and Holland to draw the main British and French forces north so that Rundstedt can hit their flank. Neither the Belgians nor the Dutch have given the Allies any real cooperation in planning a joint defense because they do not wish to compromise their neutrality or provoke the Germans into attacking. The Allied Plan D is consequently less well elaborated than the German scheme. It provides for the First Army Group, the BEF and the Seventh Army to advance to the line of the River Dyle and the Meuse above Namur, to be joined there by the Belgian forces and on the left to link with the Dutch. General Gamelin is the Supreme Commander, General Georges commands the armies on the Northeast Front, General Billotte the French First Army Group and General Lord Gort the BEF. Gort has the right to appeal to the British government if he believes that his orders from the French leaders threaten his force.

In theory the two sides are fairly evenly matched on the ground, the Germans having 136 divisions and the four Allies together 149. In tanks the Allied strength is somewhat greater and a number are of superior quality. Of course the Germans have the advantage that all their forces come under a single command and conform to one tactical system. In the air the Germans are very much stronger, with over 3000 combat planes facing less than 2000 of the Allies to which the British home-based bombers, about 500, can be added. Later more RAF fighters and bombers will take part in the battle, both from bases in France and England. Most of the Allied planes are of inferior types. The German organization and command are immeasurably superior. Their tanks are concentrated efficiently in armored divisions which are almost invariably energetically, and sometimes brilliantly, led. The higher command is not always ready to accept armored innovation but both individually and collectively it is still superior to the rambling Allied arrangements. Gamelin will take little real control of the operations and several of the French general officers will perform inadequately. The Allied troops of all nations are often poorly equipped and poorly led at more junior levels also. The tanks, especially the powerful French force, are mostly deployed in small infantry support units and will be let down by their poor mobility and defeated in detail. Although the British believe in the idea of the armored division they have not yet deployed one in France. (The 1st Armored Division will be ordered to France, incomplete, on 11 May.)

The distribution of the Allied forces also leaves much to be desired. The strongest and best-trained units are in the force to be sent forward into Belgium with the best parts of the small reserve in support. Billotte's First Army Group includes almost all the armored units which the French army has formed. All three of the light armored divisions and two of the three heavy armored divisions are with the force which advances into Belgium and the infantry of the BEF and the French First Army are the best on the Allied side. The forces covering the Ardennes are weakest because the terrain in the sector is judged to be too difficult to allow a significant German attack. They have almost no reserves. The Maginot line forces are stronger. In effect, the flanks are strong and the center, where the German attack falls, is weak – the French forces few and poor in quality.

On the first day Rundstedt's forces immediately begin their advance through the Ardennes with the three armored corps in the van. Kleist has two Panzer corps under command, Guderian's and Reinhardt's and they are heading for Sedan and Montherme. Hoth's corps is making for Dinant. The advance is rapid and the little opposition, mostly French cavalry, is thrown aside.

Far more spectacular and a far greater claim on Allied attention are the efforts of Bock's Army Group B. There are parachute landings deep inside Holland which do much to paralyze Dutch resistance. German units cross the Maas near Arnhem in sudden early-morning attacks and, more exciting still, the fort at Eben Emael is

Left: Well-armed German troops look down over Narvik. *Below:* General Heinz Guderian, May 1940. *Right:* Map showing the balance of forces on the eve of the German invasion.

put out of action by a German airborne force which lands its gliders literally on top of it. The fort is meant to cover the crossings of the Albert Canal nearby and this is not achieved. The Luftwaffe give powerful support.

The British and French react quickly to these attacks as soon as they hear of them from the Belgians. By the evening much of the Dyle line has been occupied but the troops find that there are no fortifications to compare with the positions they have prepared along the Franco-Belgian frontier during the Phoney War. Some of the reserve is therefore committed to strengthen the line. Some of the advance forces of Giraud's Seventh Army make contact with the Germans in southern Holland and are roughly handled.

At the end of the day the German advance has gone almost according to plan and the Allies are acting in the manner best calculated to improve the German success. Already it is becoming apparent that the Belgian and Dutch armies are going to fail to hold out long enough to receive British and French help. The main blow against the British and French is yet to fall.

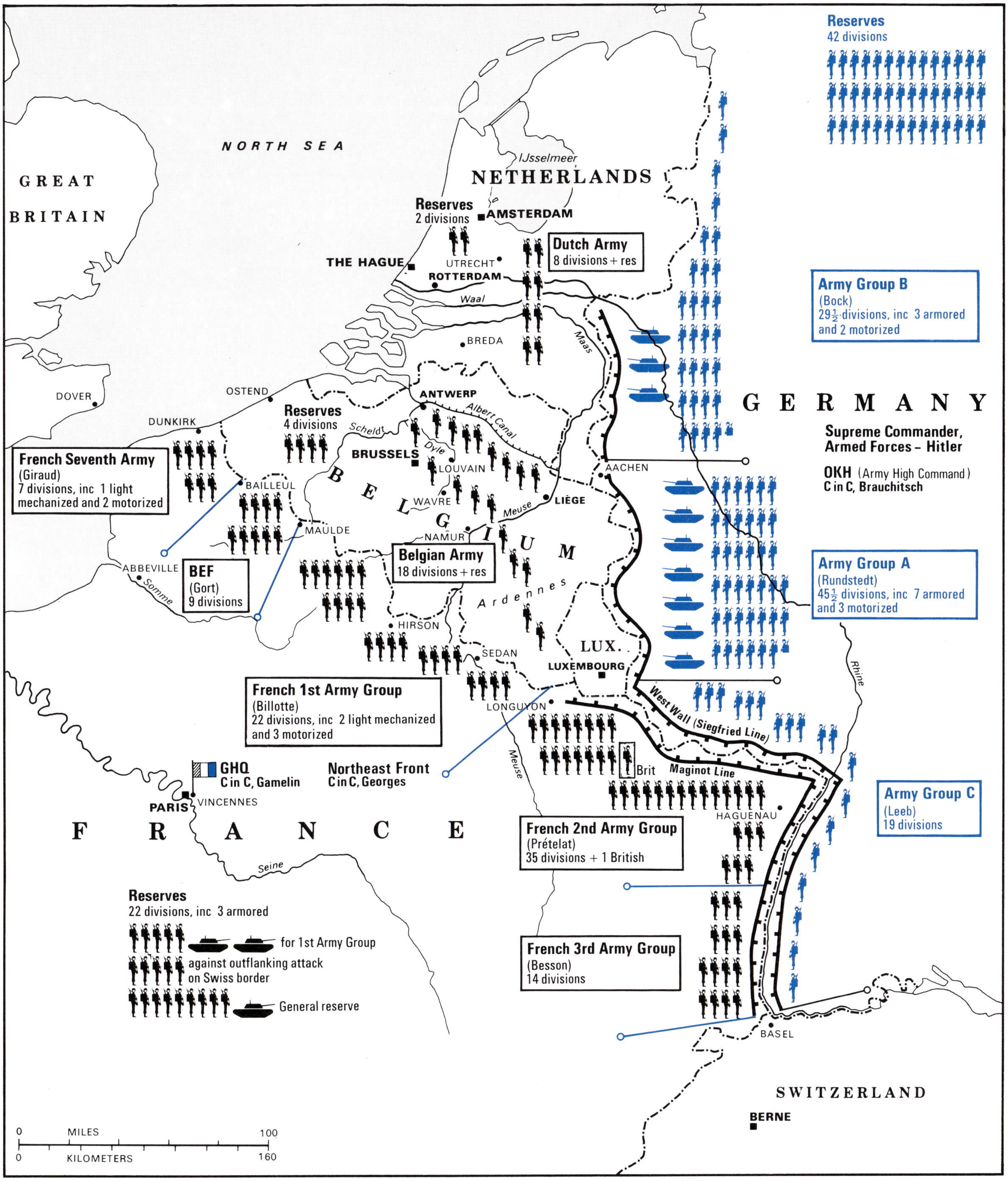

Above: Well camouflaged German assault engineers paddle across a water obstacle in their rubber boat, France, May 1940.

Above: Junkers Ju-87 Stuka dive-bombers fly toward their target, May 1940. The Stukas were an integral part of *Blitzkrieg*.

Norway British forces are sent south from Harstad to Mo-i-Rana to join the small units trying to delay the German advance to relieve the Narvik force. Some of these units are now engaged at Mosjoen.
Iceland British troops land on the island. They are the advanced elements of a force which is to set up a destroyer and scout-plane base to help in the convoy battles in the Atlantic. Equally, they will prevent the Germans using the island to aid their U-Boat campaign.

11 May 1940

Western Front The German offensive continues at high speed. The advance in Holland is very rapid and even more of the Dutch army is put out of action. In Belgium the Germans are approaching the British and French positions which are now strongly held. Eben Emael falls to German attacks after some fruitless resistance. Rundstedt's forces advance nearer to the Meuse.
Caribbean British and French troops land on the Dutch islands of Aruba and Curaçao to protect the oil installations there, and also the approach to the Venezuelan fields.

12 May 1940

Western Front The French Seventh Army advancing into Holland is engaged with the German advance near Tilburg and is thrown back. In their main armored thrust the Germans enter Sedan without a fight. The French forces in the area retire to the left bank of the Meuse where they have substantial artillery support deployed to deny the crossing to the Germans. Other tank forces reach the Meuse farther north.

13 May 1940

Western Front The German Panzer divisions cross the Meuse in two places at Sedan and Dinant. The French troops opposing them have not prepared their positions properly and are quickly demoralized and terrorized by heavy dive-bomber attacks. At Sedan Guderian is right at the front, urging his troops on and at Dinant the young commander of the 7th Panzer Division, General Rommel, is also doing well. Farther north the Germans take Liège and in Holland the defense has now been totally disrupted. The advancing German ground troops have linked with the paratroops at Moerdijk. Queen Wilhelmina and the Dutch Government are taken to London at different times during the day. Giraud's Seventh Army is in full retreat.
Norway The Allied forces start their advance toward Narvik from Harstad. The first landings on the way, at Bjerkvik 10 miles north of Narvik, are successfully carried out by French troops.
Britain, Home Front Prime Minister Churchill makes the first of a famous series of inspirational speeches in a radio broadcast. He says, 'I have nothing to offer you but blood, toil, tears and sweat.'

14 May 1940

Western Front After a surrender demand has been submitted but before it has expired, Rotterdam is very heavily bombed by the Luftwaffe. The Dutch Commander in Chief, General Winkelmans, decides that he must surrender.

The German armor pours across the Meuse at Sedan and Dinant. French tank units in both areas, but especially at Sedan fail to put in any concerted counterattacks and are brushed aside. There are considerable air attacks on the German bridgeheads by both British and French bombers. Many of the attacking planes are shot down. Once across the river the Germans drive west, cutting a huge gap between Corap's Ninth and Huntziger's Second Army. Huntziger has no orders on which way to retreat. Corap's Army is falling apart.
Britain, Home Front Recruiting begins for a volunteer home-defense force from men in reserved occupations or too old or young for military service. This force is to be called the Local Defence Volunteers. In July the far more-effective title of Home Guard is chosen.
Norway A transport carrying a large part of the British 24th Guards Brigade to join the holding forces south of Narvik is bombed and sunk by the Germans. Much equipment is lost.

15 May 1940

Western Front The Dutch army capitulates at 1100 hours. General Billotte, commanding the French First Army Group, decides to abandon the Dyle line in the face of Reichenau's attacks. His superior, General Georges, concurs with the decision and is now in fact beginning to lose his nerve. At this stage Gamelin, the Supreme Commander, remains oblivious and confident. The German tank forces push forward, urged on all the time by their commanders who are up with the leaders and in complete control of the situation. Their momentum is maintained by this leadership. The optimistic atmosphere at French GHQ is partly dispelled by the news that Guderian's tanks have reached Montcornet less than 15 miles from Laon. Guderian is ordered to halt here but after vigorous complaints he is allowed another day's march.

Britain, Planning This is a vital, symbolic day for several reasons. At crucial meetings of the Chiefs of Staff Committee and the War Cabinet, Air Marshal Dowding argues strongly against sending any more RAF fighters to France. Despite strong opposition Dowding has his way. The decision is taken also to send the first strategic bombing raid against the Ruhr. Finally on this day Churchill sends the first in a long series of telegrams to Roosevelt, signing himself as Former Naval Person. He asks consistently for American aid, works to develop a good relationship with Roosevelt and above all to bring America closer to active participation in the war. Not the least of Churchill's achievements as prime minister will be the way he cultivates this friendship. Already in this first message he presents a shopping list which includes old destroyers and aircraft as well as other arms.

16 May 1940

Western Front The British and French forces which advanced into Belgium only a few days ago, begin to retreat to their former positions behind the line of the Scheldt. Units of Hoth's XV Panzer Corps, with Rommel's 7th Division well to the fore, have reached just east of Cambrai and to the south Guderian's forces are moving on St Quentin. Again a halt order is issued to the German tank forces because some of the more conservative minds at army headquarters cannot accept that the Panzers can advance so far without exposing their flanks. In fact the speed of the advance has itself protected them and thrown the French into confusion. Perhaps the best indication of the German success is the conversation between Churchill, on a visit to Paris, and Gamelin. Churchill asks where the strategic reserve is and is appalled to receive the answer that there is none, or at least none left. Outside the room where this meeting takes place French government employees are beginning to burn secret files.

United States, Politics Roosevelt asks Congress to authorize the production of 50,000 military planes per year and for a $900,000,000 extraordinary credit to finance this massive operation.

17 May 1940

Western Front Reichenau's troops enter Brussels. Antwerp and the islands at the mouth of the Scheldt are also being abandoned but have not yet been taken by the Germans. The British and French forces in Belgium have now fallen back to the River Dendre. The Belgian government has moved to Ostend. In the main German attacks Guderian's forces, exploiting the loophole in their orders allowing reconnaissance in force, reach the Oise south of Guise. On their left flank the French 4th Armored Division led by Colonel de Gaulle sends in an attack northward from around Laon. The Luftwaffe attacks them fiercely and prevents any real gains.

General Gort is now worried by the growing threat to his right flank and rear areas and, therefore, forms a scratch force to defend this area. General Mason-Macfarlane is put in command. He has up till now been Gort's Chief of Intelligence. Gort can be criticized for weakening this important department at such a vital stage.

Norway The British cruiser *Effingham* goes aground and is lost while carrying men and stores to join the forces south of Narvik.

18 May 1940

Western Front St Quentin and Cambrai are taken by German Panzer units. Farther north Reichenau's Sixth Army takes Antwerp.

France, Politics Reynaud appoints a new Cabinet in an attempt to strengthen the French conduct of the war. He himself takes the Ministry of Defense, Marshal Pétain is deputy prime minister and Mandel is minister of the interior. General Weygand, even older than Gamelin but far more vigorous, has been recalled from the Middle East to take over the Supreme Command. Although these changes probably do strengthen Reynaud's team, especially his own new office, they will turn out to have been ill-advised. Some of the new men, Pétain in particular, will become deeply pessimistic about the outcome of the war and will in time bring Reynaud down when he himself would have preferred to fight on.

Holland, Home Front Artur Seyss-Inquart is appointed Reich Commissioner for Holland. He will take up office on 29 May.

Britain, Home Front Tyler Kent, a clerk at the US Embassy in London, and Anna Wolkoff, a Russian emigrée, are arrested on spying charges. Kent has had access to the correspondence between Churchill and Roosevelt, and Wolkoff has helped pass it to Germany via Italian diplomats. Kent's diplomatic immunity is waived by the United States ambassador. Wolkoff has had connections with a pro-Fascist oranization, the Right Club.

19 May 1940

Western Front Most of the German Panzer forces halt in positions between Péronne and St Quentin to regroup but some of Guderian's troops are still pushing forward. Rommel's 7th Panzer Division also makes a small advance in the direction of Arras. De Gaulle's 4th Armored Division again attacks north from around Laon. It makes very good progress against gradually stiffening resistance but is ordered to retire before any real gains can be achieved.

The possibility that it will be necessary to evacuate the BEF is raised for the first time in telephone conversations between London and

Below: Map showing the early stages of the German attack, May 1940.

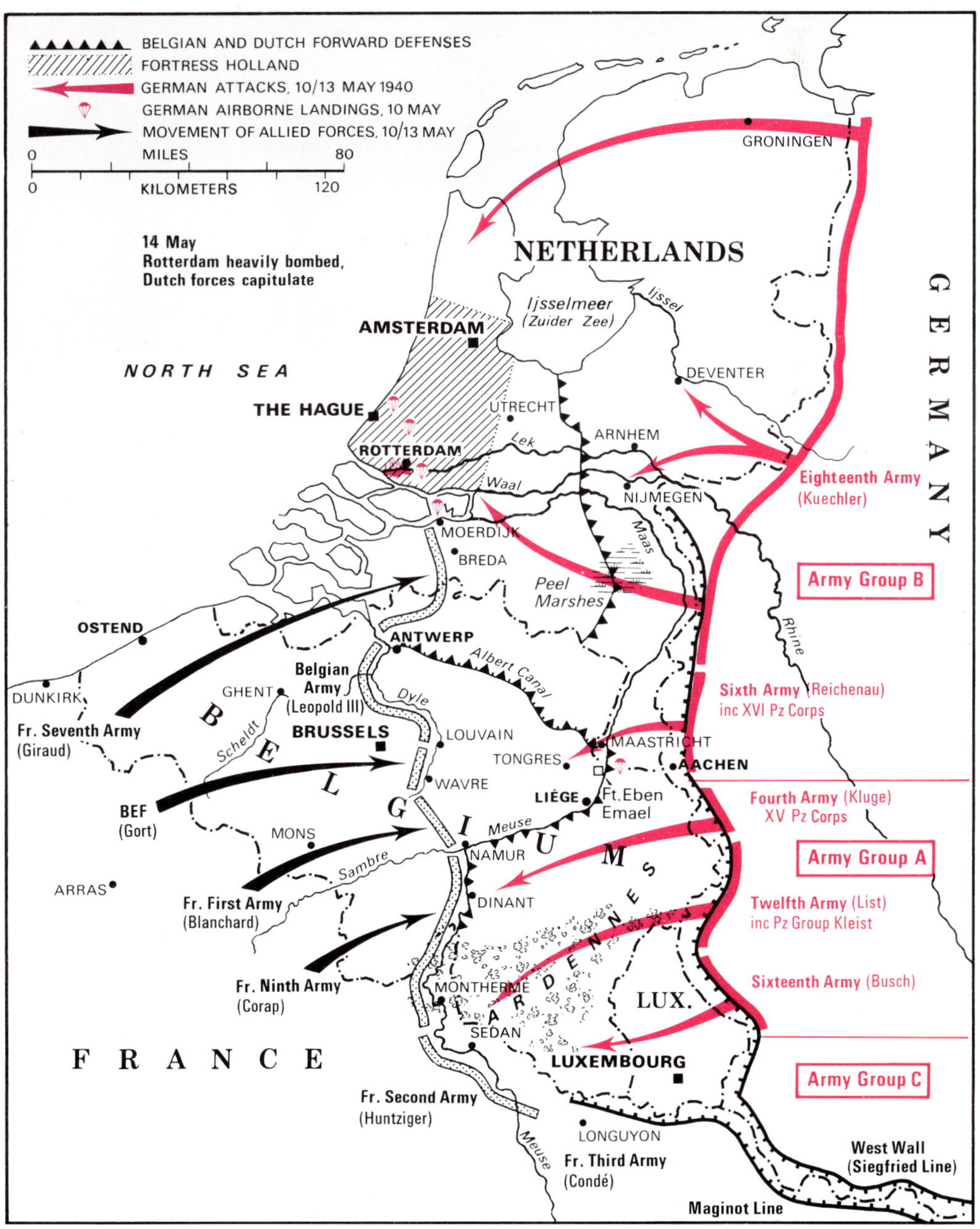

Above: A Panzer Mark III, armed with a 3.7cm main gun, advances through a devastated French village on the Aisne river.

the commanders in the field. The government are still optimistic at this stage. The main British forces are now in positions along the Scheldt.

20 May 1940

Western Front The German armored advance again makes considerable progress. The most spectacular gains are made by Guderian's XIX Corps. Amiens is taken in the morning and in the evening Abbeville is captured. Advance units even reach the coast at Noyelles. The Germans have now driven a corridor at least 20 miles wide from the Ardennes to the Channel. The obvious need is for the British and French to cut through this corridor before its walls can be strengthened to cut off irrevocably the forces to the north. Before his dismissal Gamelin was planning such an attack, but it has been cancelled following his sacking only to be revived now by Weygand. The delay imposed by these changes of mind prevents it from retaining even a slim chance of success.

21 May 1940

Western Front Rommel's division is sharply attacked around Arras by British tank forces. The attack does very well at first largely because of the comparative invulnerability of the Matilda tanks to the standard German antitank weapons. After some panic on the German side the attack is halted, principally because of the fire of a few 88mm guns. The British force is too small to repeat the advance or to shake free from this setback.

Weygand visits the commanders of the northern armies to try to coordinate attacks from north and south of the German corridor to the coast. By a series of accidents he misses seeing Gort, and Billotte, to whom he has given the fullest explanation of his plans, is killed in a car accident before he can pass them on. The attack will never take place. The small British effort has already been made. The Belgians will try to free some more British units for a later effort but this will not be possible. The French themselves, both north and south, are already too weak.

Norway The French, Polish and Norwegian forces moving in on Narvik advance another stage and gain positions on the northern side of Rombaksfiord.

Germany, Planning In a conference Admiral Raeder mentions to Hitler for the first time that it may be necessary to invade Britain. The German navy has made some preliminary studies before this but they have not been based on the availability of French bases. Little real thought is given to the possibility at this stage even after this conference.

22 May 1940

Western Front The German forces on the Channel coast turn their attacks to the north toward Boulogne and Calais. The Belgian forces retreat to the Lys.

Allied Planning Churchill is again in Paris discussing plans for an Allied offensive. Once more Weygand proposes an attempt to cut the German line to the Channel by attacks from the

Below: The drive to the Channel: map showing the Panzer breakthrough.

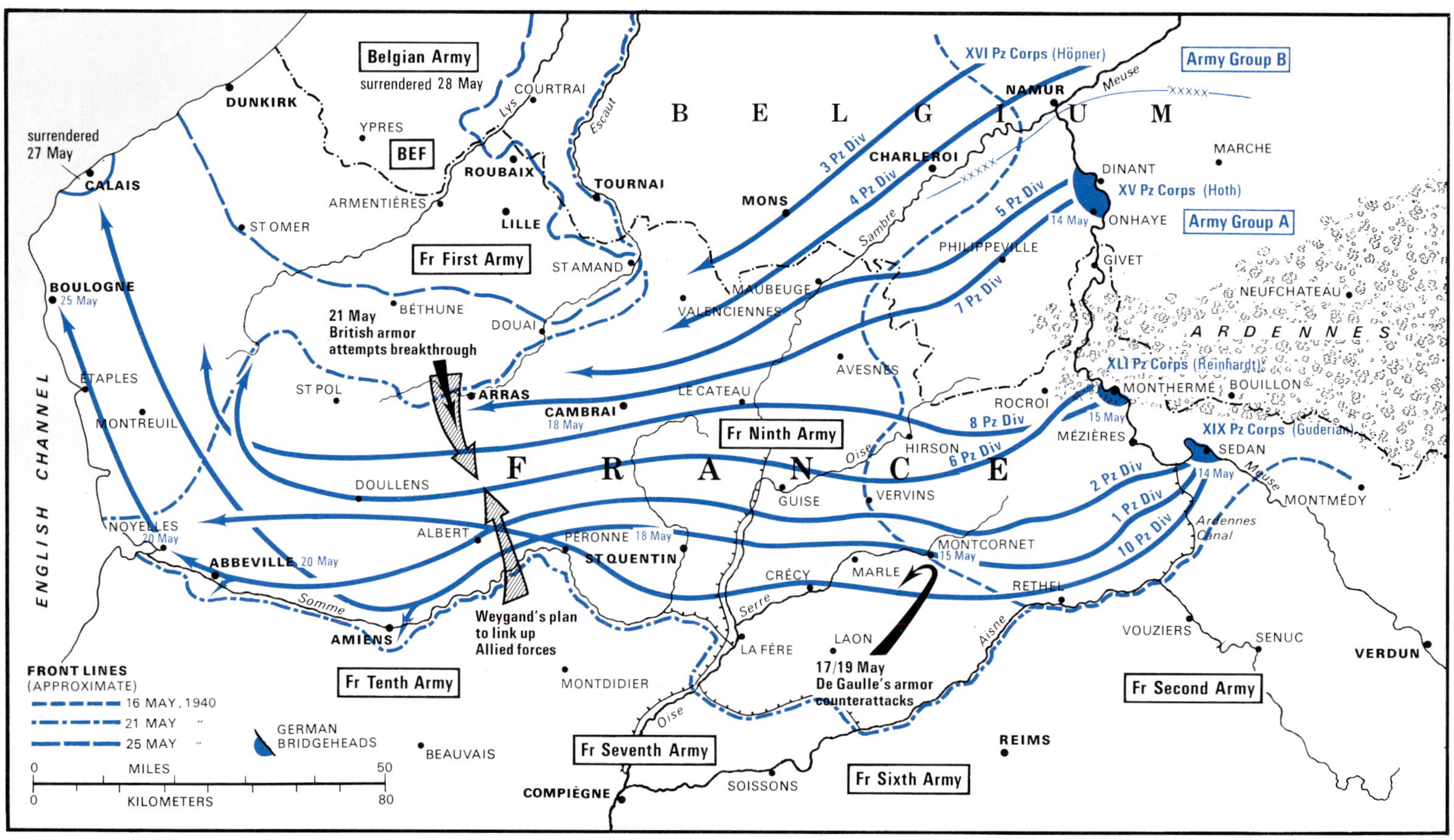

north of here is not well suited to armored action the Allied defenses are weak. The pause, which lasts until the morning of the 27th, gives the French and British time to strengthen this position and is generally seen as being the move which makes the evacuation of the BEF possible. The motives for Hitler's decision can only be guessed. Certainly the armored forces are in need of a rest. Equally, Goering is pressing for the Luftwaffe to be given a bigger share of the action and the consequent glory. There may also be some truth in the suggestions that Hitler is deliberately being soft on the British in the hope that they can be persuaded to come to terms in the near future.

Allied Planning The Supreme War Council decides to end its involvement in Norway. They agree to capture Narvik and destroy the port facilities before they will evacuate. Ironically the airfield at Bardufoss has only just received its first complement of British aircraft and already the campaign is seeming less one-sided, showing what might have been done. The Norwegians are not yet told of the decision to leave.

Above: French troops lay down their arms in Lille, cut off from the coast by the speed of the German advance. *Right:* British troops wade out to be taken on board a waiting rescue ship at Dunkirk, May 1940.

north and south. It is agreed that this should be attempted but in reality there is little with which to implement the plans.

Britain, Home Front Parliament passes an Emergency Powers Act giving the government sweeping powers over the persons and property of British citizens.

23 May 1940

Western Front General Rundstedt, commanding Army Group A, orders his tank forces to halt their advance. Despite this order 2nd Panzer Division are attacking Boulogne and inland the British evacuate Arras. Owing to this retreat the planned Allied counteroffensive is postponed. It is becoming clear to the British generals in France that an evacuation by sea is probably going to be necessary.

Britain, Home Front The former leader of the British Union of Fascists, Sir Oswald Mosley, is arrested. Also detained is a Member of Parliament, Captain Ramsay. Ramsay has been connected with the Right Club (*see* 18 May).

United States, Politics President Roosevelt wins the Democratic primary in Vermont and is now certain to receive his party's nomination.

24 May 1940

Western Front The German attacks on Boulogne continue. Farther along the coast they are also attacking Calais. The Royal Navy is active in support of the British forces in both towns. During the day and later in the night destroyers are used to evacuate 5000 men from Boulogne and over the next three days two light cruisers and seven destroyers are in support near Calais. There are also German attacks on the line of the Lys and around Tournai. The plans for an Allied counteroffensive depend on the Belgians being able to take over a longer section of the front but with this pressure they will not be able to do so.

The partial halt of the main German armored forces already made by Rundstedt is confirmed by Hitler. They have reached the line Gravelines-Omer-Béthune. Although the ground

25 May 1940

Western Front The Belgian forces are driven out of Menin by attacks of units from Army Group B. The last pockets of resistance in Boulogne are eliminated.

At 1700 hours Gort cancels the preparations he has been making to join Weygand's offensive. Later in the day Weygand in turn cancels the whole scheme, blaming Gort for this decision. In fact the French forces on the Somme have not made any attacks, as has been claimed, and the French forces with the northern armies are in no condition to do so.

26 May 1940

Westen Front, Dunkirk The position of the Belgian army is becoming increasingly grave. It is clear that it is unable to stay in the fight for much longer. The British forces are beginning to fall back on Dunkirk and in the evening the order is issued to begin Operation Dynamo, the evacuation from Dunkirk. Admiral Ramsay, who commands the Royal Navy forces based at Dover, is appointed to command the operation. The scope of the operation is not made clear to the local French commanders at first and they feel, with some justice, that they are being abandoned.

Norway The British cruiser *Curlew* is sunk by air attack off Harstad.

British Command General Dill becomes Chief of the British General Staff. His predecessor General Ironside takes over as Commander in Chief of Home Forces.

Below: The Dunkirk perimeter, showing the steady German advance.

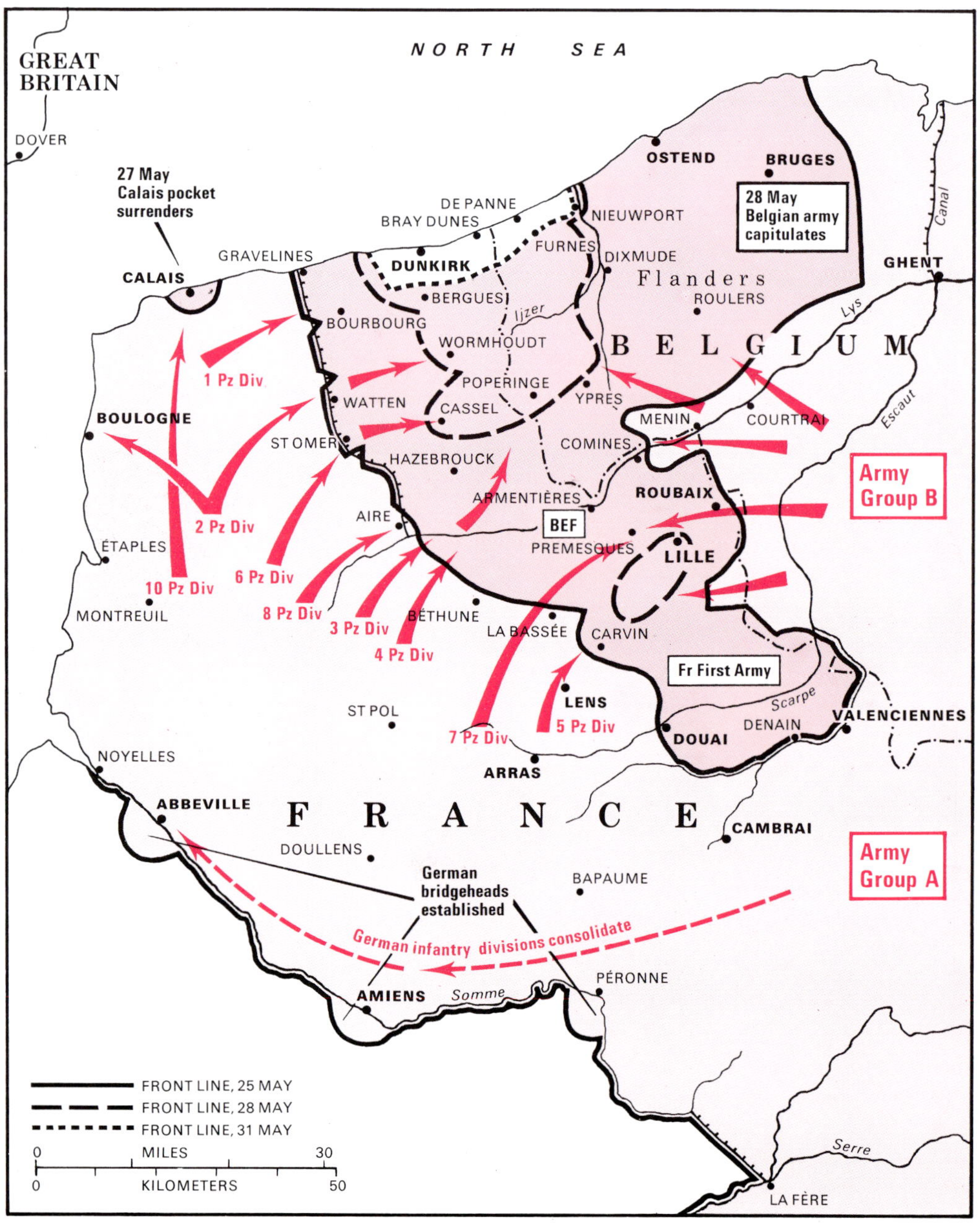

27 May 1940

Western Front, Dunkirk The German armor resumes its attacks, trying to cut off the British and French forces around Lille. A desperate defense, most notably by the French First Army around Lille, enables most of them to get away to positions nearer the coast. There is also trouble nearer the coast where the Belgian resistance is becoming increasingly weak. At Dunkirk, to date, only a little is achieved with less than 8000 men being landed in Britain.

27-28 May 1940

Norway The Allied assault on Narvik gets under way. The attacking troops are led by the French General Béthouart. The town is taken after a brisk fight. When bad weather at the Bardufoss airfield grounds the Allied fighters, the attack is briefly held up because the ships providing bombardment support then have to fight off the Stukas alone.

28 May 1940

Western Front, Dunkirk King Leopold agrees to the surrender of the Belgian army without consulting the other Allies or his government (now in Paris). The capitulation becomes effective at 1100 hours and it is only by a desperately hurried redeployment of the British and French forces that the Germans are prevented from reaching Nieuport, and from there the Dunkirk beaches. A corps of French First Army is holding out in Lille but they are now cut off from the main British and French forces in the evacuation area. There is fierce fighting around Cassel and Poperinghe where Rundstedt's men again press forward. The evacuation continues, with 17,800 men being brought off at a cost of one destroyer and several other less important vessels.

29 May 1940

Western Front, Dunkirk The German forces continue to press all round the contracting Dunkirk perimeter. By the end of the day most of the remaining British troops and a large proportion of the French are inside the final canal positions. The evacuation from Dunkirk and over the beaches goes on. The Luftwaffe increases the strength of its attacks despite the efforts of the RAF to give protection. A further 47,310 men are evacuated but three destroyers are sunk. The French are now beginning to allow their troops to be evacuated and have sent some ships to assist. Owing to the destroyer losses and the demand for them in other operations the Admiralty decides that the more modern types must be withdrawn.

30 May 1940

Western Front, Dunkirk There is something of a lull in the land battle around Dunkirk because of confusion and disagreement in the German command. The Panzer forces begin to withdraw from the front line to take up positions to the south for the next stage of the Battle of France. The evacuation, of course, continues with 53,823 men being taken off. The small ships over the beaches do most of the lifting but transfer their loads to larger vessels for the trip to England. One destroyer is sunk during the day, the French *Bourrasque,* three others are hit and at least nine of the smaller ships are also sunk. This total does not include the smallest vessels whose losses are also considerable. General Brooke, who has commanded the British II Corps with distinction, is one of the evacuees.

31 May 1940

Western Front, Dunkirk This is the most successful day of the Dunkirk evacuation, with 68,014 men being taken to Britain. The ships lost include one destroyer and six more are damaged. General Gort returns to Britain after handing over command of the remnant of the BEF to General Alexander as ordered. There are considerable air battles over the beaches at various stages during the day in which the RAF claim to shoot down 38 German aircraft for the loss of 28.

Norway The British blocking force is evacuated from Bodo.

Britain, Home Front A series of measures, including the removal of all direction signs from crossroads, is taken to counter worries about fifth-column and parachute attacks.

United States, Politics President Roosevelt introduces a 'billion-dollar defense program' which is designed to boost the United States' military strength significantly.

June 1940

Battle of the Atlantic Allied shipping losses this month increase dramatically to 140 ships of 585,500 tons. A considerable proportion of these losses occur at Dunkirk and during other evacuation operations. The normal shipping routes are also less protected because many vessels suitable for escort work have to be used in the evacuations.

The Atlantic convoys can now be given escorts as far as 15 degrees West. U-Boats sink 58 ships of 284,100 tons.

1 June 1940

Western Front, Dunkirk Despite increased Luftwaffe attacks a total of 64,429 men are evacuated from Dunkirk. However, German planes sink four destroyers and damage five more as well as several of the Channel ferries and other ships, which form the backbone of the evacuation fleet. The RAF sends eight large patrols to give cover but most of the damage is done in the intervals between them. On the ground the Germans increase their efforts, breaking the defensive perimeter along the canals at Bergues and forcing retreats in other sectors also. During the night the British authorities decide that the air attacks have made the evacuation too dangerous to continue by day.

Norway The British and French tell the Norwegians that they are about to begin their evacuation. They have delayed giving this information on the grounds of security but by doing so they have encouraged the Norwegians to openly resist the Germans, which can only be costly when the Allies leave.

2 June 1940

Western Front, Dunkirk During the day the Dunkirk perimeter, now manned entirely by French forces, is largely driven in but the Germans still cannot penetrate to the town. The beach area is only about two miles long after this advance, however. Both before dawn and after dark the evacuation continues, with 26,256 men being taken off, including the last British units to leave. Just before midnight the evacuation dies to a trickle. There are still plenty of ships but the French troops have not been given proper orders about where to go and which piers are in use. Many more have gone to earth in and around the town.

3 June 1940

Western Front, Dunkirk During the day the German attacks around Dunkirk continue. Again they force forward, contracting the perimeter, and despite a brave counterattack they reach to within two miles of the harbor. The British and French naval authorities are led to believe that there are only about 30,000 soldiers left in the beachhead and plan the night's operations accordingly. In the course of the night 26,175 men are evacuated but as the rearguard are marching down to the ships an enormous crowd of French stragglers begins to appear out of cellars and other hiding places. When the last ship leaves at 0340 hours on 4 June there are still 40,000 men left for the Germans to capture.

4 June 1940

Western Front, Dunkirk Early in the morning the Germans enter Dunkirk and capture all the remaining French soldiers. The official figure for those evacuated is 338,226 of which 112,000 are French. Almost all heavy equipment has been lost and many of the troops are without rifles and basic kit. Against the original expectation that a maximum of perhaps 50,000 men might be taken off it has been something of a triumph, but at some cost. The British and French navies have lost at least 80 merchant craft and warships as well as many small vessels. Nine destroyers have been sunk. From a force of 180 in September 1939 the Royal Navy now has only 74 destroyers not in dock for essential repairs. The Home Fleet has three capital ships and eight cruisers under repair also, although this is not because of Dunkirk. The credit for the unexpected success of the operation must lie in part with the British land and naval commanders but the Germans must also be included. Despite the brilliance of their campaign, many of the most senior commanders have not fully realized the potential of their armor and have handled it hesitantly, granting vital time for Gort and his subordinates to redispose their force. The RAF has also suffered heavily, with 80 pilots being killed in the operation. The German losses in the air have been a little heavier but German reserves are, of course, much larger.

Britain, Home Front Churchill delivers perhaps the most famous of his great wartime speeches. His message is, 'We shall fight on the beaches . . . We shall never surrender.' Already he is talking of the time when '. . . The New World, with all its power and might, steps forth to the rescue and the liberation of the Old.' This message seems to suggest that France will be beaten, leaving Britain to fight alone. This is not perhaps the best way to encourage the French to fight on.

4-8 June 1940

Norway The Allied evacuation gets under way. During these days the Harstad force is taken off. The total number evacuated is 24,500. The considerable base organization which has been built up has to be dismantled.

5 June 1940

Western Front The German attack on the line of the Somme begins. The French have used the

Below: Relieved British soldiers arrive in Dover after their rescue from the Dunkirk beaches.

period of the Dunkirk battle to make some defensive preparations but not enough to compensate for the weakness of their forces. These are now organized as Army Groups Three and Four. Army Group Three holds the Somme near the coast and Army Group Four the line of the Aisne. The German attack is code named *Fall Rot.* Their tank forces, now organized in two Panzer Groups and one Panzer Corps, are given the leading role. The heaviest fighting at first is in the sector between Amiens and the sea where Hoth's Panzer Corps is heading the drive.

France, Politics In a Cabinet reshuffle Daladier is dropped and the newly promoted General de Gaulle is made Under-Secretary for Defense.

6 June 1940

Western Front The French line along the Somme between Amiens and the coast is broken by the attacks of XV Panzer Corps after a vigorous struggle. Rommel's 7th Panzer Division makes the largest gains. Between Amiens and Péronne Kleist's Group is still being held, but farther inland Guderian's divisions are seizing bridgeheads over the Aisne in preliminary attacks.

7 June 1940

Western Front In their advance on the coastal sector the Germans take Montdidier, Noyon and Forges-les-Eaux. They are now only 20 miles from the Seine at Rouen.

Norway The British cruiser *Devonshire* carries the king of Norway and his government from Tromso to Britain.

8 June 1940

German Raiders The German battlecruisers *Scharnhorst* and *Gneisenau* operate off the Norwegian coast. Their aim is to attack the various convoys carrying the evacuation from Norway to Britain. They sink three empty ships and then find the aircraft carrier *Glorious* and two destroyers. Despite a gallant defense by the destroyers there is no time for *Glorious* to escape or launch her aircraft, and although *Scharnhorst* is damaged all three British ships are sunk. The British Admiralty has been careless in providing too few escorts for these waters, and it is by no means inconceivable that *Scharnhorst* and *Gneisenau* might have achieved a still greater victory by intercepting the simultaneous troop convoys. Admiral Marschall, in command of the German operation, decides to return to base because of the damage to *Scharnhorst.*

9 June 1940

Norway The king and his prime minister order the loyal Norwegian forces to cease fighting at midnight.

Western Front The German forces reach the Seine at Rouen and take the city. Dieppe and Compiègne are both captured. Guderian's forces are now in full attack against the French positions around Reims. They have been joined by Kleist's Panzer Group who have been switched east after being held between Amiens and Péronne. In the fighting the French defenders manage to hold most of their positions but take heavy losses.

10 June 1940

Italy Unable to resist the opportunity to take a share of the glory, Mussolini issues declarations of war to Britain and France. Neither the Italian economy nor the Italian people are particularly well prepared for war. Their fleet is, however, of considerable strength and strategic significance. They have two battleships immediately available, with four more modern ships nearly completed. They also have a powerful force of cruisers and destroyers and the largest submarine force in the world, 116 strong. These forces, when all the battleships are available, will be comfortably stronger than the British and French forces in the Mediterranean, the more so when Britain is fighting alone. The only class of ship which the Italians do not have is the aircraft carrier. Two British ships of this type are in the Mediterranean at this time.

The Italian army is not as formidable as the fleet. Although of considerable size its units are usually understrength and, as the coming battles will show, badly led and dreadfully equipped.

Diplomatic Relations Prime Minister Reynaud appeals to President Roosevelt to intervene in the war in Europe. This appeal is repeated on 13 June but without success.

Norway The Allied campaign comes to an end. Strategically the campaign has been most significant for the naval losses on each side and the transformation it has helped to bring about in the potential of the available bases for the German fleets. The Allies have lost one carrier, two cruisers, nine destroyers and many smaller craft, also many ships were damaged. These losses do nothing to help the British ability to protect the trade routes. The Germans have lost three cruisers, 10 destroyers and several submarines. This forms a large proportion of their fleet and this loss cannot be replaced at all quickly. It certainly subtracts considerably from the Kriegsmarine's limited ability to help protect, for example, an invasion of Britain.

Manpower losses in the Norwegian campaign are about 5600 for the Germans and 6100 military deaths for the Allies as well as many civilian casualties.

Western Front The Germans are across the Seine west of Paris. Elements of the French Tenth Army are still fighting around St Valéry along with some British forces. Some of these units are evacuated from the town. East of Paris the German advance is also very rapid. Evacuations also begin at Le Havre. In the next three days 11,059 British and some French will be taken off, some to go to Cherbourg but the bulk is bound for Britain. East of Paris the German forces begin to gain ground south of the Aisne.

11 June 1940

Western Front Paris is declared an open city. Most of what remains of the French forces are retreating in confusion south of the Seine and Marne. The German tank forces take Reims

Mediterranean The first actions of the war in this theater are some air skirmishes in North Africa and over Malta.

11-13 June 1940

Allied Diplomacy Churchill is again in France meeting Reynaud and Weygand at Briare. Churchill is unable to instill much of his own fighting spirit into the French leaders. Reynaud would prefer to fight on but has little support. The British are determined to prevent the Germans from obtaining control of the French navy, and are prepared to use force against their former ally, if necessary.

12 June 1940

Mediterranean A British cruiser and destroyer force shells the Italian base at Tobruk. The main force of Admiral Cunningham's Mediterranean Fleet is in support. An Italian force of cruisers is sent to engage the bombardment group but does not make contact. In a different action off Crete the cruiser *Calypso* is sunk by an Italian submarine. Turin and Genoa are bombed by the RAF.

Western Front Guderian's troops take Châlons-sur-Marne. Here and elsewhere the German advance continues to be very rapid. St Valéry on the Channel coast is taken. A large part of the British 51st Highland Division is captured.

Below: British Prime Minister Winston Churchill (left) talks to the French General Georges, commander of the North-East Front, 1940.

12-22 June 1940

Baltic States On 12 June the Soviet government issues an ultimatum to Lithuania demanding territory and the establishment of a new government. Kaunas and Vilna are occupied by Soviet troops on 15 June and a new government installed on 16 June. Similar demands are made of Estonia and Latvia. These are met on 20 and 22 June respectively. There have been Soviet garrisons based in the Baltic States since October 1939.

13 June 1940

Western Front The French forces west of Paris are now retreating to the Loire. The British decide to abandon attempts to rebuild a BEF in France and begin to evacuate the British and Canadian troops which still remain in the country.

United States, Politics Roosevelt signs a new $1,300,000,000 Navy bill providing for much extra construction.

Arms Supply In response to Churchill's pleas in his telegrams to President Roosevelt, surplus stocks of artillery weapons and rifles have been assembled from US government stores. The first shipment now leaves the USA on the SS *Eastern Prince* for the voyage to Britain. The US Neutrality Laws have been subverted by first 'selling' the arms to a steel company and then reselling them to the British government.

Left: Italian Fascist leader Benito Mussolini in heroic pose. On 10 June 1940, he declared war on Britain and France. *Below:* German horse-drawn artillery passes beneath the Arc de Triomphe in Paris.

14 June 1940

Western Front Paris falls to the Germans. New instructions are issued to the German armies. While most of the armored forces are to continue their advance into the center of the country, Guderian's two corps are to swing east to cut off any attempt by the Maginot garrisons to retreat. Army Group C, General Leeb, attacks and breaks through the Maginot defenses in some sectors, proof of the inadequacy of the French defensive system.

Mediterranean A force of French cruisers and destroyers shells the Italian ports of Genoa and Vado.

15 June 1940

Western Front Strasbourg and Verdun are taken in the converging German advance on the Maginot defenses. On the Channel coast evacuations begin from Cherbourg. In the next three days 30,630 British and Canadian troops are taken off without loss.

United States, Politics Another Navy bill passes into law. This provides for a much-expanded air corps, with 10,000 planes and 16,000 more aircrew.

Above: German Army trumpeters celebrate the fall of France, June 1940.

Top: Hitler (center) marches toward the railway carriage at Compiègne to impose his terms on the French. *Above:* General Huntziger (second from right) and his French colleagues leave the railway carriage, 22 June 1940. The completeness of the French humiliation is underscored by the ceremony at Compiègne.

16 June 1940

Western Front Dijon is taken and to the east Guderian's units have reached the Saône. The Maginot Line is breached near Colmar in Alsace. On the Channel coast there are more evacuations. From St Malo during the next two days 21,474 Allied troops are taken off and from Brest 32,584. The evacuations from St Nazaire and Nantes take three days and carry 57,235 away but over 3000 are lost when the *Lancastria* is sunk by German bombers.

Allied Diplomacy France asks Britain to be released from the obligation not to make a separate peace. In return the British make an offer to establish a state of union between the two countries, but this rather wild scheme is rejected by the French. Reynaud has lost the support of his Cabinet and resigns. Pétain is chosen to replace him.

17 June 1940

Western Front Pontarlier, almost on the Swiss border, is reached by Guderian's forces. Other units have nearly reached the Loire and still more are advancing in Brittany and Normandy.

France, Politics The Pétain Cabinet takes office. Weygand is Minister of Defense. They announce that they are asking Germany for armistice terms. The British government understands that these will only be accepted on the condition that the French Fleet does not fall into German hands. Equally it is the German policy to stop the French Fleet and colonies from joining Britain and this is the reason for their comparative leniency in allowing the establishment of Vichy as a focus for loyalty for the French. French representatives in the USA do allow the British to take up arms orders they have made under the 'Cash and Carry' rules.

Britain, Home Front Churchill broadcasts saying that the Battle of France is over and that the Battle of Britain is about to begin. His message is 'Let us so bear ourselves that, if the British Empire and Commonwealth last for a thousand years, men will still say, "This was their finest hour."'

18 June 1940

Western Front The Germans advance continues inexorably. The 7th Panzer Division takes Cherbourg, 5th Panzer Brest. Among the other towns captured are Le Mans, Briare, Le Creusot, Belfort, Dijon and Colmar.

Europe, Air Operations The RAF bomb Hamburg and Bremen.

France, Politics General de Gaulle, as yet comparatively unknown to the majority of his countrymen, broadcasts from London urging the French to fight on, saying that only a battle and not the whole war has been lost.

19 June 1940

Western Front On the Loire Nantes and Saumur are taken. In Brittany Brest falls and in central France, between the Saône and the Loire, the Germans are approaching Lyons. There are more evacuations from the west coast. In the following week 19,000, mostly Poles, are taken off from Bayonne and St Jean-de-Luz. Since Dunkirk 144,171 British, 18,246 French, 24,352 Poles, 4938 Czechs and a few Belgians have got away.

20 June 1940

German Raiders The German battlecruiser *Gneisenau* is seriously damaged in a torpedo attack by the British submarine *Clyde* off Trondheim.

Western Front Lyons and Vichy are captured.

Diplomatic Relations The French delegation sets out for the armistice talks which are to be held at Compiègne in the same railroad carriage and on the same site as the negotiations which ended World War I.

United States, Politics President Roosevelt strengthens his Cabinet by bringing in two prominent Republicans. Henry Stimson becomes Secretary for War and Frank Knox becomes Secretary for the Navy. Stimson is strongly against America's isolationist tradition and will be a champion of Lend-Lease.

21 June 1940

Diplomatic Relations The German armistice terms are given to the French delegation. The Germans will permit no discussion. In addition to the provisions for establishing a vestigial French State and for demobilizing the French Armed Forces there are stringent financial clauses. The French are allowed to consult briefly with their government.

Western Front There are Italian attacks in some of the Alpine passes which are easily beaten off despite the weakness of the French forces which are left in these areas.

War in the Air R V Jones, who heads British Scientific Intelligence, gives evidence to an important investigating committee concerning a German radio navigation aid code named *Knickebein.* Churchill gives orders for countermeasures to be developed. Vital progress in this field is soon made and plays a large part in mitigating the effects of the German Blitz in the coming months. Henry Tizard, who, more than any other, has been responsible for organizing the British use of radar, resigns because his advice is disregarded. His resignation confirms the position of the less reliable Frederick Lindemann (Lord Cherwell) as Churchill's principal scientific advisor.

22 June 1940

Diplomatic Relations General Huntziger, who leads the French delegation, signs the armistice with Germany in the Compiègne railroad carriage specially taken out of its museum. It is perhaps appropriate that Huntziger, who led the Second Army at Sedan at the start of the campaign, should be involved in the final act. The French forces which have been driven out of the Maginot Line but are still resisting, finally surrender on Weygand's order.

23 June 1940

France, Politics Pierre Laval is appointed Deputy Premier by Pétain. De Gaulle is officially cashiered by General Weygand.

24 June 1940

Diplomatic Relations The Franco-Italian armistice is concluded.

24-30 June 1940

United States, Politics In the Republican Party convention at Philadelphia Wendell Willkie is selected as the presidential candidate after the sixth ballot by a margin of 654 to 318 over Senator Taft. The convention is overwhelmingly in favor of a policy of nonintervention in the war.

25 June 1940

United States, Home Front New considerably increased taxes are introduced which bring an additional 2,200,000 people into the tax roll who have never formerly payed income tax. These increases of course reflect the armament expenditure.

Diplomatic Relations The Franco-German armistice comes into force.

The Japanese put pressure on the French authorities in Indochina to block the transit of

Below: Map showing the advance of German forces into central France.

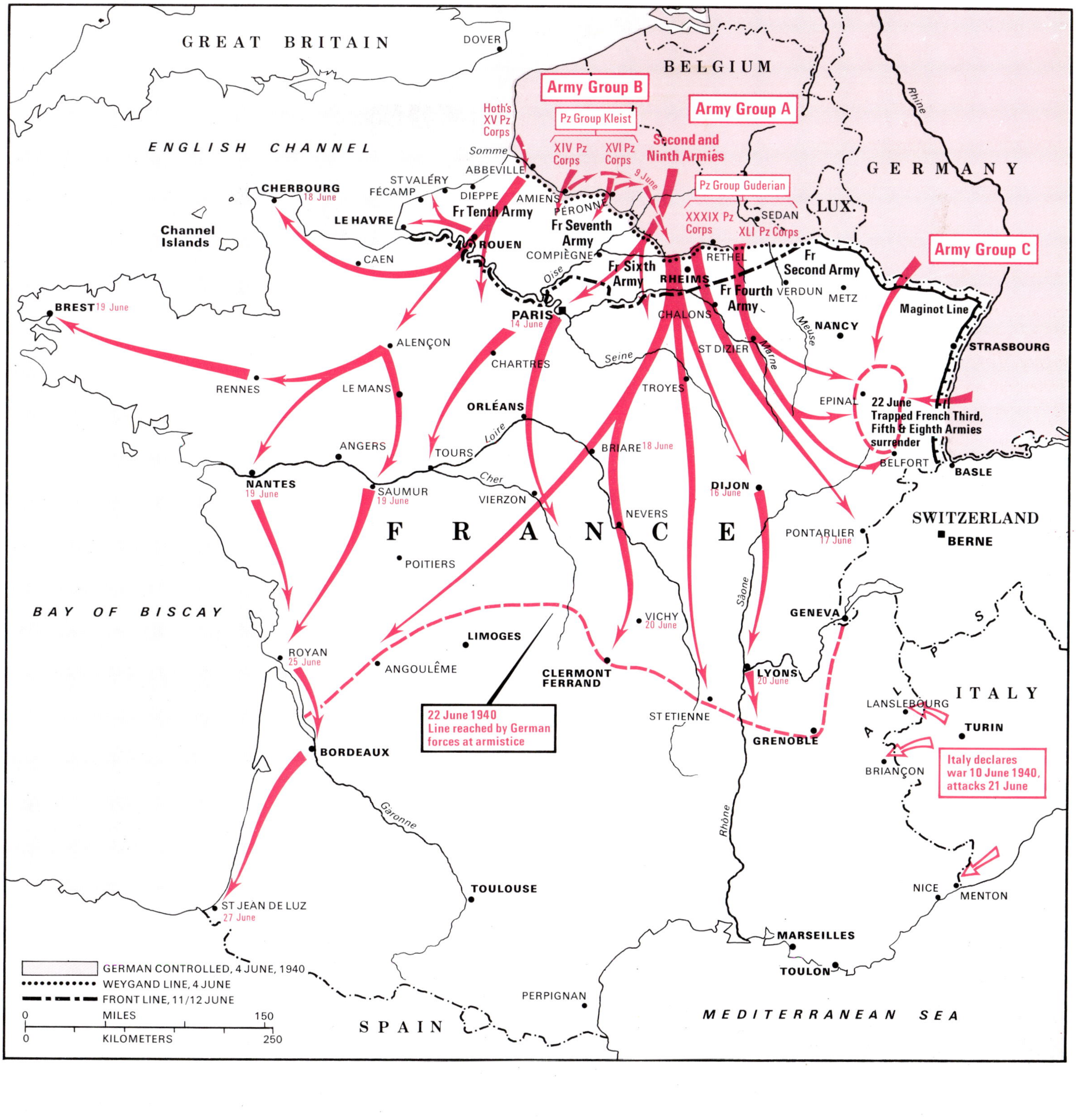

supplies to the Chinese Nationalists. They wish the rail line into China to be closed and a Japanese mission to be allowed in to inspect this.

26 June 1940

Rumania The Soviets present an ultimatum to Rumania demanding the cession of territory in Bessarabia and Northern Bukovina. Germany reluctantly intervenes to help persuade the Rumanians to give in. They do so on 27 June.

27 June 1940

Diplomatic Relations A confidential meeting is held between British and Australian representatives and the United States' Secretary of State Cordell Hull. The British and Australians ask for help in standing up to Japan. They wish the USA to take economic measures or to move more units of the fleet to Malaysian and Philippine waters or to offer to mediate between China and Japan. Hull is unable to agree to any of these moves which would involve a more active foreign policy than the American public is prepared to contemplate at this time.

28 June 1940

France, Politics General de Gaulle is recognized by Britain as 'Leader of All Free Frenchmen.'

North Africa Marshal Balbo, Italian Governor and Commander in Chief in Libya, is killed by 'friendly' antiaircraft fire while flying over Tobruk during a British air raid. Marshal Graziani is appointed to replace him.

30 June 1940

Western Front The German forces begin to occupy the Channel Islands, the only British territory which they will conquer.

July 1940

Battle of the Atlantic The period between now and October 1940 will become known to the U-Boat crews as *Die Gluckliche Zeit* (the Happy Time). During these months each submarine will sink an average of eight Allied ships each patrol. (By early in 1941 this figure will be down to two and will only rise again briefly early in 1942.) This is the period when the U-Boat ace commanders will make their names. Endras, Prien, Schepke and Kretschmer will be the best known. Almost exactly two-thirds of the U-Boat successes will be among 'independents.'

From 17 July all convoys bound for the British west coast are routed north of Ireland and any ships going to the east coast will travel north of Scotland. Of course, such radical changes cause problems of organization for the escort forces and congestion in the ports now emphasized.

In July the U-Boats sink 38 of a total Allied loss of 105 ships. There are now 28 operational U-Boats with 23 more in training.

1 July 1940

United States, Politics Roosevelt signs a further Navy bill providing for the construction of 45 more ships and providing $550,000,000 to finance these and other projects.

2 July 1940

Germany, Strategy An Armed Forces High Command, OKW, order is issued entitled 'The War Against England.' It begins 'The Fuehrer and Supreme Commander has decided that a landing in England is possible.' In response to this order Goering gives instructions for an intensified air blockade with especial attention to be given to attacks on shipping.

War at Sea/Home Front The British merchant ship *Arandora Star* is sunk off the coast of Ireland by a U-Boat. Of the 1200 people aboard 800 are drowned. They are among the 8000 'enemy aliens' who are to be deported from Britain for internment abroad.

As in the later cases of Japanese-Americans in the United States, the British internment policy is both harsh and foolish. Among those interned in Britain are many Jewish refugees from Hitler, including important scientists and many more who want to work for Britain. Hysterical fears of a Fifth Column are the main reason for the internment policy. It is gradually relaxed after August 1940, however, when more sensible views slowly begin to prevail.

3 July 1940

Britain, Planning There have been some suggestions, supported by Admiral Pound, the First Sea Lord, that the British Fleet should be withdrawn from the Eastern Mediterranean. The idea is squashed by Churchill. This is a brave decision when it has not yet been established that the Italians are likely to misuse their considerable resources and when the problem of the French Fleet has not yet been resolved.

War at Sea The British government and Admiralty are desperately worried by the status of the French navy and fear that it will fall into German hands. They therefore take action to prevent this. At Plymouth and Portsmouth two French battleships, nine destroyers and many smaller ships are taken over with a little bloodshed in some minor skirmishes. At Mers-el-Kebir near Oran there is an entirely different story. Here the British Admiral Somerville has been sent with the two battleships and one battlecruiser of Force H supported by an aircraft carrier. Somerville has been ordered to present various alternative schemes for the demobilization of the French ships and their removal to distant ports. The French Admiral Gensoul has four battleships and a large complement of supporting vessels. The deadline in Somerville's orders expires before the negotiations have achieved an agreement and he feels compelled to open fire. The *Bretagne* is sunk and two more battleships badly damaged. The *Strasbourg* and five destroyers steam out of the port and succeed in getting away to Toulon. Negotiations are proceeding in Alexandria between the British and French commanders there.

4 July 1940

East Africa The Italians advance from Abyssinia into the Sudan occupying Kassala and Gallabat just over the border. The Italians use more than two brigades at Kassala which is defended by only two companies of the Sudan Defense Force.

Rumania A new Cabinet is formed. The prime minister is Gigurtu and the Foreign Minister Manoilescu who represents the Iron Guard. On 5 July Rumania adheres to the Axis system. The policies of the new government are clearly pro-German and anti-Semitic.

Battle of Britain The Luftwaffe attacks a Channel convoy south of Portland and the Stuka bombers sink five of the nine ships involved.

5 July 1940

France, Politics Marshal Pétain's government, now based in Vichy, breaks off diplomatic relations with Britain because of the action taken against the French navy. There is an attempt to raid Gibraltar with torpedo planes but without success.

6 July 1940

Mediterranean The carrier *Ark Royal* sends planes to attack the battleship *Dunkerque*, lying damaged at Mers-el-Kebir. Further hits are achieved. *Dunkerque* and the escaped *Strasbourg* are the principal concern of the British since these are modern ships built specifically to be superior to the German pocket battleships.

6-10 July 1940

Mediterranean There are various convoy operations covered by the main forces of each side. The Italian squadron, led by Admiral Campioni, has two battleships active along with eight heavy and 12 light cruisers. Admiral Somerville's Force H is still stronger than usual from the Mers-el-Kebir operation with three battleships and one carrier and Admiral Cunningham's Mediterranean Fleet has at this stage a similar strength. All the convoys pass safely. There is some action on 9 July however. Force H is attacked by high-altitude bombers without loss and Cunningham's force and the Italian squadron are involved in a brief surface action in which the battleship *Giulio Cesare* is damaged by a hit from the *Warspite* after which the Italians break off.

7 July 1940

War at Sea The French commander in Alexandria, Admiral Godefroy, agrees to allow his ships to be demobilized. The French force here consists of the battleship *Lorraine*, three heavy cruisers, one light cruiser, three destroyers and a submarine.

7-8 July 1940

War at Sea The battleship *Richelieu* is attacked in Dakar Harbor during the night by a small British unit. On 8 July the damage done is increased by a hit from a torpedo bomber from

Below: Reichsmarschall Hermann Goering, head of the German Luftwaffe.

Above: Admiral Erich Raeder, Commander in Chief of the German Navy.

the carrier *Hermes*. The *Jean Bart* in Casablanca is also attacked. The regrettable, though necessary, attacks on the French fleet represent a low-point in Anglo-French relations. De Gaulle criticizes the British for these actions. This is the first sign that he will maintain French independence and be a stormy partner.

9 July 1940

France, Politics Marshal Pétain is granted powers to make and alter the constitution by vote of the French parliament. He is opposed by only four votes, three in the Chamber and one in the Senate.

10 July 1940

Battle of Britain There are more actions over the Channel in which there are losses on both sides. The Germans also send 70 planes to raid dock targets in South Wales. In the British reckoning this is the first day of the battle.

11 July 1940

France, Politics President Lebrun resigns and Pétain becomes head of state after an overwhelming vote in his favor in parliament. His first decree shows his new style and pretensions. It begins 'Nous, Philippe Pétain.'

11-24 July 1940

Battle of Britain The principal events are attacks by aircraft from Luftflotten 2 and 3 against shipping in the Channel. The RAF responds cautiously to these probing actions and the losses are 48 for the RAF and 93 for the Luftwaffe. On balance this favors the RAF because of the time granted to improve aircraft stocks, but in fighters alone the casualties are about equal and the Luftwaffe has superior numbers.

13 July 1940

Germany, Planning Hitler issues Directive 15 on the air war with Britain. The offensive is to begin at full strength on 5 August. Goering in fact will not be able to have his plans ready by this date. This lack of efficiency will waste vital days of the fine summer weather. The RAF is to be rapidly driven from the skies and the air supremacy necessary if an invasion is to be attempted is to be achieved.

In a conversation with some of his generals Hitler makes his first real mention of the future necessity to attack Russia. He suggests that England is only fighting on because of the hope of Soviet help.

13-15 July 1940

East Africa The Italian forces in Abyssinia move over the border into Kenya to attack the small town of Moyale. After a brief resistance the outnumbered garrison withdraws.

15 July 1940

Baltic States Plebiscites conducted in Estonia, Lithuania and Latvia are announced to show a unanimous desire for union with the USSR.

15-18 July 1940

United States, Politics In the Democratic Party convention at Chicago Roosevelt is nominated as the presidential candidate without any real opposition. Henry Wallace is chosen to run for vice-president.

16 July 1940

Germany, Planning Hitler issues his Directive 16. It begins, 'I have decided to begin to prepare for, and if necessary to carry out, an invasion of England.' It goes on to explain the importance of the air battles for the achievement of this aim. Some commentators think that the tentative phrasing of the Directive indicates uncertainty in Hitler's mind over the desirability of the operation. It is certainly true that it could have been issued sooner after the end of the Battle of France. At this stage in the planning the German army's views are dominant. They wish the Channel crossing to take place on a wide front with landings all along the south coast of Britain. They envisage that the force to be employed will be at least 25 and perhaps 40 divisions. They hope that the crossing can be protected by the Luftwaffe and mines on its flanks. This is not a very realistic plan.

Japan, Politics Prime Minister Yonai resigns because of military pressure and on 17 July a new Cabinet headed by Prince Konoye is appointed. Matsuoka is the new Foreign Minister and will be very influential. The Cabinet also includes a number of supporters of a more aggressive policy. The most important is General Tojo who becomes Minister of War.

18 July 1940

Diplomatic Relations In response to Japanese pressure and because of their present weakness, the British government closes the Burma Road to the passage of supplies to the Chinese Nationalists. The monsoon season is just beginning in Burma, so there is little real loss to the Chinese, and the road will be reopened in October when the better weather begins.

19 July 1940

Britain, Home Front General Brooke is appointed to be Commander in Chief, Home Forces replacing General Ironside. This is purely an army position and does not give authority over the other services as the title might suggest. Brooke is more of a success in the job than Ironside and produces more realistic plans for dealing with invasion. Ironside is promoted to field marshal.

Diplomatic Relations In a speech to the Reichstag Hitler issues what he describes as 'a final appeal to common sense,' urging that Britain make peace. The British Foreign Secretary, Lord Halifax, replies on 22 July 'we shall not stop fighting till freedom for ourselves and others is secure.'

United States, Politics President Roosevelt signs the 'Two-Ocean Navy Expansion Act.' This orders construction of 1,325,000 tons of warships and 15,000 naval planes. Including the existing ships, the fleet will comprise 35 battleships, 20 carriers and 88 cruisers.

Mediterranean There is an action between two Italian cruisers and the Australian cruiser *Sydney* and five destroyers. The Italian *Bartolomeo Colleoni* is damaged by *Sydney* and then sunk by destroyer attack. Later *Sydney* is hit by *Bande Nere* before the Italians flee.

21 July 1940

Germany, Planning In an OKH conference Hitler again says that Germany must prepare to attack the Soviet Union. Although the generals would prefer to deal with Britain first, they raise no objections. Later in the month Jodl tells an OKW planning section that Germany will attack in the east in the spring of 1941 and that planning for the movement of the armed forces to Eastern Europe should be begun.

Baltic States The Soviet Union formally annexes all three states and they become constituent republics of the USSR.

22 July 1940

Britain, Planning The British government believes strongly that there will be uprisings against Hitler's rule that will contribute greatly to the overthrow of his power and will make a British return to the continent possible. The Special Operations Executive (SOE) is created to work clandestinely to encourage these developments. Although events will not turn out as the British imagine, SOE will make a considerable contribution to the development of the various resistance movements in occupied Europe. Officially SOE is to be a part of the Ministry for Economic Warfare. The later American OSS will be modelled partly on SOE and partly on MI6.

23 July 1940

Allied War Production The British Purchasing Mission in the United States reaches agreement that it will be allowed to buy up 40 percent of the United States' production of aircraft.

Czechoslovakia, Politics A provisional government is formed in London and is recognized by Britain. Dr Beneš is president and Mgr Šramek is prime minister.

25 July 1940

United States, Policy The United States prohibits the export of oil and metal products in certain categories, unless under license, to countries outside the Americas generally and to Britain. This move is seen as an anti-Japanese measure, particularly because of Japan's needs for foreign oil. From this time Japanese fuel stocks begin to decline. There are similar problems with other raw materials. Japanese attention is, therefore, drawn south from China to the resources of the Netherlands East Indies, and Malaysia.

Above: A Messerschmitt Bf-110 twin-engine fighter flies over the White Cliffs of Dover during the summer of 1940.

25-29 July 1940

Battle of Britain There are various attacks on British convoys in the Channel. On the 25th aircraft from Kesselring's Luftflotte 2 attack one convoy in the Dover Straits very fiercely. They have help from German light naval forces. These are driven off during the day but return to do damage during the night. The British lose 11 of the 21 ships in the convoy. On 26 July the British Admiralty order that no ships are to pass Dover during daylight. This is not a direct response to the previous day's losses but has been under preparation for some time because of the extra organization involved. On 27 July Kesselring sinks two destroyers and damages one in Channel operations. On 28 July all destroyers are withdrawn from Dover to Portsmouth. This is a significant achievement for the Luftwaffe implying that they may be able to dominate the Channel Narrows during the hours of daylight. On 29 July another destroyer is sunk and the whole eastern half of the Channel is placed out of bounds for RN destroyers in daylight. Minesweeping operations continue, however, ensuring that access can be gained if necessary. In the air operations the RAF loses 18 planes and the Germans 52.

26 July 1940

Japan, Policy The Japanese government formally adopts policy documents giving top priority to solving their China problem by blocking supplies reaching the Chinese through Indochina and to securing their own raw materials by a more aggressive stance in the Dutch East Indies.

28 July 1940

War at Sea There is an engagement in the South Atlantic between the German auxiliary cruiser *Thor* and the similar but less well-armed British merchant cruiser *Alcantara*. *Thor* is only lightly hit but *Alcantara* is forced to break off and head for Rio. Only proper British cruisers are adequate to catch and fight such useful German vessels.

31 July 1940

British War Production Fighter output for July is found to be 50 percent above the target figures. Since 1 May 1200 have been produced. This is more than have been made in Germany and the RAF is therefore closing the Luftwaffe's advantage.

August 1940

Battle of the Atlantic Changes are introduced in the British naval codes which, for a time, set back the work of B Dienst, the German cryptanalysis service, which has previously been able to glean a considerable quantity of very up-to-date and useful intelligence from the British radio transmissions. The British work on the German Enigma coding machine is not yet giving the results that will be achieved later.

The German potential for Atlantic operations is strengthened by the entry into maritime service of long-range Condor aircraft from bases near Bordeaux. On the 17th Hitler declares a total blockade of the British Isles in which neutral ships may be sunk at sight. In the month's operations the U-Boats sink 56 ships of 267,600 tons out of a total Allied and neutral loss of 397,200 tons. One minor consolation for the British is the first sinking of a U-Boat by a depth charge dropped by a plane (*U.51* on 16 August). These modified weapons will not come into widespread use until the spring of 1941 until which time the less effective antisubmarine bombs will be used.

1 August 1940

Germany, Planning Hitler issues his Directive 17 on the invasion of Britain. The army plans have now been revised to take some note of naval problems and on account of these it is laid down that preparations are to be complete by 15 September for the operation to take place between the 19th and 26th. The order is to be given about 14 days after the main Luftwaffe offensive to gain air supremacy has begun.

Japan, Politics A public policy declaration is made concerning Japan's support for a 'New Order' in East Asia.

1-10 August 1940

Battle of Britain On each day there are German attacks on shipping in the Channel. The air fighting is heaviest on 8 August when the Germans lose 31 planes and the RAF 20. Overall the losses are less favourable than on that occasion for the Luftwaffe with the RAF total loss being 27 planes and the Luftwaffe's 62.

2 August 1940

Mediterranean The carrier *Ark Royal* with Force H attacks the Italian base on Sardinia at Cagliari. The old carrier *Argus*, which is also based on Gibraltar, is at sea to fly off a cargo of Hurricanes to Malta.

Britain, Politics Lord Beaverbrook, Minister of Aircraft Production is taken into the inner circle of Churchill's War Cabinet.

3 August 1940

East Africa The Italians invade British Somaliland. In Abyssinia the Italians have a total force of 350,000 men of whom 70 percent are native troops. The British forces in East Africa, also including many colonial troops, are less than 25,000 men of whom only four battalions are in Somaliland. The Italians allot seven times this force to the invasion along with an overwhelm-

Below: RAF pilots 'scramble', rushing toward their Hawker Hurricane fighters in response to a German attack.

ingly superior artillery contingent. General Nasi is in command. There are three main lines of advance: toward Zeila in the north, Hargeisa in the center and Odweina on the right.

5 August 1940

Germany, Strategy The first operational plans for the German invasion of the Soviet Union are presented to General Halder, the Chief of Staff at OKH, by one of his officers, General Marcks. They envisage a two-pronged attack with the major effort being directed toward Moscow and a minor advance being made toward Kiev. Work continues on the plans at both OKH and OKW (*see* 17 September).
East Africa Zeila in the north of British Somaliland and Hargeisa on the main road to Berbera are both taken by the Italians.

15-16 August 1940

East Africa The British forces pull out of their positions around Tug Argan in British Somaliland after a notable defense.

16 August 1940

Battle of Britain The Luftwaffe flies 1715 sorties and the RAF 776. In the fighting the Germans lose 45 planes and the British 21 in the air and a number on the ground. Among the targets attacked by the Germans are several Fighter Command airfields and these are quite heavily damaged.

Hitler intervenes in the quarrel between his army and naval staffs as to whether the invasion of Britain should be conducted on a broad front, as the army prefers or the narrow front more suited to naval limitations. He orders them to reach a compromise. The army has previously talked of using 40 divisions in the first three days of the operation, but now consider using 13.
Italy The RAF sends attacks against the Fiat works in Turin and the Caproni works in Milan.
United States, Politics Roosevelt announces that there have been conversations with the UK on the acquisition of bases for western hemisphere defense. He does not disclose as yet that Britain wants some old US destroyers in return.

16-19 August 1940

East Africa In British Somaliland the British forces embark at Berbera for evacuation to Aden. Altogether nearly 5700 service personnel and civilians are taken off by RN cruisers and destroyers.

The British have suffered 260 casualties in the brief campaign and the Italians 2050. Churchill criticizes the performance of the British forces despite this balance. They are defended, however, by General Wavell, whose Middle East command they are part of. Wavell has recently been in London and has made a bad impression on Churchill and the arguments about this issue do not improve Churchill's feeling toward him.

17 August 1940

North Africa Admiral Cunningham leads three battleships and several other vessels of the British Mediterranean Fleet to bombard the Italian positions at Bardia and Fort Capuzzo. Air attacks on the ships are beaten off.
Europe, Air Operations The RAF sends a raid against the armament works at Leuna. Although at this stage of the war the RAF intends to hit only military targets, it cannot achieve the necessary accuracy in night bombing.
Greece Following recently increased tension with Italy, the Greek armed forces are partially mobilized with a call-up in some districts. Among the provocations is the sinking of the Greek cruiser *Helle* by an Italian submarine.
Battle of Britain There are no major German attacks even though the weather is reasonably good. In response to pleas from Dowding the Air Ministry agrees to give Fighter Command some extra pilots from other RAF branches and to shorten the training period for new pilots even though this has obvious disadvantages.

18 August 1940

Battle of Britain The Germans make another big effort. Their targets are still mostly airfields but not all the attacks are well organized. Biggin Hill escapes comparatively lightly, but Kenley is so disrupted that part of the fighter force has to be withdrawn to another airfield. The Germans lose very heavily, 71 aircraft to Fighter Command's 27. The British originally claim that 155 have been shot down. Owing to heavy losses the Stuka is withdrawn from attacks on targets inland.

20 August 1940

Britain, Home Front Churchill produces another of his famous fighting speeches. His message is a tribute to the RAF fighter pilots:

Below: A German U-Boat commander returns to port after a successful cruise against British and Allied shipping during 1940.

Below: The view through the periscope of a German U-Boat. *Bottom:* A British freighter is hit by a torpedo in the Atlantic.

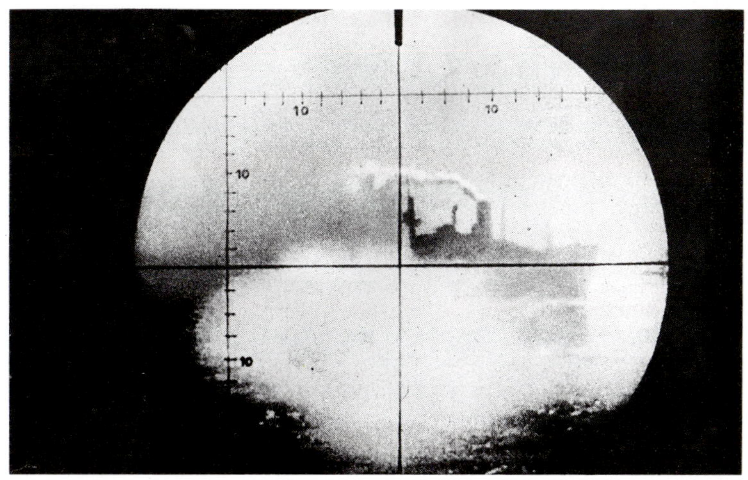

Above: British civilians rush to view the remains of a Messerschmitt Bf-109 fighter.

'Never in the field of human conflict was so much owed by so many to so few.'

Of more concrete importance to the course of the war is an official announcement that bases will be leased to the United States.

21 August 1940

World Affairs Leon Trotsky is assassinated in Mexico. Trotsky has been an enemy of Stalin throughout the latter's career, and it seems that the assassin has been working on Soviet orders.

24 August 1940

Battle of Britain After a lull of five days of poor weather the Germans again resume major operations. Their bombers now have really strong escorts and it is in consequence very difficult for the British fighters to get among the formations. The small airfield at Manston is so badly damaged that it cannot be used. There is also a damaging attack on Portsmouth. The losses for the day are nearer the figures required by the Germans, with the Luftwaffe losing 38 and the RAF 22. During the night the Germans continue their efforts, sending 170 bombers on various missions. Some of these, unable to find their targets, scatter their bombs aimlessly on South London despite specific orders to avoid this – a serious and significant error. During the night only two German bombers are lost.

25 August 1940

Battle of Britain The main German attack is against the fighter airfield at Warmwell. The attack is heavily escorted and, despite powerful British fighter forces being sent, the Germans only lose one bomber and each side loses 11 fighters. In total the Germans lose 20 aircraft and the British 16. This ratio favors the Germans in the long run. During the night the Germans attack Birmingham and other targets.

In response to the events of the previous night the RAF bombs Berlin. This is something of a shock to the German leaders who have claimed extravagantly that this is impossible.

26 August 1940

Battle of Britain The German attacks continue. They send three major raids against RAF airfields and one on Portsmouth. One of the airfield raids gets through almost undamaged but all the others are engaged heavily by the RAF. The day's losses are 31 RAF fighters and 19 German bombers and 26 fighters. According to the original timetable Hitler ought to decide now whether the invasion should be attempted.

27 August 1940

Battle of the Atlantic The Coastal Command of the RAF establishes an air base on Iceland to help in convoy protection. At this stage there are only outdated Fairey Battle aircraft situated there, but this base will soon be expanded.

28 August 1940

Battle of Britain After a lull on the 27th, the Germans attack again. They lose 30 aircraft and Fighter Command 20. One attack is made by fighters alone and the British commanders are tricked into engaging it on the assumption that it is a mixed formation. During the night there is the first of a series of four raids on Liverpool. Around 160 aircraft are sent each night.

Battle of the Atlantic The British AMC *Dunvegan Castle* is sunk by a U-Boat.

29 August 1940

Battle of Britain There are more German fighter sweeps but no major efforts by the day-bomber force. The losses are 17 German and nine British aircraft.

30 August 1940

Battle of Britain The Germans attack airfields in Kent and an aircraft factory at Luton. The important Biggin Hill sector station is severely hit as is the Luton airport. The Germans lose 36 planes and the RAF 26. Hitler announces that he will make a decision on Operation Sealion about 10 September. This will mean that the landings will be on 21 September.

Diplomatic Relations In the Balkans, Hungary and Bulgaria have been recently trying to pick a quarrel with Rumania so that, following the example of the Soviet Union, they can seize portions of Rumanian territory. The Germans do not wish their grain and oil supplies to be threatened by a Balkan war and, therefore, intervene to adjudicate the dispute. A conference is called at Vienna and by the Vienna Award Hungary is given a large part of Transylvania and Bulgaria is given southern Dobruja. Rumania can only acquiesce.

31 August 1940

Battle of Britain The Germans maintain their concentrated attacks on the British airfields. Biggin Hill is almost put out of action and Debden and Hornchurch are severely hit. The RAF loses 39 aircraft in the air and several more are hit on the ground. The Luftwaffe losses are 41. Goering is now in measurable distance of achieving his objective of superiority over south-east England. The RAF airfields at Biggin Hill, Manston, West Malling, Lympne and Hawkinge are all more or less out of the fight. There are only two RAF sector stations in commission south of the Thames and three more airfields which might be used for that role. There is no reason why these might not be similarly damaged, three having been already hit. This is the RAF's most difficult period of the battle.

September 1940

Battle of the Atlantic British problems in coastal waters increase when German E-Boats now begin major operations off the east coast. (There have been a few E-Boat sorties earlier in the summer.) The majority of sinkings by U-Boats are still occurring off the Irish coast with 70 percent being achieved by surface attack by night. The U-Boats sink 59 ships out of a total loss of 100 of 448,600 tons.

1 September 1940

East Africa In Kenya the Italians capture the small town of Buna in the northeast of the country.

1-6 September 1940

Battle of Britain The German attacks on the British airfields continue but with less strength than in the two previous days. Effort is wasted on less vital aircraft factories. On 4 September they attack a bomber factory at Weybridge and on 6 September a more important plant at Brooklands. By the end of this period the RAF fighters are flying more sorties per day than the combined total of the German bombers and fighters. The RAF loses 120 planes and the Luftwaffe 148. If the RAF losses on the ground are added or if some allowance is made for German planes crashing on the way home it seems that the Germans are getting the better of the fighting. However, it is clear that Park is keeping his force in existence through the troubles and is not yet beaten. There are also night attacks on Bristol, Liverpool and London.

2 September 1940

United States, Policy Following the agreement made in July and later detailed negotiations, a deal is now ratified between Britain and the USA by which Britain gets 50 old destroyers, veterans of World War I, but desperately needed for escort work, in return for bases granted to the United States in the West Indies and Bermuda. The first of the ships is taken over by a RN crew on 9 September and reaches the UK on the 28th. Considerable modification will be necessary to make the ships ready for service although even then they will have only a limited naval role. More important, however, is that this is an important stage in Roosevelt's efforts to develop a more active foreign policy and accustom the American public to actively supporting the Allies.

Mediterranean Admiral Cunningham's fleet is reinforced by the battleship *Valiant* and the carrier *Illustrious* from Gibraltar. He now has three battleships and two carriers. The composition of the Gibraltar based Force H varies greatly from time to time because of the uncertainty regarding the behavior of the remains of the French Fleet. The Italians now have five battleships in commission, including two modern ships.

3 September 1940

Germany, Planning The operational orders for the invasion of Britain are issued. It is confirmed that the decision to go will be taken 10 days before the invasion is to take place. S-Day is now scheduled for 21 September.

The Sealion plan now provides for elements of 11 divisions to make the assault. Two airborne divisions are to be sent in at once, but the other nine will start 6700 strong and will only reach full strength after several days. About 250 tanks are to accompany the assault. Four divisions of the Sixteenth Army with airborne support are to land near Folkestone, two of the Ninth Army near Eastbourne and three more of the Ninth Army, also with airborne support, at Brighton. These beachheads will not be mutually supporting in the early stages.

At this time the defending British forces have only made a partial recovery from the equipment losses at Dunkirk. There are perhaps four divisions fully equipped and about eight more in a reasonable state. In addition, there are various mobile brigade groups. There are about 350 cruiser and heavy tanks in the country and about 500 antitank guns.

4 September 1940

United States, Policy The United States warns the Japanese government against making aggressive moves in Indochina.

4-6 September 1940

Rumania There are political upheavals following the recent losses of territory by the Vienna Award. On the 4th King Carol gives General

Below: A Heinkel He-111 bomber flies over the London dockland during a daylight raid, September 1940.

Above: Luftwaffe crews study maps of England alongside a Messerschmitt Bf-110 fighter.

Above: A Supermarine Spitfire of No. 72 Squadron flies above the Channel.

Antonescu full powers. Parliament is dissolved on the 5th and the constitution suspended, and on the 6th the king abdicates in favor of Prince Michael. Later in the month it is announced that the fascist Iron Guard is to be the only legal political party.

7 September 1940

Battle of Britain The British authorities decide that they have information that a German invasion is likely in the next few days and accordingly they issue an invasion warning. This warning is in the form of the signal word Cromwell which means that invasion is imminent and its issue causes some wild measures to be taken. In fact this signal has been chosen because its true meaning corresponds most nearly to the needs of bringing about a higher state of readiness. No other code word has this effect.

The Germans alter the tactics of their air offensive and send a major daytime raid against London. This gives the RAF a welcome respite from the airfield attacks which have been so damaging during the last few days. The German attack on London follows from a suggestion of Hitler which coincides with Goering's own theories. The German tactic is that the RAF will be forced to commit its carefully hoarded reserves and that they can then be destroyed. Kesselring's 2nd Air Fleet is to attack London by day with its 500 bombers (including some brought from Norway and Denmark) and 600 fighters. Sperrle is to attack by night with about 300 bombers, as all his fighters have been switched to Kesselring. In addition there are about 100 Me 110s and over 200 Stukas. The British have about 350 aircraft in their frontline squadrons with more in reserve. Park is modifying his tactics slightly to cope with the bigger German formations and now intends pairing his squadrons where possible.

In the afternoon the Germans send 300 bombers and 600 fighters to attack targets in the London dock area. The British interceptions are not well managed because the change of tactics comes as a surprise. The Luftwaffe loses 41 aircraft and Fighter Command 28 shot down and several more damaged. The bombing is most effective. During the night Sperrle follows up the attack with 250 bombers with the still-blazing fires to guide them to their target. The damage is very serious. There is little the RAF can do at night to achieve interceptions although the first airborne radar sets are coming into operation. Despite the damage done it is clear that the casualties and the disruption of civilian life are not as great as prewar fears suggested. There is no question of the Germans achieving a decisive result in these operations. These attacks become known as 'The Blitz' by the British people.

8 September 1940

Battle of Britain There is relatively little activity, but the day is important because of a decision by Dowding that the Fighter Command units in southeast England should have the right to select the best pilots to keep their experienced squadrons up to strength despite the effects this will have on the other parts of the Command and on planning for the future.

9 September 1940

Battle of Britain The Germans send about 200 bombers, well escorted, to bomb London. They are intercepted by strong RAF forces and many are compelled to drop their bombs before reaching their targets. The air battle is very fierce. The British lose 19 planes and the Germans 28.
United States, Politics A new $5,500,000,000 appropriations bill becomes law in the United States. Contracts are placed for 210 new vessels for the navy, including seven battleships and 12 carriers.
West Africa Six French warships leave Toulon bound for Dakar. They are reported to the British forces too late, and reach Dakar despite the efforts of the squadrons now en route to Dakar to attack on behalf of the Free French.

10 September 1940

Battle of Britain Hitler decides that the Luftwaffe has not yet won clear air supremacy and puts off his decision on Sealion until 14 September, which means that the invasion is now scheduled for 24 September. In the air this is a quiet day.

10-20 September 1940

Albania The Italians increase their force in Albania by 40,000 men in preparation for their proposed attack on Greece.

11 September 1940

Battle of Britain The air fighting goes well for the Germans. They send a raid to London which gets through to the target and they also do significant damage to a Spitfire factory at Southampton. In the fighting the RAF comes off worst, losing 25 aircraft to the German loss of 29. Buckingham Palace is hit by a bomb but none of the Royal family is hurt. In fact, this is of benefit to national morale since it gives the impression that punishment is being shared fairly.

13 September 1940

North Africa The Italian forces begin a cautious offensive from Libya into Egypt. They have five divisions in the attack with another eight in rear areas in Libya. Marshal Graziani is in command. The British Western Desert Force of two divisions is led by General O'Connor. On the first day the Italians occupy Sollum as the British pull back.

During the months since the Italian declaration of war there have been no actions of any size, but the Italian numerical superiority has been morally undermined by much offensive patrolling by the British forces. These harassing tactics are now employed to good effect against the Italian offensive.
Battle of Britain The British bring heavy units of the Royal Navy nearer to the likely invasion area. The battleships *Nelson* and *Rodney* join the *Hood* at Rosyth and the *Revenge* is at Plymouth. There are, of course, strong cruiser and destroyer forces in relevant positions.
East Africa Italian troops from Ethiopia penetrate up to 20 miles into Kenya in a tentative advance.

14 September 1940

Battle of Britain Hitler decides that Goering needs four or five consecutive days of fine weather to hammer home his advantage.

Accordingly he defers his decision on the invasion once more, until 17 September, which in turn means that the invasion cannot take place until 27 September. This is a final date because 8 October might be the only day when conditions will be suitable for the landing; this is dangerously near winter for the exploitation stage of the invasion. There can almost certainly be no further postponement.

The daytime attacks on London are repeated again after two quieter days. The night attacks have been continuing without respite. The fighting goes well for the Luftwaffe with 14 planes lost on either side. With some justification it appears to the Luftwaffe leaders that the RAF is almost beaten.

15 September 1940

Battle of Britain Kesselring makes another great effort against London. He plans two main raids but they cannot be timed to catch the RAF fighters refuelling because his strength is sufficiently reduced that he must send the same fighters on both occasions. He can muster about 400 fighters but less than 200 bombers in the morning attack. The fighting is very heavy with the Germans being harried all the way to London, then being heavily engaged over London and all the way back to the coast. The bombers are not able to drop their loads with any accuracy at all. The afternoon shows a similar story but the fighter battles are more intense and the bombers bomb nearer to their targets as a consequence. Although the fighter combats have gone about equally the German bomber losses are very severe, bringing the German loss for the day to 60 aircraft for a bag of 26 from the RAF. Many more German bombers have been damaged or have crewmen dead or wounded. Their morale suffers as they meet up to 300 RAF fighters in one raid after their leaders have told them that the RAF as a whole has less than this number. Although it is not apparent at the time or for several weeks afterward, this is the last real attempt by the Luftwaffe to destroy the resistance of Fighter Command. The Battle is turning in favor of the RAF.

USSR, Home Front The USSR modifies its conscription laws. From now on 19-20 year olds will be conscripted.

Canada, Home Front Following legislation passed in August single men between 21 and 24 are called up.

16 September 1940

North Africa The Italians take Sidi Barani as their cautious advance into Egypt begins to grind to a halt.

United States, Home Front The Selective Service Bill becomes law. It permits compulsory induction into the armed forces for all males between the ages of 21 and 35.

16-17 September 1940

Mediterranean Aircraft from the carrier *Illustrious*, escorted by the battleship *Valiant*, attack Benghazi during the night. Four Italian ships are sunk in the harbor, including two destroyers. The cruiser *Kent* is detached from the force while returning to Alexandria in order to shell Bardia and is badly damaged in an attack by torpedo planes.

Above: High-ranking Italian officers discuss the finer points of a military problem during an Italian advance.

Below: View from the nose of a Dornier Do-17 twin-engine bomber, part of a stream heading toward Britain, summer 1940.

17 September 1940

Battle of Britain Hitler postpones Operation Sealion until further notice. The German invasion flotillas are attacked during the night by RAF Bomber Command and a fair degree of damage is done. The German night attacks include a raid on Clydeside in which the cruiser *Sussex* is damaged.

Germany, Planning General Paulus, the Deputy Chief of the Army General Staff, presents a further plan for the attack on the Soviet Union. This version envisages three thrusts for Leningrad, Moscow and Kiev, but the emphasis is still on the central advance to the Soviet capital. Further consideration over the coming weeks confirms to the General Staff that this priority is correct (*see* 5 December).

18 September 1940

North Africa The advance of the Italian Tenth Army comes to a halt, officially because of supply difficulties. They occupy themselves building various fortified camps and make little effort to keep in touch with the British forces which have pulled back before their superior strength.

Battle of Britain During the day there is a German attack by 50 bombers on targets in London. There is heavy fighting in which the RAF loses 12 planes and the Luftwaffe 19.

19 September 1940

Battle of Britain The German invasion fleet begins to disperse from the Channel ports. The later reports of the German navy show that 1918 barges have been assembled, of which 214 have been sunk or damaged. Similarly 21 out of 170 transports have been lost.

Axis Diplomacy Ribbentrop meets Mussolini and Ciano in Rome and warns them not to attack

Above: British civilians shelter from Luftwaffe bombing in the London Underground, winter 1940. This was a regular routine.

Greece or Yugoslavia. The Italian leaders dutifully reply that they will conquer Egypt first.

19-24 September 1940

Battle of Britain The German attacks continue with minor raids in which they lose 59 planes and shoot down 22.

20-22 September 1940

Battle of the Atlantic The convoy HX-72 is successfully attacked by a U-Boat group. Altogether 12 ships of 78,000 tons are sunk, seven of them during the night of 21-22 September by Schepke's *U.100*.

21 September 1940

Australia, Politics The election results are declared. Menzies remains prime minister. Labor is the largest party in both the House and the Senate but has no overall majority.

It is announced that a 9th Australian Division will be raised.

The Blitz As the night attacks on London continue, the government officially allows the Underground (or subway) stations to be used as air-raid shelters. This has been happening for some time.

22 September 1940

Indochina The Japanese enter Indochina after concluding a long period of negotiation with the Vichy government. The Japanese aim is to prevent aid reaching the Chinese through Indochina. There are to be 6000 troops stationed in the country and they are to have transit rights. Completely powerless, the Vichy government is forced to acquiesce to every Japanese demand.

Finland Finland agrees to allow transit rights to German troops en route to north Norway in return for arms supplies.

23-24 September 1940

Europe, Air Operations During the night the RAF bombs Berlin.

23-25 September 1940

French West Africa British and Free French forces try to bring the port of Dakar over to the Allied cause. The operation is code named Menace. The British are led by Admiral J Cunningham and the French by General de Gaulle. The forces involved include three small Free French warships but the main power is provided by two British battleships and one carrier. There are 3600 Free French troops aboard the various transports and a further 4300 British who, for political reasons, are not to be used unless absolutely necessary. The Vichy forces include the battleship *Richelieu* (unfinished), two cruisers and some destroyers and submarines. Admiral Landriau commands these vessels and Governor Boisson is in overall charge. On the first day of the operation there are talks between de Gaulle and the Vichy representatives, but these fail to reach any agreement and the Vichy warships begin an exchange of fire. There is damage done on both sides and one Vichy submarine sunk. An attempt by the Free French forces to land in Rufique Bay is beaten off. On 24 September the battleship *Resolution* is hit by shellfire and on 25 September is seriously damaged by a torpedo. On 25 September the *Barham* takes a 15-inch hit from *Richelieu*. Following these setbacks the operation is abandoned on Churchill's orders.

24-25 September 1940

Mediterranean As a retaliation for the events at Dakar, Vichy air forces attempt on both days to raid Gibraltar. Little damage is done.

25 September 1940

Norway Terboven, the Reichs Commissioner, deposes the King of Norway formally and appoints Quisling to lead the new Norwegian government.

25-30 September 1940

Battle of Britain The German attacks in this period are sent mostly against aircraft factories. Factories in Bristol, Southampton and Yeovil are all hit but the defending fighters exact a high price. The RAF loses 82 planes and the Luftwaffe 143.

26 September 1940

United States, Policy An embargo is imposed on the export of all scrap iron and steel to Japan.

27 September 1940

Axis Diplomacy Germany, Italy and Japan sign an agreement promising that each will declare war on any third party which joins the war against one of the three. It is stated that this agreement does not affect either Germany's or Japan's relations with the USSR. This treaty is known as the Tripartite Pact. All the signatories hope that the pact will deter the United States from joining the war in Europe or taking a more active line in the Far East.

October 1940

Battle of the Atlantic During the month the British shipping losses are 103 ships of 443,000 tons of which the U-Boats sink 352,400 tons. Convoys are now provided with escorts as far as 19 degrees west (about 300 miles west of Ireland). The Canadian forces provide similar cover in their waters. There are, however, still very few escorts and the cover is not strong. Following a few earlier attempts to coordinate operations by a group of U-Boats the wolf-pack tactics now begin to be widely used. There is little that can be done against these or against the U-Boats' favorite technique of attacking on the surface from within the center of a convoy at night. The submarines present only a small, insignificant, profile to visual search and radar is not yet advanced enough to conquer this deficiency. The listening devices with which escorts are equipped are not able to discern the difference between the sound of a submarine and the sound of the ships of the convoy, and Asdic (Sonar) is only effective against submerged submarines. Even if they are sighted, the U-Boats are often able to escape into the darkness because they are faster on the surface than the corvettes which form a large part of the escort forces.

Battle of Britain The Germans only send in a few raids by bombers in daylight. They do, however, send sweeps by fighters and fighter-bombers at altitudes which make interceptions difficult for the RAF and at which the Me 109 is superior to both the Spitfire and Hurricane. The night attacks of the Blitz continue, with London still bearing the brunt, but Liverpool, Manchester and Birmingham are also attacked.

By the end of the month bad weather is beginning to put an end to the day operations, and in fact 31 October is regarded by the British as the end of the Battle of Britain.

Germany, Planning To aid their preparations for an attack on the Soviet Union, German reconnaissance planes begin flights over Soviet territory at great altitude to spy out troop dispositions.

1 October 1940

Finland The Germans and Finns reach another agreement strengthening their ties. The Germans promise arms and the Finns grant rights to the Germans to purchase their nickel production from the mines near Petsamo.

3 October 1940

Britain, Politics Neville Chamberlain resigns his position in the War Cabinet. His offices are taken up by Herbert Morrison, Lord President of the Council, and Sir John Anderson, Home Secretary. Kingsley Wood and Ernest Bevin are brought into the War Cabinet.

4 October 1940

Axis Diplomacy Hitler and Mussolini meet. Hitler warns Mussolini against undertaking new campaigns and offers help in Africa, which Mussolini declines.

British Command Sir Charles Portal is chosen to be the new Chief of the Air Staff. The former chief, Sir Cyril Newall, becomes governor of New Zealand.

5 October 1940

United States, Politics The Tripartite Pact is condemned by Navy Secretary Knox and he announces that he is calling up some of the naval reserve.

6 October 1940

Rumania Antonescu assumes command of the Iron Guard, adding further strength to his position. On 7 October German troops enter Rumania ostensibly to help reorganize the army. Hitler's main aim is in fact to protect the oil fields.

7 October 1940

France The Germans order all Jewish people in the occupied part of France to register immediately with their authorities.

9 October 1940

Britain, Politics Following Chamberlain's resignation Churchill is chosen as the new leader of the Conservative Party. This is an impressive achievement because he was little liked by many in the party at the time of his selection as prime minister. He has succeeded in winning their loyalty despite the hard times he has presided over. His attention to party affairs illustrates his concern for the forms of parliamentary democracy.

9-20 October 1940

Battle of the Atlantic During this time there are 11 German submarines operating in the North Atlantic and they succeed in sinking 39 ships. Convoy SC-7 of 30 ships is attacked between 17-19 October and loses 21 vessels and HX-79 of 49 ships loses 12 between 19-20 October. Following these losses the British decide to increase their convoy escorts and this can only be done by dismantling some of the anti-invasion measures.

10 October 1940

Luxembourg The Germans run a plebiscite in Luxembourg. When the results are counted they find that 97 percent of the population is opposed to their occupation. The experiment is not repeated elsewhere.

11 October 1940

The Blitz Liverpool is heavily attacked in the continuing German bombing campaign. Four ships in the port are sunk and other damage is inflicted.

Finland The demilitarization of the strategically important Åland Islands is agreed in a Finnish-Soviet convention.

France, Politics Pétain broadcasts to the French people, advocating that they abandon their traditional ideas on who are their friends and who are their enemies.

Below: German, Italian and Japanese representatives sign the mutual alliance soon to be known as the Axis Pact, 27 September 1940.

Above: Officers relax on the conning tower of a U-Boat as it approaches the safety of its base in occupied France.

11-12 October 1940

Mediterranean The British light cruiser *Ajax* is attacked during the night by first three then four Italian destroyers. Two of the attackers are sunk and two damaged.

12 October 1940

Germany, Planning Operation Sealion is deferred until the spring of 1941. It will never take place.

15 October 1940

Italy, Planning The Italian War Council makes the final decision for an attack on Greece. Hitler is not to be told beforehand and instead is to be presented with a *fait accompli.* The Italians hope for the campaign to be over within two weeks. Operations will start at the end of the month.

Germany, Planning Goering issues orders to give priorities for the German night offensive against Britain. The priorities are firstly London, secondly aircraft factories and third industry in the Midlands and all air bases.

16 October 1940

United States, Home Front Registration begins for the draft according to the provisions of the Selective Service Act. The first drafts will be balloted on 29 October.

16-19 October 1940

Diplomatic Affairs There are discussions between the Japanese and the authorities in the Dutch East Indies concerning the supply of oil. It is agreed to supply the Japanese with 40 percent of the production for the next six months. There are British attempts to block this agreement.

18 October 1940

China The Burma Road is reopened to the passage of supplies to Chiang Kai-shek's forces.

Vichy France Anti-Semitic laws are introduced whereby Jews are to be excluded from public service and from positions of authority in industry and the media.

20 October 1940

Persian Gulf Italian planes from bases in East Africa bomb oil refineries in Bahrain and Saudi Arabia.

20-21 October 1940

Red Sea There is a surface action between four Italian destroyers and the escorts of a British convoy. The convoy is escorted by a light cruiser, one destroyer and five smaller vessels. The Italians lose one ship.

23 October 1940

Axis Diplomacy Hitler meets General Franco at Hendaye in southern France. Hitler tries to persuade Franco to join the war and offers as bait the allocation of Gibraltar and territory in North Africa. Franco is uncertain about how to proceed and successfully muddles the issue, leaving Hitler no better informed as to what is Spanish policy but without causing offense.

24 October 1940

Belgium, Politics An exile government is established in London. Its leading members include Camille Gutt, Hubert Pierlot and Paul-Henri Spaak.

26 October 1940

Battle of the Atlantic The 42,000-ton liner *Empress of Britain* is damaged by a bomb attack off the coast of Ireland. On 28 October *U.32* completes the job and sinks the damaged ship.

27 October 1940

Axis Diplomacy At 2100 hours the Italians tell the Germans of their decision to invade Greece.

28 October 1940

Greece and Albania An Italian ultimatum is presented to the Greeks during the night. It amounts to a declaration of war. At dawn, before the ultimatum expires, the Italians begin to cross the border into Greece. Patras is bombed.

General Prasca leads eight of the 10 Italian divisions in Albania in the advance. They attack along three lines with the main effort being in the center from the Dhrina and Vijosë valleys. General Papagos, the Greek Commander in Chief, has not deployed his main forces close to the border to avoid giving any provocation to the Italians. He too hopes to use eight divisions with the possibility of reinforcements being brought from the troops otherwise watching the Bulgarian border.

The greatest obstacle to the Italians for the first two or three days is the very bad weather which grounds their air support. The Italians have chosen a very unwise time of the year for their attack.

Hitler and Mussolini meet at Florence. Hitler conceals his anger at not being kept informed of the Italian plans and says that German troops are available if it is necessary to keep the British out of Greece and away from the Rumanian oil.

France, Politics Laval becomes Foreign Minister of the Vichy government.

November 1940

Battle of the Atlantic The German submarine force has now been joined in the Atlantic by 26 Italian vessels, but this strong force proves to be very inefficient. The shipping losses are 97 ships of 385,700 tons of which U-Boats account for 32 ships.

The Blitz Among the targets for the German air raids this month are Coventry, Birmingham, Southampton, Bristol and Liverpool. London continues to be hit also. Civilian casualties are 4500 dead and 6200 seriously hurt.

Europe, Air Operations Among the RAF targets are Berlin, Essen, Munich, Hamburg and Cologne. Bomber Command drops 1300 tons of bombs.

1 November 1940

Greece and Albania The Italian advance reaches the Kalamas River in the Epirus district. A small British bomber unit is sent to help the Greeks. This force is increased at Churchill's order during the next few days. About half the RAF strength from Egypt is sent. The British government believes that it is vital to fulfill the guarantees given to Greece to bolster neutral opinion, especially in the Balkans and Turkey.

3 November 1940

The Blitz This is the first night since 7 September that there is no raid on London. There have been 57 consecutive nights of attack and after tonight 10 more will follow. An average of 165 planes has attacked each night dropping 13,600 tons of high explosive and many incendiaries.

Battle of the Atlantic Two British AMCs, the *Laurentic* and the *Patroclus* are sunk by Kretschmer's *U.99*.

4 November 1940

Greece and Albania The first Greek counterattacks begin in the northern sector of the front. The Italian offensive, despite its numerical strength, is already in difficulties.

5 November 1940

United States, Politics President Roosevelt is elected for an unprecedented third term. His majority in the popular vote is 10 percent – 27,000,000 to Willkie's 22,000,000. In the Congressional elections the Democrats lose four Senate seats and gain eight seats in the House. They retain their majority in both chambers.

Battle of the Atlantic The German pocket battleship *Admiral Scheer* finds the British convoy HX-84 of 37 ships while on a sortie into the Atlantic. At this point in its route the convoy is only escorted by a single AMC, the *Jervis Bay*, which, although totally outgunned, engages the *Scheer* to gain time for the convoy to scatter. *Jervis Bay* is sunk but only five ships of the convoy fail to get away. The British suspend convoy sailings until 17 November but their pursuit fails to find the German ship which has moved toward the south Atlantic.

Scheer had left port on October 23 and will return on 1 April 1941 after sinking 16 ships of 99,000 tons in addition to *Jervis Bay.*

6 November 1940

Greece and Albania The Italian advance in the coastal sector reaches Igoumenitsa.

6-7 November 1940

East Africa General Slim's 10th Indian Brigade attacks and captures Gallabat from the Italians on the 6th but withdraws again on the 7th after losses to the supporting tanks and in the air. The Italians reoccupy the position.

7 November 1940

West Africa Colonel Leclerc leads a Free French force in landings north of Libreville. There is some fighting but by 14 November French Equatorial Africa has been brought over to the Free French.

8-10 November 1940

Greece and Albania The Italian 3rd Alpini Division is trapped in the area of the Pindus Gorges by the Greek counterattacks. The Greeks take over 5000 prisoners.

9 November 1940

Britain, Politics Neville Chamberlain, the former prime minister, dies at the age of 71.

10 November 1940

Greece and Albania The Italian Undersecretary for War, General Soddu, replaces General Prasca as the Commander in Chief in Albania.

11 November 1940

Battle of Britain In a postscript to the main actions a force of Italian bombers, protected by biplane fighters, is sent to attack Harwich. They are intercepted and lose six planes for no loss to the RAF. The Italians make other attacks, mostly by night, on east-coast ports during the next nine weeks.

11-12 November 1940

Mediterranean The British Mediterranean Fleet attacks the Italian base at Taranto. During the night 21 Swordfish aircraft attack in two waves and gain three torpedo hits on the brand new battleship *Littorio* and one each on *Caio Duilio* and *Conte di Cavour*. Two other ships are damaged. The aircraft have come from the carrier *Illustrious* and only two are lost. This brilliant attack will certainly be studied by other navies and the potential for such an attack on an enemy fleet in harbor is clear to the Japanese who, in fact, make a close study of the raid.

In other operations in the few preceding days the Mediterranean Fleet has carried troops to Malta and been strengthened by another battleship, making five in all. The Gibraltar based Force H attacked Cagliari with aircraft from *Ark Royal* on 9 November.

12 November 1940

Germany, Planning Hitler issues Directive 18. Although talks are being conducted with the Soviets (Molotov is in Berlin), the planning for the attack on the Soviet Union is to continue as are the preparations for the attack, code named Marita, on Greece, and Felix, the advance through Spain to Gibraltar.

12-13 November 1940

Dutch East Indies Agreements are concluded between the Japanese and the principal oil companies whereby the Japanese are to receive 1,800,000 tons of oil annually from the Dutch East Indies.

14 November 1940

British Command The new British Commander in Chief for the Far East, Air Marshal Brooke-Popham, arrives in Singapore.

The Blitz There is an especially heavy and effective German attack on Coventry involving 449 planes. Factories and historic buildings are badly damaged. Some historians have since suggested that, by a combination of scientific and cryptographic Intelligence, the British authorities were able to take precautions against this raid but that they did not do so in order to protect their sources. This is not the case. Warning has been received during the afternoon of the 14th and the few precautions possible at this short notice have been taken by the relevant authorities.

14-16 November 1940

Greece and Albania By the 14th all the Greek forces are in full attack against the Italian invaders.

British aid to Greece begins to arrive. Four cruisers ferry 3400 troops and airfield staff from Alexandria to Piraeus.

15 November 1940

Atlantic US flying boats begin patrols from bases in Bermuda.

Greece and Albania The Greek counteroffensives continue with especial success for the advance from western Macedonia in the area around Mount Morava.

17 November 1940

British Command Air Marshal Dowding is replaced at Fighter Command by Air Marshal Sholto Douglas. Dowding is sent to work for the Ministry of Aircraft Production in the section dealing with orders for American planes. Later he will be denied the promotion to Marshal of the Royal Air Force which his distinguished services during the Battle of Britain more than entitle him to expect. Air Marshal Park will also be treated in a shabby fashion and will shortly be replaced at 11 Group by Leigh Mallory. Park will receive no comparable command in the future. A new RAF Command for Army Cooperation is created, to be led by Air Marshal Barratt.

18-19 November 1940

Battle of the Atlantic In an Atlantic operation a U-Boat approaching a convoy is detected by a

Below: The British aircraft carrier HMS *Illustrious* enters harbor in Malta.

Sunderland flying boat fitted with an Air to Surface Vessel (ASV1) radar set. This is the first time such a location has been achieved by airborne radar in operational conditions.

19 November 1940

Greece and Albania The Greeks claim to have driven the Italians back behind the Kalamas River. There is heavy fighting near Koritza.

20 November 1940

Hungary Prime Minister Count Teleki and Foreign Minister Cśaky agree in Vienna to bring Hungary in to the Tripartite Pact's provisions.

21 November 1940

Greece and Albania The Greeks enter Koritza. They capture 2000 prisoners and some heavy equipment. Almost all the invading Italian forces have now been driven back to Albania.
United States, Home Front The Dies report on German and Communist espionage and subversive activities is published. As in the similar investigations which have been made in Britain, the strength of these disruptive elements is wildly overestimated and accompanied with calls for preventive measures.
Australia, Politics The government presents its war budget for the coming year. Twenty percent of the national income is to be devoted to war expenditure and is to be financed by considerable increases in taxation.

23 November 1940

Britain, Production and Supply The new British Ambassador to the United States, Lord Lothian, talks in New York of the possibility of Britain running out of ready money and securities to pay for arms and says that Britain will need financial help in 1941. In fact by April 1941 British reserves of gold and dollars will be as low as $12,000,000 – a mere pittance when set against arms expenditure.
Balkans, Politics In a meeting in Berlin Antonescu agrees to join the Axis powers. There are also talks on preparation for a German attack on Greece by the forces based in Rumania. Germany has been putting pressure on all the Balkan states since the Italian invasion of Greece in an attempt to ensure the stability of food and oil supplies. Hungary succumbed to the pressure on 20 November. Bulgaria and Yugoslavia have not joined the Tripartite Pact but progress has been made in the talks.

24 November 1940

Balkans, Politics The prime minister of the German puppet state of Slovakia, Tuka, joins the Tripartite Pact powers in a meeting in Berlin.

26 November 1940

Poland, Home Front Work begins on the creation of a Jewish ghetto in Warsaw in which the Germans intend to herd the local Jewish population under dreadful living conditions. The Germans describe the move as a 'health measure.'
Mediterranean Aircraft from the British carrier *Eagle* raid Tripoli. In another operation the carrier *Illustrious* attacks targets on Rhodes.

27 November 1940

Mediterranean There is a naval battle off Sardinia. Admiral Somerville, who is covering a Malta convoy, has the *Renown, Ark Royal,* four cruisers and nine destroyers. He will be joined later by *Ramillies,* three cruisers and five destroyers. Admiral Campioni leads two battleships, seven heavy cruisers and 16 destroyers. There is a brief gun battle in which the cruiser *Berwick* and one Italian destroyer are hit. Despite their superior gunpower the Italians then break off the action.

27 November-4 December 1940

Rumania, Home Front There are riots and other civil disturbances. The Iron Guard begin the trouble with the arrest and execution of various prominent persons including the former Prime Minister Jorga. The army later clamps down with German help.

30 November 1940

China, Politics Japan officially recognizes the puppet Nanking government led by President Wang Ching-wei.
Greece and Albania The Greek advance from Macedonia continues. They win an important victory near Pogradec.

December 1940

War at Sea Bad weather hampers the main U-Boat operations with only one convoy, HX-90, being attacked during the month. There are some successes for the U-Boats off Portugal and West Africa. They sink 37 ships out of a total loss of 82.
The Blitz British civilian casualties this month are 3800 dead with 5250 injured. German targets include London, Sheffield and Liverpool. The attack on London on 29/30 December is heavy and destructive.

2 December 1940

British Command Various changes for the Royal Navy are announced. Admiral Tovey is to succeed Admiral Forbes as Commander in Chief, Home Fleet. Forbes goes to Plymouth Command. Admiral Harwood becomes Assistant Chief of the Naval Staff.

3 December 1940

Britain, Production and Supply Britain announces that it has placed a first order with US yards for the construction of 60 merchant ships.

4 December 1940

Greece and Albania The Greek forces continue their advance and enter Premeti.

5 December 1940

Germany, Planning An outline plan for the attack on the Soviet Union is presented to Hitler by the army. As in the last version it provides for a three-pronged attack, with the center force moving toward Moscow being strongest. Hitler agrees to allow planning to go ahead on this basis but suggests some modifications (*see* 18 December). He also orders planning for the attack on Greece to continue.

6 December 1940

Italian Command Marshal Badoglio resigns his post as Italian Commander in Chief. His successor is General Count Cavallero.
Greece and Albania The Greek advance north along the coast continues to go well. Sarandë is taken.

8 December 1940

Greece and Albania The Greek forces capture Argyrocastro and Delvino.

9 December 1940

North Africa The British begin an offensive in the western desert. General O'Connor leads two divisions, 7th Armored and 4th Indian, in the attack. They are supported by 7th Royal Tank Regiment (RTR) against whose Matilda tanks the Italians will have no answer. General Wavell is in Supreme Command in Egypt. The British force has few reserves and therefore the attack has comparatively limited objectives at first. General Graziani is the Italian Commander in Chief and he has deployed the seven divisions of General Gariboldi's Tenth Army in forward positions in Egypt. O'Connor's men began their advance from Mersa Matruh, 70 miles from the Italian front, three days previously and achieve complete surprise when they make their attack. The Italians have done little since mid-September but build a series of fortified camps in which they now sit. These camps do not give any real

Below: A building collapses in Queen Victoria Street, London, in the aftermath of a German bombing raid, December 1940.

support to each other and will be very easily isolated.

The British attack is in the form of a left hook around behind the Italian coastal positions and owes much to the careful training which the troops have received in desert warfare. The Matildas are used to break into first the Nibeiwa camp and then the Tummar West camp which both fall during this first day.

Italian Command There are command changes and redistribution of ships and squadrons in the Italian navy. Admiral Riccardi replaces Admiral Cavagnari as Undersecretary of State and Head of Supermarina. Admiral Iachino replaces Campioni as Fleet Commander in Chief.

Greece and Albania Pogradec falls to the Greek advance.

10 December 1940

United States, Policy Roosevelt announces an extension of the export-license system. Iron ore, pig iron and many important iron and steel manufactures are brought within the system. Like previous measures this is aimed at Japan. The changes come into effect at the end of the year.

Germany, Strategy OKW issues a directive ordering the transfer of X Fliegerkorps to south Italy and Sicily. Field Marshal Milch has been in Rome during the past few days to discuss the measures to help the Italian navy.

North Africa Sidi Barrani falls to the British attack. There are 20,000 prisoners already in the offensive. The coast road to the west has been cut by 7th Armored Division at Buq Buq.

11 December 1940

North Africa Sollum is bombarded by ships from Cunningham's fleet. O'Connor's attacks have ruined five of the seven Italian divisions they have met and they are all rapidly retreating from Egypt. Some 14,000 more prisoners are taken, many of whom come from the Catanzaro Division which is expelled from positions near Buq Buq.

12 December 1940

North Africa Wavell is not able to follow up his success as vigorously as he would have wished because 4th Indian Division is about to be withdrawn for service in the Sudan.

Balkans, Politics A treaty of friendship is signed in Belgrade by Yugoslavian and Hungarian representatives. By this token of good relations with a German client the Yugoslavs hope to improve their own relations with Germany.

13 December 1940

Germany, Planning Hitler issues Directive 20 giving orders for the further preparation of the invasion of Greece, Operation Marita. The German forces in Rumania are accordingly increased.

Vichy, Politics Pétain dismisses and arrests Laval and appoints Flandin as foreign minister in his place. Laval is released on 17 December after the German ambassador has intervened.

North Africa A small British force has entered Libya and now cuts the road leading west from the important Italian position at Bardia.

16-24 December 1940

Mediterranean There are further British and Italian fleet operations. Valona in Albania is shelled by the British battleships *Valiant* and *Warspite*. The Italians are also active in support of their armies in Albania with Lukova, just north of the Corfu Channel being shelled. The British carrier *Illustrious* attacks airfields on Rhodes and sends strikes against Italian convoys.

Above: Rumanian leader Ion Antonescu (third from right) agrees to the terms of the Axis alliance in a meeting with Hitler, 23 November 1940.

17 December 1940

United States, Politics President Roosevelt gives a press conference outlining a scheme which he plans to introduce to bring further aid to Britain which he will call Lend-Lease. His argument is that if a neighbor's house is on fire it is only sensible to lend him a hose to stop the fire spreading to your own house, and that it would be stupid to think of asking for payment in such circumstances.

North Africa The British forces occupy Fort Capuzzo, Sollum and three other Italian positions near the Egypt-Libya border. The Italian garrisons of these places have withdrawn to the Bardia fortress.

18 December 1940

Germany, Planning Hitler issues Directive 21. Its message is simple: 'The German Armed Forces must be prepared, even before the conclusion of the war against England, to crush Soviet Russia in a rapid campaign.' The projected operation is given the code name Barbarossa.

Hitler has modified the draft plans prepared by the army in one important respect. Although three lines of attack are still suggested, Hitler's scheme reduces the importance which has been laid on the advance to Moscow. He suggests that after the first battles the center group should swing north to help clear the Baltic States and Leningrad before moving on the capital. The preparations are to be ready by 15 May 1941.

19 December 1940

Finland, Politics President Risto Ryti takes office. His predecessor, Dr Kallio, dies suddenly the same day.

20 December 1940

Bulgaria, Politics New anti-Semitic laws are introduced. Bulgaria's Jewish population at this point is about 50,000 people. There are also measures against Free Masons and other so-called secret societies.

23 December 1940

Britain, Politics Lord Halifax becomes British ambassador to the United States. Anthony Eden takes over as foreign secretary. David Margesson becomes secretary for war (army minister).

Greece and Albania The Greeks continue their advance, occupying Himarra.

25 December 1940

German Raiders The German cruiser *Admiral Hipper* meets and attacks a British troop convoy 700 miles west of Cape Finisterre. The escort for the convoy consists of three cruisers and the carriers *Argus* and *Furious*. In the engagement which develops, the British cruiser *Berwick* is hit but the *Hipper* is forced to withdraw to Brest with engine trouble, sinking one ship on the way. This is the only return for a cruise lasting one month.

27 December 1940

German Raiders The German raider *Komet* shells the phosphate production installations on the island of Nauru in the Central Pacific while flying a Japanese flag. Both *Komet* and *Orion* have been active in this area for some days and have sunk several of the ships engaged in the specialized phosphate trade.

28 December 1940

Greece and Albania The Greeks bring their offensive to an end for the moment in order to consolidate their gains and improve communications with the front.

29 December 1940

United States, Home Front In one of his famous 'fireside chat' broadcasts President Roosevelt describes how he wishes the United States to become the 'arsenal of democracy' and to give full aid to Britain regardless of threats from other countries.

1941

January 1941

Battle of the Atlantic There are now 22 operational submarines in the German fleet but there are 67 more on trials or in training. A total of 21 ships of 126,800 tons is sunk by U-Boats in January. A large proportion of this success is achieved after the convoys have dispersed, usually beyond 20 degrees west. German aircraft are also very active, both in scouting for the U-Boats and in their own right. They sink 15 ships themselves. The total shipping losses for the Allies are 76 ships of 320,200 tons. The first types of radar sufficiently sensitive to detect submarines on the surface are beginning to be used by the British escort forces but it will take some time for all problems to be ironed out.
The Blitz The principal targets for the German bombing this month are London, Bristol, Cardiff and Portsmouth.
British Air Operations Among the targets for the RAF this month are Bremen, Hamburg, Brest and Wilhelmshaven.

1 January 1941

Balkans, Politics Ribbentrop, the German foreign minister, meets Filov, the Bulgarian prime minister, in Berlin to discuss arrangements for allowing the passage of German troops across Bulgaria. No agreement is reached but Bulgaria is now nearer to acquiescing to German pressure to join the Tripartite Pact.
Mediterranean The strength of the German X Fliegerkorps in Sicily is now 96 bombers and 25 fighters. At full strength there will be 270 bombers, 150 of them Stukas, 40 fighters and 20 scout planes. At this time the RAF has only 15 Hurricanes in Malta.

2 January 1941

United States, Production Roosevelt announces a program to produce 200 7500-ton freighters to standardized designs. They will be known as Liberty ships.

Previous page: The devastation at Pearl Harbor, 7 December 1941. *Below:* The Bank of England and Royal Exchange, following a German raid, 11 January 1941.

3 January 1941

North Africa The Allied force, renamed XIII Corps, has been increased by the arrival of the 6th Australian Division to replace the 4th Indian Division previously withdrawn to the Sudan. The new force leads the attack on Bardia which now begins. The 16th and 17th Brigades provide the assault units. They have considerable tank and artillery support. In addition three battleships of the Mediterranean Fleet also shell the Italian positions. The attack goes in against the west and southwest of the fortress and progress is very rapid. Around 30,000 prisoners are taken in the first 24 hours. This campaign will prove beyond doubt the inability of the Italian Army to successfully wage a modern war.

4 January 1941

Albania The Greeks begin a new offensive. They drive westward toward Valona from their positions in the mountains. The Greeks are, however, outnumbered by the Italians and find it difficult to make significant gains.

5 January 1941

North Africa Bardia is taken along with 40,000 prisoners and large numbers of guns, tanks and other vehicles. General Bergonzoli is withdrawing toward Tobruk with the still considerable remnants of his force. There have been less than 500 Allied casualties in the attack.

6 January 1941

United States, Home Front President Roosevelt, in his State of the Union message, talks of four essential freedoms, of speech and worship and from fear and want. He again refers to the United States as the 'arsenal of democracy.'
North Africa Advance units of the Allied force reach the outer defenses of Tobruk after taking El Adem airfield to the south. The encirclement of Tobruk will not be complete in any strength, however, until 9 January. Patrols to examine the Italian defenses begin immediately. The Tobruk garrison is 25,000 men with 220 guns and 70 tanks. General Mannella is in command. There are other Italian units still in positions farther west in Libya.

8 January 1941

United States, Politics Roosevelt presents his budget to Congress. It outlines total expenditure of $17,500,000,000 with $10,800,000,000 going on defense.
Albania The Greeks begin to attack Klisura in their continuing offensive. Their progress farther north is less good, especially around Berat.
Mediterranean There is a British air raid on Naples by Wellington bombers in which the battleship *Giulio Cesare* is badly hit while moored in the harbor. The *Vittorio Veneto* is hit also but scarcely damaged.

10 January 1941

United States, Politics The Lend-Lease Bill is introduced to Congress. There is considerable opposition. Among the prominent opponents of the bill are Senators Wheeler and Nye, former Ambassador Kennedy and Charles Lindbergh. (*see* 11 March).
Mediterranean Off Pantelleria a British convoy is attacked, first by two Italian torpedo boats, one of which is sunk for no loss to the convoy, and then by 40 German Stuka and Ju 88 bombers. The carrier *Illustrious* is hit six times by dive bombers. *Warspite* dodges several attacks but other ships are also damaged. This is the first action by the German X Fliegerkorps. *Illustrious* retires to Malta. All the British forces from Gibraltar and Alexandria have been out covering convoys for Greece and Malta. More troops and 18 fighters are brought to Malta.
Axis Politics Soviet-German pacts on frontiers in Eastern Europe and on trade are signed in Berlin and Moscow. Food and raw materials are to be exchanged for industrial equipment. The economic benefits to Germany of the agreement with the Soviet Union will continue until the very day that Operation Barbarossa begins.
Albania The Greek forces take Klisura after the four Italian divisions in that sector have been pulled back.

11 January 1941

Mediterranean The British cruisers *Southampton* and *Gloucester* leave Malta for Gibraltar. *Gloucester* is damaged and *Southampton* sunk by a Stuka attack.
Germany, Planning Hitler issues Directive 22 outlining his plans for limiting British gains in the Mediterranean. It includes the order for the establishment of the Afrika Korps.

12 January 1941

Malta British aircraft based on Malta attack Catania airfield on Sicily in an attempt to prevent German and Italian planes from attacking Malta while temporary repairs are carried out on the crippled aircraft carrier *Illustrious*.

14-15 January 1941

Greece General Wavell and Air Marshal Longmore are in Athens for talks with Prime Minister Metaxas and the Greek Commander in Chief, General Papagos. The Greeks ask for nine divisions and a substantial air component to be sent to support their forces. The Greeks have the equivalent of 13 divisions facing the larger Italian force in Albania and four facing the Bulgarians. At this stage the Germans have 12 divisions in Rumania and more in Bulgaria. To meet such a force Wavell is able to offer only a small contribution now, but more later.

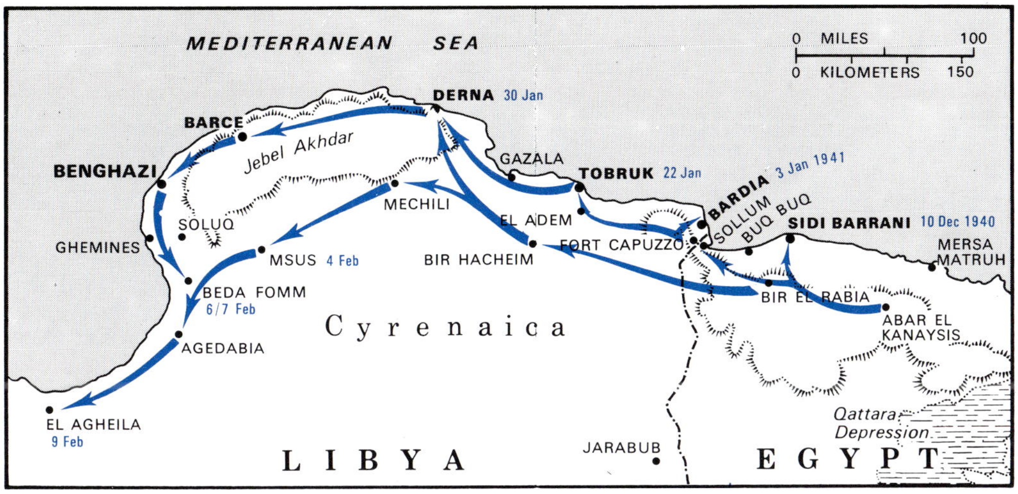

Above: Map showing the advance of British units from Egypt to El Agheila.

16-19 January 1941

Mediterranean There are German and Italian attacks on Malta and especially the damaged carrier *Illustrious.* On 16 January a force of about 80 Stukas attacks and, although 10 are shot down, they hit the carrier again as well as the cruiser *Perth.* The harbor facilities are also badly hit. On 18 January the attacks are repeated but the island's airfields are the principal target. On 19 January slight damage is done to *Illustrious.* On 23 January the emergency repairs are complete and the ship is able to make for Alexandria with 24 knots available if necessary. Later the *Illustrious* will proceed to the United States for full repairs. Even as a neutral power the United States is providing Britain with essential support services for the Royal Navy.

19 January 1941

East Africa The British forces in the Sudan begin their offensive against the Italians in Eritrea. The British force is led by General Platt and includes 4th and 5th Indian Divisions and units of the Sudan Defense Force. The Italian troops in the various border positions amount to 17,000 men and are led by General Frusci. There is the equivalent of four more divisions in the interior of the country. Kassala is taken immediately.

19-20 January 1941

Axis Politics Hitler and Mussolini meet at the Berghof. Mussolini is unwilling to accept German help in Albania but is prepared to accept some aid in Africa. Hitler says that he will attack Greece if it seems that Britain is going to come in.

20-24 January 1941

Rumania, Home Front There is a revolt of the Iron Guard which is put down on the order of General Antonescu with the help of the Rumanian and German armies.

21 January 1941

North Africa The 6th Australian Division begins the attack on Tobruk. The town is already isolated by the advance of the British 7th Armored Brigade which is heading for Martuba and Mechili. The southeast corner of the Italian position is assaulted and after a heavy bombardment the Italian defense is quickly broken. Fort Palastrino is taken later in the day and General Mannella also captured.

22 January 1941

North Africa The remainder of the garrison of Tobruk surrenders after demolishing some of the harbor facilities. There are 27,000 prisoners. Much equipment is also captured and in fact it will prove possible to put the port into service fairly quickly. The Allied casualties have been less than 500 men.
East Africa In Eritrea the Italian forces are falling back toward Agordat in the face of Platt's attacks. There is also some skirmishing along the border between Kenya and Italian Somaliland.

23 January 1941

Balkans, Politics The Bulgarian prime minister agrees to bring his country into the Tripartite Pact as soon as military arrangements with the Germans can be completed.

24 January 1941

North Africa There is a brief tank engagement near Mechili. The British 4th Armored Brigade and the Italian force suffer about equal losses before the Italians retire. The Italian forces in Libya are now split, with one group around Mechili and one on the coast at Derna. These positions do not give each other any support. The 19th Australian Brigade is moving on Derna while Mechili is to be encircled by 4th and 7th Armored Brigades.

26 January 1941

North Africa The Italians pull out of Mechili. The British blocking force from 4th Armored Brigade is carelessly handled and does nothing to prevent their escape.
Albania There is an Italian counterattack near Klisura which has a slight local success.

27 January 1941

Albania Ciano and other senior members of the Italian government arrive in Albania to take up active army commands. This bizarre measure is presumably designed to boost morale.
East Africa The British advance into Eritrea reaches Agordat and a battle gradually develops in this area.

29 January 1941

Greece, Politics Prime Minister Metaxas dies. His successor is Alexander Korizis. Korizis is less decisive than Metaxas and does not have as good a relationship with the Greek Commander in Chief, General Papagos. Although he is, if anything, more ready to accept British help this change does not contribute to the smooth running of the discussions with the British.
North Africa The Italians pull out of Derna and begin a precipitate retreat toward the west along the coast road.
East Africa Allied forces cross the border from Kenya into Italian Somaliland. General Cunningham is in command and his forces are 11th and 12th East African Divisions and 1st South African Division. The main attack will not begin until 10 February.

29 January-27 March 1941

Allied Planning There are secret staff talks in Washington between British and American representatives. They produce conclusions code

Below: A British 25-pounder field gun bombards Italian positions at Tobruk, January 1941, preparatory to an infantry assault.

Above: Australian troops in captured Italian tanks prepare to enter Tobruk, on fire after an RAF raid, January 1941.

named ABC1 which state that Allied policy in the event of war with Germany and Japan should be to put the defeat of Germany first. In March an American mission visits Britain to select sites for bases for naval and air forces in case of war with Germany. Preliminary work to equip these bases will begin later in the year. The talks mark an important stage in the development of cooperation between the US and Britain. As well as their important decisions they accustom the staffs to working with each other.

30 January 1941

North Africa Derna is taken by the 19th Australian Brigade.

31 January 1941

Germany, Planning After consultations with army and army group staffs the Army High Command has now prepared the first operational plans for the German invasion of the Soviet Union. The deployment plan for the forces is also ready. These schemes are presented to Hitler at a conference on 3 February. He again tries to draw attention away from the central drive toward Moscow which the Army planners think essential.

February 1941

Battle of the Atlantic Although the operational U-Boat strength is at its lowest mark of the war at 22 vessels, the sinkings increase this month to 39 ships of 196,800 tons. Aircraft are also more effective, sinking 27 vessels. The total Allied shipping loss is 403,400 tons. More than half of the U-Boat successes are stragglers from convoys or independents. This reflects the growing strength and deterrent effect of the convoy escorts. On 6 February Hitler issues orders confirming the aims of the offensive. There are changes in the British organization. On 7 February the Western Approaches Command HQ is moved to Liverpool where it will be in closer touch with the organizations controlling merchant shipping and better able to supervise the training of the escort forces. On the 17th Admiral Noble takes over the command.

British Air Operations Among the targets for the RAF this month are Dusseldorf, Wilhelmshaven, Brest and Cologne. Only 1400 tons of bombs are dropped in these operations – a mere fraction of later efforts.

The Blitz The German attacks continue. Their range of targets includes heavy attacks on Swansea for the first time. The civilian casualties are 789 dead and 1068 injured.

1 February 1941

East Africa In Eritrea Agordat falls to Platt's forces after a vigorous three-day battle. Frusci's troops are falling back to the mountain positions around Keren after suffering some losses. To the south Barentu has also been captured by the Indian troops.

United States, Command There is a major reorganization of the US Navy. It is now to be formed in three fleets, the Atlantic, the Pacific and the Asiatic. Admiral King is appointed to command the new Atlantic Fleet. There is to be a significant strengthening of the forces in the Atlantic.

Japan, Home Front Japan announces that it will be necessary to introduce rice rationing.

1-14 February 1941

War at Sea The heavy cruiser *Admiral Hipper* goes on a commerce-destroying raid in the north Atlantic from Brest. The convoy SLS-64 of 19 ships is attacked on 12 February. Seven of the ships are sunk. One independent is also attacked. *Hipper* then returns to Brest.

2 February 1941

North Africa The Australian forces have already advanced well to the west of Derna on the coast and are discovering that the Italians are withdrawing at speed. Wavell agrees with O'Connor that 7th Armored Division should be sent hurrying across the center of Cyrenaica in an attempt to cut the Italians off. Supplies are being assembled to support this move but because the Italian retreat is so rapid the advance will have to start before the preparations are complete.

East Africa The British carrier *Formidable*, on her way to the Mediterranean to replace the damaged *Illustrious*, sends its planes to attack the harbor installations at Mogadishu.

3 February-22 March 1941

German Raiders The German battlecruisers *Scharnhorst* and *Gneisenau* go on a commerce-destroying expedition in the Atlantic under the command of Admiral Lutjens. On the night of 3 February they pass through the Denmark Strait. On 8 February they approach the convoy HX-106 but do not attack because the escort includes the old battleship *Ramillies*. Similarly, on 8 March SL-67 escapes because the battleship *Malaya* is present. Hitler has ordered that no risk of damage to the ships is to be run if this can be avoided. On 22 February five ships from a dispersed convoy are sunk and on 15-16 March 16 more are destroyed. During this encounter the British battleship *Rodney* comes up but cannot close the range and engage.

After this the British hunt is extensive but the Germans reach French waters on 22 March. As well as the dispersing convoys found, one other ship has been sunk, bringing the total to 22 ships of 115,600 tons. Considerable disruption to the British convoy system has been caused, but as ever the U-boats are the main threat.

4 February 1941

North Africa The British advance across Cyrenaica has now begun. Msus is taken and the forces then move toward Antelat. In the north the Italian retreat is continuing.

East Africa The British forces begin to attack the strong Italian positions around Keren. There are 30,000 Italian troops in this area. In the first phase of the battle, which lasts until 7 February, the 11th Indian Brigade manages to take Cameron Ridge but is thrown back from other positions by Italian counterattacks.

5 February 1941

North Africa The first British armored units reach the coast road near Beda Fomm with armored cars and light tanks after their drive across Cyrenaica. Heavier tank units are following rapidly. The retreating Italian columns are engaged and about 5000 men are captured. In the north the Australians take Barce.

6 February 1941

North Africa Benghazi is taken by Australian units following the Italian retreat. The Italian forces are streaming back along the coast road to Beda Fomm and during the day they make desperate attacks on the British blocking force there. These attacks are repulsed with heavy loss but the small British force is compelled to give some ground.

7 February 1941

North Africa Large-scale surrenders begin at Beda Fomm after the Italians have made fruitless attempts to break through to continue their retreat. Eventually about 25,000 more Italians will be taken, along with 200 guns and 120 tanks. Since the start of the campaign two months previously a force of no more than two divisions has destroyed 10 Italian divisions and taken 130,000 prisoners for the loss of 555 dead and 1400 wounded. Many of the British vehicles now desperately need repairs. This will have an important effect later. In the evening Agedabia falls to the British forces.

8 February 1941

Balkans, Politics The German and Bulgarian staffs agree on the detailed arrangements for German troops to enter Bulgaria.

Above: Field Marshal Lord Wavell, Commander in Chief Middle East.

9 February 1941

North Africa The British advance comes to a halt at El Agheila. There is little Italian opposition to prevent a further move, but Wavell is being compelled to withdraw troops which will be sent to Greece. He is also responsible for the campaign in East Africa and for making some provision for the defense of Palestine. In the near future, this will demand more of his attention because of German activity in Iraq and Syria.
Mediterranean In an audacious attack the battleship *Malaya* and the battlecruiser *Renown* from Force H bombard the harbor at Genoa. The carrier *Ark Royal* also takes part in the operation, sending aircraft to attack Leghorn and La Spezia. Five ships in Genoa are sunk and 18 damaged. The Italians fail to attack the British force.

10 February 1941

Britain, Strategy Churchill formally instructs Wavell to regard help for Greece as having a higher priority than exploiting the success in Africa. He mentions the important effect on American opinion of being seen to fulfill promises to smaller nations. Colonel Bill Donovan has recently been on a tour of the Balkans on Roosevelt's behalf and is known to value the idea of fighting the Germans there. The British also hope to make a good impression on Turkey and perhaps even establish a Balkan coalition against Hitler.
East Africa The attacks of 4th Indian Division at Keren go on with renewed effort. The fighting is fierce over the next two days but Italian counterattacks prevent the Indian troops from making any gains. A long lull follows for the rest of the month while the British commanders bring up more forces and supplies for the formal offensive which will be necessary to break the Italian positions.

11 February 1941

East Africa General Cunningham's forces extend their advance from Kenya into the Italian Somaliland and take Afmadu.
France, Politics Darlan is nominated to be successor and deputy to Pétain. He is to hold office as Foreign Minister, Minister of the Interior and Minister of Information as well as his rank as Commander in Chief of the Navy.

12 February 1941

North Africa General Rommel arrives in Tripoli. Nominally more important is the appointment of the new Italian Commander in Chief for Libya, General Gariboldi. The first units of what will become the Africa Korps begin to land at Tripoli on 14 February. The advance guard is a battalion of light infantry and an antitank unit. Field Marshal Kesselring is in Rome as the German representative.
Soviet Command General Zhukov is appointed Chief of the General Staff and Deputy Commissar for Defense. General Meretskov is now to lead the Red Army's training directorate.

13 February 1941

East Africa The carrier *Formidable* attacks Massawa. This raid is repeated on 21 February and 1 March because the *Formidable* cannot pass through the Suez Canal to join the Mediterranean Fleet owing to mines which have been dropped by German planes. These are being cleared.

14 February 1941

Balkans, Politics Hitler meets the Yugoslav Premier Cvetkovič and his foreign minister at Berchtesgaden to urge them to join the Tripartite Pact. They still refuse to commit their country, in the hope that Hitler will soon be preoccupied with relations with the Soviet Union and that they can get aid from Britain and the USA.
East Africa The 22nd East African Brigade takes Kismayu with fire support from the cruiser *Shropshire* and other smaller vessels. Elsewhere in Somaliland the British advance is also rapid.

16 February 1941

East Africa In Italian Somaliland the 1st South African Brigade begins an important battle to seize crossings over the lower reaches of the river Juba.

17 February 1941

Balkans, Politics Under German pressure Turkey and Bulgaria sign a friendship agreement by which Turkey accepts that the movement of German troops through Bulgaria is not an act of war. This more or less confirms that there is no possibility of Turkey being persuaded to ally with Britain.

18 February 1941

East Africa In Abyssinia South African forces advancing from Kenya attack the town of Mega. It is quickly captured along with 1000 prisoners.

19 February 1941

East Africa Emperor Haile Selassie, who was brought back to Abyssinia in January to help organize resistance to the Italians, arrives at Dangilla along with Wingate's Gideon Force. During the next two weeks they harass the Italian troops around Bahrdar Giorgis and Burye

Below: Italian troops man a sandbagged defensive position in the wastes of the North African desert, early 1941.

Above: A Handley Page Halifax B-II four-engine bomber of No. 35 Squadron, Bomber Command. This aircraft was lost over Nuremberg in 1942.

with considerable success. The Italians have four brigades in the area and the Gideon Force is only 1700 strong.

19-23 February 1941

Greece On 19 February Eden, Dill (the Chief of the General Staff) and the local commanders, Wavell and Cunningham, meet in Cairo to discuss whether they can send help to Greece and if so how much. The British political leaders are strongly in favor of sending all that can be spared and Wavell, the military commander who is responsible, believes that this can be done effectively and is, therefore, prepared to recommend it.

On 22 February the British leaders are in Athens to meet King George and Premier Korizis. On 23 February the Greeks agree to accept a force which at this stage is intended to be 100,000 men with suitable artillery and tank support. The Greeks are very reluctant to accept anything less since it would not be enough to fight the Germans off and would only encourage them to attack. The disposition of the British and Greek forces is also discussed. The British prefer a position along the line of the Aliakmon River but the Greeks are unwilling to give up the territory which this line does not cover. No final decision is made – a serious omission in the light of later events.

20 February 1941

North Africa The British and German patrols make contact for the first time in the desert, near El Agheila. The first brief action is on the 24th.

21 February 1941

Soviet Union, Politics Changes in the Central Committee of the Communist Party are announced. Among those to be dismissed are the foreign minister and former ambassador to the United States, Maxim Litvinov.

23 February 1941

East Africa In Somaliland the main Italian forces defending the line of the Juba River have been defeated. General Cunningham's troops are now advancing very rapidly toward Mogadishu. There is a small Free French landing in Eritrea.

25 February 1941

East Africa Mogadishu is taken by the British forces after an advance of over 230 miles in the past three days. Considerable stocks of fuel and other supplies are captured.

Mediterranean The Italian light cruiser *Diaz* is sunk by a British submarine while forming part of the escort for a Naples-Tripoli convoy.

26 February 1941

Balkans, Politics Eden and Dill continue their Middle East mission with a visit to Ankara, but they get no real response to their efforts to interest the Turks in an alliance.

27 February 1941

War at Sea The Italian merchant cruiser *Ramb I* is sunk by the New Zealand cruiser *Leander* off the Maldive Islands. *Ramb I* sailed from Massawa on 20 February.

28 February 1941

East Africa Asmara, Eritrea, is bombed by British planes. The RAF has now established superiority in this area.

March 1941

Battle of the Atlantic The threat posed by the German attacks is formally recognized by Churchill when he issues his Battle of the Atlantic Directive on 6 March. Measures are immediately put in hand to strengthen the British forces and a high-level Battle of the Atlantic Committee begins meeting to monitor progress. It includes political, military and scientific leaders and will be important in bringing about better coordination between these specialities. Although enemy submarines and aircraft both sink 41 ships during the month and although the total of 139 ships of 529,700 tons is comparable with the worst times of the previous German offensive in 1917, there is some compensation in the sinking by the escort forces of six U-Boats, one fifth of the operational fleet (*see* 7 and 16-17 March).

Churchill's later comment on the events of the following months is most revealing: 'How willingly would I have exchanged a full-scale attempt at invasion for this shapeless, measureless peril, expressed in charts, curves and statistics.'

British Air Operations The Halifax bomber comes into service with Bomber Command. Among the targets for the RAF this month are Kiel, Hamburg, Bremen and Brest, of special interest because of the entry of the German battlecruisers later in the month. Bomber Command flies about 1900 sorties, 39 aircraft fail to return and 36 more crash.

The Blitz The strength of the German attacks increases again with the coming of better weather. London is the target for three major raids. Merseyside is attacked twice, and Glasgow, Bristol and Plymouth are also heavily hit. In the first three months of the year the Luftwaffe has lost 90 bombers. The British night fighters and AA defenses are becoming stronger.

1 March 1941

United States, Preparations The US Navy forms a Support Force for the Atlantic Fleet. The main part of this unit is made up from three destroyer squadrons of 27 ships.

Balkans, Politics Prime Minister Filov brings Bulgaria into the Tripartite Pact.

North Africa Kuffra in southeast Libya is taken by a Free French force from Chad. Colonel Leclerc is in command. The French force has received some help from units of the British Long Range Desert Group.

2 March 1941

Balkans Following the treaty agreement on the previous day German troops begin to move into Bulgaria in force. These German units are part of List's Twelfth Army, which will be used to invade Greece.

4 March 1941

Norway There is a British Commando raid on the Lofoten Islands. The 500-strong force is carried by naval units which include two light cruisers and five destroyers. Ten ships are sunk in the operation and 215 German prisoners taken. There are also 300 Norwegian volunteers who are taken to Britain. The operation is a success but the Germans take fierce reprisals when the British force withdraws. Many members of the Norwegian resistance movement do not approve of such raids for this reason.

Balkans Hitler meets Prince Paul of Yugoslavia secretly at Berchtesgaden to ask him once again to join the Tripartite Pact. Paul returns to Yugoslavia convinced that he must decide very soon between Britain and Germany. Talks in the next few days convince him that Britain has little help to offer.

General Wilson, who is to command the British force being prepared for Greece, arrives in Athens to arrange the final details with the Greek staff. A major convoy is about to leave Alexandria with the first large contingent. The British have only just discovered that the Greek forces in Macedonia have not retired to the Aliakmon Line and will not be able to persuade them to do so because of the damage to morale that would result if territory is obviously given up without a fight after the German move into Bulgaria. Although understandable, this is not a very realistic attitude. Wilson is further hindered by the Greek insistence that he remains incognito inside the British Embassy in order not to provoke the Germans. In fact the German consulate in Piraeus overlooks the port area which will be used to land the British forces, so they are well aware what is happening.

6 March 1941

Holland, Resistance Following strikes during February over the arrest of Jews and attempts to force workers to jobs in Germany the Germans condemn 18 Dutch resistance members. These are the first such victims in Holland. The Communists have played a notable part in organizing the strikes.

7 March 1941

Battle of the Atlantic The British destroyer *Wolverine* sinks the German submarine *U.47* in a convoy engagement. The *U.47* is commanded by the ace captain, Prien, one of three leading U-Boat captains who will be killed or captured in the next few weeks.

9 March 1941

Albania The Italians launch an offensive along the front between the Rivers Devoli and Vijosë. There are a few local successes initially. The Italians have assembled 12 divisions for the attack and Mussolini himself has crossed to Albania to supervise its progress. There is little subtlety in the tactical plan and much that is reminiscent of World War I. The Greek intelligence of the direction of the attack is good and their defenses well prepared.

10 March 1941

East Africa Since taking Mogadishu General Platt's troops have advanced 600 miles north from there into Abyssinia and only now come into contact with any Italian forces. Their encounter is at Dagabur, only 100 miles south of Jijiga.

11 March 1941

United States, Politics The Lend-Lease Bill becomes law when signed by President Roosevelt. It passed the House on 8 February by 260 votes to 165, and passed the Senate on 8 March by 60 to 13. Important amendments have been made by Congress. A time limit has been placed on the operation of the act – until June 1943 – but a motion originally passed in the House forbidding US warships to give convoy protection to foreign ships has been defeated. Also to be allowed are transfers of ships to other countries solely on the presidential authority without reference to Congress.

Essentially the act means that Britain can continue to order American materials without necessarily having the cash to pay for them. They are to be paid for after the war. At this stage it makes little difference to the quantity of supplies going to Britain. British war production is greater than America's and will continue to be so until some time after Pearl Harbor. Most of the items supplied for the rest of 1941 will in fact be paid for in cash. There is little difference too in the quantity supplied when compared with 1940 but in some commodities, such as food and fuel oil, the United States' contribution will be of very great value.

Although justly described as one of the most generous acts of any nation's history, Lend-Lease is not entirely disinterested. Britain is compelled to go on paying cash for as long as this is possible and this means that many British assets in the United States must be sold at well below their true value. Britain is also forbidden to export anything containing materials supplied under Lend-Lease nor can items wholly produced in Britain be exported if equivalent items are being supplied under Lend-Lease. These restrictions and the keenness with which they are enforced will do much to destroy the little that remains of Britain's export trade. Although there will be some relaxation of the rules in 1944, a considerable barrier will have been placed against a British postwar economic recovery.

12 March 1941

United States, Politics President Roosevelt presents an Appropriations Bill for Lend-Lease to Congress for $7,000,000,000. It passes into law on 27 March.

13 March 1941

Albania The Italian attacks toward Klisura continue but are now being held comfortably by the Greek defense.

Germany, Planning Hitler issues a directive for the invasion of the Soviet Union which gives administrative control of captured territory to the SS. This and later orders concerning the treatment of commissars and ordinary prisoners will lead to many dreadful atrocities. It also ruins the previously quite good chance that the Germans will receive worthwhile support from those who have reason to bear Stalin's government no love.

14 March 1941

East Africa Wingate and Haile Selassie establish new headquarters at Burye. The main Italian force in their area is now at Debra Markos. The Italians are negotiating with a local chief called Ras Hailu and are preparing an attack with him.

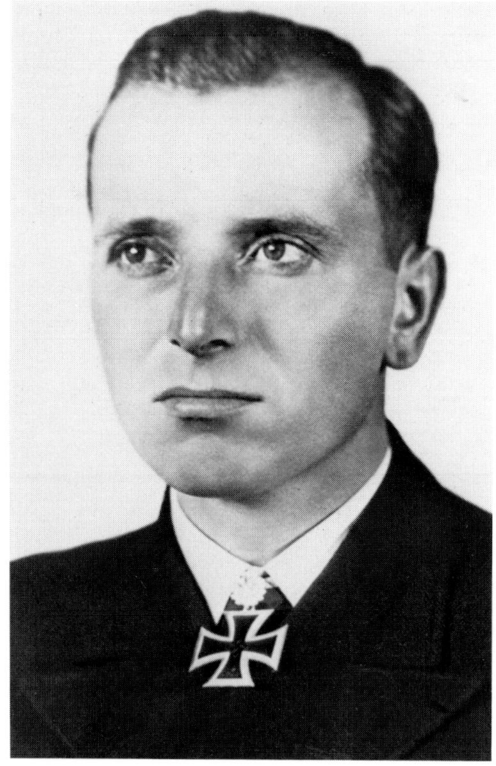

Above: U-Boat ace Otto Kretschmer, captured by the British, 27 March 1941.

15 March 1941

East Africa The British attacks toward Keren, Eritrea, are renewed. Both 4th and 5th Indian Divisions are now involved. The first attacks by 4th Indian go fairly well but not all the gains can be held.

United States, Politics In an important speech Roosevelt promises that the United States will supply Britain and the Allies 'aid until victory' and that there will be an 'end of compromise with tyranny.'

16 March 1941

East Africa A small British force arriving by sea from Aden in two light cruisers, two destroyers and seven other vessels lands and captures the port of Berbera. The capture takes only a little time and immediately afterward they begin to advance inland. There are also British gains in the battle around Keren. The 5th Indian Division, which has been unable to advance on the first day, now takes the Dologorodoc position south of the Keren road. The next five days are dominated by Italian efforts to mount counterattacks.

Albania The Italian offensive is called off. In the past few days they have incurred 12,000 casualties and taken absolutely no ground. However, the Greeks have been compelled by the Italian offensive to do nothing to strengthen their forces which face the German threat elsewhere.

16-17 March 1941

Battle of the Atlantic Kretschmer's *U.99* and Schepke's *U.100* are both sunk in a convoy battle. These sinkings, combined with the loss of Prien 10 days previously, are a severe blow to the morale of the U-Boat crews as well as a serious military loss because of their unusual ability. The sinking of *U.100* is symbolic as being achieved with the aid of new radar equipment. Kretschmer is captured after his ship is sunk.

17 March 1941

East Africa General Cunningham's northward advance reaches Jijiga which has been evacuated by the Italians.

19 March 1941

Balkans, Politics The Germans repeat their demands on Yugoslavia. They now give the Yugoslavs five days to make a decision.

Battle of the Atlantic The British battleship *Malaya* is seriously damaged by a torpedo from *U.106* when with a convoy in the Atlantic. The *Malaya* goes to New York for repairs – the first major British warship to receive such help.

20 March 1941

Balkans, Politics In a meeting of the Royal Council in Belgrade it becomes clear that Regent Paul is ready to agree to Hitler's demand that Yugoslavia join the Tripartite Pact and allow free passage of German troops. Four ministers resign in protest.

East Africa The British force advancing from Berbera takes Hargeisa.

21 March 1941

East Africa Troops of the 11th African Division attack Italian positions in the Marda Pass west of Jijiga. After some resistance the Italians fall back despite the strength of their position.

22 March 1941

East Africa In the advance west from Jijiga the Allied forces overrun another defensive position at the Babile Pass.

24 March 1941

North Africa El Agheila is recaptured from the British by Rommell's forces. General O'Connor and his experienced desert troops have been withdrawn and General Neame has been left to hold Libya with the understrength and inexperienced 2nd Armored Division, 9th Australian Division and an Indian Brigade. The tanks available are mostly old and more or less worn out. Collectively the Allied units have neither the desert experience of O'Connor's veterans nor the professionalism of Rommel's troops. Rommel has one German division, 5th Light, with a strong tank component and part of four Italian divisions. Rommel has been forbidden to attack by the German High Command and has been told that he will receive no extra forces. He will ignore his instructions.

Above: An Australian 25-pounder gun crew practise firing in the North African desert, 1941. It is unlikely that they are in action.

Below: Vice-Admiral Sir James Somerville (right), RN commander in the western Mediterranean.

25 March 1941

Balkans, Politics The Yugoslav Prime Minister Cvetkovič and the Foreign Minister Cincar-Markovič sign the Tripartite Pact in Vienna. The reality of the situation and the influence of German pressure is made only too clear by the cold tone of the occasion. Germany agrees to respect Yugoslav sovereignty and not to demand passage for troops. There are disturbances in Belgrade when the agreement is known.

East Africa The 5th Indian Division renews its advance toward the Italian blocking position on the Keren road.

26 March 1941

Mediterranean A night attack by explosive boats of a special Italian unit penetrates Suda Bay in Crete and sinks one tanker and cripples the British cruiser *York*.

East Africa The British forces occupy Harar, Abyssinia.

26-29 March 1941

Mediterranean Battle of Cape Matapan. Following claims by German aircraft to have sunk two of the British Mediterranean Fleet's battleships and with the promise of German air support and reconnaissance, Admiral Iachino leads the Italian Fleet in a sortie into the Aegean to disrupt the British convoys to Greece. He has one battleship, six heavy cruisers, two light cruisers and 13 destroyers. They leave port on 26 March. On 27 March the British forces set out. Admiral Pridham-Wippell leads four light cruisers and four destroyers from the Piraeus and Admiral Cunningham the main body of three battleships, one carrier and nine destroyers from Alexandria.

On 28 March there is a long-range engagement between Pridham-Wippell's force and some of the Italian cruisers. The Italians suspect that a large British force is present and begin to retire. In the afternoon Swordfish aircraft from the *Formidable* attack the Italian ships, hitting the battleship *Vittorio Veneto* and the cruiser *Pola*. The *Vittorio Veneto* is able to proceed at reduced speed but the *Pola* is stopped. In the evening Iachino sends the cruisers *Zara* and *Fiume* and four destroyers back to help the *Pola*. The British ships are pressing on in pursuit hoping to come up with the damaged *Vittorio Veneto* when, during the night, they find the three Italian cruisers and their escorts on their radar. The British approach to close range, without being sighted in return, and in a brief gun battle the cruisers and two of the destroyers are shot to pieces and sunk before they have the chance to fire a shot.

In the whole operation the British lose two aircraft. The training of the British forces pays off superbly and the steady process of British success over the previous months has now achieved a position of almost complete moral superiority which will inhibit any further Italian initiative.

26 March-4 April 1941

East Africa The Italian forces and their new local allies attack Wingate's Gideon force around Burye – they are beaten off, however.

27 March 1941

Balkans, Politics There is a coup in Yugoslavia. The council of Regency and Prince Paul are deposed and the 17-year-old King Peter takes over nominal charge of the government. The rising is led by air force officers and their Chief of Staff, General Simovič, who becomes the new head of government. British agents have had a hand in bringing the rising about. The change is very popular among the Serbian sections of the population (almost all the leaders of the armed forces are Serbian) but less so among the Croats. In an immediate angry response to the change of government Hitler issues Directive 25 which orders planning for the invasion of Yugoslavia to begin. It is to be mounted as soon as possible and the invasion of Greece is to take place at the same time. Hitler accepts that it may be necessary to defer Barbarossa to allow these new operations to take place.

East Africa The Allied advance clears the Italian road blocks in the Keren position. The Italian force begins to withdraw toward Asmara. The Indian divisions have lost 4000 casualties in the Keren battles and the Italians 3000 dead as well as many wounded.

28 March 1941

Balkans, Allied Planning The British Chief of Staff, General Dill, is in Belgrade for talks with the Yugoslav authorities, but there is little he can offer them and no agreements of any importance are reached.

29 March 1941

East Africa Cunningham's South African troops take Diredawa, Abyssinia, in their advance west to Addis Ababa. The local Italian population has appealed to the British for help because of atrocities committed by deserters from the native forces after the Italian part of the garrison has withdrawn.

30 March 1941

North Africa Correctly discerning that the British forces are weakly dispersed in positions which prevent mutual support, Rommel brings his forces forward from El Agheila toward Mersa Brega. Only part of 2nd Armored Division is ready to oppose him. The bulk of the Australian Division is near Benghazi and the remainder is back at Tobruk.

Germany, Planning Hitler approves the army plans for the attack on Yugoslavia, to begin on 6 April. Hitler also speaks to a conference of 250 top commanders who will have important parts in the Barbarossa operation. He makes it plain to them that the war in the east is to be conducted along different lines to any previous operation. There is to be no talk of proper 'knightly' behaviour and commissars and Communists are to be treated with utmost severity.

United States, Politics The United States takes German, Italian and Danish ships into 'protective custody,' effectively confiscating them.

31 March 1941

North Africa Rommel's forces attack the positions of infantry units from the British 2nd Armored Division at Mersa Brega. A fierce battle develops, in which the British come off worst but are able to halt the German advance for the moment. The few tanks with 2nd Armored Division do not join the battle.

Mediterranean The British cruiser *Bonaventure* is sunk by a torpedo-boat attack in the Eastern Mediterranean.

April 1941

Battle of the Atlantic The German U-Boat fleet now has 32 operational boats which means that about 20 are on patrol at any one time. There are a further 81 boats on trial or in training in the Baltic. In the Atlantic the trend is for the U-Boats to hunt farther west looking for unescorted ships to attack but the British are countering this by providing escorts as far as 35 degrees West (more than halfway across). Fuelling bases for the British escorts have now been established on Iceland. The number of aircraft based on Iceland has also been increased to give even more protection. On 15 April RAF Coastal Command is brought under the operational control of the Admiralty which will lead to an increase in its effectiveness in the battle against the U-Boats. This month the U-Boats sink 43 ships of 249,000 tons but only 10 of these are from convoys. The only convoy battles are round SC-26 and HX-121. It is a good month for German aircraft – they sink 116 ships in all theaters. The total Allied loss from all causes is 195 ships of 687,000 tons.

The Blitz There are two very heavy German attacks on London on 16/17 April and 19/20 April with about 700 planes being involved in each raid. Other targets are Plymouth, Coventry and Birmingham. Some Luftwaffe units are withdrawn for service in the Balkans.

British Air Operations Brest is attacked seven times by RAF bombers and among the other targets for Bomber Command are Kiel, Wilhelmshaven, Emden and Mannheim.

1 April 1941

North Africa The British withdraw from Mersa Brega, abandoning almost the only available defensive position before the wide open spaces of the Cyrenaica Plateau.

East Africa Asmara, the captial of Eritrea, is taken by the British forces led by General Platt.

1-3 April 1941

Iraq, Politics On 1 April a coup begins and by 3 April a new government has been installed. The Regent Faisal escapes to Transjordan. The coup is led by the nationalist politician Rashid Ali and a group of officers calling themselves the 'Golden Square.' They are opposed to the British presence in the country. The British react quickly and soon troops are being sent from India and the Middle East to ensure access to the vital oil supplies.

2 April 1941

North Africa The German advance begins to gather momentum. Agedabia is taken and the Germans now have the option of striking out across Cyrenaica on various routes or following the coast. In fact they will split their force and follow almost all these options. The German units divide into three columns taking two main routes to Msus and Mechili. Italian forces and a small German unit are sent along the coast to Benghazi under a German commander. Rommel flies from column to column in his scout plane, urging the advance on.

Wavell comes up to the front from Cairo and decides that O'Connor must be brought back from convalescence to replace Neame. In fact when he arrives O'Connor agrees to act only as an adviser. The exiguous British tank force is split up on Wavell's order and is further weakened by breakdowns, giving the Germans every opportunity to continue their advance.

Mediterranean The carrier *Ark Royal* flies a small contingent of Hurricane fighters to Malta.

Hungary, Politics Prime Minister Count Teleki commits suicide because he does not wish to lead his country in collaboration with Germany. The regent, Admiral Horthy, and the new prime minister, László Bárdossy, continue to work with the Germans.

United States, Politics Roosevelt orders the transfer of 10 coastguard cutters to the Royal Navy. These are very useful vessels for escort work, having a long range and good seakeeping qualities – superior in almost every way to the Royal Navy's own escort corvettes. They will be in RN service by June.

Below: A British oil tanker blazes furiously after being torpedoed in the North Atlantic. The crew are unlikely to have survived.

4 April 1941

North Africa Rommel's offensive develops further. There are three main lines of advance. Benghazi, on the coast, is taken by the Italian forces and the accompanying German battalion. The force heading for Msus is making only slow progress but the third group, the most southerly, with part of 5th Light and the Italian Ariete Division, is going well toward Mechili.
United States, Politics Roosevelt agrees to allow RN warships to be repaired in the US. Among the first ships to benefit from this order are the battleships *Malaya* and *Resolution*. RN warships are also to be allowed to refuel in the US when on combat missions.
German Raiders The German raider *Thor* meets and sinks the British AMC *Voltaire* in the central Atlantic.

5 April 1941

Yugoslavia A Soviet-Yugoslav Nonaggression Pact is agreed and is signed in the early hours of the 6th but is too late to have any effect in halting the imminent German attack.
North Africa The Axis advance continues. On the coast Barce is taken while inland Tengeder falls and Mechili is threatened.

6 April 1941

Balkans German forces invade Yugoslavia and Greece. The attack begins with advances by List's Twelfth Army from Bulgaria and with bombing raids on Belgrade and targets in Greece. The initial forces from the Twelfth Army will be joined over the next few days by Kleist's First Panzer Group also part of Twelfth Army, Weich's Second Army and other German, Hungarian and Italian forces. As well as infantry forces the Germans employ six armored and four motorized divisions. The Yugoslav Army has 28 infantry and three cavalry divisions but these are widely dispersed in a cordon defense of the frontier and only five infantry and two cavalry units will do any real fighting. The Germans also have overwhelming air support of around 1000 planes from Fliegerkorps IV and VIII. Apart from the forces facing the Italians in Albania, in Greece the Allies have seven weak Greek divisions, the New Zealand Division, part of the 6th Australian Division and one British armored brigade. There are about 80 RAF planes. General Wilson commands the British and Anzac forces which are based on positions known as the Aliakmon Line. There is a mixed tank and infantry force holding the route into Greece from Yugoslavia by the so-called Monastir Gap. Some of the Greek force are also on the Aliakmon Line but rather more are in frontier positions known as the Metaxas Line in Macedonia and Thrace.

The main German attack on the first day falls on these advanced Greek troops. One German corps, XXX, attacks the center and right of the line. A second corps attacks the left of the line but sends more of its force into Yugoslavia toward Strumica. The third corps moves into Yugoslavia farther north heading for Skopje. There is heavy fighting on the Greek border but the Yugoslav frontier is crossed easily by the Germans. During the night of the 6th there is an important air raid on the port of Piraeus in which a British ammunition ship blows up, sinking many other vessels and extensively damaging the port installations.
North Africa The German and Italian advance is maintained. On the coast the Australian Division is beginning to pull back to Tobruk from Derna. General O'Connor has now arrived at the front to advise Neame but both are captured during the night by a German patrol. O'Connor, the architect of Beda Fomm, is an especially serious loss.
War at Sea The German battlecruiser *Gneisenau* is badly hit by a British torpedo plane while on exercise just outside the port of Brest. On the night of 10/11 April the same ship is hit another four times by bombs during a British raid. The *Scharnhorst* is also in the port undergoing engine repairs. Neither battlecruiser will be able to join the *Bismarck* in its cruise in May.
East Africa Addis Ababa, Abyssinia, is taken in the continuing Allied advance. The Duke of Aosta is withdrawing to the north toward Amba Alagi with the remains of the main Italian force. General Frusci is in tactical command of these troops. Elsewhere in the country the Italians have about 80,000 more men. General Nasi commands in the Gondar area with half this force and General Gazzera in the south and southwest with the rest. The port of Massawa in Eritrea is attacked by the Allied forces with support from British naval vessels lying offshore.

Below: Yugoslav troops surrender to a German reconnaissance unit, April 1941. The Yugoslavs were no match for *Blitzkrieg*.

7 April 1941

Greece As well as the frontal pressure on the Metaxas Line its left flank is being threatened by a German armored division which is moving south into Greece after having reached Strumica in the advance in Yugoslavia. The Greek Commander in Chief, General Papagos, further weakens the Aliakmon Line by sending forward a Greek force from it to try to block this last German advance.
Yugoslavia After a rapid advance troops from XL Panzer Corps enter Skopje late in the day.
Battle of the Atlantic US naval and air bases open in Bermuda. The carrier *Ranger* and other ships are to be based there as the Central Atlantic Neutrality Patrol. These forces will be considerably increased by three battleships and two carriers later in April and during May and June.
North Africa On the coast Derna is overrun in the continuing Axis advance. Inland near Mechili an armored battle begins between the German 5th Panzer Regiment and the remnants of the British 2nd Armored Division.

8 April 1941

Yugoslavia The German offensive is extended with the start of attacks by Kleist's First Panzer Group. They advance west over the Bulgarian border and by evening have destroyed the Yugoslav forces on the frontier and have advanced as far as Nis.
East Africa Massawa falls to the Allied forces. Seventeen large Axis merchant ships are taken in the port along with many smaller military and civilian vessels. The 4th Indian Division, which has played a large part in the Allied campaign in Eritrea, is immediately prepared for shipping to Egypt where the Allied forces are under great pressure. The priority in the East African campaign is now to clear the road between Asmara and Addis Ababa. Forces are being sent to this task from both ends of the road.
North Africa Mechili falls to the German attacks in the morning and Rommel immediately begins to organize an advance to Tobruk.

9 April 1941

Greece The resistance of the Greek forces in the Metaxas Line has been weakened on the 8th and now collapses. Thessaloniki is taken by the 2nd Panzer Division. The Greek Second Army, the force defending the Metaxas Line, surrenders. Other German units have taken Monastir in Yugoslavia and are moving south through the Monastir Gap. It will not be possible to hold a strong attack here, although Wilson has strengthened the defending force and it will, therefore, be necessary to withdraw from some of the Aliakmon positions. This is discussed with Papagos and he concurs.
Yugoslavia The German Second Army joins the attack on Yugoslavia. Two corps move south over the Austrian border, quickly taking Mari-

bor. The third corps, XLVI Panzer, is based in Hungary and begins to seize crossings over the Drava. The two corps from Kleist's force which began the attack on Yugoslavia have now moved through the southern part of the country and into Greece.

10 April 1941

Yugoslavia The advance of the German Second Army gathers speed. Zagreb is captured. The German advance is helped by the desertion of many Croat troops from the Yugoslav army. During the day Zagreb radio proclaims the establishment of an independent Croatian republic. The Croatian nationalist leader, Pavelić, is in Rome.

North Africa Rommel's troops begin to attack Tobruk with a small improvised force but are beaten off.

10-12 April 1941

Greece On the 10th the Germans begin their attacks through the Monastir Gap. The attacks are repeated with growing strength over the following two days and on the 12th the defending British and Australian forces pull back. The Germans have very powerful air support throughout. During this time the Allied forces to the east are pulling back from the Aliakmon Line to a position hinging on Mount Olympus.

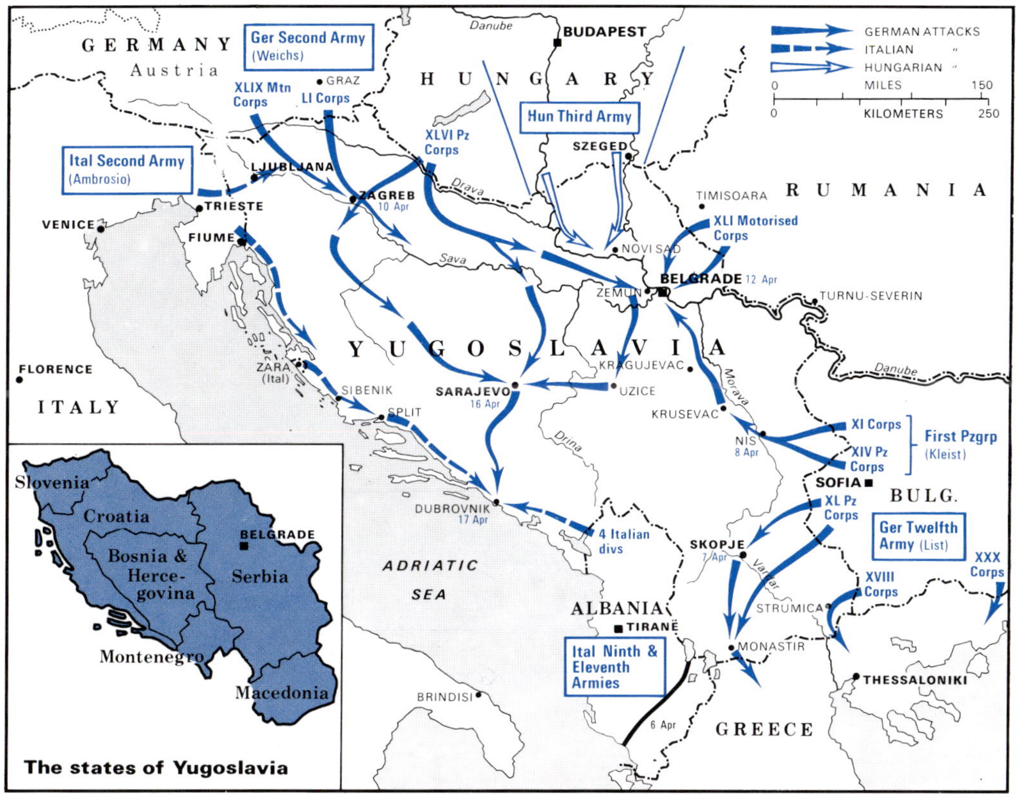

Above: Map showing the German advance into Yugoslavia and northern Greece, April 1941.

11 April 1941

Yugoslavia The Italian Second Army, led by General Ambrosio, begins a cautious advance from the Trieste area toward Ljubljana but Weich's forces arrive there first. Other Italian units begin to advance south along the Dalmatian coast. The German XLI Corps also begins an advance over the Rumanian border toward Belgrade. The Hungarians also join in with an advance from the Szeged area toward Novi Sad. They are held up more by resistance from Yugoslav civilians than by the Yugoslav army.

North Africa The isolation of Tobruk is now complete, all the remainder of the Allied force having retreated to the Egyptian border. The German attack on Tobruk continues but the combination of Australian infantry and British artillery defending proves too strong for them and they fail to break through.

War at Sea Roosevelt tells Churchill that the US Navy will extend the American Defense Zone up to the line of 26 degrees West. The Red Sea is declared to be no longer a 'combat zone' and under the terms of US law US ships may now carry cargos to ports there including supplies for the British in Egypt.

United States, Politics President Roosevelt creates the Office of Price Administrations under the direction of Leon Henderson. It is given the task of controlling prices and profits and balancing civilian and defense needs. This bureau will play an important part in holding back many increases in prices and containing inflation.

12 April 1941

Yugoslavia In the evening Belgrade surrenders to General Kleist's forces who have advanced down the Morava valley from Nis. They only reach Belgrade a little before other German units from the north and east.

13 April 1941

Diplomatic Affairs The USSR and Japan sign a five year Neutrality Agreement. For Stalin this

Below: A Panzer Mark III of the *Afrika Korps* fires at a distant target in North Africa, 1941. It is ideal tank country.

Above: U-Boat crew members, battle pennants announcing the scale of their recent success, wait to dock at the port of St Nazaire.

is an invaluable piece of diplomacy which, backed by secret information from Soviet spies in Tokyo, will allow him to transfer forces from Siberia to face a possible German attack. These moves begin now and will be particularly important during the final German advance on Moscow later in the year.

The agreement represents a complete change in Japanese policy and marks the growing concern of the Japanese military leaders and statesmen to look south to the resources of the East Indies. The agreement has been negotiated almost alone by Foreign Minister Matsuoka, in Moscow on the way back from a European visit. Although it conforms well to the other Japanese leaders' ideas, they are upset at Matsuoka's brash and independent attitude.

Greece Although the withdrawal to the Mount Olympus position is not yet complete the British and Greeks decide that they must retreat farther to shorter lines near Thermopylae.

13-17 April 1941

North Africa There are more German and Italian attacks on Tobruk but again they are beaten off. The Italian Ariete Division performs particularly badly in these operations.

14 April 1941

Yugoslavia, Politics King Peter leaves Yugoslavia and flies to Athens. The Simović government joins him there on the 15th.

Diplomatic Affairs There are secret talks in New York between the Americans and the Icelandic consul. The Icelandic officials agree to do nothing to resist an American occupation to replace the present British force.

14-18 April 1941

Greece From the 14th the Allied forces on the Olympus position are attacked by the advancing Germans. In the Monastir Gap the rearguards are also under pressure throughout this time as they try to retire through Kozani. On 16 April Wavell gives orders, on the basis of the situation both in North Africa and Greece, that the sailing of the 7th Australian Division and the Polish Brigade from Egypt is to be cancelled. This is effectively a decision to abandon the Greek campaign and indeed Papagos is already suggesting that the British leave Greece in order to minimize the damage to his country. On the 18th the Greek Prime Minister Korizis commits suicide. The campaign continues however, with the Olympus position having been abandoned on that day. The rearguard will be considerably harried by the Luftwaffe as they fall back to Thermopylae.

15 April 1941

United States, Politics Harry Hopkins is appointed to be Roosevelt's personal representative in charge of running the Lend-Lease program.

16 April 1941

Yugoslavia Ante Pavelić is sworn in to head the new Croat republic. Over the next few months his Ustaše followers, Roman Catholic Croats, will murder about 500,000 people, most of them Orthodox Serbs, who will be presented with a choice between rebaptism and death. Many Jews are also killed. Unusually the local Catholic priests will be involved in the massacres. Elsewhere in Occupied Europe the Catholic clergy will generally have a good record in resistance work.

Mediterranean An important German convoy of five transports escorted by three Italian destroyers is attacked by four British destroyers near Kerkinnah Island. One of the British ships is sunk in the engagement but all the Axis vessels go down. About 1250 of the 3000 German troops are rescued by Axis forces.

17 April 1941

Yugoslavia On the Dalmatian coast the Italians enter Dubrovnik.

The former prime minister, Cincar-Marković (deposed 27 March), signs an armistice with the Germans. In the course of overrunning the country the Germans have lost less 200 dead.

19 April 1941

Iraq A British convoy begins to land troops from the 20th Indian Brigade at Basra. A small British contingent has already been sent in by air to protect the air base at Shaibah, near Basra. Later in the month this force will be sent on to the Habbaniyah airfield. By a treaty of 1930 the British are entitled to send troops across Iraq to and from Palestine and with no prospect of immediate German help of any size Rashid Ali's new government cannot object at first to the British landings. In diplomatic exchanges they unsuccessfully oppose any addition to the British force. British reinforcements in fact arrive at Basra on the 29th. By this time the Iraqis will have decided to fight.

Britain, Home Front The first registration of women for war work under a new Employment Order begins.

19-21 April 1941

Greece On the 19th Wavell is in Athens to meet General Wilson and General Blamey, the commander of the Australian forces. They decide that it will probably be necessary to evacuate their troops from Greece, but promise the Greeks that they will keep fighting as long as the Greeks themselves do so. On the 21st Papagos recommends that the Allies leave and permission for the evacuation is given from London.

On the ground the Allied forces still active have all passed through the Thermopylae position by the 20th. On that day, however, the Greek forces in Epirus that have been fighting in the Albanian campaign are forced to surrender to the SS Adolf Hitler Brigade.

19-22 April 1941

East Africa The 1st South African Brigade has been sent north from Addis Ababa along the road to Asmara in Eritrea and now comes up to Italian positions south of Dessie. The fighting lasts for four days before the Italians fall back before the advance.

21 April 1941

North Africa Three battleships from the Mediterranean Fleet shell Tripoli on their return from escorting a Malta convoy. Cunningham has only undertaken this operation under protest and with direct orders from Churchill. At first Churchill wished to try to block the port by sinking the battleship *Barham* in the entrance to Tripoli Harbor.

22-24 April 1941

Greece The German forces begin to arrive at the Thermopylae position on the 22nd but do not mount a large attack until the 24th when they are held off. By the 24th the position has largely served its delaying function and during the night of the 24th the defending troops fall back, leaving a further rearguard at Thebes. On the 23rd King George and his government are evacuated to Crete and on the night of the 24th the main evacuation begins, with 11,000 men being taken off.

23 April 1941

German Raiders The German raider *Thor* returns to Brest after a cruise of 322 days in which 11 merchant ships and one British auxiliary cruiser have been sunk and two more auxiliaries damaged. Although it is the German U-Boats that do the most destruction, the surface raiders are a problem for the Allies.

24 April 1941

United States, Politics Roosevelt formally orders US warships to report the movements of German warships west of Iceland. This is happening unofficially already. The information is usually passed one way or another to the British.

25 April 1941

Germany, Planning Hitler issues Directive 28 giving the order for Operation Merkur, the airborne attack on Crete.

25-29 April 1941

Greece There is little fighting until the 26th when the main German advance is again halted by the Allied rearguard, this time at Thebes. There are, however, two German attempts to move into the Peloponnese to interfere with the evacuations going on there. A paratroop force is dropped at Corinth to take the vital canal bridge but it is blown up before they can do so. At the west end of the Gulf of Corinth there is more success for the Germans as the Adolf Hitler Division begins to cross over to Patras. The Thebes rearguard falls back during the night of the 26th and the Germans enter Athens on the 27th.

Meanwhile the evacuation of the Allied forces has been going on. The few port facilities and the beaches at Rafina, Nauplia, Monemvasia and Kalamata are all used, as well as other sites. The British Mediterranean Fleet provides a force of six cruisers, 20 destroyers and about 30 other ships. The evacuation generally goes very well except for incidents at Nauplia and Kalamata. On the 27th a transport is bombed off Nauplia and two destroyers that come to the rescue are also sunk. Many of the soldiers on all three ships are lost. Also at Nauplia a burning merchant ship blocks the pier on the last night and 1700 men have to be left behind. At Kalamata a German force bursts into the town on the 28th but is eventually defeated by the 7000 troops waiting for evacuation. The naval force off the port sees the fighting and withdraws before the Germans are subdued. About 5000 troops are taken off on the 28/29th, the last night, bringing the total evacuated to just over 50,000 at a cost of two destroyers and four transports. It has taken Germany less than a month to overrun Greece and Yugoslavia.

The strategic importance of the German campaign lies particularly in its relationship to the preparations for the attack on the USSR. It has often been suggested, although probably incorrectly, that the Balkan campaign delayed Barbarossa during a period of fine summer weather that might have been invaluable to the Germans later in the year. As well as questions of equipment, training and the weather in Poland that probably contributed most to the timing of the attack, it should be noted that the campaign in Greece was part of the long-intended German strategic program and that any disruption to the program was caused by the independent Yugoslavian situation. The 'postponement' of Barbarossa which Hitler ordered in response to the Yugoslav coup did not change the date fixed for the attack, but changed the date by which preparations were to be complete – a rather different thing. Very few of the forces employed in Yugoslavia were irreplaceable in the Barbarossa order of battle, and there is evidence to suggest that after the Yugoslavian campaign they were only sent back to their Barbarossa positions slowly. If an earlier Barbarossa attack had been required, the units used in Yugoslavia could have taken part or been replaced, temporarily, from the reserve.

26 April 1941

East Africa The Allied forces take Dessie with 8000 Italian prisoners.

27 April 1941

North Africa General Paulus arrives in North Africa on an inspection tour of Rommel's force. He has orders from OKH to try to bring Rommel under control and sort out a situation which, from Germany, seems very confused. He immediately halts preparations for more attacks on Tobruk. German reconnaissance units enter Egypt and occupy the Halfaya Pass, one of the few routes from Egypt by which the Cyrenaica plateau can be reached.

Mediterranean The carrier *Ark Royal* flies a further 23 Hurricanes to Malta. A small convoy also arrives at the island with some supplies from Gibraltar and some reinforcements which are to join the Mediterranean Fleet at Alexandria.

29 April 1941

East Africa Advance forces from 5th Indian Division reach the north side of the Italian position at Amba Alagi, in Abyssinia.

30 April 1941

North Africa After General Paulus has decided to allow a further effort against Tobruk the heaviest German attack yet goes in after a bombardment by artillery and many Stuka bombers. A salient in the western sector of the perimeter around the Ras el Madauar hill is gained by the attack but vigorous defense halts it there.

May 1941

War at Sea Partly because of captures made during the month, the British code-breaking service begins to be able to decipher German naval messages regularly and promptly. This is not a continuous process, however. The code is altered daily and major changes are made every month. The keys to these changes are given only a limited issue and thus a U-Boat setting out for a planned six-week cruise would only be given the machine settings for a little more than this period. Captures are, therefore, of very limited value as well as being very difficult to achieve.

A new Newfoundland Escort Force, largely provided by the Canadian Navy, is established and after HX-126 and OB-318 have lost heavily in mid-ocean, a continuous escort is provided for eastbound convoys from Halifax. This begins with HX-129 which sets out on 27 May. The escort is provided in stages from Canada, Iceland and finally from Britain. Obviously these new requirements increase the strain on the escort forces and call for very careful organization so that, for example, destroyers with a comparatively limited margin of endurance are not kept waiting at a rendezvous for a convoy which has been delayed by bad weather or attack. The Allies lose 58 ships of 325,500 tons to the U-Boats during May, more than half of which fall to a six-strong group operating in the weakly protected waters off Freetown. During this operation *U.107* sinks 14 ships in one patrol – a record total for the whole war. The total Allied shipping loss is 139 ships.

The Blitz In the first week there are several heavy attacks on Liverpool in which 18 vessels are sunk in the harbor and 25 badly damaged. The port installations are reduced to 75 percent of their normal handling capacity. Belfast and the Clyde ports are also attacked. The raid on London on the night of 10-11 May is the last major attack for three years. The Houses of Parliament are damaged in this attack, the heaviest made on a British city in the whole campaign. On the night of 30-31 May Dublin is bombed in error by the Luftwaffe.

British Air Operations Among the targets for Bomber Command this month are Brest, Hamburg, Bremen and Cologne. Bomber Command is now able to send over 350 sorties on selected nights. In the month's operations 2690 sorties are flown, 2840 tons of bombs are dropped and 76 aircraft are lost.

Europe, Resistance The first three British Special Operations Executive (SOE) agents to become active are parachuted into France.

1 May 1941

Iraq Fighting begins when Iraqi soldiers make a small attack on the British outpost at Rutba (west of Baghdad, about 125 miles from the Transjordan border).

Iraqi forces are also established in positions

Below: Archibald Wavell (center), C in C Middle East, lands in Greece to inspect Allied defences, 1941, following the arrival of British troops.

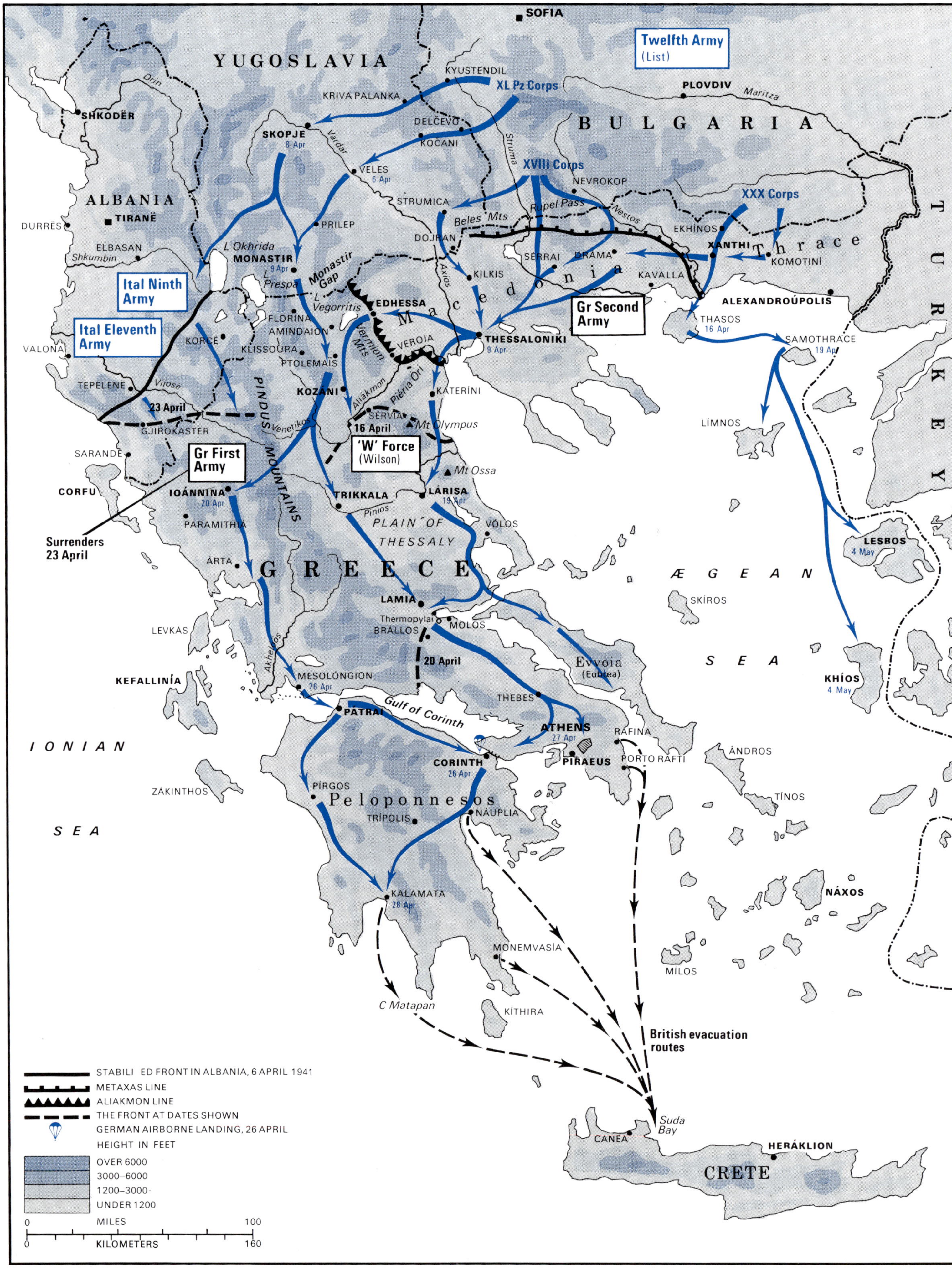
SOFIA
Twelfth Army
(List)
YUGOSLAVIA
KYUSTENDIL
XL Pz Corps
KRIVA PALANKA
PLOVDIV
Maritza
SHKODËR
Drin
SKOPJE
8 Apr
DELČEVO
KOČANI
Vardar
Struma
BULGARIA
VELES
6 Apr
XVIII Corps
NEVROKOP
ALBANIA
TIRANË
STRUMICA
Rupel Pass
XXX Corps
DURRES
PRILEP
Beles Mts
Nestos
EKHINOS
TURKEY
ELBASAN
Shkumbin
L Okhrida
MONASTIR
9 Apr
DOJRAN
XANTHI
Thrace
SERRAI
DRAMA
KOMOTINÍ
Ital Ninth Army
L Prespa
Monastir Gap
Axios
KILKIS
Macedonia
KAVALLA
Vegorritis
EDHESSA
ALEXANDROÚPOLIS
Ital Eleventh Army
FLORINA
Gr Second Army
AMINDAION
Vermion Mts
THASOS
16 Apr
VALONA
KORÇE
VEROIA
THESSALONIKI
9 Apr
SAMOTHRACE
19 Apr
KLISSOURA
PTOLEMAÏS
TEPELENE
Vijose
KOZÁNI
Piéria Ori
KATERÍNI
23 April
Aliakmon
SERVIA
PINDUS MOUNTAINS
16 April
Mt Olympus
LÍMNOS
GJIROKASTER
Venetikos
SARANDE
Gr First Army
'W' Force
(Wilson)
Mt Ossa
CORFU
IOÁNNINA
20 Apr
TRIKKALA
LÁRISA
19 Apr
Pinios
PARAMITHIA
PLAIN OF THESSALY
VÓLOS
Surrenders
23 April
LESBOS
4 May
ÁRTA
GREECE
ÆGEAN
SKÍROS
LAMIA
Thermopylai
BRÁLLOS
MOLOS
LEVKÁS
20 April
SEA
Evvoia
(Euboea)
Akhelóos
KHÍOS
4 May
KEFALLINÍA
MESOLÓNGION
26 Apr
THEBES
PATRAI
Gulf of Corinth
ATHENS
27 Apr
RAFINA
IONIAN
CORINTH
26 Apr
PIRAEUS
PORTO RAFTI
ÁNDROS
ZÁKINTHOS
PÍRGOS
Peloponnesos
NÁUPLIA
TÍNOS
SEA
TRÍPOLIS
KALAMATA
28 Apr
NÁXOS
MONEMVASÍA
MILOS
C Matapan
KÍTHIRA
British evacuation routes
Suda Bay
CANEA
HERÁKLION
CRETE
STABILIZED FRONT IN ALBANIA, 6 APRIL 1941
METAXAS LINE
ALIAKMON LINE
THE FRONT AT DATES SHOWN
GERMAN AIRBORNE LANDING, 26 APRIL
HEIGHT IN FEET
OVER 6000
3000–6000
1200–3000
UNDER 1200
0 MILES 100
0 KILOMETERS 160

Far left: The Axis advances into Greece. *Above:* British troops in Iraq.

around the Habbaniyah airfield. The Iraqi forces amount to about four divisions in total. Two are in the Baghdad area.

North Africa Rommel's attack on Tobruk continues. He attempts to widen and deepen the gap already won in the defenses but the Australian forces largely contain the attacks.

2 May 1941

Iraq The British airfield at Habbaniyah is attacked by considerable Iraqi ground forces. The British have about 80 obsolescent aircraft at Habbaniyah, many of them training types. Despite their age and unsuitability they are immediately employed against the Iraqi forces with considerable success. The British are, therefore, encouraged to hold Habbaniyah although their ground force there is very small.

There are also some skirmishes at several points near the Persian Gulf, especially at Basra where there are riots and some shooting in opposition to further British landings.

North Africa The fighting at Tobruk continues with little change in the positions on either side.

3 May 1941

East Africa The British forces begin attacks from the north against the Italian positions at Amba Alagi. These positions guard passes in the road between Asmara and Addis Ababa. They are based on a number of steep and rugged hills and there are numerous caves. The position is very strong.

Iraq There are British attacks on the Iraqi positions around Habbaniyah and by air on the Iraqi Rashid airfield.

4 May 1941

North Africa Rommel halts his attack on Tobruk. The Germans will continue to hold the enclave in the perimeter that they have just won but will not be able to extend it at any time later in the siege. For both sides life at Tobruk settles down into a style not unlike the trench warfare of World War I. The ground is very hard, however, and this makes digging particularly difficult so that trenches are often shallow at first. This means that their occupants must stay virtually motionless throughout the burning heat of the day. Neither side is well placed with regard to supplies or other personal comforts. Both sides soon adopt a policy of offensive night patrolling which means that there can be no relaxation.

Iraq The main events are again British air operations. An airfield at Mosul which is being used by a small German force is one RAF target. The German force is receiving supplies from and via Syria with the cooperation of the Vichy authorities.

East Africa The Italian forces around Amba Alagi are driven off three hills in the west of their position by attacks from the 29th Indian Brigade.

5 May 1941

East Africa Emperor Haile Selassie triumphantly returns to his capital, Addis Ababa. In the battles at Amba Alagi the Italian Middle Hill position is taken.

5-6 May 1941

North Africa Supplies are brought to the besieged garrison in Tobruk by destroyer for the first time. From now until the end of the siege two destroyers will be used on such missions on most nights and at about weekly intervals reinforcements will be brought in and the wounded evacuated.

6 May 1941

Iraq The British forces consolidate their hold on Habbaniyah airfield, driving the Iraqis back from Sin el Dhibban toward Fallujah, nearer the capital. The 21st Indian Brigade arrives at Basra.

Soviet Union, Politics The Praesidium of the Supreme Soviet nominates Stalin President of the Council of People's Commissars. Previously Stalin has been content to hold only the office of general secretary of the Communist Party.

6-12 May 1941

Mediterranean For the first time for many months the British try to run a convoy through the Mediterranean from Gibraltar to Egypt. Churchill is the driving force behind this decision and has ordered the operation because he wishes the supplies and tanks carried in the ships to form the basis of an offensive in the desert as soon as possible.

The operation is code named Tiger. There are five transports. On 6 May they pass Gibraltar and are joined by one battleship, a carrier from Force H and another battleship which is to go on to join the Mediterranean Fleet. With these heavy units are four cruisers and seven destroyers. Six more destroyers join the convoy from Gibraltar on 6 May. Also on 6 May two convoys leave Alexandria for Malta with an escort of five cruisers and three destroyers.

Cunningham takes the whole of the Mediter-

Below: Rommel's first advance into Libya.

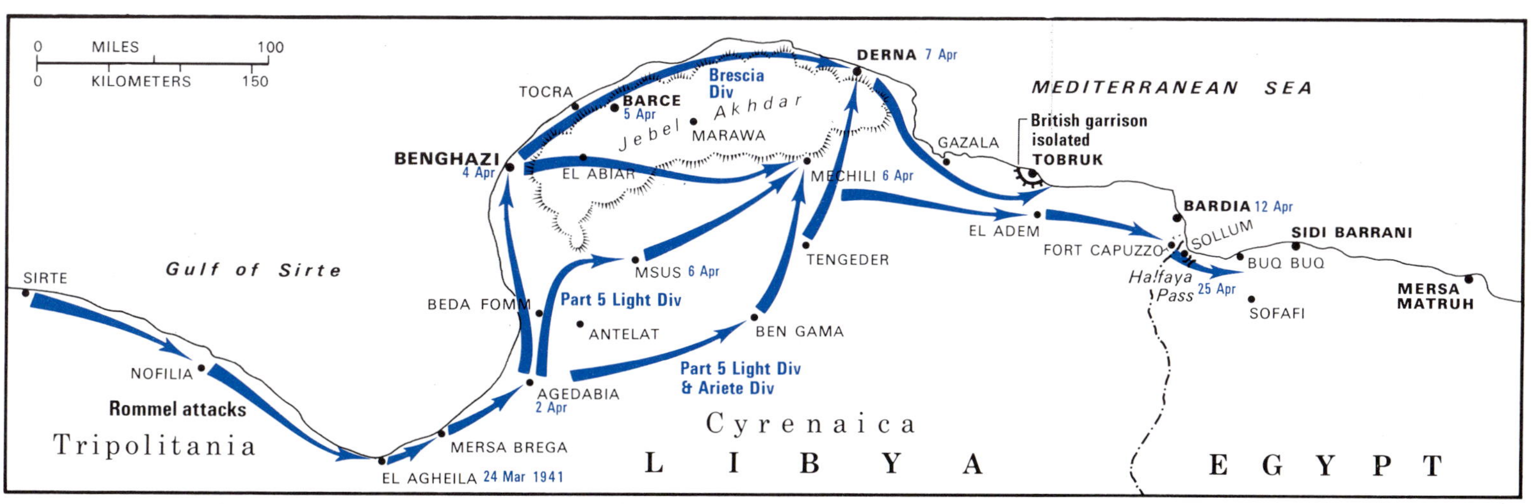

Above: General Rommel, commander of the *Afrika Korps*, in front of Tobruk, June 1941.

ranean Fleet out in support with three battleships, his single carrier, three cruisers and 19 destroyers. On the night of 7/8 May part of Cunningham's force shells the harbor at Benghazi, sinking two ships.

On 8 May there are air attacks on the eastward and westward bound convoys. The carrier with each convoy engages the attacking Italian planes. On 9 May one of the Tiger transports sinks on a mine. Force H begins to return to Gibraltar. On the night of 10/11 May Benghazi is again shelled. By 12 May all the ships have reached their destinations. Tiger has brought 238 tanks and 43 Hurricanes to Egypt for the loss of 57 tanks.

7 May 1941

Battle of the Atlantic In a special operation mounted for the purpose the German trawler *München*, a weather ship, is captured northeast of Iceland and secret papers relating to the Enigma coding machine are taken. Although Allied intelligence was already supplied with the basic details of Enigma, any new information was a vital bonus to the code breakers.

Iraq General Quinan takes command of the British forces in Iraq.

8 May 1941

German Raiders The British heavy cruiser *Cornwall* finds and sinks the German raider *Pinguin* near the Seychelles. The *Pinguin* has sunk 28 ships of 136,550 tons during its cruise.

8-10 May 1941

East Africa The Amba Alagi fighting continues. On the 8th the Indian forces take the Falagi Pass and three small peaks south of Amba Alagi itself. On the 10th the Gumsa position is taken.

9-11 May 1941

Battle of the Atlantic After sinking two ships from the convoy OB-318. *U.110* is forced to surface by a depth-charge attack and is boarded and captured. Code books and an Enigma cipher machine are recovered. As well as providing useful information for general code breaking work, in this case the books are of considerable use in the imminent operations involving the *Bismarck* and her supply ships. On 11 May *U.110* sinks from the depth charge damage while on the way to Iceland. Throughout the war the Germans do not discover that *U.110* has been captured. (It should be noted that the code details captured do not include the main code which will be used by the *Bismarck*. None of the *Bismarck*'s messages will be successfully decoded by the British at the time.)

10 May 1941

Iraq British-led forces from the Jordanian Arab Legion take Rutba. A stronger detachment, Habforce, is being prepared for a move to Rutba. Part of this force, to be known as Kingcol, will then move on to relieve the town of Habbaniyah.

10-11 May 1941

Diplomatic Affairs Rudolf Hess, the deputy leader of the Nazi Party and second in line to Goering as heir to Hitler, flies to Britain on a bizarre peace mission. He lands by parachute at Eaglesham near Glasgow, hoping to contact the Duke of Hamilton whom he met at the 1936 Olympics. He believes that there is a considerable body of British opinion that is opposed to Churchill but is also anti-Communist and therefore prepared to consider making common ground on these terms with Germany. He is immediately disowned by the German authorities (he has left a note explaining himself to Hitler) and this prompt reaction detracts from the propaganda value that the episode might have had for the British.

13 May 1941

Germany, Politics Martin Bormann is appointed to take Hess' former position. He is given the title of party chancellor, an important step in his rise to power.

Middle East, Politics The exiled Mufti of Jerusalem broadcasts from Baghdad summoning all Islamic countries to join the fight against Britain.

14 May 1941

East Africa The South African force advancing north from Addis Ababa has now joined the Amba Alagi battle and moves to attack the Italian Triangle position. The attacks are held during the day but the Italians retire at night. Italian morale is now very low, largely because of the fierce and undisciplined conduct of some of the Ethiopian guerrilla forces supporting the Allies.

15 May 1941

Yugoslavia, Politics An independent Kingdom of Croatia is established with Italian backing. On 18 May the Duke of Spoleto is proclaimed king. He will never visit his kingdom. The Axis dismemberment of Yugoslavia was a deliberate policy designed to encourage regional and sub-national rivalries within the new state.

Iraq and Syria The British government announces that German planes are arriving in Syria and using Syrian bases to move on to Iraq. The RAF, therefore, bombs Palmyra and Damascus airfields. These attacks continue over the next few days.

15-16 May 1941

North Africa In preparation for the major offensive which the tanks from the Tiger convoy (*see* 6-12 May) will allow, Wavell begins an operation code named Brevity. It is designed to capture Halfaya Pass and gain ground leading to the more open areas of the Cyrenaica Plateau. Churchill's habit of describing the recently arrived tanks as 'Tiger Cubs' indicates the importance which he attaches to the coming offensive and foreshadows the rigor with which he will punish failure. The information which has been received from the interception of German signals, especially from the recent reports of General Paulus on the situation in Africa, has convinced Churchill that the German forces are weak and overextended.

General Gott commands the Brevity opera-

Below: Rudolph Hess, Hitler's Deputy. In May 1941 he made his bizarre flight to Britain.

tion. His plan calls for mixed columns to advance to Halfaya Pass and Fort Capuzzo and for a tank force to move to Sidi Aziz. On the first day the forces on the coast reach and capture Halfaya, but the 22nd Guards Brigade is held up in heavy fighting at Capuzzo. The tank force on the left makes good ground initially but the approach of the German 8th Panzer Regiment makes the British decide to withdraw on the 16th.

15-19 May 1941

Crete There are powerful German air attacks on the island. These are, of course, in preparation for the coming landing and are designed to subdue the garrison and compel the RAF to withdraw its few aircraft from Crete.

18 May 1941

Iraq After outflanking an Iraqi blocking force the British relieving group, Kingcol, reaches Habbaniyah airfield.

Syria General Dentz broadcasts, warning his troops in Vichy-controlled Syria to meet force with force. Airfields in Syria are bombed again by the RAF.

18-22 May 1941

Battle of the Atlantic On 18 May the battleship *Bismarck* leaves Gdynia in company with the heavy cruiser *Prinz Eugen* for an Atlantic cruise under the command of Admiral Lutjens. Various supply ships are already at sea. On 20 May the two ships are reported in the Kattegat. The information reaches London with the cooperation of Intelligence officers of the Swedish navy.

On 21 May British reconnaissance aircraft find the German ships near Bergen. Later in the day the battleship *Prince of Wales* and the battlecruiser *Hood* put to sea from Scapa Flow. On 22 May British planes report correctly that the Germans have also put to sea and the Commander in Chief of the British Home Fleet, Admiral Tovey, therefore sets out with the battleship *King George V* and the carrier *Victorious*. The battlecruiser *Repulse* joins this force later in the day. Tovey plans to reinforce the patrols watching the Faeroes-Iceland passage while Holland in the *Hood* goes to give further strength to the forces in the Denmark Strait (*see* 23-27 May).

19 May 1941

East Africa The Duke of Aosta surrenders with the 7000 remaining Italian troops at Amba Alagi. The Allied forces have now killed or captured 230,000 of the Italian East Africa force. About 80,000 remain.

Iraq The British forces based at Habbaniyah airfield begin to operate more aggressively, attacking and capturing Fallujah. The British airfield is bombed by German planes.

20 May 1941

Crete The German attack begins. There are airborne landings by forces of 7th Paratroop Division from Fliegerkorps XI. General Student is in command and has 5th Mountain Division in reserve. There is massive air support from Fliegerkorps VIII which has over 400 bombers and 200 fighters. Altogether the Germans employ about 23,000 troops. The garrison consists mostly of troops recently evacuated from Greece. There are strong Australian and New Zealand contingents among the 32,000 British and Empire troops and about 10,000 Greeks. All units are short of equipment and heavy weapons. General Freyberg is in command.

The attack begins with heavy air raids and these are followed in the morning by airborne landings at Máleme and Caneá. In the afternoon there are further landings at Rétimo and Heráklion. It is clear to both Allies and Germans that the battle for the island depends on control of the airfields and it is round these that the German attack concentrates. There is heavy fighting in all sectors, with the German forces suffering heavy losses. At Rétimo and Heráklion the defending forces are successful in holding off the Germans and although fighting in these areas continues for several days it will not effect the outcome of the battle. The German forces near Caneá are made to retreat inland but are not neutralized. At Máleme the fighting is very fierce and by the end of the day the airfield is virtually no man's land. The commander of the New Zealand battalion holding the airfield is slightly out of touch with the situation of his whole force, through no fault of his own, and decides to withdraw during the night. This comparatively minor move effectively decides the whole battle. The Germans recognize their lack of success in the other sectors and soon rush reinforcements in to the Máleme airfield – the tide of battle has turned in the Germans' favor.

The British Mediterranean Fleet is cruising off the island to prevent any German force arriving by sea. This, of course, makes the Fleet vulnerable to German air attack.

Battle of the Atlantic The US merchant ship *Robin Moor* is sunk in the Atlantic by a U-Boat. On 21 May Roosevelt describes the incident as 'an act of intimidation' to which 'we do not propose to yield.'

21 May 1941

Mediterranean The carriers *Ark Royal* and *Furious* fly off a cargo of 48 Hurricanes to Malta. In the air fighting since January the Germans have lost 62 aircraft and the Italians 15. The British losses in the air have been 32 machines, as well as an equal number destroyed on the ground.

21-23 May 1941

Crete During the 21st the Germans consolidate their hold on Máleme. The first troops of the 5th Mountain Division are flown in. During the night the nearby New Zealand forces counter-attack and although they have some success they do not penetrate to the airfield. There is little change in the Allied positions during the 22nd but in the face of the growing strength and complete air superiority, Freyberg cancels a further counterattack on the night of the 22nd and orders a withdrawal instead. During the 23rd the Germans continue to exploit their hold on Máleme, sending in artillery units and fighter aircraft.

In the naval battles offshore one British destroyer is lost to air attack on the 21st, but during the night a German convoy attempting to reach the island is intercepted and turned back without loss by a force of cruisers and destroyers. On the 22nd a second convoy is turned back but is not pursued far because the Luftwaffe intervenes. In various actions during the day the battleship *Warspite* is badly damaged and two cruisers and one destroyer are sunk. Admiral Cunningham, ashore in Alexandria, orders the fleet to return after being wrongly informed that ammunition for the battleship's antiaircraft guns is in very short supply. During the night of 22/23 May the Máleme airfield is bombarded by Lord Mountbatten's 5th Destroyer Flotilla but the destroyers *Kelly* and *Kashmir* are sunk on the 23rd by the Germans while they are withdrawing. King George of Greece is evacuated from the island to Egypt on 22/23 May.

23-27 May 1941

Battle of the Atlantic The German battleship *Bismarck* and her consort, *Prinz Eugen*, are sighted in the Denmark Strait by the patrolling British cruisers *Norfolk* and *Suffolk*. British radar equipment plays an important part in the interception. On 24 May the *Hood* and the

Below: The Duke of Aosta (saluting), Governor of Italian East Africa, marches into captivity, April 1941.

Prince of Wales come up and engage the German ships. The *Hood* is sunk very quickly and a short while later the *Prince of Wales* breaks off the action after receiving some damage. Only three men from the *Hood*'s complement of 1416 are saved. Various theories try to explain how the *Hood* was destroyed so quickly. Certainly the ship's armor was inadequate by 1941 standards and the *Hood* was long overdue for her planned modernization. It is possible that a shell from the *Bismarck* penetrated the magazine but a more plausible explanation is that a shell set fire to some antiaircraft rocket ammunition and that this fire spread to the magazine.

The *Prince of Wales* is very new and has sailed from Scapa with some dockyard men still aboard working on the guns. In the action one of the guns jams and cannot be used. This contributes to the decision to break off the action. There has been no time for the crew to train properly and this state of affairs will prevail for the rest of the ship's life. Although the ships of the *King George V* Class are generally sound, they all require a generous working-up period before they are fully efficient.

However, the defects of the ships are not the only reasons for the *Bismarck*'s success. Admiral Holland led his ships into the battle in such a way that not all their heavy guns could bear, nor does he seem to have made full allowance for the possible effects of plunging long-range fire on the comparatively thin deck armor of the *Hood*.

After the action the British cruisers continue to shadow the German ships. The *Bismarck* has been hit three times, which has caused the loss of some fuel and the contamination of more. Lutjens therefore decides to put in to Brest. The British battleships *Rodney* and *Ramillies* leave the convoys they have been escorting to join the hunt. Force H, with the battlecruiser *Renown* and the carrier *Ark Royal,* puts to sea from Gibraltar. During the night of 24-25 May aircraft from the Home Fleet carrier *Victorious* attack, and hit *Bismarck* with one torpedo. The damage is negligible. Later in the night *Prinz Eugen* slips away to operate independently, and later still contact is lost between the shadowing British cruisers and the *Bismarck*. For much of 25 May, therefore, the British commanders are in the dark as to *Bismarck*'s position but Lutjens breaks radio silence to report and is picked up on the British direction-finding equipment. This information is passed to Admiral Tovey but is at first misinterpreted, perhaps because the radio bearings are plotted on an unsuitable navigation chart. Tovey now has *King George V* and *Rodney,* but both are short of fuel and by this mistake they lose their chance of meeting the *Bismarck* unless her speed can be reduced. During the operation the British have been most worried to protect the convoy lanes and block the *Bismarck*'s return home by the northern routes. The best dispositions to prevent the *Bismarck* reaching Brest have not been made. Nonetheless Force H has been hurrying north over the past few days and when on 26 May a Catalina aircraft finds *Bismarck* only 700 miles from Brest it is clear that the aircraft of the *Ark Royal* offer the best chance of slowing the German ship so that she can be caught. The first strike launched from the *Ark Royal* finds and attacks the British cruiser *Sheffield* by mistake owing to the bad weather. The attack fails because of defects in the magnetic exploders of the torpedoes, so simple contact types are substituted for a second strike. The 15 Swordfish find the correct target and score two hits. One hit wrecks the German battleship's steering and practically brings her to a halt. During the night the *Bismarck* is further harried by torpedo and gunfire attacks by five British destroyers. It is not clear whether they score any torpedo hits. On 27 May *Rodney* and *King George V* come up and in a gun battle lasting less than two hours, the *Bismarck* is reduced to a hulk. She is finished off with torpedoes from the cruisers *Dorsetshire* and *Norfolk.*

Above: The German battleship *Bismarck* fires her main armament. The destruction of the *Bismarck* in May 1941 was a welcome British victory.

Below: Junkers Ju-52 transports on Maleme airfield, Crete, May 1941. Although successful, the German invasion of Crete was costly.

24 May 1941

Crete The Allied forces in the Caneá area are now in positions around Galatas. The German buildup at Máleme continues.

East Africa In southern Abyssinia Soddu falls to the Allied forces. In this area General Gazzera leads seven weak Italian divisions. The attacking Allied force is made up of the 11th and 12th African Divisions.

25-26 May 1941

Crete The German forces begin to advance westward toward Galatas. The fighting is very intense and the town changes hands several times during the two days. Toward the end of the 26th Freyberg raises the question of a withdrawal from the island. During the night of the 26th most of the Allied forces withdraw from the Galatas position amid some confusion about the exact nature of their orders. On the 26th aircraft from the carrier *Formidable* attack the Stuka base at Scarpanto in the Italian Dodecanese. The carrier is hit twice by air attacks.

27 May 1941

Crete The Germans take Caneá and Suda. The Allied forces are now largely split up and moving in a disorganized manner in the direction of Sfakia to be evacuated. The evacuation is authorized by Wavell after he has consulted with London.

North Africa Rommel has reinforced his troops on the Egyptian border and his two panzer regiments retake Halfaya Pass in a converging attack. The Germans begin work to fortify their new position, especially by digging in their 88mm guns.

Iraq British forces begin to advance from their positions around Habbaniyah and Fallujah toward the capital, Baghdad.

28 May 1941

Iraq The Allied forces occupy Ur. The 20th Indian Brigade has made this advance from Basra but can go no further for the moment because repairs to roads and railroad tracks are needed.

Above: A *Sturmgeschütz* (StuG) III assault gun enters Athens, 27 April 1941, signaling the end of the campaign in Greece.

Above: Survivors of the *Bismarck* are picked up by the British cruiser HMS *Dorsetshire*, 27 May 1941, at the end of an epic sea battle.

28 May-1 June 1941

Crete The Allied forces fight some small rearguard actions to cover their retreat to the evacuation beaches at Sfakia. Evacuations from Sfakia take place each night. Also, on the night of 28/29 May, the Heraklion garrison of 4000 men is taken off by a force of cruisers and destroyers. These ships are heavily attacked while withdrawing. Two destroyers are sunk and the two cruisers involved are hit. During 1 June the cruiser *Calcutta* is also sunk by the German aircraft. Altogether 18,600 men are taken off but casualties and prisoners in the battle for the island amount to another 15,000 from the land forces and 2000 from the navy. About 600 more men will escape from the island by various routes later. The largest groups of prisoners are the 5000 men who are captured when the Germans take Sfakia on 1 June and the garrison of Rétimo who do not receive evacuation instructions because of a communications breakdown. The ships lost include three cruisers and six destroyers. In addition, two battleships, one carrier and numerous cruisers and destroyers have been hit. In all the operations in Greece and Crete 44 transports are lost. The Germans admit casualties of 7000 from their force – a very high proportion of them deaths – and Hitler decides that such large-scale airborne attacks should not be repeated even although the result has been a brilliant success.

30 May 1941

Iraq Although the main Allied force is held up at Ur and the small British force from Habbaniyah is only advancing very slowly, Rashid Ali gives up the struggle and flees to Iran. An armistice is agreed on the 31st. The British right to station troops in the country is confirmed and the Iraqis undertake to do nothing to help the Axis.

June 1941

Battle of the Atlantic German submarines sink 61 ships of 310,000 tons this month. Owing to the diversion of German aircraft to take part in Barbarossa there is a drop in Allied shipping losses to air attack. The total Allied loss from all causes is 432,000 tons (109 ships). The first escort carrier, the *Audacity*, enters British service. Five more ships of this class are being converted in the UK and six in the USA under Lease-Lend arrangements. The work on these British ships will provide useful information for the construction of later US vessels of this class. The U-Boats' task is also being made more difficult by Allied scientists. Radar working on the 10cm wavelength is now gradually coming into service. This is sufficiently sensitive to detect a submarine periscope over 1000 yards away in the best conditions.

Atomic Research The British Maud Commit-

Below: A Royal Navy seaman signals with an Aldis lamp to another convoy ship.

tee reports that they believe that it will be possible to make an atomic bomb using the isotope Uranium 235. Research in the US is also proceeding, as yet at a more gentle pace but substantial funds will be authorized later in the year. Following the Maud report, the British soon move to set up a formal research program under the code name Tube Alloys (*see* 18 June 1942).

The Blitz Manchester is the target for almost the only major German attack during the month. Much of the strength of the Luftwaffe is being withdrawn early in the month to be ready to support the attack on the Soviet Union.

British Air Operations Brest is attacked five times during the month, as are targets in the Ruhr, the Rhineland and ports in northwest Germany. RAF Fighter Command conducts a series of fighter sweeps over northern France.

1 June 1941

Iraq British forces enter Baghdad. Regent Emir Abdul Illah, the uncle of King Faisal, returns to the country.

North Africa Air Marshal Tedder takes command of the RAF forces in the Middle East. The majority of the German 15th Panzer Division has now joined Rommel's force.

Battle of the Atlantic The US Coastguard begins patrol operations off the southern Greenland coast. Only four ships are involved at this stage.

Britain, Home Front It is announced that measures for clothes rationing are being prepared.

2 June 1941

North Africa Vichy grants the Axis powers the use of the port of Bizerta for unloading nonmilitary supplies for their forces stationed in North Africa.

3 June 1941

Iraq British forces enter Mosul. A few German pilots are captured.

Above: Vichy French troops, many of them wounded, march into captivity under British guard, Syria, July 1941.

3-23 June 1941

German Raiders British forces successfully intercept and sink nine German supply ships. Seven of them have been sent to sea to cooperate with the *Bismarck* and the remaining two have been working with the merchant raiders. These interceptions all occur because of the British ability to decode some German signals.

4 June 1941

World Affairs The former Kaiser of Germany, Wilhelm, dies at home in Doorn, Holland.

Iraq A new Iraqi Cabinet is formed under British auspices. British forces are now moving through the country establishing control of key points. Some of the British troops will be ready to move into Syria later in the month.

5 June 1941

United States, Politics The US Army Bill for 1942 is introduced into Congress. It calls for appropriations amounting to $10,400,000,000. It will be passed on 28 June.

Below: The price of German victory on Crete, May 1941: a dead German paratrooper.

6 June 1941

United States, Politics A new law comes into force allowing the government to take over foreign ships laid up in the United States.

Mediterranean The carriers *Ark Royal* and *Furious* again carry a cargo of Hurricanes from Gibraltar to within flying distance of Malta.

8 June 1941

Syria At 0200 hours British and Free French forces invade Syria. The British have been increasingly worried by reports of a German presence in Syria in recent weeks. In fact, although German aircraft did use Syrian bases during the fighting in Iraq, they have all now left at the request of the Vichy authorities. The Allied attack goes in nonetheless.

The attacking force is commanded by General Wilson and includes 7th Australian Division, 4th Indian Brigade and Free French units. The defending Vichy forces are rather stronger, with 45,000 men under the command of General Dentz. The Allied force advances along several lines from positions in Palestine and Transjordan. There is little resistance at first.

General Catroux, who has been appointed by General de Gaulle to head the Free French forces, issues a proclamation calling optimistically for Dentz and his men to change sides. The British announce that they seek no territorial gains.

9 June 1941

Syria The Allied advance continues to make good progress. Tyre, Marjayoun and El Quneitra are all taken in the advance from Palestine.

There is a naval battle off the Syrian coast between forces which eventually include four British and two Vichy destroyers. The French are forced to retire but inflict some damage.

10 June 1941

Syria Australian forces advancing along the coast north of Tyre begin improvising crossings over the Litani River. A commando raid on the 9th failed to take an important bridge in this sector.

East Africa An Indian battalion lands and captures Assab, the last Red Sea port held by the Italians. There is fighting southwest of Addis Ababa near Galla Sidamo.

13 June 1941

War at Sea The German pocket battleship, *Lützow*, is damaged by a torpedo attack from a British Beaufort aircraft off the Norwegian port of Lindesnes. *Lützow* returns to port and will be in dock until January 1942.

Syria On the coast the Australian forces begin attacks around Sidon. The town falls on the 15th.

Vichy France The Vichy government announces that more than 12,000 Jews have been arrested and are 'interned' in concentration camps because of a 'Jewish plot' to hinder Franco-German cooperation. The anti-Semitic laws in Vichy are being extended to include the expropriation of Jewish businesses.

Soviet Union, Politics The news agency Tass issues an official denial that there is tension between Germany and the USSR. It states that 'there could be no misunderstanding between the two countries.'

14 June 1941

Mediterranean The carriers *Ark Royal* and *Victorious* fly another cargo of Hurricanes to Malta. Of the 47 sent 43 arrive.

United States, Politics President Roosevelt freezes all German and Italian assets in the United States.

15 June 1941

North Africa A major British offensive, Operation Battleaxe, begins. The aim is to relieve Tobruk. Wavell is still reluctant to attack, largely because the tanks which recently arrived on the Tiger convoy have had many mechanical faults and the time taken for repairs means that the troops have had a very short training period. Although the two divisions involved, 4th Indian and 7th Armored, are both experienced formations, they are not at full strength and have been further weakened by changes in command. Beresford-Pierse is in charge of the attack.

Three columns are sent forward, one to Halfaya Pass, one to Capuzzo along the edge of the escarpment and one inland to Hafid Ridge. The attack of Matilda tanks is beaten off at Halfaya by the emplaced 88s, and without tank support the infantry units there can achieve nothing. A force of lighter cruiser tanks similarly loses heavily at Hafid Ridge. Some success is achieved at Capuzzo, however.

The German radio intelligence gives them excellent tactical information and their dispositions of 5th Light forward and 15th Panzer watching Tobruk are more than adequate. On the whole Rommel is content to defend on the first day and, indeed, by the end of the day the British tank losses already leave them at a disadvantage.

Syria A counterattack by the Vichy forces succeeds in retaking part of the town of Marjayoun and some nearby positions. However, both to the west on the coast, where Sidon is taken, and to the east in the approaches to Damascus, where Kiswe falls, the Allied advance is still going well.

16 June 1941

North Africa Nominally the British attack continues but the initiative has really passed to the Germans. The British 7th Armored Brigade loses heavily in a running battle with 5th Light while 4th Indian Division has to fight hard to hold off 15th Panzer. Halfaya remains in German hands.

Syria The Vichy counterattacks continue. El Quneitra is retaken.

United States, Politics President Roosevelt orders that all German and Italian consulates in the country should be closed, along with the offices of other German agencies. On 19 June Italy and Germany take similar action regarding American offices in their countries.

17 June 1941

North Africa Rommel attempts to move his tank forces together early in the day to threaten the now-weakened British armor guarding the inland flank. After some confusion the whole British force begins to withdraw and Wavell is left to signal the failure of Battleaxe to Churchill.

Syria Australian troops take Jezzine, just inland from Sidon. The Habforce group, which had an important role in the fighting in Iraq and is now made up of a cavalry brigade and some small infantry units, is ordered to begin an advance from Iraq due west along the main oil pipeline leading to Palmyra.

Germany, Planning Hitler decides that the attack on the Soviet Union will commence on 22 June 1941.

18 June 1941

Diplomatic Affairs A German-Turkish treaty of friendship for 10 years is concluded by the Turkish government and the German ambassador in Ankara, von Papen.

19-20 June 1941

Syria There is heavy fighting just outside Damascus at Mezze where the Vichy forces manage to cut off and eventually eliminate an Indian battalion.

20 June 1941

Finland, Politics All reservists under the age of 45 are called up.

Battle of the Atlantic A German U-Boat sights the American battleship *Texas* within the area that Germany has declared is the operational area for U-Boats. However, after checking with the U-Boat Command, the *Texas* is not attacked.

21 June 1941

East Africa British forces take Jimma, southwest of Addis Ababa. About 15,000 prisoners are taken. Although Jimma has been General Gazzera's main base, he escapes capture with a small part of his force. A further 4000 prisoners were taken earlier after an action at crossings of the Omo River, and many more were rounded up in smaller groups.

Syria Damascus falls to the Allied forces after

Below: The scourge of the Desert War: a German 8.8cm flak/anti-tank gun fires at a distant target.

Above: Afrika Korps resupply: Panzer Mark III tanks, armed with 5cm main guns, are offloaded in Tripoli harbor, 1941.

Above: As a U-Boat dives, a crew-member hastily closes the watertight hatches to the conning tower. Delay under attack could be fatal.

the Vichy garrison has been evacuated. Habforce begins to advance into Syria from Iraq.

22 June 1941

Eastern Front Operation Barbarossa, the German attack on the Soviet Union, begins. Despite the massive preparations spread over many months and the numerous indications Stalin receives from many sources, the Soviet forces are taken almost completely by surprise and lose very heavily in the first encounters.

The Germans have assembled almost 140 of their own divisions (figures vary in different sources), including 17 Panzer and 13 motorized units. Army Group North, commanded by Field Marshal Leeb, has 26 divisions and includes two infantry armies and Hoeppner's Fourth Panzer Group. Field Marshal Bock leads the largest German force, Army Group Center, with 51 divisions in two infantry armies and Guderian's Second and Hoth's Third Panzer Groups. Army Group South is led by Field Marshal Rundstedt and includes 41 German divisions in three armies and one Panzer Group as well as 14 Rumanian and two Hungarian divisions. German units from Norway in General Falkenhorst's Norway Army will join the attack in alliance with the 21 divisions of the Finnish army who are keen to regain the territory lost to the USSR in 1940. There are more German units in general reserve and others allocated for security duties in captured territory. Altogether, the Germans deploy over 3,000,000 men, 7100 guns and 3300 tanks. Each army group has support from a complete Luftflotte. The total strength is 2770 aircraft, almost the same as in France but now spread over a much larger front. Of the 3300 tanks deployed in the attack only 1400 are Mark III or IV types. This is a rather greater proportion of high-grade machines than in 1940 but Hitler's wish to have many of them armed with better guns has not been met. The increase in the number of Panzer divisions compared with 1940 has been achieved by a reorganization made in September 1940, when tank establishment was halved so that the number of divisions could be doubled. The strongest Panzer division in May 1940 had 300 tanks; now the strongest has 199. The new Panzer divisions have made considerable demands on scarce supplies of other vehicles also. As well as the tank force there is now a significant number of assault guns (250), mustered in special infantry-support battalions. The assault guns are formidable machines but they are administered and commanded by the artillery rather than the Panzer arm and will come to compete with the true tanks for scarce production resources.

The logistic preparations for Barbarossa have been particularly difficult for the German High Command. It has only been possible to assemble even a bare sufficiency of motor transport by using German, French and other captured types, which will, of course, cause many problems with spares and maintenance. The captured vehicles, especially the French, will be found to be notably unreliable. In addition to the motor transport the forces moving into the USSR still employ 625,000 horses. A further difficulty for the Germans is that the Soviet railroad system runs on a different gauge and must be converted if German rolling stock is to be used in captured areas. The Soviet forces also have their problems. Out of a total Red Army strength of over 230 divisions, about 170 are in the western part of the Soviet Union and 134, 32 of them armored, are with the formations facing the Germans. The total Soviet tank strength is around 24,000 machines but only a quarter of these are in running order. The Red Air Force has about 8000 aircraft facing the Germans but, again, many are obsolete or in poor repair. In all classes of equipment the most modern Soviet designs are simple and durable and at least as good as the German equivalent.

There are important gaps in the Germans' information about Soviet strength and equipment. They underestimate badly the manpower the Soviets have available and take too little account of the speed with which the Soviets will prepare new army and militia units. They also believe that the Soviets have a total of 10,000 tanks and they have no real information about the superior T34 and KV1 tanks. There are 1475 of these in the various armored divisions. The KV type is almost invulnerable to the German tanks' guns.

However, the considerable Soviet resources are less formidable than their extent suggests. Following the purges of the late 1930's a large part of the remaining senior leadership of the Red Army has been made up from the 'Cavalry Army' clique, old associates of Stalin not always distinguished for their military talents. Marshal Budenny typifies this group, perhaps owing his preferment to his position as one of Stalin's favorite drinking companions.

The Winter War with Finland exposed many weaknesses within the Red Army and led to many changes. Some, like the re-creation of the mechanized corps in September 1940, are undoubtedly sensible but others have been wasteful. All the changes, sensible or not, have been made in an atmosphere of haste which has made assimilating them more difficult. Training has also been poor. Some of the tank drivers and mechanics have had about an hour's instruction altogether on their new T34s and KV1s. Soviet deployment is also very weak. Some units which are supposedly part of the front line are as much as 200 miles away in barracks or on training grounds. Other formations, Tenth Army of the Western Front is the best example, are too far forward in dangerously exposed salients. Plans are under way to bring reinforcements from the units deployed in the Far East but these have not yet become effective. Thus, despite Soviet manpower resources and useful stocks of equipment, the weakness of their tactical system, training and deployment means that they could hardly be worse placed.

Marshal Timoshenko is Commissar for Defense and General Zhukov is Chief of the General Staff. In the line from north to south are Kuznetsov's Northwest Front, Pavlov's West Front, Kirponos' Southwest Front and Tyulenev's South Front. The balance of forces differs from the Germans in showing a slight preponderance in the south. Kuznetsov, Pavlov and Kirponos will all be replaced early in the campaign.

The German plan is for an advance by all three army groups. Leeb is to go for Leningrad, Bock for Smolensk and Rundstedt for Kiev. Army Group Center is to be prepared to give support to the flanks of the thrust rather than to press toward Moscow after Smolensk. This decision has been Hitler's own and is generally regarded by later military critics as unsound. Equally controversial is the timing of the attack. Since the war it has often been argued that despite errors in Hitler's direction of the campaign, the main reason why the German army did not reach Moscow and win the war in the autumn and early winter was the weather and that, if Barbarossa had been begun earlier in the year, Moscow would have fallen. However, it is by no means certain that even with a few weeks' grace the Germans would have been able to finish off their Moscow attack. Also, it is almost certain that Barbarossa could not have been started any earlier. The Greek campaign did not cause any delay and the Yugoslav campaign almost none (*see* 25-29 April). The real causes of delay were that the winter and spring of 1940 were particularly wet, flooding the rivers of Poland and softening the ground. Even in early June the Bug was well over its banks in many places on the front of Army Group Center. It should not be forgotten also that any delay meant that the Germans could add tanks and lorries to their units. All this discussion is somewhat academic. The Germans were in no particular hurry because they believed that they could win in a matter of weeks, and foreign military opinion agreed with them. The Red Army proved everyone wrong.

On the first day of the attack almost everything goes the German way. The attack begins at 0300 hours with advances on the ground and simultaneous air strikes. The Luftwaffe begins its operations very early in order to be over the Soviet bases exactly at zero hour. By noon the

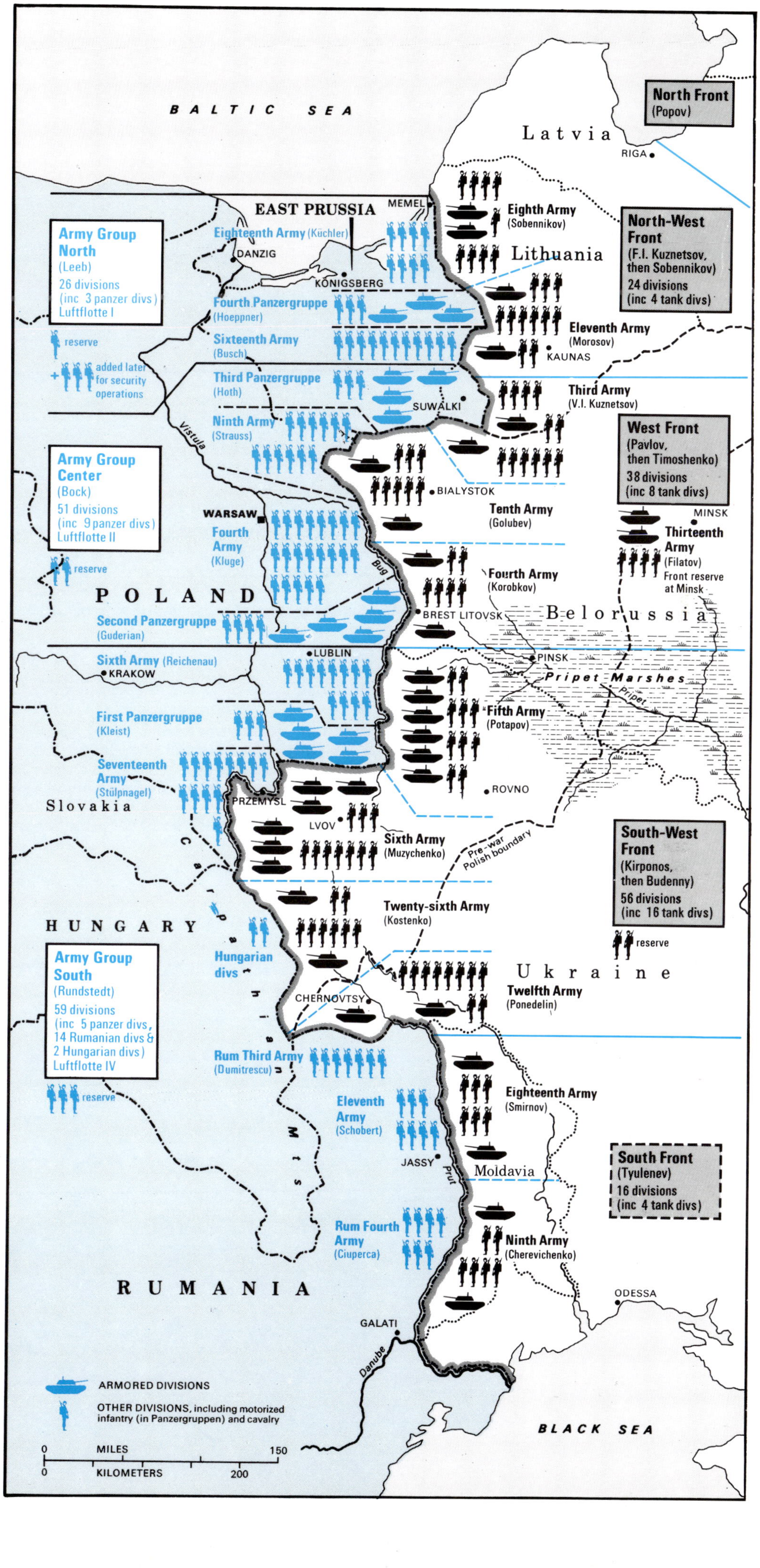

Right: The balance of forces on the Eastern Front on the eve of Germany's attack on the Soviet Union – Operation Barbarossa, 22 June 1941.

Soviet Air Force has lost around 1200 planes. The land battle is equally successful. Army Group North's Panzer spearhead advances 40 miles during the day and Army Group Center captures most of the Bug bridges intact. During the first four days Manstein's LVI Panzer Corps with Army Group North will advance 185 miles: Guderian's Panzer Group will make 270 miles in the first week. Other forces will do equally well. One setback for Army Group Center is that, although they win control of the town of Brest Litovsk, they will not be able to take the medieval citadel or use the communications network centering there for several days.

Britain, Politics Churchill broadcasts saying that help will be given to the Soviet Union. He says, 'Any state who fights Nazism will have our aid . . . It follows therefore that we shall give whatever help we can to Russia.'

22-29 June 1941

Syria There is heavy fighting in and around Marjayoun in which the Australians eventually drive the Vichy forces into retreat.

23 June 1941

Eastern Front The German attacks continue to make astonishing progress. The tank and motorized forces are already forging ahead. In the north Fourth Panzergruppe has advanced almost 50 miles. Hoth's forces have gone a little farther and taken bridges over the Niemen. Guderian's tanks have done slightly less well but have still made deep penetrations on either side of Brest Litovsk. Kleist's First Panzer Group has made some ground also but the Soviet defense in their southern sector is stronger. The Luftwaffe continues to batter the Red Air Force and disrupt Soviet communications.

Syria The advance of the British force from Iraq reaches Palmyra but the Vichy garrison holds out.

23-29 June 1941

War at Sea The largest convoy battle to date occurs around HX-133. Ten U-Boats are concentrated to attack the convoy, which at first has four escorts. The escort group is later reinforced by nine more ships from other convoys (which, partly in consequence, lose two freighters) and in the ensuing battles HX-133 loses five ships. Two U-Boats are sunk. This ratio of losses would be favorable to the British in the long run if it could be repeated.

24 June 1941

Eastern Front The German attacks continue to make rapid gains. Vilna and Kaunas have been taken and Brest Litovsk, which is now far behind the front line, is also assaulted.

United States, Politics At a press conference President Roosevelt announces that he intends to send aid to the USSR.

25 June 1941

Eastern Front Already the Germans are threatening to complete the first of their great encircling operations. The Soviet salient around Bialystok, containing forces of Third and Fourth Armies, is menaced by an envelopment southwest of Grodno while a far deeper cordon is to be drawn closed at Minsk in a few days.

Sweden, Politics The government announces that it will allow the Germans to move forces up to one-division strong through Sweden from Norway to Finland.

Eastern Front In the north Daugavpils is taken in the German advance and Hoeppner's forces begin working to take bridgeheads over the Dvina. In the advance of Army Group Center the first encirclement is closed by Hoth's and Guderian's forces near Baranovichi.

26 June 1941

Diplomatic Affairs Finland declares war on the USSR.

26-30 June 1941

Mediterranean In two operations, first by *Ark Royal* alone and then by *Ark Royal* and *Victorious* together, 57 Hurricanes are flown off to Malta. More planes are embarked but cannot be sent because of malfunctions in the launching equipment of the carriers.

27 June 1941

Diplomatic Affairs Hungary declares war on the USSR.

29 June 1941

Eastern Front Hoth's and Guderian's forces join up near Minsk, completing the isolation of another huge pocket around Gorodische. Elsewhere the German armies are maintaining their advances and the Soviet position is further stretched by the start of joint German-Finnish attacks in the Karelian Isthmus and farther north near Petsamo.

30 June 1941

Eastern Front Bobryusk is taken by Second Panzer Group and operations begin to cross the Berezina. Troops from Army Group South take Lvov while to the north other units make deeper advances toward Kiev.

Soviet Union, Politics The formation of a new State Committee of Defense is announced in Moscow. The members will be Stalin, Molotov, Voroshilov, Malenkov and Beria. Stalin is very much in charge.

July 1941

Battle of the Atlantic Allied shipping losses are much less severe this month. Only 22 ships of 94,200 tons are sunk by U-Boats out of a total of 121,000 tons. The strength of the U-Boat fleet is increasing, however. There are now 63 boats operational and a further 93 in training. About 20 new boats will be commissioned during the month and only one of the operational fleet will be lost. The strength of the British escort forces is increasing also. Outward convoys to North America and convoys to West Africa can now be given continuous escort and the Gibraltar convoys have their escorts strengthened. Until this time the U-Boats have been able to take supplies from German ships sheltering in the Canary Island harbors but British diplomatic pressure on the Spanish government now brings this to an end.

On the technical side the British ability to track U-Boats from their radio messages is becoming greater. A U-Boat which finds a convoy must signal to assemble a pack for an attack but if the position of the sighting U-Boat can be plotted by radio direction finding it may perhaps be driven away or sunk and the whole pack left blind. There is no way the Germans can avoid this. Indeed, this remains one of the central problems for the German *Kreigsmarine* throughout the war; it is never solved.

British Air Operations There are several attacks on general targets in the Ruhr and the Rhineland. Berlin is also hit. There are more operations against ports in France and Germany (*see* 24 July). RAF bombers drop 4380 tons – the highest total achieved until mid-1942. Over 3800 sorties are flown and 188 aircraft are lost.

1 July 1941

Middle East General Auchinleck is appointed to command the British forces in the Middle East. General Wavell takes Auchinleck's old post as Commander in Chief in India. Churchill has finally tired of Wavell with the failure of the Battleaxe offensive. The British government recognizes that the Commander in Chief, Middle East, has had heavy political responsibilities up to now in addition to his military duties and to avoid the distraction which this has caused in the past Oliver Lyttelton is appointed minister of state, resident in the Middle East.

Below: Graveyard for the Russian fighter arm, June 1941. Pre-emptive attacks on the enemy's air force were a vital part of Blitzkrieg.

Eastern Front Units of Army Group North take Riga while to the south other German troops are already well beyond the Dvina, making for Ostrov. West of Minsk the Berezina has been crossed and the advance continues.
Syria Troops from General Slim's 10th Indian Division move into northern Syria from Iraq.
Battle of the Atlantic Aircraft from the United States Navy start antisubmarine patrols from bases in Newfoundland.

2 July 1941

Japan, Policy An Imperial Conference (a meeting of Japanese government and military leaders and the Emperor to explain policy to the Emperor and nominally to take important decisions – in fact these are already taken at the Liaison Conferences between the politicians and the military leaders) records the decision that attempts should be made to take bases in Indochina even at the risk of war. The US authorities very soon know of this determination through their code-breaking service which has managed to work out the key to the major Japanese diplomatic code and some other minor operational codes. The information gained from the diplomatic code is circulated under the code name Magic.
Eastern Front After a rapid concentration and regrouping Hoeppner's Fourth Panzer Group attacks with renewed vigor toward Ostrov.

In the south the Rumanian Third and Fourth Armies and the German Eleventh Army begin full-scale attacks.

3 July 1941

Soviet Union, Home Front Stalin broadcasts for the first time since the German invasion. The reason for his delay in responding is not clear. He calls for total effort and a policy of scorched earth before the German advance, and guerilla warfare in their rear. He defends the 1939 nonaggression pact on the grounds of his desire for peace. The broadcast is the first of many to emphasize patriotic nationalism.
East Africa In southern Abyssinia the Italian resistance comes to an end with the surrender of General Gazzera and 7000 troops to a Belgian unit. In the northwestern Gondar area there are more Italian surrenders around Debra Tabor.
Syria Deir el Zor falls to the troops from 10th Indian Division. The Vichy fort at Palmyra surrenders to Habforce after a long defense.

4 July 1941

United States, Home Front In an Independence Day broadcast Roosevelt says that the United States 'will never survive as a happy and fertile oasis of liberty surrounded by a cruel desert of dictatorship.'

5 July 1941

Eastern Front The German Sixth Army breaches the Soviet defense line west of Zhitomir. Kleist's First Panzer Group begins to move through the gap but is somewhat held back by orders from Hitler. Farther north in the attacks east of Minsk the German advance reaches the Dniepr.

6 July 1941

Eastern Front Rumanian forces take Chernovtsy and are welcomed by the civilian population on entering the city. The Soviets claim to have carried out successful counterattacks in Latvia and in Belorussia.

7 July 1941

Iceland American forces land on the island to take over the task of garrisoning it and protecting nearby shipping from submarine attack. The US troops are from General Marston's 1st Marine Brigade and the transport ships are from Admiral Breton's TF 19, which also includes two battleships, two cruisers and 12 destroyers.

8 July 1941

Yugoslavia The Germans and Italians formally announce their plans for the dismemberment of Yugoslavia. Croatia is to be 'independent.' The province of Ljubljana, part of Dalmatia and some of the Adriatic islands are to be annexed by Italy. Bosnia is to be under Italian protection. Germany takes Montenegro, Carinthia and Cariola. Hungary also takes some territory.
Eastern Front In the advance on Leningrad, Hoeppner's Fourth Panzer Group takes Pskov.

8-10 July 1941

Syria There is a series of sharp fights just inland from Sidon at Jezzine and Mazzrat-ech-Chouf.

9 July 1941

Eastern Front The pockets earlier surrounded by Army Group Center have now all been wiped out. At least 300,000 prisoners have been taken and more than 40 divisions have been eliminated from the Soviet Order of Battle. Second and Third Panzer Groups are united to form Fourth Panzer Army and the forces of this new formation have now crossed both the Dniepr and the Dvina, aiming to encircle Smolensk.
Syria The Australian troops advancing north along the coast take Damour. There is now no obstacle blocking their approach to Beirut. Homs also falls to the Allied advance. General Dentz asks for an armistice on behalf of the Vichy forces.

10 July 1941

Eastern Front Units of the Soviet Fifth Army counterattack southwest of Korosten. Kleist's Panzer Group holds the attack amid heavy fighting. Four Italian divisions leave Italy bound for the Eastern Front.
United States, Politics Roosevelt submits new appropriations measures to Congress. He asks for $4,770,000,000 for the army. On 11 July he asks for $3,323,000,000 for the navy and the Maritime Commission.

11 July 1941

Syria Despite instructions from Vichy forbidding him to do so, General Dentz accepts the Allied armistice terms. The cease-fire begins 2100 hours. The casualties in the campaign have been about 2500 on the Allied side and 3500 from the Vichy forces. In addition the Vichy authorities have had a number of prisoners flown out to Europe including a few after the armistice terms forbidding this have been agreed.
Eastern Front First Panzer Group renews its advance toward Kiev and reaches to within 15 miles of the city. The Soviet State Defense Committee establishes three new command areas for the Red Army. Marshal Voroshilov is to command in the north (Northwest Front), Marshal Timoshenko the central West Front, and Marshal Budenny the Southwest Front.
United States Roosevelt appoints William

Above: General Sir Claude Auchinleck, appointed C in C Middle East in June 1941.

Donovan to head a new civilian intelligence agency with the title 'coordinator of defense information.' This appointment will lead to the creation of the Office for Strategic Services (OSS) which will in turn develop into the modern CIA.

12 July 1941

Eastern Front Moscow is bombed for the first time.
Diplomatic Affairs Britain and the Soviet Union sign an agreement in Moscow providing for mutual assistance and forbidding the making of a separate peace.
North Africa General Bastico replaces General Gariboldi as Commander in Chief of the Italian, and nominally the German, forces in North Africa.

14 July 1941

Eastern Front The German advance continues and the Luga River is reached in the northern sector.
Mediterranean A force of German Ju 88 bombers attacks Suez from bases in Crete causing damage to harbor installations and to ships unloading.

15 July 1941

Eastern Front The Soviets counterattack for the next three days in the Lake Ilmen area to gain time for the building of further fortifications round Leningrad. The attacking forces lose heavily in their efforts because the troops are very inexperienced.

16 July 1941

Eastern Front The Finnish attacks north of Lake Ladoga take Sortavala and reach the lake to the southeast of the town, cutting off Soviet forces to the west. The Soviets will be able to get some of their troops away by boat. The German attacks by Army Group South surround a Soviet pocket south of Uman.
Germany, Planning At an important meeting Hitler, Goering, Bormann and Rosenberg decide on plans for the exploitation of the terri-

tory being captured from the Soviets. Rosenberg is put in charge of a new ministry with the task of organizing the new lands for Germany's economic benefit and eliminating Jews and Communists.

Vichy, Politics General Weygand is appointed Governor General of Algeria.

16-18 July 1941

Japan, Politics In order to remove Matsuoka from the Foreign Ministry, Prince Konoye resigns on 16 July and re-forms his Cabinet on 18 July with Baron Hiranuma as deputy prime minister and Admiral Toyoda as foreign minister. Already personally unpopular, Matsuoka is removed because he has been urging that the Neutrality Agreement with the Soviets should be abandoned and that Japan should join with Germany in the attack on the USSR. The other Japanese leaders do not wish to take such a decisive step, and have decided that without Matsuoka and his known liking for Hitler they have a better chance of reaching an agreement with the US over the pressing problem of the oil resources.

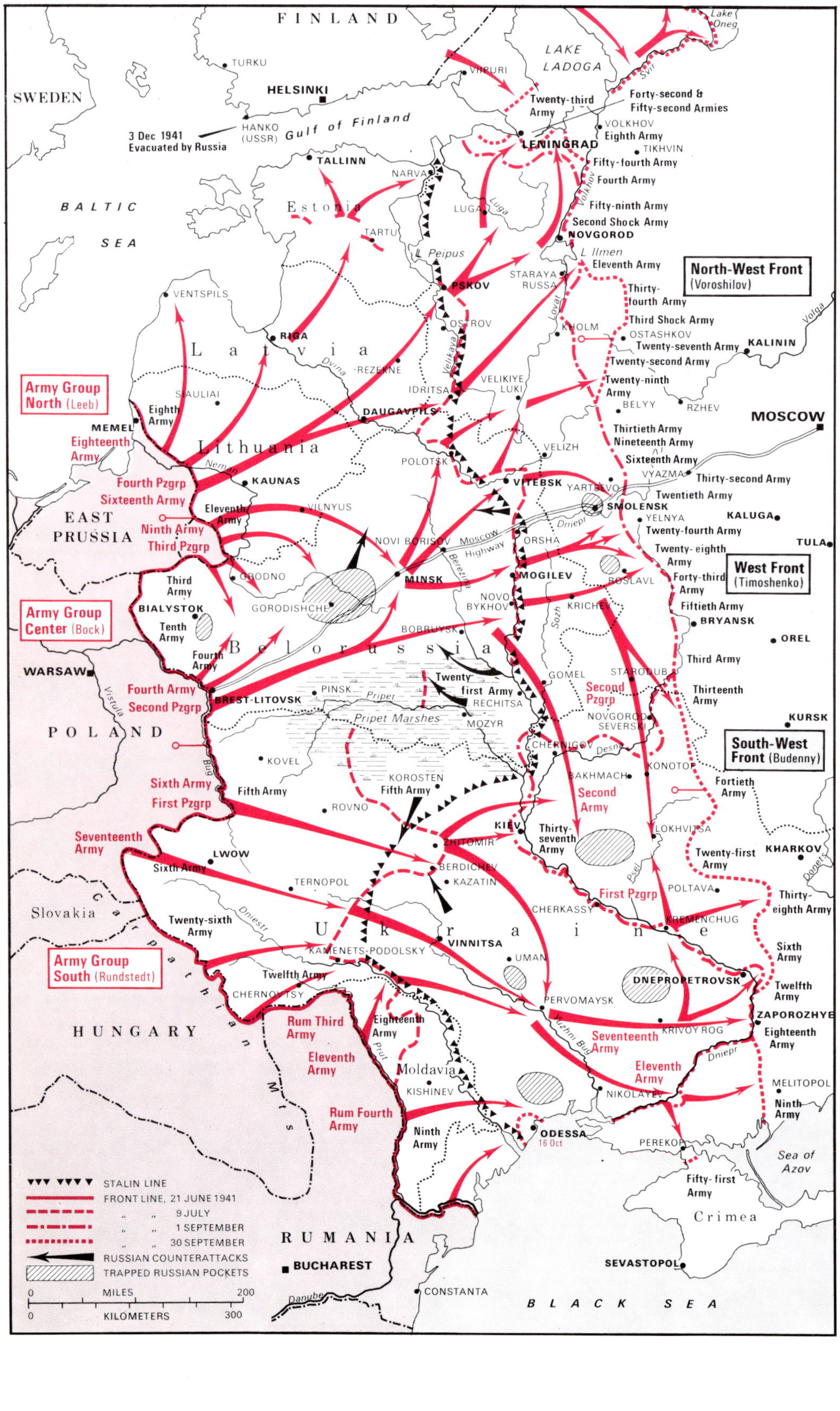

Below: Map showing the main thrusts of German advance in Russia, June-September 1941.

17 July 1941

Eastern Front The Germans develop an important bridgehead over the Dniepr.

In an attempt to stiffen resistance the political commissars are restored to the Soviet army and navy units.

18 July 1941

Czechoslovakia, Politics Britain formally recognizes the Beneš government as the legal provisional government. A friendship and mutual assistance agreement between the Czechs and the Soviets is signed in London.

19 July 1941

Eastern Front Guderian receives orders that after the Smolensk battle is over he is to move his force south to join the Kiev battle. This proposal is very much Hitler's idea. Guderian objects strongly, arguing that it will be far better to continue the attack toward Moscow.

Battle of the Atlantic The United States Atlantic Fleet forms TF 1 for the protection of the American forces on Iceland and support for convoys bound there. The carrier *Wasp* flies a cargo of P-40 fighters to the island. Early in August flying boats begin patrols from Iceland. The USN commits up to 25 destroyers to the Iceland operation as well as heavier forces. They are ordered to provide escorts for ships of any nationality sailing to and from Iceland.

Europe, Resistance At midnight there is a BBC broadcast by 'Colonel Britton' urging the creation of resistance forces with the slogan 'V for Victory.' The BBC has been introducing programs to Europe with the Morse signal for V for some time. Following this resistance members paint V signs on walls and German posters and it becomes a symbol for all Western European resistance movements.

21 July 1941

United States, Politics Roosevelt asks Congress to extend the draft period from one year to 30 months and to make similar increases in the terms of service for the National Guard. These measures pass the Senate on 7 August and the House on 12 August only after considerable debate. Indeed, the Bill is only passed by one vote (203-202) in the House, so it would be wrong to say that American political opinion is strongly in favor of a more militant policy at this stage.

Eastern Front There are more German air attacks on Moscow. The Soviet authorities announce that they have withdrawn their forces from the line of the Dniestr.

21-27 July 1941

Mediterranean A major operation, code named Substance, is mounted by the British Gibraltar forces to bring supplies to Malta. There are seven transports in the convoy and they are covered by Force H which has been specially reinforced for the occasion. In addition to *Renown*, *Ark Royal*, a cruiser and eight destroyers, the Home Fleet has sent *Nelson*, three cruisers and nine destroyers. The whole force sets out on 21 July. On 22 July part of the convoy is located by Italian planes but the Italian fleet stays in port, expecting only a repeat of the previous carrier operations to fly planes to Malta. On 23 July one destroyer is sunk and one cruiser and three destroyers are hit in Italian air attacks. On 24 July one transport is hit before entering Malta. Empty ships from previous trips join

Force H for the return to Gibraltar where they arrive on 27 July.

24 July 1941

Japanese Policy In line with the Imperial Conference decision of 2 July, the Japanese presented an ultimatum to the representatives of the Vichy government on the 19th demanding bases in southern Indochina. This demand is now conceded. The Japanese forces begin to occupy the bases on the 28th. It is very clear that the main

Right: German artillery is deployed to root out the last vestiges of Soviet resistance. *Below right:* German troops of Army Group South advance eastward. *Bottom right:* Russian T-34/76 tanks lie abandoned in marshy terrain, July 1941. *Below:* The invasion of northern Russia.

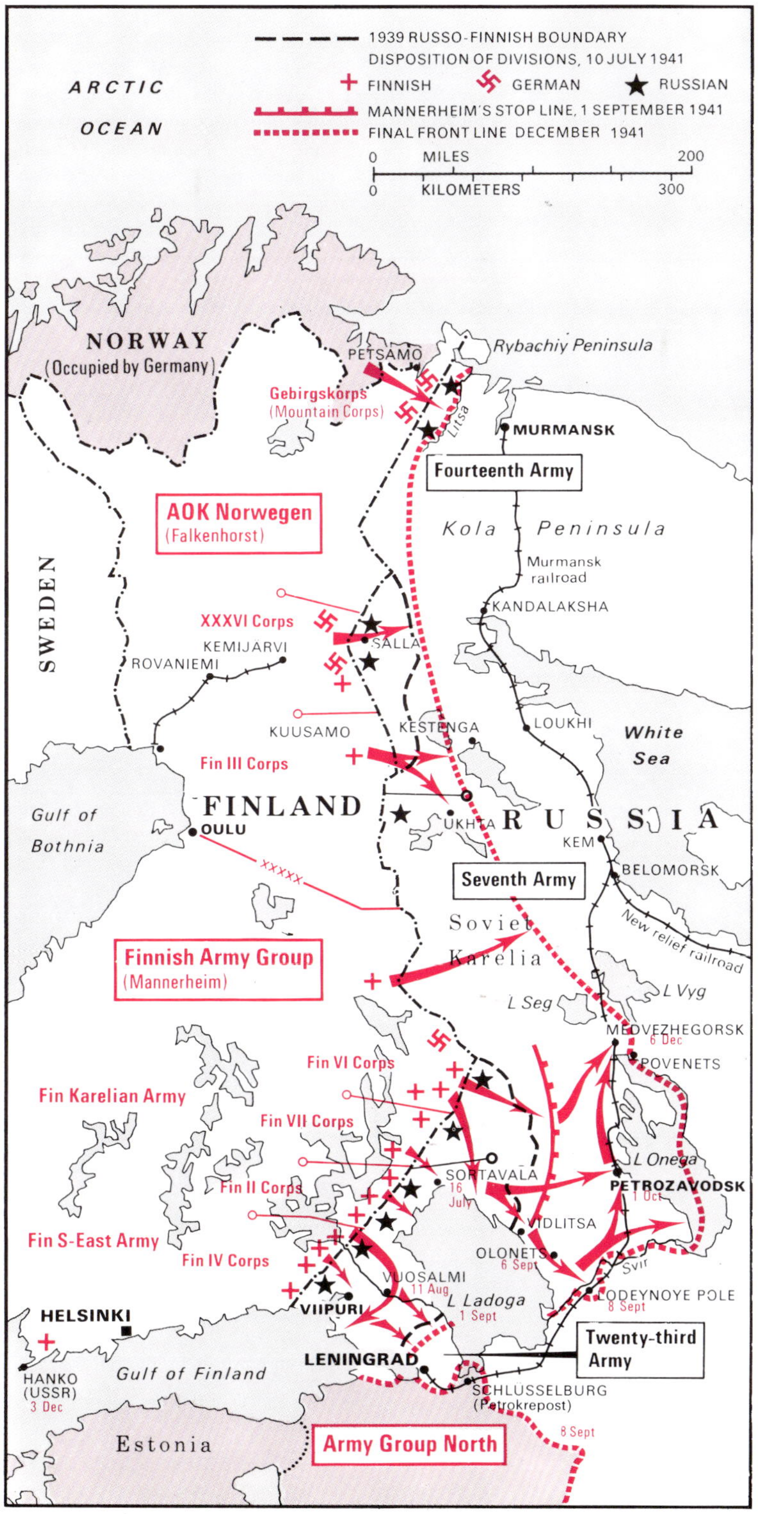

Above: Mussolini and Hitler (right) confer with Goering and Himmler, Chief of the SS (left), July 1941.

use for such bases would be in an invasion of Malaya, the East Indies or the Philippines.

British Air Operations The *Scharnhorst* is hit five times by bombs from a force of 15 Halifax bombers while lying in the port of La Pallice. The repairs will not be complete until 1942. Since *Prinz Eugen* has been hit earlier in the month and *Gneisenau* is under repair, this means that none of the German heavy ships in and around Brest is fit for operations in the near future.

26 July 1941

Diplomatic Affairs Japanese assets in the United States and Britain are frozen. On 28 July Japan retaliates with similar measures. Also on 28 July Japanese assets in the Dutch East Indies are frozen and oil deals cancelled. On 29 July Japan freezes Dutch assets. This means that almost 75 percent of Japan's foreign trade is at a standstill and that 90 percent of its oil supplies have been cut off.

Philippines Roosevelt orders that the Philippine army be entirely incorporated in to the US Army. MacArthur, who has been leading the Filipino forces, is appointed to command the US forces in the area as well.

27 July 1941

Eastern Front The Soviet forces in and around Smolensk are cut off by the German pincer movement. In the north the Baltic port of Kallinn is attacked by the Germans.

30 July 1941

China The US gunboat *Tutiula* is damaged by an attack by Japanese bombers in Chungking. Japan apologizes for the incident but it does nothing to ease the strained relations between the two countries.

30 July-4 August 1941

Norway On 30 July planes from the British Home Fleet carriers *Victorious* and *Furious* attack German shipping and installations near Kirkenes and Petsamo. Little damage is done and 15 of the 57 attacking aircraft are lost to anti-aircraft fire and the German fighters.

31 July 1941

Eastern Front Sixteenth Army from the German Army Group North continues the advance reaching the south side of Lake Ilmen. In southern Finland Finnish attacks toward Viipuri and Vuosalmi begin.

North Africa The Axis forces are reorganized. General Cruewell now commands the Afrika Korps (DAK) with Rommel in charge of the new Panzer Group Africa. The 5th Light is renamed as 21st Panzer Division and Rommel, therefore, has two Panzer divisions and one German infantry division in his force. In addition there are seven Italian divisions.

31 July-4 August 1941

Mediterranean There is a small British supply operation from Gibraltar to Malta. Force H gives cover. While on this operation destroyers from Force H and aircraft from the *Ark Royal* attack Alghero in Sardinia. When the operation is complete the battlecruiser *Renown* returns to the UK for a refit. *Nelson* remains as Admiral Somerville's flagship.

August 1941

Battle of the Atlantic This is another month of moderate success for the German U-Boat fleet. They sink only 23 ships of 80,300 tons for the loss of three of their number. The U-Boat effort in the North Atlantic is now concentrated rather closer to the UK than has been the recent practice because of the longer patrols this allows the smaller boats. The total Allied shipping loss is 41 ships of 130,700 tons.

British Air Operations Bomber Command raids many towns in Germany including Hanover, Frankfurt, Mannheim, Hamburg, Berlin and Karlsruhe. There are also sweeps by fighters and fighter-bombers over northern France and the Low Countries. Rotterdam is among the targets for these operations.

It has recently become apparent that the results of the British bombing offensive have been very poor. The Butt Report is prepared from studying photographs taken at the moment of bomb release during the June and July operations. This report is presented during August. It shows that on moonlit nights, of the planes which claim to have bombed their targets, only 40 percent have dropped their bombs within five miles. On dark nights less than seven percent have achieved this 'accuracy.' As there are no navigational aids available to overcome the problem yet, the whole policy of precision attacks is seriously questioned.

1 August 1941

Diplomatic Affairs President Roosevelt forbids the export of oil and aviation fuel from the United States except to Britain, the British Empire and the countries of the Western Hemisphere. This decision hits very hard indeed against Japan because Japan has no oil of her own and is left with only strictly limited stocks. The position is such that Japan must either change her foreign policy very radically or decide very quickly to go to war and try to gain access to the oil of the East Indies. Roosevelt's

Below: U-101, a Type VIIB U-Boat, comes alongside a resupply vessel during crew training in the Baltic Sea.

decision confirms the steps taken recently when Japanese assets were frozen.
Eastern Front The fighting is especially heavy near Vitebsk and Orsha. The Soviets attack along the northern edge of the Pripet Marshes from west of Gomel with the aim of striking into the German rear areas. In most sectors the Germans can withstand the attacks.

2 August 1941

Eastern Front The German forces in the northern sector begin to attack Staraya Russa just south of Lake Ilmen on the right of their drive toward Leningrad.
United States, Politics US Lend-Lease aid begins to be sent to the Soviet Union.

3 August 1941

Eastern Front In the south another German encircling move closes near Pervomaysk on the River Bug.

5 August 1941

Eastern Front The fighting around Smolensk comes to an end. The Germans claim to have taken 310,000 prisoners and to have killed many of the 700,000-strong Soviet force. The Soviets admit far lower losses. The German figures are probably more accurate.
Vichy, Politics Admiral Darlan is promoted to be in charge of Vichy policy in North Africa. The veteran General Weygand is to be his subordinate.

6 August 1941

Diplomatic Affairs The Japanese government presents proposals involving some concessions in China and Indochina to the US, asking in return for the end of the freeze on Japanese assets. The proposals are not acceptable to the US and when the rejection is made known to the Japanese they propose that Konoye and Roosevelt meet to discuss the issues at stake. This question is not resolved until after Roosevelt and Churchill meet at Placentia Bay (*see* 9-12 August).

7-8 August 1941

Soviet Air Operations During the night the Soviets raid Berlin with a small force. Berlin is bombed on six more occasions by the Soviets in this month.

9 August 1941

Eastern Front Army Group South, with forces from Eleventh and Seventeenth Armies, begins attacks along the River Bug.

9-12 August 1941

Allied Diplomacy Churchill and Roosevelt meet at Placentia Bay in Newfoundland. Both are accompanied by their military staffs. The discussions cover the situation in Europe and the Far East. It is agreed to send strong warnings to the Japanese and it is understood that America will almost certainly enter the war if Japan attacks British or Dutch possessions in the East Indies or Malaya. A message is also sent to Stalin, proposing a meeting in Moscow to make formal arrangements for the provision of supplies to the Soviet Union.

The conference is best remembered for the agreement later called the Atlantic Charter. This is a statement of the principles governing the policies of Britain and America and states that all countries should have the right to hold free elections and be free from foreign pressure.

Although its noble intentions will have comparatively little influence on the course of the war it is important as setting out the reasons why the United States might go to war and as a description of the aims of such a war.

The conference is important also because of the opportunity it gives the British and American staffs to get to know each other and to work together

11 August 1941

Eastern Front The Finnish attacks south of Lake Ladoga reach Vuosalmi.

12 August 1941

Eastern Front Hitler issues Directive 34. Army Group North is ordered to continue its efforts in the direction of Leningrad. Army Group South is to begin the battle for the Cri-

Below: A Fairey Albacore torpedo-bomber takes off from the deck of the carrier HMS *Indomitable* during a convoy run to Malta, 1941.

mea, Kharkov and the Donets. Army Group Center is to halt for the moment to bring help to the other forces.

Vichy, Politics In a broadcast Marshal Pétain says that Germany is fighting 'in defense of civilization' in the war against the Soviet Union. He announces new measures for the suppression of political parties and the creation of a stronger police force and special courts. Admiral Darlan is to be appointed to the Ministry of Defense.

12-18 August 1941

North Africa The Australian government has been pressing for their troops in Tobruk to be relieved and so in various night operations 6000 fresh troops from a Polish Brigade are sent in and 5000 of the Australians brought out. The fast minelayers *Abdiel* and *Latona* are prominent in these moves. A cruiser and two destroyers are also employed.

14-17 August 1941

Eastern Front The Soviets evacuate their Black Sea naval base of Nikolayev. Eight destroyers of the Black Sea Fleet cover the operation. Of the ships under construction in the port, 13 are far enough advanced to be towed away but one battleship and 10 other vessels on the stocks have to be blown up. The Black Sea Fleet is very active in support of land operations whenever possible.

Above: President Franklin D Roosevelt (left) and Prime Minister Winston Churchill meet at Placentia Bay, August 1941.

Below: The exhaustion of a speedy advance: German motor-cycle troops in Russia grab what rest they can.

17 August 1941

Diplomatic Affairs The United States presents a formal warning to the Japanese along the lines agreed at Placentia Bay. The text of the note has been toned down somewhat from the draft originally agreed with the British and Dutch, so they do not present their notes in order not to be seen to disagree with the American line. No decision has yet been taken on the Japanese proposal of a meeting between Roosevelt and Konoye, but on 3 September the Japanese will be told that it cannot take place. The Americans are worried that Konoye would not be able to make the Japanese military keep to any agreement that might be made.

Eastern Front The attacks of Army Group South reach the Dniepr at Dnepropetrovsk. The town is captured. In the northern sector Novgorod on the shores of Lake Ilmen is also taken.

18 August 1941

Eastern Front Budenny, commanding the Soviet southern armies, begins to withdraw as many of his troops as possible behind the line of the Dniepr. In the north the Germans take Kingisepp, on the Luga west of Narva. In this sector there is also heavy fighting near Novgorod. In the central sector there are fierce engagements near Gomel.

19 August-10 September 1941

Arctic There are various British naval operations. The population of Spitsbergen is evacuated and the Norwegians taken to Britain and the Soviets to the USSR. The first small supply convoy is sent from Iceland to the Soviet Union. The carrier *Argus* also brings a cargo of Hurricanes to the Soviet Union, complete with RAF pilots who will fly them in combat for the first few weeks. The carrier *Victorious* sends air attacks against German installations in and around Tromso on both 3 and 7 September but little damage is done.

21 August 1941

Eastern Front In the north the Germans take Chudovo, northeast of Novgorod, cutting the main rail link between Leningrad and Moscow. In the Finnish attacks farther north Kexholm is taken from the Soviets. In the central sector the Soviets pull out of Gomel after a long struggle and a series of counterattacks.

23 August 1941

Eastern Front Second Panzer Group and Second Army from the German Army Group Center begin attacks south to link up east of Kiev with the forces of Army Group South. Most of the German generals are opposed to this move and would prefer to maintain the drive toward Moscow but Hitler insists on this change in strategy.

German Raiders The German merchant cruiser *Orion* returns from its cruise and arrives in the Gironde Estuary. The cruise has lasted 510 days and six ships of 39,000 tons have been sunk, as well as seven more in company with the raider *Komet*.

24 August 1941

Eastern Front General Konev leads a new Soviet counterattack in the Gomel area. It makes little progress. In the north the Finnish attacks continue to press forward.

24-25 August 1941

Mediterranean Force H carries out another offensive operation. Aircraft from *Ark Royal* attack the Italian airfield at Tempio in northern Sardinia. Mines are also laid off Leghorn. The

Above: German heavy artillery is moved towards the front in Russia, 1941. Tractor-drawn units were essential on the rudimentary roads.

battleship *Nelson* is in support. The Italian battleships *Vittorio Veneto* and *Littorio* also come out but they move against a suspected Malta operation and there is no contact. The cruiser *Bolzano* is torpedoed by the submarine *Triumph.*

25 August 1941

Iran British and Soviet forces move into Iran. They have been worried by reports of German 'tourists' being in the country and have decided to demand that Iran accept their 'protection' of its oil supplies. The British land forces are led by General Quinan and their naval support by Admiral Arbuthnot. They advance in two areas, to seize the oil installations near Abadan, and from northeast of Baghdad to take similar sites around Kermanshah. The Soviet forces advance in three columns under General Novikov's command. One column moves on Tabriz while the other two advance on either side of the Caspian. There is little opposition to either the British or the Soviet forces.

There are British landings at Bandar Shapur, Abadan and Khoramshahr in the Persian Gulf area. Two small Iranian warships are sunk and several Axis merchant ships are seized. The British forces moving on Kermanshah, commanded by General Slim, and all three Soviet columns soon make good progress. The Soviets bomb Tabriz.

26 August 1941

Eastern Front There is a brief, unsuccessful Soviet counterattack against the German positions near Velikiye Luki.

26 August 1941

Iran The British forces take complete control of the Abadan area while the Soviets moving down from the north enter Tabriz. The Soviets bomb Teheran.

27 August 1941

Eastern Front The Germans begin full-scale attacks against the Baltic port of Tallinn.
Iran In the advance on Kermanshah the British take Shahabad and in the south they are preparing to attack Ahwaz. The Iranian government resigns.
Battle of the Atlantic While on an operation south of Iceland *U.570* surfaces immediately below a Coastal Command Hudson bomber and is captured. *U.570* is taken to Iceland and eventually will enter British service as HMS *Graph.*
Vichy, Politics Laval and a prominent pro-German newspaper editor are shot and wounded near Versailles by a young member of a resistance group. This incident is taken as an excuse by the Vichy government to round up many of its opponents, describing them as communists.

28 August 1941

Iran, Politics A new government led by Ali Furughi takes office and gives orders to cease fire. Negotiations with the British and the Soviets are under way.
Eastern Front The Soviets announce that the great dam over the Dniepr at Zaporozhye has been destroyed.

28-29 August 1941

Eastern Front The Soviets evacuate their garrison, X Rifle Corps, from Tallinn by sea. Several convoys attempt to get through to Kronstadt but losses to mines and air attacks are very severe on both days. Almost all the transports are sunk, along with many of the escorting vessels from the Baltic Fleet. On 29 August the Finnish forces farther north take Viipuri. The Finns are preparing to halt their advance when they reach their former frontier positions. This decision will contribute much to the Soviet ability to defend Leningrad.

29 August 1941

Iran The fighting comes to an end. On 31 August the Soviet and British troops link up at Kazvin. The final terms are agreed by the Iranian government on 9 September. The British and Soviets are to occupy certain key points but agree to keep out of Teheran.
Yugoslavia General Milan Nedić is appointed to lead the puppet Serbian government backed by Germany.

30 August 1941

Eastern Front In the Leningrad sector the Germans take Mga, cutting the last railroad link between Leningrad and the rest of the USSR.

September 1941

War at Sea Allied shipping losses increase this month to 84 ships of 285,900 tons. U-Boats

Below: Manhandling torpedoes on board a Type VII U-Boat in the Atlantic, 1941.

account for 53 ships of 202,800 tons. There are important convoy battles around SC-42, which loses 20 ships and one escort. SL-97 and HG-73 suffer heavily also. Some U-Boats are sent to the Mediterranean later in the month.

During the month there are several important developments in the maritime policy of the United States.

British Air Operations Among the targets for Bomber Command this month are Stettin, Hamburg and Cologne. The north German ports and Brest are again hit because of their naval value but little damage is done to the ships, which are the main targets. The usual daylight sweeps by light forces over northern France continue.

North Africa Italian agents of the Servizio Informazione Militare steal the 'Black Code' from the US Embassy in Rome. This theft is to be of great value because the US Military Attaché in Cairo, Colonel Fellers, is accustomed to send accurate and detailed reports to Washington concerning the Eighth Army's plans and dispositions.

Yugoslavia Tito's Partisans begin active resistance operations in southwest Serbia.

Mihajlovič gets word out to the west that he is organizing resistance and is hailed as a hero by the Allied press.

Above: Rommel surveys the battlefield from his command car, North Africa, 1941. The tank is an Italian M13/40.

1 September 1941

Eastern Front The attacking German forces are now within artillery range of Leningrad itself. To the east of the city the advance is nearing the south shore of Lake Ladoga.

Battle of the Atlantic The US Atlantic Fleet forms a Denmark Strait patrol. At first two heavy cruisers and four destroyers are allocated to this duty, but this force is increased later. The US Navy is now allowed to escort convoys in the Atlantic comprising ships of any nation provided an American merchant ship is present.

4 September 1941

Battle of the Atlantic In a convoy operation the US destroyer *Greer* is attacked by a German U-Boat but is not damaged and in return attempts to sink the submarine with depth charges. In fact the *Greer* has been brought into action by the reports of a British aircraft and has been mistaken, not unreasonably, for a British ship by the German commander. Roosevelt, however, presents the incident to the American public as an example of German aggression.

Below: Obergruppenfuehrer Reinhard Heydrich, head of the German security service.

6 September 1941

Japan, Policy Konoye gives in to military pressure and an Imperial Conference decides that, in view of the declining oil stocks, war preparations should be completed by mid-October and that if no agreement is reached by then that the decision to go to war should be taken. Konoye continues to make some conciliatory proposals to the US but is judged insincere despite the advice of Grew, the Ambassador in Tokyo, that if no agreement is reached the moderate Konoye may be replaced by a military dictatorship.

Occupied Europe By order of Heydrich, who heads the German security services (SD, a division of the SS) and the security police, all Jews over the age of six are to wear a distinguishing Star of David badge. This measure is only one token of the increasing barbarity with which the Jews are being treated. Experiments are being conducted at the Auschwitz concentration camp with various methods of exterminating large numbers of people. The gas Cyclon-B is being tested. The extermination camps will not begin full-scale operations until early in 1942.

8 September 1941

Eastern Front Between Lake Ladoga and Lake Onega the continuing Finnish attacks cross the Svir and take Lodenoye Pole, cutting the railroad track south from Murmansk. At this time of year it is still possible to use Archangel as the extrepôt for British and American supplies to the Soviet Union but later in the winter the Soviets will be unable to fulfill their promise to attend to the icebreaking. It will, therefore, be necessary to build a railroad track to Murmansk.

8-14 September 1941

Mediterranean A further 69 Hurricanes are flown to Malta in two operations by Force H, involving first the *Ark Royal* alone and then both the *Ark Royal* and *Furious.*

9 September 1941

Eastern Front A Spanish volunteer 'Blue Division' arrives to begin service on the Leningrad Front with the German forces.

10 September 1941

Eastern Front Guderian's southward attack on the Soviet forces east of Kiev reaches Konotop. Kleist's First Panzer Group begin to break out of their bridgehead over the Dniepr around Kremenchug.

11 September 1941

Battle of the Atlantic Owing to the *Greer* incident on 4 September, Roosevelt is able to order US warships to 'shoot on sight' in waters 'the protection of which is necessary for American defense.' In fact this is more or less what is happening already.

12 September 1941

Eastern Front Guderian's and Kleist's forces link up near the small town of Lokhvitsa, cutting off the huge Soviet forces in the pocket between there and Kiev, 100 miles to the west. At least 600,000 men are encircled. North of Kiev Chernigov, on the banks of the Desna, is evacuated in the face of attacks by the German Second Army.

The first snowfall on the Eastern Front is reported.

Norway, Home Front The Quisling government bans the Boy Scouts and other youth organizations. Boys are to be obliged to join youth sections of the Nasjonal Samling Party.

12-22 September 1941

North Africa There is another series of relief operations to Tobruk. The fast transports bring in about 6300 men and a large quantity of supplies, and take out 6000 of the Australian garrison. The new troops are from General Scobie's 70th British Division.

15 September 1941

Eastern Front The Germans capture Schlüsselburg on the south shore of Lake Ladoga, east of Leningrad, completely isolating the city from overland contact with the rest of the Soviet Union. Some supplies can still be carried in by boat across Lake Ladoga. There are sufficient stores for only about one month in the city even with very poor ration allowances. The siege will not be raised fully until early in 1944 and several hundred thousand civilians will die of starvation in the city.

United States, Politics The Attorney General rules that the Neutrality Act does not prevent US ships from carrying war material to British possessions.

16 September 1941

Iran The Allies have decided to occupy Teheran because the Shah has not done enough, in their view, to expel all Axis nationals from the country. The Shah abdicates in favor of the Crown Prince, Mohammad Reza Pahlavi. The British and Soviet forces arrive in the capital on 17 September.

17 September 1941

Battle of the Atlantic The US Navy increases its commitment to escort Atlantic convoys. It takes over responsibility for some of the Halifax-UK convoys and for most of the Iceland traffic. Canadian forces are escorting the others as far as 22 degrees west when the British take over on all routes.

Eastern Front There is heavy fighting with some German successes in the outskirts of the Ukrainian capital of Kiev.

18 September 1941

United States, Politics Roosevelt asks Congress for an additional $5,985,000,000 for Lend-Lease.

19 September 1941

Eastern Front Kiev finally falls to the Germans after more than 40 days of fighting. The Soviet losses in this battle have probably been in excess of 500,000 men. The Germans have lost about 100,000.

Yugoslavia, Resistance Tito and Mihajlovič meet to discuss resistance but they quarrel. Mihajlovič sees Tito as an anti-Royalist troublemaker who wants to muscle in on the Serbian territory that Mihajlovič regards as his own preserve. Tito in turn sees Mihajlovič as a bourgeois representative of an already discredited officer corps. They meet again on 26 October but cannot resolve their differences. Their supporters soon begin fighting.

20 September 1941

Battle of the Atlantic An aircraft from the British escort carrier *Audacity* shoots down an Fw Condor which is trying to shadow the convoy OG-74. This is the first success for the escort-carrier class. Escort carriers will not be readily available for convoy operations until the spring of 1943. Even with the *Audacity* in escort, OG-74 loses six from 27 ships.

Mediterranean Italian midget submarines are sent to attack shipping in Gibraltar harbor and succeed in sinking two ships, a triumph for Italy's amphibious forces.

23 September 1941

United States, Politics At a press conference Roosevelt announces that the United States is thinking of arming its merchant shipping against possible German attacks.

24 September 1941

Mediterranean The first German U-Boat to enter the Mediterranean passes Gibraltar. Six boats of the first group will arrive in the next two weeks. Later in the year about half the German U-Boat force will be engaged in the Mediterranean. Their most notable successes will be the sinking of the battleship *Barham* and the carrier *Ark Royal*.

Eastern Front The advance of the tank forces of Army Group South reaches to within 40 miles of Kharkov.

Allied Diplomacy Fifteen governments sign the Atlantic Charter at ceremonies in London and Washington. They include the UK, USA, USSR, the countries of the British Empire and many of the exiled governments of Europe.

24-30 September 1941

Mediterranean Operation Halberd is launched in a major effort to carry supplies from Gibraltar to Malta. There are nine transports in the convoy and their escorts and covering force include three battleships, one carrier, five cruisers and 18 destroyers. On 26 September Admiral Iachino leads two battleships, six cruisers and 14 destroyers of the Italian Fleet out to intercept. The remainder of the Italian Fleet stays in port, ostensibly because of fuel shortage. On 27 September both sides fail to find the main enemy force by air reconnaissance. The British battleship *Nelson* receives slight damage by a hit from an Italian torpedo plane, but the heavy ships do not make contact. One transport is sunk by air attack but the rest reach Malta with a close escort of cruisers and destroyers. Pantellaria is shelled by part of the British force and an Italian submarine is sunk by a destroyer. Among the 50,000 tons of supplies brought to Malta is enough food to last for several months.

25 September 1941

Eastern Front The Germans have now isolated the Soviet forces in the Crimea and begin attacks near Perekop with support from parachute troops.

27 September 1941

Eastern Front In the fighting in the approaches to the Crimea the Germans take Perekop.

East Africa The 4000-strong Italian garrison at Wolchefit surrenders to the besieging 25th East African Brigade. The Italians here have been very short of food because they have been isolated from their main body at Gondar by guerrilla activity.

Czechoslovakia, Home Front Von Neurath, the German governor of Bohemia and Moravia, resigns his post. Heydrich replaces him. On 28 September Heydrich imposes martial law on six districts. On 29 September Prime Minister Elias is arrested. There are many more strict measures

Below: Yugoslav Cětnik partisans, photographed in 1942. Initially opposed to the Axis occupation, they later fought the communists under Tito for control of Yugoslavia.

Above: Field repairs on a Panzer Mark IV in Russia: the mechanics are in the process of an engine overhaul.

taken at Heydrich's order and he quickly gains a justly vile reputation.

United States, Production The first batch of 14 Liberty ships is launched in the various constructing yards. Another 312 are on order. The total tonnage of these vessels is 2,200,000 tons.

28 September-1 October 1941

Allied Planning The conference suggested at Placentia by Churchill and Roosevelt takes place in Moscow. Harriman is the United States' representative and Beaverbrook the British delegate. Molotov takes the leading part on the Soviet side. On 1 October a joint declaration is made that the Soviet Union will continue to receive an increasing amount of help from both Britain and America.

29 September-11 October 1941

Arctic The convoy PQ-1 passes from Iceland to Archangel with 10 merchant ships escorted by one cruiser and two destroyers. There is no German attack. At the same time QP-1 passes from Archangel to Scapa Flow. This is the start of the regular traffic.

30 September 1941

Eastern Front Now that the Kiev battle is complete, Guderian's Second Panzer Army has been moved north again to form the right wing of the German attack on Moscow. Guderian's troops now begin this attack with an advance from around Glukhov northeast toward Orel and Bryansk.

In the south Kleist's Panzer Group attacks east of the Dniepr from Dnepropetrovsk. The Soviet line is quickly broken. Some of the attacking units head toward Donetsk while others move in a more southerly direction toward the Sea of Azov at Berdyansk.

October 1941

Battle of the Atlantic German U-Boat strength is now 198 vessels of which 80 are operational. This month they sink 156,500 tons of Allied shipping out of a total loss of 218,300 tons. The diversion of U-Boats to the Mediterranean continues and this partly accounts for the lower Allied loss than in September.

British Air Operations Hamburg, Stuttgart, the Ruhr towns and several of the north German ports are the main targets for Bomber Command this month. Over 2600 sorties are flown, 3000 tons of bombs dropped and 126 planes lost.

1 October 1941

Eastern Front The Finnish attacks west of Lake Onega capture Petrozavodsk.

2 October 1941

Eastern Front The German attack on Moscow, Operation Typhoon, officially begins. Hoth's Third and Hoeppner's Fourth Panzer Groups, Second, Fourth and Ninth Armies all join the advance, which was started two days previously by Guderian's forces on the right wing. The Germans have considerably superior forces on the ground and an even greater preponderance in the air. The main efforts are by the tank units. Guderian's force is already making good progress toward Bryansk and Orel while Hoth and Hoeppner plan an encircling movement to link at Vyazma. Along with Guderian, Hoth and Hoeppner are considered to be the finest tank generals on the Eastern Front.

Australia, Politics The Country Party government falls. The new prime minister is John Curtin of the Labor Party.

4 October 1941

Eastern Front Units of Hoeppner's Panzer Group attack near Vyazma from the south while Hoth's forces are attacking the still-intact Soviet line between Vyazma and Rzhev. On the right wing of the attack Guderian's forces are increasing their threat to Orel and Bryansk. Large Soviet forces west of Bryansk and Vyazma are in danger of being cut off.

6 October 1941

Eastern Front In the south the right wing of Kleist's attacks reaches Berdyansk, on the Sea of Azov, cutting off more than 100,000 Soviet troops. The German Eleventh Army is attacking along the coast to link with Kleist's force. The German advances in the Moscow sector continue.

The Soviet position around Vyazma and Bryansk grows more desperate. Large pockets have been isolated and are being reduced south of Bryansk and west of Vyazma. Other German forces are attacking well to the east of both these towns.

8 October 1941

Eastern Front The Germans occupy Mariupol on the Sea of Azov. In the Moscow sector the Vyazma and Bryansk battles continue. In these engagements about 600,000 Soviet troops will be taken, along with massive quantities of equipment. The main German efforts are now in northeasterly attacks toward Tula and Kaluga in the south and Rzhev and Kalinin in the north. Heavy rain begins to fall along the front. This will prove to be an ever-increasing hindrance to the German mobile operations.

9 October 1941

United States, Politics Roosevelt asks Congress to allow US merchant ships to be armed and to repeal certain sections of the Neutrality Act.

10 October 1941

Eastern Front General Zhukov returns to Moscow from his duties at Leningrad to take control of the defense of the capital.

12 October 1941

Eastern Front The German advance on Moscow continues with the capture of Kaluga despite the poor weather and the increasing determination of the Soviet defenders. The Soviets evacuate the town of Bryansk but the fighting round the isolated pockets nearby continues.

12-26 October 1941

North Africa There is a further series of relief operations to Tobruk. Just over 7000 troops are taken in to the fortress and just under 8000 are taken out. The minelayer *Latona* is lost to a Stuka attack and one destroyer is damaged.

13 October 1941

Eastern Front The Soviet forces are driven out of Vyazma and the resistance of the nearby pocket is almost over.

Below: A Focke Wulf Fw-200 Condor long-range maritime reconnaissance aircraft, used by the Germans as an effective means to spot Allied convoys in the North Atlantic.

14 October 1941

Eastern Front The German attack northwest of Moscow reaches Kalinin. The Soviet defense between here and Tula, southwest of the capital, is very stubborn.

15 October 1941

Poland, Home Front The German authorities decree that any Jews found outside the ghettos will be executed automatically.

15-16 October 1941

Eastern Front The Soviets evacuate Odessa, which has been holding out although for several weeks it has been well behind the German lines. About 35,000 men from three divisions are taken off. One transport is sunk by air attack on 16 October but the rest reach Sevastopol safely. Two cruisers and four destroyers and many smaller craft are involved. Most units of the Black Sea Fleet are now based in Sevastopol.

The 16 October is remembered in Moscow as a day of panic. Foreign diplomats and much of the government staff are moved to Kuibyshev. Many senior party members lead a less official exodus in cars and on the trains.

16 October 1941

Japan, Politics Prime Minister Konoye resigns and is replaced by War Minister Tojo. Tojo himself takes the offices of prime minister, war minister and home affairs minister. Shigenori Togo is foreign minister and Admiral Shimada is navy minister. These changes mark the increasing ascendency of the party which intends to go to war. The decision to go to war has not yet finally been taken, and it has been suggested that Tojo has taken the Home Affairs Ministry himself in order to be able to prevent any violent opposition if a decision for peace is reached.
Vichy Politics Daladier, Reynaud and Blum, all former prime ministers of France, are arrested on Pétain's orders to face charges that they were responsible for the French defeat.

16-17 October 1941

Battle of the Atlantic During the night *U.568* hits the US destroyer *Kearny* with a torpedo in a convoy battle involving British, Canadian and United States' ships.

18 October 1941

Eastern Front In the continuing German advance on Moscow, Mozhaysk is taken by troops from Fourth Panzer Group.

18-21 October 1941

Mediterranean On 18 October Malta's air forces are augmented by a force of strike planes flown in from Gibraltar. On 21 October two cruisers and two destroyers arrive in Malta to add their efforts to the threat which Malta poses to the Axis supply lines to Africa. For the next few weeks, as the British prepare for a new offensive in North Africa, an increasing portion of the Axis supplies will be lost.

19 October 1941

Eastern Front Stalin announces that he is remaining in Moscow, although most of the government has left, and that the city will be defended with every effort. Harsh punishments are to be imposed on looters and defeatists. Work is proceeding at a hectic pace on three fixed defense lines around the city. In the south the German advance along the coast of the Sea of Azov reaches Taganrog.

Above: A German horse-drawn artillery unit struggles through the Steppes of southern Russia. Such units rarely kept up with the tanks.

20 October 1941

Eastern Front In the Moscow sector there is heavy fighting near Mozhaysk and at Malayaroslavets.

In the south the German attacks also make progress capturing Donetsk (also known as Stalino).
France, Resistance The German commander in Nantes is shot by resistance workers. Fifty hostages are shot in reprisal. There is a similar incident similarly punished in Bordeaux on 22 October.

23 October 1941

Eastern Front The Soviet command system is reorganized. Zhukov takes over responsibility for the northern half of the front and Timoshenko for the south.

24 October 1941

Eastern Front A joint attack by the German Sixth and Seventeenth Armies succeeds in taking Kharkov.

25 October 1941

War at Sea The British battleship *Prince of Wales* leaves the Clyde for the Far East. Admiral Phillips is aboard on the way to take command of the new Far East Fleet which is to be created around *Prince of Wales*. On 28 November *Prince of Wales* and *Repulse* both arrive at Colombo. The carrier *Indomitable* is intended to join them, but will be accidentally damaged on 3 November in the West Indies while training.

27 October 1941

Eastern Front In the south the Germans capture Kramatorsk.

28 October 1941

Eastern Front Most of the German attacks toward Moscow are now being halted, partly by their own weakness but even more by the weather. By day the soft and muddy ground hinders movement, and by night the severe frosts weaken the inadequately clad German troops and damage and halt their vehicles. The final major effort of this phase of attacks is a push by Guderian's forces near Tula, but this makes little progress. Farther north another brief German attack manages to take Volokolamsk.

29 October 1941

Eastern Front The first of the Soviet reserve divisions from Siberia go into the line west of Moscow.

30 October 1941

Eastern Front The German offensive in the Moscow sector comes to a halt until the winter weather sets in fully, giving permanently hard ground and restoring some mobility to the German tank forces.

31 October 1941

Battle of the Atlantic While forming part of the escort of the convoy HX-156 the US destroyer *Reuben James* is sunk by a U-Boat. This is the first sinking of a US warship and 100 sailors are lost.

November 1941

Battle of the Atlantic Allied shipping losses are the lowest of the war so far at 104,600 tons. U-Boats only sink 13 ships of 62,200 tons. At the start of the month there are 10 U-Boats in the Mediterranean with more on the way. Ironically the sinking of the *Ark Royal* by two of the U-Boats makes submarine operations near Gibraltar more difficult since the carrier's surviving aircraft are based ashore and used solely for antisubmarine work. British air strength on the main convoy routes is now being augmented by Catapult Aircraft Merchant Ships (CAMS). The first action by an aircraft from one of these is on 1 November.
British Air Operations The targets for RAF Bomber Command include Kiel, Hamburg and Emden. British aircraft losses have been high and have risen in recent weeks; in the light of the Butt Report (*see* August) the practicality of the bomber offensive is being increasingly questioned. On the night of 7/8 November these problems come to a head when, of a force of 400 planes sent to Berlin, the Ruhr, Cologne and

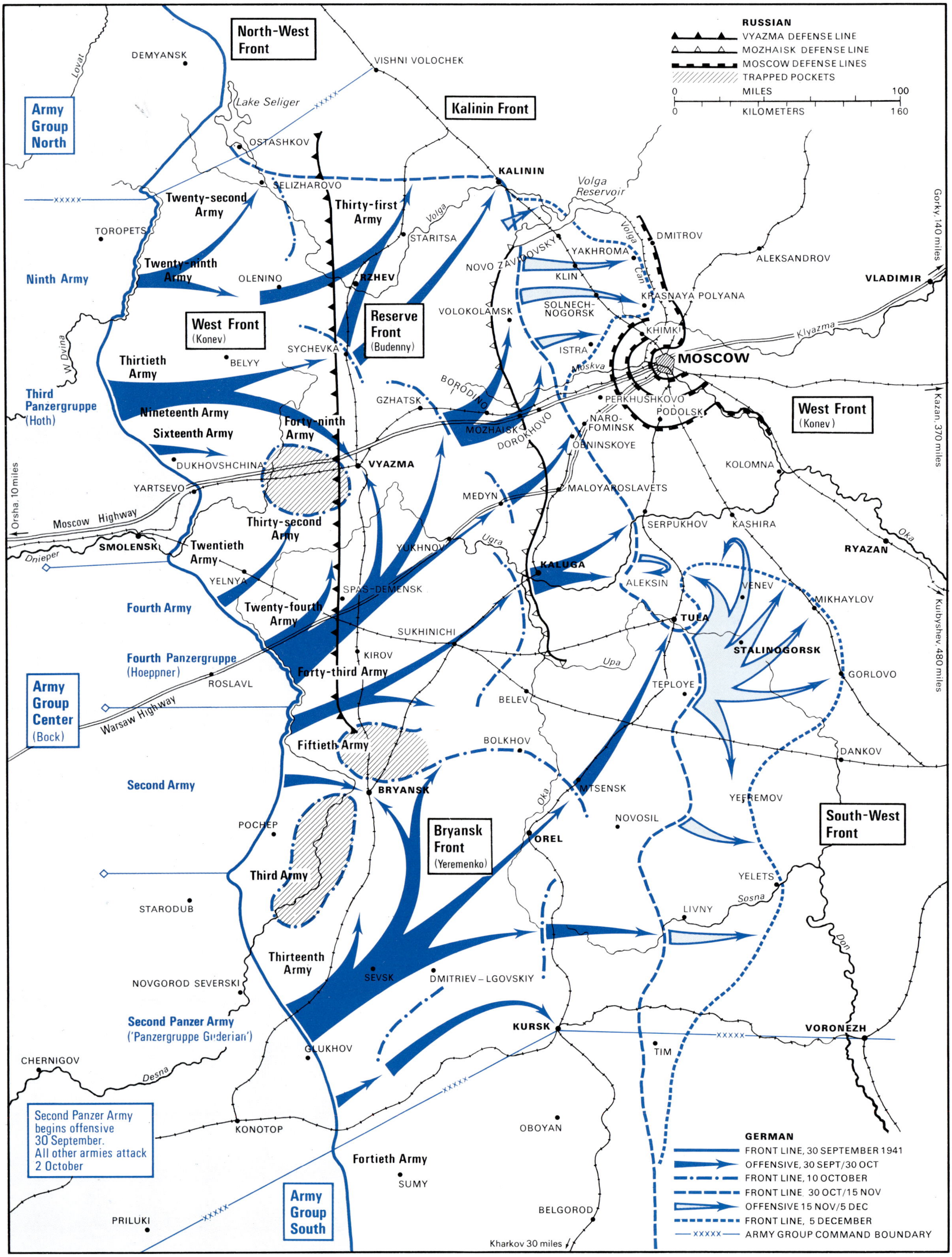
North-West Front
Kalinin Front
West Front (Konev)
Reserve Front (Budenny)
West Front (Konev)
Bryansk Front (Yeremenko)
South-West Front
Army Group North
Army Group Center (Bock)
Army Group South
Ninth Army
Third Panzergruppe (Hoth)
Fourth Army
Fourth Panzergruppe (Hoeppner)
Second Army
Second Panzer Army ('Panzergruppe Guderian')
Twenty-second Army
Twenty-ninth Army
Thirty-first Army
Thirtieth Army
Nineteenth Army
Sixteenth Army
Forty-ninth Army
Thirty-second Army
Twentieth Army
Twenty-fourth Army
Forty-third Army
Fiftieth Army
Third Army
Thirteenth Army
Fortieth Army
MOSCOW
KALININ
VYAZMA
BRYANSK
OREL
KURSK
TULA
KALUGA
SMOLENSK
RZHEV
VOLOKOLAMSK
MOZHAISK
MALOYAROSLAVETS
SERPUKHOV
KASHIRA
STALINOGORSK
YEFREMOV
YELETS
VORONEZH
RYAZAN
VLADIMIR
KOLOMNA
PODOLSK
Second Panzer Army begins offensive 30 September. All other armies attack 2 October
RUSSIAN
VYAZMA DEFENSE LINE
MOZHAISK DEFENSE LINE
MOSCOW DEFENSE LINES
TRAPPED POCKETS
0 MILES 100
0 KILOMETERS 160
GERMAN
FRONT LINE, 30 SEPTEMBER 1941
OFFENSIVE, 30 SEPT/30 OCT
FRONT LINE, 10 OCTOBER
FRONT LINE 30 OCT/15 NOV
OFFENSIVE 15 NOV/5 DEC
FRONT LINE, 5 DECEMBER
ARMY GROUP COMMAND BOUNDARY

Boulogne, 37, or nearly 10 percent, fail to return. After this Churchill gives orders to conserve the bomber force until the spring brings better weather and equipment. In the last few months it is probably true to say that more Bomber Command personnel have been killed than German civilians.

Mediterranean/North Africa More than 60 percent of the Axis supplies sent to North Africa are lost in transit. Only about 30,000 tons arrive, compared with an average over the past few months of more than 70,000 tons. Both Rommel and Auchinleck are hoping to prepare for an offensive and the supply situation is crucial.

Yugoslavia, Resistance Throughout the month the Germans are very active in anti-Partisan operations. This is their first major drive against the resistance forces in Yugoslavia.

1 November 1941

Eastern Front In the Crimea Simferopol, an important communications center, falls to the German Eleventh Army.

Marshal Shaposhnikov becomes Chief of Staff of the Soviet forces.

2 November 1941

United States, Politics The coastguard is placed under the control of the navy.

3 November 1941

Eastern Front In the Leningrad sector there are further German attacks in the continuing effort to complete the isolation of the city. Their aim in this phase is to take Tikhvin, an important railroad center, 100 miles east of the city. During this battle there will be repeated Soviet counter-attacks but they will be foolishly directed against some of the strongest German positions.

At the junction between Army Group Center and Army Group South, Kursk falls to the Germans.

4 November 1941

Eastern Front In the Crimea the German attacks are now making good progress. Feodosia is captured by the 170th Division.

5 November 1941

Diplomatic Affairs After discussion the Japanese decide to make further peace attempts, setting their deadline for the end of any negotiations at the end of November. The terms they offer are rejected by the United States because they contain no repudiation of the Tripartite Pact and because the Japanese intend to maintain bases in some parts of China. The outcome of the Japanese discussions and their diplomatic plans continue to be intercepted by the US codebreaking service.

6 November 1941

Production and Supply President Roosevelt announces that a loan of $1,000,000,000 is to be given to the USSR to help finance the acquisition of Lend-Lease supplies.

German Raiders The German blockade runner *Odenwald,* carrying a cargo of rubber from Japan, is captured in the American Security Zone off the Brazilian coast by the US cruiser *Omaha.*

Left: Map showing Operation Typhoon, the German attack on Moscow, September-December 1941.

Above: A Short Sunderland flying boat flies over a troop convoy in the eastern Atlantic. Air cover for Allied convoys was not always available.

Soviet Union, Home Front In a major public speech delivered to celebrate the anniversary of the 1917 Revolution, Stalin calls on the peoples of the Soviet Union to increase their efforts to defend 'holy Russia.' He claims that the German forces are worn out having taken almost 5,000,000 casualties compared to 1,800,000 for the Red Army.

8-9 November 1941

Mediterranean In a night battle the British Force K from Malta, two cruisers and two destroyers, attacks an Italian convoy sinking all seven transports and one of its escorts. The Italian covering force of heavy cruisers and destroyers does not engage.

9 November 1941

Eastern Front In the Leningrad sector Tikhvin is taken by the Germans, cutting the rail route into the city. In the Crimea Yalta falls to the German attack.

10 November 1941

World Affairs In a public speech Churchill announces that 'should the United States become involved in war with Japan, a British declaration of war will follow within the hour.'

11 November 1941

East Africa The final battle to eliminate the Italian presence in Abyssinia begins. The regular Allied forces, aided by local guerrillas, attack Chilga to the west and Kulkaber to the southeast of the main Italian Gondar position. The attacks are beaten off for the moment

12 November 1941

Eastern Front There is an important conference of German commanders at Orsha at which General Halder presents plans for continuing the attack on Moscow. The generals who will have to execute the scheme are not entirely happy with it but their opposition is fairly half-hearted and the plan is agreed. Three Panzer groups and three infantry armies are to take part.

12-14 November 1941

Mediterranean A further 34 Hurricanes are flown off from the British carriers *Argus* and *Ark Royal* to Malta on the 12th. On the 13th the force is returning to Gibraltar when two U-Boats, *U.81* and *U.205,* make attacks. *Ark Royal* is hit once and badly damaged. It seems at first that the damage has been brought under control but on the 14th, when the carrier has been brought to within 25 miles of Gibraltar, a fire breaks out and she is abandoned to sink. As in some carrier losses early in the Pacific war, poor damage control seems largely to have been responsible.

13 November 1941

United States, Politics Changes in the Neutrality Laws pass Congress. US merchant ships may now be armed and enter war zones. These administration-sponsored measures only pass by a small margin even after the *Kearny* incident and other developments in the Atlantic have been carefully presented as German aggressions. The small margin shows that the US is not yet ready to go to war.

15 November 1941

Eastern Front The German Moscow offensive is renewed. The main effort is to be made by the tank forces which are to drive converging attacks toward the capital from just to the north and to the south. Guderian's Second Panzer Group attacks from around Tula to the south of the capital, while just north of the city both Third and Fourth Panzer Groups are involved in the advance toward the Moscow-Volga Canal. The infantry armies on the flanks, and particularly

Above: The reality of German occupation: four Russian prisoners, accused of partisan activities, are publicly hanged.

Fourth Army occupying the front between the armored thrusts, are to make supporting holding attacks.

The Soviet strategy for this winter period is to try to build up reserves for a counterattack from the forces that are being brought from Siberia, while doing just enough to hold the German advances. To some extent, therefore, the inward movement of the German tank attacks will be permitted during the next few days while the Soviet reserves are built up on the outer flanks.

All the German units are very seriously under strength both from the losses in the fighting since June and from the more recent ravages of the weather. This winter will turn out to be the most severe in the Soviet Union throughout the period for which records have been kept and the German troops and their equipment are badly prepared for it. Losses of manpower through frostbite and of equipment through other effects of the cold – lubricating oil freezing solid and metal parts like rifle bolts becoming brittle and breaking – have already helped reduce Panzer divisions to tank strengths appropriate for battalions. The losses will continue.

16 November 1941

Eastern Front The German forces continue to overrun the Crimea. Kerch falls to one wing of the attack while Sevastopol is now being besieged by other forces. The Soviet resistance in Sevastopol will become very stubborn.

In the Moscow sector the new German drive makes some slow advances.

17 November 1941

Eastern Front Rosenberg, the Nazi Party 'racial expert' and ideologist, is appointed to head a new Reich Ministry for Occupied Eastern Territories. His jurisdiction includes the Baltic States and White Russia and his task is to exploit these areas for German economic benefit and to rid them of the 'undesirable elements' of their populations, such as Jews and Communist supporters. Throughout their occupation the German authorities treat the population with ever-increasing brutality. This plays into the hands of the Soviet authorities who are trying to organize partisan bands and ensure the continued loyalty of the people to the Soviet state.

In the fighting at the front the advance of First Panzer Group continues to go well in the southern sector near Rostov, but the Soviet Ninth and Thirty-seventh Armies begin a counterattack on the flank of the German drive. General Timoshenko is in overall charge of the Soviet forces in the south. One of the Red Army commanders in the Russo-Finnish War, Timoshenko had developed as an able commander and as a firm disciplinarian.

18 November 1941

North Africa A new British offensive, Operation Crusader, begins with an advance by XXX Corps over the Egyptian border into Libya. The British forces in the desert are now organized as Eighth Army with General Cunningham in command. They have about 450 cruiser tanks and 132 infantry models in their main forces with more in the Tobruk garrison. They also have good reserve stocks of all equipment. The cruiser tanks are concentrated in XXX Corps which leads the British attack. There are problems with the reliability and gun power of the British tanks and, far more importantly, defects in the tactical training of their armored units. General Cunningham has no experience of commanding tank units. The Germans have about 180 Mk III and IV tanks with another 220 of the much weaker Italian and other German models. On or near the frontier there are garrisons in fortified areas on the coastal routes to west and east with 21st Panzer supporting them. The bulk of the Italian force is farther back, around Tobruk and to the south. 15th Panzer and the German Afrika Division are also near Tobruk. Rommel was intending to attack Tobruk on 21 November and has, therefore, enough supplies for a short sharp battle, but not for the prolonged brawl which will in fact ensue. The British deception measures have been good and because of this and his determination to attack Tobruk, Rommel will not react promptly to the British attack. He is in fact returning to North Africa from Rome when the British moves begin.

The rather vague British plan is to advance round the inland flank to the area of Gabr Saleh and Sidi Rezegh, draw the Germans into making

Below: A Messerschmitt Bf-110 fighter takes off from a desert airstrip. By 1941 the Bf-110 was largely confined to a night-fighter role.

Above: British Matilda tanks advance through the desert near Tobruk, 1941. Although fast and manoeuvrable, the Matilda was undergunned.

attacks and destroy their tank forces. On the first day 7th Armored Division and other XXX Corps units advance virtually unmolested to Gabr Saleh.

Eastern Front One of Guderian's infantry divisions loses heavily in fighting near Venev in a counterattack sent in by one of the fresh Soviet Siberian divisions. There is a series of similar brief Soviet attacks against Guderian's force during the next few days which do much to confine the German attempts to advance.

Pacific A force of 11 Japanese submarines leaves their home ports to go to take up stations off Hawaii or to take part in other scouting missions. A further nine vessels sails toward Hawaii from Kwajalein.

British Command General Brooke is chosen to replace General Dill as Chief of the Imperial General Staff (the British Army Staff). General Dill will go to Washington to lead the British military mission there and General Paget becomes Commander in Chief, Home Forces in place of Brooke. These appointments take effect in December.

19 November 1941

North Africa The British 7th Armored Brigade advances easily to Sidi Rezegh but the other parts of 7th Armored Division are heavily engaged. The 4th Armored Brigade loses heavily to an attack by part of 21st Panzer and 22nd Armored Brigade equally heavily in a wasteful, unnecessary and badly conducted attack on the Italian Ariete Division at Bir el Gubi. Both British and Germans would have done better to concentrate their forces. The British have more than 40 tanks out of action already whereas the Germans have lost only a handful.

German Raiders The Australian light cruiser *Sydney* finds a suspicious ship in an area about 170 miles west of Western Australia. After an exchange of signals the *Sydney* rashly approaches close to the ship which opens fire with guns and torpedoes crippling the cruiser with the first salvo. The ship is in fact the German raider *Kormoran. Sydney* manages to fight back and both ships later sink. The *Kormoran* has sunk 11 ships of 68,300 tons during its cruise. News of the battle only becomes known when some of the crew of the *Kormoran* are found later. There are no survivors from *Sydney.*

20 November 1941

North Africa Both British and Germans still fail to concentrate their tank forces properly. The British 4th Armored Brigade is again mauled, this time by 15th Panzer. The 7th Armored Brigade is still active around Sidi Rezegh and 22nd Armored Brigade is moving to join 4th Armored. General Cunningham feels sufficiently in control of the situation to order the Tobruk garrison to begin break-out attacks, but in fact Rommel is beginning to appreciate the extent of the British aims and orders his panzer divisions toward Sidi Rezegh at the end of the day.

Vichy, Politics It is announced that General Weygand has returned from his post in North Africa. He has been removed after German pressure.

20-25 November 1941

Diplomatic Affairs The Japanese make proposals for an interim settlement with the United States. The proposals are unacceptable but Secretary Hull prepares a negotiating reply. This is not delivered because Chiang Kai-shek's government are successful in making the British and Dutch worried about the concessions offered to the Japanese in China.

21 November 1941

North Africa Both German tank divisions attack the 7th Armored Brigade at Sidi Rezegh and by the end of the day the British force has about 20 tanks left. A break-out attempt by the Tobruk garrison is brought to a halt when the expected help from 7th Armored Brigade cannot arrive. The British 4th and 22nd Armored Brigades are moving toward Sidi Rezegh.

East Africa The Allied attacks on Kulkaber southeast of Gondar are renewed with greater force and after a stout resistance the Italian defenders surrender. The Italians are now confined to the immediate area of Gondar.

21-22 November 1941

Mediterranean There are considerable Axis convoy operations because of the growing supply difficulties of their forces in North Africa. Two of the escorting cruisers are badly hit, one by a British torpedo plane and the other by submarine attack. The British Malta naval forces search for the Italian ships but cannot find them.

22 November 1941

North Africa There is a very confused tank battle around Sidi Rezegh in which 21st Panzer forces the British 7th and 22nd Armored Brigades to withdraw away from Tobruk. The 4th Armored Brigade loses heavily in a separate action with 15th Panzer. The New Zealand Division, part of XIII Corps, begins to move into the battle to help the British tanks. The Germans now hold the initiative, however, since they have over 170 tanks left and the British less than 150.

German Raiders The raider *Atlantis* is found and sunk by the cruiser *Devonshire* while replenishing a U-boat off the West African coast. *Atlantis* has sunk 22 ships of 145,700 tons during her cruise. On 1 December the German supply ship *Python* is also sunk in this area by a British cruiser. Doenitz had hoped to send a force of U-Boats to work off South Africa but with the loss of these sources of supply this will not now be possible. The British successes are based on code-breaking information.

23 November 1941

Eastern Front In the Moscow sector the German offensive continues to make gradual gains. Progress is made on a 50-mile front northwest of the city. In these attacks Klin is captured by three of Hoth's Panzer Divisions. Some of the German forces are less than 35 miles from Moscow.

North Africa There are more violent battles southeast of Sidi Rezegh. The fighting is especially fierce in the afternoon when both German panzer divisions and the Ariete Division make a headlong charge against the British armor and

Below: German troops wait for the order to attack, North Africa, 1941.

two South African Brigades which have now joined the tanks. The losses on the German side bring their force down to less than 100 tanks. German infantry casualties are also heavy. To the Afrika Korps the day becomes known as '*Totensonntag*,' 'the Sunday of the Dead.' The British losses are also high and General Cunningham has now lost confidence in the outcome of the battle. This brings Auchinleck, the more resolute British Commander in Chief, forward to take more interest in the tactical moves. Rommel does not take part in the day's main fighting but is involved farther north around Gambut where the New Zealand infantry capture the Afrika Korps Headquarters and much of Rommel's communication equipment.

23-25 November

Mediterranean An Axis convoy bringing fuel from Greece to Benghazi is attacked by the Malta-based Force K and loses two freighters. The British Mediterranean Fleet puts to sea to cover the operation and on the 25th the battleship *Barham* is torpedoed and blows up in an attack delivered by *U-331.*

24 November 1941

Eastern Front The Germans evacuate Rostov because of the threat to their rear from the continuing Soviet counterattacks in this sector. Field Marshal Rundstedt is personally responsible for this move which has been expressly forbidden by Hitler.

North Africa Rommel believes that the British armor has largely been destroyed in the fighting of the 23rd and, ignoring the New Zealand infantry, decides to collect his armor and advance along the Trigh el Abd to the Egyptian frontier. This move becomes known as 'the dash to the wire.' Although it causes some panic (the 'Matruh Stakes') in Eighth Army's rear echelons, the German forces take some losses from harrying attacks and more significantly have loosened their grip on the British tank units. Rommel and the senior generals with him are out of touch with the situation.

Battle of the Atlantic The British cruiser *Dunedin* is sunk by *U.124* in the central Atlantic.

Above: German troops travel through the desert in their *Kubelwagen* reconnaissance car.

Below: A British Valentine tank lies disabled in the desert, a dead crew member alongside.

25 November 1941

Eastern Front In the Moscow sector, northwest of the capital, the Germans take Istra.

Pacific The US Navy begins to establish compulsory convoying of merchant vessels.

East Africa The British forces take Tadda Ridge, seven miles from Gondar.

25-26 November 1941

North Africa The German panzer divisions dissipate their strength in attacks on British positions around Capuzzo and Sidi Aziz. Toward the end of the 26th Rommel realizes that the British armor is quietly regrouping in the Sidi Rezegh area and that the New Zealand infantry are continuing to move toward Tobruk. He therefore begins to move his tank forces back in that direction. On the 26th also General Cunningham is relieved of Eighth Army. Auchinleck's Chief of Staff, General Ritchie takes over from Cunningham.

26-27 November 1941

Diplomatic Affairs Roosevelt and Hull decide to present a stiff 10-point note of final terms to the Japanese. It demands that the Japanese leave China and Indonesia and recognize the Chinese Nationalist Government. The Americans promise in return to negotiate new trade and raw materials agreements.

On the 26th the Japanese carrier force leaves its bases to move across the Pacific to Pearl Harbor. On the 27th the US authorities issue a war warning to their overseas commanders.

27 November 1941

Eastern Front In the southern sector the Soviet forces have now reoccupied Rostov as their offensive goes on. The German First Panzer Group are retreating toward Taganrog.

In the Moscow sector Guderian's forces have been fighting around Kashira for three days, but it is agreed that they cannot continue their drive toward Moscow unless reinforced. This is as close as they will get. They will be able to maintain limited attacks for a few days, however.

North Africa The advance of the 4th and 6th New Zealand Brigades links up with forces from the Tobruk garrison at El Duda early in the day. Later on there are evenly fought tank engagements in the Sidi Rezegh area.

The German Afrika Division is renamed 90th Light Division. The famous trio of 15th Panzer, 21st Panzer and 90th Light, which are together associated with the name Afrika Korps, is thus complete.

27-28 November 1941

East Africa Early on the 27th the Allied attack on Gondar goes in and quickly makes progress despite the very rugged terrain. General Nasi, commanding the Italian forces, decides to ask for terms. These was agreed and the 22,000 Italians surrender on the 28th. Mussolini's East African Roman Empire has ceased to exist.

28-30 November 1941

North Africa There is renewed heavy fighting around Sidi Rezegh with the German tank forces trying to wipe out the link between the New Zealand infantry and the Tobruk garrison. By the end of the 30th, after a very confused battle and

losses on both sides, one of the New Zealand brigades has been forced out of the fight.

29 November 1941

Eastern Front In the Moscow sector German tank forces commanded by General Reinhardt reach the Moscow-Volga Canal and manage to cross it in the Dmitrov area. The Germans here are coming up against some of the fresh Siberian units and more of the German tank force is being tied down here because of the fierce Soviet resistance.

Mediterranean The British forces in Malta are strengthened by the arrival of a further two cruisers and two destroyers.

29 November-1 December 1941

Japan, Policy On 29 November a Japanese government liaison conference decides that the final terms are unacceptable and that Japan must go to war. This decision is confirmed on 1 December at a meeting in the presence of the Emperor Hirohito. As Japanese custom requires, he remains silent throughout the meeting merely giving his assent to his ministers' decisions.

30 November 1941

Eastern Front Field Marshal Rundstedt is relieved of his command of Army Group South for refusing to cancel his orders for retreat in the Rostov sector. Reichenau is the new commander. On the Soviet side Stalin gives his approval to Zhukov's plans and preparations for the coming counteroffensive in the Moscow sector.

Pacific & East Indies Japanese naval forces are reported to be on the move by British units based in Borneo. There are various other reports during the next few days of Japanese movements, which lead to an increase in tension in Malaysia and the East Indies but draw no eyes toward Hawaii.

German Raiders The raider *Komet* arrives back in Hamburg after a cruise of 516 days in which three ships of 31,000 tons have been sunk along with seven more in company with *Orion*.

Battle of the Atlantic A British Whitley bomber sinks *U.206* in the Bay of Biscay with the aid of Air-to-Surface-Vessel radar (ASV). This is the first success achieved with this equipment. It also marks a period of greater British efforts to interfere with the German traffic across the Bay.

December 1941

War at Sea At the beginning of the war with Japan, total Allied shipping losses soar this month to 285 ships of 583,700 tons. More than 430,000 tons is lost in the Pacific. It is again a poor month for the German submarines with much of their effort being still devoted to the comparatively unrewarding waters of the Mediterranean and off Gibraltar. (*See* 14-23 December for one important Gibraltar convoy.) Ten U-Boats are lost during the month.

During 1941 Allied shipping losses have been 1229 ships of 4,300,000 tons. Britain has received just over 30,000,000 tons of dry cargo during the year compared to a peacetime average of around 50,000,000 tons. As well as the losses, ships in convoy tend to sail slower, by longer routes, and are often unavoidably sent to crowded ports, unsuitable for their particular cargo. The British have already imposed strict rationing controls, of course, but the continuing shortfall in imports means that these must be made even more rigorous if the war effort is to continue.

Occupied Europe The '*Nacht und Nebel*' (Night and Fog) Decree is issued to the German secret services. This allows them to arrest and hold anyone they judge is a danger to German security, without being required to give any information about who they are holding or why. In future those arrested by the Gestapo will virtually vanish leaving their friends and relations with the terrible dilemma about whether to inquire and risk being implicated in their 'crimes.'

British Air Operations The bomber effort is less intense this month but Aachen, Cologne, Bremen and Brest are all attacked while light forces are active over northern France.

1 December 1941

North Africa Rommel's forces manage to make the remaining New Zealand force at Sidi Rezegh retreat, but the German units are now becoming very tired and have had many of their senior officers captured or killed. Although Eighth Army has been severely mauled it is still very much in the fight and unlike the Axis units it is still receiving generous supplies and replacement tanks.

Above: British destroyer HMS *Hotspur* prepares to act as escort to a convoy in the Atlantic. It was a tough job.

Eastern Front There is a brief Soviet counterattack in the Moscow sector near Tula.

Malaya The British authorities declare a State of Emergency following reports of Japanese preparations for an attack.

2 December 1941

Eastern Front In the Moscow sector some small German forces reach the northern suburbs of the capital and come within sight of the Kremlin less than 20 miles away. There are renewed efforts, on Hitler's direct order, by Kluge's forces to the west of the city. The weather continues to grow colder with blizzards being added to the previous hard frosts and heavy snow. Both Bock, commanding Army Group Center, and Brauchitsch, the Commander in Chief, are ill and unable to perform their duties fully effectively.

Pacific A special code order 'Climb Mount Niitaka' is transmitted by Japanese naval headquarters to the ships of the carrier force steaming across the ocean to Hawaii. The order confirms that negotiations have broken down and that the carriers are to execute the Pearl Harbor attack.

East Indies The British battleship *Prince of Wales* and the battlecruiser *Repulse* arrive in Singapore.

2-6 December 1941

North Africa The very confused fighting continues. Rommel's forces are trying simultaneously to maintain the confinement of the Tobruk garrison in fighting around El Duda, to inflict losses on the British armor regrouping farther south toward Bir el Gubi and to send some help to the Axis garrisons at Bardia, Sollum and Halfaya Pass which are still holding out against XIII Corps' 4th Indian Division. The Germans are not strong enough to accomplish all this and their efforts only increase their weakness.

Above: Malta comes under renewed air attack: the view from a rooftop as bombs burst around the entrance to the harbor.

4 December 1941

Britain, Home Front A new National Service Bill is passed by Parliament. Its provisions include compulsory direction and conscription for female labor.
South China Sea The Japanese landing force bound for Malaya sets out from Hainan.

Below: With crew members on the conning tower, a U-boat ploughs through the Atlantic swell. Movement on the surface saved the batteries.

5 December 1941

Eastern Front Hitler agrees that the German Moscow offensive should be halted, as the growing weakness of the German forces prevents there being any possibility of further gains.
Mediterranean Hitler orders the transfer of the whole of Fliegerkorps II from the Eastern Front to the Mediterranean. The aim is to reduce the effectiveness of the attacks of the British Malta forces on the Axis supply convoys and by this and more direct intervention to help the forces in North Africa.
Allied Diplomacy General Sikorski, the head of the exiled Polish government is in Moscow to see Stalin. A friendship and mutual aid agreement between the Soviets and the Poles is signed by the two leaders.

6 December 1941

Eastern Front In the early hours the Soviets begin a major counteroffensive all along the 500 miles of the Moscow sector. Fresh troops and tanks have been added to the Kalinin, West and Southwest Fronts. Among the units prominent in the attack are First Shock and Twentieth Armies in the advance against the Klin area and Tenth Army which leads the move against Guderian's troops east of Tula. The Soviet intention with these attacks, and others on their immediate flanks, is to cut through the panzer wings of Army Group Center and then to isolate and destroy it. Among the Soviet commanders in the attack are Zhukov, who has planned and commands the whole effort, Rokossovsky, Kuznetsov and others who will be among the Red Army's best war leaders in all the years to come. From the beginning the attacks meet with considerable success against the weak and overextended German forces.
Diplomatic Affairs President Roosevelt makes a final appeal to the Japanese Emperor for peace. This is misunderstood and resented by the Japanese leaders who believe it wrong for the Emperor to be given the burden of such decisions. There is no Japanese reply. Late in the day the Japanese begin transmitting what is to be their final message to the US Government. The first 13 parts of the note are intercepted by the US code-breaking service, quickly translated and passed to the president. Although the crucial 14th and last part is not yet available, Roosevelt correctly interprets the message as meaning

Below: German infantry, supported by a Panzer Mark IV tank, advance through the snow toward a Russian-held village.

war. The message is not seen at this stage by General Marshall or Admiral Stark.

It is also known in the US that a Japanese agent in Honolulu has been asked for a special situation report on the US Pacific Fleet, but since similar requests to agents elsewhere have also been intercepted no special interpretation is put on this order.

Pacific Japanese forces leave Palau bound for the attack on the Philippines.

7 December 1941

Diplomatic Affairs The 14th part of the Japanese signal, stating specifically that relations are being broken off, reaches Washington in the morning and is decoded by the US authorities around 0900 hours. A little after 1000 the order to the Japanese Embassy in Washington to deliver the main message at 1300 is similarly intercepted by the Americans. It is quickly realized that this timing coincides roughly with dawn at Pearl Harbor. Various delays ensue while General Marshall is found (it is a Sunday and he has gone for a morning ride) and then there are errors in the method of transmission of the warning message. It arrives in Headquarters in Oahu just before midday local time, when it is far too late.

There are also delays in the preparation of the Japanese note at their Embassy in Washington. The decoding and translation proceeds at a leisurely pace until the order giving the time for delivery arrives – the Embassy has had no previous hint that urgency is required. There is also delay in obtaining an appointment for the ambassador to see Secretary Hull. He eventually does so and delivers the message at 1430. Hull has, of course, already seen the American version and has just received first reports of events at Pearl Harbor.

The British receive no official indications of what is afoot from the Japanese until three hours later, when their Ambassador in Tokyo is given a copy of the Japanese note. Both the British and US ambassadors in Tokyo are given declarations of war a further three hours later.

Pearl Harbor At 0755 local time, Japanese carrier aircraft attack the main base of the US Pacific Fleet at Pearl Harbor. There is complete tactical and strategic surprise.

The Japanese have sent six carriers, *Akagi*,

Below: Map showing the Russian counterattacks around Moscow in the winter of 1941-42.

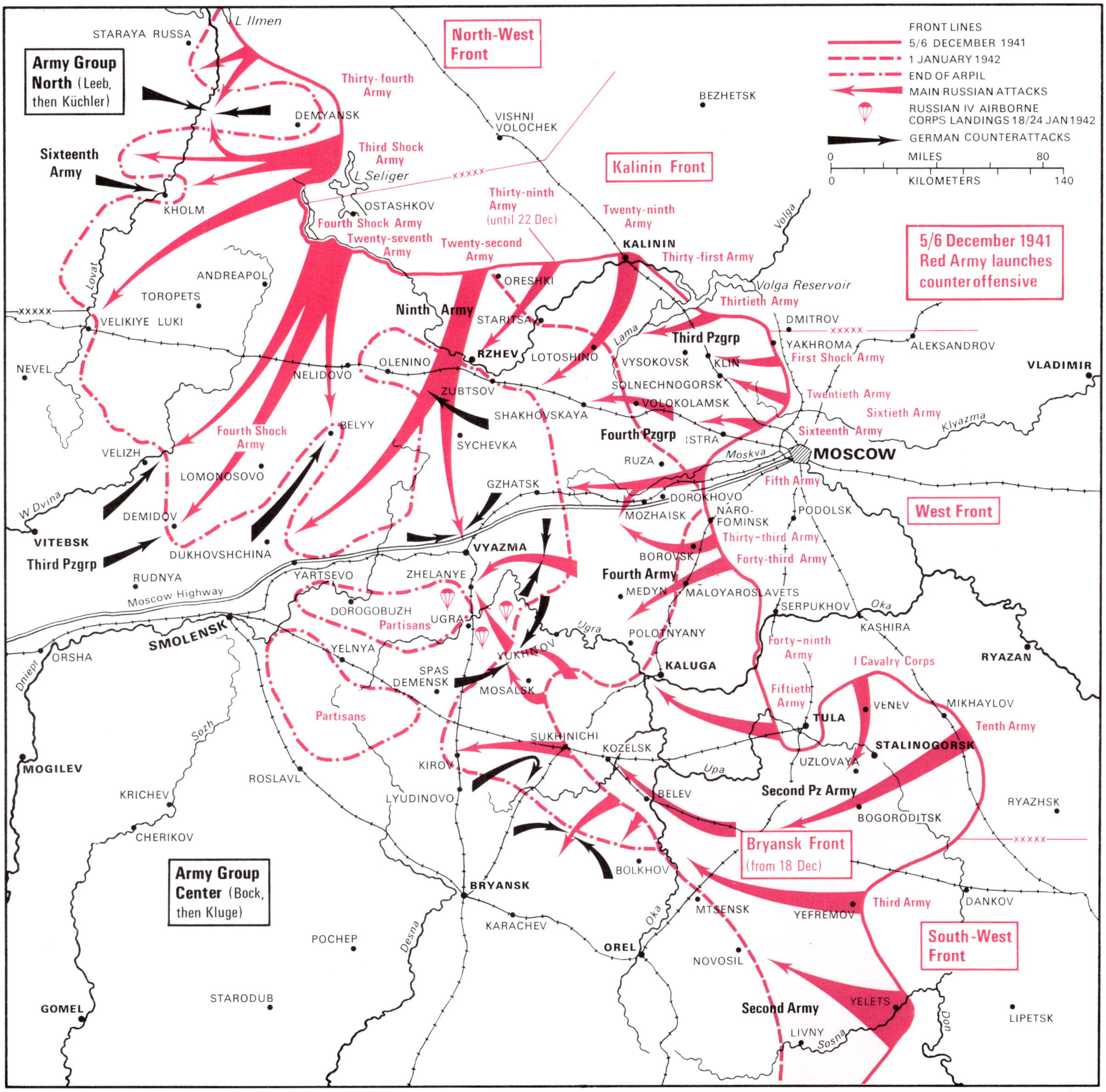

Above: Japanese sailors cheer as the bombers take off from the Pearl Harbor attack force, 7 December 1941.

Kaga, Hiryu, Soryu, Zuikaku and *Shokaku*, with a total of 423 planes embarked to make the attack. The pilots are brilliantly trained and their equipment is good. Admiral Nagumo commands and he has, in addition to the carriers, two battleships and two heavy cruisers in his force along with destroyers and other supporting vessels including tankers.

Two waves of attacks are sent in. Commander Fuchida leads the first strike with 40 torpedo bombers (with special shallow running torpedoes), 51 dive bombers, 50 high-level bombers and 43 fighters. The second wave is of similar total strength but with extra dive bombers replacing the torpedo aircraft. All eight US battleships in port are damaged, five of them sinking. (*Arizona* is a total loss; *Oklahoma* will be raised but scrapped; *California, Nevada* and *West Virginia* will be rebuilt and will rejoin the fleet later in the war.) Three cruisers and three destroyers are also sunk. The Americans lose 188 aircraft from the island's airfields. The Japanese lose 29.

Although what is regarded at the time as the main force of the US Pacific Fleet has been destroyed, it is perhaps more relevant to recount what escapes the Japanese attack. By a combination of coincidences all three carriers serving with the Pacific Fleet at this time are absent when the Japanese attack, and of necessity they will become the major element in the USN forces. The base installations at Pearl Harbor including the massive oil storage tanks also escape unhurt because Nagumo unwisely disregards the advice of his staff to send in a third attack. The Americans are, therefore, left with their base intact and the nucleus of a more modern fleet still in being.

One aspect of the Japanese attack plan is a complete failure. They have sent off five midget submarines to try to penetrate the American anchorage but all of these are lost. One is attacked by the destroyer *Ward* at about 0630 but, since it has not been unknown for destroyers to make false submarine reports, no great stir is caused. When compared with the wonderful successes of their airmen, the failure of the Japanese submarine service is especially disappointing and this has a disproportionate effect on the later Japanese naval effort. The submarine service will find its work devalued and there will be no Japanese equivalent of the U-boat offensive in the Atlantic. The tactical doctrine of the Japanese submarine service is also faulty in its emphasis on attacking enemy warships and disregarding commerce destroying. It will be the US Navy which will mount an increasingly effective submarine offensive, destroying a growing proportion of the Japanese merchant marine and preventing the Japanese gaining anything like the desired benefit from the resources of Malaysia and the East Indies because of their inability to ship the raw materials back to Japanese factories and refineries. It is ironic that access to these resources is the principal Japanese war aim and that, although they will be taken, they will be of disappointingly little use. It should be noted that it will be some time before the US submarine campaign begins to be effective because of depth keeping and fuse defects in their torpedoes which will take time to remedy. (The Germans had similar trouble off Norway in 1940.)

The sighting report of the *Ward* is not the only warning received by the US authorities. Even more exact warning comes from one of Oahu's five radar stations. Two conscientious operators stay on watch for longer than the prescribed early morning period and just after 0700 they detect the Japanese strike approaching. Their reports are disregarded by the junior officer they contact who believes that they must be American aircraft. To add to this is the information from the diplomatic radio traffic that a deadline for action is imminent, and a mass of lower level radio information that some Japanese moves are about to take place. No radio intelligence is received concerning the position of the Japanese carriers, but no sinister interpretation is placed on this silence. A similar radio pattern has occurred during previous Japanese moves against Indochina in which the carriers were not involved. It is, therefore, easy to assume that, although the Japanese may be up to something, the carriers may not be involved. The US commanders at the Pearl Harbor base have been kept fully informed of the intelligence situation, and their general conclusion has been that, since none of the evidence points more specifically to Pearl Harbor than elsewhere, it is unnecessary to order a very high state of readiness. Instead, US aircraft are found parked wingtip to wingtip on the island's airfields; there are no torpedo nets to protect the fleet anchorage; partly because is a Sunday officers and crew from the ships are ashore and few antiaircraft guns are manned; many ammunition boxes for AA guns are kept locked because peacetime custom decrees that every round must be accounted for. Admiral Kimmel, Commander in Chief US Pacific Fleet, and General Short, commanding US Army forces in Hawaii, will be dismissed for this catalog of errors.

At the highest level of the US command criticism is also deserved. The proverbially poor relations between the US Army and Navy are one cause of the difficulty. More understandably the misguided audacity of the Japanese is a very real surprise. The American leaders all find it easier to believe that the Japanese might attack Singapore, for example, since this would leave the US Government with the political problem of whether it could declare war to help Britain defend colonies, when the whole idea of empire is ideologically obnoxious to American opinion and without an attack on American territory.

The Pearl Harbor attack leaves the Allies with the three US carriers and the two doomed British battleships at Singapore as the only active capital ships left to face the Japanese. Counting Dutch and Free French ships the

Above right: A Japanese view of the attack on Pearl Harbor, 7 December 1941. 'Battleship Row' can clearly be seen, with an aircraft above.
Right: Aerial view of the US Pacific Fleet base at Pearl Harbor, October 1941.

Note. The chronological account of the war in the Pacific is made considerably more complicated by the International Date Line and the many time zones. Events will normally be listed under the appropriate local date and time. A comparison of the local, Washington and London times of the opening events of the Japanese offensive shows the high degree of co-ordination involved.

	Local time	Washington time	London time
Landings in Malaya	0100, 8 Dec	1230, 7 Dec	1730, 7 Dec
Pearl Harbor	0755, 7 Dec	1255, 7 Dec	1755, 7 Dec
Opening attack on Hong Kong	0800, 8 Dec	1900, 7 Dec	2400, 7 Dec
First air attack on Luzon	0930, 8 Dec	2030, 7 Dec	0130, 8 Dec

The first military act of the Pacific war was several hours before the Japanese landings in Malaya when a British reconnaissance plane was shot down near the Japanese invasion force.

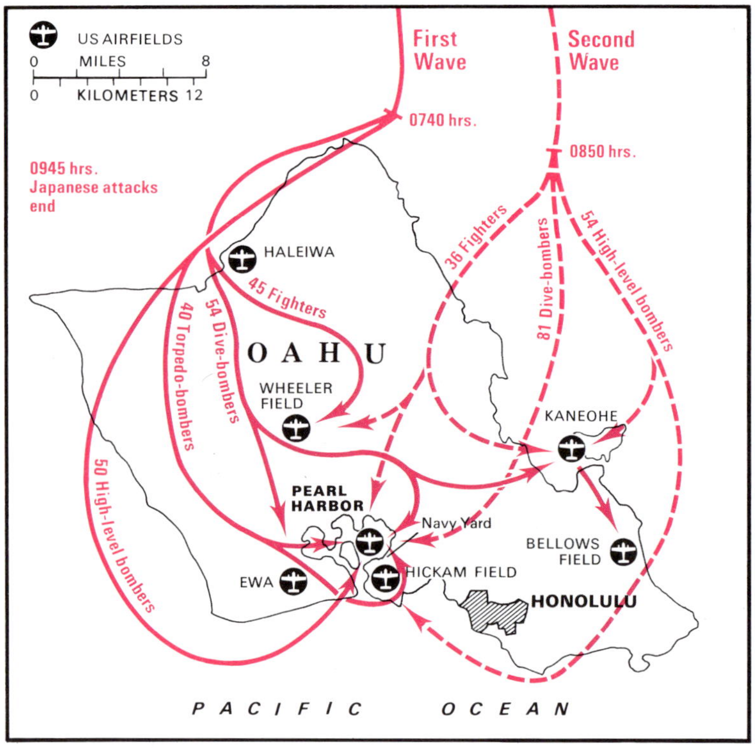

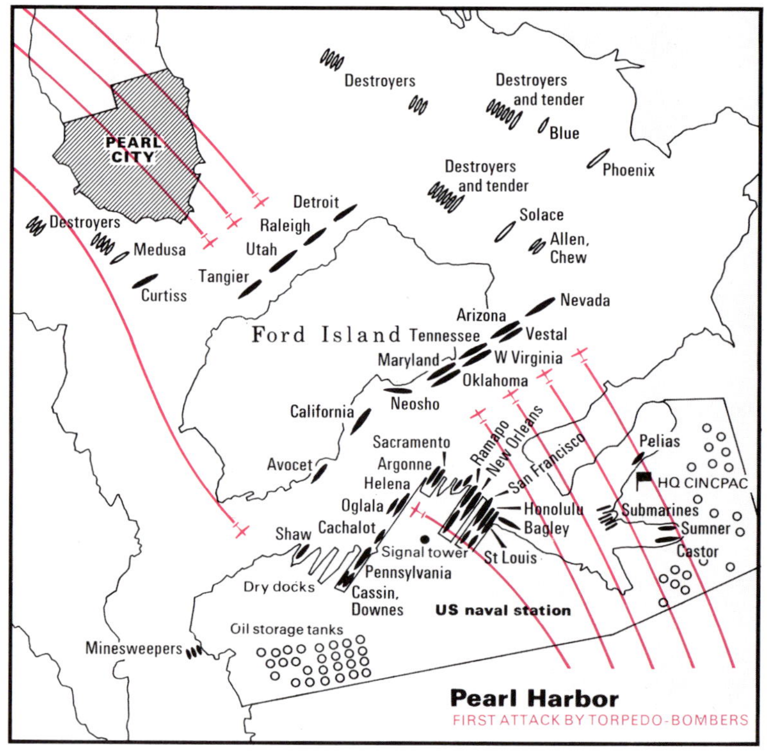

Above: Map of the Japanese attack routes. *Above right:* Map of Pearl Harbor.

Allies have only a slight inferiority in cruisers, destroyers and submarines, but the Allied forces are widely dispersed and there will be problems of coordination and command.

Japanese Forces and Plans The Japanese Army has 51 divisions of which 11 can be spared from duties in China, Indochina and at home to join the offensive against the Allies. The Japanese navy has 10 battleships, six large and four smaller carriers, 36 cruisers, 113 destroyers and 63 submarines. There is no independent air force but the navy has about 1000 aircraft, half of them carrierborne, which will be committed along with about half of the army's 1500 planes.

Below: American battleships burn at Pearl Harbor: from left to right, USS *West Virginia, Tennessee* and *Arizona.*

It is clear that with such forces the Japanese cannot hope to win an all-out war against the United States and the British Empire. Instead their aim is to take advantage of the distraction provided by the war in Europe and seize the resource producing areas of Malaya and the East Indies. They will then be self-sufficient and will hope to defend a fortified perimeter around their conquests so fiercely that Britain and the United States will make peace. As well as the economic and militaristic pressure supporting the plan, there is also an element of broader Asian nationalism which sees value in the Asian Co-Prosperity Sphere which is to be created.

The attack on Pearl Harbor has been planned to disable the US Navy for the time required for the creation of the defensive perimeter. Admiral Yamamoto, who commands the Japanese Combined Fleet and has been responsible for the planning of the attack, is, however, deeply pessimistic about the eventual outcome. He sees the Pearl Harbor success as illusory and as granting only six months respite before Japan is swamped by US production. In greater detail the plan provides in the first phase for four divisions of Twenty-fifth Army to advance into Malaya to take Singapore after landing in Thailand; for two divisions of Fifteenth Army to move into Burma from Thailand; for two and a half division of Fourteenth Army to take the Philippines; and for other units to take Hong Kong, Guam, Wake and the Makin Islands. The second and subsequent phases will see the same forces being regrouped and moving on to Borneo, Sumatra and Java; the Bismarcks and New Guinea; and into Burma in strength.

Pacific As well as the Pearl Harbor attack there are Japanese air raids on Guam and Wake and a bombardment of Midway.

Eastern Front Already stricken by illness and now demoralized by the Soviet counteroffensive, Brauchitsch offers his resignation to Hitler. No formal acceptance of the resignation is made, but Brauchitsch will take no more important decisions.

8 December 1941

World Affairs The United States and Britain declare war on Japan. In his address to Congress President Roosevelt describes the events at Pearl Harbor as forming part of 'a date which will live in infamy.' Roosevelt does not ask Congress to declare war on Germany and Italy. Australia, New Zealand, the Netherlands, the Free French, Yugoslavia and several South American countries all declare war on Japan also. China declares war on Germany, Italy and Japan.

Philippines The Japanese offensive here begins in the morning with air attacks and a landing on Batan Island north of Luzon by a small force who soon overcome the tiny garrison and begin work on an airfield. The main air attacks come in about midday, having been delayed by fog over the Japanese airfields in Formosa. Almost 200 aircraft are involved and they catch most of the defending aircraft on the ground and destroy about 100, leaving 17 B-17 bombers and less than 40 fighters in operating

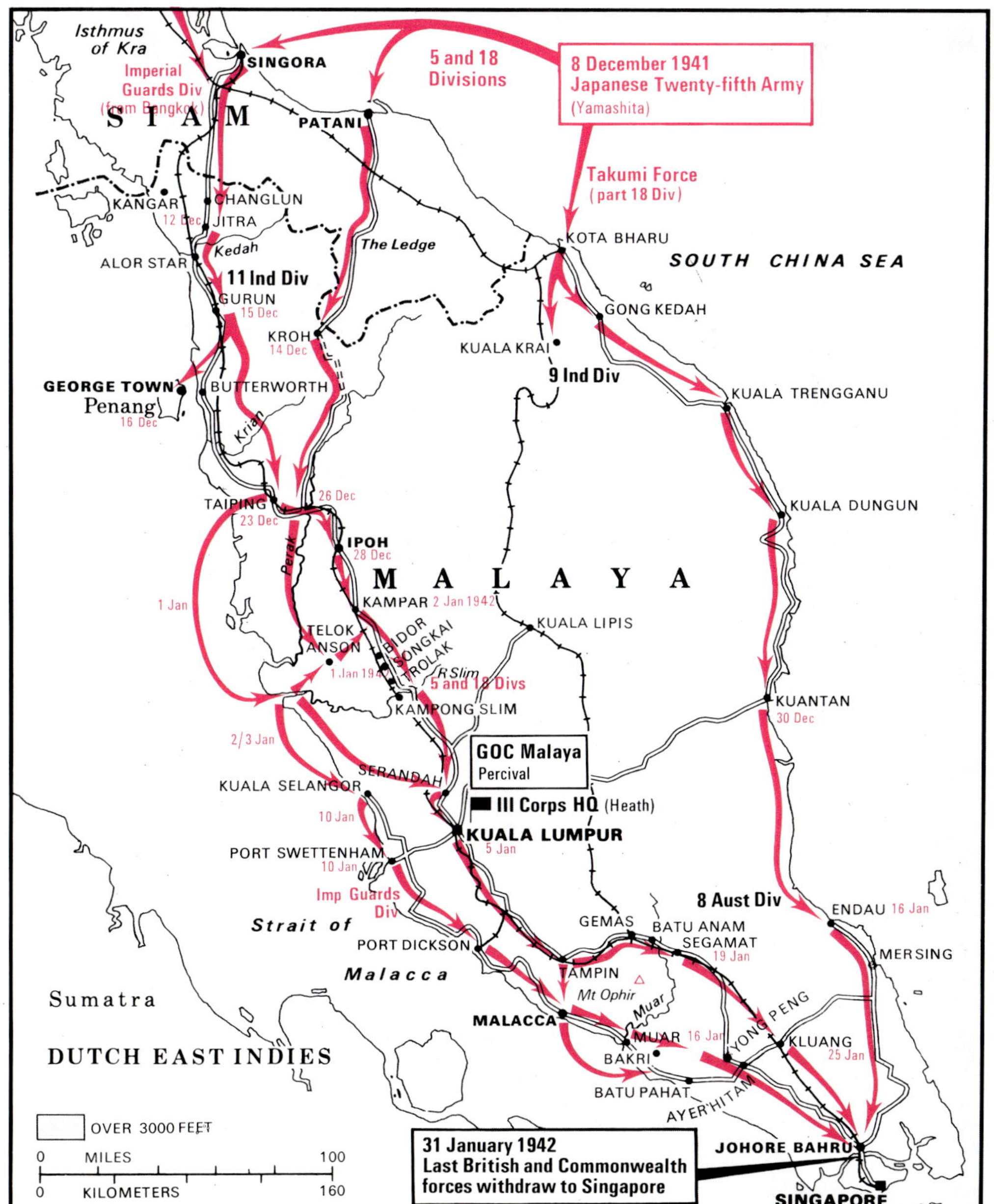

Above: Pearl Harbor, the aftermath. *Above right:* USS *West Virginia* burns furiously as the Japanese attack is at its height. *Right:* The Japanese invasion of Malaya and the fall of Singapore, December 1941-February 1942: a major British defeat.

condition. There are also attacks by 22 planes from the carrier *Ryujo* against Davao on Mindanao. The first of the Japanese landing forces bound for the Philippines leaves Palau. General MacArthur commands the 130,000 strong Allied force on the Philippines. About 20,000 of his men are American, the rest being from the Philippine army. They are comparatively poorly equipped and trained. Many are unavoidably dispersed to garrisons on the various islands. The largest units are on Luzon as part of either Wainwright's North Luzon Force or the smaller South Luzon Force led by General Parker. MacArthur had hoped to use his aircraft to delay and disrupt Japanese landings which he recognizes his ground forces are too weak to repel. He then plans to retreat into the Bataan Peninsula and to hold out there until help can be brought from the main forces of the Pacific Fleet. The losses at Pearl Harbor and his own losses in aircraft mean that neither part of this plan can work properly.

Malaysia Not long after midnight Japanese transports appear off Kota Bharu and landings begin. Before dawn there is also a small bombing raid on Singapore and by early morning the Japanese have also begun landings at Singora and Patani in Thailand. Units of the Japanese 5th Division land here while at Kota Bharu the troops are from 18th Division. Tank units are landed at Singora and Patani also. The British have almost no tanks in Malaya. In Malaya the British have three divisions and numerous fortress troops but only one division is free for active operations against the Japanese, since the other units are guarding possible landing places or airfields. The British force is poorly trained and too dependent on movement with motor transport by road. General Percival is in command. The RAF has 158 planes in Malaya when

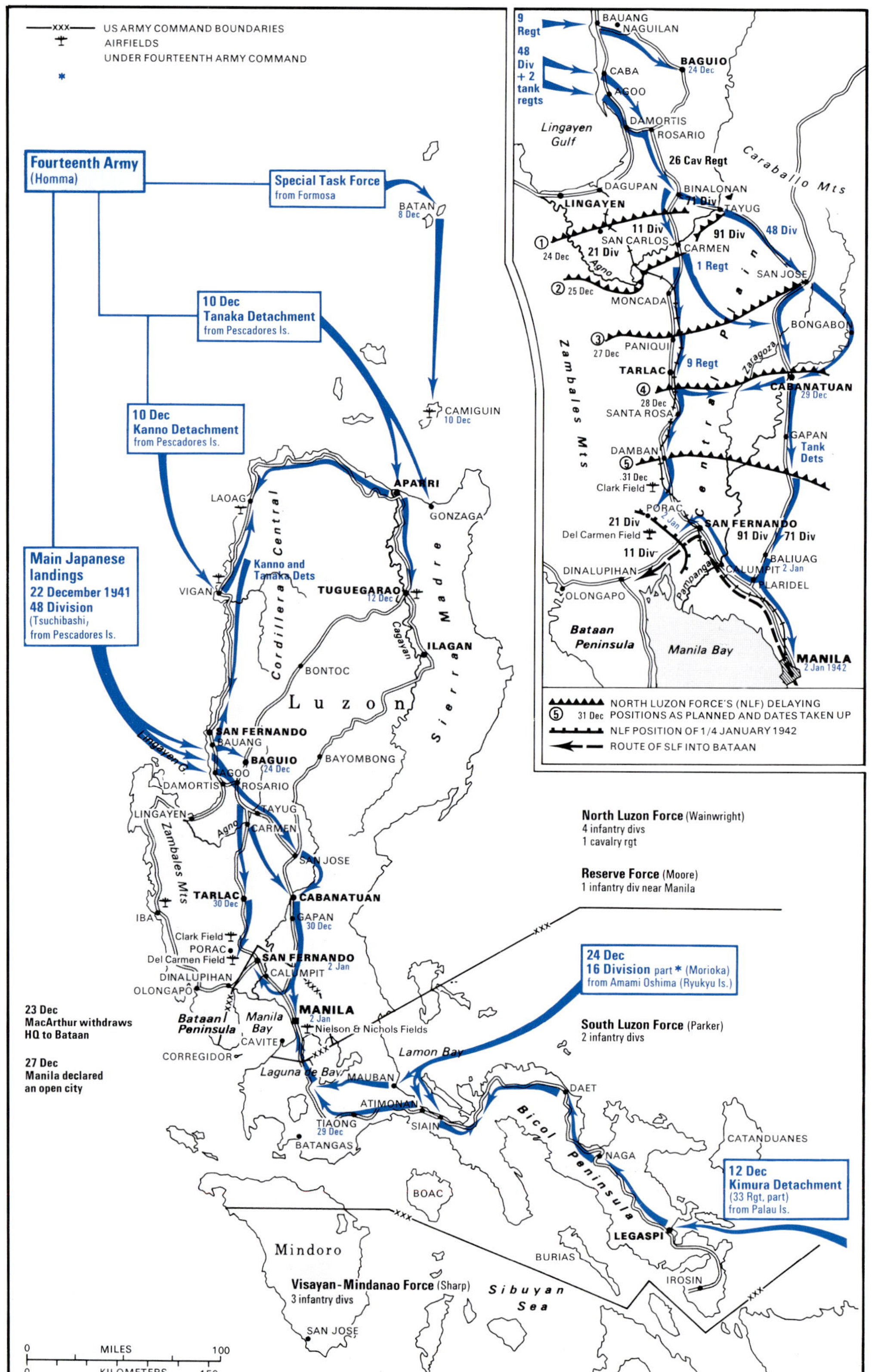

Above: Japanese troops race into Hong Kong, December 1941 to achieve the first of a series of stunning victories against the British. *Right:* Map showing the Japanese invasion of the Philippines.

operations begin but many are lost on the first day. The airfield at Kota Bharu is also abandoned on the first day, but the runway is left untouched and stocks of fuel and bombs are not destroyed. The capital ships *Prince of Wales* and *Repulse* sail from Singapore with four destroyers on the afternoon of the 8th. Admiral Phillips is in command. The Japanese have two battleships and six heavy cruisers covering their landings as well as many smaller ships. Admiral Kondo is in command.

The British have hoped to forestall Japanese landings at Singora and Patani by an advance into Thailand, but have not ordered this before the Japanese attack because such an advance into a neutral country could have upset opinion in the United States. Once the Japanese land it is too late to begin this plan and so a more limited alternative involving delaying actions at Jitra in northern Malaya and an advance into Thailand to a position known as The Ledge is ordered. There is delay in putting the plan into operation and more delay is imposed by the resistance of the Thai border guards who know nothing of events farther north. Thus by the end of the day the Japanese are well ashore at all three of their landing places and the British have been delayed in their counter moves and have lost heavily in the air.

Wake Island There are Japanese air attacks on the island on the 8th and over the following two days. A small Japanese landing force leaves Kwajalein on the 8th, escorted by a cruiser and six destroyers.

Hong Kong The Japanese 38th Division begins an attack at 0800 hours local time. General Maltby commanding the garrison has only six battalions and 28 guns with which to make a defense. His plan is to fall back from the border to a line across the neck of the Kowloon Peninsula known as the Gindrinkers Line and to try to hold out there for as long as he can. Delaying actions will be fought for the first two days to cover the retreat to this line.

Shanghai The Japanese occupy the whole of the city and capture the small US garrison in the American sector.

Eastern Front The Soviet counteroffensive in the Moscow sector continues to make considerable headway despite desperate German defense. The Red Army forces are advancing successfully in the Leningrad sector also.

8-11 December 1941

North Africa On the 8th Rommel decides to give up attempts to stay in the fight around Tobruk. There are only about 40 tanks left in the German divisions and 90th Light is down to a strength equivalent to two battalions. The German retreat is well controlled and the whole force is back around Gazala on the 11th. The siege of Tobruk is raised completely on the 10th. About 34,000 men have been taken in to replace the garrison during the siege and a similar number taken out as well as 7000 wounded and 7000 prisoners. In the various supply operations two destroyers have been lost and many other ships sunk or damaged. For the British, the successful defense of Tobruk is one of the few bright spots in an otherwise disastrous month.

9 December 1941

Eastern Front In the Moscow sector the Soviet drive against Guderian's forces succeeds in reaching and capturing Elets. In the Leningrad sector the Soviets retake Tikhvin and force the Germans into a brief but hurried retreat. General Meretskov commands the Soviet forces here. Although tremendous efforts are being made by the citizens and garrison of the city and by Meretskov's forces outside, only the merest trickle of supplies is getting in. Rations are already well below starvation level and during this month perhaps 50,000 of the population will die.
Malaysia There are more Japanese landings at Kota Bharu, Singora and Patani. In Thailand the Japanese occupy Bangkok.

9-10 December 1941

South China Sea On the afternoon of the 9th *Prince of Wales* and *Repulse* are sighted by a Japanese submarine while heading north toward the Japanese landing areas. They turn back later in the day when Japanese aircraft are sighted, since Admiral Phillips knows that no British fighter protection will be available farther north. About midnight reports of a Japanese landing at Kuantan are sent to Admiral Phillips and he alters course in that direction. He decides not to signal his intentions to avoid giving away his position, believing that the staff at Singapore will realize that he will make this move and send fighters to Kuantan at first light. In the early hours of the 10th the British ships are sighted and attacked by a Japanese submarine. The attack is not noticed and the submarine later reports their position. In the morning the landings at Kuantan are found not to exist and just before midday Japanese aircraft from Indochina find and attack Phillips' force. About 90 Japanese planes are involved and in two hours both British capital ships have been sunk. This disaster leaves the Allies without a battleship active in the whole Pacific theater.
Gilbert Islands On the 9th small Japanese forces occupy Tarawa and on the 10th Makin.

10 December 1941

Philippines There are Japanese landings and air attacks on Luzon. The naval base at Cavite is badly hit and important weapon stocks destroyed in the air attacks. On the north coast, at Aparri, 2000 men of the Tanaka Detachment land from one cruiser, six destroyers and other ships while in the northeast of the island at Vigan a similar number, the Kanno Detachment, also goes ashore covered by a slightly larger naval force.
Marianas A Japanese force commanded by Admiral Goto lands and captures the island of Guam which is defended by only 300 US troops.
Hong Kong The Japanese forces have now advanced up to the main defense line and succeed in capturing an important position at its west end.
Malaysia The British force which has advanced into Thailand from Kroh reaches The Ledge position where they are to prepare to meet the Japanese advance, only to find that the Japanese have arrived first and are stronger. The British attack is thrown back.

11 December 1941

World Affairs Germany and Italy declare war on the United States. Congress replies with declarations of war and votes that US forces may be dispatched to any part of the world. The term of service for those enlisted under the Selective Service Act is extended until six months after the end of the war. The German declaration of war can only be regarded as one of Hitler's greatest mistakes, since without it US participation in the European war has still been in doubt.
Eastern Front The Soviet propaganda machine begins to announce the Red Army's successes in the Moscow counteroffensive. The gains on the ground continue to be impressive with Guderian's troops being forced back from Stalinogorsk. Many of the already weakened German units have suffered so heavily in the few days of the Soviet offensive that they are virtually out of the fight.
Wake Island An attempted Japanese landing is beaten off and two destroyers sunk by the small defending force of 450 marines. Admiral Kimmel prepares to send his carriers to bring help and more aircraft to the island.

11-12 December 1941

Malaya The positions of the 11th Indian Division at Jitra are attacked by the Japanese units which have advanced from Singora. The Indian division has already lost heavily in some outpost actions and the Jitra position is abandoned after a further brief fight.

12 December 1941

Philippines The Japanese Kimura Detachment, 2500 men of the 16th Infantry Division, lands in south Luzon at Legaspi. There are further Japanese air attacks on the few remaining US aircraft on the island.

13 December 1941

Hong Kong The British forces withdraw from their positions on the mainland to Hong Kong island.
Burma The British evacuate their airfield at Victoria Point in the extreme south of the country on the Kra Isthmus. The Japanese move in.

13-16 December 1941

North Africa Some of the British forces have closed up to the Gazala position by the 13th but lose heavily to sharp German counterattacks. Rommel realizes that, despite these successes, he cannot make a permanent stand here because of the weakness of his forces. He therefore begins the long retreat through Cyrenaica to the next defensible position at El Agheila. The withdrawal begins on the 16th.

13-19 December 1941

Mediterranean There is much naval activity by both sides. On the 13th two Italian cruisers carrying a cargo of fuel to North Africa are attacked and sunk off Cape Bon by three British and one Dutch destroyer. Also on the 13th the Italians begin a major convoy operation to bring supplies to Benghazi covered by their main fleet including four battleships. Two transports are sunk by a British submarine on the 13th and the *Vittorio Veneto* similarly damaged on the 14th. The Italians abandon this effort. On the 15th *U.557* sinks a cruiser off Alexandria. Later on the 15th the British begin an operation to bring supplies to Malta from Egypt. Including the forces that set out from Malta six cruisers and 16 destroyers are involved. On the 16th the Italians start a second convoy again covered by four battleships with five cruisers and 21 destroyers also in the escort. Admiral Iachino commands the Italian force and Admiral Vian the British. On the 17th the British Force K from Malta joins with Vian's Force B from Alexandria. On the night of the 17th the covering forces of the two convoys meet in an action known as the First Battle of Sirte, but the fighting is indecisive because most attention is paid to protecting the convoys. On the 18th the British convoy reaches Malta, and Force B turns back to Egypt while Force K searches for the Italian ships. During the night, however, Force K runs into a minefield and loses one cruiser and one destroyer and has both the other cruisers present damaged. On the same night three Italian midget submarines penetrate into the Mediterranean Fleet anchorage at Alexandria, taking advantage of the net defenses being opened to allow Force B to return. Their charges are placed under the battleships *Queen Elizabeth* and *Valiant*. Both ships sink to the bottom of the harbor, but because it is comparatively shallow and they come to rest on an even keel the Italians do not realize the extent of their success. Thus, in the actions of one night, the Mediterranean Fleet is deprived of its Malta striking force and of both its battleships. As well as being a serious blow to British strength in the Mediterranean it compounds the Allied lack of capital ships for all theaters.

14 December 1941

Malaya The Japanese forces from Patani have now pushed on beyond The Ledge to Kroh.

14-23 December 1941

Battle of the Atlantic On the 14th the convoy HG-76 sails from Gibraltar for the UK. There are 32 ships in the convoy and the escort includes the escort carrier *Audacity* and 12 other ships. The escort is led by perhaps the most famous of the British escort leaders, Commander (later Captain) Walker. During the convoy's passage 12 U-Boats are involved in attacks, but five are sunk and in addition two Condor aircraft are shot down. This success is tempered by the sinking of the *Audacity* on the 21st. One destroyer and two merchant ships are also lost to the attacks which are called off by Doenitz on the 23rd.

15 December 1941

Eastern Front In their attacks northwest of Moscow the Soviets have reached Klin and Kalinin and they claim to have taken both towns. Elsewhere the remorseless pressure of their offensive continues to wear the defending German units out.
Malaya The British forces have fallen back to Gurun and once more lose heavily to a Japanese attack. The Japanese cannot take Gurun, however.
Hong Kong The Japanese attempt to ferry a small force over to Hong Kong Island from Kowloon but are pushed back.

16 December 1941

Borneo Early in the day there are Japanese landings at Miri, Seria and Lutong. The oil plants are set on fire before the small British and Dutch forces retreat. The Japanese force is from 16th Infantry Division and they have considerable naval support.

16-17 December 1941

Malaya There is a second wave of Japanese landings. Over the next few days the 5th and

Above: Japanese troops approach the landing beaches in Lingayen Gulf, north of Manila, in the Philippines, 22 December 1941.

18th Divisions will be brought up to full strength and the Imperial Guards Division will begin to arrive. On the 16th the British forces withdraw from Penang on the west coast and on the 17th they pull back from their main defensive position at Gurun. They will now retreat south of the Perak River fighting delaying actions on the way.

17 December 1941

Eastern Front In contrast to the continuing Soviet attacks on all other fronts, in the Crimea German attacks by LIV Corps begin against the fortress city of Sevastopol.

United States Command Admiral Nimitz is appointed to command the US Pacific Fleet relieving Admiral Kimmel. It will be a few days until Nimitz can arrive in Hawaii, and Admiral Pye takes temporary command until he does so. These changes do not help with the attempts to relieve the beleagured US positions on Wake Island, which are under way.

Battle of the Atlantic The British cruiser *Dunedin* is sunk by a U-Boat.

18 December 1941

Eastern Front Following Rundstedt's dismissal at the beginning of the month, a second of the German army group commanders is replaced. Field Marshal Bock has been ill like Brauchitsch and is replaced by Kluge.

18-19 December 1941

Hong Kong During the night there are Japanese landings on Hong Kong Island along a front between North Point and the Lei U Mun Channel. The attacking force gets well established and British counterattacks over the following days, especially on the 20th, are unsuccessful.

19 December 1941

German Command Hitler formally removes Brauchitsch from his post of Commander in Chief of the army. Hitler directly assumes the responsibilities of the post himself, telling Halder that 'anyone can do this little matter of operational command.'

At first Hitler is remarkably successful, applying his considerable talents to mastering a range of detailed information relating to his task. It is generally agreed that his orders to stand fast, which he repeats throughout this winter campaign on the Eastern Front, will help save the German Army from an even more disastrous defeat.

The Germans will be able to retreat into admittedly isolated defensive localities based around what shelter can be obtained in the many villages. The Soviets will be unable to prevent Luftwaffe supply operations and will lack the heavy weapons or tanks necessary to break into the German defenses.

Hitler's clear perception of his own place in this defensive success will only serve to convince him further of his own ability as a general and of the useless weakness of the army leaders. He will also remain convinced to the end that no retreat is a sufficient tactical answer to any attack in any circumstances. His belief in the army's failure also encourages him to expand the forces of the Waffen SS. Although these units will almost always fight fanatically in the German cause, their leaders sometimes lack the training and experience of their army counterparts, and more significantly their expansion will lead to the situation of their being a 'second German army' with its attendant problems of organization and supply. As resources become increasingly scarce toward the end of the war there are many clashes between army and SS for priorities in obtaining weapons and equipment.

North Africa The Axis retreat through Cyrenaica continues.

United States, Manpower The Selective Service Act is amended, making it compulsory for all men 18-64 to register and for those 20-44 to be subject to military service.

19-20 December 1941

Philippines During the night the Japanese land near Davao on Mindanao. The carrier *Ryujo* is in support and the landing force is made up of 500 men from the 56th Infantry Regiment.

19-25 December 1941

Eastern Front In the Crimea the German attacks on Sevastopol continue, and by the 23rd the outer ring of forts around the town has been captured after heavy fighting. The garrison is being strengthened, however, in various Soviet naval operations during this time. Altogether over 14,000 men are brought in as well as supplies.

20 December 1941

Eastern Front In the Moscow sector the Soviet offensive continues to inflict considerable losses on the defending forces. Northwest of the capital Volokolamsk is retaken.

United States Command Admiral King is appointed to be Commander in Chief, US Fleet.

Germany, Home Front Goebbels broadcasts an appeal for contributions of winter clothing for the troops serving in the USSR.

21-23 December 1941

Philippines There are Japanese landings on Luzon at Lingayen Gulf. The landing force is made up from 48th Infantry Division specially reinforced with other units including tanks. They have considerable air and naval support. The defending forces are not able to make a very strong resistance and the Japanese soon establish a strong perimeter for their beachhead.

22-23 December 1941

Wake Island The Japanese return to the attack with stronger forces. Wake has been bombarded from the air since the first successful defense, with planes from the carriers *Hiryu* and *Soryu* joining in on the 21st and 22nd. Just before midnight on the 22nd the Japanese are able to land some 200 men on the island and, although the garrison fights back, they are compelled to surrender later on the 23rd. The carriers of the US Pacific Fleet have been sent on a mission to Wake but they are still several hundred miles away when the island surrenders.

Below: The British counterattack in the desert, November-December 1941.

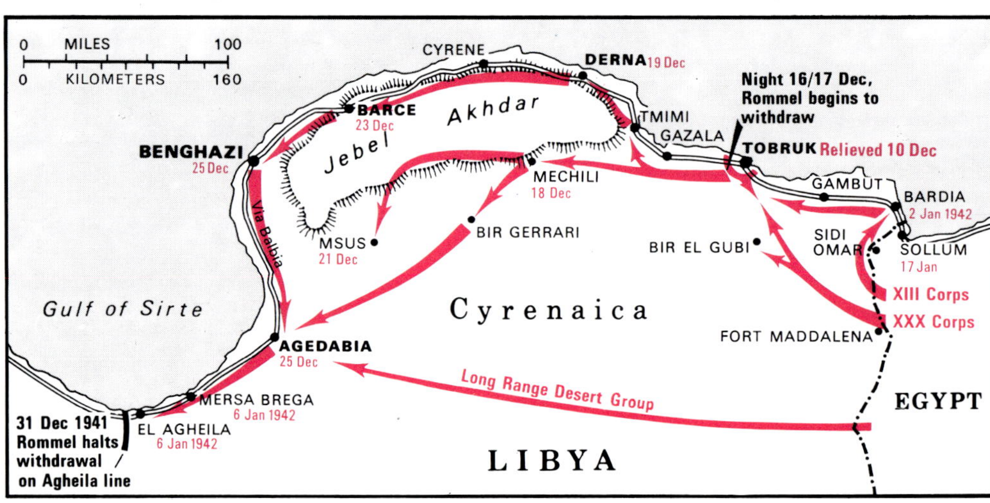

22 December 1941-7 January 1942

Allied Planning The British and American leaders meet in Washington at the Arcadia Conference. There are long discussions between Churchill and Roosevelt, their Chiefs of Staff and other political leaders from both countries. The two main conclusions of the conference are to confirm the policy of beating Germany first agreed early in 1941 and to establish the Combined Chiefs of Staff as the directing body for the whole Allied military effort. The idea for the Combined Chiefs of Staff is General Marshall's and arises from his belief that a Supreme Commander should be appointed to control the operations against the Japanese in the East Indies and Malaysia. Wavell will be selected for this task (*see* 3 January) and it is decided that he should be responsible to a combined Allied authority. The Combined Chiefs of Staff will meet in Washington. The American Chiefs will participate personally and General Dill will lead the British Military Mission. The general strategic program is agreed also. This provides for a US buildup in Britain in preparation for future land operations against Germany. The bomber offensive is to continue. It is accepted that there will be further losses in the Pacific but these are to be held to a minimum by stout defense. The British come to the conference rather better prepared than the Americans, not unnaturally since they have been fighting longer. The American military delegation is also a little unbalanced since Admiral King has only just taken over at the head of the US Navy. The US military leaders will feel afterward that they have been unfairly dominated and will also worry about Churchill's personal influence on Roosevelt.

23 December 1941

Burma There are the first Japanese air attacks on Rangoon. The Allied air forces in Burma only have two fighter squadrons at this stage, one from the RAF, and one from Chennault's American Volunteer Group. Not surprisingly they are only able to offer token resistance to the hordes of Japanese Zeros.
Borneo There are Japanese landings at Kuching, the capital of Sarawak. Two transports are sunk and two damaged by a Dutch submarine. A second submarine sinks a Japanese destroyer but is then sunk in turn. The small British force at Kuching resists until 25 December and then withdraws.
North Africa The Axis forces evacuate Benghazi. The Allied advance has reached Barce.

24 December 1941

Philippines The Japanese land 7000 men of the 16th Infantry Division at Lamon Bay in southeast Luzon. In north Luzon the American forces have taken up the first of five delaying positions planned to block the advance of the Japanese from Lingayen Gulf toward the Bataan Peninsula. MacArthur's intention from the first has been to retire to this area and await help and reinforcements from across the Pacific. Such help cannot now arrive but MacArthur has no other options open.

24-25 December 1941

Sulu Archipelago Japanese forces land on Jolo.

25 December 1941

Eastern Front The Soviet offensives continue to achieve successes. The German forces are now down to 75 percent of their strength in June. Their losses in tanks have been especially severe. Guderian has less than 40 tanks in his whole command. In Hoeppner's Panzer Group only one of the four armored divisions has more than 15 tanks.
North Africa The advancing Allied forces reach Benghazi and Agedabia as the Axis retreat continues.
Hong Kong The British forces in Hong Kong capitulate in the evening.
Philippines The US forces in north Luzon are attacked on their second line of defense at the Agno River.

26 December 1941

Eastern Front The German attacks on Sevastopol are continuing, but other German units of Eleventh Army are threatened by Soviet landings in the eastern Crimea at Kerch.

26-28 December 1941

Arctic There is a British commando raid on the Lofoten Islands. On December 26 a force of 260 men is landed on Moskenesoy to destroy the fish-oil factory there. On 27 December there are landings on Vaagso and Maaloy nearby by almost 600 troops. Again fish factories and radio stations are the targets. The raids are a success with various merchant and patrol craft being sunk and 243 volunteers being taken to join the Norwegian forces in Britain. The raid also contributes to fears of Hitler's about a British invasion of Norway. In the short term Doenitz will be ordered to station U-Boats to guard against this and in the long term considerable German forces will be sent to idle in Norway.

27 December 1941

Philippines Manila is declared an open city by the American authorities while in the fighting to the north the American forces have now fallen back to their third line running east and west from Paniqui.
British Command General Pownall replaces Air Marshal Brooke-Popham as Commander in Chief Far East. This command will shortly be superseded by Wavell's ABDA to which Pownall will become Chief of Staff.

21 December 1941

Eastern Front The German attacks on Sevastopol make some gains in the Fort Stalin area where 22nd and 24th Divisions are leading the offensive. The Germans, under the command of General Manstein, believe that they will soon take the city.
Philippines The US forces have now fallen back to the line Tarlac-Cabanatuan and are attacked there.
Malaya The British forces withdraw from Ipoh under pressure from the Japanese advance. The next defended positions will be at Kampar and the crossings of the River Slim.
Burma General Hutton is appointed to command the British forces.

28-30 December 1941

North Africa In a series of brisk engagements the British 22nd Armored Brigade takes severe losses as the retreating Germans turn and counterattack. The German performance in this retreat through Cyrenaica and in their retreat after Alamein, contrasts strongly with the behaviour of the British and Allied forces when they have the same experience. In March 1941 and January 1942 when the Allied front breaks there is great confusion and often panic in the rear areas. The Afrika Korps in retreat is well planned and orderly.

Above: British soldiers face the humiliation of surrender to the Japanese in Hong Kong, December 1941.

29 December 1941

Eastern Front There are new Soviet landings in the eastern Crimea at Feodosia. The forces moved to here and Kerch will be a serious threat to the German Eleventh Army and it will be compelled to halt attacks on Sevastopol while it deals with them. The Soviet units involved are Fifty-first and Forty-fourth Armies.

30 December 1941

Philippines The US forces fall back from Tarlac to their last prepared line before the Bataan Peninsula. They must attempt to hold this position just north of Clark Field so that the troops retiring before the Japanese landings in south Luzon can pass through Manila to Bataan.
Eastern Front The continuing Soviet advance on the Moscow sector recaptures Tula.
Malaya The Japancsc advance has now reached nearly to Kampar in the west and Kuantan in the east.

31 December 1941

Eastern Front Although the battles since June have seen huge losses for the Red Army – at least 5,000,000 casualties, 3,000,000 prisoners, 20,000 tanks and 30,000 guns destroyed – the Soviets are still very much in the fight. They will maintain the initiative until well into the spring of 1942, but by then the resources that have been carefully assembled during the autumn of 1941 will have been dissipated in attacks. Although the Germans have already lost severely in the winter offensive and will continue to do so, there will be no Soviet breakthrough and instead a gradual growth in German manpower and equipment levels.
United States Command General Brett takes command of US forces in Australia.

1942

January 1942

Battle of the Atlantic The German U-Boat fleet now has 91 vessels operational with another 158 on training missions or on trials. The operational boats are distributed with 64 in the Atlantic theater, 23 in the Mediterranean and four in the Arctic. This month Allied shipping losses in all theaters amount to 106 ships of 419,900 tons; 48 ships are sunk in the Atlantic and 62 ships fall to Axis submarines of all nations. From later in the month until March Doenitz is compelled by Hitler to deploy a significant number of his fleet off Norway to guard against an invasion. This is one useful result for the Allies of the British commando raid on the Lofotens at the end of 1941. The most important development in the maritime war during the month is the move of the German submarines to the East Coast of America (*see* 13 January 1942).
British Air Operations RAF Bomber Command makes many attacks during the month. Targets include Emden, Hamburg, Bremen and Brest (aimed at the *Scharnhorst, Gneisenau* and *Prinz Eugen*).
Mediterranean Fliegerkorps II makes heavy attacks on Malta throughout the month, ensuring that British forces based there can do little against the Axis supply routes going to North Africa. In any case the Italians provide very strong (up to four battleships and many cruisers) escorts for all convoys sent to North Africa. The British send three small convoys to Malta.

1 January 1942

World Affairs The first step is taken toward the establishment of the United Nations when representatives of 26 countries meet in Washington to endorse the principles of the Atlantic Charter. They agree (1) to employ all their resources against the Axis powers and (2) to make no separate peace.
Eastern Front German forces counterattack near Kerch in the Crimea. The attacks of the Kalinin Front retake Staritza.

2 January 1942

Eastern Front In the advance of the West Front south of Moscow Maloyaroslavets is retaken from the Germans.
North Africa The Axis garrison of Bardia on the Egyptian border surrenders. It has held out since almost the start of the Crusader offensive.
Philippines Japanese forces occupy Manila. Their American and Filipino opponents establish themselves on the approaches to the Bataan Peninsula.
Malaya British and Empire forces continue to be compelled to retreat southward. The 15th Indian Brigade is forced back from around Kampar.

3 January 1942

Allied Command By the authority of the Arcadia Conference Chiang Kai-shek is named Commander in Chief of Allied forces in China. General Wavell is appointed to the newly established ABDA (American-British-Dutch-Australian) Command. His task is to hold the 'Malay Barrier' (the line from Malaya through the Dutch East Indies to Borneo).

4 January 1942

Malaya The 11th Indian Division prepares to attempt to hold the line of the River Slim but is coming under increasingly heavy Japanese air attack as the new Japanese bases in Thailand become operational.
New Britain Japanese air forces attack Rabaul.

5 January 1942

Eastern Front Stalin refuses advice from Zhukov and his other military advisers and orders offensives on all fronts rather than concentrating against Army Group Center. Zhukov has argued that Soviet resources are not sufficient to allow such diverse operations and that, although early successes may be achieved, there will be no reserve of strength to break into German fortified positions. This will turn out to be an accurate prediction.
Philippines Late in the day American forces begin to make final withdrawals to the main Bataan position.

6 January 1942

North Africa The British 1st Armored Division becomes operational in Cyrenaica. The inexperience of this formation is to be an important factor in the coming operations. The German retreat through Cyrenaica comes to an end. The British advance has reached Mersa Brega and El Agheila.

7 January 1942

United States, Politics President Roosevelt submits the budget for 1943 to Congress. The total of the appropriations is $59,000,000,000. Production in 1942 is to be 60,000 planes, 45,000 tanks and 8,000,000 tons of shipping; in 1943, 125,000 planes, 75,000 tanks and 11,000,000 tons of shipping.
Malaya Japanese tanks and infantry totally disrupt the defenses of 11th Indian Division around Trolak and Kampong Slim. The two brigades most heavily engaged are reduced to about 20 percent of their normal strength.

8 January 1942

Malaya General Wavell, visiting Singapore, orders the Allied forces to withdraw to positions south of the Muar River where the next stand is to be made.
Eastern Front West of Moscow the Soviet forces are now attacking Mozhaysk.

8-10 January 1942

Malaya There is a third wave of Japanese landings bringing in more troops. There is the usual lavish escort for the convoys.

9 January 1942

Eastern Front The Soviet Northwest, Volkhov and Kalinin Fronts launch a new offensive in the Valdai Hills area west and northwest of Moscow. The Soviet advance is very rapid at first despite fierce German resistance.
Philippines The first period of Japanese attacks on Bataan begins.

11 January 1942

East Indies Japanese forces begin their invasion of the Dutch East Indies. They make landings on the small islands of Tarakan and Minahassa. General Yamashita and Admiral Takahashi are in command.

The Japanese plan for the invasion of the East Indies envisages a three-pronged attack. The landings at Tarakan are from the Central Force which is to take Borneo. The Western Force will advance from Sarawak and make landings on Sumatra and Java. The Eastern Force is to begin with landings on the Celebes and at Amboina, before attacking Bali, Timor and the eastern part of Java.
Pacific The carrier *Saratoga* is severely damaged in an attack by the Japanese submarine *I.6* near Hawaii, one of the few major successes of the Japanese submarine arm.

Previous page: An RAF Short Stirling bomber.
Below: General George C Marshall (left) discusses plans with Secretary of War Henry L Stimson.

12 January 1942

North Africa Rommel agrees with a proposal from his subordinates that they should prepare a surprise counteroffensive against the British. To preserve security neither the German nor Italian High Command are told of the plans. Even during the retreat in December the Germans were receiving new supplies of tanks and more arrived on 5 January. The British forces are going to be reduced by the withdrawal of the two Australian divisions to face the Japanese, and 7th Armored Brigade will also go. Other units earmarked for Eighth Army will be diverted in transit.

Yugoslavia, Politics General Simovič resigns and Professor Yovanovič becomes Premier of the exile government with Colonel Mihajlovič as Minister of War.

East Indies After fierce fighting Tarakan is taken by the Japanese. Tarakan and Manado in the Celebes are quickly made into air bases to support the Japanese advance.

13 January 1942

Battle of the Atlantic The German U-Boats begin operations off the US East Coast. The move is code named Paukenschlag (Drum Roll). Doenitz has faced arguments from his superiors in the German Navy who do not favor the operation, and he has had the difficulty that only the larger 740-ton U-Boats are really suitable for such long-range patrols. When Doenitz gives the order for the attack to begin there are 11 U-Boats in position and 10 more en route, and together they sink 150,000 tons during the first month. Intelligence sources have given reasonable warning of the attack but the U-Boats find virtually peace-time conditions in operation. Ships sail with lights at night; lighthouses and buoys are still lit; there is no radio discipline – merchant ships often give their positions in clear language; there are destroyer patrols (not convoys with escorts) but these are regular and predictable and their crews are naturally inexperienced. The US Navy refuses to take the advice on trade protection offered by the British, and the British are annoyed that many of their ships making for the convoy assembly points in Nova Scotia are among the victims.

Philippines Japanese attacks on Bataan continue and, although they make progress on the east side of the peninsula, they are still held in the west.

War Crimes Allied representatives meeting in London announce that Axis war criminals will be punished after the war.

Above: Admiral Karl Doenitz, C in C of the U-Boat arm, inspects sailors belonging to a destroyer flotilla on the Atlantic coast.

15 January 1942

Arctic The German battleship *Tirpitz* is moved to Norwegian waters.

Burma Units of the Japanese 55th Division move into Burma north of Mergui.

Malaya Japanese forces have now penetrated south of Malacca. The Japanese 5th Division is heavily engaged with Australian troops at Batu Anam on the River Muar. Troops from the Japanese Imperial Guards Division break into

Below: Japanese troops march past the remains of a British Bren-gun carrier, Burma, 1942.

the coastal section of the Allied position where 45th Indian Brigade is stationed.

16 January 1942

Eastern Front Field Marshal Leeb is removed from command of Army Group North and replaced by General Kuchler. All three German Army Group commanders have, therefore, been removed since the start of December; two of the Panzer Group commanders, Guderian and Hoeppner, have also gone, as well as 33 other officers commanding divisions or higher formations. All have been removed because of Hitler's annoyance over their requests to make withdrawals. Hitler now completely dominates German military planning and decision making.
Malaya The fighting on the Muar continues with more Japanese gains.
United States, Politics Donald Nelson is appointed head of the newly created War Production Board.

17 January 1942

South Africa, Politics The South African Parliament rejects a motion calling for independence from Britain and accords General Smuts a vote of confidence.
Eastern Front Field Marshal von Reichenau dies of a stroke while returning to Germany from the Eastern Front – one of the many German generals to die on active service.
North Africa British forces take Halfaya and capture 5500 German and Italian troops. The garrison at Halfaya has been isolated since the start of the Crusader offensive, but has held out under the command of a remarkable German leader, Major the Reverend Bach.
Arctic The convoy PQ-8 is attacked by U-Boats. This is the first such attack on an Arctic convoy. One destroyer and one merchant ship are sunk by *U.454*.

Below: Japanese Type 89 medium tanks cross a bridge just outside Manila in the Philippines, early in 1942.

18 January 1942

Eastern Front Russian South and Southwest Fronts provide the attacking units and the aim is to cross the Donets and wheel south to the Sea of Azov, trapping German units against it. The German Sixth and Seventeenth Armies are the defending units.

In the Moscow sector the Valdai Hills offensive is still going well for the Red Army. They have reached to within 70 miles of Smolensk and also threaten Velikiye Luki. In the Crimea the German forces are recovering from the disruption caused by the Soviet landings at the end of December and have resumed their attacks to take Feodosia.

19 January 1942

Eastern Front Von Bock is appointed to succeed von Reichenau in command of Army Group South. The Russians recapture Mozhaysk in the central sector after a fierce street battle. There are also Soviet paratroop landings south of Smolensk now and over the next few days. The paratroops will help establish partisan groups to strike at German rear areas.

20 January 1942

Occupied Europe At a conference held in Berlin, which will become known as the Wannsee Conference, Heydrich presents plans to Hitler for the 'Final Solution' to the 'Jewish Problem.' These plans provide for the transportation of all Europe's Jews to extermination camps. Hitler gives his approval. Eichmann will be in charge of the department of the SS responsible for the execution of the plan (*see* March 1942).
New Britain Japanese aircraft from four carriers make major attacks on Rabaul.

21 January 1942

North Africa Rommel's second offensive begins. Cautious German advances quickly reveal faulty British dispositions. The German attacks are therefore pressed home with great success. This ability to respond quickly to fleeting opportunity is one of the secrets of the Afrika Korps' strength. The Germans employ about 100 tanks in their drive with the German tank units advancing to El Agheila on the inland flank while German and Italian infantry move along the coast. The British forces in the forward defensive positions are a Guards Brigade and part of 1st Armored Division. They are taken by surprise.
Malaya The Allied forces are beginning to retreat south of the Muar after taking heavy losses. The 45th and 15th Brigades have been virtually destroyed in the fighting. Japanese air raids on Singapore increase in intensity. The few defending Hurricane fighters are outmatched by the Japanese Zeros.
China General Stilwell is nominated as Chief of Staff to Chiang Kai-shek.

22 January 1942

North Africa The German attack gathers pace, taking Antelat and Agedabia. The Axis troops in Africa are formally renamed Panzer Army Africa.

23 January 1942

Pacific There are Japanese landings at Rabaul in New Britain, at Balikpapan in Borneo, near Kavieng on New Ireland and on Bougainville in the Solomons. After Rabaul is taken it becomes a major Japanese naval base.

24 January 1942

Eastern Front In the Soviet offensive south of Kharkov the advance has now crossed the Donets. Barvenkovo is taken.
Philippines On the Bataan Peninsula the US forces begin withdrawals to a second defense line.
East Indies Four Dutch and American destroyers attack the Japanese transports off Balikpapan, sinking five ships. There are Japanese landings at Kendari in the Celebes where an important airfield is captured.

25 January 1942

North Africa The British 2nd Armored Brigade is largely destroyed in fighting around Msus as the German advance continues.
Burma General Wavell, visiting Rangoon, gives orders for the defense of Moulmein although the local commander would prefer to retire.
Malaya Batu Pahat, the last defensive position near the Muar River, is abandoned by the Allied forces. Wavell has authorized Percival to retreat to Singapore.

26 January 1942

United States, Politics The Board of Inquiry established to investigate the Pearl Harbor disaster publishes its findings. Admiral Kimmel (then Commander in Chief US Fleet) and General Short (then Commander in Chief Hawaiian Department) are judged guilty of dereliction of duty. Both have already been dismissed.
North Africa Rommel's offensive recaptures Msus.
Western Europe The first American troops arrive in the British Isles.

27 January 1942

Britain, Politics Churchill opens a major House of Commons debate with a report of re-

Above: German Junkers Ju-52 transports take on supplies on a snowy airfield near Smolensk, February 1942.

cent negotiations of measures for Allied cooperation. He describes the Combined Chiefs of Staff Committee, the Pacific Council and the plans for US land forces to come to Britain. The debate clears the air of various criticisms of the conduct of the war and a vote of confidence is opposed by only one member.

Eastern Front Timoshenko's troops continue their advance into the Ukraine and capture Lozvaya. They now threaten Dnepropetrovsk which is the main supply base for Army Group South. The German defense is now stiffening and by 31 January the Soviets will be halted.

Borneo A Japanese force lands and captures Pemangkat and the nearby airfield.

27-28 January 1942

Malaysia The British carrier *Indomitable* flies a cargo of 48 Hurricane fighters to Java. From here they will move on to reinforce the defenses of Singapore. The 22nd Indian Brigade is cut off in fighting near Layang Layang south of Kluang.

Below: Map showing Rommel's counterattack in North Africa, January-February 1942.

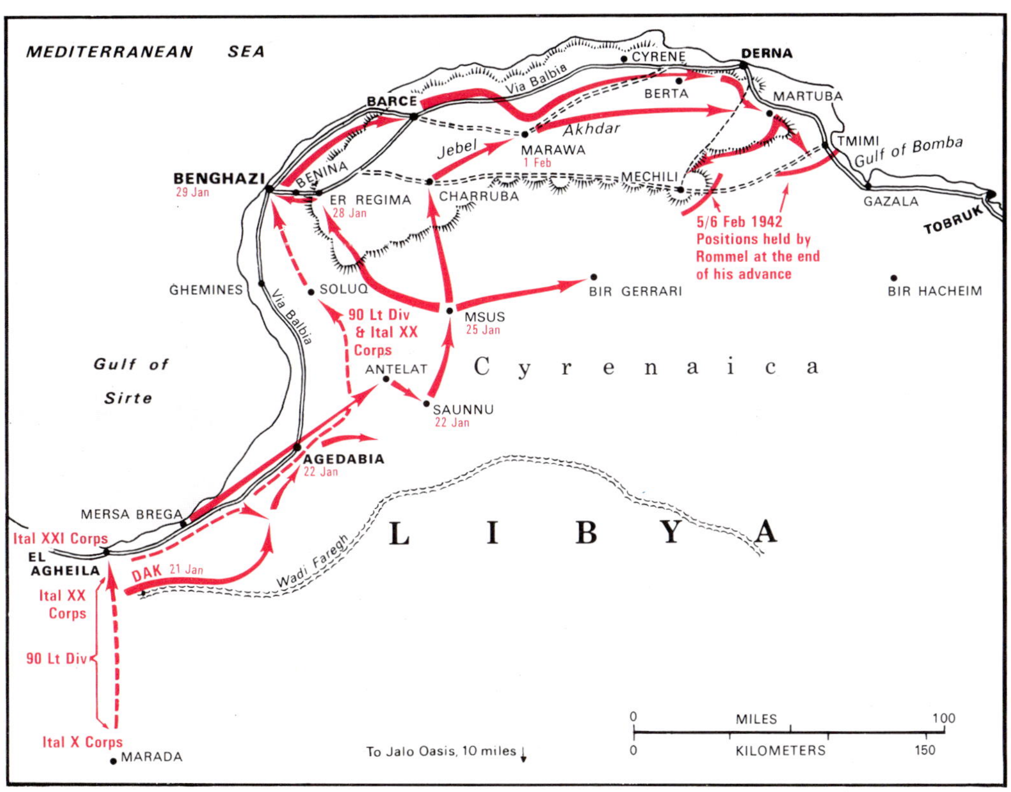

29 January 1942

North Africa Rommel retakes Benghazi and continues to advance.

Diplomatic Affairs Britain and the USSR sign a treaty of alliance with Iran. Many supplies from the Western Allies later use this route to Russia.

United States, Command General Harmon becomes Chief of Staff, USAAF, succeeding General Spaatz who will now lead Air Force Combat Command.

30 January 1942

Philippines Japanese pressure on the American positions on Bataan is maintained. As well as striking against the main defense lines, amphibious landings have been made at various points on the coast. Amboina, the second largest naval base in the Dutch East Indies, is attacked by the Japanese.

Burma The Japanese 55th Division begins attacks on Moulmein.

31 January 1942

Malaya The last Australian-British forces are withdrawn to Singapore.

Burma In Burma there is more heavy fighting at Moulmein causing British troops to retire northward. The town falls to the Japanese.

February 1942

Battle of the Atlantic On 1 February the Germans begin to use a new cipher, Triton, for the radio traffic to their U-Boats operational in the Atlantic. This will not be broken by the British until almost the end of the year. Since the German codes were first broken regularly, however, the British have improved their radio direction finding techniques and their photo-reconnaissance capabilities. They are still able to read most of the other German naval codes and, from all these sources and the insight their long period of knowledge has given, are still able to make useful guesses about the German moves.

The submarine campaign off the United States continues with great success and is being extended to take in the Caribbean also. One of the few battles about this time is around ON-67 when five U-Boats sink eight ships in three days – with six of the casualties being large tankers. Altogether Axis submarines sink 85 ships of 476,500 tons this month out of a total Allied loss of 154 ships of 679,600 tons (54 ships of 181,200 tons are sunk in the Pacific).

British Air Operations RAF bombers mount various attacks on targets in Germany and France, especially in the middle and at the end of the month. Kiel, Mannheim and Cologne are among the targets. (*See* 14 and 22 February for important developments.)

Mediterranean Malta is bombed on many occasions, day and night, throughout the month. The problems of supplying the island and keeping the forces there up to strength are now more difficult now that the airfields of Cyrenaica are in German hands, preventing air cover being given to convoys. Equally, without Cyrenaican airfields the RAF finds it more difficult to strike at Rommel's supplies.

1 February 1942

Pacific American naval task forces under Halsey and Fletcher attack air bases in the Marshall and Gilbert Islands. The aircraft carrier USS *Enterprise* is damaged.

Norway, Politics Quisling is appointed to head the Nazi puppet government.

North Africa General Ritchie orders Eighth Army to withdraw to the Gazala line.

Above: Japanese troops are welcomed by the citizens of a town in Burma. Their enthusiasm would not last long, however.

3 February 1941

East Indies The Japanese begin major attacks on Java. Surabaya and other Dutch bases are hit. All defending aircraft are destroyed. In New Guinea, Port Moresby is bombarded.
North Africa British forces evacuate Derna.

4 February 1942

East Indies Japanese aircraft repel Dutch and American ships attempting attacks in the Makassar Straits. Two American cruisers are damaged. The Japanese have now completed the capture of Amboina despite brave resistance by the mixed Australian and Dutch garrison.
Malaya Japanese demands for the surrender of Singapore are rejected. British reinforcements continue to arrive despite the desperate situation. Wavell hopes that the island can be held for some time while Allied forces elsewhere in the East Indies are being built up.

Below: The German battlecruiser *Scharnhorst*, photographed from the deck of the *Prinz Eugen* during the 'Channel Dash', February 1942.

6 February 1942

Allied Planning The first meeting of the Combined Chiefs of Staff takes place in Washington. (*See* Arcadia Conference, 22 December 1941.)
Philippines Japanese reinforcements land on Luzon. The fighting on Bataan has been less severe for a few days.

7 February 1942

Germany, Production The German minister of munitions, Todt, is killed in an air crash. Speer, Hitler's architect, is appointed to replace him. The German war industries have been fairly inefficiently run until Todt's brief appointment when more sensible priorities were established. At this time, when compared with Britain or the USSR, Germany is not well mobilized for war. As yet the German people have had no real cuts in their standard of living when compared with peace-time conditions. This is gradually changing under the impetus of Todt's measures and the effect of the first defeats in the USSR. Speer will prove to be brilliant at continuing and extending the process.
North Africa Rommel's forces stop their advance near Gazala. In a lightning campaign they have recovered almost all of the ground so dearly won by the British at the end of 1941. They have completely disrupted the British 1st Armored Division and severely damaged Eighth Army morale.
Eastern Front The Soviet forces attack Rzhev in the battles west of Moscow.

8 February 1942

Philippines General Homma, commanding Japanese forces on Luzon, discontinues his main attacks and awaits further reinforcements. However, heavy fighting continues on some sectors for several weeks.
Malaya After dark and following a considerable bombardment, Japanese troops of the 5th, 18th and Imperial Guards Divisions make successful landings on Singapore. The landings are made in the northwest of the island in the sector defended by 22nd Australian Brigade. The garrison of the island is about 85,000 strong, including administrative units. The attacking Japanese force is considerably smaller. The guns of the Singapore fortress can only make a small contribution to the defense because their positions and the ammunition supplied are designed with a seaborne attack in mind.

10 February 1942

Malaya The fighting on Singapore Island continues. Owing to a confusion of orders, the Allied forces fall back further than is necessary and abandon some good defensive positions on the Jurong Line.
Burma Japanese troops begin to cross the Salween near its mouth at Martaban and Pa-an. Reinforcements are ready to follow.
Allied Planning There is the first meeting of the Pacific War Council in London. Representatives of Britain, New Zealand, Australia and Holland are present.

11 February 1942

Malaya A final Allied counterattack on Singapore Island is driven off with heavy losses and the Allied troops begin to pull back to their final perimeter around the town itself.

11-12 February 1942

English Channel The German battlecruisers *Scharnhorst* and *Gneisenau* and the heavy cruiser *Prinz Eugen* run home from Brest up the English Channel. By a combination of luck and the slackness of British forces only a few piecemeal attacks are made. Both battlecruisers are damaged by mines, however. The damage to *Scharnhorst* is serious, and when *Gneisenau* is in

dock to have her slighter hurts repaired she is seriously hit in a bombing raid. The operation is code named Cerberus and Admiral Ciliax is in command. Although it is a notable insult to British power, the British strategic position is improved since it is easier to guard against any attack from German ships when they are in German or Norwegian bases.

13 February 1942

Eastern Front The Russian offensives continue in all sectors against increasing German resistance. Despite this Russian spearheads have now reached White Russia.

Germany, Planning Operation Sea Lion, the invasion of Britain, is finally formally cancelled by the German High Command. (Until now it has merely been postponed).

14 February 1942

British Air Operations The Area Bombing Directive is issued to RAF Bomber Command. The attacks 'should now be focused on the morale of the enemy civil population and, in particular, of the industrial workers.' It is understood that the aiming points for the attacks will be the inflammable residential districts rather than the factories, and that the desired effects will be produced by destroying the workers' houses rather than the means of production.

East Indies Japanese paratroops land at Palembang on Sumatra. Other units of Admiral Ozawa's Western Force are en route to Sumatra by sea.

15 February 1942

Malaya The Allied forces are now confined into a small area around Singapore town. Certain categories of ammunition are in short supply and there is little water because the Japanese hold the reservoir area. The Allied commanders decide to seek terms. General Yamashita accepts General Percival's surrender. The Japanese losses in the whole Malayan campaign have been less than 10,000 men. The British have lost 138,000. Japanese forces have been far better trained and led, and have had the crucial advantages of overwhelming air power and the few tanks present. They have expected to complete the campaign in 100 days; they have taken 70. The Malayan campaign has been the greatest disaster in British military history.

East Indies The Japanese forces attacking Palembang receive reinforcements and compel the garrison to retreat before they have finished destroying the great oil refinery.

Burma Because the Japanese are now over the Salween in force, the outpost units of 17th Indian Division are pulled back.

16 February 1942

Japan, Politics General Tojo outlines Japanese war aims to the Diet. He speaks of 'a new order of coexistence and coprosperity on ethical principles in Greater East Asia.'

Battle of the Atlantic German U-Boats shell important oil installations at Aruba.

16-19 February 1942

Burma There is fighting along the Bilin River as the Japanese continue to attempt to advance.

19 February 1942

United States, Command General Eisenhower is appointed Chief of the War Plans Division of the US Army General Staff.

Vichy, Politics General Gamelin and two former prime ministers of France, Reynaud and Blum are put on trial at Riom by the Vichy authorities, charged with being responsible for the French defeat in 1940. The defendants are largely successful in shifting the blame as it appears from the evidence toward the whole of the military establishment. This is a victory because a large part of the Vichy government is taken from such sections of society. The trial is never concluded.

Britain, Politics Churchill announces changes in his War Cabinet. Sir Stafford Cripps, formerly ambassador in Moscow, replaces Arthur Greenwood and Sir Kingsley Wood.

Australia One hundred and fifty carrierborne aircraft attack Darwin in Northern Australia, damaging the harbor installations and sinking a number of warships. Four carriers from the Pearl Harbor force lead the attack.

East Indies The Japanese invade Bali.

20 February 1942

East Indies The aircraft carrier USS *Lexington*, escorted by cruisers and destroyers, attempts to attack Rabaul but is driven off by Japanese forces. Portuguese Timor is invaded by the Japanese.

21 February 1942

Burma The 17th Indian Division begins to fall back to the Sittang through Kyaikto.

Arctic The pocket-battleship *Admiral Scheer* and the cruiser *Prinz Eugen* leave Germany for bases in Norway.

22 February 1942

British Air Operations Air Marshal Harris is appointed to lead RAF Bomber Command. He will become a controversial figure but his early record will be good. He will succeed in reviving Bomber Command morale and developing a policy suited to the limitations of the force. He will be especially good at the public relations side of his job. The bomber offensive will be the only weapon with which Britain can strike directly at Germany until 1944, and it will be important to convince the British people and the leaders of the USSR that as much as possible is being done.

Philippines General MacArthur is ordered to leave the Philippines and establish his headquarters in Australia.

Burma Japanese troops attack the positions of 17th Indian Division around Mokpalin on the River Sittang. There is heavy fighting near the one bridge over the river.

23 February 1942

Burma The only accessible bridge over the Sittang is demolished, leaving a large part of the 17th Indian Division cut off on the east bank. Most of the men managed to escape but all heavy equipment is lost.

24 February 1942

Wake Island An American task force led by Admiral Halsey in the USS *Enterprise* successfully attacks Wake Island.

Eastern Front The German resistance to Russian attacks grows firmer, but in the northern sector the Russians have surrounded II Corps of the German Sixteenth Army just south of Lake Ilmen in the Demyansk area. Air supply (an average of 270 tons a day) will enable this unit to hold out until relieved in April.

Above: A German soldier digs a shallow foxhole in the desert.

25 February 1942

Burma and East Indies The ABDA Command is dissolved. General Wavell again becomes Commander in Chief India. The Dutch General Ter Poorten takes command in Java.

26 February 1942

Allied Politics Litvinov, speaking in Washington, demands effort from the Allies, saying that, 'only by simultaneous offensive operations on two or more fronts can Hitler's armed forces be disposed of.'

Eastern Front The Soviets inflict heavy casualties on the German Sixteenth Army around Staraya Russa.

Burma The Japanese infiltrate west of the Sittang. They now threaten the Rangoon-Mandalay railroad.

27-29 February 1942

Battle of the Java Sea An Allied squadron, commanded by Admiral Doorman, comprising five cruisers and 11 destroyers of four nationalities, tries to intercept an invasion force bound for Java and, in a series of running battles, is almost totally eliminated. The Japanese, aided by their superior torpedo equipment and night-fighting skills, suffer only slight damage. Their force includes four cruisers and 14 destroyers. Admiral Takagi is in command.

28 February 1942

France British troops raid the German radar station at Bruneval, taking away equipment for examination.

March 1942

Battle of the Atlantic The U-Boat campaign off the United States is stepped up. Of the 111 operational U-Boats 80 are deployed for the Atlantic. Axis submarines sink 95 ships this month, 35 of them in US or West Indian waters.

Of these 35 ships half are large tankers. Two U-Boats off Freetown sink 11 ships. Toward the end of the month the first submarine tanker or *milch cow* leaves Lorient to join the U-Boat fleet. During the next few months there will be two or three of these on station at any time, effectively doubling the radius of the German U-Boats. Total Allied shipping losses are 273 ships of 834,200 tons of which 534,000 tons are sunk in the North Atlantic. In the war against Japan 252,000 are lost. The US Navy is still arguing against British advice and saying that the weak convoys that would be all they would be able to organize would be worse than none. Many of the US forces deployed in the Atlantic before December 1941 are now, of course, in the Pacific, but about 35 British escorts and some Coastal Command aircraft are now operating off the US or in the Caribbean.

British Air Operations There are several important landmarks for Bomber Command this month. The *Gee* navigational aid comes into large-scale service (it has been tested in 1941). The Lancaster bomber is first used on operations in the raid on Lubeck on the 28th, which is itself important as being the first demonstration of Harris' new policy. Lubeck is chosen because it is a medieval town with narrow streets and timber framed houses and will, therefore, burn well. Other RAF targets include Essen, Cologne and Kiel.

War Crimes The large-scale transportation of Jews to the Nazi extermination camps gets fully under way. The five extermination camps, Auschwitz, Chelmno, Treblinka, Sobibor and Belsen-Bergen, should be distinguished from the 'ordinary' concentration camps. The extermination camps mission is to kill, whereas the concentration camps expect to work their inmates to death amid foul conditions and rations much less than the minimum for survival.

Auschwitz, the largest of the extermination camps, will be able to deal with over 12,000 people in a day. The occupants of the Polish ghettos will form the largest proportion of the camps' victims during the first months – 2,600,000 of Poland's 3,000,000 Jews will be killed during the war. For German occupied territory as a whole at least 5,500,000 will be murdered by the Nazis or their local accomplices. Alongside the Jews some 3,000,000 other 'undesirables' will be murdered, mainly Communists, socialists, gypsies and other dissidents to the Nazi regime.

Mediterranean German air attacks on Malta continue throughout the month, as do British efforts to transport supplies to the island (*see* 6 and 20-23 March).

United States, Home Front The American authorities begin to transport almost 100,000 Japanese-Americans from their homes on the West Coast to internment camps in the midwest. This measure is in fact almost totally unnecessary as the performance of some Japanese-American regiments later in the war, particularly in Italy, shows only too well.

Eastern Front The mud of the spring thaws checks movement all along the front. Both Russians and Germans are becoming too exhausted to make important gains.

Above: A German parachutist uses his flamethrower to clear a way forward through a Russian village, February 1942.

1 March 1942

Burma The Chinese Fifth Army is being concentrated around Toungoo, on the Sittang 150 miles from Rangoon. Chennault's 'Flying Tigers', who have done sterling work in the defense of Rangoon, move to the RAF bomber base at Magwe.

Eastern Front A new Soviet push begins in the Crimea. In a staff analysis General Halder estimates that German losses in the war with the USSR have reached 1,500,000. Losses as high as this represent a serious drain on German manpower, especially as many of those killed are amongst the Army's best troops.

East Indies The remainder of Doorman's squadron, retreating from Java, fight actions in the Sunda Strait in which they lose three cruisers and four destroyers. There are almost unopposed Japanese landings on Java at Kragan, Merak and Eretenwetan.

Below: Japanese soldiers advance through a rubber plantation in southern Malaya, early 1942. This was the period of the greatest success for the Japanese Army.

Above: A US Navy guard stands in front of sandbag defenses around Manila's biggest bookstore, the Philippine Educational Company.

2 March 1942

Philippines Japanese troops land on Mindanao. Targets on Mindanao, Cebu and Negros are also bombarded by Japanese warships.
Burma The Japanese begin to cross the Sittang in force.
East Indies Japanese troops capture Batavia on Java.

3 March 1942

Eastern Front German announcements mention the difficulties of the Sixteenth Army which is still partially encircled.

4 March 1942

Central Pacific Halsey's task force attacks Marcus Island.
China General Stilwell establishes US China Headquarters at Chunking.

5 March 1942

British Command General Brooke replaces Admiral Pound as Chairman of the British Chiefs of Staff Committee. Brooke works well with Churchill and his all-round qualities are an improvement on Pound's naval viewpoint.
Burma General Alexander arrives in Rangoon to take command and orders counterattacks.
New Guinea Japanese invasion forces leave Rabaul bound for New Guinea.

6 March 1942

Burma Counterattacks fail to relieve Pegu. Alexander confirms the order for the evacuation of Rangoon.
Mediterranean The carrier *Eagle* ferries 18 Spitfires to Malta. Seven Blenheim bombers are also flown in. These Spitfires are the first of Britain's best fighter planes that can be spared for service overseas.

6-12 March 1942

Arctic While the convoy PQ-12 is sailing to the USSR the German battleship *Tirpitz* makes a sortie from Trondheim to try to attack it. The British Home Fleet with the carrier *Victorious* is out also and, although it is given accurate instructions from the Admiralty, there is no contact between the various forces. This is one instance when it has been correct for the Admiralty to 'interfere' in the conduct of operations in the way that will attract criticism concerning the PQ-17 operation.

7 March 1942

East Indies On Java, Japanese troops take Surabaya and Lembang.
New Guinea The Japanese invasion fleet begins landings on New Guinea in the Salamaua area.
Burma Rangoon is evacuated. British troops retiring north from here and Pegu have to fight through road blocks on the way. As Rangoon is the only significant port in Burma, all supplies for the Allies must now come overland from India. Late in the day units of the Japanese 33rd Division occupy Rangoon.

9 March 1942

United States, Command Admiral Harold Stark is appointed to command US naval forces

Below: The Japanese advance and conquest of Southeast Asia.

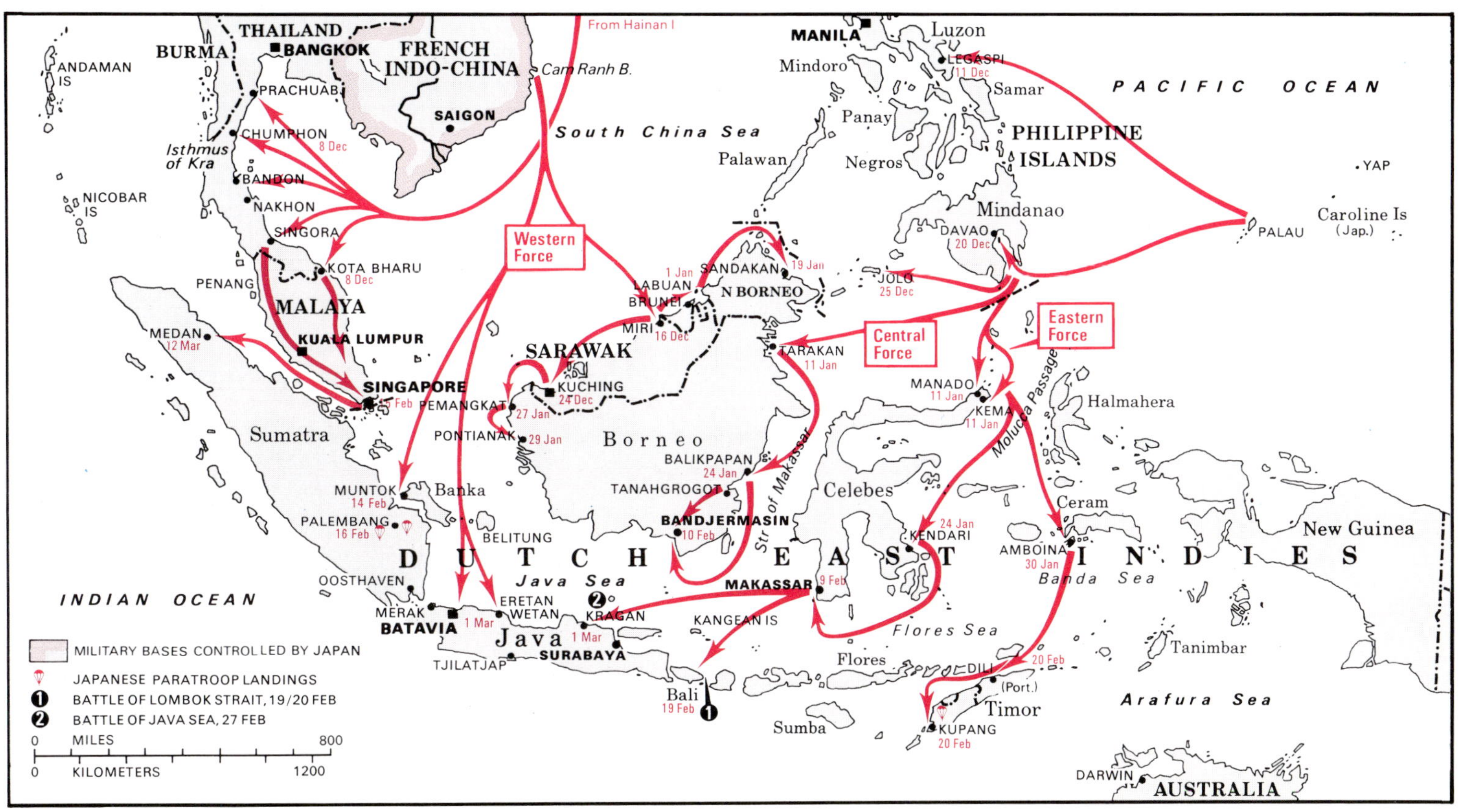

in European waters. He relives Admiral Ghormley. Admiral King, Commander in Chief of the US Navy, takes over Stark's work as Chief of Naval Operations on 26 March.
East Indies The Japanese army in Java has virtually complete control of the island. The Dutch government has been evacuated and General Ter Poorten has agreed to surrender the 100,000 Allied Troops.

10 March 1942

New Guinea Japanese naval units are attacked near Lae by aircraft launched from the carriers USS *Lexington* and *Yorktown*.

11 March 1942

Philippines General MacArthur leaves Luzon with the famous declaration 'I shall return!' On orders from Washington he hands over his command to General Wainwright.
Burma General Stilwell is appointed to command the Chinese Fifth and Sixth Armies (the equivalent of European divisions) presently concentrating around Mandalay and in the Shan States.
Mediterranean The British cruiser *Naiad* is sunk by *U.565* 50 miles north of Sollum.

12 March 1942

Pacific American forces land at Noumea in New Caledonia to garrison the island and build a base. They include the first 'Seabees' to see active service.

The Japanese consolidate their conquests in the Solomon Islands.
East Indies The Dutch forces formally surrender to the Japanese. Units of the Japanese Imperial Guards Division land in northern Sumatra.

14 March 1942

Australia US troops begin to arrive in Australia in large numbers.

15 March 1942

Eastern Front Hitler announces that Russia will be 'annihilatingly defeated' in the coming summer campaign. German casualties since the start of the year have now reached 250,000.

17 March 1942

Allied Command General MacArthur arrives in Australia to take Supreme Command of Allied Forces in the Southwest Pacific.

19 March 1942

Burma General Slim arrives in Burma to take operational command of the British forces now to be reorganized as I Burma Corps.

20-23 March 1942

Mediterranean There is an important British convoy operation to supply Malta, but because of British losses in late 1941 and the demands of the Far East there is only a relatively small escort. Four merchant ships are in the convoy and the escort, led by Admiral Vian, has five light cruisers and 17 destroyers to face perhaps the whole Italian navy. On the 22nd the Italians send out the battleship *Littorio*, two heavy cruisers, one light cruiser and eight destroyers. They attack the convoy during the afternoon but, despite their very superior strength (one of the British cruisers and several of the destroyers must stay as close escort and AA defense for the convoy), they are beaten off in an action involving smoke screens and torpedo attacks. Because of the German and Italian air attacks only 5000 tons of cargo is landed in Malta from the three ships that reach port.

21 March 1942

Eastern Front The units of the German Sixteenth Army surrounded at Demyansk begin attempts to break out.

24 March 1942

Burma General Alexander and Chiang Kai-shek meet to discuss plans for the cooperation of Chinese and British forces. Japanese troops attacking near Toungoo achieve considerable success.
Philippines Japanese artillery and aircraft again attack American positions on Bataan and Corregidor.

27 March 1942

Burma RAF aircraft and the remainder of the volunteer American squadrons are withdrawn from Burma. Japanese attacks on the Chinese 200th Division at Toungoo continue.
British Command Admiral Somerville takes command of the British Far East Fleet based in Ceylon.
Australia, Command General Blamey arrives back in Australia with some of the troops from North Africa. He is appointed to command Allied land forces in Australia.

28 March 1942

France British commandos raid St Nazaire. At considerable cost the dock gates are badly damaged. The St Nazaire dock is the only one in western France capable of accommodating the *Tirpitz*.

29 March 1942

British Air Operations An unusually successful raid on Lübeck causes Hitler to order reprisals. These 'Baedeker Raids' begin in April.
Burma At the request of General Stilwell, British forces attack Boungde to relieve pressure on the Chinese at Toungoo.
Arctic A British convoy for Murmansk is engaged unsuccessfully by German surface forces. The *Tirpitz* and the other heavy units of the German fleet are now based in Norway posing a further threat to convoys.

30 March 1942

Pacific, Command The joint Chiefs of Staff divide the Pacific into two commands. Admiral Nimitz is to control the Pacific Ocean Zone and General MacArthur the Southwest Pacific (including Australia, New Guinea, the Bismarcks and the Solomons). This division presages the later controversy between the two as to how the reconquest should be attempted.

31 March 1942

Indian Ocean Admiral Somerville's Eastern Fleet sails from Ceylon to avoid the coming attack by the main Japanese carrier forces of which intelligence has been received. Somerville is well aware that the aircraft from his three carriers are not a match for the Japanese in an open fight. However, they have been well trained in night operations (at this stage of the war neither Japanese nor American are similarly trained) and have radar mounted in planes to assist target acquisition. Somerville therefore plans to avoid action by day and search for the Japanese each night.
Burma Chinese forces withdraw from Toungoo.

April 1942

Battle of the Atlantic The U-Boat campaign off America continues to score many important successes. The loss of tankers is especially worrying. On 1 April a partial convoy system off the US East Coast is begun. The number of Halifax-UK convoys sailing has to be reduced so that more British and Canadian escorts can be sent to join the US forces. Axis submarines sink 74 ships during the month out of a total Allied loss of 132 ships of 674,500 tons. Only seven ships are sunk in the Pacific while in the Indian Ocean 150,000 tons is lost largely because of the foray early in the month by the Japanese carrier force.
Eastern Front In the course of the month the German forces receive considerable aid from

Below: Hans-Joachim Marseille, one of the leading German fighter aces of the Desert War, stands beside one of his victims – a Hurricane.

RAF force in Malta loses 126 planes on the ground and 20 more in the air. Very few are left. The converse of Malta's weakness is that Rommel loses only one percent of the supplies shipped to Africa by the Axis. He receives 150,000 tons.

1 April 1942

Philippines The Japanese resume major attacks on Bataan. The American and Filipino forces have 24,000 men sick because of short (one-quarter) rations and tropical diseases.
Mediterranean, British Command The Italian cruiser *Bande Nere* is sunk by the submarine *Urge* north of Sicily.

Admiral Cunningham leaves the command of the British Mediterranean Fleet to serve on the Combined Chiefs of Staff Committee in Washington.
Burma The Chinese troops near Toungoo are forced to continue their retreat. The British at Prome are also heavily attacked.
New Guinea There are Japanese landings on New Guinea at Sorong and Hollandia. As yet there is almost no opposition to the Japanese forces on New Guinea which continue their buildup for about three weeks.

2 April 1942

Burma The British Burma Corps retreats from Prome to avoid being surrounded.

3 April 1942

Burma Mandalay is heavily bombed. British forces continue to withdraw up the Irrawaddy Valley.
Philippines After a lull on the 2nd, the final Japanese assault on Bataan begins. There is a long bombardment before the attack goes in and the exhausted defenders are thrown back.

4 April 1942

Indian Ocean A Catalina seaplane from Ceylon sights the Japanese fleet of Admiral Kondo. As well as four battleships of the *Kongo* Class,

Left: A tanker burns in Malta harbour during a German air raid, June 1942. *Below:* Handley Page Hampden bombers of No 44 (Rhodesia) Squadron, Bomber Command.

their allies. Italy, Rumania, Hungary, Slovakia and Spain all send units to be added to the German Order of Battle.
British Air Operations RAF Bomber Command attacks increase in intensity this month. The range of targets includes industrial areas in Germany and France and several of the Atlantic ports in France and Norway. Cologne, Hamburg and Rostock are all heavily hit. There are also offensive fighter sweeps over occupied France practically every day. Like Lubeck in the attack during March, Rostock has been chosen for its inflammable nature and its easy-to-find position on the Baltic. It is an important pointer for the future that, although attacked four times this month, industry in Rostock is soon back at full production.
Mediterranean Air attacks, despite RAF retaliation against Sicilian airfields, make Malta's situation still more desperate. Toward the end of the month British submarines are forced to abandon their base at Malta. One destroyer is lost in the harbor and it is virtually closed because of the lack of minesweepers and the damage to the dockyard. During the month the

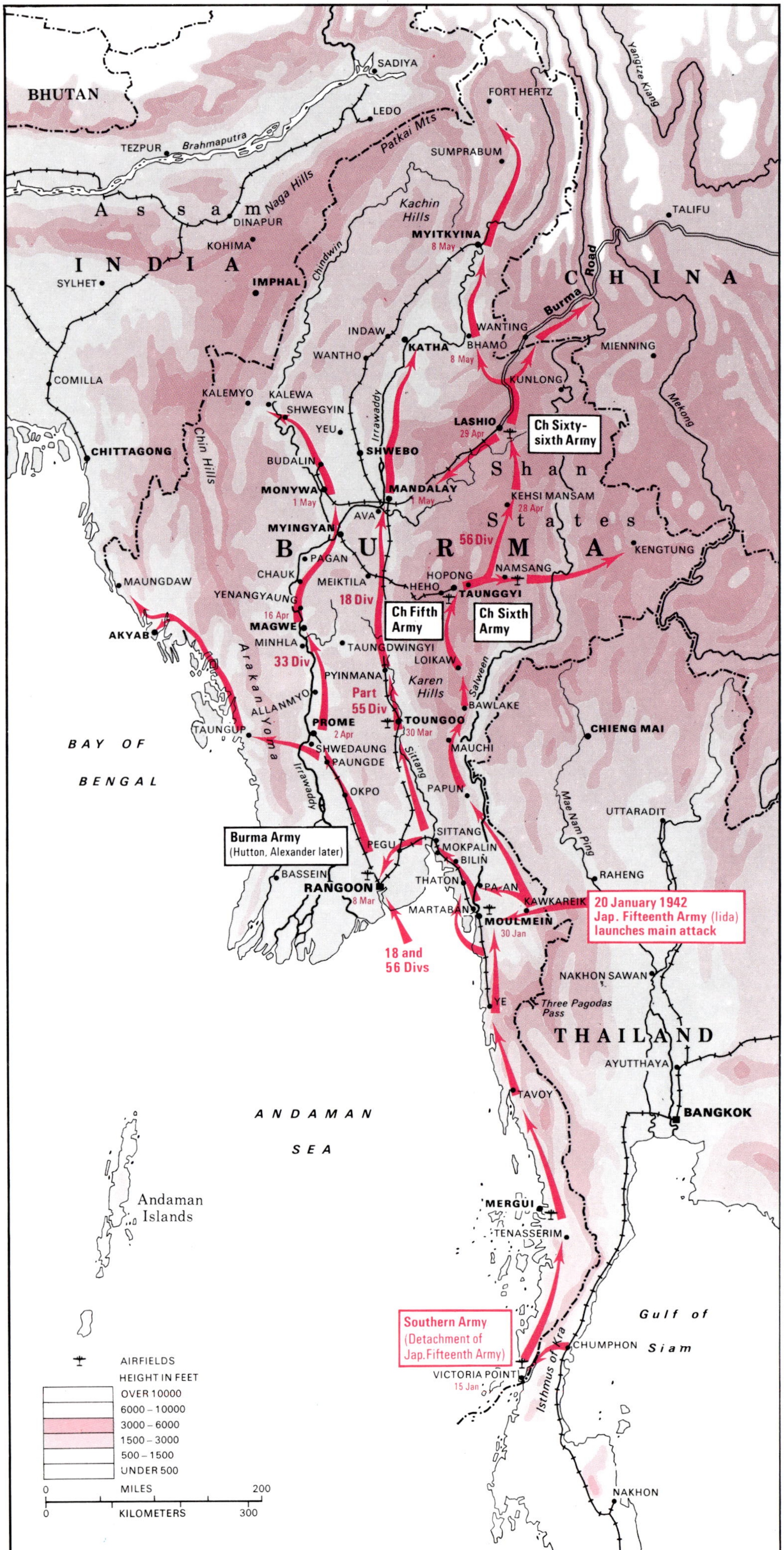

the Japanese fleet includes their main carrier forces with Admiral Nagumo leading *Akagi*, *Soryu*, *Hiryu*, *Shokaku* and *Zuikaku*. Somerville's intelligence predicted that the Japanese attack would be on 1st or 2nd and after being ready then, he has now retired to Addu Atoll to replenish. HMS *Hermes*, *Cornwall* and *Dorsetshire* have been sent on other missions. The Japanese attack cannot now be parried, so the order is given for shipping to disperse from Colombo.

5 April 1942

Indian Ocean Believing that the British will still be in port, the Japanese carriers launch 130 planes against Colombo. A small British air strike against the carriers is completely unsuccessful. Later Japanese scout planes sight the heavy cruisers HMS *Dorsetshire* and HMS *Cornwall*. New strikes are mounted by the Japanese which find and sink these ships. The Japanese squadron continues its hunt for the main British force without success.

Philippines The Japanese attacks on Bataan continue. Mount Samat is taken after heavy fighting in which the US 21st Division loses heavily. Japanese detachments leave Luzon bound for Cebu Island.

War at Sea US Task Force 39 arrives in Scapa Flow with the aircraft carrier USS *Wasp* and the battleship USS *Washington*. These forces are to aid the British Home and Gibraltar squadrons while Operation Ironclad is being carried out against Madagascar.

6 April 1942

Indian Ocean A Japanese force with cruisers and a small carrier attacks shipping in the Bay of Bengal causing heavy damage. The 83,000 tons of shipping sunk are largely the vessels dispersed from Colombo on the 4th. The attacks are extremely efficiently carried out.

Solomons The Japanese land at Bougainville.

Burma Chiang Kai-shek visits the Chinese Divisions and gives orders for the defense of positions around Pyinmana.

7 April 1942

Burma The Japanese 18th Infantry Division arrives in Rangoon by sea from Singapore.

Philippines The Japanese continue to make gains, particularly in the eastern sector of Bataan. The American and Filipino forces are now behind a line running inland from Limao. Roosevelt authorizes the commanders to take any necessary steps. Wainwright withdraws as much of his force as possible to the fortress island of Corregidor in Manila Bay.

8 April 1942

Mediterranean It is a particularly bad day for Malta. The heaviest air attacks of the war take place, the island being repeatedly bombarded by both German and Italian aircraft.

Philippines The American resistance on Bataan collapses under the fierce Japanese attacks. The destruction of equipment is ordered as a preparation for surrender.

9 April 1942

Indian Ocean Trincomalee is attacked by planes from Nagumo's carriers with damage being inflicted on the Ceylonese (Sri Lankan)

Left: Map showing the Japanese invasion of Burma and the British retreat to eastern India.

port. The small British carrier HMS *Hermes* is attacked and sunk.

In their operations in the Indian Ocean the Japanese forces have sunk 112,000 tons of merchant shipping along with one carrier, two cruisers and four smaller RN ships. This is the high-water mark of the Japanese carrier forces' success. Their limitations are now beginning to appear. It is notable that in the attacks on Colombo and Trincomalee, the efficiency of the Japanese strike has been sharply reduced by the small defense forces (even though these have been quickly overcome) when compared with the carriers' early successes.

Philippines General King unconditionally surrenders US forces on Luzon. Seventy-five thousand men are captured, 12,000 of them American. The prisoners are marched to San Fernando, 100 miles away, many thousands dying because of ill-treatment on the way.

Fighting continues in isolated areas of Luzon and the other islands with some US and Filipino units operating in a guerrilla role. General Wainwright holds out on Corregidor.

Burma The British troops take positions between Taungdwingyi and Minhla on the Irrawaddy. Both the Allies and the Japanese are preparing offensives, but the Japanese are ready first because they have been more quickly reinforced.

Eastern Front German attempts to relieve the units of Sixteenth Army trapped around Demyansk make some progress. In the Crimea renewed Russian attacks achieve little.

10 April 1942

Indian Ocean The British Far East Fleet is withdrawn from bases in Ceylon to the Persian Gulf because of the superior Japanese forces which are in fact mostly returning to the Pacific.

Philippines The Japanese land on Cebu with about 12,000 men. The small American forces retire inland.

British Air Operations The RAF drops its first two-ton bombs over Essen.

11 April 1942

Burma The new Japanese offensive begins with attacks on the British positions.

Eastern Front Russian landings in the Crimea at Eupatoriya are held by the German Eleventh Army.

12 April 1942

Burma Despite receiving help from 38th Chinese Division, the British positions on the Irrawaddy are threatened by the Japanese capture of Migyaungye.

13 April 1942

British Command Rear Admiral Lord Mountbatten, although of junior rank, has been appointed Chief of Combined Operations with a seat on the British Chiefs of Staff Committee. This appointment, only now announced, has been effective since 18 March.

Burma The Japanese achieve a breakthrough in the British defenses. Allied forces fall back to new positions at Magwe. The Chinese Sixth Army, previously positioned in the Shan States, is ordered to Mandalay.

14 April 1942

Battle of the Atlantic The destroyer *Roper* sinks *U.85*. This is the first submarine kill by an American ship.

Above: Japanese soldiers stand guard over American troops captured at Bataan. These men are about to endure the 'Death March.'

Vichy, Politics Laval forms a new government in Vichy. Pétain is to remain as head of state.

Burma The demolition of oil installations around Yenangyaung is begun in order to deny them to the Japanese.

Allied Planning The British government and its military advisers provisionally accept the American plan 'Bolero' for the American build-up in Britain in preparation for a second front.

15 April 1942

Burma Following their breakthrough on the 13th the Japanese continue to drive northward, isolating one of Slim's divisions.

16 April 1942

Philippines With Allied resistance on Cebu now crumbling, the Japanese also land 4000 troops on Panay.

Malta King George VI awards Malta the George Cross, for the collective heroism of the Maltese people in the face of the Axis air attacks.

17 April 1942

Burma Unsuccessful attempts are made by the Allies to relieve the 1st Burma Division trapped around Magwe. Further north the Japanese hold the main road in the Irrawaddy Valley at Yenangyaung. The Chinese forces in the Sittang Valley and at Mauchi come under heavy pressure.

18 April 1942

Eastern Front Von Leeb is removed from command of Army Group North attacking Leningrad.

Burma The Chinese 55th Division, retreating from Mauchi, is effectively destroyed by the Japanese 56th Division. This leaves the road to Lashio undefended for the moment. Lashio is the terminus of the Burma Road. In the Sittang Valley the Chinese are forced to withdraw.

Pacific Bombers from the USS *Hornet* raid targets in Japan. Under the command of Colonel Doolittle, 16 B-25 Mitchell bombers take off from the *Hornet* about 650 miles from Japan, raid Tokyo and other targets and fly on to China. Technically the raid is extremely difficult. The bombers fly practically unarmed because of the need to lighten them to give extra range and the ability to take off from a carrier deck. The USS *Enterprise* accompanies the *Hornet* to give fighter cover. This is not in fact needed because, although the carriers are sighted, the Japanese wait for them to come within range of the lighter bombers before launching their attack. Little material damage is done, but the raid acts as a morale-booster for the people of America by showing US forces striking back directly against the Japanese.

20 April 1942

Mediterranean USS *Wasp*, escorted by HMS *Renown*, two cruisers and six destroyers, ferries 47 Spitfire fighters to Malta. However of the 46 which arrive, 30 are destroyed immediately after landing.

Burma British and Chinese forces retreat in both the Sittang and Irrawaddy Valleys.

21 April 1942

Eastern Front The German pocket at Demyansk is relieved after being cut off from all apart from air support for two and a half months. This success for air supply will probably contribute to Hitler's decision to attempt it at Stalingrad at the end of the year.

France, Politics General Giraud reaches Switzerland after escaping from German captivity. He will return to the unoccupied part of France.

22 April 1942

Burma British forces including the 7th Armored Brigade take up positions around Meiktila. Chinese troops of 200th Division are sent from there to bolster the position at Taunggyi, but inattention of General Stilwell's orders by another formation makes this position dangerous.

Above: The Japanese carrier *Shoho* is torpedoed by US aircraft during the Battle of the Coral Sea, 7 May 1942.

23 April 1942

Burma The remains of Chinese Sixth Army begins to retreat from Taunggyi toward Yunnan Province. The Allied forces in the Sittang and Irrawaddy Valleys are forced to retreat because the Japanese 56th Division has forged on from Taunggyi toward Lashio, threatening the left flank of the Allied Armies.

24 April 1942

German Air Operations Exeter is bombed by the Luftwaffe in the first of the 'Baedeker Raids,' so called because they are aimed at historic towns selected (supposedly) from the Baedeker Guide book in retaliation for the RAF raid on Lübeck on 28 March.

25 April 1942

Burma Although the Japanese fail to hold Taunggyi which is now defended by Chinese Fifth Army, they continue to move toward Lashio. To the west, General Alexander orders that the forces around Meiktila should withdraw north of the Irrawaddy.

German Air Operations The Germans bomb Bath. In the next few days Norwich, York and Hull are all hit.

26 April 1942

Philippines Fighting continues on Mindanao where Filipino forces resist the Japanese invaders, who now receive further reinforcements.

Germany, Politics Hitler, speaking in the Reichstag, foretells major victories for Germany in the summer and calls for supreme effort. His absolute power is extended and confirmed.

28 April 1942

Burma The Chinese 28th Division, now moving from Mandalay, is ordered to defend Lashio.

29 April 1942

New Guinea Japanese preparations are now well in hand for an amphibious attack on Port Moresby (Operation Mo).

Philippines The Japanese forces continue to bombard Corregidor and on Mindanao, with reinforced strength and air support, they push back the defenders.

Burma The Japanese enter Lashio. China is now cut off by land and all supplies from the Allies must go by air.

General Alexander decides to withdraw to new positions in the Chindwin and Irrawaddy Valleys.

30 April 1942

Southwest Pacific The carriers *Shokaku, Zuikaku* and *Shoho* sail from Truk for the Coral Sea to take part in Operation Mo.

Burma After withdrawing north of the Irrawaddy, British forces destroy the bridge at Ava.

May 1942

Battle of the Atlantic The efforts of the German *milch cow* supply submarines mean that there is the large number of between 16 and 18 U-Boats off the US coast during the month. Their only easy successes are off Florida, and they are gradually moving south to the Caribbean and the Gulf of Mexico where there are as yet no convoys. British and Canadian ships are being moved to strengthen the US forces in this area, however. From the middle of the month a fairly complete convoy system covers all the US coast north of Florida. There is also one pack operation against ONS-92 on the main convoy routes. Axis submarines sink 125 ships of 607,200 tons this month out of a total of 705,000 tons.

British Air Operations RAF targets this month include Stuttgart and Mannheim as well as day and night attacks on strategic installations in France. All these operations are overshadowed by the raid on Cologne on the night of the 30th/31st.

Mediterranean Air attacks on Malta are again severe, but the defending forces are now being strengthened. The RAF attacks airfields in Sicily at Catania and Augusta on several occasions.

1 May 1942

Philippines More Japanese forces have landed on Mindanao and fighting is therefore heavy. Corregidor is bombed and shelled.

Burma Mandalay falls to the Japanese.

2 May 1942

Solomons The Australian garrison of Tulagi, a small island near Guadalcanal, is evacuated.

Battle of the Coral Sea The buildup to the Coral Sea Battle begins. The principal aim of the Japanese plan is the capture of Port Moresby. The Japanese forces are divided into five groups to accomplish this and other subsidiary tasks. These forces include the large carriers *Zuikaku* and *Shokaku* under the command of Admiral Takagi which are to provide overall cover. A second group with the small carrier *Shoho* and four heavy cruisers, Admiral Goto, is to help first with close support for the landings on Tulagi (to establish a seaplane base) and then with the main operations. Admiral Inouye commanding at Rabaul, from where the main invasion force is to set out, is in command.

Largely because of American ability to read the Japanese codes, Admiral Nimitz is able to order a concentration of Allied task forces to oppose the Japanese who in turn believe that there can be at most one enemy carrier in the area. The withdrawal from Tulagi already mentioned is designed to encourage the Japanese attacks by feigning weakness. The Allied ships come from three task forces. Task Force 17 (Admiral Fletcher) with the carrier USS *Yorktown*, Task Force 11 (Admiral Fitch) with the carrier USS *Lexington* and Task Force 44 (Admiral Crace) with Australian and American cruisers. At first only Task Force 17 is in operation.

Philippines Despite the Japanese buildup on Mindanao, they can only make slow progress with their attacks.

Arctic The cruiser HMS *Edinburgh*, already damaged by *U.456*, is sunk by destroyers in the Barents Sea while escorting the Arctic convoy QP-11.

3 May 1942

Solomons The Japanese land at Tulagi.

Philippines There are further Japanese landings on Mindanao which cannot be beaten off.

4 May 1942

Battle of the Coral Sea Aircraft from the *Yorktown*, 100 miles south of Guadalcanal, attack the Japanese forces off Tulagi. The *Yorktown* then returns south to join the rest of the Allied forces.

Philippines On Mindanao there is reduced activity, but in Manila Bay the bombardment of Corregidor becomes most intense.

Burma Akyab is evacuated by the British. Chinese forces are defeated at Wanting on the Burma Road and at Bhamo on the Irrawaddy.

5 May 1942

Battle of the Coral Sea Takagi's carriers enter the Coral Sea from the west. Fletcher is refuelling but fortunately for him the Japanese make no contact.

Madagascar British forces land near Diego Suarez supported by a battleship and two carriers. The US Government, previously sensitive to Vichy opinion, openly backs the British action as necessary to secure the island against Axis, 'especially Japanese' use.

Philippines Just before midnight the Japanese land on Corregidor. Most of the gun emplacements on the island have been put out of action by the Japanese bombardment. Nonetheless the Japanese lose heavily to the defensive fire before they consolidate their landing.

Burma General Stilwell, in Burma with his Chinese troops, learns of the true extent of the Japanese advance further north on the Irrawaddy and decides that his forces must also retire toward India, not China. Japanese forces have in fact entered China via the Burma Road.
Japan, Planning Imperial Headquarters orders the navy to prepare for an attack and landing on Midway Island.

6 May 1942

Philippines General Wainwright on Corregidor surrenders with 15,000 American and Filipino troops. On Mindanao there are further Japanese attacks.

7 May 1942

Battle of the Coral Sea Fletcher sends Task Force 44 to attack the Japanese transports bound for Port Moresby. The Japanese sight these ships and unsuccessfully launch heavy attacks on them with land-based aircraft. The Japanese also sight the American tanker the *Neosho* and the destroyer USS *Sims*. They are attacked and sunk but the *Neosho* has been mistaken for a carrier. The Americans also record a success, locating Goto's covering force and sinking the small carrier *Shoho*. An attempt by Takagi late in the day to locate and attack the American carriers is a failure, with 21 aircraft lost for no result (a small group are sufficiently confused to attempt to land on the *Yorktown*). The Japanese transports turn back to Rabaul to await the outcome of the carrier action.
Philippines General Wainwright, in Japanese custody, broadcasts from Luzon to announce the surrender of Corregidor and invites the remaining US forces in the Philippines to do likewise. Despite the US losses the campaign has not been an unqualified failure. General Homma was initially allocated 50 days to complete the campaign, but his crack troops have in fact been campaigning now for five months when they might have been employed elsewhere. One feature of the struggle has been the loyalty of the Filipinos to the US cause. This has been contrary to Japanese expectations.
Madagascar Vichy commanders at Diego Suarez surrender to Admiral Syfret and General Sturges.

8 May 1942

Battle of the Coral Sea Reconnaissance aircraft from each fleet sight their enemy virtually simultaneously and all the carriers dispatch strikes. The *Lexington* is badly hit and abandoned (she is later finished off by an American destroyer) and the *Yorktown* is damaged. The *Shokaku* is seriously hurt. The Japanese losses in aircraft have been especially severe and with them have gone irreplaceable, highly trained pilots. The Japanese are forced to abandon their attack on Port Moresby and this, the first real check to the Japanese advance means that the action can be justly described as a strategic victory for the Americans. This is the first major naval battle fought without visual contact being made between the main bodies of opposing forces.
Eastern Front The first real German attacks of the year begin slowly with an offensive by 22nd Panzer Division of Eleventh Army in the Crimea aimed at clearing the Kerch Peninsular.

9 May 1942

Mediterranean Sixty-four British Spitfires are ferried to Malta by forces including USS *Wasp* and HMS *Eagle*. On this occasion adequate arrangements have been made to have them quickly and safely refuelled and rearmed so that they are not shot up while on the ground. *Wasp* returns to the US after this operation.
Philippines The Japanese forces on Mindanao press home their attacks near Dalirig, practically finishing the defenders' resistance.

10 May 1942

Philippines General Sharp, commanding the remaining American forces, gives the order to surrender.

11 May 1942

Burma Part of the retreating British forces fight a sharp action at Kalewa before continuing on to the Imphal area.
Canada, Politics Following a referendum on 27 April the Canadian Parliament passes legislation to introduce full conscription.
Mediterranean The British destroyers HMS *Lively*, *Kipling* and *Jackal* are sunk by German aircraft from a specially trained force based on Crete.

12 May 1942

Eastern Front Russian attacks near Kharkov begin. This offensive is a renewal of the attempts made in January to trap German forces against the Sea of Azov.

Above: The crew of the American carrier USS *Lexington* abandon ship after a Japanese air strike, 8 May 1942.

13 May 1942

Burma Japanese troops, pursuing the Chinese Sixth Army, cross the Salween on the way to Kengtung.
Eastern Front Russian troops begin to withdraw from Kerch in the face of German attacks. About 80,000 manage to get away.

14 May 1942

Midway The first indications of the coming Japanese attack reach the American code breakers.

15 May 1942

Burma The first British forces reach India in the retreat from Burma. The British casualties from the campaign have been about 30,000 from a force of 45,000. Many of these 'casualties' are Burmese deserters. The Chinese losses cannot be computed, but must have been enormous. There were about 95,000 Chinese engaged and only one formation, 38th Division, remains as a

Below: Vice-Admiral Chuichi Nagumo, commander of the First Carrier Strike Force.

viable fighting unit. The Japanese losses of less than 8000 reflect their superior training tactics, equipment and air power. With the monsoon season beginning the Japanese can be well satisfied with having so rapidly overrun Burma and with cutting China off from surface communication.

Arctic The cruiser HMS *Trinidad* is sunk by German bombers while escorting an Arctic convoy.

New Guinea Australian reinforcements are dispatched to Port Moresby.

Eastern Front Troops from Manstein's Eleventh Army capture Kerch. The Russians lose 150,000 men, including many taken prisoner.

United States, Home Front Gasoline rationing begins in 17 states. The weekly ration is three gallons for nonessential vehicles.

18 May 1942

Mediterranean The carriers HMS *Argus* and *Eagle* of Force H ferry 17 Spitfires to Malta. Admiral Harwood is appointed to command the British Mediterranean Fleet.

19 May 1942

Eastern Front After strongly resisting the Russian attacks for several days, the Germans mount a major counterattack near Kharkov, in the Ukraine.

23 May 1942

Eastern Front The German Sixth Army from the north and Group Kleist (Seventeenth Army and First Panzer Army) work to encircle elements of the Russian Sixth and Fifty-seventh Armies west of the Donets.

25 May 1942

Midway Two light carriers and two cruisers leave port in Hokkaido to carry out diversionary raids in the Aleutian Islands. US forces are also on the move with submarines leaving Hawaii for patrol positions related to the Midway operation.

Burma Part of the Chinese 38th Division manage to reach India.

26 May 1942

North Africa Rommel begins a new offensive with holding attacks on the Gazala Line made by the Italian infantry. The British forces have extensively fortified this position in front, leaving their armor free to attack outflanking moves such as those now being attempted. Rommel sends all his armor, both Italian and German, in a wide right hook south of Bir Hacheim. The Italian Trieste Division gets lost and blunders into 150th Brigade between Trigh Capuzzo and Trigh el Abd.

The balance of forces is very much in the Allies' favor. The Germans and the Italians have respectively 400 and 230 tanks but are very short of infantry, especially German infantry. The British have about 850 tanks operational and 150 in reserve. About a quarter of these are the new American Grant type which at last gives the British tanks a weapon which can fire a high-explosive shell against antitank gun positions. The British dispositions are faulty, however, with the armor too widely dispersed. Throughout the war in the desert, the British use of armor compares poorly with that of the Germans in almost every respect.

Midway Admiral Nagumo's 1st Carrier Fleet leaves the Inland Sea. He has the carriers *Akagi, Kaga, Soryu* and *Hiryu*, with two battleships, cruisers and destroyers as escort. The US Task Force 16, based around the *Enterprise* and *Hornet*, returns to Pearl Harbor from the South Pacific where the Japanese believe it still to be.

Below: Short Stirling Mark I heavy bombers of No 7 Squadron, Bomber Command.

Above: Douglas Dauntless carrier-borne dive-bombers prepare to take off from the deck of USS *Ranger* in the Pacific.

27 May 1942

Midway The Midway Invasion Fleet puts to sea from Saipan and Guam with transports carrying 5000 men escorted by cruisers and destroyers. The invasion force for the Aleutians also sails in two groups from Ominato. USS *Yorktown* arrives in Pearl Harbor and repairs begin immediately.

Czechoslovakia, Resistance Resistance fighters, trained in Britain and daringly parachuted into Czechoslovakia, attempt to assassinate Reichsprotektor Heydrich in Prague. He dies of his wounds on 4 June.

North Africa Rommel's armor turns north and rapidly defeats 3rd Indian and 7th Motorized Brigades. In various engagements with British armor both sides lose heavily but the British are better able to absorb such losses. The Italian Ariete Division is meant to eliminate the Free French at Bir Hacheim but fail to do so and 90th Light swing furthest to the east in a diversionary role.

28 May 1942

North Africa The Afrika Korps is in trouble. Some of Rommel's panzers halt, out of gasoline, on the Rigel Ridge but others, although short of supplies, continue to attack toward Acroma. There is more fighting with British armor especially near Bir Harmat.

Midway The Japanese continue their preparations. The remainder of the Japanese forces set out. Admiral Yamamoto is in supreme command. Under his direct control he has seven battleships, one small carrier, cruisers and destroyers. Admiral Kondo's Second Fleet consists of two battleships, one light carrier and two seaplane carriers with escorts. Admiral Kakuta's force (*see* 25 May) has two light carriers and their escorts. The Japanese plan is complex. Kakuta is to cover landings on the Aleutians before the main operation begins in order to make sure that there are no American forces near Midway. Even without this diversion the main forces which are to attack and capture Midway are expected to achieve complete surprise and finish the conquest before any assistance can come up. Yamamoto believes that once Midway is taken, the American Fleet will come in force to dispute the capture. They can then be beaten before new American production swamps the Japanese. The plan is therefore for Nagumo's carriers to pound the Midway defenses and then await the American Fleet. Kondo is to give close support to the landings and Yamamoto's battleships are to be disposed in general reserve.

The Americans make preparations. Task Force 16 sails from Oahu with the carriers *Enterprise* and *Hornet* with escorts. Fletcher's Task Force 17 follows later with repairs to *Yorktown* completed miraculously quickly.

29 May 1942

Eastern Front The Germans complete their encirling maneuver west of the Donets. The Russians have lost 250,000 men. They have badly underestimated the German strength and preparedness. In fact the Germans had intended in any event to pinch out the Russian salient and the Russian attacks between 12 and 19 May only made this operation more worthwhile.

North Africa There is heavy fighting around the 'Knightsbridge' road junction, but the British fail to develop a coordinated attack and the German antitank guns are as usual most effective. The Italian Trieste Division which had blundered into 150th Brigade on the 26th has now managed to clear a path through their position. This path is to be a lifeline for the Afrika Korps.

30 May 1942

North Africa Rommel pulls all his tanks back into the 'Cauldron' – a tight defensive semicircle backing on to the minefields and, while holding the main British attacks, works to eliminate 150th Brigade and free his supply lines.

Midway Four Japanese submarines arrive to patrol off Pearl Harbor but too late to intercept the American carriers. Two more carry supplies to the French Frigate Shoals to help set up a seaplane base to supplement the Japanese reconnaissance but they find the Americans there first.

Below: The Fletcher-class destroyer USS *O'Bannon* shows her 5in main armament to advantage, 1942.

30-31 May 1942

British Air Operations Bomber Command sends more than 1000 bombers to raid Cologne. This enormous effort has only been made possible by scraping together every plane from operational squadrons and training units. The planes from the training units are flown by pupils and instructors. The raid is a considerable military and propaganda success. Only 40 of the 1046 bombers are lost and 45,000 people are made homeless in Cologne.

31 May 1942

Midway In a desperate attempt to reinforce the Pacific Fleet the battleships *Colorado* and *Maryland* sail from San Francisco.

31 May-1 June 1942

North Africa The Afrika Korps overruns the British 150th Brigade and frees its own supply route.

June 1942

Battle of the Atlantic Throughout the month there are about a dozen U-Boats operating in the Caribbean and some more in waters off Brazil. Doenitz is hindered in his task by orders from Hitler to watch for an Allied move to take bases in the Atlantic islands. On the British side important developments include the entry into service of aircraft fitted with Leigh lights for work in the Bay of Biscay. Some convoy escorts are now being refuelled at sea which eases routing problems since one of the previous limitations has been the restricted range of the escorts. The total Allied loss is 173 ships of 834,200 tons of which submarines sink 144 ships of 700,200 tons.

British Air Operations There are two RAF 1000 bomber raids this month on Essen and Bremen. Other targets include Emden, Osnabruck, St Nazaire, Le Havre and Dieppe. Bomber command drops 6950 tons of bombs, the largest total achieved until February 1943, flying 5000 sorties and losing 240 aircraft.

This level of losses is about the average for the rest of the year. With each crew doing a tour of 30 operations and a rate of loss of about one in 20, the prospects for those involved are clearly not good. The normal front line strength of the Command is about 420 aircraft, half of them Wellingtons. The numerical strength will remain similar for the rest of the year but quality will improve.

North Africa The British Intelligence Service contrives, late in the month, to break the 'Black Code' used by the American military attache in Cairo. The code is therefore correctly judged to be insecure (*see* September 1941) and is changed, cutting off a major source of intelligence for Rommel.

Mediterranean RAF bombers attack many targets in Italy as well as enemy ground forces in Egypt and Libya. Oil installations at Ploësti are raided by US Liberators on 12 June.

Yugoslavia, Resistance German anti-Partisan operations are conducted in Montenegro throughout the month.

Above: Douglas Dauntless dive-bombers from the carrier USS *Hornet* fly over the burning Japanese warship *Mikume*, Midway, 6 June 1942.

Below: Officers and men of the Type VIIc U-boat *U.203* prepare to leave harbor for a voyage in the North Atlantic, July 1942.

1 June 1942

Midway The USS *Saratoga* sails from San Diego after repairing the torpedo damage caused on 11 January, but it is too late to take part in the battle. Various groups of US submarines, 25 in all, are in position in the waters around Midway.

1-2 June 1942

Western Europe Essen is raided by 1036 RAF bombers. Thirty-five fail to return. The raid is not very effective.

2 June 1942

North Africa Rommel sends 90th Light and the Trieste Division south to take Bir Hacheim and free his flank. The Free French resistance there is extremely stubborn and even when 15th Panzer and Rommel's heavy artillery come up they still hold out.

Eastern Front German forces renew the bombardment of Sevastopol. Among their 1300 artillery weapons are the two 60cm (24in) 'Karl' mortars and the even more enormous 80cm (32in) 'Dora' gun. They are also supported by the Fliegerkorps VII.

Midway The US carrier groups from Pearl Harbor join forces northeast of Midway. Altogether the three carriers have about 250 aircraft, approximately the same as the Japanese main force.

Diplomatic Affairs Chinese Foreign Minister Soong and Cordell Hull sign a Lend-Lease agreement.

Aleutians Kakuta's light carriers attack Dutch Harbor, but with their knowledge of Japanese intentions against Midway, the Americans are not distracted.

3 June 1942

Midway The Midway Invasion Group and their heavy supports (Admiral Kondo) are found by air reconnaissance from Midway and are unsuccessfully attacked by a group of Flying Fortresses from the island.

Malta Another batch of 31 Spitfires is flown from HMS *Eagle* to Malta; 27 arrive safely.

4 June 1942

Midway Believing that the Americans will not yet have left Hawaii, 14 Japanese submarines patrol between Midway and Hawaii. The Japanese operations around Midway begin according to plan with 108 aircraft from the carrier force being sent to attack the island. The American forces on the island detect the strike on the way in and send off one of their own. The Japanese massacre the defending fighters but in their commander's view, fail to inflict sufficient damage on the island. He signals for a second strike to be prepared. The mixed bag of US aircraft attacking the Japanese carriers are also roughly handled, losing 17 out of 52 and scoring no hits.

The US carriers begin searching for Nagumo at dawn and the first strikes are launched around 0800. At 0700 the Japanese begin to rearm their reserve planes for a second attack on Midway but reports of the American Fleet, vague at first, begin to arrive during the next hour and a quarter. When the presence of an enemy carrier is finally confirmed, Nagumo is presented with a terrible problem. His decks are cluttered with aircraft, torpedoes and bombs, his defending fighters need fuel, having just finished repelling the attacks from Midway, and his first strike force is shortly due to return. He decides to recover all his aircraft first and then send a coordinated strike against the American ships.

At about 0930, the first American carrier planes come into action. The American strike is badly coordinated and at this stage only the 41 torpedo bombers attack. Thirty-five are shot down and no hits achieved. They have managed, however, to lure almost all the Japanese Zeros down to low level and the tight cruising formation of the Japanese ships has been disrupted, weakening their AA defense. Just before 1030, when the Japanese have at last organized their strike, the American dive-bombers arrive, and within five minutes *Akagi*, *Kaga* and *Soryu*, their decks packed with aircraft ready to take off, have all been fatally hit. *Hiryu* is at this stage undamaged and launches strikes which find and critically damage the *Yorktown*. Late in the afternoon planes from *Enterprise* and *Hornet* inflict similar damage on the *Hiryu*. All four Japanese carriers sink or are scuttled within the next 24 hours.

5 June 1942

North Africa The British mount attacks on 'The Cauldron.' One armored brigade, 32nd Army Tank Brigade, blunders into a minefield and loses 60 out of 70 of its tanks and another, 22nd Armored Brigade, loses touch with the infantry and artillery which it should be supporting. Over the next few days all these units are defeated in detail. The tank forces available to the two armies are now about equal in numbers but in quality the Germans are far ahead.

World Affairs The United States declares war on Bulgaria, Hungary and Rumania.

5-7 June 1942

Midway At first Yamamoto thinks of closing in to try and fight a surface action but abandons the idea and retreats on 6 June. *Yorktown* is sunk by a Japanese submarine on 7 June. Midway ranks as one of the most decisive victories of the war. With the lost Japanese carriers have gone many irreplaceable pilots. The only large carriers the Japanese have left are *Shokaku* and *Zuikaku* which are still refitting after the Coral Sea Battle. The American success is perhaps the clearest example of the whole war of a victory based on superior intelligence. The urgency with which the carriers were rushed from the Coral Sea and repaired and replenished at Pearl Harbor was based entirely on the code-breaking information. The Japanese, by contrast, produced an overelaborate plan with their forces wastefully dispersed. Their four 'light' carriers, for example, could carry up to 140 aircraft and the survivors from the air groups of *Shokaku* and *Zuikaku* could have brought the main force up to full strength – there was room for 50 more planes. The Japanese scouting was marred by ill-luck and poor reporting and the timing of the American attacks in the morning was most fortunate especially when they had not been well organized.

After Midway the American strategic position and the strength and quality of their forces can only improve.

6 June 1942

Aleutians The Japanese successfully land a small force on Kiska Island. On 7 June they also take Attu.

Below: The American carrier *Yorktown* is hit by a Japanese torpedo, Midway, June 1942.

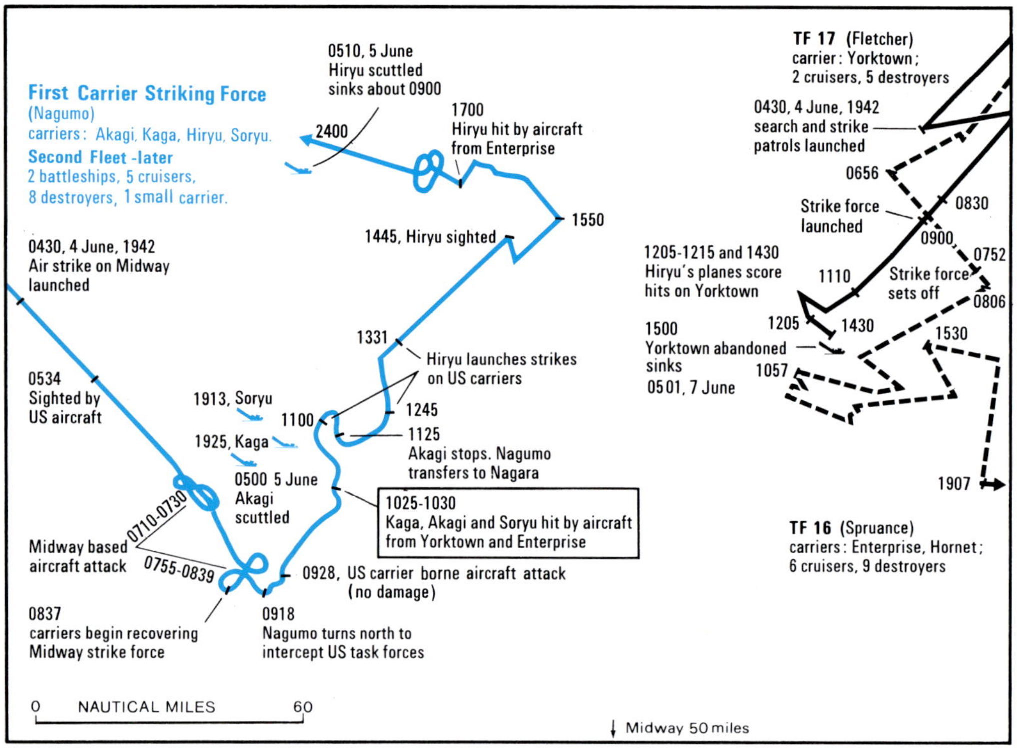

Above: Map showing the tracks of the rival fleets during the Battle of Midway, June 1942.

7 June 1942

Eastern Front Major German attacks on Sevastopol begin. The Soviet Black Sea Fleet is heavily involved in bringing supplies to the town. The Russian garrison consists of seven infantry divisions and three marine brigades, all badly under strength. The Germans have nine divisions, two of them Rumanian.

9 June 1942

Czechoslavakia The village of Lidice is obliterated as a reprisal for the assassination of Heydrich (*see* 27 May). More than 100 Czechs have already been killed and on 24 June the village of Levzasky is also destroyed. Altogether the Germans murder more than 1000 people in direct reprisals.

Mediterranean Another consignment of 32 Spitfires is flown to Malta. The number sent in during the last few weeks indicates how fierce the fighting for the island has been.

Allied Planning The British and Americans appoint Combined Boards for Production and for Food. They are to meet in Washington under the supervision of Donald Nelson and Oliver Lyttelton.

10 June 1942

North Africa During the day the Free French defenders of Bir Hacheim still hold out and at night 2700 of them are successfully evacuated.

Pacific The carrier *Wasp* and the battleship *North Carolina* with cruisers and destroyers pass the Panama Canal to join the Pacific Fleet. There are now four large US carriers in the Pacific.

11 June 1942

Allied Diplomacy Litvinov and Hull sign an additional Lend-Lease agreement in Washington.

North Africa Rommel's forces break out from 'The Cauldron' and attack the line of ridges between Knightsbridge and El Adem. Ritchie is compelled to fight there as he has foolishly left the bulk of his infantry still in the Gazala Line and because his massive base organization outside Tobruk is threatened.

11-16 June 1942

Mediterranean There are two major convoy operations to supply Malta. Admiral Curteis leads Operation Harpoon from Gibraltar and Admiral Vian Operation Vigorous from Egypt. The Harpoon force passes Gibraltar on the 11th and has six merchant ships escorted by the battleship *Malaya*, the carriers *Eagle* and *Argus*, four cruisers and 17 destroyers. Several other merchantmen sail independently. The first air attacks, by German and Italian forces, are on the 14th when one merchantman is sunk and one cruiser hit. On the 15th the convoy goes on with only a close escort of cruisers and destroyers and is engaged by a similar Italian force. There are also many air attacks and altogether two destroyers and three merchant ships are sunk and four of the escorts damaged. Two merchant ships reach Malta.

Operation Vigorous is even less successful. Admiral Vian has received reinforcements from the Eastern Fleet, so he can lead eight cruisers and 26 destroyers to cover the 11 merchant ships. The convoy sets out on the 11th and the first air attacks are on the 13th. On the night of the 14th Axis torpedo boats join in, damaging a cruiser and sinking a destroyer. On the 15th there are more air attacks in which two destroyers are sunk and a cruiser hit. The merchant convoy has now been reduced to six ships. Ammunition is running short after the many attacks and it is known that the battleships *Littorio* and *Vittorio Veneto* are approaching with a cruiser and destroyer escort. The convoy, therefore, turns back. The *Littorio* is damaged later by air attack and the heavy cruiser *Trento* sunk by a submarine, providing some consolation for the failure. Also during the operation almost all the German aircraft from North Africa have been involved in the attacks, giving Eighth Army some respite. However, on the 16th there is a further loss when the cruiser *Hermione* is sunk by *U.205*.

12 June 1942

North Africa The Guards Brigade at Knightsbridge comes under particularly heavy pressure and British counterattacks are badly directed. The British lose 100 tanks, leaving only 70 operational, half the number Rommel has. The battle is now decided. A further advantage for Rommel is that, since the Germans have taken the ground on which the battle has been fought, they are able to recover and repair many damaged tanks. This is another area where the Germans have usually been superior in the desert.

13 June 1942

North Africa The South African and British infantry begin to pull out of the Gazala Line and the Guards abandon Knightsbridge.

Below: The battlefield at Gazala, May 1942: with a burning vehicle in the background, German troops wait for orders. Gazala would be a further victory for the Afrika Korps.

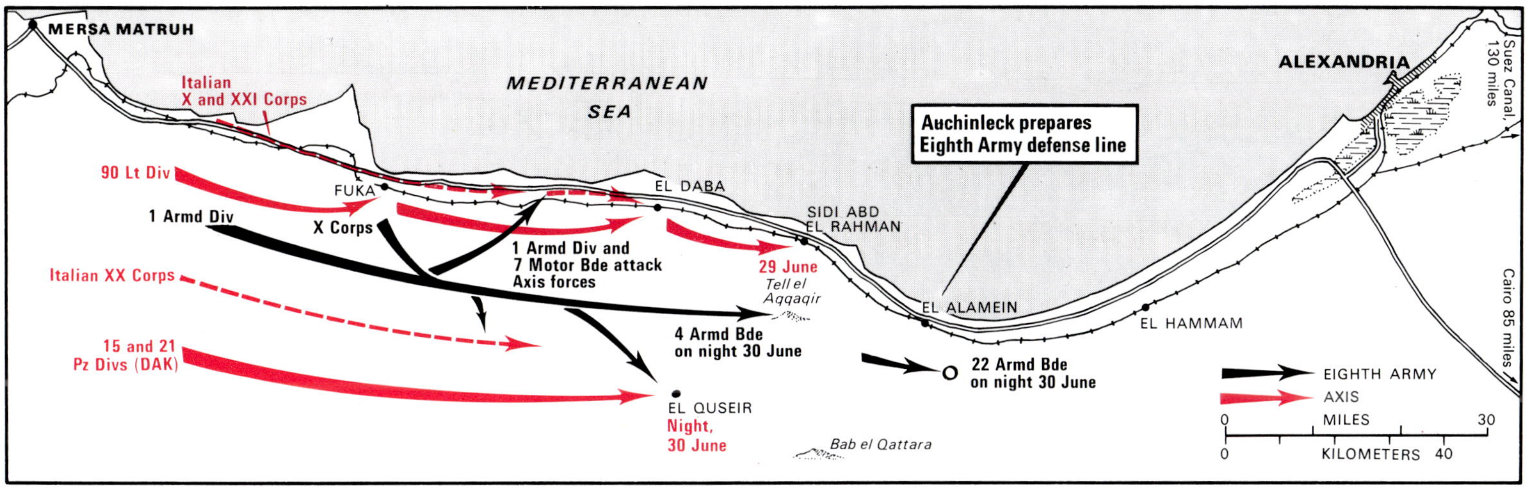

Above: Rommel's advance from Mersa Matruh toward the Alamein Line, June 1942.

15 June 1942

North Africa Early in the day part of 15th Panzer Division blocks the main road east of Tobruk just too late to catch the South African Division. In the evening the main body of 21st Panzer reaches Sidi Rezegh.

16 June 1942

North Africa The British evacuate the position of El Adem, finally conceding any chance of forming a front west of Tobruk.

17 June 1942

North Africa In an attack on the main German forces near Sidi Rezegh 4th Armored Brigade loses one-third of its tanks.

18 June 1942

Allied Planning/Atomic Research Churchill arrives in the USA for talks with President Roosevelt and his advisers. There is much discussion of the plans for a Second Front, but it is becoming clear that the conditions for Operation Sledgehammer (the Second Front in France in 1942) are going to be impossible to meet. This is confirmed during July. Churchill raises the possibility for an attack on French North Africa, to be known at first as Gymnast and later as Torch, with the president. (*See* 22 July.)

As well as the discussions on the Second Front, Churchill and Roosevelt talk about the future of atomic research. They agree that Britain and the United States should share their knowledge but that for the future the work should mostly be concentrated in the US. At a lower level relations between those involved in the project have not been good and these troubles continue, especially since the American work is now beginning to make better progress (*see* 17 September 1942).

North Africa Although his forces are now exhausted, Rommel issues orders for an attack on Tobruk to be begun on 20 June. He plans to attack in the southeast sector with 15th and 21st Panzer and Ariete and to drive straight to the harbor. Kesselring brings in every bomber available in the Mediterranean to support the attack. The garrison, though lavishly supplied, is made up of a hodgepodge of units and is not as forcefully led by the South African General Klopper as the Australians were during the former siege.

20 June 1942

North Africa Rommel's attack on Tobruk begins with fierce dive-bomber attacks early in the morning. His ground forces advance quickly and by the afternoon are through the main positions, reaching the harbor in the evening.

Eastern Front Amid bitter fighting the Germans penetrate to Sevastopol Harbor.

21 June 1942

North Africa The garrison of Tobruk surrenders to the Germans and Italians. There are 30,000 prisoners and mountains of stores of every kind. One German soldier even records how his comrades sent home parcels of Australian bully beef. More importantly the captured stores, 3,000,000 rations and 500,000 gallons of gasoline, are a vital addition to the Afrika Korps' scanty reserves. Rommel wishes to drive on to Egypt, chasing his beaten enemy. He puts this suggestion to Hitler and Mussolini despite the objections of Kesselring, who prefers to carry out Operation Herkules against Malta. Rommel has his way and, as the hero of the hour, is promoted Field Marshal by Hitler. The fall of Tobruk has one consequence that Rommel could not have foreseen, however. On the 21st,

Below: Junkers Ju-87 Stukas fly toward British lines in North Africa. Vulnerable to fighters the Stuka remained a good ground-attack aircraft.

Above: The German battleship *Tirpitz*, protected by torpedo nets, lies in Narvik Fiord, northern Norway, 1942.

while in a meeting with Roosevelt, Churchill is given the news and accepts a generous offer of immediate help. The result is that 300 Sherman tanks and 100 self-propelled guns are quickly sent off to Eighth Army and in fact play a vital role at El Alamein.

22 June 1942

Vichy, Politics Vichy Prime Minister Laval broadcasts on the desirability of a German victory and urges Frenchmen to work hard in German industry.

23 June 1942

North Africa The leading German troops cross the border into Egypt. Eighth Army meanwhile is withdrawing to Mersa Matruh in considerable confusion.

25 June 1942

Eastern Front The Soviets retreat from Kupyansk on the Oskol River east of Kharkov.
North Africa Auchinleck sacks General Ritchie from command of Eighth Army and takes direct control of the battle himself.
United States, Command General Eisenhower is appointed to command US Land Forces in Europe.

26 June 1942

North Africa The Afrika Korps has about 60 tanks and the Italian Littorio Division about 40 more. The British have about 200 tanks in operation at this moment and have several fresh formations in position around Mersa Matruh. Despite this imbalance of forces the German advance continues.
Western Europe The RAF 'thousand raid' has Bremen as its target. This is the last such raid at this time. The training squadrons must return to normal duty if the future of Bomber Command is not to be seriously disrupted.

27 June 1942

Arctic The convoy PQ-17 leaves Reykjavic for Archangel. There are 36 freighters and a tanker. The close escort consists of 6 destroyers and 13 smaller ships. The 35 ships of QP-13 have also left Murmansk and Archangel on their return journey.
North Africa The Allied forces around Mersa Matruh at first fight back strongly against the German attacks, but later in the day they are compelled to withdraw.

28 June 1942

North Africa The German 90th Light Division takes Mersa Matruh and again a large quantity of stores and equipment are captured. The Eighth Army and the German and Italian forces are intermingled in a great stream heading back toward El Alamein where Auchinleck has decided to make a stand.
Arctic The Home Fleet leaves Scapa Flow to provide distant cover for PQ-17. There are two battleships, *Duke of York* and *Washington*, and one carrier, the *Victorious*, with cruisers and destroyers.
Eastern Front The main German summer offensive gets under way. Bock's Army Group South begins to drive east from around Kursk toward Voronezh.

30 June 1942

Arctic The close cover for PQ-17 leaves Iceland with four cruisers, two American, and three destroyers. QP-13 is sighted by the Germans but is not attacked.
Eastern Front The Russian High Command orders the evacuation of Sevastopol. The Black Sea Fleet, much weakened by recent operations, attempts to comply with little success.

July 1942

Battle of the Atlantic The convoy system off the East Coast of America is extended during the month south from Florida. These convoys will be very effective in the months to come, losing only 39 ships up to December 1942. Other changes in the Allied system this month include the establishment of a CHOP (CHange of OPerational control) Line in mid-Atlantic clearly marking the boundaries of responsibility of the eastern and western routing authorities. High Frequency Direction Finding (HF/DF) sets are now being fitted in the escort vessels. These will become standard and will supplement the shore radio direction finding services. Eleven U-Boats are lost this month. Axis submarines sink 96 ships of 476,100 tons out of a total Allied loss of 128 ships of 618,100 tons. There is some return to operations in the Atlantic away from the American coast with U-Boats being active off Sierra Leone.
Allied Supply The United States finalizes arrangements with various South American countries for the supply of raw rubber to replace the sources captured by the Japanese. These agreements are extended in October.
British Air Operations RAF targets this month include Danzig, Bremen, Hamburg and the Ruhr. There are daylight attacks on targets in France in which the USAAF participates from 4 July onward. Bomber Command drops 6400 tons of bombs.

1 July 1942

North Africa The German advance reaches the defended area around El Alamein. The British 4th Armored Brigade arrives at Alam el Onsol only just before the German 90th Light Division. To the south there is particularly fierce fighting at the west end of the Ruweisat Ridge where 15th and 21st Panzer Divisions are pressing forward to Point 64. These attacks continue with little progress until 4th July.

Arctic The German intelligence service, B Dienst, has intelligence of PQ-17. Early in the day PQ-17 is sighted by *U.255* and *U.408*. Eight other U-Boats join the operation.

2 July 1942

Arctic QP-13 and PQ-17 pass each other. Reports of the sighting of both convoys and some of the covering forces are not properly reconciled by the Germans causing some confusion in their dispositions. There are unsuccessful air and submarine attacks on PQ-17. Farther south the *Tirpitz*, the *Hipper* and six destroyers leave their base at Trondheim.
Britain, Politics In the House of Commons, a motion of censure on the direction of the war is defeated by 476 votes to 25. Churchill's speech winding up the debate does much to reassure MPs. The principal criticism is that Churchill has too heavy a burden with the conduct of the war and the business of government both being his direct responsibility. Churchill's reply is that Parliament should either change the government or support it, but should not meddle with its composition.
Allied Supply The British Board of Trade announces an agreement to control the supply of wheat involving the USA, UK, Argentina, Australia and Canada.

3 July 1942

Arctic The *Lützow* and the *Admiral Scheer* leave Narvik with a destroyer escort and proceed to join *Tirpitz* at Altafiord. On the way, however, *Lützow* and three destroyers run aground.
North Africa The Italian Ariete Division, attacking toward Alam Nayil, is almost totally destroyed by 2nd New Zealand Division and their supporting artillery.

4 July 1942

Eastern Front The siege of Sevastopol comes to an end. The Germans take 90,000 prisoners and have lost 24,000 casualties. The Russian death toll is impossible to estimate.
Arctic The Germans score their first successes against PQ-17. Admiral Pound, the First Sea Lord, orders the convoy to scatter and the close cover and escort to retire. He believes that the German heavy ships will inevitably attack and, since the convoy is now comfortably within the range of German aircraft, it cannot be protected by the Home Fleet. The Admiralty messages are badly worded, but the commanders on the spot, although inclined to disobey, eventually conform to the orders.
United States Air Operations Airfields in Holland are the first targets for USAAF planes operating over Europe. Six planes join a RAF attack.

5 July 1942

Arctic Thirteen vessels from PQ-17 are sunk. The German heavy units make an abortive sortie, returning when the successes of the Luftwaffe and the U-Boats make their presence unnecessary. QP-13 in the Denmark Strait sails into a 'friendly' minefield, losing four ships.
Eastern Front Hoth's Fourth Panzer Group reaches the Don near Voronezh. On their left the attacks of Weich's Second Army also make some progress.

7 July 1942

Eastern Front The Germans capture Voronezh. Other units of Army Group South, including Sixth Army, continue to drive along the Donets Corridor.
Mediterranean British aircraft raid targets in southern Italy including Messina and Reggio Calabria.
United States Command General Spaatz is appointed to command US air forces in Europe.
Arctic Another eight ships of PQ-17 are sunk. From 9 July onward stragglers begin to arrive in Russian ports both singly and in groups. The ships which reach Russia deliver 896 vehicles, 164 tanks, 87 aircraft and 57,000 tons of general cargo. Twenty-four ships are lost altogether, with 3350 vehicles, 430 tanks, 210 aircraft and 96,000 tons of other equipment. The Germans lose five planes. There are no more Arctic convoys until September. PQ-17 has been a disaster.

Although Admiral Pound could not know of the restrictive conditions placed by Hitler on the operation of the German heavy ships his decision to order the convoy to scatter has probably been premature. The system of control from the Admiralty has not been to blame. Pound has had all the information and the necessary authority to make such a decision because he has access to the latest intelligence.

9 July 1942

Eastern Front The Germans reorganize their command system in the south. Army Group South is divided into two. Army Group A (General List) is composed of First Panzer Army, Seventeenth Army and Eleventh Army. Army Group B (General Bock) has Fourth Panzer Army, Second Army and Sixth Army. This reorganization is designed to expedite the progress of the Caucasus offensive now being prepared. The plan is for Army Group A to advance from positions south of the Donets, capture Rostov, cross the Don and after overrunning the oilfields, to come to a halt on a line from Batumi on the Black Sea to Baku on the Caspian. Army Group B at this stage is ordered to advance north of the Don and establish a protective front for Army Group A (but *see* 17 July and 29 July for changes to this plan). Army Group A's attacks begin immediately. Army Group B's forces are already under way and their advance now reaches Rossosh cutting the Moscow-Rostov railway.

10 July 1942

North Africa The Australian 9th Division, recently arrived at the front, attacks the positions of the Italian Sabratha Division around Tell el Eisa and Rommel is forced to send reinforcements. In a series of careful attacks in the next few days, Auchinleck concentrates against the weak and unreliable Italians forcing the German armor to burn precious fuel motoring to their aid.

12 July 1942

Eastern Front The Soviet High Command appoint Marshal Timoshenko to a newly constituted Stalingrad Front. The Germans reach Lisichansk and Kanteminovka.

13 July 1942

Eastern Front Misled by early success, Hitler alters the strategic plan for his summer offensive and designates Stalingrad as a major objective for Army Group B which previously has been given only a covering role. This is typical of Hitler's inability to observe the military law of 'maintenance of the objective.'

14 July 1942

North Africa There are British attacks, by units of 1st Armored Division, to the south of Ruweisat Ridge. Little ground is gained and losses on both sides are severe.

14-19 July 1942

Mediterranean Supplies are carried to Malta by submarine and fast transport. HMS *Eagle* flies 31 Spitfires to the island. Italian submarines are also engaged in supply work for their forces in North Africa which are short of supplies.

15 July 1942

India and China The first supplies flown 'Over the Hump' reach Chiang Kai-shek's forces.
North Africa In the operations south of the Ruweisat Ridge the Germans regain some ground but lose heavily to British artillery fire. The British artillery in North Africa has generally up to now been ill-organized and wastefully dispersed, so that its comparatively lavish resources have produced inadequate results. These faults are gradually remedied in the next few months.

16 July 1942

Eastern Front The Russians claim that in the fighting since 15 June, the Germans have lost 900,000 men. Although this claim is wildly

Below: Admiral of the Fleet Sir Dudley Pound, First Sea Lord and the man responsible for ordering Convoy PQ-17 to scatter, July 1942.

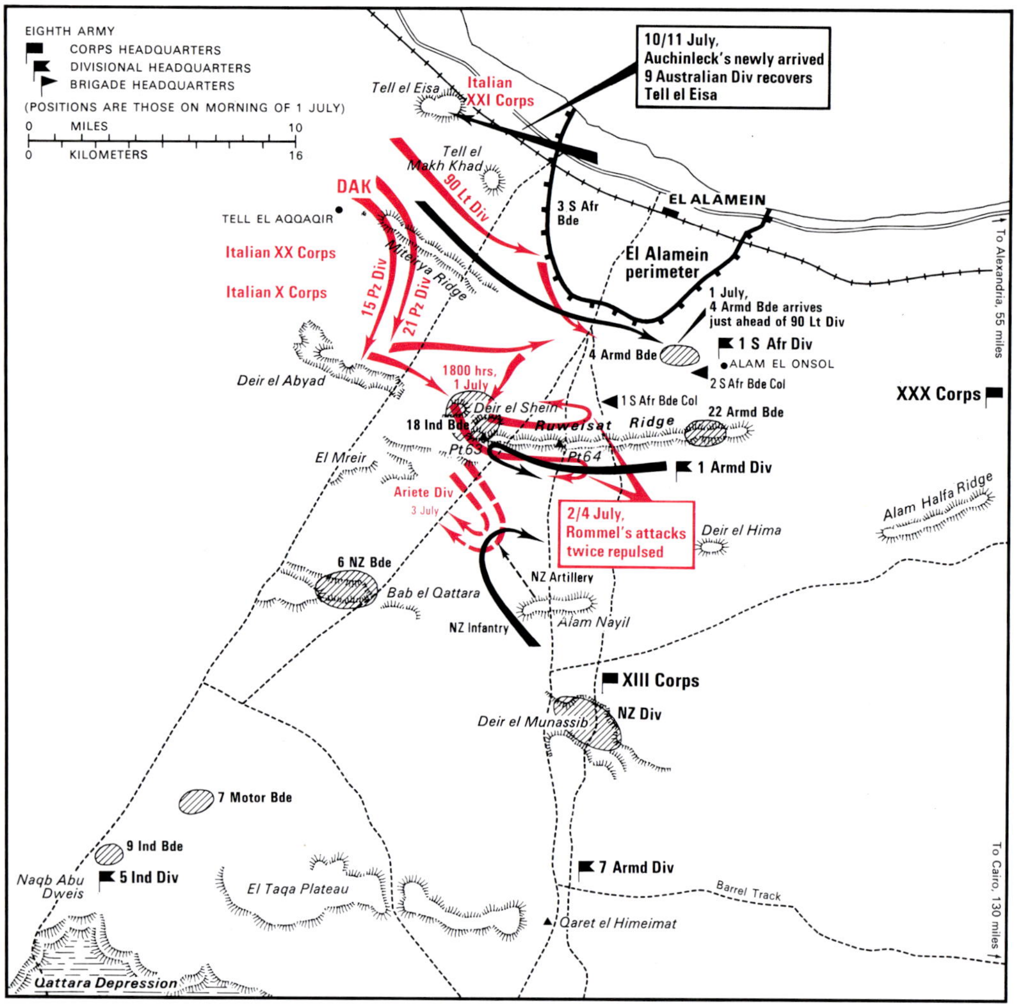

Above: The First Battle of Alamein, July 1942: Rommel's advance is halted.

exaggerated, the Russian resistance has stiffened as the Germans near Rostov.

17 July 1942

Eastern Front Hitler again interferes with the German dispositions. He fears that Army Group A will not be able to force its way across the Don, and therefore switches Fourth Panzer Army to join these operations. Naturally Army Group B, deprived of its spearhead, now makes much slower progress.

North Africa Desperate counterattacks by German and Italian forces halt a British advance around Miteirya Ridge. Rommel's supply difficulties continue to increase and he suggests a retreat to Cavallero and Kesselring.

19 July 1942

Eastern Front The German forces of Army Groups A and B continue to make rapid progress. In the last few days they have captured Kamensk and Voroshilovgrad and have reached the Don as far east as Tsimlyansky.

Battle of the Atlantic The final two U-Boats sent to operate off the United States' East Coast are ordered to other areas after a period of no success because of the improved convoy operations.

21 July 1942

New Guinea Japanese troops of General Horii's Eighteenth Army land at Gona. The Allies have also planned landings here but are forestalled.

North Africa Rommel sends reports to OKW giving details of his shortages of men, equipment and supplies. The British through *Ultra* are aware of his position and have therefore decided to mount a major attack. Eighth Army has more than 300 tanks and the Germans and Italians about 50 each. As the actions during the last two or three weeks have worn out the Italians, Auchinleck decides to complete the job by attacking the Afrika Korps directly. At first there is some progress in infantry attacks, but as happens all too often, the supporting armor fails to arrive in the right place at the right time. The Australian and New Zealand infantry especially (perhaps the best troops in Eighth Army) are growing increasingly disillusioned because of these failures.

United States Command Admiral Leahy is appointed as President Roosevelt's personal Chief of Staff.

22 July 1942

North Africa Although the British forces attacking south of Ruweisat take heavy losses, including the decimation of 23rd Armored Brigade, Rommel decides that the drain on his strength in the past fourteen days has been too great to permit further attacks. Both sides now wish a pause to rest and regroup. The British are far better placed to receive reinforcements being so close to their base in the Nile Delta. Malta too is recovering its strength to attack Axis communications.

New Guinea The Japanese forces begin to advance along the Kokoda Trail from Buna. A small Australian force prepares to defend Kokoda itself.

Allied Planning Roosevelt agrees with the British that 'Sledgehammer' (the Second Front in 1942) is not possible and instructs his negotiators in London to agree 'another place for US troops to fight in 1942.' The plan to invade North Africa, previously mooted as 'Gymnast' is adopted in talks over the next few days and renamed 'Torch.'

23 July 1942

New Guinea The advancing Japanese make contact with Australian defensive positions on the Kokoda Trail near Wosida. By 27 July the Australians have been pushed back to Kokoda itself.

Eastern Front There is heavy fighting along the Don from Rostov to Tsimlyansk, especially around Novocherkassk.

World Affairs In a broadcast US Secretary of State Cordell Hull urges the formation of an international peace-keeping organization by the United Nations after the war.

25 July 1942

Eastern Front Army Group A completes the capture of Rostov.

27 July 1942

Eastern Front Army Group B, and especially Paulus' Sixth Army, battles to clear the Don elbow of Russian troops. The important position at Kalach is attacked.

28 July 1942

Eastern Front Following the fall of Rostov, now officially admitted by the Russians, Stalin begins to implement measures to bolster the resistance of the Red Army with harsher discipline and by granting officers higher status and authority.

29 July 1942

New Guinea After heavy fighting for three days Kokoda is taken by the Japanese who have been reinforced. Help was sent to the Australians during the fight but the supply planes

Below: An anti-aircraft gun on board a British merchant ship, 1942. Protection from air attack was crucial.

turned back at the last minute when they were told incorrectly that the airstrip was in Japanese hands. Since this is the only airfield in the interior of the island, its loss is crucial.

Allied Production A combined British and American Production and Resources Board is established in London to control allocations of material and industrial priorities. Harriman, the US Lend-Lease Representative in the UK, and Lyttelton, the UK Minister of Production, are to be the senior members. Such careful planning of the Anglo-American alliance makes a strong contrast with the inefficient economic organization of Nazi Germany.

Eastern Front The attacks of Army Group A south of the Don continue to make good progress with Proletarskaya being captured. Hitler is not satisfied with the progress of Sixth Army in the Don elbow and again alters his dispositions, returning Fourth Panzer Army to Army Group B. The series of alterations to the strategic plan which Hitler has found necessary are generally held to have crippled the German chances of decisive success in this campaign. Fourth Panzer Army has wasted much effort moving from front to front and Stalingrad has gradually assumed an ever more dominant position in the German plan, leaving Army Group A with a massive, strategically vital, task and inadequate resources.

30 July 1942

East Indies The Japanese occupy some small islands between Timor and New Guinea in a move designed to support their campaign against Port Moresby.

Eastern Front German troops advancing from Rostov take Bataisk on the Don.

31 July 1942

Solomons American bombers attack targets on Tulagi and Guadalcanal.

August 1942

Battle of the Atlantic The total Allied shipping losses in all theaters are 123 ships of 661,100 tons of which submarines sink 108 ships of 544,400 tons. The U-Boats are now operating again on the main North Atlantic convoy routes. Other U-Boat concentrations are off Brazil and Venezuela, with some still in the Caribbean and the Gulf of Mexico. A further group operates off Freetown. The narrow channels in Caribbean waters mean that there are many targets for the U-Boats there, but that making attacks is difficult. The protection of traffic off Brazil is made easier by Brazil's entry into the war on 22 August following many German provocations and especially the sinking of five ships off Bahia on the 16th and 17th by *U.507*. Bases can be provided for the Allied forces in Brazil. The German prospects are improved by the fitting of Metox radar search receivers to some of their boats. These are effective against radar on the 1.5-meter wavelength.

Allied Air Operations RAF Bomber Command continues its campaign with attacks on Duisberg, Mainz and Frankfurt. The first independent raids by US bombers are made on targets in occupied France (*see* 17 August). Alto-

Left: A German Panzer Mark III crosses a river in southern Russia, summer 1942. *Below:* The German advance into the Caucasus and towards Stalingrad in the summer of 1942.

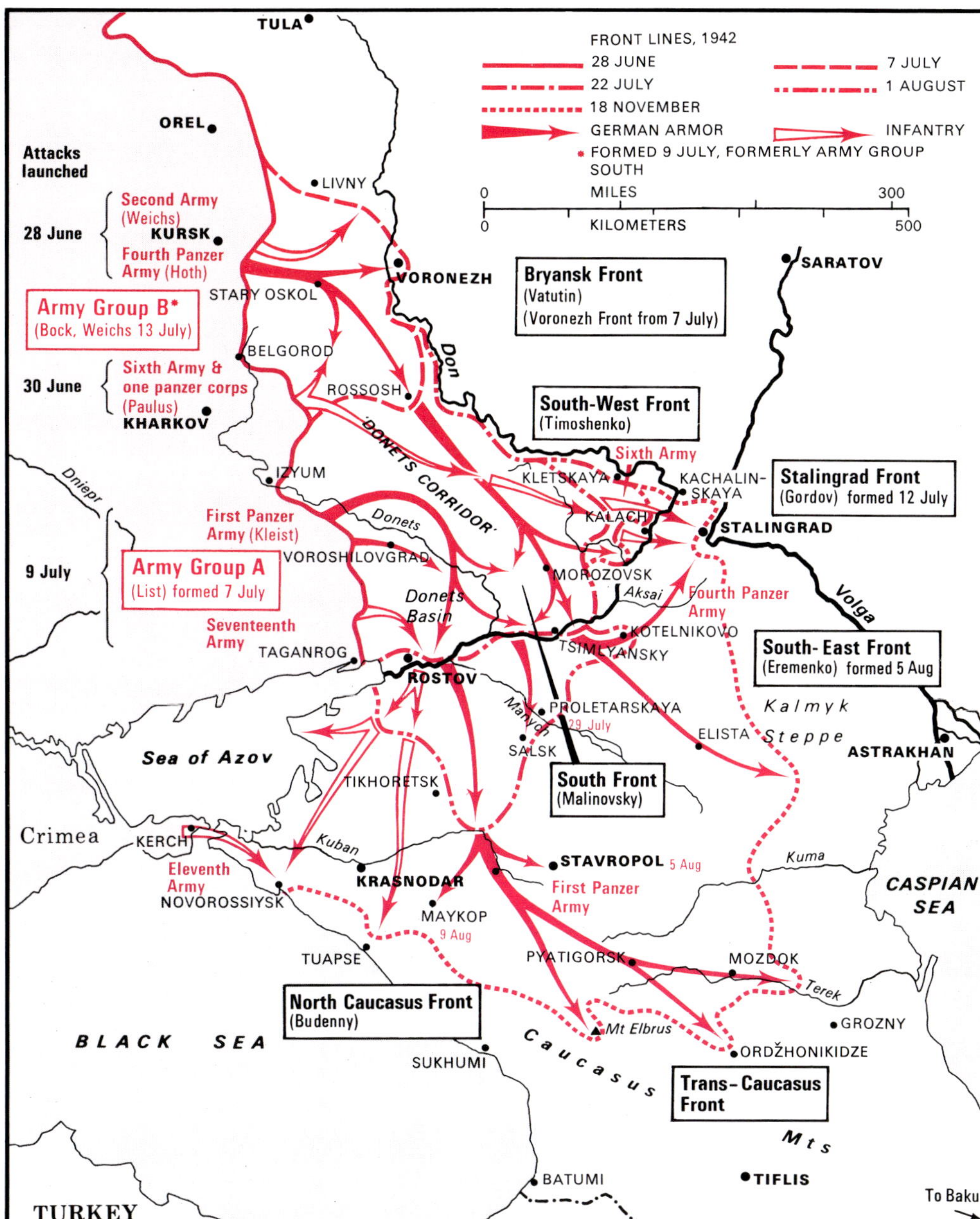

Above: Crewmen on board the carrier USS *Enterprise* load a bomb beneath the fuselage of a Douglas Dauntless dive-bomber, August 1942.

gether US planes drop 170 tons of bombs and also take a small part in the offensive sweeps made by other units of the RAF against communications targets in France.

During August a Pathfinder Force for Bomber Command is established. This unit is to have responsibility for marking targets for the main force to bomb. Although the idea of the Pathfinder Force has many critics (including Harris himself), it proves itself a success in the long term. In the short term, however, there is a setback for bombing accuracy as the Germans have now begun effective jamming of the navigational aid *Gee*. It will still be useful for homing aircraft to their bases.

Mediterranean This month the air attacks on Malta are somewhat less fierce.

United States, Production The carrier USS *Independence* and the battleship USS *Iowa* are launched – an indication of how American warship production will soon swamp the Japanese. Between now and the end of the year four more carriers and another battleship are also launched.

1 August 1942

Eastern Front The forces of Army Group A continue to advance, capturing the town of Salsk and reaching the Kuban River near Kropotkin. There is more fierce fighting in the bend of the Don near Kalach and Kletskaya.

3 August 1942

Eastern Front Army Group B continues to attack Kletskaya. Fourth Panzer Army, having crossed the Don at Tsimlyansky, is now driving east around Kotelnikovo. First Panzer Army is mounting two attacks from its position on the Kuban, east toward Stavropol and south toward Maykop.

British Command Churchill and General Brooke arrive in Cairo to investigate what is wrong with the Eighth Army and to provide new commanders. Churchill feels that with the lavish resources sent to Eighth Army far more should have been achieved.

5 August 1942

Eastern Front The German attacks continue, with Army Group A making some progress near the Kuban River.

5-13 August 1942

Battle of the Atlantic The convoy SC-94 is attacked by a U-Boat pack during its passage across the Atlantic. This marks the return of the U-Boats to large-scale operations on the main north Atlantic routes. SC-94 loses 11 ships, but two of the attacking U-Boats are sunk and four damaged.

6 August 1942

British Command After much discussion of various proposals, General Alexander is chosen to command in the Middle East and General Gott to have tactical control of Eighth Army.

Eastern Front Army Group B is beginning to wear down the Russian defenses in the Don elbow. Seventeenth Army from Army Group A manages to capture Tikhoretsk.

7 August 1942

North Africa General Gott is killed on the flight back to Cairo and General Montgomery is chosen to replace him.

Palestine Sir John Grigg announces the creation of a Palestine Regiment in the British Army. This unit will be made up of separate Arab and Jewish battalions. The training provided for service in these units will provide valuable experience for the postwar operations of both sides.

Aleutians The Japanese-held island of Kiska is bombarded by an American naval task force.

Solomons The American landings begin. An amphibious task force (Admiral Turner) carries General Vandegrift's 1st Marine Division to land on Guadalcanal. Smaller detachments also land on Tulagi and Gavutu. Admiral Fletcher with three carriers is in support. The landings on Guadalcanal meet little opposition at first. The subsidiary operations are, however, heavily opposed.

8 August 1942

Solomons The remainder of the first American wave lands on Guadalcanal. The forces advancing inland easily overrun the Japanese airstrip which is renamed Henderson Field. The capture of Tulagi and Gavutu is completed. Because of the intense air and submarine activity, Fletcher decides, probably incorrectly, to withdraw his carriers but the cruisers and transports near Guadalcanal remain.

Allied Command Roosevelt and Churchill agree that General Eisenhower shall lead Operation Torch.

Eastern Front Army Group A continues to drive south as well as consolidate its gains near the Kuban River. Army Group B captures Surovniko.

9 August 1942

Solomons Just after midnight a Japanese cruiser squadron led by Admiral Mikawa enters Sealark Channel (later renamed Ironbottom Sound) south of Savo Island. The defending allied force, led by Admiral Crutchley, is not nearly so well trained or equipped for night fighting and is decisively beaten, losing four cruisers and sinking none.

The Japanese have failed, however, in their aim of attacking the transports unloading off Lunga Point. The transports are withdrawn because of the Japanese threat. The Marines are left very short of heavy equipment and with only about half their supplies.

Eastern Front From Army Group A, First Panzer Army captures Maykop and Seventeenth Army, Krasnodar. The oil installations at Maykop have been demolished however.

10 August 1942

Solomons The Japanese heavy cruiser *Kako* is sunk by a US submarine while returning to Rabaul from the Savo Island battle.

11 August 1942

Mediterranean A large convoy of 14 merchant ships en route to Malta is sighted by Axis reconnaissance aircraft. The importance of Operation Pedestal is well shown by the massive escort provided for such a comparatively small convoy. Admiral Syfret leads two battleships, four carriers, seven cruisers, 32 destroyers and other smaller craft. As well as supplies from the convoy, more aircraft are flown to Malta from HMS *Furious* which then turns back to Gibraltar. The carrier HMS *Eagle* is sunk by *U.73*, but an air attack on the battered convoy in the evening is unsuccessful.

Below: U-582, a Type VIIc U-boat, returns to harbor. The flag belonged to the US merchant ship SS *Stella Lykes*.

New Guinea The Australian forces are pushed out of Deniki on the Kokoda Trail and retreat for five miles toward Templeton's Crossing near the summit of the Trail.
Vichy, Politics In a public speech, the Vichy Prime Minister, Pierre Laval, says, 'The hour of liberation for France is the hour when Germany wins the war.'
Eastern Front The Soviet position at Kalach on the west bank of the Don falls to the Germans.

12 August 1942

Mediterranean The convoy and the covering forces of Operation Pedestal are attacked constantly throughout the day. One merchantman is sunk in the morning, and in the early evening, shortly before the main covering force withdraws on schedule, the carrier *Indomitable* is damaged and a destroyer sunk. Later a cruiser and two freighters are sunk and two more cruisers, a transport and a vital tanker, the *Ohio*, are damaged.
New Hebrides The Americans land strong reinforcements on Espiritu Santu to build a base to support the Guadalcanal campaign.
Allied Diplomacy Churchill arrives in Moscow for talks essentially to apologize to Stalin that there will be no Second Front in 1942.

12-13 August 1942

New Guinea A strong Japanese detachment lands at Buna.

13 August 1942

Eastern Front Troops from Fourth Panzer Army advance southeast toward Elista.
North Africa Montgomery, supposedly only on a visit to the front, assumes command of the Eighth Army. Alexander replaces Auchinleck on 15 August. Montgomery starts at once to prepare his defenses for a German attack.
Mediterranean Very early in the morning the cruiser HMS *Manchester* is sunk, as are five more freighters from the Pedestal convoy. Later another two are sunk but four reach Malta and a fifth, the tanker *Ohio*, is towed into Valetta on 15 August. *Ohio* carries vital fuel for the island's defense forces.

Below: On the way to Stalingrad: a German railway unit prepares to set out, complete with musical accompaniment.

Above: A Japanese bomb explodes just aft of the 'island' of the carrier USS *Enterprise*, Battle of the Eastern Solomons, August 1942.

14 August 1942

Eastern Front Sixth Army has almost completely cleared the Don Elbow of Russian resistance, but from the German point of view too many potential prisoners have escaped to the east because of the lack of mobile forces.

15 August 1942

Eastern Front The Germans make further gains in the Caucasus, especially around Georgivesk.
Guadalcanal The Marines are busy preparing the airstrip and consolidating their perimeter around it. They receive a small consignment of supplies by sea.

16-17 August 1942

New Guinea More Japanese reinforcements for the Kokoda Trail land near Buna.

17 August 1942

Gilbert Islands A Japanese seaplane base on Makin Island is raided by US Marines.
Allied Air Operations Rouen is the target for the first all-American bombing raid over Europe.

Between now and the end of 1942 the US Eighth Air Force will fly 1547 sorties and lose 32 aircraft. This loss is less than two percent, but all the raids have British fighter escort and none penetrates Germany. The buildup of the Eighth Air Force is badly delayed by the transfer of many aircraft to north Africa after Operation Torch in November. Thus there is no real test for the theories of the American airmen that their aircraft can bomb unescorted and with great accuracy. It will emerge even in the few operations that are undertaken this year that the much vaunted Norden bombsight, although excellent in good training conditions, is less impressive in the overcast skies of Europe.
Eastern Front The Germans capture Pyatigorsk and Yessentuki in the Caucasus.

18 August 1942

Eastern Front Because partisan activity has been so intense, Hitler issues a directive ordering harsh measures and giving more power to SS Special Units.
Guadalcanal The first Japanese reinforcements land at Taivu. This detachment, about 1000 strong, led by Colonel Ichiki, immediately marches toward the American positions. At this stage the Japanese believe there are only 3000 Americans on the island. There are in fact more that 10,000 and Henderson Field is now ready to receive aircraft.

19 August 1942

Western Europe There is a major raid by Canadian and British troops on Dieppe. The troops involved are the 2nd Canadian Division (General Roberts) and Nos 3 and 4 Commando with a handful of Americans and Free French – in all 6000 men. The raid is designed to provide battle experience for the troops and to gain information about German defense methods which might be useful in the future. The raid is a disaster. Almost none of the installations marked for destruction is reached and only a proportion of the landing force can be evacuated. The casualty list is long: 3600 men, 106 aircraft, a destroyer, 30 tanks and 33 landing craft. The Germans lose about 600 men and about 50 planes. The lessons of the operation, however bitter, are very important both on the general points of how difficult is to capture a defended port, or how important is a preliminary bombardment, to the more detailed lessons relating to equipment for beach landings.

Above: Disaster at Dieppe: the scene on the beach in front of the town, 19 August 1942, complete with stranded tanks.

20 August 1942

Guadalcanal Henderson Field receives its first aircraft – a group of 31 fighters.

21 August 1942

Eastern Front Army Group A penetrates almost as far as Novorossiysk on the Black Sea. Troops from Army Group B cross the Don near Kletskaya.

Guadalcanal Ichiki's force makes a series of wild attacks across the Tenaru River in which they are eventually wiped out. The US forces receive useful shipments of supplies and some reinforcements.

22 August 1942

World Affairs Brazil declares war on Italy and Germany after several Brazilian ships have been sunk in the past week.

23 August 1942

Eastern Front Army Group B reaches the Volga on a five-mile front between Rynak and Erzovka. The Soviets continue to resist.

German mountain troops climb Mount Elbrus in the Caucasus but it is merely a propaganda victory. In terrain like this everything is on the side of a stubborn defense.

Battle of the Eastern Solomons Both the Japanese and the Americans send major warships to cover attempts to ferry supplies to Guadalcanal. The main American squadron, Task Force 61 (Admiral Fletcher) consists of the carriers *Saratoga*, *Enterprise* and *Wasp*. The Japanese are operating characteristically in several separate groups. Admiral Nagumo has the carriers *Zuikaku* and *Shokaku*, and Admiral Hara has the smaller *Ryujo*. Fletcher sends off a strike but it fails to find any targets. Both forces are now alert for the next day's fight.

24 August 1942

Battle of the Eastern Solomons In the morning American scout planes sight *Ryujo* and a strike is dispatched. While it is on its way *Shokaku* and *Zuikaku* are also sighted and Fletcher tries to redirect his attack. Only a few of his planes receive this message and most carry on to sink *Ryujo*. Shortly after this strikes from Nagumo's carriers find the *Enterprise* and although she is damaged, aircraft can still be landed on. At the end of the day both carrier groups retire without attempting to achieve a decisive result.

Germany, Home Front Hitler appoints Thierack as Minister of Justice with powers to set aside any or all written law.

24-25 August 1942

New Guinea Japanese assault troops from Buna land on Goodenough Island in preparation for a later move into Milne Bay.

25 August 1942

Eastern Front There is heavy fighting along the Terek River in the Caucasus particularly around Mozdok.

Solomons Despite the setback received on 24 August, the Japanese transports continued on toward Guadalcanal. Two are damaged and a destroyer is sunk by American aircraft and after that they turn back. The Japanese now recognize the difficulty of daylight operations because of Henderson Field's aircraft, and for the moment revert to using fast destroyers to bring in supplies during the night.

Britain, Home Front HRH The Duke of Kent (King George's younger brother), a serving officer in the RAF, is killed in a plane crash in the north of Scotland.

25-26 August 1942

New Guinea Japanese troops landing in Milne Bay are fiercely resisted by the Australian and American garrison. Despite the arrival of reinforcements on 27 August, no real progress is made by the Japanese. On the Kokoda Trail the Japanese do gain some ground near Isurava.

26 August 1942

Eastern Front The Russians announce that a successful offensive on the Moscow front began two weeks ago. Their claim of a 15- or 20-mile penetration on a 75-mile front is exaggerated however.

26-27 August 1942

Soviet Air Operations Soviet aircraft raid Berlin and other German cities. The attack is repeated on 30 August.

27 August 1942

Eastern Front Around Stalingrad the Soviet perimeter is gradually drawing in, and in the far south the Germans have crossed the River Terek and captured Prochladrii.

Solomons The aircraft carrier USS *Saratoga* is damaged in an attack by the Japanese submarine *I.26* and is out of action until the end of October. The *Wasp* is now the only operational US carrier left in the Pacific.

28 August 1942

Eastern Front There is a small Russian attack near Leningrad.

28-29 August 1942

Guadalcanal The Japanese receive important reinforcements run in during the night by Admiral Tanaka's 2nd Destroyer Flotilla now known to the Marines as the 'Tokyo Express.'

Below: An RAF Bristol Beaufighter takes off from a desert airstrip. By late 1942 the British were beginning to achieve air supremacy.

30 August 1942

Guadalcanal The American air group at Henderson Field receives 18 more fighters and 12 dive bombers.

30-31 August 1942

North Africa Rommel's forces begin a final attack designed to clear the British out of Egypt. Already, however, British preparations have been more extensive than he realizes. Much has been done to reconstitute formations shattered earlier in the summer and the British intelligence is effective, enabling Montgomery to improve on the good dispositions established by Auchinleck. Rommel has received some reinforcements, particularly the German 164th Division and a parachute brigade. He is desperately short of supplies and decides to mount his attack on the strength of promises of future shipments. As well as helping the Royal Navy strike at the supply routes, the RAF is dominant over the desert and causes Rommel many casualties.

As usual the cutting edge of Rommel's attack is the German tank formations and these are sent, shortly before midnight, to break through the British minefields between Alam Nayil and Qaret el Himeimat. Once this is done, the plan is for them to push east of Alam Halfa and then turn north. The British minefields are more elaborate and better defended than Rommel's staff have anticipated and progress is slow. Indeed, by 0800 hours in 31 August Rommel wishes to call off the attack but is persuaded not to. Instead he orders an earlier turn north and a direct attack on Alam Halfa Ridge but this is beaten off. The Afrika Korps has been bombarded all day by the improved British artillery and by the RAF. This continues day and night for the remainder of the battle, allowing the Germans no rest.

31 August 1942

United States, Home Front Claude Wickard, the Agriculture Secretary, warns that it will probably be necessary to introduce meat rationing. Roosevelt has already spoken on 28 August about the possibility of introducing a meatless day.
New Guinea General Hyakutake, commanding Seventeenth Army, decides to evacuate the troops who have landed in Milne Bay and concentrate on the Guadalcanal operation. This evacuation is completed by 7 September, but at least 1000 Japanese have died. This is the first significant setback the Japanese have received on land.
Guadalcanal General Kawaguchi and 1200 troops land on the island.
Eastern Front The Germans have thrust forward to within 16 miles of Stalingrad despite tenacious Russian resistance.

Below: German troops advance toward Russian positions on the way to Stalingrad, 1942. The man in the foreground is carrying an MG34 machine gun.

Above: The tough young soldiers of the Wehrmacht in Russia.

September 1942

Battle of the Atlantic The German U-Boats operate in much the same areas as in August. Their attacks off Trinidad remain important for the next two months, but these are the last easy gains to be made off the American coast. Convoys in this area will only be started in October. The North Atlantic convoys are reorganized to run from New York to the UK rather than from Sydney and Halifax in Canada. This makes fitting the main convoys with the coastal convoys easier. The first Support Groups are formed to aid the escort forces. These are groups of escort vessels, ideally including an escort carrier, which are to be sent to help the escort of any particularly hard-pressed convoy. They are particularly valuable for their high standard of training and teamwork. There are also increases in the number of Leigh Light aircraft in service with RAF Coastal Command. One notable convoy battle occurs around ON-127 (*see* 10-14 September).

The total Allied shipping losses during the month are 114 ships of 567,300 tons of which submarines sink 98 ships of 485,400 tons.
Western Europe Allied air attacks continue. British targets are to include Bremen, Duisburg and Wilhelmshaven. The American targets are in France and the Low Countries. Bomber Command drops more than 6000 tons of bombs during the month. As yet the USAAF can only make a small contribution (about 200 tons).
Mediterranean British naval and air forces based on Malta and Egypt sink one-third of the supply ships sent to the German and Italian forces. Rommel's supply position remains dreadfully weak and, to his fury, many of the supplies and vehicles which do land are sent to inactive Italian units in Libya. Only one-third of Italy's 1940 merchant fleet remains in operation; the rest has been either sunk or captured.

1 September 1942

Eastern Front There is fierce fighting in the Stalingrad area where German units have now reached the suburbs in some sectors. The

Above: Lt General Hyakutake, commander of the Japanese Seventeenth Army.

Russian Sixty-second Army is in danger of being cut off.
North Africa The German attack today is much weaker. One Panzer Division is out of fuel and the other, 15th Panzer, makes no real progress, although it gives the British 8th Armored Brigade an expensive lesson in the use of anti-tank guns.
Japan, Politics The Foreign Minister, Togo, resigns and his office is taken over for the moment by Prime Minister Tojo. Masayuka Tani is appointed to the Foreign Ministry on 17 September.
Eastern Front Troops of Eleventh Army cross from Kerch and land on the Taman Peninsula. There are both German and Rumanian units involved.

2 September 1942

Eastern Front Troops from Eleventh and Seventeenth Armies advance near Novorossiysk. First Panzer Army is approaching Grozny but its progress is slow.
North Africa Rommel gives orders to withdraw back to the start line and Montgomery, probably quite correctly, refuses to follow up with his own armor.

2-3 September 1942

New Guinea The Japanese Army at Buna is reinforced by 1000 more men from Rabaul.

3 September 1942

North Africa The New Zealand Division, in position around Alam Nayil, is ordered to attack southward to threaten the retreat of the German forces but fails to get far in heavy fighting during the next two days.

4 September 1942

Eastern Front Over 1000 German planes are involved in attacks in the Stalingrad sector. The Germans reach the Volga south of the city.

4-5 September 1942

Guadalcanal Again the Japanese receive reinforcements during the night. Two old American destroyers being used as transports are sunk by the Japanese destroyers.

6 September 1942

Eastern Front Army Group A captures Novorossiysk.
North Africa The battle of Alam Halfa is over and the Germans are back in their original positions. They discover that large reinforcements for Montgomery are on the way and that, unless they also receive considerable help, Eighth Army will win in the end. Rommel sets his forces to prepare elaborate fixed defenses of barbed wire, minefields and booby traps. The Eighth Army is busy regrouping, absorbing new equipment and training for the coming assault.

7-8 September 1942

Guadalcanal A force of Marine Raiders, about 600 strong, lands to attack the Japanese base at Taivu. They do considerable damage and disrupt Japanese preparation for an attack on the main American position.

8 September 1942

New Guinea The Australian forces are pushed back once more in the Owen Stanley Range. This time the position near Efogi has to be abandoned.
Vichy, Politics General de St Vincent, Military Governor of Lyons, is dismissed by the Vichy authorities for refusing to help arrest Jews in his area.

9 September 1942

Eastern Front Hitler sacks General List from command of Army Group A and from now on he directs it personally.
Guadalcanal The commander of the Japanese Seventeenth Army, General Hyakutake, lands at Tassafaronga with elements of 2nd Infantry Division.

10 September 1942

Madagascar There are renewed operations on the west coast of Madagascar. The British now intend to occupy the whole island and therefore make landings at Majunga.

10-14 September 1942

Battle of the Atlantic The skill of the U-Boat commanders is shown in the operations against the convoy ON-127. Every U-Boat from a group of 13 manages to make at least one attack. Only one U-Boat is damaged and 12 freighters and one destroyer are sunk.

12 September 1942

War at Sea *U.156*, en route to the area of the Cape of Good Hope, sinks the liner *Laconia* just south of the Equator. *Laconia* is carrying servicemen's wives and children and Italian prisoners of war. Kapitan Leutnant Hartenstein surfaces and helps the survivors and sends radio messages to the Allied authorities in plain language. *U.156* is, however, attacked by an American plane. Doenitz, therefore, gives orders that there are to be no further similar rescue attempts by U-Boats. He also arranges for Vichy ships from Dakar to be sent to finish the rescue work. This *Laconia* Order forms one of the counts against Doenitz at Nuremberg.
Eastern Front The Soviet perimeter around Stalingrad is now only about 30 miles long. In this desperate situation General Chuikov is appointed to command Sixty-second Army, soon to be besieged in Stalingrad. Chuikov performs superbly throughout the battle. His orders are responsible for the Russian close quarter style of fighting which so effectively disrupts the normally fluid all-arms cooperation of the German forces. His firm and abrasive character are also essential to the defense.
Guadalcanal The Japanese begin major attacks especially around 'Bloody Ridge'. The attacking units are from General Kawaguchi's 35th Brigade. The Americans receive valuable reinforcements of aircraft flown in from the carrier *Wasp*.

Below: The American carrier USS *Wasp* on fire and sinking after being torpedoed off the Solomons, September 1942.

13 September 1942

North Africa British units of the Long Range Desert Group attack airfields at Benghazi and Barce. There are also amphibious landings at Tobruk, which are beaten off with heavy casualties.

Guadalcanal The Japanese attacks are very fierce. They are only held off with difficulty and because of effective American artillery support.

13-18 September 1942

Arctic The convoy PQ-18 passes to the USSR with none of the disasters of its predecessor. It is provided with a large escort including an escort carrier. Thirteen ships are lost, but the Germans lose two U-Boats and 20 planes.

14 September 1942

Guadalcanal Kawaguchi's attacks peter out with 1200 casualties lost.

New Guinea The Japanese have their final success on the Kokoda Trail when they force the Australians back to Imita Ridge, only about 30 miles from Port Moresby.

Solomons The Japanese submarine *I.19* sinks the USS *Wasp* with three torpedoes. A destroyer is also sunk and the battleship *North Carolina* is damaged.

Aleutians American bombers attack the Japanese held island of Kiska. The attacks are repeated during the next few days.

16 September 1942

New Guinea The Japanese attacks are brought to a halt before Ioribaiwa and with the benefit of local air superiority and the American troops who are now arriving at Port Moresby, the Allies can plan an offensive.

Eastern Front There is heavy fighting in Stalingrad around the Mamayev Kurgan Hill. It is taken and retaken several times by each side during the next few days, and throughout the battle will be the scene of many extremely fierce confrontations.

17 September 1942

Atomic Research All atomic research in the United States is placed under military control and General Groves is appointed to direct the program. Groves is deeply worried about security; partly for this reason and partly through simple chauvinism he is strongly opposed to sharing any information with the British (*see* December 1942).

Madagascar The terms suggested by the British for an armistice are rejected by the Vichy Governor General.

18 September 1942

Guadalcanal Six transports bring supplies and the 7th Marine Regiment to reinforce the American position. The American strength is now about 23,000 men and they have adequate supplies.

New Guinea In response to superior orders and because of the difficulty of supplying the forward troops, General Horii begins to pull some of his men back to the area around Buna and Gona.

Madagascar There are British landings on the east coast at Tamatave.

20 September 1942

Eastern Front In the Caucasus the town of Terek is captured by the Germans.

21 September 1942

Sweden, Politics In the national elections the pro-Nazi candidates do very badly.

23 September 1942

Madagascar British troops take the capital, Tananarive.

North Africa Rommel flies back to Germany for medical treatment. General Stumme takes command in Africa with General Von Thoma to lead the armor. In the past few months there have been many high-level German casualties in Africa. Some of the new men have been brought in from the Russian campaign and do not fit in well with the old hands of Afrika Korps.

New Guinea The Australians go over to the attack. More American reinforcements land at Port Moresby and General Blamey (the Australian Commander in Chief) takes personal charge with orders from MacArthur to invigorate the conduct of the campaign.

23-26 September 1942

Eastern Front The Russians mount a small counterattack in the northwest of Stalingrad from the district of Orlovka. This attack makes some progress but is fiercely resisted by the German troops.

24 September 1942

German Command General Halder is dismissed by Hitler after many arguments during the summer. The new Chief of Staff at OKH with responsibility for the Russian front is General Zeitzler.

German Raiders In one of the most notable small actions of the war the Liberty ship *Stephen Hopkins*, armed with only one 4-inch gun, fights an attack by the much more powerful German raider *Stier*. Both ships sink. In its cruise *Stier* has sunk four ships of 29,400 tons.

24-25 September 1942

Guadalcanal During their habitual night supply operations, two Japanese destroyers and one cruiser are damaged – an indication of an improving US Navy.

25 September 1942

United States, Production In Washington the Maritime Commission announces that 488 cargo ships have been built in the last year.

27 September 1942

New Guinea The Japanese begin to withdraw back down the Kokoda Trail in the face of Australian attacks.

28-29 September 1942

Eastern Front In a small attack, Russian forces cross the Volga near Rzhev in the central sector.

29 September 1942

Madagascar British forces land at Tuléaron, in the southwest of the island.

Below: Map of the Battle of Alam Halfa, August-September 1942.

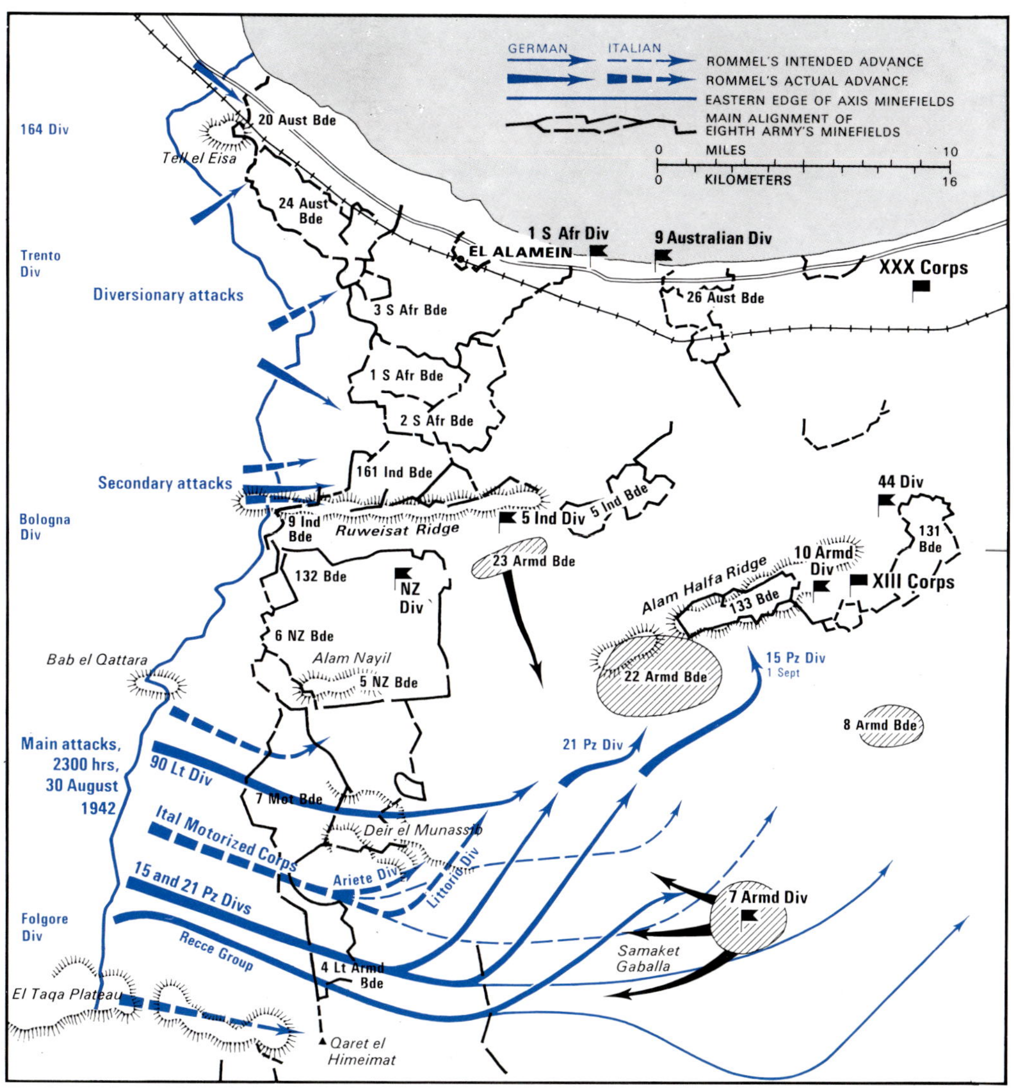

October 1942

Battle of the Atlantic Allied shipping losses increase this month to 637,800 tons from all causes. Axis submarines account for 619,000 tons, or 94 ships, of this. The increase is partly because escorts have to be diverted, especially later in the month, to cover the 10 Torch convoys on their way to Morocco and Algeria. The period of German successes off the east coast of America is coming to an end. The last good pickings for the U-Boats are in the area near Trinidad.
Allied Air Operations The Allied bomber offensive continues. Among the German targets for RAF Bomber Command are Flensburg, Essen and Cologne. British and American aircraft attack targets in France by night and day, including Le Creusot and Fives-Lille. There are heavy attacks by RAF aircraft based in Britain on targets in Italy, including Genoa, Turin and Milan. The RAF drops 4100 tons of bombs and the US Eighth Air Force 300 tons.

1 October 1942

Eastern Front There is heavy fighting along the Black Sea coast north of Tuapse. Inland the Germans are still battling toward Grozny. There are German gains in the Orlovka sector of Stalingrad.
New Guinea General MacArthur issues orders for the Allied advance on Gona and Buna. Australian forces have already begun to move forward along the Kokoda Trail. A US force is to move over the parallel Kapa Kapa Trail to join the Australians in cutting off the Japanese retreat at the Kumusi River. There are also to be landings along the north coast between Milne Bay and Cape Nelson, especially at Wanigela.
United States, Home Front Fuel oil is now rationed in most parts of the country.

2 October 1942

United States, Home Front President Roosevelt is granted power to control wages, salaries and agricultural prices from 1 November by the Stabilization of the Cost of Living Act which now becomes law.
War at Sea The British cruiser *Curaçao* is sunk off Ireland after a collision with the liner *Queen Mary* which is being used as a troop transport. Like the other giant ocean liners, the *Queen Mary* is normally unescorted for the major part of any voyage, relying on speed to keep out of trouble. Only in waters close to the British Isles are escorts provided.
South Pacific American forces begin to build a base on Funafuti Atoll in the Ellice Islands.

4 October 1942

Eastern Front Paulus begins a new series of attacks within Stalingrad – his fourth major effort. This will be the fiercest and longest lasting of the German offensives. They have been reinforced by combat-engineer and police units to increase their street fighting expertise. The Soviets are developing their skills also and will attempt to direct the German advances into specially prepared killing zones. The German attacks are sent against the Soviet posts in the Barrikady, Krasnye Oktyabr and Tractor Factories. The German forces will be dangerously worn down in this phase of the battle.
New Guinea The Australian forces following up the Japanese retreat along the Kokoda Trail take Effogi and continue the advance to Kagi and Myola.

5 October 1942

Solomons Aircraft from the carrier *Hornet* attack Japanese shipping gathering off Bougainville but only achieve slight success.

6 October 1942

United States, Production and Supply An additional Lend-Lease agreement is signed in Washington by representatives of the USA and the USSR. Between now and July 1943 it is planned to deliver 4,400,000 tons of supplies to the Soviet Union, 75 percent by sea, the rest through Iran.
Eastern Front Army Group A captures the oil-producing center of Malgobek near Mozdok, in the Caucasus. The advance continues toward the Terek.
New Guinea A small party from the US 32nd Division begins to move over the Kapa Kapa Trail. This route is about 25 miles southwest of the Kokoda Trail and the terrain is even worse.

7 October 1942

Guadalcanal The 1st Marine Division attacks west from the American beachhead in an attempt to free Henderson Field from all but the heaviest Japanese artillery fire by taking positions at the mouth of the Matanikau River.
Eastern Front In Stalingrad there are particularly fierce fights near the Tractor Factory.
War Crimes Britain and the United States announce that a United Nations Commission is to be established to investigate Axis war crimes. It is to be a condition of any armistice that war criminals are to be handed over to be tried.

7 October-13 November 1942

War at Sea A group of four U-Boats operating off the South African coast sink 170,000 tons of shipping. This is a very clear illustration of the wide scope and effect of submarine operations and of the difficulty of protecting shipping in distant waters.

8 October 1942

Guadalcanal Despite heavy rain, there is heavy fighting west of the American beachhead along the River Matanikau.
Belgium, Home Front German decrees are issued ordering the registration for war work of all males between the ages of 18-50 and of all unmarried women between 21-35. Germany's manpower crisis begins to deepen.

9 October 1942

Soviet Command The command authority of the commissars in the Red Army is taken away. They are still to have an important role in morale and propaganda, but responsibility for military decisions now rests entirely with the commanding officers.
Guadalcanal The American attacks west of the Matanikau continue and succeed in wiping out a Japanese battalion. The attacks are halted after this largely because of intelligence reports that the Japanese plan to renew their attacks on the main part of the American beachhead.
Madagascar British East African forces begin moving south from the capital, Tananarive, to link up with the troops landed in the south at the end of September.

11 October 1942

Eastern Front For the first time in almost two months there is a complete lull in the Stalingrad sector.

11-12 October 1942

Battle of Cape Esperance Both sides mount supply operations to the forces on Guadalcanal. The covering squadrons of cruisers and destroyers meet off Cape Esperance and a confused night action ensues. The American force consists of four cruisers and four destroyers led by Admiral Scott. The Japanese squadron, commanded by Admiral Goto, has three cruisers and two destroyers. Although the Americans have the crucial advantage of radar, communications between their ships are poor and their actions are not well coordinated. Likewise the Japanese are not well led and they fail to make best use of their superior torpedo equipment. At various stages in the battle both sides fire on their own ships. The Americans lose one destroyer, and two cruisers and another destroyer are seriously damaged. The Japanese come off worse, losing a cruiser and a destroyer and having their other two cruisers damaged. Their remaining two destroyers are sunk by air attack by planes from Henderson Field during 12 October.

Both sides' transports get through. On the 11th the Japanese land various supplies including artillery and tanks, and on the 13th the Americans land 3000 more men from the Americal Division.

12 October 1942

Battle of the Atlantic *U.597* is sunk in the Atlantic by a British Liberator bomber. This is the first success scored by the single RAF Coastal Command squadron of these invaluable long-range aircraft. Despite the obvious utility of these planes a second squadron is not established until March 1943, largely because the aircraft are claimed for the strategic-bomber forces.

13 October 1942

Eastern Front In the southern part of Stalingrad XLVIII Panzer Corps of Fourth Panzer Army has reached the Volga, but to the north many of the large factory buildings are still stubbornly held. There are Soviet counterattacks in the factory areas.

13-14 October 1942

Guadalcanal As the bombers based on Henderson Field have become so effective, the Japanese bring up the battleships *Konga* and *Haruna* to bombard the airfield during the night. About 50 aircraft are destroyed, more than half the complement. Taking advantage of the disruption caused to the American air cover, a group of destroyers and transports led by Admiral Tanaka lands 4500 men and large quantities of supplies at Tassafaronga. Henderson Field is shelled again. During 14 October some aircraft manage to leave Henderson Field and damage three Japanese transports.

14 October 1942

Eastern Front Hitler decides that all offensive action should be suspended except in Stalingrad and a small area of the Caucasus along the middle reaches of the Terek River. In Stalingrad the Soviet forces in and around the Tractor Factory are nearly broken by attacks from five German divisions which are assisted by heavy air support. A newly arrived Russian Guards Division joins the defending troops. Throughout the battle the Soviets will be deliberately niggardly in giving help to Sixty-second Army because they want to build up reserves.

New Guinea There is an important action on the Kokoda Trail at Templeton's Crossing.
War at Sea The German raider *Komet* is sunk in the Channel by a British force.

15 October 1942

Eastern Front In Stalingrad the German attacks in the area of the Tractor Factory continue to make ground, reaching the Volga a little to the north of the main complex.

16 October 1942

Solomons Aircraft from the carrier *Hornet* raid Japanese supply bases on Santa Isabel. On Guadalcanal the Japanese are preparing for a major attack by an increasing bombardment of the American positions.

17 October 1942

New Guinea The Australian advance along the Kokoda Trail is temporarily held up at Eora Creek by strong Japanese resistance. The Australian 16th Brigade has now taken over from 25th Brigade at the head of the advance. Once regiment of the US 32nd Division is airlifted from Port Moresby to Wanigela on the north coast.
Burma Orders are given to the 14th Indian Division, advancing slowly into the Arakan, to reach a line between Rathedaung and Buthidaung by the start of December in preparation for further operations toward Akyab.

18 October 1942

United States Command Admiral Halsey replaces Admiral Ghormley in charge of the South Pacific Command Area.
Stalingrad After two days in which the Soviets have largely succeeded in holding the German advance, renewed attacks in the Krasnye Oktyabr area make some gains.
War crimes Following some incidents in the raid on Dieppe and the more-recent, smaller landings in the Channel Islands, in which German prisoners have been shot while tied up, Hitler issues orders that all prisoners taken from Commando or other similar units are to be shot immediately.
New Guinea The American force moving over the Kapa Kapa Trail begins to arrive at Pongani. By 21 October the whole of one regiment has made this journey but after the rigors of the trip they are in no condition to fight. Its efforts have been wasted since it has proved possible to fly troops from Port Moresby to the north coast.

20 October 1942

United States, Home Front Congress passes the largest tax bill in the country's history. The measures are designed to raise $6,881,000,000.

21 October 1942

Guadalcanal The Japanese forces under General Maruyama are now 20,000 strong and begin a series of attacks against the American positions. The main units are from the 2nd Infantry Division. The plan is for the primary attacks to be delivered northward between the Lunga and Tenaru Rivers while secondary attacks are to be made on the western outposts along the Matanikau. Japanese Intelligence has little information on the strength and dispositions of the US forces. When this shortcoming is added to the difficulties of the inland approach march for the main attacks, the whole Japanese effort proves to be badly planned.

The offensive opens with a brief, unsuccessful attack across the Matanikau supported by tanks and heavy artillery fire.
Eastern Front The focus for the German effort in Stalingrad is now the Barrikady Factory and housing estate. Over the next two days over half of it is taken in a series of vicious engagements. There are German gains in the Red October area.
New Guinea The Australian troops fighting their way along the Kokoda trail have succeeded in closing up to the main Japanese positions at Eora. MacArthur issues orders trying to speed their progress but problems of supply and terrain slow their advance.

21-30 October 1942

Operation Torch Although 21 U-Boats are operating off Gibraltar and the Moroccan coast, they are engaged with the convoy SL-125 and do not sight any of the transports which are now en route. There are occasional sightings of some of the warship groups bound for North Africa, but they are sufficiently vague and scattered to prevent the Germans and Italians making a correct appreciation of the situation.

22 October 1942

Guadalcanal The Japanese against attack over the Matanikau with a strong force of tanks and

Below: The British destroyer HMS *Charity* shows her lines. Escorts such as this were vital in the Atlantic convoy battles.

infantry, but are beaten back with heavy losses inflicted largely by the well-organized American artillery.

Eastern Front The first winter snow falls at Stalingrad.

New Guinea There are Australian landings on Goodenough Island which has been largely abandoned by the Japanese since their defeat at Milne Bay.

23 October 1942

Operation Torch General Clark lands in Algeria for talks with the French General Mast and with the American diplomat Robert Murphy. Murphy has been conducting delicate negotiations with many of the French leaders in Morocco and Algeria. The most important supporters of the Allied cause are Generals Mast and Béthouart who are Chiefs of Staff at Algiers and Casablanca respectively. The Allies have had less success with the more senior French officials and soldiers and none at all with the admirals, who have remained profoundly anti-British since Mers-el-Kebir and Dakar. This particular conference is intended to confirm to Mast the importance to the Allies of his help and to ascertain that he is prepared to accept the authority of General Giraud. Giraud is still in Vichy, but is to be smuggled out before the invasion starts. Mast agrees to accept Giraud but in reality he is an unsatisfactory choice and unlikely to command widespread loyalty. Giraud prefers to be regarded as a soldier.

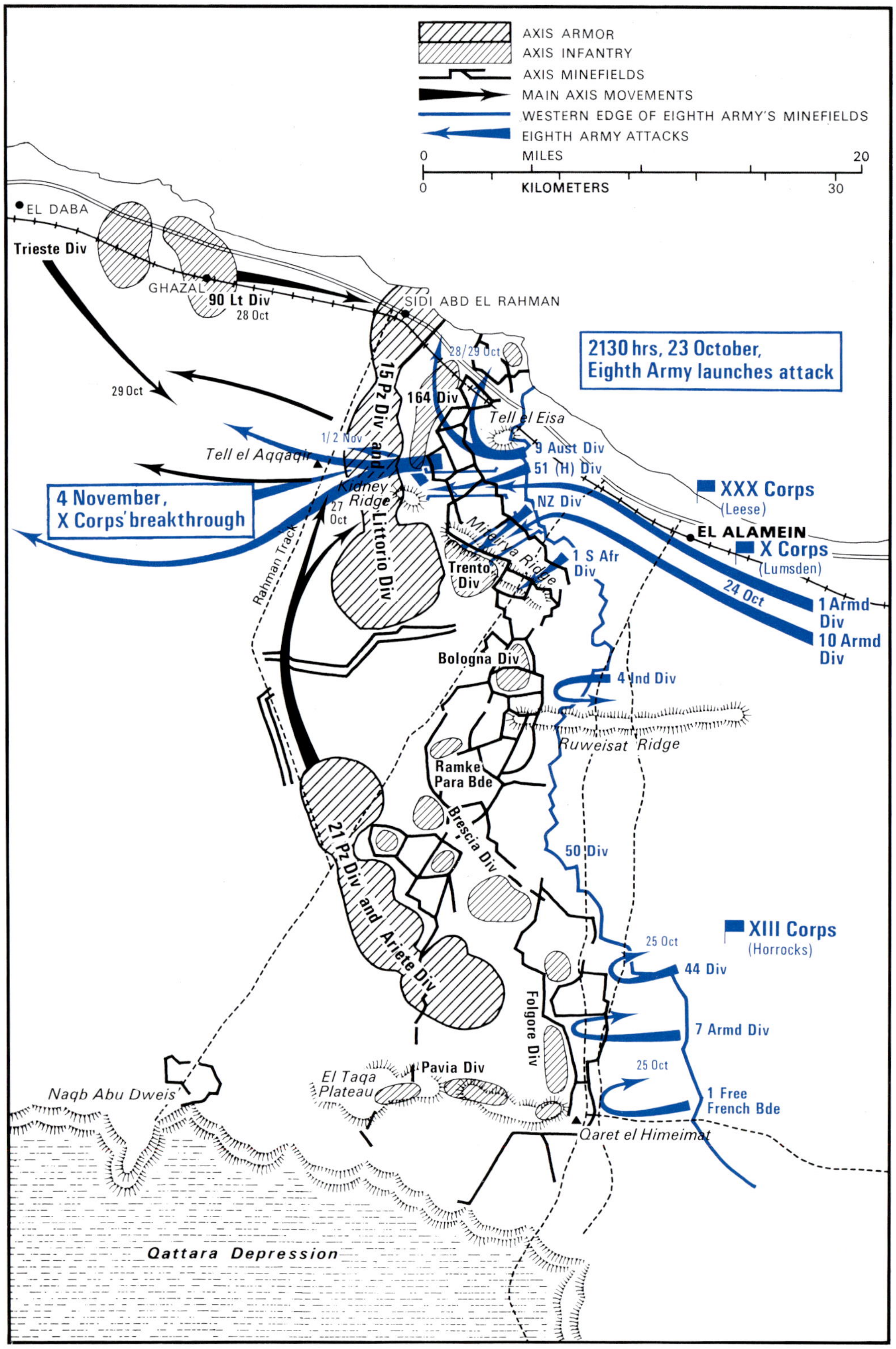

Below: The Second (and decisive) Battle of Alamein. October-November 1942.

Burma The bulk of the British force has advanced to Cox's Bazaar but forward units have reached Buthidaung. There they come into contact with a Japanese formation which has pushed up from Akyab. After a brief fight the Japanese hold the position.

23-24 October 1942

Battle of El Alamein Montgomery's attack begins shortly before midnight after meticulous preparation. Units have received precise training in night movement and mine clearance. An elaborate and extensive artillery plan has been worked out, and complicated measures of deception have been taken to confuse the enemy as to the time and place of the attack. The plan is for the infantry of XXX Corps to push through the minefields and the enemy infantry positions and then for X Corps, of two armored divisions, to move through and hold off the counterattacks while the infantry clears and widens the gap behind. In the final phase the German armor will be fought and destroyed in the open. Eighth Army has a superiority of about two to one in tanks, guns and men as well as a considerable advantage in the air. Most important, however, is the question of supplies. The German armor has been dispersed into two groups because, if concentrated, it might not have enough fuel to motor to the site of an attack. All along the front Italian and German units have been mixed so there is a reliable German contingent everywhere.

The main attack in fact falls on the German 164th Division and the Italian Trento Division who are supported by Littorio and 15th Panzer. Diversionary attacks at first make sure that 21st Panzer stays in the south. During the opening night and day of the battle the British forces make some progress but do not manage to keep to their timetable to force their armor through the minefields. General Stumme, who commands in Rommel's absence, dies of a heart attack during a visit to the front and in the very confused situation the German reaction is somewhat lethargic. On the afternoon of 24 October Rommel receives word to return from Germany.

24-25 October 1942

Guadalcanal The Japanese offensive continues. The secondary operations in the Matanikau sector continue on both days with partially successful Japanese infiltrations of the left wing of the American force. The main operations against the south of the American perimeter begin after dark on the 24th and continue throughout the night. They fail and similar unimaginative efforts on the night of the 25th are thrown back with heavy losses.

25 October 1942

El Alamein Montgomery intervenes decisively in the battle to ensure that X Corps pushes forward vigorously. Although by the end of the day they have lost perhaps 250 tanks, this can be accepted since 15th Panzer has less than 40 left. When Rommel arrives in the evening the 9th Australian Division in the north has already started attacking toward the sea. They make important gains which attract Rommel's attention.

Eastern Front After a period devoted to regrouping, the Germans renew their offensive with attacks by III Panzer Corps south of the Terek River in the Caucasus.

Battle of Santa Cruz The Japanese navy mounts a major operation in support of the offensive on Guadalcanal, sending four battleships and the carriers *Shokaku, Zuikaku, Zuiho* and *Junyo* as well as numerous cruisers and destroyers. The carriers are to send aircraft to Henderson Field once the army has captured it and only a report to that effect has brought it so close to the island. The Americans have two carriers in the operation, the *Enterprise* and the *Hornet*, but unlike the Japanese their one battleship is in close attendance to provide supporting anti-aircraft fire. As at Midway, the Japanese force is split into several groups (in this instance four). The battleships are separate from the carriers which themselves have fewer defensive guns than their American counterparts. The *Junyo*, with 55 aircraft, is even in a separate group from the rest of the carriers. A second disadvantage in the design of the Japanese carriers is that their bridges are too small to accommodate the admiral's staff necessary if no other large ships are in company. However, despite these disadvantages, the Japanese have 212 planes on their carriers and the Americans 171. Both sides will receive help, especially in scouting, from land-based aircraft.

The American patrols are first to find the enemy but a strike launched later goes astray. Both sides prepare for action on the 26th.

26 October 1942

Battle of Santa Cruz Both sides launch strikes about 0700 hours. Just after 0900 hours the Japanese attack reaches and seriously damages the *Hornet* which sinks later. The American attacks have been launched at the extreme range of the aircraft (the Japanese have longer range) and so no fuel can be used forming up for a coordinated attack. Some of the American planes attack Admiral's Abe's Vanguard Group, damaging the cruiser *Chikuma*, and the remainder inflict severe punishment on *Shokaku*. A second wave of Japanese attacks manages to severely damage the *Enterprise*, but many aircraft from this group and from a third less successful strike from *Junyo* are shot down by the massive barrage of the *South Dakota*. Although the *Enterprise* is made partially effective, Kinkaid decides to withdraw.

Although this has been an undoubted Japanese victory, leaving the damaged *Enterprise* as the only American carrier in the Pacific, the Japanese losses in aircrew have again been severe, with the undamaged *Zuikaku* virtually out of action because of this. The Japanese withdraw also, partly because of lack of fuel, and partly because their aircraft strength has been too reduced to make any attack on Henderson Field worthwhile.

El Alamein The British attack is making little progress and Montgomery halts most of his forces to regroup. Rumors of this reach Churchill and he is furious that the battle seems to be abandoned so soon. However, it is far from over. The main events of the day are German counterattacks. Rommel orders up 21st Panzer and Ariete from the south. Believing that the main Allied attack is now coming along the coast, he tries to counter there with 15th Panzer and moves 90th Light forward to support.

Eastern Front In the Caucasus the town of Nalchik falls to the Germans.

27 October 1942

El Alamein While the British command is mostly concerned with regrouping, what Rommel intends as a major counterattack by his armor is beaten off by a small British force at Kidney Ridge.

Eastern Front In Stalingrad the Germans gain ground in the area between the Red October and Barrikady Factories. From their new positions they are able to bring the landing stages on the west bank of the Volga under direct machine-gun fire. The remaining Soviet-held areas of the city are now on average about 300 yards deep. Their largest holdings are on the Mamayev Kurgan Hill and in the Barrikady Factory. The Red October Factory and almost all of the Tractor Factory are now in German hands. What remains to the Soviets, however, is very strongly held and fortified.

The Soviet policy has been to commit only small parts of divisions at a time, but German Intelligence has assumed that when these parts have been destroyed the whole unit can be written off. They thus overestimate the Soviet losses and underestimate the size of the Soviet reserves. The Soviet practice of briefly blooding newly assembled divisions in the Moscow sector also contributes to the faulty German appreciations. The Germans tend to assume that these divisions are being held in the central sector when in fact they have been moved south after a brief spell in the front line.

Guadalcanal The Japanese offensive is called off. They have suffered 3500 casualties. The various attacking groups have not been properly coordinated and, therefore, have been defeated in detail.

28 October 1942

Operation Torch Murphy tells General Mast that the invasion will take place early in November. Mast protests that he will be unable to organize the Allied sympathizers by then or arrange for Giraud to be accepted, but he promises to do his best.

28-29 October 1942

El Alamein The attacks of the Australian Division make some progress during the night in the northern sector and draw more German forces, principally from 90th Light, to oppose them. On the morning of the 29th Montgomery is persuaded to alter the direction of the next phase of his attack, Supercharge, to bear more on the Italians, now alone opposite Kidney Ridge.

28-30 October 1942

Malta The British carrier *Furious* flies off another cargo of Spitfires to Malta from Gibraltar. Malta is getting very short indeed of food and armaments, and the only supplies which are being brought in are the small quantities carried by a few submarines and one fast minelayer. The Germans and Italians are well aware that stocks are low on Malta and this knowledge contributes to their belief a few days later that the buildup of shipping in Gibraltar presages a supply operation to the island.

29 October 1942

New Guinea The Australian forces send in a final attack against the Japanese positions at Eora, forcing the Japanese out only a little before they had intended to retire. General Vasey takes over command of the 7th Australian Division from General Allen who has been judged to be insufficiently forceful.

Guadalcanal The Japanese are dismayed by their heavy losses and begin to pull some of their units back along the coast to the west of the American bridgehead. The Americans are preparing to follow up.

Madagascar East African troops take Fianarantsoa, the most important town in the south of the island, and continue their advance toward the final areas of resistance from the Vichy forces.

30 October 1942

New Guinea The Australian advance has reached Alola, about 10 miles south of Kokoda. One brigade is sent directly toward Kokoda while a second takes a more easterly route to Oivi.

30-31 October 1942

El Alamein The Australians and 90th Light continue their slogging match north and east of Tell el Eisa.

November 1942

Battle of the Atlantic This month the U-Boat operations are again more successful than the last with 729,100 tons or 119 ships being sunk.

Below: Advancing through the smoke of battle, a British soldier takes the surrender of a German tank man, Alamein, October 1942.

Above: A Russian fighter calls his comrades forward during the bitter street-to-street fighting in Stalingrad.

The total loss from all causes is 807,700 tons, of which 131,000 tons are sunk in the Pacific and Indian Oceans. This is the third best month of the war for the Axis forces. In the various operations 13 German and 4 Italian submarines are lost. The main focus of the U-Boat campaign is beginning to turn to the central North Atlantic once more despite the efforts which are made against the Allied shipping near North Africa. At the start of the month the Germans have about 100 vessels on active operations.

Allied Air Operations Bomber Command's raids on Germany are less intense this month. Among the targets are Hamburg and Stuttgart. In France Allied targets include Le Havre, St Nazaire and La Pallice. RAF bombers from Britain heavily raid Genoa and Turin four times. Airfields on Sicily and Sardinia are also raided by theater forces. The RAF drops 2600 tons of bombs in the main operations and the Eighth Air Force just over 650.

Atomic Research Work begins on the first atomic pile at the University of Chicago under the direction of Enrico Fermi.

Yugoslavia, Resistance The Yugoslav National Anti-Fascist Liberation Council meets openly at Bihać in Croatia, protected by the Partisan forces. The Partisans are now solidly enough established to begin to create the apparatus of government, with courts and other administrative bodies in operation.

1 November 1942

Guadalcanal Two Marine regiments begin to attack west across the Matanikau River. During the last few days engineers have built bridges to help supply the attack. There is fairly heavy fighting. Other American units begin to advance east of the bridgehead toward Koli Point where a Japanese landing is expected.

Eastern Front The German advance in the Caucasus region stumbles on. Alagir, an important road junction 30 miles west of Ordzhonikidze, is taken by First Panzer Army.

1-2 November 1942

El Alamein Montgomery's Supercharge Operation gets under way. The infantry attacks to clear the final minefields are held up and when the armor reaches open ground during the 2nd it takes heavy losses from the prepared positions of 15th Panzer. The British can afford these largely inevitable losses, however, since later in the day when 21st Panzer joins the battle Rommel has only about 35 tanks in action with little ammunition and less fuel. He therefore signals to Hitler that he cannot prevent a breakthrough and must withdraw.

1-12 November 1942

Guadalcanal During this period the Japanese destroyer force bringing supplies to the island is especially active. Nearly 70 missions are run by its various ships. The force is known to the Americans as the Tokyo Express. Admiral Tanaka takes command of these operations on 5 November.

2 November 1942

New Guinea Kokoda is recaptured by men of the Australian 25th Brigade. With possession of the Kokoda airstrip it will now be possible to ease the strain on the men by supplying them by air rather than having everything carried up to Kokoda over the terrible switchback terrain of the trail.

Guadalcanal The US advance to the west continues slowly with some success around Cruz Point.

3 November 1942

El Alamein The German and Italian forces begin to withdraw but some are halted because Hitler orders no retreat. In the south the Italian infantry is already committed to the move back. Rommel is astonished by the lack of pressure from the British, who are in fact trapped in confused traffic jams.

Guadalcanal During the early hours of the morning a Japanese force about 1500 strong is put ashore at Koli Point to the east of the American perimeter. It is engaged by the American force in the area but these troops are soon forced to pull back.

United States, Politics In congressional elections the Republicans make some gains but do not win control. They gain nine extra seats in the Senate, 42 in the House and four more state governorships.

4 November 1942

El Alamein The British X Corps finally reaches open ground. There is considerable fighting in which Ariete, 90th, Light and even German headquarters units all suffer heavily before breaking off to retreat. General von Thoma is captured while leading an attack. During the night, when the remnants of Rommel's forces are retreating to Fuka, the Eighth Army fails to advance at all despite Montgomery's orders to do so. The battle so far has been an almost unqualified success for the British, whatever shortcomings there may develop in the pursuit. Eighth Army has taken 30,000 prisoners, at least 1000 guns and the remains of 450 tanks. The German divisions can barely muster a regiment each and the Italian formations are ruined. The British and Commonwealth troops have about 13,500 casualties, with 150 tanks destroyed and 300 damaged.

Battle of the Atlantic The first meeting of the Cabinet Anti-U-Boat Warfare Committee takes place in London. Churchill himself takes the chair and the other members include the service chiefs, other government ministers and several important scientists in the fields of radar and operational research. This combination of the highest-level political, military and scientific personnel in one decision-making body is symbolic of the sort of coordination which the British and Americans are able to bring to their war efforts. None of the Axis powers achieves a system in any way comparable.

Operation Torch A group of 19 German and 21 Italian submarines begins to take up patrol positions in the western Mediterranean because of the shipping concentrations which have been sighted off Gibraltar. During the next two weeks they achieve some successes.

5 November 1942

North Africa Rommel retreats from Fuka. Some of the Italian infantry in particular take heavy punishment. The main pursuit is held up by lack of fuel and by an old minefield which in fact is a dummy laid months previously by the British themselves.

Eastern Front The German attacks south of the Terek in the Caucasus are being worn down, but the advance still goes on and has now reached nearly to Ordzhonikidze.

Operation Torch General Eisenhower arrives in Gibraltar and sets up his headquarters. Admiral Cunningham will command the naval forces. General Doolittle and Air Marshal Welsh will command the air forces. General Anderson will lead the British First Army which will be the main ground formation.

Madagascar The Vichy forces ask for an armistice. The terms are agreed and signed on 6 November.

New Guinea The Australian forces begin attacks against Oivi. The Japanese intend to fight a rearguard action here while their main force retires across the Kumusi River.

6 November 1942

Egypt Many of the pursuing British forces are short of fuel because not enough can be got through the chaos around Alamein. The 7th Armored Division does catch and destroy what is left of 21st Panzer, which is completely stranded and out of fuel. Later in the day heavy rain falls which means that the only practical route of advance is now along the coast road.

7 November 1942

Operation Torch General Giraud, who has been brought from southern France secretly in the British submarine *Seraph*, arrives in Gibraltar for talks with General Eisenhower. The Allies wish to involve a more prominent French figure than de Gaulle or any of the North Africans in their operation in the hope of minimizing resistance from forces loyal to Vichy. They have been told by local sympathizers that Giraud will be suitable but in fact he is not likely to command wide support. Giraud believes that he has been summoned to take command of the whole operation but Eisenhower, of course, cannot agree to this.

Guadalcanal The US Marines begin attacks to the east of their main perimeter in the direction of Koli Point. There are two columns in the advance. There are Japanese landings after dark to the west of the American holdings. The troops brought in are the first from the 38th Infantry Division.

Egypt The pursuing British forces enter Mersa Matruh but most of Rommel's divisions have slipped away, albeit in total disorder.

8 November 1942

Operation Torch The Allied invasion of French North Africa begins. There are three main sectors of operations. The Western Task Force has sailed direct from the United States and sends in landings at three places on a 200-mile front around Casablanca. There are 35,000 troops from the US 2nd Armored, 3rd Infantry and part of the 9th Infantry Divisions. General Patton commands the ground forces. The naval forces involved include two battleships, one fleet carrier, four escort carriers and numerous cruisers and destroyers, led by Admiral Hewitt. The Center Task Force, to land near Oran, is led by General Fredendall and Commodore Troubridge. There are 39,000 troops from the US 1st Infantry and Armored Divisions. The naval force includes two escort carriers as well as many smaller ships. The Eastern Task Force lands at Algiers and is led by Admiral Burrough and General Ryder. There are 52 warships and 33,000 soldiers. The troops are from the US 34th Infantry Division with parts of 9th Infantry and 1st Armored also present. The only large British assault force, 78th Division, is landed here. In support of the whole operation and on guard against the still-formidable Italian Fleet is the British Force H from Gibraltar under Admiral Syfret with three battleships, three fleet carriers and a strong force of cruisers and destroyers.

At Algiers the landings make good early progress and quickly capture the town. Admiral Darlan, who is there on a visit on private business, is captured also. At Oran the landing is not so successful and an attempt to rush the harbor costs two destroyers. By nightfall, however, the landing is well established and the airfield at Tafaraiu is in Allied hands with an American-manned Spitfire force already in position. The fighting is fiercest at Casablanca. The battleship *Jean Bart*, armed but immobile, fights a gunnery duel with the *Massachusetts*. The French destroyer flotilla in the port also fights but its ships are soon driven off or sunk. Of the other landings of the Western Task Force, those at Safi go well but at Port Lyautey there is more fighting. Altogether there are 1800 Allied casualties.

All the landings receive some help from French supporters. This help is most effective at Algiers where General Mast does much to make the French reaction hesitant enough not to hinder the actual landings. His superior, General Juin, is not actively opposed to the Allies but feels that is may be necessary for the good of the French mainland to make some show of resisting the landings. Mast and the Allied leaders are sur-

Below: Men of the US Marines 2nd Ranger Battalion storm ashore on the southern coast of Guadalcanal, November 1942.

Above: Scene on the American battleship USS *Massachusetts* during the landings at Casablanca, 8 November 1942.

prised when they learn that Darlan is in Algiers. As one of the principal leaders of the Vichy government he is likely to command widespread support, as being a representative of constituted French authority, and if his undoubted influence over the navy is also considered his importance is obvious. Negotiations with him begin immediately. In Casablanca General Béthouart is less successful in his efforts. General Noguès is less sympathetic to the Allied cause and the commanding admiral of the strong naval force, Admiral Michelier, is deeply anti-British.

Although most of the merchant shipping and naval support is provided by the British, the Allies have taken pains to present Torch to the French as mainly a US operation. Therefore almost all of the assault troops are American, and all the political and military contacts with the French have been made by the Americans. On the other hand, the British have better relations with the Spanish and Portuguese and have been responsible for ensuring that a German move through Spain to Gibraltar will not be aided by the Spanish. The various broadcasts put out during the day confirm these arrangements. Roosevelt and Eisenhower broadcast to the French, and the British lead in giving public assurances that Spanish neutrality will be respected. Although de Gaulle has not been told of the operation he buries his annoyance for the moment and also makes a suitable approving broadcast.

All U-Boats in the Atlantic with sufficient fuel (25 in all) are ordered to North Africa. Among their successes is the sinking of the escort carrier *Avenger* by *U.155* on 15 November.

Eastern Front The Soviet forces in the Caucasus have gone over to the attack on the Terek front and are threatening to cut off some units of III Panzer Corps.

9 November 1942

French North Africa At Casablanca the US forces secure their beachheads and at Port Lyautey there is more heavy fighting between French tanks and General Truscott's troops. The town of Oran still holds out, but General Anderson, who has landed to take command of First Army at Algiers, is able to send armored columns rushing to the east. Prime Minister Laval agrees to allow the Germans to use airfields in Tunisia, and the first German troops are flown in immediately. The British planners of Torch, particularly Admiral Cunningham, wished to make landings as far west as Bône and Bizerta, but this was vetoed by the American Chiefs of Staff. In retrospect this decision seems to have been an error.

General Giraud arrives in Algiers but General Clark realizes now that Darlan is likely to command more loyalty and, therefore, continues to press him to declare for the Allies. Publicly Pétain is strongly opposed to the Allied landings but secretly he is giving some encouragement to Darlan to negotiate with them.

Egypt and Libya The New Zealand Division enters Sidi Barrani, leading the pursuit of Rommel's forces.

9-10 November 1942

New Guinea The Australian 25th Brigade takes Gorari after a fierce battle. The Japanese force at Oivi is, therefore, cut off and with it General Horii.

10 November 1942

French North Africa Oran falls to the US attack and to the west, at Casablanca, Patton's men begin to move into the town. Admiral Darlan broadcasts orders to all the French forces in North Africa to stop fighting the Allies. A similar appeal to sail and join the Allies is sent to the powerful French fleet at Toulon.

Hitler, Laval and Ciano meet at Munich to discuss the situation in Africa and, as Hitler wishes, they decide to hold on to as much as possible. Churchill, speaking in London, describes recent events in Africa as marking 'the end of the beginning' of the Allied efforts.

Eastern Front In response to intelligence reports of a Soviet buildup, some German units from XLVIII Panzer Corps are sent from around Stalingrad to bolster the reserves supporting Third Rumanian Army to the north.

10-11 November 1942

Guadalcanal The Japanese forces around Koli Point are dispersed by American attacks. Attacks to the west of the perimeter are renewed on the 10th but are halted the next day when information about Japanese convoys comes in.

11 November 1942

French North Africa The French authorities sign an armistice. Casablanca is occupied. The

Below: Crew members on board the cruiser USS *Augusta* take a welcome break during the Allied landings in French North Africa.

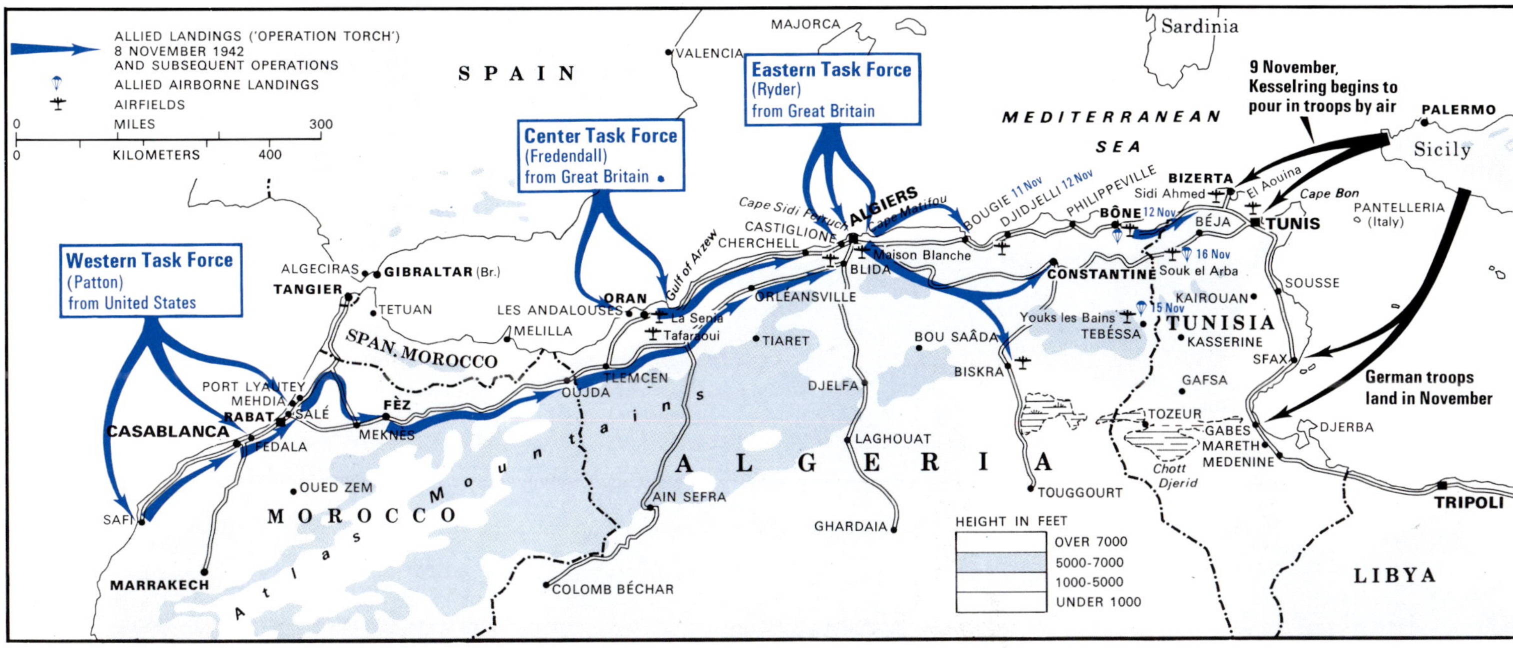

Above: Operation Torch, 8 November 1942, showing the three landing areas.

British 11th Brigade begins to move east from Algiers in strength and Bougie is taken by a landing by 36th Brigade. These forward forces have little air cover and several of the ships at Bougie carrying important equipment are sunk by the Luftwaffe during the next few days. The Germans now have over 1000 troops in Tunisia.

France Hitler orders German troops to move into Vichy.

Eastern Front In Stalingrad Paulus' last major attack begins. There is, as usual, vicious fighting with heavy casualties on both sides. Despite some new German tactics the Soviets are able to fragment the German effort so that within two days all central control is lost and the offensive degenerates into a series of unconnected actions. Some German groups are able to penetrate to the Volga while others are cut off from support. The German command is unable to follow the course of the battle and thus the Soviet small-unit expertise gradually prevails. The offensive continues for six days. The Soviets are having problems with their supplies because floating blocks of ice on the Volga are making the river crossing almost impossible.

Egypt and Libya The advance units of Eighth Army reach Halfaya Pass, move into Libya and take Bardia without opposition. The New Zealand Division is forced to halt to reorganize on the Egyptian frontier.

War at Sea Two Japanese merchant raiders attack the Indian minesweeper *Bengal* and the tanker *Ondina* in the Indian Ocean. In the ensuing action *Bengal* sinks the *Hokoku Maru* and drives the *Aikoku Maru* off despite an enormous disparity of force. Both Japanese ships have six 6-inch guns, while the *Bengal* has one 3-inch and the *Ondina* one 4-inch. This action ranks with that of the *Stephen Hopkins* as one of the most remarkable defenses made by small ships during the war.

11-13 November 1942

New Guinea The advancing Australians are heavily engaged around Gorari during this time. When the Japanese finally manage to pull back across the Kumusi River they leave behind 600

Below: The American landing beach at Oran, in French North Africa, Operation Torch, 8 November 1942.

dead. General Horii is drowned during the retreat. This battle signals the collapse of organized Japanese resistance outside their beachhead at Gona and Buna.

12 November 1942

Tunisia and Algeria A combined sea and airborne assault takes Bône and the nearby airfield. The first German supply ships begin docking in Bizerta despite the efforts of the local French commanders to block the harbor and prevent this.

Guadalcanal A large American convoy landing supplies and reinforcements is compelled to retire on the approach of large Japanese naval forces. There are many Japanese air attacks on land and shipping targets.

Libya Units of the British 1st and 7th Armored Divisions enter Tobruk.

United States, Home Front The draft age is lowered from 20 to 18. Roosevelt estimates that the US armed forces will embody nearly 10,000,000 men by the end of 1943.

12-13 November 1942

Eastern Front In the Caucasus the Germans extricate 13th Panzer Division from a brief Soviet encirclement south of the Terek but are still under considerable pressure in this sector.

13 November 1942

Algeria The Allied troops at Bône are reinforced. The British 36th Brigade has now passed Djidjelli in their advance from Algiers. A formal agreement is signed by Admiral Darlan and General Clark recognizing Darlan as head of the French civil government in North Africa. The agreement is ratified by Eisenhower, Noguès and Juin. Giraud is to command the French armed services.

Battle of Guadalcanal The Japanese send a large convoy of 11 transports carrying 11,000 men and escorted by Tanaka's 11 destroyers. To give cover to the operation and to bombard Henderson Field Admiral Abe leads two battleships, two cruisers and 14 destroyers. The Japanese carriers are at sea farther to the north providing more protection. Admiral Callaghan, with five cruisers and eight destroyers, moves to intercept Abe's squadron.

Just before 0200 hours the two forces blunder into each other. In an action lasting about half an hour two Japanese cruisers are sunk and almost all their other ships are damaged. The Americans lose two cruisers and four destroyers. Once more the Americans fail to make proper use of their radar equipment, partly because various ships have sets with different capabilities and communications are poor. The Japanese transport convoy turns away. Later in the day the battleship *Hiei*, badly damaged during the night, is torpedoed by American aircraft and has to be scuttled.

14 November 1942

Tunisia The French commander, General Barré, begins to move his troops away from the coastal towns in preparation for going over to the Allies.

14-15 November 1942

Battle of Guadalcanal Tanaka turns south with his destroyers and transports early on the 14th and immediately comes under heavy attack. Seven of the transports and two warships are lost. The attacking aircraft mostly come from Henderson Field but some are from the carrier *Enterprise*. Tanaka continues his advance, however, and during the night there is a further battle off Savo Island. The Japanese covering force is now led by Admiral Kondo with the battleship *Kirishima*, four cruisers and nine destroyers. The Americans have brought up TF64 (Admiral Lee) with the battleships *Washington* and *South Dakota* with four destroyers. Shortly before midnight the engagement begins. *South Dakota* is hit and forced out of the battle but later a devastating seven-minute burst of fire from *Washington* sinks *Kirishima*. Control of the seas round Guadalcanal is now passing gradually to the Americans but in this case Tanaka's remaining transports manage to reach Tassafaronga. Of the troops who have survived the earlier attacks more are killed while landing. After this defeat the Japanese are forced to make considerable use of submarines to transport supplies. Already many of their men are ill and hungry.

Below: Junkers Ju-87 Stuka dive-bombers approach their targets in Stalingrad, late 1942. The city was devastated during the battle.

15 November 1942

Tunisia and Algeria The British 36th Brigade captures Tabarka on the coast road to Bizerta. US paratroops take the airfield at Youks les Bains near Tebéssa. The German buildup has been very rapid and there are now 10,000 troops taking up positions in Tunisia. They have over 100 combat planes in bases long established by the French, convenient for the front and with all-weather runways. The Allied air forces are forced to use temporary landing grounds farther from the front.

New Guinea Having built rudimentary bridges over the Kumusi the Australians are able to advance to take Wairopi and Ilimow.

16 November 1942

Tunisia A British parachute battalion takes Souk el Arba and 36th Brigade farther north takes Djebel Abiod. Late in the day the paratroops have reached nearly to Béja.

General de Gaulle announces that he and his Free French supporters do not accept Darlan's authority. Many British politicians are worried, too, about cooperating with a former member of the Vichy government. The Americans have been always much more ready to favor Vichy than the British and, therefore, see nothing wrong with such a useful arrangement.

17 November 1942

Libya The vanguard of Eighth Army has reached Derna on the coast and Mechili inland.

New Guinea A Japanese convoy lands 1000 fresh troops at Buna. The Japanese positions around Gona, Buna and Sanananda have been strongly fortified since September and are now well garrisoned also.

Burma General Wavell decides to cancel the proposed major amphibious operation against Akyab and instead, on 19 November, issues orders for a more limited advance by 14th Indian Division down the Mayu Peninsula perhaps to be followed by a shorter seaborne operation against Akyab.

17-20 November 1942

Malta A convoy, code named Stoneage, passes from Gibraltar to the island. None of the four freighters is lost and of the three cruisers and 10 destroyers which form the escort only one vessel is hit. The long period of heavy attacks on the island is over and the siege has at last come to an end.

18 November 1942

Guadalcanal The US forces begin moving west from their perimeter once more. The attacks are not particularly forceful but do continue for five days before the next lull. The Americans are not again compelled to close up to their original perimeter.

Tunisia The British Brigade at Djebel Abiod drives off a German attack. The parachute force is now as Sidi Nsir.

Vichy, Politics Pétain grants power to Laval allowing him to issue decrees solely on his own authority. Pétain is gradually becoming less and less important in the Vichy government, although his enormous prestige remains.

Above: A Scottish soldier guards German prisoners taken at Alamein.

19 November 1942

Eastern Front The Soviet winter offensive begins along the Don. The German forces throughout the southern Soviet Union are hopelessly overextended. Stalingrad has drawn German troops like moths to a candle while both on their left and right are unreliable allies. The Soviets have been planning a grand attack with fresh divisions for weeks. They intend a pincer move with armies from the Southwest Front (Vatutin) and the Don Front (Rokossovsky) attacking southward from the Don, especially between Kletskaya and Kotovskiy, and the Stalingrad Front (Yeremenko) whose armies are to attack westward from south of the city. Zhukov is in overall command. Only the northern claw of the pincer attacks at this stage. The Soviets have assembled more than 500,000 infantry, 900 new T34 tanks, and have the support of masses of artillery and over 1000 attack planes. The units deployed in the northern pincer are Fifth Tank Army, Twenty-first Army and part of the First Guards Army. The unfortunate victims are the seven divisions of the Rumanian Third Army who come under murderous pressure and can do little to prevent a major breakthrough around Kletskaya. In the Caucasus the Germans are in trouble also. The Soviets win an important engagement near Ordzhonikidze. Bad weather largely ends major operations here but the Soviets manage a series of small gains in the next few weeks.

Tunisia French forces at Medjez el Bab resist German attacks and are reinforced by the British and Americans. The Germans, now led by General Nehring, have brought forward tanks and infantry.

Libya Eighth Army enters Benghazi.

New Guinea The US troops from Pongani begin their attack on Buna, believing it to be only lightly held. In reality the Americans are easily pushed back by the well-prepared Japanese forces. The Australians are closing up to Gona and a mixed Allied force is moving on Sanananda.

Battle of the Atlantic Admiral Horton takes over the British Western Approaches Command from Admiral Noble. Although Noble has been an able leader, he does not have the forceful spirit which Horton brings to the job. The German U-Boat leaders soon notice the change.

20 November 1942

Eastern Front The southern claw of the Soviet pincer round Stalingrad begins its attacks. The attacking units are from Fifty-first, Sixty-fourth and Fifty-seventh Armies. The principal victims here are the Rumanian Fourth Army and part of the German Fourth Panzer Army (the other part is in the city and will be surrounded). The attack is held up for a time by energetic counterattacks by the 29th Panzergrenadier Division, but eventually the Soviet numbers tell.

Below: A Douglas Dauntless dive-bomber flies over burning Japanese transports on the coast of Guadalcanal, November 1942.

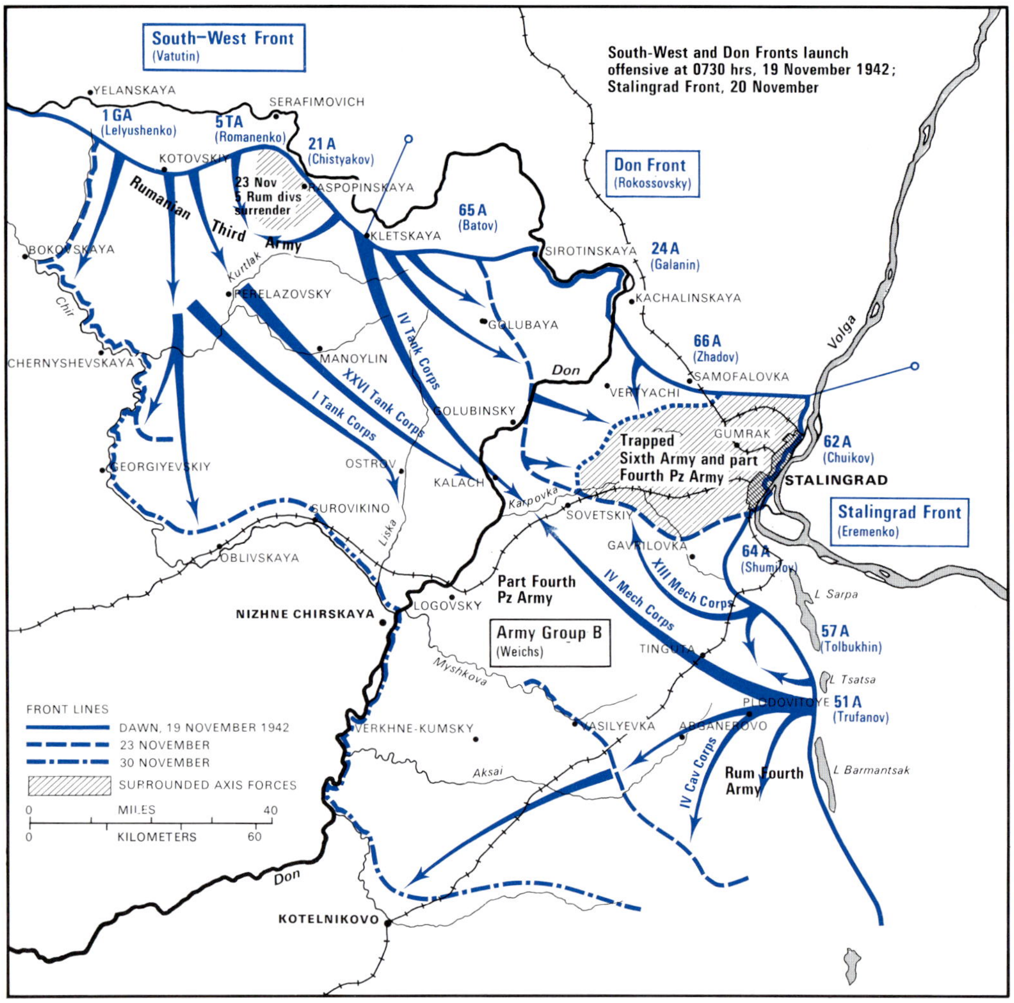

Above: Map showing the Russian counterattack at Stalingrad, November 1942.

Vichy, Politics Laval broadcasts once more in support of Germany. He says that Germany will win the war and that the alternative is to be ruled by 'Jews and Communists.' At a press conference on 13 December he confirms these views announcing, 'I must say without any ambiguity, that I want Germany's victory.'

New Guinea An Australian advance succeeds in breaking into the Japanese position at Gona but the attacking force is later driven out. The Australian and American attacks on the Japanese positions continue intermittently for the next 10 days, but with small success.

21 November 1942

Eastern Front The Rumanian Third Army is in a desperate condition. The Soviets have 34 divisions in the advance and have broken through on a 50-mile front. Tank units from Rokossovsky's Don Front are advancing rapidly toward Kalach. The German command is disorganized. Sixth Army's staff is being forced to move because of the Soviet advance and General Manstein, who has been ordered to take command of a new Army Group Don, is making a long train journey to take up his post.

23 November 1942

Eastern Front The important bridge over the Don at Kalach is captured by Soviet forces coming from the north in a surprise attack. After crossing this bridge advance units link up with tank forces of Fifty-first Army and the encirclement of Stalingrad begins. The Soviets believe that they have about 85,000 Germans cut off in the city when in fact the total is nearer 300,000. Five Rumanian divisions of Third Army's seven surrender around Raspopinskaya.

The Soviets intend, as their first priority, methodically to destroy the Stalingrad garrison before continuing their offensive to the west. Zhukov supports this unambitious scheme because he is well aware of the limitations of the Soviet forces in wide-ranging operations. Despite this priority, the false assessment of German positions leaves the siege forces short.

Libya After a sharp action around Agedabia the Axis troops fall back to the El Agheila position. Montgomery halts his advance to reorganize his forces, which have now chased their enemy almost 600 miles in 14 days. The British advance has been perhaps too cautious although German demolitions and booby traps have been one cause of delay.

France, Politics Darlan announces that French West Africa now accepts his authority.

24 November 1942

Eastern Front Manstein arrives at Army Group A Headquarters. He has been summoned south from Leningrad to restore the situation but the forces allocated to him to create Army Group Don are either practically nonexistent or shut in Stalingrad. The whole of Sixth Army and most of Fourth Panzer Army are surrounded, and have orders from Hitler to maintain their positions with the help of air supply. Five of the seven divisions of the Third Rumanian Army have surrendered. Almost the only significant German unit available to Manstein is a division holding the important position at Elista which

Below: American troops advance through French North Africa, ensuring that any forces loyal to Vichy know who is coming.

Above: A German infantry officer briefs his men prior to a patrol in the Stalingrad sector, 1942. The men are obvious veterans of a tough war.

ought to be maintained as a link with Army Group A in the Caucasus. The other German Army Group commanders and the High Command cooperate with Manstein's request for reserves only with reluctance and his buildup is slow.

It is not at all clear to Manstein how he should proceed even when his forces are assembled. The Soviets already have over 1000 antitank guns in positions round Stalingrad and with such opposition a breakout may be impossible. Even if a breakout is possible Manstein cannot be sure that it is desirable. Since the Soviets would have no need to continue to invest the city they could devote their forces to further wide encirlements, to which the Germans would be especially vulnerable with Sixth Army and the relieving force concentrated at the tip of an exposed salient. In this situation the whole of Manstein's forces and also Army Group A in the Caucasus might well be endangered. In fact this large threat will not materialize for the moment because of the more limited Soviet intentions, but it must remain in Manstein's thoughts.

Hitler's orders to hold on to Stalingrad are based on a wild claim by Goering that Stalingrad can be supplied by air. Sixth Army would need at least 700 tons of supplies each day and for this 500 planes would be necessary as well as good weather and low losses. There are 300 planes available and their airfields are in poor condition and under threat from the Soviet advance. There is no possibility of Goering keeping his promise although the attempt will be made and almost 500 planes lost before the end of the siege. They will manage to take out 42,000 wounded men and some important specialists.

In the central sector, west of Moscow, there are Soviet attacks around Rzhev.

25 November 1942

Greece, Resistance Led by British SOE agents, resistance workers from two rival Greek organizations join forces to blow up an important viaduct on the Athens-Salonika railroad at Gorgopotamos. Many of Rommel's supplies have in the past used this route.

26 November 1942

Eastern Front The Soviets claim to have taken Krasnoye, Generalov and Selo on the Don. For the next few days there is something of a lull on the outer ring round Stalingrad. The Soviets are concentrating on the German pocket inside and the Germans are busy assembling strength for a counterattack.

Tunisia The Germans are driven out of Medjez el Bab by the British 78th Division. The German-held airfield at Djedeida is raided by a US tank battalion.

26-27 November 1942

New Guinea Despite losing a destroyer to air attack the Japanese manage to reinforce their troops at Buna.

27 November 1942

France The German II SS Panzer Corps occupies Toulon but the French Fleet is scuttled by order of Admiral Laborde. Three battleships, seven cruisers and 62 other craft go down, including 16 submarines.

Tunisia Tebourba, 15 miles west of Tunis, is captured by the Allied forces while another column approaches Bizerta.

28 November 1942

Eastern Front The Soviets make considerable gains on the central sector near Rzhev.

Tunisia British and American forces at brigade strength take Djedeida, but German troops are moving on their rear from St Cyprien.

Indian Ocean Free French forces occupy the island of Réunion.

29 November 1942

Tunisia A British parachute battalion lands at Depienne and moves toward Oudna. The Allied forces occupying Djedeida come under heavy pressure and begin to fall back. As ever, the German infantry proves a most formidable opponent when on the defensive.

Churchill broadcasts from London, warning the Italian people that they must chose between a full-scale Allied attack and a revolt against Mussolini.

Below: The French Fleet lies scuttled in Toulon harbor, November 1942; a French response to the German takeover of Vichy.

30 November 1942

New Guinea The American forces attacking Buna make their first real gains.

Burma The advance of the British 123rd Brigade in the Arakan has now reached Bawli Bazar. Terrible weather, which would normally be expected to clear during November, has been impeding the advance and making road construction difficult.

German Raiders The German raider *Thor* is destroyed by fire in Yokohama Harbor. In a cruise lasting from January to October 1942, *Thor* sank 10 ships of 56,000 tons.

30 November-1 December 1942

Battle of Tassafaronga The regular night run of the Tokyo Express again develops into a major battle. Tanaka has eight destroyers and the US Admiral Wright has five heavy cruisers and seven destroyers. Although radar helps Wright get off the first shells and torpedoes the American fire is ineffective, with one Japanese destroyer sinking later. In the Japanese reply one cruiser is sunk and three very seriously damaged. Despite these successes Tanaka is reprimanded for failing to deliver his supplies to the starving Japanese forces on the island.

December 1942

Battle of the Atlantic This month the U-Boats sink 60 ships of 330,000 tons in the Atlantic convoy battles. The most important development during the month is the change in the standard of the Allied intelligence information that occurs in the second week when the U-Boat cipher Triton is broken for the first time. For several months there will be delays, often of three or four days or sometimes as much as a week, before new settings on the code machine can be broken. Even when messages can be decoded promptly it will not always be possible to route convoys away from U-Boat concentrations. One problem here is the shortage in Britain of bunker fuel for the merchant fleet. There are only two months' reserves outside RN stocks.

Below: Sailors on board the British corvette HMS *Dianthus* reload a depth-charge thrower.

During 1942 Allied shipping losses have been 7,790,000 tons of which less than 7,000,000 tons have been replaced by new construction. The German U-Boat strength has increased to 212 operational boats despite a shortfall of 15 percent in production. Eighty percent of the Allied loss has fallen to submarines. British resources in shipping and British needs for imports and the transport of supplies to forces overseas remain greater than those of the US for the moment. During Torch Britain has been lending more shipping to the US than she has been borrowing. During 1942 Britain has consumed 2,400,000 tons of supplies more than has been landed. The year 1943 will see the American production begin to show fruit and will see a complete change in the patterns of Allied shipping and losses.

Allied Air Operations British bomber targets in Germany include Frankfurt, Duisburg and Munich. In France American attacks are made on Abbeville and Rouen as well as other joint British and American raids with lighter forces. RAF bombers from bases in Britain attack Turin on three occasions while targets raided by the British and American forces from North Africa include Naples (five times), Palermo and Taranto. RAF Bomber Command drops 3000 tons in these operations and the US Eighth Air Force based in Britain drops 370 tons.

The navigational aid *Oboe* comes into service with the RAF. It gives accurate and reliable results, but its range is comparatively limited, reaching only as far as the Ruhr from bases in Britain. Only a very limited number of planes can be operated on the system at a time so it is used mostly for target marking. Theoretically it is very vulnerable to jamming, but the Germans only begin this in August 1943. More advanced versions of *Oboe*, which enter service from late in 1943, remain almost immune to interference until the end of the war.

1 December 1942

French North Africa In Tunisia there is a strong German counterattack near Tebourba which the Allies manage to beat off after taking heavy casualties. German forces in Tunisia are now 15,000 strong. The buildup is to continue. Two German infantry divisions and most of 10th Panzer Division will arrive soon. The Italians have shipped 90,000 tons of supplies to Tunisia since Operation Torch began and the German air-transport fleet is also very active. Allied attacks are taking a considerable, and increasing toll of these shipments. The efforts made to strength Tunisia also mean that Rommel is forced to make do with a poorer allowance for his troops to the east.

Darlan broadcasts from Algiers announcing that, because the Chief of State, Marshal Pétain, is a prisoner, he has assumed the responsibilities of the French government.

General Spaatz is transferred to command the Allied Air Forces in Northwest Africa. General Eaker takes his place with Eighth Air Force in Britain. Many of the supplies which would otherwise have come to Eighth Air Force are now being sent to North Africa where Twelfth Air Force will be established.

Britain, Home Front The House of Commons receives the Report on Social Insurance prepared by the Beveridge Committee. The report proposes far-reaching measures of social reform which are designed to eliminate poverty in Britain. The laws which will emerge from the consideration of the report are the foundation of Britain's modern welfare system.

United States, Home Front Gasoline rationing is introduced throughout the country.

1-2 December 1942

Mediterranean Axis supply problems are well illustrated by events during these two days. There are four Italian convoys at sea which are threatened by a British squadron of three cruisers and two destroyers. Three of the convoys are recalled. The four freighters and one of the escorts of the fourth convoy are sunk and two more escorts damaged. The British later lose one destroyer to an air attack. During December the Italians will try to convoy over 200,000 tons of cargo to Tunis and Tripoli, but of this 90,000 tons (32 ships) will be lost to British and Allied naval and air attacks.

2 December 1942

Atomic Research The first manmade, self-sustaining chain reaction is achieved in the atomic pile at Chicago University.

New Guinea The Australians capture part of the Gona defenses. A further Japanese reinforcement convoy for Buna is turned away by air attacks but the troops carried are landed along the coast to the west. General Eichelberger has been sent by MacArthur to investigate the lack of progress at Buna and he decides to relieve General Harding of command of the US forces there.

3 December 1942

Tunisia Djedeida and Tebourba are taken by German troops from 10th Panzer Division after a series of attacks.

3-4 December 1942

Guadalcanal Tanaka leads 10 destroyers in a supply operation. Only about 300 of the 1500 containers dropped reach the Japanese forces ashore.

4 December 1942

Italy The US Ninth Air Force attacks Naples, sinking two cruisers in the harbor and causing

Above: Japanese soldiers lie dead in the mud of the Tenaru river after a vicious battle with US Marines, Guadalcanal, 1942.

other damage. This is the first US raid on the mainland of Italy.
United States, Politics Roosevelt receives a petition from 244 Congressmen supporting the establishment of a Jewish homeland in Palestine.

5 December 1942

New Guinea There is a strong US attack on Buna which is halted by defensive fire after a few scattered gains have been made.

6 December 1942

Tunisia The Allied forces are pushed back near Medjez el Bab by renewed German attacks which continue for the next four days.
New Guinea After more vicious fighting the Allied troops manage to reach the beach on the east side of Buna. The Australian forces again attack at Gona but with little success. Japanese attempts to push a relieving force along the coast from farther west make some progress.

7 December 1942

New Guinea There are fierce Japanese counterattacks at Buna which are only just beaten off by the US forces.
Eastern Front There are several Soviet attacks to gain bridgeheads over the River Chir and threaten the German airfields which are the bases for the supply operation to Stalingrad. The German 11th Panzer Division is in the area and in a sequence of maneuver battles it brings the Soviet advance to a halt, but only at considerable cost.

7-8 December 1942

Guadalcanal A Japanese supply operation, involving seven destroyers led by Captain Sato, is abandoned because of attacks by American PT boats.

8 December 1942

Tunisia German forces led by General Gause occupy Bizerta, capturing four French destroyers, nine submarines and three other warships.
Britain, Home Front Parliament lowers the age for conscription by six months, to 18. Already, Britain is feeling a manpower shortage.

8-9 December 1942

New Guinea In yet another hard-fought engagement the Japanese positions at Gona are stormed by Australian troops from 21st Brigade.

9 December 1942

Guadalcanal The exhausted 1st Marine Division is relieved by General Patch's XIV Corps. The Marines begin to leave for Australia and, as not all Patch's force is assembled, there is a continued lull in the land fighting.

10 December 1942

Eastern Front A small German counterattack in the Rzhev area makes a little ground.

10-11 December 1942

Tunisia In the continuing German attacks Medjez el Bab is now the objective but the advancing columns are finally beaten off. The Allied force is still very thin on the ground and many of the troops are showing their inexperience.

11 December 1942

Libya Eighth Army begins to advance once more.

11-12 December 1942

Guadalcanal Tanaka again leads a Japanese supply operation with 11 destroyers. One destroyer is sunk, and of 1200 containers dropped overboard to float in to the island, only 200 are collected by the Japanese forces. The remainder are mostly punctured and sunk by machine-gun fire from American PT boats.

12 December 1942

Eastern Front Although the Germans have a bridgehead over the Don at Nizhne Chirskaya, only 25 miles from the nearest forces trapped in the Stalingrad pocket, Manstein has decided to begin his relieving attack farther south around Kotelnikovo. The code name for the operation is *Wintergewitter* (Winter Storm). General Hoth is in tactical charge of the attack which, with initial armor superiority, makes good progress at first. The Germans have assembled a total of 13 divisions for the operation, including three Panzer units. The Soviet line, held by Fifty-first Army, is comparatively weak because its next major moves are planned both farther north and farther south. In fact, Second Guards Army, which is intended to participate in the next attack to the north, is quickly summoned to take up positions on the Myshkova River. This reinforcement for the Soviet rear cannot arrive for a few days, and Fifty-first Army is left to delay the German advance.
Tunisia Italian midget submarines sink four ships in Algiers Harbor. There is more heavy fighting near Medjez el Bab.

13 December 1942

Libya Eighth Army captures Mersa Brega. Rommel begins to pull out of the El Agheila position.
Tunisia There are heavy US air raids on Bizerta and Tunis. On the ground the fighting dies down for the moment.

14 December 1942

Eastern Front The German relieving attack toward Stalingrad is still making good progress. The airlift to the city today supplies 180 tons. This is the largest effort which will be managed on any day during the siege.
Libya The El Agheila line is attacked by 7th Armored Division while the New Zealanders attempt an outflanking maneuver.
New Guinea Japanese reinforcements land about 30 miles west of Gona and begin to march along the coast toward the Australians' flank. There are renewed US attacks on Buna village which is taken easily after a brief Japanese resistance. The far tougher obstacle of the Buna Government Station still remains in Japanese hands.
Madagascar Eden and de Gaulle agree that the administration of the island should be handed over to the Free French. General le Gentilhomme will be High Commissioner.

15-25 December 1942

Solomons In addition to their usual duties Tanaka's flotilla carries out several missions to help build an airfield on Munda (New Georgia) to support the operation on Guadalcanal.

16 December 1942

Eastern Front The Soviets begin the next phase (*Saturn*) of their winter offensive even though the German drive toward Stalingrad is still going forward slowly. The Soviet blow falls on the Italian Eighth Army on the middle Don and this force is almost immediately shattered. As in the Soviet offensive in November, there are very few German units in the immediate area of the attacks. There are also Soviet attacks along the Chir against Army Detachment Hollidt. The German relieving attack toward Stalingrad is still going well but the Soviet breakthrough to the north threatens the sort of wide

Above: Italian troops suffer the effects of a Russian winter: the cold can almost be felt!

encirclement that has been particularly worrying to Manstein for the past few weeks.
Libya Because of the progress of the New Zealanders to their rear, the Axis force at El Agheila splits into small groups to break away.
Guadalcanal The Tokyo Express is again in operation. The destroyer *Kagero* is damaged by US dive bombers. On land the US forces begin to move on Mount Austen.
Burma In the Arakan the British forces have assembled two brigades to attack the Japanese lines between Maungdaw and Buthidaung, but the Japanese forces pull out before the blow can fall. They move south to a shorter, more defensible line between Gwedauk and Kondan.

17 December 1942

Eastern Front The Volga freezes over and the Soviets are able to send supplies easily to Sixty-second Army on the west bank in Stalingrad. This has been difficult for the past few weeks because of fast-moving blocks of ice floating down river. Hoth's attacks to relieve the city are still going fairly well, with his leading tank units now having reached the Aksai River.
Libya Rommel leaves a rearguard to cover his main forces while they consolidate at Buerat.
Tunisia There are heavy US air attacks on Tunis and Gabes and other German air bases.

18 December 1942

New Guinea Cape Endiadere, east of Buna, is taken by the Allies. Australian forces are now leading the attack here, and with newly arrived tank support they are able to come to grips with the Japanese defenses on more favourable terms than in the recent past. The battle continues.
Libya There is a brisk engagement at Nofilia.

19 December 1942

Eastern Front The Soviets take Kontemirovka. The Italian Eighth Army has practically ceased to exist as a fighting formation. Owing to the success of this attack, Paulus is ordered by Manstein to attempt a breakout immediately, but he refuses. The chief of staff of Sixth Army, General Schmidt, an ardent Nazi, is instrumental in bringing about this decision. General Hoth's attacks to relieve the city are gradually making less and less ground. They are now being held near the Myshkova River.
Guadalcanal The American forces on Mount Austen meet heavy resistance.

20 December 1942

Eastern Front The Soviets claim to have reached nearly to Millerovo, 70 miles northeast of Voroshilovgrad. The Rostov-Voronezh railroad has been cut and severe pressure is now being brought to bear on Army Detachment Hollidt, the northern wing of Manstein's force. Manstein tries to get Zeitzler at OKH to arrange for a breakout by Paulus. Zeitzler gives little help and Paulus now pleads that he is too short of fuel to attempt it in any case. There is some truth to this argument, but not to make some sort of effort is senseless.

21 December 1942

Eastern Front The Red Army makes a deep advance with the troops of General Golikov's Voronezh Front. Manstein appeals to Hitler to order Paulus to break out, but Hitler quotes Paulus' reports of fuel shortages and refuses.
Burma The British forces advancing toward Akyab capture Alethangyaw.

22 December 1942

Eastern Front The Soviet advances are very rapid and they retake several towns, including Morozovsk, Nikolkoe and Fydorovka.
Tunisia The British V Corps of First Army begins an attack just north of Medjez el Bab. The fiercest fighting centers around Longstop Hill. There is very heavy rain which does much to hinder the attack.
Burma General Lloyd orders his 47th Brigade to advance down both sides of the Mayu Peninsula while the 123rd Brigade is to send the bulk of its force toward Rathedaung. A small detachment is to move farther inland in the direction of Kyauktaw. These dispositions are less than ideal because of the dispersion they bring about.

23 December 1942

Eastern Front While Manstein has been fighting to have Paulus ordered to break out, Hoth has been dutifully battling his way forward. Today, however, the Soviet defense line on the Myshkova River finally wears Hoth's attacks to a halt. The troops in Stalingrad can hear the fighting but it comes no closer.

Below: Panzer Mark IV tanks, armed with long-barreled 7.5cm main gun, stand guard close to Tunis, December 1942.

24 December 1942

Eastern Front The Soviets drive Hoth back. Despite stubborn resistance Generalovsky is taken. In Stalingrad fresh forces attached to Sixty-second Army retake the Red October Factory.

French North Africa Admiral Darlan is shot in his office by a fanatic called Bonnier de la Chapelle who supports both royalist and Gaullist politics.

The fighting in Tunisia continues. Although Longstop is once again taken by a British Guards battalion, Eisenhower, Anderson and Allfrey (commanding V Corps) decide to end their attacks for the moment.

New Guinea The Allied forces break into the new defensive positions of the Japanese near Buna, but the casualties are heavy and the last serviceable tanks of the small group which has been in support for the last few days are also lost.

Burma Japanese advances in two areas of the Chin Hills are repelled by Allied troops.

25 December 1942

Libya The Axis garrison of Sirte, already outflanked, withdraws because of pressure to the front.

New Britain The Japanese base at Rabaul is attacked by bombers from Guadalcanal, causing damage to harbor installations.

Tunisia The German forces retake Longstop Hill. There is continued sporadic activity for the next few days, but this soon dies down with bad weather and supply problems hindering both sides.

Burma Patrols from the 123rd Brigade reach Rathedaung and report that the Japanese have moved out. In fact this is not the case and Japanese reinforcements are on their way.

26 December 1942

Eastern Front Manstein's forces are in full retreat south of the Don and the Soviet advance nears Kotelnikovo.

France, Politics General Giraud is chosen as French high commissioner for North Africa. Darlan's assassin is executed.

27 December 1942

Guadalcanal The US attacks on Mount Austen are restarted. The attacking troops, from the 132nd Infantry Regiment, lose heavily and are brought to a halt despite considerable artillery preparation.

Eastern Front As well as their continuing advance on the Stalingrad fronts, the Soviets are also on the move in the Caucasus, especially around Nalchik where there are six armies attacking under the command of Maslennikov and Tyulenev. Von Kleist is beginning to withdraw, fearful of being cut off if the advance of the Stalingrad armies reaches Rostov to the north.

Under German auspices the captured General Vlasov forms the Smolensk Committee to organize Russian opponents of Stalin. This body will later become known as the Liberation Army. The Germans give little real support to Vlasov and fail to understand his position as both a patriotic Russian and an opponent of Stalinism.

27-28 December 1942

Burma Part of the 123rd Indian Brigade tries to occupy Rathedaung but is thrown back by the recently reinforced Japanese forces there.

28 December 1942

Atomic Research Roosevelt confirms the policy of noncooperation with the British that his advisers have been recommending. He orders that no information should be given to the British unless it happens to be in an area in which British scientists are directly involved. Among the American worries is the question of the postwar peaceful use of atomic energy and the fear that the British may be too concerned with using American research for this. That one of the leading British workers is also research director for a major British chemical and industrial company only confirms this fear.

The British are upset at Roosevelt's decision feeling that it contradicts former agreements and does not recognize the important early work done by the British. Churchill raises the matter with Hopkins at the Casablanca conference and again with Roosevelt in Washington in May. (*See* 20 July for further developments).

Vichy, Politics In a broadcast Pétain describes the Free French leaders as having betrayed French Africa to the British and Americans.

29 December 1942

Eastern Front The Soviets recapture Kotelnikovo after a bitter fight and make other gains all along the front.

Libya The advance elements of Eighth Army come to a halt before the Axis' Buerat position.

30 December 1942

Eastern Front The Soviets retake Remontnoe, 40 miles northwest of Elista.

30-31 December 1942

Battle of the Barents Sea The Germans send heavy surface ships to try to intercept the Arctic convoy JW-51B. On 30 December Admiral Kummetz sets out from north Norway with the pocket battleship *Lützow* and the heavy cruiser *Admiral Hipper* with an escort of six destroyers. The British escorts for the convoy are in three groups. Captain Sherbrooke commands the close escort of seven destroyers and five other warships. Admiral Burnett leads a close-covering force of two light cruisers and two destroyers. Admiral Fraser is also at sea with the battleship *Anson* and an escort, but is forbidden to risk air attack near Norway and will not take part in the action.

On 31 December the *Hipper* and the *Lützow* move toward the convoy on separate courses. *Hipper* approaches three times and *Lützow* twice, but Sherbrooke's destroyers use smokescreens and the threat of torpedo attack to keep the German ships ineffective at a distance. One British destroyer is sunk and one badly damaged. Burnett's cruisers are able to intervene during the *Hipper*'s third approach, damaging the German ship and sinking one destroyer. After this the German force withdraws. The German leaders have been hampered by instructions not to risk serious damage to their ships and have, therefore, shown a disastrous lack of initiative despite their overwhelming strength. The enterprise with which the British ships have been handled has done the rest.

31 December 1942

Eastern Front Troops of the Soviet Fifth Shock Army, driving southwest from Nizhne Chirskaya, expel the Germans from Tormosin. Army Detachment Hollidt can do little to halt such strong attacks.

Guadalcanal The Japanese High Command decide to evacuate the island. The orders are issued on 4 January.

Libya A Free French force under the command of General Leclerc advances from Chad into the South Fezzan. They will continue to move north and join up with Eighth Army during January 1943.

Below: Maj General Alexander Vandegrift, commander of the US 1st Marine Division on Guadalcanal, August-December 1942.

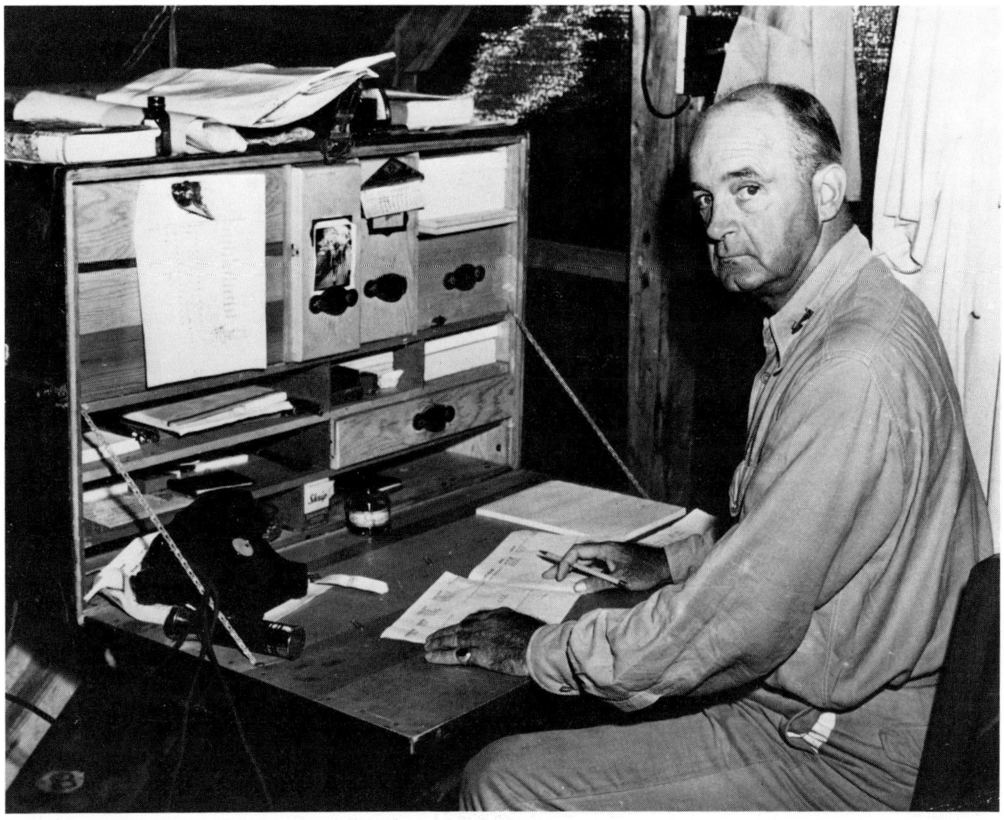

383

1943

January 1943

Battle of the Atlantic The German U-Boat fleet now has 212 operational boats and a further 181 on training or trials missions. This month the Allied shipping losses are fairly moderate at 50 ships of 261,400 tons of which total submarines account for 37 ships of 203,100 tons. Bad weather in the Atlantic and effective evasive routing by the convoy authorities helps keep the losses down. One successful action for the Germans is against the tanker convoy TM-1 which loses seven of its nine ships in attacks just to the south of the Azores. Radar failures hamper the escort. At the end of the month Liberators in Coastal Command service begin to be fitted with 10-centimeter ASV radar. This offers an enormous improvement in performance over the earlier types and cannot be detected by the search receivers presently fitted in the U-Boats. It is similar to the H2S radar entering service with the strategic bomber forces.
Allied Air Operations The Allied air offensive is directed this month principally against the German U-Boat bases and production centers. Among the manufacturing towns attacked are Essen, Cologne and Dusseldorf. The first USAAF raid on Germany is against Wilhelmshaven on 27 January. Targets in France for the USAAF include St Nazaire and Brest. Altogether the Americans drop 547 tons of bombs. The British effort is still much greater. The RAF drops more than 1000 tons in four raids on Lorient alone. The navigational aid H2S is used for the first time over Hamburg on 30/31 January. There is also the first daytime raid on Berlin, by a force of RAF Mosquitoes on the 30th. The Casablanca Directive sets forth future bombing policy for both the British and American strategic forces.

The average daily availability of Bomber Command aircraft is now about 515 compared with about 500 a year before. The quality of the force has much improved. There are now 178 Lancasters and 104 Halifaxes in the heavy bomber force and 17 Mosquitoes are also in service. The number of Wellingtons is now down to 128. The navigational aids, Gee, Oboe and H2S are all available and will be improved. General Eaker's Eighth Air Force has about 80 bombers and is gradually gaining experience.

Below: The communist leader Josip Broz (Tito) stands in the center of these Yugoslav partisans.

Previous page: The landings at Salerno, September 1943. *Above:* Luftwaffe mechanics prepare a reconnaissance aircraft.

January-April 1943

Yugoslavia, Resistance The German forces mount their fourth offensive against Tito's Partisans. There are actions throughout Hercegovina, Montenegro and in Dalmatia. Although Tito's forces lose heavily and there is much destruction of the homes and livelihood of his supporters, the Partisans remain in the fight.

New Guinea Heavy attacks against the Japanese positions at Buna continue. Some of the garrison withdraw as the situation becomes hopeless.

1 January 1943

Eastern Front After vicious street fighting the Soviets recapture Velikiye Luki in the central sector. Other important positions taken include Elista and Chikola.

2 January 1943

New Guinea Troops from Eichelberger's I Corps storm the Japanese posts at Buna. Fighting continues, however, around Sananada.
Guadalcanal Once again the Americans mount a formal attack on the Japanese positions on Mount Austen. Some progress is made but the Gifu strongpoint remains in Japanese hands.

3 January 1943

Eastern Front The Soviet Caucasus offensive is now well under way. Mozdok and Malgobek are both retaken by troops from Fifty-eighth and Forty-fourth Armies. Farther north Manstein is fighting hard to keep the Soviets from cutting Kleist off in the Caucasus and at Stalingrad Sixth Army continues to suffer. The inadequate attempts to ferry supplies in by air are proving very costly indeed and the route to Stalingrad is littered with wrecked German transport aircraft.

4 January 1943

Eastern Front The Soviet advance goes on. They capture Nalchik in the Caucasus and Chernyshkovskiy on the River Chir.
New Georgia The Japanese base at Munda is bombarded by the US TF 67 (Admiral Ainsworth). A second group of cruisers and des-

troyers is in support. Proximity fuses for AA ammunition are used for the first time by one of the bombarding vessels.

5 January 1943

Tunisia British forces make small gains near Djebel Azzag west of Mateur.
Eastern Front The Russians capture Prokhladny in the Caucasus and consolidate their gains farther north by taking Morozovsk and Tsimlyansk.
Guadalcanal The Americans are unaware that the Japanese are beginning to execute their planned withdrawal. The Japanese stand on Mount Austen continues despite the growing American strength.
Tunisia The US Fifth Army led by General Clark becomes operational.

6 January 1943

German Command Following the fiasco of the attack on the convoy JW-51B (*see* 30-31 December 1942), Admiral Raeder resigns his post as Commander in Chief of the navy.

7 January 1943

Guadalcanal The Americans send fresh troops against Mount Austen and begin to make new advances.
New Guinea A Japanese convoy lands supplies and reinforcements at Lae despite air attacks.

8 January 1943

Eastern Front Rokossovsky, commanding the Don Front Armies besieging Stalingrad, and Voronov, the Stavka representative, issue a summons to surrender to the Germans. Paulus' sense of resistance is stiffened by his chief of staff, Schimdt, a convinced Nazi, and he ignores the demand. In terms of manpower the German defenders are if anything superior, but the Russians are well fed and clothed and have adequate supplies of fuel and ammunition. The Germans have virtually nothing and are already weakened by hunger and cold. Farther south Zimovniki falls to Russian attack.
Madagascar The Free French take over the administration of the island.

9 January 1943

New Guinea The Australian 17th Brigade is airlifted to Wau to establish a forward base for the next phase of the Allied offensive which will take place when the capture of Buna and Sanananda is achieved and consolidated. In that sector the Americans take Tarakena village but are held up when they try to advance nearer to Sanananda.

10 January 1943

Eastern Front The Russians begin an offensive all round Stalingrad. They nominally have seven armies and the Germans the equivalent of two, but Russian armies are only the same size as a German corps. Sixty-second and Sixty-fourth on the east and southeast of the circle are particularly under strength. All the Russian forces move to the attack but the main effort is by Sixty-fifth and Twenty-first Armies to the west. The attack goes in after the usual fierce barrage and the Germans are soon on the retreat.
Guadalcanal An American offensive begins, accompanied by heavy air and artillery bombardments. The Gifu strongpoint is again attacked by the 35th Infantry Regiment. The Americans now have well over 50,000 men on Guadalcanal and the Japanese less than 15,000, all of whom are desperately short of food. During the night eight Japanese destroyers attempt to bring supplies. One is damaged by PT boats.
New Guinea The American forces make some progress in their drive on Sanananda and make a smaller advance near Tarakena.

11 January 1943

Eastern Front The siege of Leningrad is partially broken. A narrow corridor is opened south of Lake Ladoga by concerted attacks by the Leningrad garrison and the troops of the Volkhov Front.

In the Caucasus the Russians take Georgivesk, Pyatigorsk and Mineralnye Vody. Slightly farther north Kuberle, on the railroad line from Zimovniki to Proletarskaya, also falls.
Guadalcanal The Americans take the Japanese 'Sea Horse' position but the Gifu strongpoint continues to hold out.

12 January 1943

Aleutians Amchitka Island is occupied by a small American force (General Jones), but the destroyer *Worden* is lost in an accident.
New Guinea The Japanese positions north and west of Gona are attacked by Australian infantry and tanks.
Eastern Front The Soviet Voronezh and Bryansk Fronts (Generals Golikov and Reiter) attack the Hungarian Second and the German Second Army respectively. The Hungarian defenses are quickly shattered and the Russians are soon driving toward Kharkov. Farther south, Manstein's Army Group Don is also under heavy pressure as the Russians attempt to cut off the Caucasus by an advance to Rostov. Even more dangerous for the Germans is the possibility that the Russians may be able to drive south from around Kharkov, cutting off both Manstein and Kleist. Almost all the supplies for these German units have to come through Dnepropetrovsk.

13 January 1943

Eastern Front The Soviet attacks in the Stalingrad sector are making good progress and reach the Rossoshka River late in the day.
Guadalcanal The Americans develop their offensive farther, advancing westward along the north coast as well as attacking parallel to this advance farther inland.
New Guinea The American General Eichelberger takes overall command of the fighting troops.

14 January 1943

Libya and Tunisia The personnel of 21st Panzer Division are withdrawn from Rommel's defense line and are sent to Gabes to re-equip. They are to be used to defend Tunisia from the western attack.
Eastern Front The Soviets capture Pitomnik airfield, the larger of the two which have been held by the Germans in Stalingrad. The Soviet forces have advanced across the Chervlennaya and Rossoshka Rivers. On the Voronezh Front, the Red Army advance continues but could be more forceful if more troops were available. The sacrifices of Sixth Army are not, therefore, entirely valueless.
Guadalcanal A small group of Japanese reinforcements lands near Cape Esperance to prepare positions in that area to cover the planned evacuation.

14-24 January 1943

Allied Planning Churchill and Roosevelt meet in Casablanca accompanied by their Chiefs of Staff. There is some danger of a split between the British and Americans. The Americans feel, with some justice, that the British are doing too little against the Japanese, and the British believe, also with reason, that the Americans are gradually abandoning their commitment to the Germany-first policy. After several days' dis-

Below: Churchill holds court in North Africa, along with the major commanders of both the British and American armed forces.

Above: Men of the US Army 1st Ranger Battalion cross hilly terrain in Tunisia, January 1943.

cussion between the Chiefs of Staff, these differences are smoothed over and broad guidelines agreed. The fact that the agreement is produced principally by the Chiefs of Staff is important because the American military has felt previously that Churchill has been able to convince Roosevelt to adopt policies with which they have not been in full agreement (Torch is the best example). The U-Boat offensive and supplies for Russia are now to have first priority and preparations for a landing in Europe are to be continued but this is unlikely to take place before 1944. The operations in the Pacific are to continue also and once North Africa is cleared the forces there are to move on to Sicily and Italy rather than be idle. The attack on Germany is also to be carried on by strategic bombing and an important directive ordering this is issued. At a press conference on 24 January Roosevelt announces that the Allies are fighting for the 'unconditional surrender' of Germany, Italy and Japan and this stand is immediately endorsed by Churchill. This policy has since been criticized as perhaps having helped prolong the war. This is uncertain but it is clear that neither leader has at this stage given much thought to considering the implications of the idea. The main failing of the conference is not at first apparent. All the plans are based on false estimates of the available quantity of shipping. Shipping shortages very soon affect British plans for Burma and later this is also a problem for Mediterranean operations.

15 January 1943

Libya Montgomery is now ready to advance again and the Germans are quickly forced to retire from the Buerat position.

16 January 1943

Eastern Front There is continuous heavy fighting in all sectors. In the Caucasus, Kleist's Army Group A continues to pull back in good order. Manstein is still fighting to defend Rostov, and in the north the Russians continue to try to clear and widen the supply route to Leningrad. This route is nowhere wider than six miles and it is so much under German fire that it becomes known as the 'corridor of death.' At Stalingrad the Germans now hold only about 250 square miles of territory, about half as much as five days ago.

Guadalcanal A new phase of American attacks begins. The advance goes west and southwest of the American perimeter. Japanese positions overlooking the upper part of the Matanikau River are captured.

New Guinea In converging attacks near Sanananda the American 163rd Infantry Regiment and the Australian 18th Brigade both make progress.

17 January 1943

Eastern Front Again there are Russian gains along the front from Orel to the Caucasus. Millerovo and Zimovniki are captured. Around Stalingrad there is a slight lull as the Russians regroup for the final push.

New Guinea The Australians penetrate the Japanese position at Sanananda but the Japanese continue to resist here and against the Americans at Giruwa.

18 January 1943

Eastern Front The Russians succeed in clearing the supply corridor into Leningrad but can do nothing to extend it. In the Caucasus they take Cherkessk and Divnoe (70 miles east of Elista).

Burma Troops from 14th Indian Division attack the Japanese positions at Donbaik in the Arakan without success.

Tunisia Tiger tanks are used for the first time in this theater at Bou Arada. Neither the British nor the Americans have anything which can face them on equal terms.

18-19 January 1943

Aleutians Two American cruisers and four destroyers bombard Attu Island.

19 January 1943

Eastern Front The Russian offensive on the Voronezh Front continues to make rapid progress. Valuyki and Urazavo are captured, while in the rear a pocket of Hungarian troops are driven from Ostrogozhsk. So far the Russians have taken more than 50,000 prisoners on this front but only 2500 are German.

New Guinea General Yamagata orders his forces to pull out of Sanananda but fierce fighting continues.

Libya Eighth Army's offensive continues. Tarhuna is captured and the German defense line between there and the sea is outflanked.

20 January 1943

Eastern Front Army Group A is forced back all along its lines and the Soviets take Nevinnomyssk and Proletarskaya.

Below: Map showing the Russian counterattack, November 1942-March 1943.

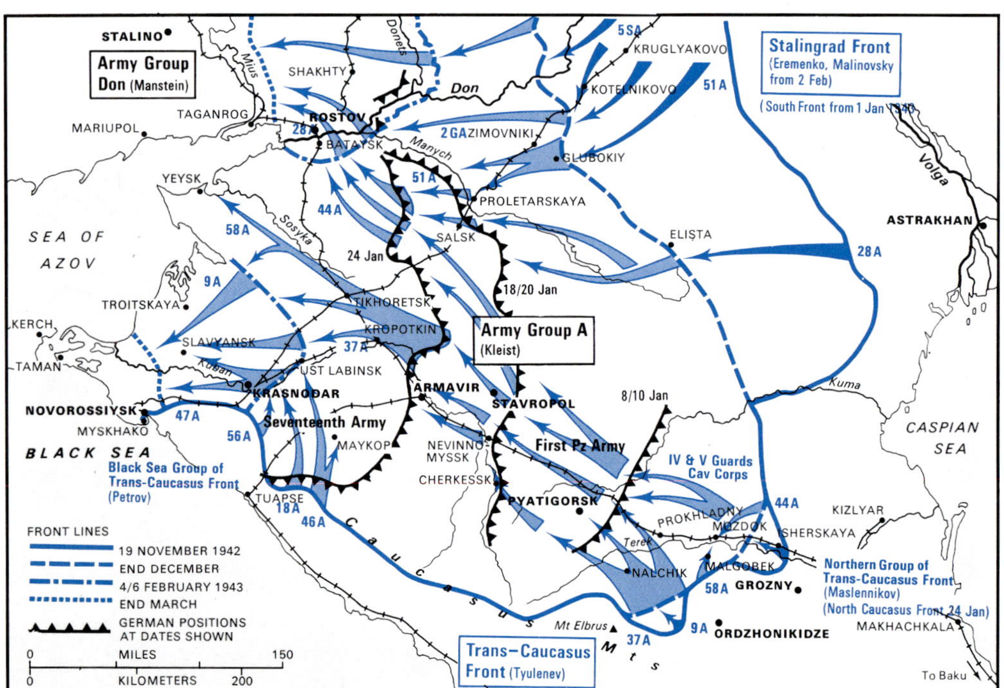

Guadalcanal The Japanese resistance on Mount Austen weakens. The garrison of the Gifu strongpoint has lost heavily to artillery fire.
Libya Troops from 51st Highland Division take Homs as the Germans fall back.

21 January 1943

Allied Strategic Bombing The Casablanca Directive is issued to the British and American strategic bombing forces in Europe by the Combined Chiefs of Staff. It sets out the priorities for the continuing Allied attacks. Most of the reasoning is in line with the precision bombing ideas of the American leaders. As yet the US Air Forces have too few resources to carry out the full scheme and RAF Bomber Command as a whole is not able to attack with enough accuracy. The RAF Command will continue its area of bombing policy, in line with the views of its Commander in Chief Sir Arthur Harris.
Eastern Front The Soviets recapture Voroshilovsk between Stavropol and Armavir. In Stalingrad the Germans lose Gumrak Airport and are now completely cut off.
New Guinea The Japanese resistance at Sananda and Giruwa is now almost completely overcome, and the Australians and Americans have only a few pockets left to wipe out.

22 January 1943

Eastern Front The final phase of the Red Army assault on Stalingrad begins characteristically with a massive bombardment followed by infantry attacks.

In the Caucasus, Salsk falls to the Russians.
Guadalcanal The American attacks are renewed and begin to make progress, especially toward Kokumbona. The Japanese fight well but the American aircraft, artillery and naval forces combine in a fierce and telling bombardment.
Libya The retreating German forces pull out of Tripoli after evacuating large quantities of stores and destroying many of the port installations.
New Guinea The last Japanese are cleared from Papua by Allied forces. The Japanese have lost about 7000 killed in the campaign, and the Allies about half this number.

23 January 1943

Libya Eighth Army enters Tripoli and is able to start using the port by the end of the month.
Eastern Front Golikov's forces try to extend the front of their advance northward by attacking Voronezh with increased strength.

Armavir in the Caucasus is taken by the Soviet forces.
Guadalcanal The Americans begin to make more rapid gains but fail to realize that this is mainly because of Japanese withdrawals toward the Cape Esperance position. The Gifu strongpoint finally falls to the Americans.

24 January 1943

Eastern Front Manstein asks Hitler's permission to order Paulus to surrender since it has now become clear that the mobile forces of Army Group A will be able to escape from the Caucasus whatever happens at Stalingrad. Permission for the surrender is refused. Farther west, troops from Vatutin's Southwest Front capture Starobelsk.
Solomons A US naval task force attacks Kolombangara Island in the New Georgia group.

Above: US reinforcements arrive in Guadalcanal, January 1943. The campaign is almost over, the Japanese defeated.

On Guadalcanal the Americans push forward to the west of Kokumbona.

25 January 1943

Tunisia American forces advance to Maknassy, threatening Sfax and Gabes.
Eastern Front The attacking Russian forces meet in the middle of Stalingrad. There are two pockets of German resistance remaining, holding 36 square miles in all.

Farther north, Voronezh also falls to the Russians.

26 January 1943

Libya and Tunisia After a series of quarrels with the Italian High Command, to whom he is nominally responsible, Rommel is told that he is to be relieved by the Italian General Messe. Rommel, however, does not hand over the command at this stage.

27 January 1943

Allied Air Operations Fifty-five US bombers raid Wilhelmshaven, losing three of their num-

Below: A soldier of the Argyll and Sutherland Highlanders takes a well-earned smoke break, Tunisia, January 1943.

ber but claiming to have shot down 22 German planes. This is the first raid by the USAAF over a German target; previously they have been allocated easier objectives in France while they gained experience.

The American bomber leaders believe that their Fortress and Liberator aircraft will be able to defend themselves in unescorted daylight missions over Germany and that they can bomb specific industrial targets with considerable and damaging accuracy. The fortunate results of this first raid help to confirm these erroneous beliefs for the moment.

28 January 1943

Eastern Front The Soviets take Kastornoye east of Voronezh, thereby ensuring a detachment of German Second Army is cut off.

Germany, Home Front A decree for the further mobilization of civilian men and women is issued by Sauckel, the Director-General of Labor.

New Guinea The Japanese carry out an unsuccessful attack on the detachment of the Australian 3rd Division at Wau.

29 January 1943

Germany and Occupied Europe, Home Front The Austrian Ernst Kaltenbrunner is appointed to head the SD. (The previous chief was Heydrich, assassinated in June 1942 – see above).

Eastern Front The Russians continue their advances on all the southern fronts. Kropotkin in the Caucasus and Novy Oskol north of Valuyki are captured.

29-30 January 1943

Solomons The US TF 18 (Admiral Giffen), covering a supply operation to Guadalcanal, is attacked by Japanese aircraft off Rennel Island and the heavy cruiser *Chicago* is sunk.

Below: Russian engineers cut the wire around a German strongpoint on the Eastern Front, early 1943. Mortar bombs explode in the background.

30 January 1943

Eastern Front The Russians take Tikhoretsk in the Caucasus and clear the Maykop oilfields. Seventeenth Army in the Kuban Peninsula is now becoming separated from First Panzer Army which is managing to retreat toward Rostov.

In Stalingrad the Russians find Paulus' Headquarters in the southern pocket and begin to surround them. Paulus is created Field Marshal by Hitler.

Germany, Home Front It is the tenth anniversary of Hitler's régime and special speeches are made in Berlin by Goebbels and Goering to mark the occasion. The RAF also mark the occasion by mounting the first daylight raid on Berlin by a group of Mosquito bombers whose attacks are timed to coincide with the speeches.

German Command Doenitz is appointed as Commander in Chief of the German navy.

Guadalcanal The US advance continues but the Japanese resistance, especially along the River Bonegi, is very heavy.

Tunisia The re-equipped German 21st Panzer Division makes easy gains around Faid, throwing back inexperienced French and American troops.

France, Home Front The Vichy régime begins the formation of a paramilitary organization called the Milice, which rapidly acquires an odious reputation. Under the command of Joseph Darnand the Milice works closely alongside the German Gestapo.

31 January 1943

Italian Command Marshal Cavallero resigns and General Ambrosio takes over as Chief of the Italian General Staff.

Eastern Front Paulus surrenders himself and the southern pocket of Germans in Stalingrad. General Strecker's group still holds out.

February 1943

Battle of the Atlantic Allied shipping losses increase to 73 ships of 403,100 tons in all theaters. Submarines sink 63 ships of 359,300 tons. There are now about 100 U-Boats at sea in the Atlantic at any one time. In the month's operations the Germans lose 19 vessels. During the month the first success is recorded for the new 10cm radar. However, Coastal Command has only one squadron of modified VLR Liberator bombers for the main convoy routes; although Bomber Command makes many attacks on U-Boat pens, this is not an adequate substitute for the transfer of aircraft to maritime service since the pens can not be penetrated with the bombs available at this time. During the month Air Marshal Slessor takes command of RAF Coastal Command (*See* 4-9 and 21-25 February for typical convoy actions).

Allied Air Operations Targets for the Allied bomber offensive are again mostly connected with the U-Boat war. Lorient and St Nazaire are most heavily raided and other targets include Hamburg, Bremen and Wilhelmshaven. Allied bombers based in the Mediterranean attack Turin, Spezia, Milan, Palermo and Naples.

1 February 1943

Eastern Front The Russians capture Svatovo between Kupyansk and Starobelsk as their drive toward Kharkov continues.

Guadalcanal An American force lands at Verahue near Cape Esperance, but despite this interference the Japanese evacuation begins. The Americans are aware of the Japanese naval activity but believe that it heralds a new offensive. Instead 5000 men are evacuated by a force of 20 destroyers, one of which is sunk by air attack.

Burma In the Arakan the British forces renew their attack on Donbaik but can make no progress.

2 February 1943

Eastern Front The last German troops in Stalingrad surrender. Of the approximately 280,000 Germans originally surrounded in the city, 90,000 are prisoners and about 40,000 have been evacuated, mostly seriously wounded. The Luftwaffe has lost 500 transport planes in the

Above: Field Marshal Paulus, commander of the encircled German troops at Stalingrad, surrenders to the Russians, 31 January 1943.

fruitless supply operation and other equipment losses have been huge. The Soviets later announce that they have removed 147,000 German and 47,000 Soviet corpses from the city for reburial. The prisoners are indifferently treated by the Russians, and only 5000 ever return to Germany, the last in 1955. On the Russian side much of the credit for the success of the operations in the city must go to Chuikov for his forceful leadership and the street-fighting tactics he has developed. Zhukov's has been the dominant influence over the wider strategic plans.
Guadalcanal The Americans succeed in crossing the Bonegi River at the coast.
Mediterranean The British submarine *Turbulent* sinks an Italian tanker near Palermo thereby preventing essential fuel supplies reaching the Italian naval squadron based on Sicily.

3 February 1943

Eastern Front The Russians capture Kuschevka on the Soskya River 50 miles south of Rostov. In the drive to Kharkov, Kupyansk is taken.
Germany, Home Front The loss of Stalingrad is announced. Three days of national mourning begin on 4 February.
Guadalcanal The US forces consolidate their lines running inland from Tassafaronga. Patrols penetrate much nearer to Cape Esperance.

4 February 1943

Eastern Front The Russian advance continues on all fronts. Shcigny, 40 miles east of Kursk, is taken as is Kanevskaya, only 30 miles from the Sea of Azov to the east of Tikhoretsk. The German Seventeenth Army is now cut off in the Kuban and must be supplied by sea from the Crimea.
Libya and Tunisia The first units of the Eighth Army cross the border into Tunisia.
Guadalcanal A squadron of one cruiser and 22 destroyers led by Admiral Koyanagi manages to evacuate 5000 more Japanese troops from the island. Four ships are damaged by air attacks. On the ground the American 147th Regiment advances west of Tassafaronga.

4-9 February 1943

Battle of the Atlantic The convoy SC-118 is attacked by 20 U-Boats and loses 30 of its 63 ships. The convoy escorts sink three submarines and badly damage two more.

5 February 1943

Italy, Politics Mussolini dismisses Count Ciano from the Foreign Ministry and takes over responsibility for it himself.
Eastern Front The Russians take Stary Oskol and Izyum. In the Caucasus they make several landings successfully at Myoshako, but are driven off at Anopa.

6 February 1943

United States Command Europe and North Africa are separated in the US command structure. General Andrews is appointed to the new European Theater Command and General Eisenhower remains in charge in North Africa.
Eastern Front In the Caucasus the Russians reach Bataysk south of Rostov and capture Yeysk on the Sea of Azov. Lisichansk on the Donets also falls and the Russians cross the river farther upstream at Izyum and reach Barvenkovo. Manstein flies to see Hitler, who eventually agrees to allow a retreat behind the River Mius.

7 February 1943

Eastern Front The Russians take Azov at the mouth of the Don and in the Ukraine they also capture Kramatorsk just south of Slavyansk.
Guadalcanal The US 161st Regiment continues to lead the American advance but for the moment moving cautiously.

8 February 1943

Burma The first Chindit raid begins. This force, more properly called 77th Indian Brigade, is led by General Orde Wingate and its task is to penetrate behind enemy lines, causing damage and disruption. Above all the expedition is designed to demonstrate that the British and Indians can take on the Japanese in the jungle. The expedition begins at Imphal and sets out toward Tamu.
Eastern Front The Russians capture Kursk.

9 February 1943

Eastern Front The Russians take Belgorod and the small town of Shebekino to the southeast.
Guadalcanal The American 161st and 132nd regiments link up at Tenaro too late to stop the last Japanese forces leaving the island. The final 2000 men have been evacuated by 18 destroyers on 8 February.

In the campaign the Japanese have lost about 10,000 killed to the Americans' 1600. The losses in ships and planes have been about equal but in effect this favors the Americans. Strategically it has been a major Japanese defeat, but only a fraction of the Japanese army has been involved, and, judging by their resistance, the next American campaigns will be very hard indeed.

10 February 1943

Eastern Front The Russians capture Volchansk and Chuguyev only 20 miles east of Kharkov.

11 February 1943

Eastern Front Lozovaya falls to Vatutin's troops from the Southwest Front.

12 February 1943

Eastern Front The Soviet progress is still rapid. In the Caucasus they take Krasnodar. North and west of the Don Shakhty, Kommunarsk and Krasnoarmeskoye are all captured.

13 February 1943

Eastern Front The Soviets capture Novocherkassk.

14 February 1943

Tunisia The Axis forces begin a major attack on US II Corps positions west of Faid. The attacking troops are mostly from 10th and 21st Panzer Divisions from General von Arnim's Fifth Panzer Army. General Zeigler is in direct command. This attack is only begun after considerable high-level debate. Rommel is still

Below: Russian civilians begin to clear the rubble in the streets of Kursk after the liberation of the city, 8 February 1943.

Above: American infantry march into the Kasserine Pass, Tunisia, scene of bitter fighting in February 1943.

holding command of what is now known as First Italian Army and he and Arnim have both produced plans of attack. Rommel urges an aggressive attack toward Tébessa but Arnim's more limited plan is the one adopted at this stage. In the attack the inexperienced American forces around Sidi Bou Zid are given a vicious lesson.
Burma The Chindits cross the Chindwin in two groups at Auktaung and Tonhe. Wingate is leading the larger northern group.
Eastern Front The Russians capture Rostov and Voroshilovgrad and among other less important gains they take Drasny Sulin, north of Shakhty.

15 February 1943

Tunisia Rommel joins in the Axis attack, sending a detachment of 15th Panzer and some Italian armor against Gafsa which is taken. Most of Rommel's forces have had to be left in the Mareth line where the last of his rearguard is now arriving from Libya.

16 February 1943

Eastern Front After fierce fighting for several days, the Russians complete the capture of Kharkov when Hausser's II SS Panzer Corps are forced to withdraw despite an order from Hitler to hold on.
Tunisia Some of Montgomery's forward units capture Medenine on the approaches to the Mareth line.

17 February 1943

Tunisia Both von Arnim's and Rommel's attacks are making good progress. The northern wing is now approaching Sbeitla, having virtually destroyed two-thirds of US 1st Armored Division including two tank battalions. Rommel, to the south, enters Fériana. The limited attack that von Arnim envisaged has certainly come off: he diverts 10th Panzer Division toward Foundouk, which has in fact been abandoned, instead of pressing on vigorously toward Sbeitla. Having observed the weak American command and the understandable inexperience of the American troops, Rommel wants to be more ambitious. He puts his plans to the Italian and German High Command, who fail to make a quick decision.
Eastern Front Hitler flies to Manstein's Headquarters at Zaporozhye. He stays until 19 February and is eventually persuaded to agree to Manstein's plan for a major counterattack.

18 February 1943

Southwest Pacific A new American Army becomes operational, the Sixth, led by General Krueger.
Tunisia The Germans enter Sbeitla, already abandoned by the Allies. The debate over what to attempt next continues in the Axis camp.

18-19 February 1943

Aleutians A US Task Group (Admiral McMorris) with two cruisers and four destroyers shells Japanese positions on Attu Island.

19 February 1943

Solomons American reinforcements are being landed on Guadalcanal in preparation for the next move to the Russell Islands which are now reported abandoned by the Japanese.
Tunisia The next phase of the Axis attack begins. It is to be more ambitious than the first, but on the orders of the Italian High Command it is to be directed toward Le Kef, as the Allies in fact expect, and not Tébessa, as Rommel wishes. There are two wings to the assault. One, involving units of 15th Panzer, goes in from Kasserine toward Thala, and the other by 21st Panzer is already beyond Sbeitla aiming north for Sbiba. Rommel has managed to have Arnim ordered to put 10th Panzer under his command, but Arnim does not release the whole division and keeps back the Tiger battalion. The Allies have prepared to meet attacks in both passes, and as a result resistance is fairly strong.

20 February 1943

Eastern Front The Russians capture Pavlograd and are involved in fierce fighting at Krasnograd. They fail to realize that, although they are making rapid progress toward the Dniepr, they are in fact driving in to a salient which is strongly held on both flanks.
Tunisia The German attacks on Sbiba are held by the defending British and American units of which the most prominent is a British Guards Brigade. The attack through Kasserine Pass is held at first, but later the detachment of 15th Panzer is joined by units from 10th Panzer and the assault goes home. Later in the day the Germans drive to within 10 miles of Thala despite the resistance of the British 26th Armored Brigade which has come up.

The Allied command in the theater is reorganized and General Alexander is appointed to lead the newly constituted 18th Army Group.

21 February 1943

Solomons In Operation 'Cleanslate' troops from General Hester's 43rd Division occupy Banika and Pavuvu in the Russell Islands without resistance from the Japanese. By the end of the month there are 9000 American troops on these islands.

21-22 February 1943

Tunisia Rommel is at the front urging 10th Panzer on in its advance toward Thala, but the British armor holds out well during the day despite inferior tanks and by the evening the front is still three miles south of the town. A detachment of 15th Panzer is sent on a diversionary move toward Tébessa, but it too is held by units of the US 1st Armored Division. The Sbiba attack achieves nothing.

During the night a fierce fight develops in the British position before Thala in which both sides lose heavily. Also during the night an American artillery regiment (General Irwin) arrives in support after an 800-mile march from Oran accomplished in four days. At dawn this new support and a small counterattack by the British convince Rommel that the Allied reserves are arriving too quickly, and in the afternoon he pulls back. Rommel's attack has come very close to a major success, and it is interesting to speculate what might have been achieved if his own, less expected, plan had been chosen. The German troops have been astonished at the lavish scale of equipment of the American units they have overrun. Although the inexperience of the Americans has been very obvious, it is clear that they are learning very quickly, and already their artillery is formidably well organized. One factor in the battle which is to recur in other campaigns is the difference in the Allied performance from 22 February onward when the weather improves for flying. The British system for controlling air support has been well worked out and is adopted by the Americans from now on, generally with excellent results – another example of the Americans' ability to learn quickly from experience.

On the Axis side the operation has been hampered by divided command and the desert veterans of 15th and 21st Panzer Divisions have proved less able than usual in the unfamiliar mountain terrain. Rommel is certainly worn out and perhaps they are too.

21-25 February 1943

Battle of the Atlantic The convoy ON-166 is attacked and loses 14 ships of 85,000 tons. One U-Boat is sunk by escorts.

22 February 1943

Eastern Front Manstein's counteroffensive begins. However, in the salient the Russians continue to press forward, one unit even coming within 12 miles of Manstein's headquarters before running out of fuel. All the Russian units have advanced so quickly that they are very short of both fuel and ammunition. By brilliant handling of his reserves, Manstein has assembled considerable forces for the attack despite being outnumbered by about seven to one. First and Fourth Panzer Armies are to attack northward from a line to the west of Krasnoarmeskoye, and Group Kempf, including principally II SS Panzer Corps, comprising three full-strength panzer divisions, is to drive south from Krasnodar.

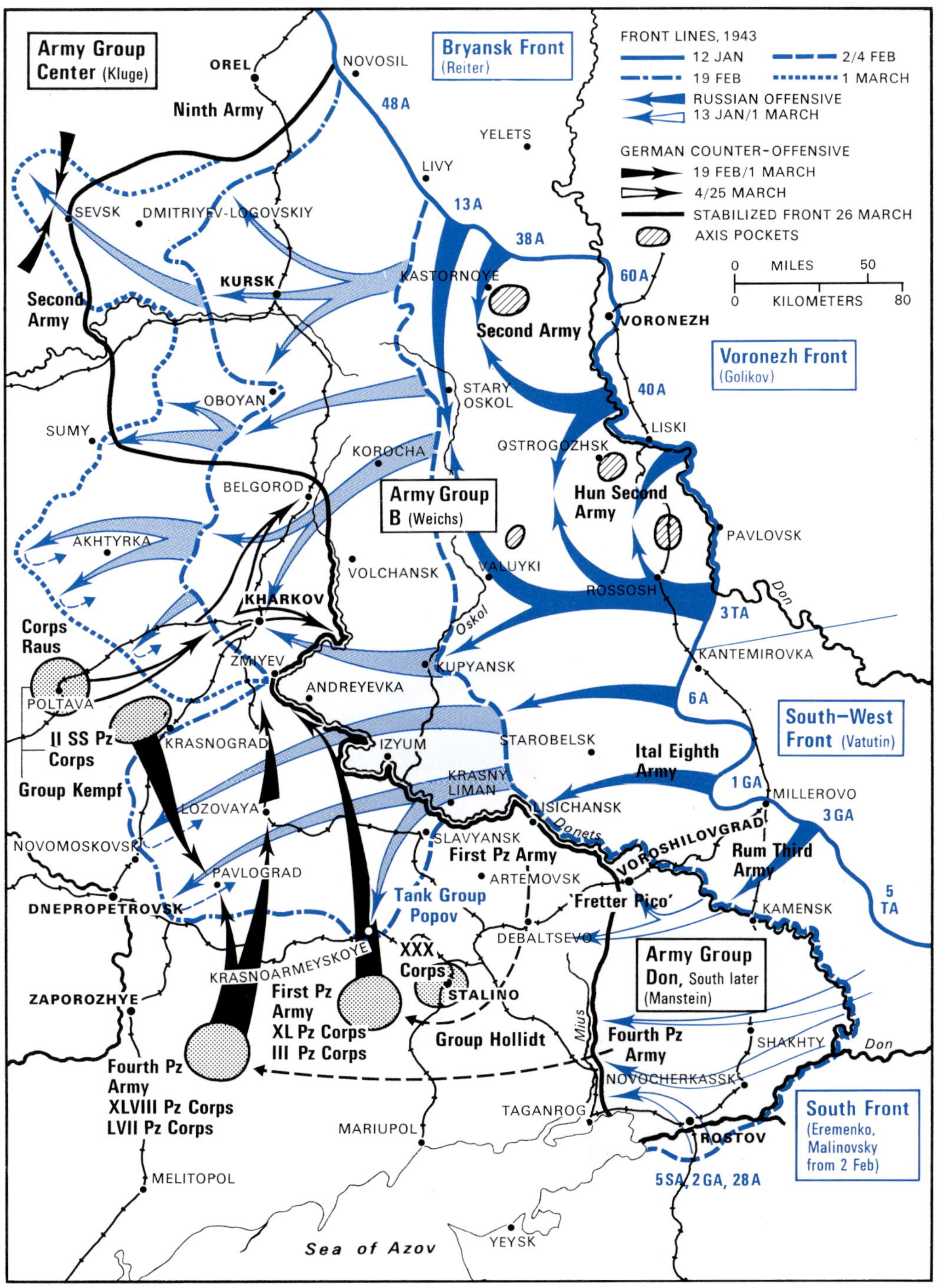

Above: General Heinz Guderian visits the Eastern Front, February 1943.
Left: Map showing the Russian attack toward Kharkov and the German counterattacks, January-March 1943.

23 February 1943

Eastern Front The Russians capture Sumy and Lebedin northeast of Kharkov, but farther south the German counteroffensive is beginning to make real progress, especially with the attack toward Barvenkovo by XLVIII Panzer Corps.

24 February 1943

Tunisia Rommel is appointed to command Army Group Afrika which is to include von Arnim's Fifth Panzer Army and the First Italian Army of General Messe. This is a remarkable choice because, although a single commander is clearly required, Kesselring for one has certainly detected Rommel's tiredness. On the ground the Germans are pulling back skillfully to the Eastern Dorsale, leaving behind booby traps.

25 February 1943

Eastern Front The Soviet attack in the Caucasus continues and east of Krasnodar Mingrelsk is captured.

26 February 1943

Tunisia Units from 10th and 21st Panzer Divisions under von Arnim's command attack the British positions at Medjez el Bab. This comes to nothing but prevents Rommel from concentrating as quickly as he wishes for an attack on Eighth Army before the Mareth line. At this stage Montgomery only has two divisions forward because his supply organization has not yet been completed. Montgomery knows that he is vulnerable and has only advanced so far as a diversionary move to help with the Kasserine operations.

27 February 1943

Eastern Front Manstein's forces attacking from the south are now on a line from Lozovaya to Kramatorsk.

28 February 1943

Norway, Resistance The Norsk Hydro power station near Ryukan is badly damaged by a sabotage team of Norwegian soldiers who have been parachuted in from Britain. This plant is known to be being used by the Germans to produce 'heavy water,' vital in atomic research.

March 1943

Battle of the Atlantic In later British Admiralty appreciations, the first 20 days of this month are described as the period when the Germans came closest to defeating the convoy system and winning the battle. The total Allied shipping loss for the whole month is 120 ships of 693,400 tons, of which submarines sink 627,400 tons. Of the 108 ships falling to submarines, 72 are in North Atlantic convoys. The German U-Boat fleet loses 15 boats but only six of these in convoy battles. The fiercest actions are around HX-229 and SC-122 (*see* 14-20 March). One problem for the Allied forces is the change in the German coding machine introduced on 8 March. By adding a fourth rotor to the standard Enigma machine the number of different settings is increased and the Germans hope that this will confirm the security of their communications. In fact the Allied coding services begin to operate as successfully as before after a brief delay. On the Allied side important developments are the reorganization of the slower north Atlantic convoys, shifting their terminus from New York to Halifax, and the return of the support groups to the Atlantic after their service with Operation Torch. The first operation by a support group is that around the convoys immediately after HX-229 and SC-122. By the end of the month there are five support groups available, including three escort carriers. A fourth escort carrier, *Dasher,* is lost in an explosion on the 27th.
Allied Air Operations RAF Bomber Command mounts 10 major attacks on targets in Germany, dropping more than 8000 tons of bombs. Berlin and Essen are heavily hit. The attacks on U-Boat facilities continue. The American targets include Vegesack and Wilhelmshaven while the RAF again hit St Nazaire very hard. The navigational aid 'Oboe' is used for the first time in the raid on Essen on 5-6 March when 442 aircraft attack with considerable effect. This raid marks the beginning of what Air Marshal Harris calls the 'Battle of the Ruhr.' This is the first of three 'battles' which Bomber Command will fight during the next year.

1 March 1943

Eastern Front The Russians are on the offensive north of Moscow and capture the important town of Demyansk.
Burma The Chindit force is making slower progress than has been hoped, partly because it has been concerned to find clearings for supply drops, when in fact it later discovers that it is possible to recover supplies dropped in jungle areas.

2 March 1943

Tunisia American forces re-enter Sbeitla and move on to Fériana. Farther north the British hold off German attacks.

2-4 March 1943

Battle of the Bismarck Sea A Japanese convoy of eight transports carrying 7000 troops of General Nakano's 51st Division, escorted by eight destroyers and led by Admiral Kimura is sighted en route from Rabaul to Lae. It is attacked by planes from General Kenney's Fifth Air Force on all three days, but especially on 3 March. PT-Boats join the attack on 4 March. All the transports and four destroyers and at least 3500 men are lost. In the air the Australians and Americans lose five planes but shoot down 25. The Japanese regard the battle as a major disaster and a serious setback to their prospects in New Guinea.

3 March 1943

Eastern Front The Red Army enters Rzhev as the Germans pull out after several days of fierce fighting. They also capture Lgov on the River Seim west of Kursk. The first phase of Manstein's counteroffensive is over in the south. The Russians have been pushed back behind the Donets everywhere south of Zmiyez, and have lost heavily. Their casualties include approximately 20,000 dead so far, but only 9000 prisoners. From this a deeper truth becomes evident – the Germans are now too short of manpower to hold the ring strongly when they do manage to encircle large Soviet units. Manstein still has the initiative, but there is little time before the spring thaw halts movement all along the front.
Tunisia There is a small skirmish between 15th Panzer and the British forces at Medenine as both sides try to scout the opposing lines.
Burma After a setback on 2 March, the southern Chindit group succeeds in cutting the Mandalay-Myitkyina railroad just north of Kyaikthin.

4 March 1943

Tunisia Montgomery is able to bring a second infantry division and an armored brigade up to Medenine where the British position is now fairly secure. A formal defense line has been established, backed by a strong antitank gun screen and including some of the new and very effective 17-pounder weapons. Intelligence has warned of the coming Axis attack, and this is confirmed when 10th and 21st Panzer are sighted moving up.
Eastern Front The Soviets take Olenino and Chertolino to the west of Rzhev and in the Kursk area they take Sevsk and Sudzha. The next phase of Manstein's offensive begins and now the objective is Kharkov and the Soviet troops nearby. Part of the SS Panzer Corps attacks westward from Poltava and units of Fourth Panzer Army attack northward from a line on the Berestovaya River west of Izyum.

5 March 1943

Strategic Bombing Bomber Command sends 443 aircraft to attack Essen. Fourteen aircraft are lost. This is the first attack of Air Marshal Harris' Battle of the Ruhr, and from now until 12 July 1943 when the battle ends there will be 43 major attacks mounted by Bomber Command in which 1000 aircraft will be lost. If nothing else, the Allied air offensive against Germany will be a drawn-out war of attrition.
Eastern Front Hoth's Fourth Panzer Army inflicts heavy casualties on three Russian Corps west of Izyum, but cannot continue its attack because the Donets is blocked by floating ice which prevents bridging operations.

Above: Field Marshal Erich von Manstein, instigator of the brilliant counterattack to retake Kharkov, March 1943.

6 March 1943

Eastern Front In the central sector the Russians capture Gzhatsk on the approaches to Vyazma south of Rzhev.
Tunisia In the morning the Germans mount a major attack on Medenine but are driven off. In the afternoon the attack is renewed half-heartedly but to no effect. The British and New Zealanders are surprised by the inept performance of their veteran opponents – for the antitank gunners it has been almost like shooting on a range. The Germans lose 50 of their tanks for absolutely nothing and now have only about 100 left. Rommel had not wanted to attack now and has little to do with the planning. He would have preferred to withdraw to Wadi Akarit.
United States, Home Front Roosevelt appoints a top-level committee to look into the manpower problems of US industry.
Burma The Chindits make a series of demolitions on the railroad between Nankan and Bongyaung.
Solomons The Americans send three cruisers and seven destroyers to bombard the Japanese airfields at Munda and Vila. Little damage is done to these targets, but two Japanese destroyers are met and sunk.

7 March 1943

Eastern Front Fourth Panzer Army has been shifted slightly westward and now begins to attack northeast from around Krasnograd, joining the newly formed but battle experienced SS Panzer Corps.

8 March 1943

Eastern Front The Soviets take Sychevka on the central sector between Rzhev and Vyazma.

9 March 1943

Tunisia Rommel leaves Africa for good. On his way home he meets Mussolini in Rome and Hitler in East Prussia but is not able to persuade either of them to withdraw from Africa.
Eastern Front Hausser's SS troops begin to attack Kharkov from the west and north. South of the city the small town of Taranovka is strongly held by the Soviet 25th Guards Division despite vicious attacks by LXVIII Panzer Corps.
New Guinea There are heavy Japanese attacks on Wau as a prelude to a spell of intensive effort in the air.

10 March 1943

Burma The Chindits are now operating in several columns and cross the Irrawaddy in two places, at Tagaung and Tigyaing farther north.
Tunisia The Germans organize an attack with air support on the Free French outpost at Ksar Rhilane southeast of Mareth but are beaten off by Leclerc's men.
United States Command Chennault is promoted and his command in China is to be enlarged and named Fourteenth Air Force.

11 March 1943

United States, Politics The Americans extend the Lend-Lease agreements for another year. Their value for the two years until the end of February 1943 is reported to have been $9,632,000,000.
Eastern Front The SS Corps enters Kharkov in force and penetrates to the center of the town after fierce fighting.

12 March 1943

Eastern Front While fighting continues in Kharkov, the Germans send a unit east to Chuguyev to cut off some of the Red Army forces south of the city. In the central sector the Germans are retreating on a wide front and the Soviets retake Vyazma without a fight.
Tunisia The 2nd New Zealand Division and the 8th Armored Brigade are secretly moved south from Medenine, and begin to concentrate west of Wilder's Gap in preparation for an outflanking move round the Mareth Line across the Dahar region.

14-20 March 1943

Battle of the Atlantic In a series of convoy battles, the largest during the war, 21 ships of 140,800 tons are sunk from the convoys SC-122 and HX-229. The slower SC convoy is sailing in front and gradually to two coalesce into one mass of about 100 ships. About 20 U-Boats out of a pack of 40 manage to make attacks and, despite the efforts of the escort, no U-Boats are sunk. The German intelligence service, B Dienst, has provided good information on the routes of these convoys.

15 March 1943

New Guinea The US Seventh Fleet (Admiral Carpender) is formed to control naval operations around the island.
Eastern Front The Gemans complete the conquest of Kharkov when the last Red Army defenders withdraw from the tractor factory. In the central sector the Soviets take Kholm and Zharkovskiy, respectively north and east of Velikiye Luki. The SS victory at Kharkov elevates them to a favorable new position, so pleased is Hitler with their performance.

Above: Brigadier Orde Wingate (center, in solar topee), the charismatic leader of the Chindits in Burma.

16-17 March 1943

Tunisia Eighth Army is involved in sharp skirmishes on the approaches to the Mareth Line as it clears the way for its coming full-dress attack.

17 March 1943

Burma The 123rd Indian Brigade is attacked by the Japanese just north of Rathedaung in the Arakan and is forced to fall back. General Koka leads the Japanese attack with units of 55th and 33rd Divisions being involved.

18 March 1943

Eastern Front Troops from the *Gross Deutschland* Division attack Belgorod in the last act of Manstein's offensive. In this phase the Soviets have lost 40,000 casualties and at least 600 tanks. The whole operation has been an unqualified technical success for the Germans, but cannot make up for their 1,000,000 dead since November 1942. As activity begins to die down all along the front in the mud of the spring thaw, German and Soviet attention begins to be drawn toward the Soviet salient around Kursk.
Tunisia General Patton's II US Corps takes Gafsa and pushes forward toward El Guettar.
Burma Wingate's column crosses the Irrawaddy south of Inywa, the last group to do so. The Japanese have now assembled considerable forces to hunt the Chindits and their operations are being increasingly circumscribed. In the Arakan the more regular British operations are not going well either. Htizwe falls to a pincer attack and on the Mayu Peninsula a British attack on Donbaik fails.

19 March 1943

Tunisia The New Zealand Corps begins to move off toward Ksar Rhilane.

20 March 1943

Tunisia The New Zealanders speed up their march, abandoning concealment, and reach the Tebaga Gap in the evening. During the night the main attack on the Mareth Line begins with a heavy bombardment of the positions of the Young Fascist Division near the coast, followed up rapidly by the assaulting infantry of 50th Division.

The Mareth Line is held by the usual mixture

Below: SS General Paul Hausser, divisional and corps commander on the Eastern Front.

Above: Italian soldiers, captured during the British assault on the well-defended Mareth Line in Tunisia, March 1943.

of German and Italian units with the 30 tanks of 15th Panzer in reserve. The Americans at Gafsa are being watched by 10th Panzer, and 21st Panzer is at Gabes in general reserve.

21 March 1943

Tunisia The New Zealanders at Tebaga are held up by a mixed Italian force. In the main attack by morning the British have managed to establish a small force across the natural antitank obstacle of Wadi Zigzaou, but ground conditions prevent any real buildup during the day.

22 March 1943

Tunisia Although the British have managed to reinforce their bridgehead over Wadi Zigzaou during the night, a counterattack by 15th Panzer causes heavy losses, effectively ending the attack there. At the Tebaga Gap 21st Panzer and 164th Light Divisions are more than enough to hold the New Zealanders.

Eastern Front The Soviets capture Durovo to the northeast of Smolensk.

23 March 1943

Tunisia For the moment the Germans halt the American advance near El Guettar, but 10th Panzer Division loses heavily in trying to exploit early successes. Already the American tactical performance is much improved. Montgomery decides to transfer his main attack to the Tebaga Gap and therefore sends 1st Armored Division and General Horrocks off to join the New Zealanders. This move is slowed by traffic problems.

24 March 1943

Burma The various Chindit columns join up between Baw and Pago, but Wingate is ordered to break off the operation and return to India. His forces split up into small groups and most succeed in reaching base by early April. One returns later via China. Losses have been heavy – about one-third of the force – but many lessons have been learned and the value to morale and propaganda has been high.

Tunisia Montgomery sends 4th Indian Division on a short outflanking move toward Ksar el Hallouf and then Beni Zelten. In difficult terrain their progress is too slow to affect the outcome of the battle, however.

25 March 1943

Tunisia By nightfall 1st Armored Division has nearly reached the Tebaga Gap. Von Arnim is worried about this attack and the threat from the Americans at Maknassy, and therefore begins to pull his German and Italian infantry out of the Mareth Line.

26 March 1943

Vichy, Politics Laval organizes a cabinet reshuffle to consolidate his power.

Tunisia Throughout the day the Axis forces in the Tebaga Gap are fiercely attacked from the air and on the ground. By the evening the German defenses have been worn practically to nothing and 1st Armored Division heads for El Hamma by the light of the moon.

Bering Sea Admiral McMorris' squadron of two cruisers and four destroyers meets a considerably superior Japanese force of four cruisers and five destroyers (Admiral Hosogaya) off the Komandorski Islands. In a traditional gun engagement a cruiser from each side is badly damaged before Hosogaya breaks off the fight, just when his superiority is beginning to tell.

27 March 1943

Tunisia In the early hours of the morning the Germans manage to construct a weak defensive front around El Hamma which holds the British off until the Axis infantry from Mareth escape toward Wadi Akarit. There is also a new American attack near Fondouk.

28 March 1943

Tunisia The German and Italian forces are arriving at the Wadi Akarit position from Mareth. The Italian formations are least weakened but have lost heart completely. Of the Germans, 90th Light is in fairly good order, 21st and 15th Panzer have both lost heavily and 164th Light is very weak indeed. The Mareth battle stands as probably the most imaginative of Montgomery's actions and has only been marred by some confused leadership on 27 March when Horrocks and Freyberg were uncertain as to who was to take charge.

29 March 1943

Tunisia The last Axis units reach Wadi Akarit as the New Zealanders enter Gabes. General Messe reports to the Italian High Command that the Akarit position, although naturally probably the strongest in North Africa (at least in Rommel's opinion), has not received much preparation and may be vulnerable to a rapid attack. Characteristically Montgomery does not attempt this.

31 March 1943

New Guinea A US battalion occupies positions around Morobe.

Eastern Front The Soviets take Anastasyevsk in the Kuban north of Novorossiysk.

April 1943

Battle of the Atlantic There are various changes in the Allied situation. The north Atlantic convoys become solely a British and Canadian responsibility from 1 April while the US Navy is to look after the more southerly routes. The British aircraft strength is augmented both for operations over the Bay of Biscay and in VLR aircraft for the main convoy routes. There are no VLR aircraft operating from western Atlantic bases.

The German submarine strength has now become 425 boats of which 240 are operational. The Allied losses are 64 ships of 334,700 tons in total and to submarines, 56 ships of 327,900 tons. There is something of a lull at the start of the month, but among the later operations are attacks on ONS-5 (*see* 28 April-6 May) and HX-233 which loses only one ship and sinks one U-Boat with the help of a support group. There is some success toward the end of the month and in early May for a small group off Freetown. Fifteen U-Boats are lost during the month.

Allied Air Operations The Allied bomber offensive continues to increase in intensity. Bomber Command mounts 10 major attacks on Germany, dropping close to 10,000 tons of bombs. Essen and Duisburg are most heavily hit. Attacks on U-Boat bases continue also. Lorient, St Nazaire and Brest are the main targets. The US Eighth Air Force drops nearly 1000 tons of bombs altogether.

In the Mediterranean Allied forces are again active. La Spezia is heavily attacked in connection with the U-Boat offensive. Allied aircraft strike at communications in Italy and Sicily and shoot down numerous transport aircraft flying to North Africa. Italian and German naval units are also involved in the supply operations. Despite Allied attacks 28,000 men are landed along with 19,000 tons of supplies and other equipment.

Below: A U-Boat heels over in the swell of a mid-Atlantic storm, May 1943. The tide of war was now turning against the U-Boats.

3 April 1943

Tunisia The Germans continue to hold off the attacks by Patton's troops around El Guettar.

5 April 1943

Burma The Japanese on the Mayu peninsula continue to advance northwestward, in the direction of Indin.

5-6 April 1943

Tunisia In his usual methodical style Montgomery is now ready to attack the Wadi Akarit Line. The defenses there have been improved in the past few days and are now occupied mostly by the Italian infantry with 15th Panzer and part of 90th Light in reserve. Most of the Axis armor is farther north, engaging Patton's Corps around El Guettar. Montgomery has been persuaded to begin his attack with a silent night advance by 4th Indian Division against the Djebel Fatnassa position. This gets under way on the evening of 5 April and soon makes good progress. The follow-up attack in the morning is badly coordinated, however, and an untidy battle develops during the day as the Axis reserves are drawn in.

7 April 1943

Solomons In an attempt to set back American preparations, Yamamoto decides to mount an all-out air offensive to be known as Operation I. The Eleventh Air Fleet based on Rabaul, Kavieng and Buin is reinforced by the pilots and aircraft from the carriers *Zuikaku*, *Shokaku*, *Junyo* and *Hiyo*, leaving the fleet with almost no trained pilots. The attacks begin with a raid against Guadalcanal and Tulagi by 180 planes in which a destroyer and two other vessels are sunk.

Tunisia The Axis forces are retreating rapidly from the Wadi Akarit position. Advance units of Eighth Army meet patrols from Patton's Corps on the road toward Gafsa.

7-11 April 1943

Axis Planning Hitler and Mussolini meet at Salzburg. Among the subjects for their discussion is, of course, the situation in North Africa, but they decide they must hold on – a disastrous decision.

Above: Chindit leader Orde Wingate, photographed on board a Dakota transport plane.

8 April 1943

United States, Home Front In an attempt to combat inflation Roosevelt forbids certain wage and price increases and orders workers not to change their jobs in some industries unless this is beneficial to the war effort.

Burma General Kawabe replaces General Iida in command of the Japanese forces, now to be organized as the Burma Area Army. The Japanese are planning to extend their hold on northern Burma and among the logistic preparations that accompany this is the construction of new rail lines. About 60,000 Allied POWs are employed on this work – about 15,000 of them die through ill treatment.

9 April 1943

Tunisia British troops from Eighth Army take Mahares, 50 miles north of Gabes, as the Axis forces continue to retreat.

10 April 1943

Tunisia The leading elements of Eighth Army enter Sfax as the Axis retreat continues apace. The British IX Corps only now succeeds in breaking out from Fondouk Pass too late to cut the retreat.

Sardinia A force of 84 Liberator bombers raids La Maddalena sinking the heavy cruiser *Trieste* and damaging the *Gorizia*.

11 April 1943

New Guinea There are vigorous Japanese air attacks on Allied shipping, especially in Oro Bay where two freighters are sunk.

Eastern Front The Germans are now planning in earnest for an attack on the Kursk salient. The idea is too obvious for any hope of surprise, and so it is clear that a massive attack must be prepared if there is to be any chance of success. The German generals are divided in their opinions. Kluge, commanding Army Group Center, and Zeitzler and Keitel of the General Staff are in favor. Guderian, now Inspector-General of Armored Troops, and Manstein who in fact originally suggested the idea, are opposed to it.

Above: Australian prisoners work in a lumber camp in Thailand under the watchful gaze of a Japanese guard.

12 April 1943

War Crimes The Germans announce the discovery of a group of mass graves in the Katyn Forest. The bodies of 4100 Polish officers, murdered by the Soviets, are found.
Tunisia The retreating Axis forces are now reaching Enfidaville where they will halt.
New Guinea In the continuing Japanese air offensive Port Moresby is attacked by 174 aircraft, but little significant damage is done.

14 April 1943

Tunisia The Axis forces are now established in their final defensive positions of the campaign. They occupy the ring of hills around Bizerta and Tunis from about Cape Serrat to Enfidaville. The Eighth Army units coming up from the south begin to put pressure on Djebel Garci and Takrouna.
New Guinea A Japanese raid on shipping in Milne Bay marks the end of the recent flurry of air activity. Two transports are sunk. The Japanese air forces have lost heavily.

15 April 1943

Aleutians America begins preparations for an attack on Attu Island. It is to be carried out by 7th Division which has in fact been training for North Africa.

16 April 1943

War Crimes The Polish government in London issues a statement on the Katyn massacre asking for Red Cross investigation.

17 April 1943

Eastern Front The only real activity is in the Kuban Peninsula where the Russians continue to press Seventeenth Army back.
Allied Air Operations In one of the Eighth Air Force's largest operations yet 115 B-17 bombers are sent to attack Bremen aircraft factories. Sixteen aircraft fail to return.

18 April 1943

War Crimes The Russians make an announcement on the Katyn massacre alleging predictably that the Germans have concocted the whole story.
Tunisia A massive convoy of 100 transport planes leaves Sicily with supplies for the Axis forces, but at least half are shot down by Allied fighters.
Bougainville An aircraft carrying the Commander of the Japanese Combined Fleet, Admiral Yamamoto, is shot down by Lightning fighters over Bougainville. Yamamoto is killed. The operation is only possible because of the interception of a coded message announcing a visit by Yamamoto. The decision to try to intercept his plane goes to the highest level. In fact the Japanese do not deduce that their codes are insecure so the risk is worthwhile. As well as suffering the loss of their leading strategist, the Japanese national morale suffers when the death is announced in May. The Americans, of course, make no announcement, since this would obviously suggest to the Japanese how they got the information that Yamamoto was aboard that particular plane. Technically it has been a very difficult operation well performed.

19 April 1943

Tunisia Another German effort to fly in supplies suffers disastrous losses.
Poland, Resistance The remaining population of the Warsaw ghetto rises against the Germans. In October 1940 there were probably almost 500,000 Jews who had been herded into the ghetto. By July 1942, when the extermination policy began in earnest, there were 380,000 left, and by October 1942, 70,000 left. Most of the rest have been taken to be murdered in Treblinka.

20 April 1943

Japan, Politics The Japanese Cabinet is reorganized, with Shimegitsu becoming Foreign Minister.
Tunisia Montgomery mounts a series of attacks on the Axis positions near Enfidaville, but these are very strong and the attacks fail with heavy casualties.

21 April 1943

Japanese Command Admiral Koga is appointed to succeed Yamamoto in command of the Japanese Combined Fleet.
Tunisia A German attack around Medjez el Bab is driven off with loss.

22 April 1943

Tunisia A series of Allied attacks begins on the various German hill positions. The US II Corps, now led by Bradley, attacks Hill 609 in 'Mousetrap Valley,' intending to advance to Mateur. The British V Corps attacks 'Longstop' and 'Peter's Corner' and the British IX Corps also attacks between Goubellat and Bou Arada. Montgomery has been ordered to stop his attacks along the coast. Another German air supply effort is severely mauled – 30 transports are shot down.

23 April 1943

New Guinea Australian troops occupy positions around Mubo without opposition.

24 April 1943

Poland, Resistance The SS begins all-out operations against the Jews in the Warsaw ghetto. Buildings are burned or blown up but resistance continues among the rubble or in the sewers. Any Jews captured are either shot immediately or sent off to the extermination camps.

26 April 1943

Aleutians The Japnese-held harbors on Attu are bombarded by an American squadron led by Admiral McMorris.
Allied Diplomacy The Russians break off relations with the Polish exile government because of the allegations concerning the Katyn massacre. Relations have been poor for some time in any case as Stalin's attitude toward a postwar Poland has become more clear. On 30 April in an attempt to patch up the quarrel, the Poles drop the call for a Red Cross enquiry.
Tunisia Longstop Hill is taken by British V Corps, much aided by the excellent cross-country performance of their Churchill tanks.
South Pacific New plans are agreed for the American Solomon Islands operations, code named 'Cartwheel.' Halsey's South Pacific Area forces are to advance through New Georgia and Bougainville. MacArthur's Southwest Pacific

Below: Admiral Isoroku Yamamoto, shot down and killed by US fighters in April 1943.

Area is to continue its advance northwest along the coast of New Guinea until he and Halsey can join to isolate the Japanese bases at Rabaul and Kavieng.

27 April 1943

Tunisia The British take Djebel Bou Aoukaz after a vicious battle.

28-29 April 1943

Tunisia There is heavy fighting around Djebel Bou Aoukaz in the British sector as the German 8th Panzer Regiment counterattacks. In the American sector some progress is made in the Mousetrap Valley.

28 April-6 May 1943

Battle of the Atlantic There is a series of engagements around the convoy ONS-5. The convoy has 42 merchant ships and is attacked by 51 U-Boats; in running battles most of the way across the Atlantic it loses 13 vessels. Of the attacking U-Boats seven are sunk and five seriously and 12 slightly damaged. This is an important success for the escorts since the ratio of one U-Boat for two merchantmen is very acceptable. There has been little air support for the convoy, unusual for such a successful operation.

30 April 1943

Operation Husky As part of the deception plan for the invasion of Sicily (Operation Husky), a British submarine, *Seraph,* releases a corpse into the sea off the Spanish port of Huelva hoping that it will be picked up and the papers carried passed to the Germans. The body purports to be that of a Major Martin of the Royal Marines and he is carrying letters from General Nye, Vice-Chief of the British General Staff, and Admiral Mountbatten, Chief of Combined Operations, to Eisenhower, Alexander and Cunningham referring to Allied plans for an invasion of Greece. The Germans do receive the information and it contributes to their lack of appreciation of the true Allied strategy.

Tunisia The Germans retake Djebel Bou Aoukaz but at heavy cost to their armor. Farther north the Americans gain a foothold on Hill 609. Alexander decides to switch veteran units from Eighth Army to join a renewed attack between Bou Aoukaz and Ksar Tyr.

May 1943

Battle of the Atlantic Allied shipping losses decline again to 58 ships of 299,400 tons, of which submarines sink 50 ships of 264,900 tons. The Germans lose 41 U-Boats and on 22 May Doenitz decides to withdraw his forces from the north Atlantic routes (*see* 22 May). Typical convoy battles might be those of HX-237 which loses three ships but sinks three U-Boats helped by the escort carrier *Biter,* or SC-129 which loses two and sinks two, again with *Biter*'s help. From the German side the month has looked hopeful at the start, with four groups, 13-17 strong, on patrol in the Atlantic and another 18 in the Mediterranean. Doenitz is being forced, because of increasing British air operations, to order his boats to reverse their previous procedure while crossing the Bay of Biscay and to surface by day and try to fight the air attacks.

On the Allied side one important change of organization is the creation of the US Tenth Fleet under the direct command of Admiral King to supervise US antisubmarine operations. This unit has no ships of its own but is important in coordinating the actions of the various US commands.

Allied Air Operations The Battle of the Ruhr continues. More than 2000 tons of bombs are dropped on Dortmund on 23/24 May, the heaviest raid yet, and other major targets include

Below: The final Allied attacks in Tunisia, April-May 1943.

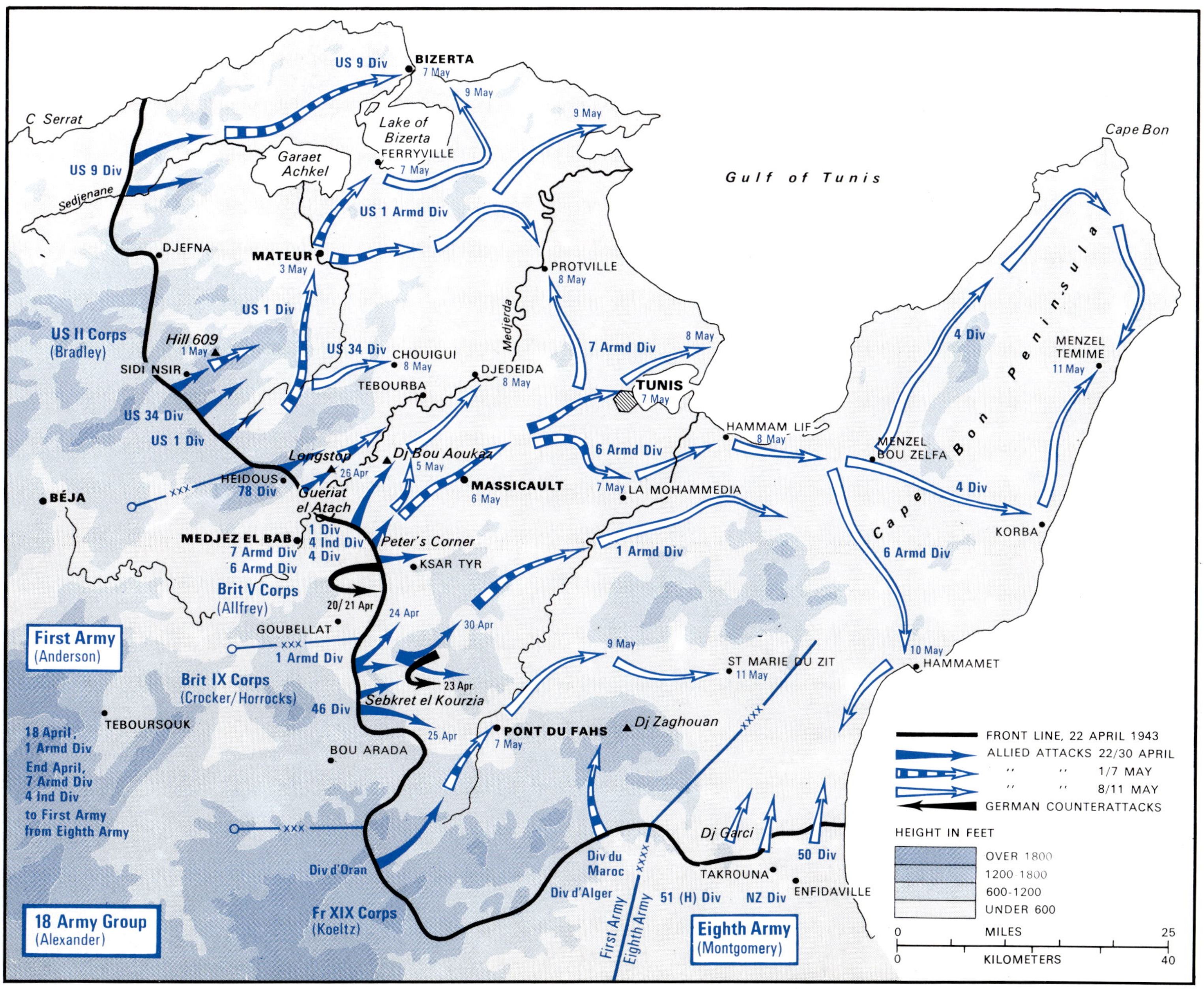

Above: A British infantry patrol, armed with Tommy guns, rifles and a Bren, advance through a damaged town in Tunisia, May 1943.

Essen, Duisburg, and Wuppertal. The USAAF concentrates on the U-Boat war dropping 2800 tons of bombs on a range of objectives including St Nazaire, Antwerp and Kiel. A specially trained RAF squadron attacks the Möhne and Eder Dams (*see* 16-17 May).

Allied aircraft based in the Mediterranean fly about 25,000 missions in support of operations in Tunisia (until the German surrender) and against targets in Sicily, Sardinia and southern Italy.

May-June 1943

Greece, Resistance The British and the Americans encourage the Greek resistance to increase its operations as part of the plan to draw German attention away from Sicily and Operation Husky. Two extra German armored divisions are sent to Greece. Once they have arrived an important viaduct on the Athens-Thessaloniki railroad is destroyed, so that if the tanks are moved away they will have to do so under their own power at the cost of much wear and tear. SOE agents help the resistance workers. The rail line is blocked for four months.

1 May 1943

Tunisia The Americans manage to complete the capture of Hill 609 but are held there.

3 May 1943

Tunisia The American 1st Division finally fights its way out of Mousetrap Valley and captures Mateur, but the Germans manage to improvise a new defense line and the advance is halted.

United States, Command General Andrews, US General commanding the European Theater, is killed in an air accident. General Devers is selected to replace him.

4 May 1943

Burma The Japanese have now infiltrated between Buthidaung and Maungdaw, disrupting British communications.

5 May 1943

Eastern Front In the Kuban the Soviets advance once more, capturing Krymsk and Neberjaisk.

Tunisia Late in the day Djebel Bou Aoukaz is taken once more by the British forces. The V Corps is now commanded by Horrocks and includes 6th and 7th Armored Divisions and 4th Indian Division.

6 May 1943

Tunisia Supported by a massive artillery and air bombardment, V Corps destroys what is left of 15th Panzer and breaks through toward Tunis. Farther north the Americans are also on the move, heading for Bizerta, Ferryville and Protville in three separate thrusts. The French XIX Corps are approaching Pont du Fahs.

7 May 1943

Tunisia The Allied forces burst forward all along the line. Tunis and Bizerta are both captured at about the same time in the afternoon by the British and Americans respectively.

Solomons US forces lay mine barrages in the waters around New Georgia to isolate it from Japanese supplies. Three destroyers are sunk by these mines on 8 May.

Burma The British are forced to retire from Buthidaung, which is taken by the Japanese.

8-9 May 1943

Tunisia The Axis forces are trying to retire to the Cape Bon Peninsula for a final stand, but during the night 6th Armored Division drives from Hammam Lif toward Hammamet, right in among the retreating troops and completing their disorganization.

10 May 1943

Eastern Front Hitler gives his consent for Operation Citadel, the attack on Kursk, to go ahead despite news of Soviet defensive preparations. Later Hitler defers the starting date from 13 June to early July in order to allow extra Panther tanks to be supplied.

Tunisia The last organized Axis resistance is overcome. There is no hope of evacuation and wholesale surrenders begin.

11 May 1943

Aleutians The American 7th Division (General Brown) begins to land on Attu supported by Admiral Kinkaid's Task Force 16. All units get ashore safely but are held up by the Japanese and the difficult terrain when they try to advance inland. There are strong naval forces in support including three battleships, one escort carrier and numerous cruisers and destroyers.

The ships provide effective fire support throughout the operation.

Burma The British pull 26th Division back from Maungdaw which the Japanese occupy on 14 May. The 1943 Arakan campaign is over. The British have lost 3000 killed and seriously wounded, more than twice as many as the Japanese. Above all the morale of the British force could hardly be poorer and their health is also weak. Generals Irwin and Lloyd are relieved and Slim is appointed to command Fourteenth Army on 15 May.

12 May 1943

Tunisia General von Arnim surrenders to the Allies as the mopping up continues. General Messe is promoted to Field Marshal by Mussolini in the hope that he will be encouraged to hold out.

Solomons Admiral Ainsworth leads four cruisers and seven destroyers in two groups to shell Vila and Munda. Other vessels also lay mines near New Georgia.

12-25 May 1943

Allied Planning Roosevelt and Churchill meet in Washington for the 'Trident' Conference. The Americans come to this better prepared for detailed argument than they have been in the past and are determined to get a firm commitment by the British to a cross-Channel invasion. The British feel that their commitment to this has never been in doubt and that the American insistence in planning so formally so far ahead will deprive the Allies of any strategic flexibility, especially in the Mediterranean. The invasion of Sicily has already been agreed but the British wish to be able to exploit this on the Italian mainland and perhaps also to act in the Balkans. The Americans feel that this is motivated by dubious postwar political aims and their Chiefs of Staff are opposed on strategic grounds as well. Admiral King has always wanted and striven for priority to be given to the Pacific, and Marshall is worried about doing anything which might detract from the cross-Channel operation which he believes is essential.

From the British point of view a major complaint is that despite the agreed Germany-first policy, the Americans have committed a larger share of their army and airforce to the Pacific as well as the bulk of their navy. The British feel that the shortage of shipping which is the major limiting factor for European operations can be put down to this. (In fact an important contributory element of this shortage is the decision taken at Casablanca in January to give priority to the building of escorts for the Battle of the Atlantic and not to landing craft.)

Compromises are reached on all headings. The Americans do not have to accept any real limitations on their Pacific operations and the British get a provisional agreement to exploit any Italian successes. Perhaps the most significant decision taken by the conference is to set a target date for D-Day – 1 May 1944. The British

General Morgan, is appointed to prepare plans for the invasion. He is given the designation COSSAC (Chief of Staff to the Supreme Allied Commander).

13 May 1943

Tunisia Marshal Messe orders the surrender of the remaining German and Italian troops. Altogether 250,000 have been captured in the last few days, half of them German.

Aleutians The American forces are still being contained virtually in their landing areas although they now outnumber the Japanese by about four to one. Bad weather has been hindering the US air support and the terrain is very difficult.

15 May 1943

Eastern Front The Germans attempt a small attack in the Leningrad sector but fail to make any progress.

Aleutians One American attack at Massacre Bay is beaten off, but a second in the north of Attu does better although there are casualties from badly aimed American bombing as well as Japanese fire.

Soviet Diplomacy The Soviet authorities decide to dissolve the Comintern to 'prove' to the West that Russia no longer has any expansionist aims. The dissolution is announced on 22 May.

16 May 1943

Aleutians The Americans continue their attacks near Holtz Bay on Attu. The Japanese are forced to pull back by weight of numbers.

Poland, Resistance In the last act of the extermination of the Warsaw ghetto, the SS blow up the synagogue. Stroop, the SS commander, boasts that since the rising began 14,000 Jews have been killed in the ghetto and a further 40,000 have been sent to Treblinka to be exterminated.

Above: Free French armored cars edge forward on the road to Tunis, May 1943: the North African campaign is almost over. *Below:* The Moehne Dam in the Ruhr, breached by Lancaster bombers of No 617 Squadron, Bomber Command, 16-17 May 1943. Popularly known as the 'Dambusters' raid it was one of the epics of Bomber Command's history.

16-17 May 1943

The Dambusters Raid During the night a specially trained RAF squadron, No 617, led by Wing Commander Guy Gibson, undertakes a precision attack on the dams on the Möhne and Eder Rivers. They use specially designed bombs and unique techniques to attack targets which are reckoned to supply the majority of the electricity used in the Ruhr and a great deal of the water. A third target, the Sorpe dam, is not attacked. The operation has only been possible by training an elite squadron for this one mission and the losses, eight of nineteen planes, are too high to bear repetition. The damage is far slighter than has been hoped and both dams are fairly quickly repaired.

16-25 May 1943

Eastern Front The Germans mount a series of counterattacks in the Kuban area but these are fairly comfortably held by the Soviet forces.

17 May 1943

Yugoslavia, Resistance The Germans begin their fifth major offensive against Tito's Partisans, code name Operation Schwarz and commanded by General Lüters. The main striking forces for the operation are to be provided by the SS Division Prinz Eugen and two formations specially brought in, 1st Mountain Division and 4th Brandenburg Regiment. Various other Axis formations are to hold an encircling ring and altogether there are 120,000 against Tito's 20,000 at most.

18 May 1943

Aleutians On Attu the American forces advancing from the north and south of the island link up and prepare to attack what they believe are the last Japanese positions on the approach to Chicagof Harbor.

World Affairs A United Nations Food Conference begins in Hot Springs, Virginia. It sits until 3 June and produces various resolutions calling for fairer distribution of resources in the postwar world.

19 May 1943

Aleutians On Attu the Americans advance along Clevesy Pass toward Chicagof.

20 May 1943

Aleutians Fighting continues on Attu in the Clevesy Pass area where the Japanese hold the high ground and have to be prised out of every position.

21 May 1943

Free French Forces Admiral Godefroy, commanding the small French squadron interned in Alexandria, decides to join the Allies.

21-25 May 1943

United States, Home Front More than 150,000 people are made homeless as rivers in the Mississippi system burst their banks.

21-27 May 1943

Aleutians The Americans make some progress on Attu each day. The fighting is especially fierce from 24-27 May when the Japanese are gradually driven off a feature known as Fish Hook Ridge. On 27 May work is begun on an airfield at Alexai Point.

22 May 1943

Battle of the Atlantic Doenitz orders all U-Boats on patrol in the north Atlantic to break off operations against the convoys. The losses have grown too high and although the Germans continue to hope for a revival of their fortunes by technical developments, the battle has effectively been won. Some boats are moved south to the Caribbean and to waters off the Azores. It is only by diverting his operations to less vital areas that Doenitz is able to continue his campaign, even at a reduced level.

The causes of the Allied victory are several: radar, aircraft and code-breaking information figure prominently. The U-Boats can perform their operations best on the surface and when they are able to signal to each other. Air cover prevents them reaching their patrol positions quickly and they cannot shadow a convoy on the surface and signal its position without being detected and attacked. Messages from the U-Boat Command can be decoded and U-Boat patrols avoided and the favored tactics for night attacks are made difficult when radar ends the U-Boats' concealment. Altogether the Allies' performance has been impressively coordinated, with scientists designing and airmen and sailors operating the weapons so quickly produced by industry. The only question over the Allied performance has been the way the maritime air services have had to compete with the strategic bomber forces for long-range aircraft. The Germans have been slow to realize the potential of their submarine force as the rate of building even as late as 1941 shows. Equally, they have been slower in fitting scientific developments into their operations.

26 May 1943

Canada, Home Front Meat rationing is introduced throughout the country.

27 May 1943

Allied Planning Churchill and General Marshall leave Washington for North Africa for talks with General Eisenhower on what is to be attempted in the coming Italian campaign. Marshall wishes to avoid any commitment that could interfere with a later cross-Channel operation, while Churchill is keen for opportunities in the Mediterranean to be exploited and Italy knocked out of the war.

Yugoslavia, Resistance British officers are dropped to rendezvous with Tito's Partisan forces in Montenegro near Mount Durmitor. For some time the SOE have been receiving reports that General Mihajlović and his Četniks are cooperating with the Germans, but only now are they able to contact Tito and the real resistance. Tito's forces are in trouble at this time. They are hemmed in by superior German, Italian and Bulgarian forces and have been under attack for 10 days but are beginning now to concentrate their force in preparation for fighting their way out. One reason for this slowness has been the desire to keep the appointment with the British.

France, Resistance The Comité National de la Résistance meets secretly in Paris for the first time. This nationwide organization for the various resistance groups has largely been the achievement of de Gaulle's lieutenant, Jean Moulin. Politically this is of considerable benefit to de Gaulle's position with the Allies.

Eastern Front In the Kuban another Soviet attack goes in but fails to penetrate the German defenses.

29 May 1943

Aleutians On Attu the Japanese mount a final fanatical attack on the Americans who are now established in Chicagof. The fighting is extremely vicious.

30 May 1943

Aleutians The Americans complete the capture of Attu. The Japanese have lost 2350 killed including many suicides and only 28 wounded have been captured. The American losses are also fairly heavy, 600 dead and 1200 wounded in capturing what is really a very unimportant position.

Below: German troops pause to read anti-fascist slogans during a sweep against partisans in Yugoslavia, scene of some of the most bitter fighting of World War II.

Important changes are introduced in the British naval codes which almost completely end the ability of B Dienst to intercept British messages. The Germans still remain convinced that their codes are secure, preferring to blame radio direction finding and spies in the French ports for any lack of security.

Allied Air Operations RAF Bomber Command drops more than 15,000 tons of bombs, principally on targets in the Ruhr. Dusseldorf is the victim of one particularly heavy raid on 11 June and Oberhausen, Mulheim and Cologne are also strongly attacked. The US Eighth Air Force drops 2500 tons on Bremen, Kiel, Wilhelmshaven and Cuxhaven. During the month the BBC issues several warnings to the population in France and the Low Countries to stay away from factories producing goods for Germany. In the Mediterranean the main Allied bombing effort is directed early in the month against Pantelleria and Lampedusa. Later Sicilian and Sardinian targets are most common.

1 June 1943

United States, Home Front More than 500,000 coal miners go on strike after protracted wage negotiations break down. Most return to work by 7 June when talks resume. A further strike begins on 21 June but most of the men have returned to work by early July.

3 June 1943

France, Politics De Gaulle and Giraud agree on the composition of a Committee of National Liberation under their joint presidency. The members are to include Massigli, Jean Monnet and André Philip.

France, Resistance The Michelin tire works at Clermont-Ferrand are badly damaged in a sabotage operation.

4-11 June 1943

Mediterranean Pantelleria is very heavily bombarded by air and from the sea.

8 June 1943

Pacific The battleship *Mutsu* sinks in Hiroshima Bay after an internal explosion.

Above: The ruthless reality of German anti-partisan operations in Yugoslavia. *Right:* General Dwight D Eisenhower (left) meets the US Chief of Staff, General George C Marshall in Algiers to plan the Sicily invasion.

France, Politics De Gaulle arrives in Algiers for talks with General Giraud to reconcile their differences.

31 May 1943

Mediterranean Pantelleria is shelled by a British cruiser and two destroyers. It has already been bombed several times in the past few days.

June 1943

Battle of the Atlantic The German U-Boats operate principally in waters west of the Azores against US-Gibraltar convoys. The U-Boats are now sailing in groups across the Bay of Biscay to improve their chances of beating off air attacks but this tactic is not successful and from the middle of the month they are ordered to submerge while on passage except when charging their batteries. Seventeen U-Boats are sunk during the month but Allied losses to submarines are only 20 ships out of a total 28.

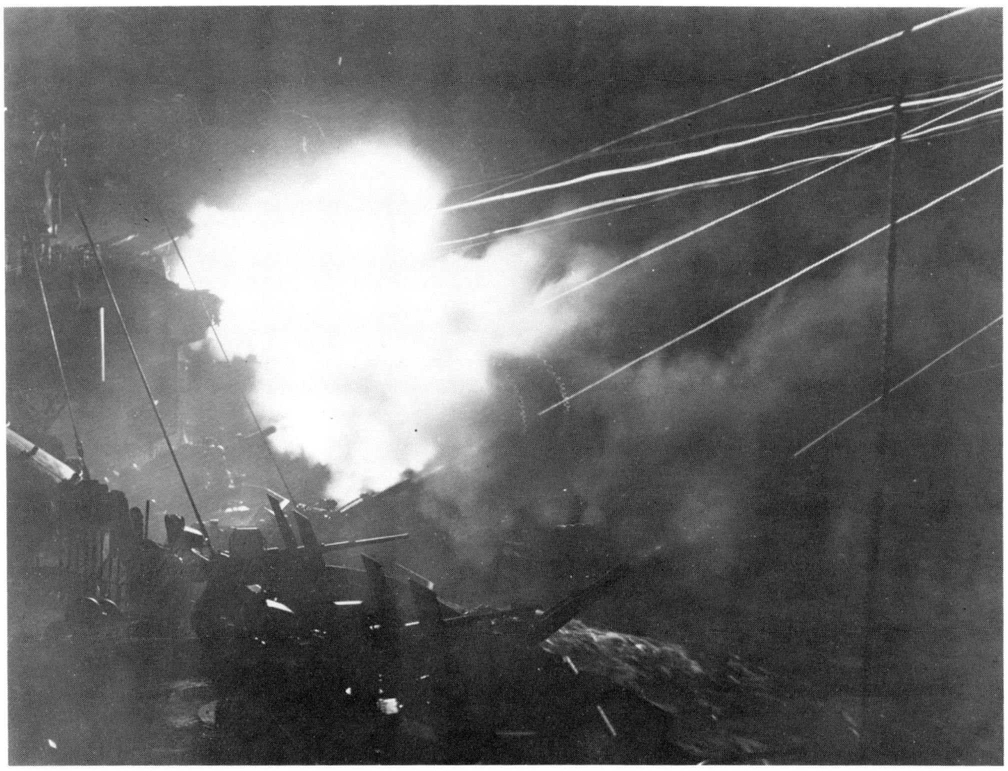

Above: The Brooklyn-class cruiser USS *Boise* shells the coast of New Guinea in support of land operations, February 1943.

9 June 1943

Eastern Front There is a Soviet attack on the Mius River sector which gains some ground. The Germans are repulsed in a similar limited effort near Lisichansk.

10 June 1943

Strategic Bombing The Joint Chiefs of Staff issue the Pointblank Directive to the commanders of the British and American heavy bomber forces in Europe. It sets out formal instructions for the priorities and aims of the bomber offensive which will last until D-Day. The instructions mostly reflect American thinking on precision attacks on specific target systems with particular reference to the German aircraft industry. There is also some mention of attacks to damage civilian morale. The leaders of the US Air Forces and Air Marshal Harris are all able to read into the directive permission to continue with their favored types of operations. There will be little coordination between the British and American forces. The American daylight precision attacks will not come near achieving their objectives until the advent of the Mustang escort fighter and the British night area bombing will also have disappointing results. German industrial production will prove to be astonishingly resilient and the morale of the workers will not suffer notably despite the damage to their homes. It is being discovered in Germany that factories that seem badly hit will often be untouched in their vital machinery and that once the rubble is cleared production can be resumed almost immediately.

11 June 1943

Mediterranean Pantelleria's 11,000-strong Italian garrison surrenders without a fight on the approach of an Allied assault force. More than 5000 tons of bombs have been dropped on this one small island in the last month and although the damage has been great, it has been far less than has been expected. This is an important indication of the difficulties in store for the main strategic-bombing campaign.

12 June 1943

Mediterranean King George VI arrives in North Africa to visit the troops. He visits Malta on 20 June.

The island of Lampedusa surrenders to the Allies. Like Pantelleria it has been heavily bombarded. The smaller islands of Linosa and Lampione are surrendered on 13 and 14 June respectively.

Solomons There is a major air battle near Guadalcanal in which the attacking Japanese forces lose heavily.

16 June 1943

Solomons US fighters from Henderson Field claim to have shot down 93 aircraft from a Japanese force attacking shipping assembled for the coming operations against New Georgia.

Operation Husky The first convoys for the invasion of Sicily leave the United States. On 17 June the first units of the supporting naval force set out from the British Home Fleet base at Scapa Flow.

18 June 1943

British Command The British government announces that General Wavell is to be the next viceroy of India in succession to Lord Linlithgow in October. General Auchinleck becomes Commander in Chief in India immediately but a separate East Asia Command is to be created. By these 'promotions' Churchill is planning to remove Wavell and Auchinleck from important military responsibility because he has lost confidence in them.

20 June 1943

New Guinea General Krueger establishes his Sixth Army HQ at Milne Bay. A Japanese attack on 17th Australian Brigade in the Mubo area is unsuccessful.

20-24 June 1943

Allied Air Operations RAF bombers attack Friedrichshaven on the night of 20/21 June, fly to Africa, and attack Spezia on the way back on 23/24 June. This is the first such 'shuttle-service' attack.

21 June 1943

New Georgia The 4th Marine Raider Battalion lands at Segi Point at the southern tip of New Georgia. There is no Japanese garrison there and the marines are reinforced without incident on 22 June.

22 June 1943

France, Politics After several days of hard bargaining the Committee of National Liberation decide that Giraud will retain command of the French forces in North Africa and that de Gaulle will lead elsewhere. This is in effect a victory for de Gaulle.

23 June 1943

Australia, Politics In the House of Representatives a censure motion on the government is beaten by one vote. Prime Minister Curtin announces that he will advise the Governor General to dissolve Parliament.

23-24 June 1943

New Guinea There are American landings on Woodlark Island.

26 June 1943

New Guinea The Allied force at Morobe prepares for an amphibious move along the coast.

27 June 1943

New Georgia The marines are ferried slightly farther up the coast from Segi Point to begin an overland advance on Viru Harbor.

28-29 June 1943

New Guinea Kiriwina and Woodlark are occupied by further US forces who start work immediately on airfield construction.

29 June 1943

Solomons A squadron of cruisers and destroyers shells the Japanese base at Shortland while other vessels lay mines in the area. Some of the US convoys bound for New Georgia are sighted by the Japanese but they mistakenly believe that they are merely carrying supplies to Guadalcanal.

30 June 1943

Solomons There are American landings on several islands in the New Georgia group, particularly Rendova. The forces involved come principally from General Hester's 43rd Division and are supported directly by Admiral Turner's Task Force 31 and by land-based aircraft commanded by Admiral Fitch. All landings are successful but resistance is heavy on Vangunu and progress is difficult.

New Guinea A mixed Australian and American unit known as McKechnie Force lands at Nassau Bay near Salamaua from Morobe and immediately is involved in heavy fighting to consolidate and extend a bridgehead.

Eastern Front There are numerous small-scale engagements in many locations all along the front. The armies are becoming more active again as the ground hardens and the winter's losses are being made good as far as is possible.

Above: Australian Prime Minister John Curtin (left), with Brendan Bracken, Minister of Information in Churchill's Coalition government.

July 1943

Battle of the Atlantic The British offensive over the Bay of Biscay is stepped up and succeeds in sinking 20 U-Boats out of the 37 lost this month. There are also successes for US hunter-killer escort groups sent to the Gibraltar and Azores area. These are based around the escort carriers *Bogue, Santee* and *Cove*. The Germans achieve some successes off Brazil, southeast and West Africa. Allied losses are 61 ships of 365,400 tons in all theaters, 46 ships falling to submarines.

Europe, Air Operations This month RAF Bomber Command drops about 16,000 tons of bombs and Eighth Air Force about 3600. Hamburg is the principal target. Essen and other cities in the Ruhr are also attacked by the RAF. American objectives include towns in France, Norway and Germany.

In the early part of the month the main target of the Allied Mediterranean air forces is Sicily. Later, Naples, Bari and Rome are among the objectives. The raid on Rome on 19 July is particularly heavy – 1100 tons of bombs are dropped by 700 aircraft. In all the raids on Italian cities leaflets are dropped urging an Italian surrender.

China, Air Operations Targets for the Fourteenth Air Force include Hankow, Pailochi, Hainan and Hong Kong.

Below: Field Marshal von Manstein (left) greets the Rumanian leader Ion Antonescu during the latter's visit to Army Group Don, in the summer of 1943.

1 July 1943

Axis Diplomacy Marshal Antonescu comes to visit Mussolini to suggest that Italy, Rumania and Hungary should leave the war together. This would clearly be a sensible policy for Mussolini to attempt but he is afraid to give any lead and in meetings with Hitler over the next few weeks he is too frightened to speak out.

New Guinea The marines from Segi Point capture Viru.

2 July 1943

Solomons The American buildup on Rendova continues but the Japanese garrison still holds out. During the night a Japanese naval force bombards the American positions on the island with little effect.

3 July 1943

New Guinea After heavy fighting in the Mubo area, the Australians advancing from Wau join up with the Americans from the Nassau Bay landing force in the region of the Bitoi River.

New Georgia US forces land at Zanana about eight miles east of Munda. There is no Japanese resistance and the beachhead is quickly consolidated.

4 July 1943

Solomons The American force advancing from Zanana toward Munda is held up by heavy Japanese resistance. The Japanese land 1200 men from three destroyers at Vila on Kolombangara.

Poland, Politics General Sikorski is killed in an air crash near Gibraltar. Mikolajczyk replaces him as prime minister of the London exile government and General Kukiel becomes Commander in Chief. Neither of these men is as capable as Sikorski. The commander of the Polish Home Army, Grot-Rowecki, was arrested by the Germans in Warsaw on 30 June. His replacement is Bor-Komorowski who, although personally a fine man, is less suited for the job.

5 July 1943

Eastern Front Both sides have assembled huge ground and air forces for what is to be the largest tank engagement of the war, the Battle of Kursk. The Germans hope to cut off the Kursk salient and create a huge gap in the Soviet front which can then be exploited. The Soviets are well aware of the general German intentions from local reconnaissance and high-level espionage information and have decided, after much debate, to follow Zhukov's advice and stand on the defensive rather than attack first themselves.

Altogether the Soviets and the Germans have concentrated 2,000,000 men, 6000 tanks and 5000 aircraft to take part in the operation with the Soviets having a slight numerical superiority in all categories. In artillery the Soviets have a significant advantage. As far as the quality of the equipment is concerned, in every class the Red Army is receiving newer and better designed weapons than has been the case in the past. The excellent T-34 tank, already in service, is being supplemented by new assault gun models. These qualitative improvements are particularly significant for the Red Air Force, which now has much more advanced fighter and ground-attack aircraft. The Germans have delayed the planned starting date of the battle at Hitler's command, in order to allow larger numbers of the new Panther tank to be supplied to the units taking part. The heavy Tiger tanks and the even more

Above: German Panzer Mark VI Tiger tank, armed with an 8.8cm main gun, lends support to SS troops at the Battle of Kursk, July 1943.

massive Elefant assault guns are also to have an important role in the attack. All these models are basically very effective designs but the conditions of the battle, and minor design errors and teething troubles for the new Panthers and Elefants, will limit their performance and to some extent set aside the advantage of skill which the German tank crews and small-unit commanders still maintain.

The northern wing of the German pincer is led by General Model and is spearheaded by XLVII Panzer Corps of Ninth Army. The somewhat stronger southern wing is commanded by General Hoth and includes Fourth Panzer Army and Operational Group Kempf. Manstein and Kluge are in overall charge of the southern and northern army groups respectively. Model's attack falls on Rokossovsky's Central Front and Hoth's on Vatutin's Voronezh Front. Konev's Steppe Front is in reserve to carry out the planned counteroffensive when the Germans have shot their bolt. Zhukov is supervising the defense in the north and Vasilievsky in the south.

In all areas the Soviets have prepared elaborate fixed defenses of minefields, other obstacles and antitank guns. Even before the German attack starts they fire a disruptive bombardment which causes the Germans considerable loss. When the attack is launched at dawn on 5 July the progress made is slow in both sectors and many tanks are lost. Soviet casualties are also considerable.

5-6 July 1943

Solomons During 5 July a further US force of regimental strength lands in the north of New Georgia at Rice Anchorage. The fighting on the Zanana-Munda track continues. During the night a force of Japanese destroyers brings almost 3000 more troops to Vila. Admiral Ainsworth, with three cruisers and four destroyers, engages a part of the Japanese squadron and sinks a destroyer but loses the cruiser *Helena*. A second Japanese destroyer is sunk by aircraft on 6 July. Bougainville is also raided by US bombers on 6 July. In New Georgia the fighting along the Barike River continues to be fierce.

6 July 1943

Eastern Front The bitter fighting of the Battle of Kursk continues. In the north the Germans make about six miles. The Elefant assault guns employed here suffer heavily from infantry attacks as their support is destroyed and their lack of machine guns prevents effective self-defense. In the south excellent artillery and air support helps achieve rather more – about 10 miles are gained. A heavy downpour restricts the advance here a little, especially on the left on the lower ground allocated to the front of XLVIII Corps.

Aleutians The Japanese positions on Kiska are bombarded by four cruisers and four destroyers led by Admiral Giffen. This attack is repeated several times by smaller forces over the next few days.

7 July 1943

Eastern Front In the northern sector of the Battle of Kursk the Germans can only make a very small advance. For the rest of the battle Model is able to push forward less than a mile a day. In the south the Germans come close to a breakthrough on the front of XLVIII Corps around Syrtzevo but Soviet armored counterattacks arrive in time to hold the Germans up in what soon becomes a slogging match.

New Guinea The Japanese positions at Mubo are heavily bombed and are further threatened by the Australian capture of Observation Hill about one mile away.

8 July 1943

Solomons On New Georgia the US forces make some progress near the Barike River.

Eastern Front The fierce fighting in the Battle of Kursk continues. The position in the south is still quite hopeful for the Germans despite their considerable losses but gradually their force is being worn down and in the very confused situation command and weapon-handling skills are becoming devalued.

North Atlantic Strong forces of the British Home Fleet cruise off Norway but they are not noticed by the Germans. This operation is designed to draw attention away from Mediterranean operations.

9 July 1943

Eastern Front The vicious attrition at Kursk continues, with the Germans becoming more and more bogged down in local encircling operations against stubborn strongpoints and at the same time having to fight off increasing Soviet tank forces which are beginning to arrive.

Sicily The Allied landing force for Operation Husky is being concentrated around Malta but the bad weather is proving troublesome. The defense of Sicily is entrusted to General Guzzoni's Italian Sixth Army. He has about 240,000 men, of whom a quarter are German. The Italian troops are all demoralized and poorly equipped,

Below: A jeep belonging to the US 82nd Airborne Division is loaded on board a Waco glider for the landings in Sicily, July 1943.

Above: Air Marshal Sir Arthur Tedder, Air Officer Commanding in the Middle East, 1941-43. *Right:* The Battle of Kursk, July 1943 – the last major German offensive on the Eastern Front.

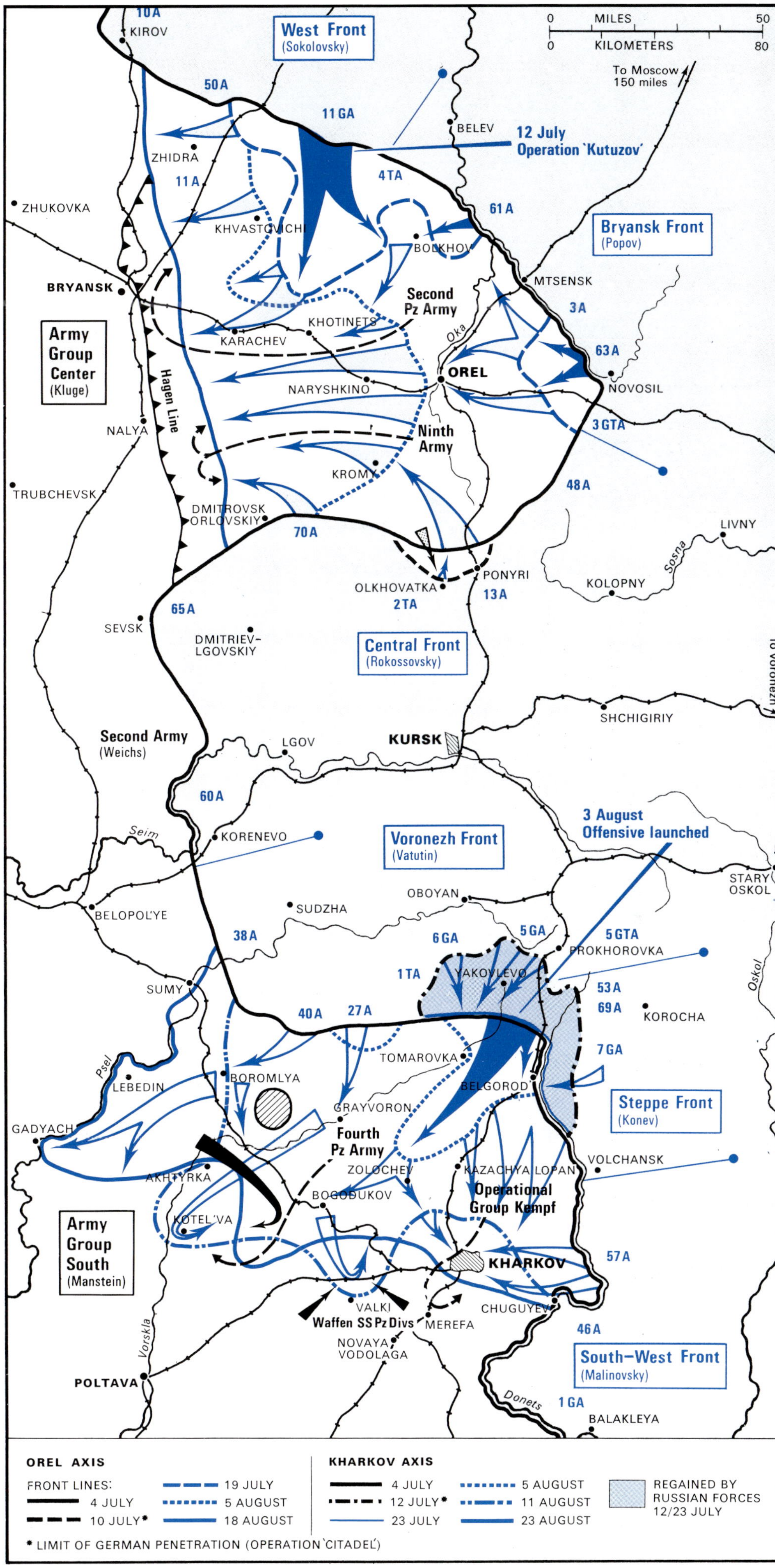

and many are tied down to fixed coastal defenses. The Allies have about 1200 transports and 2000 landing craft which will land elements of eight divisions (more than on D-Day). By the third day 150,000 will be ashore and eventually 480,000, of whom slightly more than half will be British will be landed. General Eisenhower is the Supreme Commander and his deputy, General Alexander, will lead 15th Army Group. This is composed of Patton's Seventh Army and Montgomery's Eighth Army. The naval commander is Admiral Cunningham with Admirals Ramsay and Hewitt controlling the British and American landings respectively. Tedder commands the Allied air forces which provide 3700 aircraft for direct supporting operations.

The Allies have mounted a considerable deception operation pointing both to Greece and Sardinia (*see* 30 April 1943 for one famous incident). This has been fairly successful. Hitler believes that Sardinia will be the target and has moved an airborne corps to the south of France to guard against this as well as taking precautions in Greece. Mussolini correctly expects that Sicily will be next but he is reluctant to call for the German help necessary to strengthen the defenses there.

The attack begins on the night of 9 July with airborne landings. Partly because of the strong winds and partly because of inexperience, the paratroops from General Ridgway's 82nd Airborne Division are scattered over a huge area. Although the paratroops in the British sector are dropped more accurately many gliders are released too early and more than a third come down in the sea. The airborne troops are not able, therefore, to seize all their objectives but they do cause considerable disruption.

Solomons The Americans on New Georgia are able to begin formal full-scale attacks toward Munda. The Japanese defend fiercely, however, and only a small advance is made. The Americans send reinforcements to Rendova and the Japanese to Kolombangara.

Above: A Russian gun crew prepare to fire, Kursk, July 1943. Artillery played a major role in the Russian defenses.

10 July 1943

Eastern Front In the north Model's attacks finally grind to a halt in the Battle of Kursk. In the south the unrelenting German pressure has seriously worried Vatutin and help is sent from Konev's Steppe Front – principally the Fifth Guards Tank Army.

Sicily The main Allied landings for Operation Husky begin. Patton's Seventh Army lands in the Gulf of Gela between Licata and Scoglitti. They meet only slight opposition and quickly take Gela, Licata and Vittoria. The British landings between Syracuse and the southwest tip of the island are unopposed and Syracuse is taken by the end of the day.

The bad weather has helped put the Italian coastal divisions off their guard and the Allied bombardment has helped complete their demoralization. New equipment has also been used, including LSTs and LCTs which enable the armor to be put ashore with the assaulting infantry.

Solomons The American advance on New Georgia is largely being held by the Japanese and because of the difficult terrain supply is becoming a problem for the combat troops.

New Guinea The Australians and Americans manage to link up in another sector, cutting the Japanese in Mubo off from Salamaua.

11 July 1943

Eastern Front The vicious fighting continues in the southern sector in the Battle of Kursk. It is now more strictly a tank battle with the air and other supporting forces unable to intervene effectively. Visibility on the battlefield has become so poor because of dust and smoke that the Germans can make nothing of their advantage in long-range gunnery.

Sicily The British continue to advance almost unopposed. Palazzolo is taken and on the coast the only halt is late in the day at Priolo. The Americans are more seriously attacked, however. The Hermann Goering Panzer Division moves down toward Gela from its positions around Caltagirone. The American landings have suffered rather more than the British from the weather and few tanks and antitank guns have been landed. It is, therefore, only with the help of naval gunfire that the German attack is beaten off when it has almost reached to the beaches. British battleships and cruisers are also in action shelling Favignana and Marsala during the night.

12 July 1943

Eastern Front In the Battle of Kursk the Fourth Panzer Army, led by the II SS Panzer Corps, makes one final effort in the direction of Prokhorovka but cannot break through the fresh Soviet forces. Army Group South is now being threatened near Taganrog and Stalino, and in the north of the salient a Soviet counter-offensive begins toward Orel even as Kluge orders Model to withdraw some of his panzers to meet such a threat. At the end of the day Hitler orders that the battle be discontinued. This new Soviet attack involves troops of the West and Bryansk Fronts in two thrusts west from Novosil and south from between Kozelsk and Sukhinichi.

In this battle the Germans have conceded the strategic initiative to the Soviets for good. Their shortage of manpower has compelled them to attack on a limited front and to commit almost all of their tank force to one effort. The Soviet losses in the battle so far have probably been rather greater than the German's but they can afford it. The Luftwaffe losses have been severe and its dominance is now over. The Germans must also send troops to Italy but Hitler still forbids his Generals to make necessary withdrawals.

Sicily In the morning the Hermann Goering Division continues its attack on the American positions without success and in the afternoon is drawn off to face the more threatening British advance. However, the Americans are now coming under increasing pressure from elements of 15th Panzergrenadier Division which have been brought from the west of the island.

In the British sector the advance on Augusta continues against German and Italian resistance. Lentini is captured.

12-13 July 1943

Solomons Admiral Ainsworth's Task Force with three cruisers and 10 destroyers meets a Japanese squadron of one cruiser and nine destroyers led by Admiral Izaki off Kolombangara. The Japanese make good use of their torpedo equipment, sinking one destroyer and damaging two cruisers. However, the Japanese cruiser is virtually blown out the water by the radar-directed gunfire of the American cruisers.

13 July 1943

Solomons The Americans continue to reinforce their troops on Rendova and New Georgia. On New Georgia their attacks make a little more progress against fierce resistance.

New Guinea The Japanese positions at Mubo are overrun and their force is practically wiped out.

13-14 July 1943

Sicily Augusta is captured by the British 5th Division on 13 July and other British units are engaged by the Hermann Goering Division around Vizzini. During the night Dempsey's XIII Corps begin a major effort to reach Catania, attacking from around Lentini. Commandos and paratroops are sent in to capture two vital river bridges. The commandos land by sea and manage to take the nearer bridge but the paratroops suffer heavy casualties and are driven off on 14 July. By coincidence the German 1st Paratroop Division is dropped near the commandos' position and can therefore begin its task of strengthening the Axis front immediately. On 14 July the main British and American forces succeed in advancing fairly evenly all along the

front. American units take Biscani airfield and Niscemi and the British capture Vizzini.
Eastern Front Despite the formal order to abandon the battle, Hoth's forces continue to make local efforts in the southern part of the Kursk salient. To the north both of the Soviet pincers make good progress toward Orel.

15 July 1943

United States, Politics Roosevelt creates a new office of economic warfare, headed by Leo Crowley, to replace the previous board.
Eastern Front Rokossovsky's Central Front goes over to the offensive, joining the attacks toward Orel. In the south of the Kursk salient Manstein's forces begin to pull back to their start lines followed up all the time by Soviet pressure.
Sicily General Patton forms a provisional corps to move on the west of the island while Bradley's II Corps drives north. In Catania the Axis forces fall back behind the Simeto River.
Solomons General Griswold replaces General Hester in charge of the operations in New Georgia. There is a fierce air battle over Rendova in which the Americans lose three aircraft and shoot down more than 40.

16 July 1943

Diplomatic Affairs Roosevelt and Churchill issue a special joint statement calling for an Italian surrender and suggest to the Italian people that they get rid of Mussolini. In Italy some of the Fascist politicians are beginning to plot to accomplish exactly this.
Sicily The American 3rd Division attacks Agrigento and Porto Empedocle. The Canadian 1st Division takes Caltagirone and advances on Piazza Armerina against strong resistance. Units of the British 50th Division succeed in crossing the Simeto River and later are reinforced by armor.

Above: A British battleship fires its main armament in support of ground operations around Catania, Sicily, 17 July 1943. *Left:* SS Panzer Grenadiers move forward at Kursk. The soldier in the front has a sniper mask around his neck.

17 July 1943

Eastern Front The Soviet drive north and west of Orel is gradually slowed down by German tank forces. In the south of the Kursk salient the German fighting withdrawal continues. Farther south still, Malinovsky's Southwest Front opens attacks around Voroshilovgrad.
Solomons The Americans mount a large air raid on Bougainville. Shipping offshore and the airfields between Buin and Faisi are attacked. One destroyer is sunk.
New Guinea Units from the Australian 3rd and the American 41st Divisions move toward Salamaua. This is merely a holding action in preparation for a later move against Lae and the Markham valley.
Sicily The Americans take Agrigento and Porto Empedocle.

18 July 1943

Sicily The Americans capture Caltanisetta and push on north to cut the Palermo-Enna road. To the east of Enna the Canadians take Valguarnerna. On the east coast strong German resistance halts Dempsey's force just north of the River Simeto.

19 July 1943

Axis Politics Hitler and Mussolini meet at Feltre in northern Italy. Hitler hardly lets Mussolini speak and does little but demand more effort from the Italians. Mussolini realizes that Italy cannot fight much longer, but face to face with Hitler he will not admit it. Italian criticism of Mussolini's government following the heavy Allied air raids on Rome illustrates the Italian war weariness.

Sicily The American forces advance quickly to north and west, meeting little resistance. On the east coast the British attack is held and Montgomery therefore directs the weight of his attack somewhat further inland toward Gerbini, Agira and Leonforte.

Eastern Front The Soviets continue to push forward in both sides of the Kursk salient. In the north they threaten Bolkhov.

20 July 1943

Atomic Research Roosevelt issues a firm order that atomic information should be shared with the British. Discussions between the British and American staffs follow and in August at the Quebec Conference, a formal agreement is signed by which Britain and the United States agree to share their knowledge, not to use atomic weapons against each other, not to use atomic weapons without the other's consent and not to give information to any third party. The British deny any right to exploit atomic knowledge after the war except to the extent judged fair by the US President (*see* September 1944).

Sicily On the south the Americans reach Menfi and in the center of the island Enna is captured by the Canadians who also advance to Leonforte.

Eastern Front Troops of Popov's Bryansk Front clear the Germans out of Mtsensk.

Solomons On New Georgia fresh American forces arrive in the front line. The supply problem is not so acute now because of new road construction. Two Japanese destroyers are sunk while on a supply mission.

Above: American B-17 Flying Fortress bombers fly over Hamburg during the firestorm raid of July 1943. *Right:* Marshal Pietro Badoglio, Italian soldier and statesman.

21 July 1943

Italy The Allied advance on Sicily continues. The British take Gerbini, the Canadians Leonforte and the Americans Corleone and Castelvetrano. The Italian naval base at Crotone on the mainland is bombarded.
Eastern Front The Soviets capture Balkhov.

21-22 July 1943

Solomons A small American force is sent to Vella Lavella to examine the possibility of major landings, thus by-passing Kolombangara. On New Georgia, Griswold lays plans for a large offensive.

22 July 1943

Sicily The Americans enter Palermo and have now cut off 50,000 Italian troops in the west of the island but the mobile forces including most of the Germans are escaping to the northeast corner.
Aleutians Major US naval forces bombard Kiska. Two battleships and four cruisers as well as lighter forces are involved.

23 July 1943

Sicily The Americans occupy Trapani and Marsala and on the north coast they reach Termini Imerese.
Eastern Front In the south of the Kursk salient the Germans are now back in their original positions.

24 July 1943

Italy, Politics The Fascist Grand Council meets for the first time since December 1939. The debate and voting go against Mussolini but it is not yet clear what is to happen next.
Sicily On the north coast the American 45th Division takes Cefalu and inland other American units advance toward Nicosia.

24 July-2 August 1943

Europe, Air Operations Hamburg is raided in the most effective attacks of the European campaign. The RAF mounts major operations on four nights: 24/25 July, 27/28 July, 29/30 July and 2/3 August. On the first three of these nights about 780 bombers drop 2300 tons of bombs each night and on the fourth night 425 bombers drop 940 tons. The USAF joins in on 25 and 26 July and the RAF sends small forces on every other night. Altogether about 50,000 civilian deaths are caused and as many injuries. About 800,000 people are made homeless. The attack on 27/28 July includes many incendiary weapons and a fire storm is raised for the first time. A fire storm occurs when the fires in a given area become so intense that they devour all the oxygen nearby and suck more into themselves, creating hurricane-force winds which both feed the fires and move them along at great speed. The Allied bombers only raise firestorms on a handful of occasions during the war including the atomic bomb attack on Hiroshima on 6 August 1945.

Tactically the raids are important for the RAF as they are the first time that 'window' is used. This consists of strips of metal foil dropped from supporting aircraft which confuses the German radar system by giving false echoes. It is very successful at first but improved radar nullifies some of its benefits during later months. A token of the growing strength of Bomber Command is that it is able to mount major attacks on other targets even during this period. The attacks on Hamburg and other later efforts make up the second of Air Marshal Harris' 'battles.' In fact, the success of the Hamburg battle encourages Harris to push for the third of his battles, that against the German capital of Berlin. Longer distances and improved German anti-aircraft defences will ensure that, unlike Hamburg, this battle will be a hard and costly one.

This period also sees intensive operations by the US forces against other targets, including many German aircraft factories. The Eighth Air Force loses 88 planes in these operations.

25 July 1943

Italy, Politics Mussolini is summoned to a meeting with the king in the afternoon and is told that he is being relieved of his offices. He is arrested on leaving the meeting. Marshal Badoglio is chosen to form the new government.
Sicily The Americans in the north are now meeting stronger resistance. In the center the British and Canadians are attacking Agira from two directions. Allied reinforcements are being brought over to the island from North Africa including the US 9th and the British 78th Divisions.
New Georgia The American offensive begins with units of the 25th Division supplementing the efforts of 43rd and 37th Divisions. Little progress is made, however, except near a feature called Bartley Ridge.

26 July 1943

Italy, Politics Marshal Badoglio forms a new cabinet and declares martial law throughout Italy. He professes his loyalty to the Axis but in reality he is looking for a way to end the war.
New Georgia The American attacks continue to make slow progress with heavy air and artillery support. Tanks and flame throwers are also employed.

27 July 1943

Sicily There is heavy, but inconclusive, fighting at Agira and Nicosia.

28 July 1943

Aleutians Late in the day the Japanese evacuate almost all the remainder of the Kiska garrison without being spotted. The Americans bombard Kiska on three occasions between now and their landing on 15 August as well as dropping 1300 tons of bombs.
Sicily The Americans take Nicosia and the Canadians Agira.
Solomons On New Georgia the American attacks continue, now directed principally toward Horseshoe Hill. Two Japanese destroyers are sunk by aircraft near Rabaul.

29 July 1943

Britain, Home Front The Minister of Labor, Ernest Bevin, announces that women up to 50 must now register for war work. This is a sign of the strain on manpower resources produced by Britain's more complete mobilization for war production. As the war continues this will become more pronounced and will be an important factor in Britain's negotiations with the Allies.
Sicily The British 78th Division arrives at the front and attacks toward Paterno.
Eastern Front The III Panzer Corps counterattacks the Soviet positions on the River Mius north of Taganrog but with little effect. This is another confirmation of the growing tactical and numerical power of the Red Army.

30 July 1943

Sicily The American forces are heavily engaged on the outskirts of Santo Stefano and Troina. On the British front Catenanouva is taken. Off the west coast the Egadi Islands surrender.

31 July 1943

Sicily The US 45th Division takes Santo Stefano. The British and Canadians are now moving toward Regalbuto and Centuripe.

August 1943

Battle of the Atlantic A further 25 U-Boats are sunk this month although U-Boat activity is at a lower level. Among the casualties in July and August are 10 U-Tankers which are important

Below: American B-24 Liberator bombers fly over the Rumanian oilfields at Ploesti in a daring but costly daylight raid, 1 August 1943, a triumph of long-distance planning.

Above: A German 2cm quadruple anti-aircraft (flak) gun prepares for action against the Allied invaders, Sicily, July 1943.

for the distant operations which now form the main effort of the German submarine command. One development is the German attempt to fight back against the Allied forces in the Bay of Biscay. Long-range fighters will be sent from Britain to try to counter this. Allied shipping losses for the month are not much over 100,000 tons.

Europe, Air Operations The heavy-bomber forces of the USAAF and the RAF concentrate on German targets. The RAF attacks on Hamburg continue intermittently; between now and November there are 14,500 sorties in 30 major raids. This month Bomber Command drops 19,000 tons and Eighth Air Force 3600 tons. Among the targets are Nuremberg, Berlin and Bochum. Milan, Turin and Genoa are also hit by bombers based in Britain. Milan is attacked four times; 4000 tons of bombs are dropped altogether. There are particularly important attacks on Schweinfurt and Peenemunde (*see* 17-18 August). Lighter aircraft of both Allies attack communications and airfields in Occupied Territory.

Italian communications are the main targets in many fairly small raids in the Mediterranean. Major efforts are also made against Rome and Foggia and on 1 August Ploesti in Rumania is hit by a strong American Liberator group but losses are heavy. From a force of 177 bombers, 50 fail to return.

1 August 1943

France, Politics The Free French reorganize their leadership. Giraud will now preside in the National Liberation Committee only when purely military matters are discussed. De Gaulle is to be president of the Committee at all other times.

Japan, Politics Tokyo announces that Burma is now independent and has declared war on the United States and Britain. The head of the puppet government, Ba Maw, signs a secret treaty with the Japanese.

Sicily There is heavy fighting around Troina, Regalbuto and Centuripe. The terrain in the northeast of the island is very rugged which greatly helps defense.

2 August 1943

Aleutians The Americans bombard Kiska with battleships and cruisers, yet again unaware that the Japanese have gone.

Sicily The Canadians take Regalbuto and the British 78th Division fights its way into Centuripe.

Solomons The Americans on New Georgia are now fighting on the edge of the Munda airfield. The Japanese have decided not to reinforce the island any more and are concentrating instead on Kolombangara. They are able to withdraw some of their forces to Kolombangara from New Georgia.

Eastern Front On the Orel front the Soviets take Znamenskaya.

4 August 1943

Eastern Front The Soviets enter Orel and to the south of the Kursk salient Konev's and Vatutin's forces have completed their regrouping and begin to attack toward Belgorod. The attack falls on the junction between Fourth Panzer Army and Eighth Army.

Sicily The British attack Catania while the Americans are still battling to take Troina.

4-5 August 1943

Solomons The Americans complete the capture of Munda and its airfield.

5 August 1943

Eastern Front The attacks of Konyev's armies make rapid progress, capturing Belgorod and advancing to the southwest. In the Orel sector the Germans are also being pushed back after Second Panzer Army suffered such heavy losses that it has been incorporated in Ninth Army.

6 August 1943

Sicily The American 1st Division finally captures Troina after a bitter fight. The British are now attacking the important position of Adrana.

Eastern Front The Soviets capture Zolochev, northwest of Kharkov.

6-7 August 1943

Solomons Six US destroyers meet four Japanese destroyers carrying men and supplies to Kolombangara in Vela Gulf. Three of the Japanese ships are sunk.

6-8 August 1943

Axis Politics German and Italian representatives meet at Verona. Foreign Ministers Ribbentrop and Guaniglia and the Chiefs of Staff Keitel and Ambrosio are present. The Italians try to assure the Germans that they are not negotiating with the Allies.

7 August 1943

Sicily The British capture Adrana and advance toward Bronte.

8 August 1943

Sicily In an amphibious operation supported by one cruiser and three destroyers, the Americans land a small force east of Sant Agata. The Germans pull back and Sant Agata falls to the main US forces, as does Cesaro inland. On the British sector Bronte and Acireale are taken.

New Georgia Although Munda has been captured, fighting on the island continues. The Americans are trying to prevent more Japanese escaping to Kolombangara.

9 August 1943

Denmark, Resistance Scavenius, the Danish prime minister, refuses to accept the German demand that saboteurs be tried in German courts.

10 August 1943

Eastern Front Khotinets, east of Orel, falls to the Soviets. Their offensives farther south continue to make good progress despite skillful German defense.

10-11 August 1943

Sicily The cruiser *Philadelphia* and six destroyers support another amphibious operation on the north coast. The landing is east of Cape Orlando, at Brolo, but again the Germans fall back quickly.

11 August 1943

Eastern Front The Soviets manage to cut the Poltava-Kharkov railroad about 30 miles west of Kharkov.

12 August 1943

Eastern Front In the Kharkov sector Chuguyev falls to the Soviets. The threat to Poltava is more serious, however, for if it is taken not only will the garrison of Kharkov be almost certainly cut off, but the German forces farther south will also be in grave danger. The III Panzer Corps is therefore brought back north from the Taganrog area. By this stage of the war the Germans are forced to employ their panzer divisions as a mobile reserve to cover weak spots in their defenses.

13 August 1943

Borneo The US Fifth Air Force sends 380 planes to raid the oilfields at Balikpapan from its bases in Australia.

Eastern Front The Soviet are now very close to Kharkov, having taken Bolshaya and Danilovka. A new offensive has been begun in the Smolensk area and Spas-Demensk, west of Kirov, is taken.

13-24 August 1943

Allied Planning The British and American military leaders meet in Quebec and are joined by Roosevelt and Churchill.

General Morgan's plans for the invasion of Europe are presented and accepted as the basis of more detailed work. Britain is committed to producing Mulberry Harbors – artificial ports which will be placed off the French beaches. Churchill accepts that the Supreme Commander for the invasion should be an American. In the Mediterranean the British are pleased that some exploitation of the defeat of Italy is provided for. The Pacific operations will continue, as agreed before, with the US authorities in full control. There is some difficulty in devising plans for Burma, however. It is decided to prepare another Chindit operation and to continue with the policy of sending aid to Chiang Kai-shek. Admiral Mountbatten is selected to lead a new Southeast Asia Command (SEAC).

14 August 1943

United States, Home Front New regulations for the draft come into force. There is a revised list of important occupations and, together with having dependents, will now be the deciding factor in any deferment of call up.

Sicily American and British units converge on Randazzo and capture it. The Allies are now advancing rapidly in most sectors.

15 August 1943

Eastern Front On the Bryansk Front, Karachev falls to Popov's troops after a fierce fight.

Aleutians An American assault force supported by three battleships lands 34,000 US and Canadian troops on Kiska. The Japanese have gone.

Solomons Vella Lavella is occupied by 4500 men from General McLure's 25th Division. The naval force is commanded by Admiral Wilkinson who leads Task Force 31.

New Guinea Japanese aircraft attack Tsili Tsili where the Allies now have an air base.

Sicily On the east coast the British enter Taormina as the Allied advance continues. A further American amphibious operation on the north coast arrives after the Germans have pulled back.

16 August 1943

Sicily The British attempt a small seaborne attack on the east coast but it is too late to cut off any of the retreating Germans. In the evening US forward patrols reach the outskirts of Messina.

Eastern Front The Soviets take Zhidra, northeast of Bryansk.

16-23 August 1943

New Guinea The Japanese airfields around Wewak are subjected to a series of attacks by planes of Fifth Air Force from Australia. Many Japanese aircraft are destroyed on the ground for small losses to the attackers.

17 August 1943

Solomons A small force of Japanese reinforcements is landed on Vella Lavella and there is a small inconclusive action between American destroyers and the Japanese transport force.

Sicily General Patton's troops enter Messina a few hours before the British. The campaign in Sicily is over. One disappointment for the Allies is the extent of the evacuations the Germans and Italians have managed. They have shipped 40,000 German troops with 50 tanks, 100 guns and a large quantity of supplies as well as 62,000 Italians across the Messina Strait. The Germans have lost about 10,000 men killed or captured plus many wounded. The British and Americans have suffered about 7000 killed and 15,000 wounded. More than 100,000 Italians have been taken. Although the campaign has been a political success in as much as Mussolini has been brought down, the escape of so many Germans makes the campaign in Italy a daunting prospect. Critics have suggested that the Allies could have made more imaginative use of their sea

Below: American industrial might was crucial to the Allied war effort: this is the scene at the Bethlehem-Fairfax shipyard, Baltimore, 1943.

power, not only around the island but in attacks on the Italian mainland. It has been suggested also that the Allies would have done better to follow up their success on Sicily with an immediate move to the Italian mainland. Although this is a plausible idea, it does not take account of the wider strategic debate between the British and Americans.

17-18 August 1943

Europe, Air Operations The Americans mount a large daylight raid on the ball-bearing manufacturing centers at Schweinfurt and Regensburg on 17 August. Fifty-one aircraft are lost, one-fifth of the attacking force. Such losses are insupportabe. During the night the German rocket research and manufacturing establishment at Peenemunde is attacked by nearly 600 RAF bombers. Forty-one are lost but important damage is done. The setback to the rocket program has been estimated variously but was probably about two months. This raid provides a good example of the effectiveness of 'window.' A decoy force of Mosquitos dropping 'window' cause about 200 fighters to operate over Berlin.

18 August 1943

Italy US cruisers and destroyers bombard Palmi and Gioai Taura on the Italian mainland.

19 August 1943

Diplomatic Affairs The Italians have made approaches to the Allies to negotiate surrender.

Below: Map showing the Russian offensives after Kursk towards the Dniepr river and Smolensk.

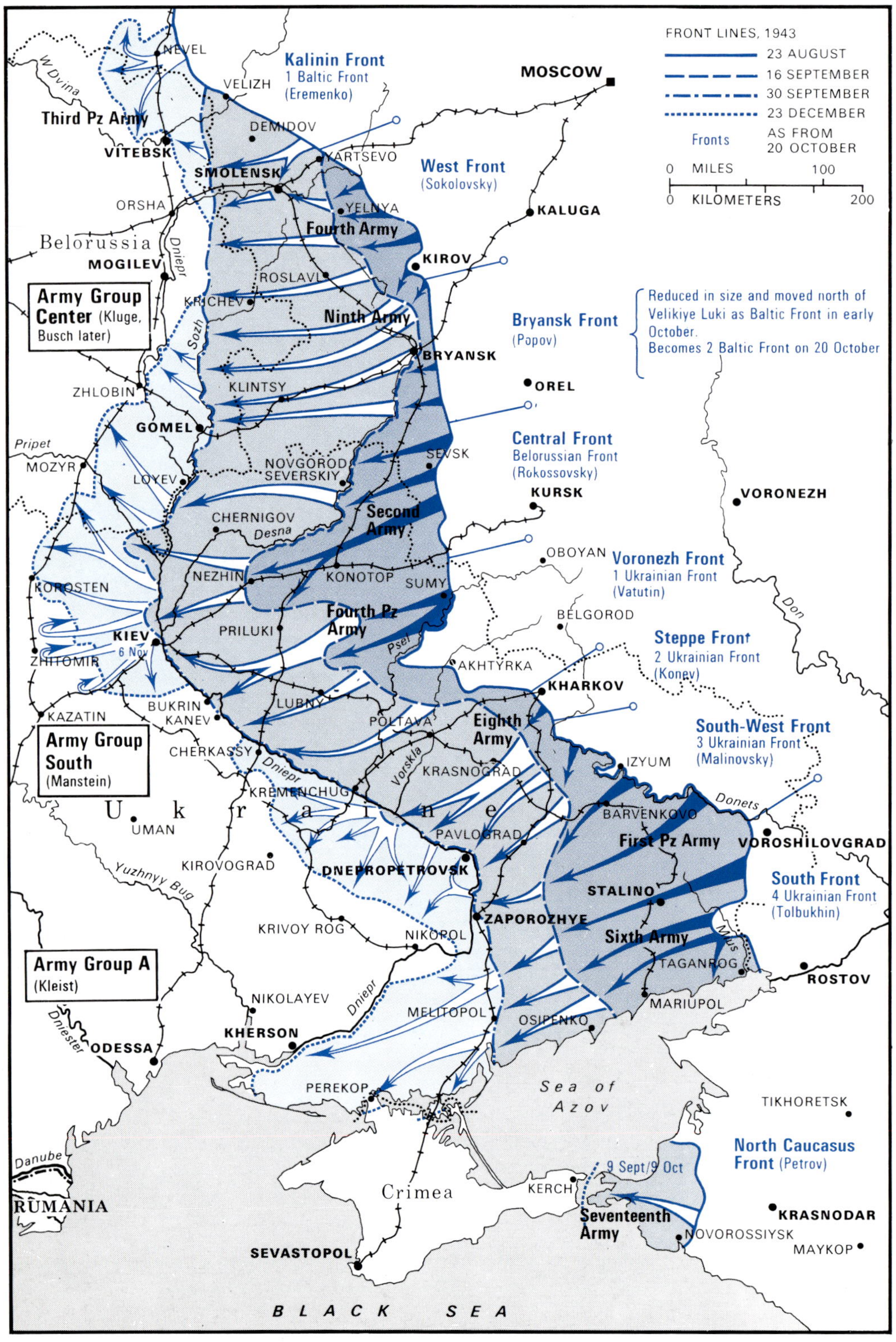

General Bedell Smith, Eisenhower's Chief of Staff, and General Strong, his chief of Intelligence, arrive in Lisbon to continue the talks with approaches to the British ambassador there, Sir Samuel Hoare. The leading Italian representative is General Castellano. (*See* 3 and 8 September.)

German Command The Chief of Staff of the Luftwaffe, Jeschonnek, commits suicide after being criticized for the effects of the attacks on Peenemunde and Schweinfurt.

20 August 1943

Eastern Front The Soviets take Libedin, to the west of Kharkov.

New Guinea Allied forces fight fiercely to take Babdubi Ridge, southwest of Salamaua.

21 August 1943

Australia, Politics Premier Curtin's Labor Party wins the election.

New Guinea Australian troops occupy Komiatum, six miles southwest of Salamaua.

22 August 1943

Eastern Front The Germans begin to pull out of Kharkov after a stubborn defense. Manstein, commanding Army Group South, refuses to hold out any longer because he believes that it would sacrifice Army Detachment Kempff in a rerun of the very costly Stalingrad offensive. Manstein has again managed to persuade Hitler against a 'stand firm' policy.

22-28 August 1943

Central Pacific US forces occupy various islands in the Ellice group, including Nukufetau and Namumea, without opposition. Work is begun on airfields.

23 August 1943

Eastern Front There are special Soviet celebrations to mark the capture of Kharkov. Farther south the Soviets are pushing forward beyond Voroshilovgrad.

23-24 August 1943

New Guinea Four American destroyers bombard Finschhafen in support of air operations against Wewak.

24 August 1943

Germany, Politics Himmler is appointed Minister of the Interior. Neurath resigns his post as Protector of Bohemia and Moravia. Frisch replaces him.

24-25 August 1943

Denmark, Resistance There are several bomb incidents in Copenhagen and many strikes in the shipyards.

25 August 1943

Battle of the Atlantic German Hs 293 glider bombs are used unsuccessfully for the first time against an escort vessel hunting U-Boats in the Bay of Biscay. The attack is repeated on 28 August with better results.

Solomons The battle for New Georgia is over. The last Japanese resistance at Bairoko is wiped out. However, many of the Japanese have succeeded in getting away to Arundel or Kolombangara.

Eastern Front The Soviets capture Zenkov and Akhtyrka to the west and northwest of Kharkov respectively.

26 August 1943

Diplomatic Affairs The United States, Britain and Canada give limited recognition to the French Committee of National Liberation. On 27 August the Soviet Union and China follow suit.

27 August 1943

Solomons US forces land on Arundel. Troops of 43rd Division occupy the Nauro Peninsula in the southeast of the island without a fight.
Eastern Front In the continuing Soviet offensives, Kotleva is captured by Vatutin's troops and Sevsk by Rokossovsky's Central Front.

28 August 1943

Denmark, Resistance The Danish government refuse to accept a German ultimatum and resign. The German commander, General von Hanneken, takes over. On 29 August he proclaims martial law and there is some fighting in various parts of the country. The Germans manage to capture one or two of the Danish Navy's few small ships but most are scuttled and a few are sailed to Sweden. The Danish govenment has been very successful until now in mitigating the effects of the German occupation while rigorously avoiding collaboration.

29 August 1943

Eastern Front The Soviets take Lyubotin, just west of Kharkov.

30 August 1943

Eastern Front The Soviets announce two more important captures. Sokolovsky has taken Yelna, on the approach to Smolensk, and in the south Taganrog has also fallen.

31 August 1943

Eastern Front Advancing south of Sevsk the Soviets capture Glukhov and Rylsk.

31 August-1 September 1943

Central Pacific US carriers attack Marcus Island. The carriers *Independence*, *Essex* and *Yorktown* are involved. Losses on both sides are slight. The carriers are from the newly formed Fast Carrier Task Force. At last the new American ships are beginning to come into action in large numbers.

September 1943

Battle of the Atlantic Doenitz sends his forces back to the North Atlantic convoy routes. New groups are sent out equipped with new radar search receivers, better AA armament and acoustic homing torpedoes. They have orders to try to sink convoy escorts rather than merchant ships. In the new operations six merchantmen and three escorts are sunk but so are three U-Boats. The U-Boat commanders give highly optimistic reports of the effectiveness of the new torpedoes because of their tendency to explode at the end of their run whether they have hit anything or not. The Allies also have an acoustic torpedo in service and soon develop a device known as 'foxer' which causes the German type to head into a ship's wake. Nine U-Boats are sunk during the month in all operations and the Allied shipping losses are 29 ships of 156,400 tons.
Pacific US submarines sink 160,000 tons of Japanese shipping. This is by no means an unusual monthly total. The drain on Japanese reserves is becoming ever more noticeable.
Europe, Air Operations Bomber Command drops 14,000 tons of bombs on various targets including Berlin, Mannheim and Hanover. American heavy bombers drop 5400 tons and their objectives include Paris, Stuttgart and

Above: Japanese Patrol Boat 39 sinks beneath the waves, Pacific, 23 April 1943. *Below:* Part of the rocket research plant at Peenemünde.

Above: Admiral of the Fleet Sir Andrew Cunningham.

Nantes. US medium bombers drop 2800 tons on airfields and marshalling yards in Occupied Europe. The deceptive effect of 'window' is now being augmented by electronic countermeasures against the German radar.

The Mediterranean forces make more than 15,000 sorties over Italy, concentrating on airfields and communications targets. During the first few days of the Salerno operation more than 1000 sorties per day are flown.

1 September 1943

Central Pacific US forces land on Baker Island and within a week have prepared an airstrip to support their coming campaign in the Gilbert Islands.
Solomons The US force on Vella Lavella is making good progress and reaches Orete Cove.
Eastern Front The Soviets capture Dorogobuzh, midway between Smolensk and Vyazma. They also make progress in the south around Taganrog.

2 September 1943

Eastern Front The Soviets announce a number of important gains in the Donets sector. Lisichansk, Kommunarsk and other important centers are taken. There are also significant advances on the Bryansk Front with Glushkovo and Sumy being captured.
Italy The British battleships *Valiant* and *Warspite* shell the Italian mainland defenses around Reggio.

3 September 1943

World Affairs General Castellano signs the Italian surrender at Cassibili in Sicily. No announcement is made until arrangements to forestall a German takeover can be worked out.
Italy At dawn units of XIII Corps from Montgomery's Eighth Army land on the Italian mainland to the north of Reggio after a heavy bombardment. There is almost no resistance. By the end of the day Reggio, Catona and San Giovanni are taken by the main forces and Mélito and Bagnara by commandos.
Eastern Front The Soviets take Putivl to the northeast of Konotop. They have now cut the Bryansk-Konotop railroad. In the south, in the Donets basin, Ilovask is taken.

4 September 1943

New Guinea The Allies land on Huon Gulf, east of Lae. The troops are 20th and 26th Brigades from 9th Australian Division. There is little Japanese resistance. The naval forces include 10 US destroyers, led by Admiral Barbey.
Solomons The US forces on Arundel which have so far been quietly consolidating their beachhead now begin to move out. They expect to meet fierce Japanese resistance.

5 September 1943

Eastern Front The main Soviet drives in the Bryansk and Donets sectors make considerable gains. Artemovsk in the south and Khutov and Mikhailovsky farther north are all in Soviet hands.
New Guinea The US 503rd Parachute Regiment lands in the Markham Valley at Nadzab, in the rear of Lae. They are joined by Australian units from Tsili Tsili. The complete Australian 7th Division is to be flown in.

6 September 1943

Italy The Eighth Army continues to advance slowly up the toe of Calabria, capturing Palmi and Delianuova. There is little German resistance but demolitions cause much delay.
Eastern Front It is another successful day for the Red Army in the south and on the Central Front. Makeyevka, just west of Stalino, Kromatorsk and Slavyansk are taken as is the important railroad town of Konotop.
Solomons The Japanese on Arundel begin to fight back strongly.
New Guinea Two brigades of the Australian 9th Division advancing west toward Lae meet strong Japanese resistance on the river crossings. The third brigade of the division, 24th Brigade, is landed.

6-9 September 1943

Arctic The *Tirpitz* and *Scharnhorst* make a sortie to bombard Spitzbergen, successfully destroying the few small installations there. The base is re-established on 15 October.

7 September 1943

Italy The Eighth Army take Bova Marina.
Eastern Front The Soviets take Baturin, east of Konotop, and Zvenkov in the Kharkov sector. The Germans begin to evacuate Stalino.

8 September 1943

Italy The Eighth Army takes Locri and land at Pizzo.
World Affairs The Italian surrender is announced, first by Eisenhower and then by Badoglio. The main body of the Italian Fleet sails from La Spezia and Genoa with three battleships, six cruisers and nine destroyers. They are to be surrendered to the Allies.
Eastern Front The Soviets move in to occupy Stalino and also take Yasinovataya nearby and Krasnoarmeisk.
Solomons Both the Americans and Japanese reinforce their troops on Arundel as the fighting there continues.
New Guinea The Australians advancing on Lae from the east win an engagement at Saingaua but are held for the moment on the line of the River Busu. The Japanese begin to withdraw from Salamaua as the Australians push forward in that sector also. Lae is shelled by four US destroyers.

9 September 1943

Italy The Allies land at Salerno and Taranto. The British 1st Airborne Division lands by sea at Taranto and seizes the port without opposition but the main landings at Salerno are more difficult. The landing forces are from General Clark's Fifth Army. On the left flank groups of US Rangers and British Commandos land respectively at Maiori and Vietri, with orders to advance north and capture passes through the hills toward Naples. Both landings are successful. The British X Corps under General McCreery, made up of 46th and 56th Divisions, lands

Below: Men of the 2nd Cameronians (Scottish Rifles) advance into the Italian town of Rosarno, 7 September 1943.

on the beaches immediately to the south of Salerno. There are some mistakes made and German resistance is strongest here but the troops manage to get ashore fairly well. The Southern Assault Force is taken from General Dawley's VI US Corps with the 26th Division forming the first wave and landing north and south of Paestum. American losses on the approach are fairly heavy because they adhere more strictly than the British to Clark's order that there is to be no supporting bombardment. Once they land, however, the resistance is less intense.

The landings at Taranto are covered by Admiral Power with the battleships *Howe* and *King George V* and an Allied cruiser squadron led by Commodore Agnew. The Salerno landings are much more complex. Admiral Cunningham commands the whole operation and the main covering force is led by Admiral Willis with four battleships and two carriers. Admiral Vian leads a support group of five small carriers and Admiral Hewitt is in direct command of the landings.

In the south Eighth Army continues to advance fairly slowly because of demolitions and poor roads.

Italian Surrender The battleship *Roma* is sunk by a glider bomber launched from a German aircraft while en route to Malta with the main body of the Italian Fleet. Several other ships are damaged by similar attacks. Admiral Zara sails from Taranto with the battleships *Andrea Doria* and *Caio Duilio* as well as other vessels. There is some fighting in the Rome area between Italian and German troops but the Italian plans have not been well prepared and the government has to leave the city, allowing the Germans to take over.

Eastern Front Advancing westward beyond Konotop, the Soviets take Bakhmach after a brisk fight. The German Seventeenth Army begins to pull out of its forward position in the Kuban.

New Guinea The Australians manage to force some small units across the Busu River.

10 September 1943

Malta The Italian fleet, including five battleships, arrives to surrender. Many smaller craft reach other Allied ports and some are scuttled in their home ports.

Italy The American sector of the Salerno landings is fairly quiet today, with the front being pushed further inland. In the British sector Montecorvino airfield and Battipaglia are occupied in the morning but the Germans concentrate most of their local reserves here, including a number of tanks from 16th Panzer Division and retake the positions by nightfall.

The German forces south of the beachhead, including those engaging Montgomery, withdraw north to reinforce the German cordon. They rely on small parties, demolitions and Montgomery's natural caution to hold up Eighth Army's advance.

Aegean Castelrosso in the Dodecanese is occupied by the British. Two British officers are dropped on Rhodes to contact the Italian commander there, General Campione. However, on 11 September he surrenders to the German forces on the island.

Eastern Front The Soviets mount a seaborne attack in the Sea of Azov and capture Mariupol. Inland on the Donets sector they take Barvenkovo, Volnovakha and Chaplino. They also land troops in Novorossiysk and a major engagement begins there.

New Guinea The Australian 7th Divison is now in position at Nadzab and begins to advance on Lae. Forward elements have reached Heath's Plantation.

Solomons The Americans are having to fight unexpectedly hard for Arundel Island and therefore send more reinforcements to their troops there.

10-30 September 1943

Corsica and Sardinia On 10 September the Germans begin to evacuate their garrison from Sardinia, moving first to Corsica and then the Italian mainland. Several of the transport ships are sunk on 21 September by Allied air and submarine attacks. Various fairly small French contingents land on Corsica from 14 September onward. They harass the retreating Germans and inflict some damage.

11 September 1943

Italy The pattern of the previous day is repeated at Salerno. Early on both the British and American Corps advance with some success but both are later pushed back. The German reinforcements are beginning to come up and in the bridgehead morale is poor because of the lack of progress.

There are major German air attacks on the landings throughout the day despite the efforts of the Allied air forces. The cruiser *Savannah* is badly damaged by a glider bomb.

Troops from British 1st Airborne Division take Brindisi without opposition. These units and those at Taranto have been sent simply to seize the ports and have virtually no transport to enable them to push north. The only opposition in that direction is the understrength German 1st

Below: Map showing the whole of the Allied campaign in Sicily and Italy, July 1943-May 1945.

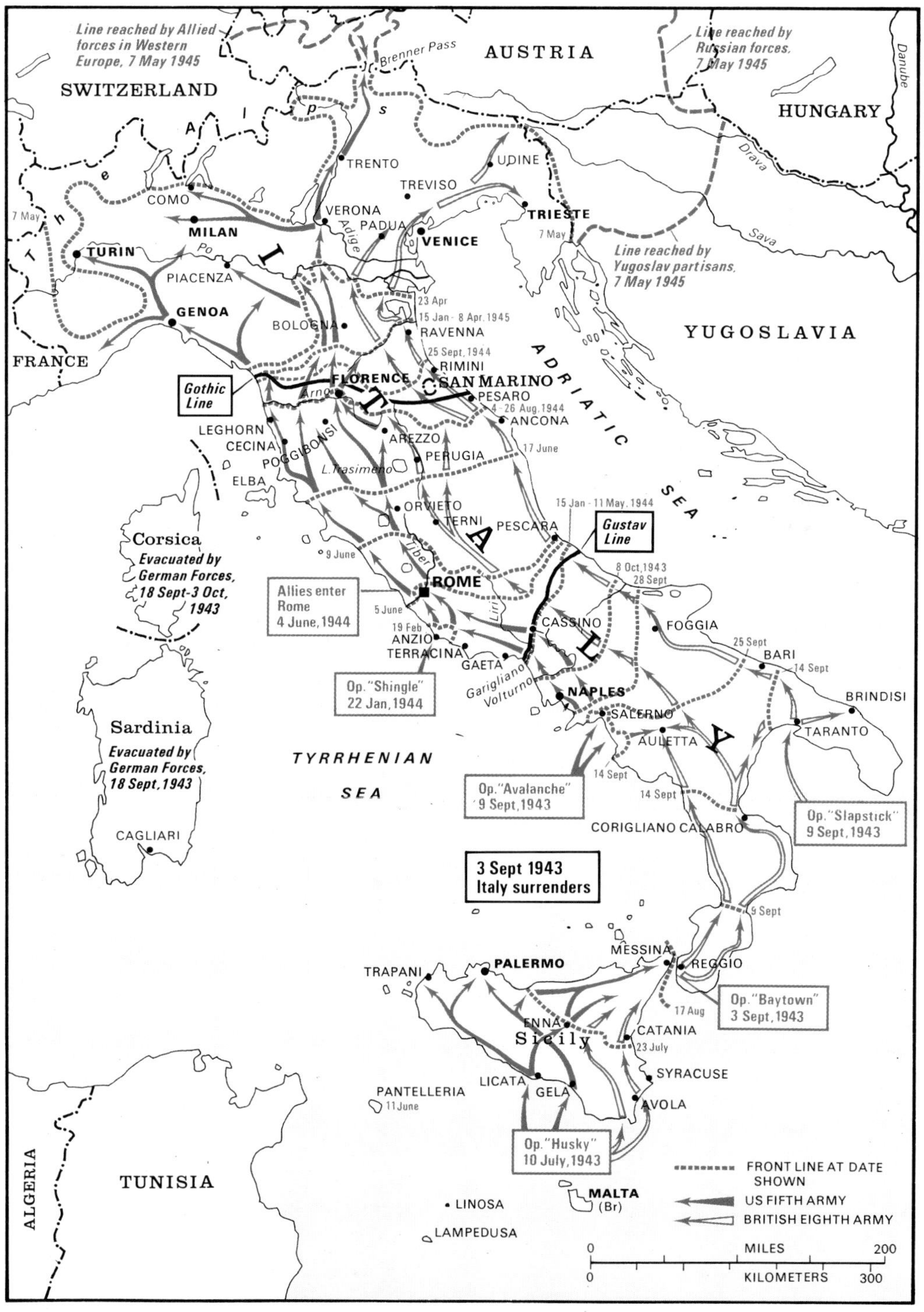

Above: The Gran Sasso Hotel, scene of the daring rescue of Mussolini by German paras under Skorzeny, September 1943.

Parachute Division, which is about a quarter of the British strength. The main forces of Eighth Army move into Catanzaro and advance toward Crotone.
Solomons The American 27th Infantry Regiment lands on Arundel.
New Guinea As the Japanese garrison of Salamaua pulls back the Australians take the airfield and enter the town.

12 September 1943

Italy Eighth Army takes Crotone and continues its advance. At Salerno the first major German counterattacks begin late in the day. The British are driven out of Battipaglia once more and in Molina Pass the unit which has replaced the Commandos is under heavy pressure from the Hermann Goering Panzer Division.

Mussolini is rescued from Gran Sasso in the Abruzzi Mountains by a German parachute detachment led by Otto Skorzeny. He is taken to Germany. The Germans have been trying to organize such an operation since Mussolini was arrested but he has never been kept for long in one place. The operation even now is technically very difficult and is executed with great daring.
Eastern Front The Soviet attacks continue in all sectors but with renewed vigor near Bryansk. On the Donets front Stary Kermenchik is taken. The Germans begin to evacuate Seventeenth Army from the Kuban. Altogether 255,000 troops, 27,000 civilians and army supplies are withdrawn by 9 October.
New Guinea Salamaua is taken by troops from the Australian 5th Division. Farther north the Japanese at Lae are beginning to be hemmed in.

13 September 1943

Italy There are now signs that a wedge can be driven between the British and American beachheads at Salerno and so the Germans now attack the US sector as well with units from 16th Panzer and 29th Panzergrenadier Divisions. The US forces are driven out of Persano and the line is penetrated in several places. In one area the Germans reach within a mile of the beaches. Naval gunfire from Allied ships anchored offshore is important in preventing the attacks from achieving a decisive success. The cruiser *Uganda* is damaged by glider bombs. Unloading from the ships in the southern sector is stopped and hurried plans are made for evacuation. Alexander and Eisenhower are extremely annoyed at this and make arrangements for more rapid reinforcement. Therefore, part of General Ridgway's 82nd Airborne Division is dropped on the beaches in the evening. The remainder drop on 14 September. Farther south Montgomery's forces continue to push forward. Cosenza is taken.
China, Politics Chiang Kai-shek becomes president of China.
Solomons The Americans land a small force on Sagekarasa.

13-22 September 1943

Greece The Italian Acqui Division resists the Germans in Cephalonia and surrenders only when 1500 have been killed and the Germans then kill 5000 more and deport the rest to labor camps.

14 September 1943

Italy The Germans maintain pressure on the Salerno beachhead but Allied air support and, even more importantly, naval gunfire prevent any significant success. Eighth Army is still driving forward in the south, having reached Bari in the east and beyond Belvedere in the west.
Solomons On Vella Lavella the US and New Zealand attacks make good progress but it is necessary to reinforce the battalion on Sagekarasa because of Japanese attacks.
Eastern Front The Germans announce the evacuation of Bryansk but fighting there continues. In the south there is also heavy fighting for the Kuban town of Novorossiysk.

15 September 1943

Italy There is something of a lull at Salerno as the Germans regroup. They now have available the equivalent of about four divisions, including perhaps 100 tanks. The Allies have seven division and twice as much armor and can now make practical plans to expand the beachhead. The battleships *Valiant* and *Warspite* join the bombarding forces. Alexander visits the beachhead on the morning of the 15th and firmly squashes any remaining ideas of withdrawal. He decides, too, to replace General Dawley in charge of VI Corps.

Eighth Army's advance continues, gradually quickening in pace. A group of war correspondents actually drives on ahead by minor roads and tracks and eventually manage to make contact with Fifth Army.

The island of Procida in Naples Bay is taken by the Allies.
Italy, Politics Mussolini issues a proclamation resuming his authority.
New Guinea The Australians have now crossed the Busu in force and built bridges. The front line is within two miles of Lae.
Aegean Cos in the Dodecanese is occupied by British paratroops and a squadron of Spitfires flown in.
Eastern Front Rokossovsky's forces take Nezhin, on the railroad from Konotop to Kiev. To the north of Bryansk the Germans are pushed out of Dyatkovo.

Below: Men of a US Navy Beach Battalion hug the sand as the Salerno beachhead comes under kattack from German fighter-bombers, September 1943.

16 September 1943

Italy Vietinghoff orders another attack on the British between Salerno and Battipaglia but it is driven off. By midday Kesselring has authorized a withdrawal to the Volturno line. In the afternoon the battleship *Warspite*, which has been providing gunnery support, is hit by two glider bombs and seriously damaged. Forward units of Fifth and Eighth Armies join up but the bulk of Eighth Army is well behind and busy transferring to the east side of the peninsula. The battle for Salerno is over but it has been a very close thing.

Aegean British forces occupy Leros and Samos.

Eastern Front The Soviets take Novgorod Seversky and Romny, north and south of Konotop respectively, on the flanks of their advance toward Kiev. Lozovaya, a railroad junction northeast of Pavlograd, is taken and Novorossiysk, in the Kuban, falls to the Soviets after a terrible struggle.

New Guinea Lae is taken by the converging attacks of Australian 9th and 7th Divisions. Many of the Japanese garrison are able to slip away into the jungle, and head for the north coast of the Huon Peninsula. In a major air attack on Wewak the Japanese lose many planes.

17 September 1943

Eastern Front The Soviets complete the capture of Bryansk. They also take Bezhitsa, a little to the north, and Trubchevsk, to the south, as they advance across the River Desna on a broad front. In the south on the Sea of Azov, Berdyansk is taken.

Italy Fifth Army is beginning to push out the boundaries of its beachhead once more. Altavilla and Battipaglia are attacked again by the Germans in order to cover their withdrawal which is now beginning.

Yugoslavia, Resistance A senior British liaison mission arrives and is sent to visit Tito. It is led by Brigadier Fitzroy Maclean who is Churchill's personal representative. It is to follow up the reports of the representatives sent in May and June and to confirm that Tito is doing more against the Germans than Mihajlović.

Below: German troops in Greece embark for movement to the Dodecanese Islands in the Aegean, recently occupied by the British.

17-19 September 1943

Central Pacific Tarawa is attacked on the 17th and 19th by land-based Liberator bombers. On the 18th aircraft from the carriers *Lexington*, *Princeton* and *Belleau Wood* (Admiral Pownall) also carry out attacks.

18 September 1943

Aegean British forces occupy Simi, Stampalia and Icaria. The Germans attack Antimachia airfield on Cos.

Eastern Front In the drive toward Kiev, Priluki, Lubny and Romodan are taken. Farther south there are gains all along the front, including Pavlograd, Krasnograd, Pologi and Nogaysk.

Solomons The fighting continues on Arundel. General Barrowclough, a New Zealander, takes command on Vella Lavella.

19 September 1943

Eastern Front In the Smolensk sector the Soviets take Yartsevo and Dukovschina to the northeast of the city.

Italy Auletta is captured by 5th British Division, Eighth Army.

20 September 1943

New Guinea The Australians advancing up the Markham Valley take Kaiapit.

United States, Home Front In the continuing debate about the drafting of fathers of families, General Marshall and Admiral King tell a Senate Committee that failure to do so will probably prolong the war.

Eastern Front Yeremenko's troops take Velizh, northwest of Smolensk, and Kholm, farther north.

Italy Canadian troops from Eighth Army enter Potenza after being held up by a tiny German force. General Lucas takes over command of VI Corps from Dawley.

20-21 September 1943

Solomons The Americans on Sagekarasa find their enemy have been evacuated on the 20th, and on Arundel a similar discovery is made on the 21st.

21 September 1943

Eastern Front The Soviets take Demidov, north of Smolensk. Troops from Central Front take Chernigov and Sinelnikovo, a little to the east of Dnepropetrovsk, is also captured.

Italy Fifth Army wheels to the left as Eighth Army moves to the east side of the country. The Germans are falling back everywhere except in the vital passes leading to Naples.

22 September 1943

Arctic Six British midget submarines are sent to attack *Tirpitz* in Altenfiord. Only two manage to place their charges but *Tirpitz* is put out of action until March 1944.

Eastern Front The Soviets take Anapa in the Kuban and Novomoskovosk, just north of Dnepropetrovsk. There is fierce fighting at Poltava as the Germans begin to pull out.

Italy Eighth Army is reinforced by 78th Division and 8th Indian Division who land at Bari and Brindisi but they cannot immediately advance up the coast in any great strength. Fifth Army is preparing to advance also. The British X Corps has the task of clearing the way to Naples and the US VI Corps moving in the first instance toward Benevento.

New Guinea The Australian 20th Brigade are landed at Katika, just north of Finschhafen. The landing is supported by a naval bombardment. Admiral Barbey leads the naval force and a strong air group also provides cover.

23 September 1943

Corsica Free French forces occupy Bonifaccio. They now control more than half of the island.

Italy The British X Corps begins formal attacks to clear the passes toward Naples. Although more than three divisions are employed against little more than a regiment, the terrain and tenacious German defense prevent very much progress. The attacks continue.

Italy, Politics Mussolini proclaims the foundation of the Italian Social Republic. Parts of northern Italy are given up to wholly German control by this administration.

Eastern Front The Soviets take Poltava and to the north, between Bryansk and Gomel, they enter Unecha east of Klintsy.

New Guinea The Australian 20th Brigade advances south toward Finschhafen and reaches a Japanese defense position on the River Bumi.

24 September 1943

New Guinea The Australians break the Japanese defenses on the River Bumi. Finschhafen airfield is captured. Offshore Japanese aircraft attempt to attack supply convoys but achieve little.

Eastern Front The Soviets capture Borispol just east of Kiev and farther north the Germans begin to evacuate Smolensk and Roslavl.

25 September 1943

Britain, Politics There is a Cabinet reshuffle because of the death on 23 September of Sir Kingsley Wood, then Chancellor of the Exchequer. Attlee becomes Lord President of the Council, Sir John Anderson Chancellor, Lord Cranbourne Dominions Secretary and Lord Beaverbrook Lord Privy Seal.

Allied Diplomacy A Lend-Lease agreement is signed by United States and Free French representatives at Algiers.

Solomons The Japanese begin to evacuate Kolombangara. Their garrison there has been made useless by the American capture of the other islands in the New Georgia group.

Above: A Junkers Ju-88c-6b night-fighter, equipped with FuG 202 *Lichtenstein* air-intercept radar in the nose.

Eastern Front The Soviets take Smolensk and Roslavl – arguably their most important success since the end of the Kursk battle. From here to the south the Germans are retreating behind the Dniepr, where they have been ordered to make a stand by Hitler. This retreat has been entirely forced and so there has been less benefit than if it had been done earlier as Manstein recommended.

26 September 1943

Corsica The Free French occupy Ghisonaccia airfield.
Italy The attack of the British X Corps today meets no resistance because the Germans have withdrawn, having won enough time for their forces father inland to pull back. They have left behind many demolitions and booby traps which prove a real hindrance. To the east, patrols from XIII Corps (Eighth Army) enter Canosa on the Ofanto River.
New Guinea The Japanese mount a series of counterattacks on the Australians around Finschhafen but they are unsuccessful.

27 September 1943

Corfu The Germans take full control of the island, having practically wiped out the Italian garrison.
Eastern Front The Red Army moves into the suburbs of Dnepropetrovsk and in the Kuban the German enclave is further reduced with the capture of Temryuk, the last port they have held.
Italy Advance detachments of Eighth Army enter Foggia and capture the airfields without a fight. Melfi is taken by Canadian units. The main body of Eighth Army is still not ready.

27-28 September 1943

New Guinea On both days there are heavy Allied air attacks on the Japanese airfields around Wewak.

27-30 September 1943

Italy, Resistance The people of Naples rise against the Germans and fight them for three days, taking heavy losses. The battle only ends as the Allied armies approach.

28 September 1943

Italy Units of British X Corps emerge into the plain of Naples at Nocera and push on. Inland US VI Corps is advancing near Avellino and has taken Teora despite having to advance over difficult roads.

29 September 1943

Italy The US 3rd Division begins to attack Avellino. In the X Corps sector the advance reaches beyond Pompeii.
World Affairs General Eisenhower and Marshal Badoglio sign the full armistice agreement aboard HMS *Nelson* at Malta.
Eastern Front The Soviet forces take Kremenchug after the usual fierce battle. Farther north, Rudnya on the Smolensk-Vitebsk railroad, is taken.

30 September 1943

Italy Advance units of X Corps reach the outskirts of Naples. Inland the Americans take Avellino.
Eastern Front The Soviets take Krichev on the River Sozh.

October 1943

Europe, Air Operations Bomber Command drop 13,000 tons of bombs in nine large operations. Targets include Munich, Kassel and Frankfurt. Heavy bombers of Eighth Air Force drop 4700 tons on targets including Emden, Bremen and Anklam. The USAAF raid on Schweinfurt is very significant (*see* 14 October). USAAF medium bombers drop 850 tons on various French airfields. RAF medium and light forces are also active against railroads and airfields. The last Wellington bombers are taken out of front-line service with RAF Bomber Command and are replaced by four-engined heavy bombers.
Pacific, Air Operations There are many Allied attacks in all areas. Rabaul is perhaps the target most heavily hit, being raided five times. In all operations Allied pilots claim to have shot down 780 Japanese aircraft. This is an exaggeration but gives some idea of the extent of the attacks.
China, Air Operations During the month the US Fourteenth Air Force attacks Haiphong, Hainan, Kwanchow and Quangyen.
Battle of the Atlantic From early in the month the Allies are able to use bases in the Azores and thus cover areas of the Atlantic which their land-based aircraft have been unable to patrol previously. The efforts of the newly equipped U-Boats continue, especially against the convoys ONS-18 and ON-202 but have little success. The U-Boat fleet is still large at 175 operational boats and 237 in training but a further 26 are lost during the month. In September and October nine merchant ships have been lost in north Atlantic convoys and 25 U-Boats have been sunk while attempting to attack.

1 October 1943

Italy Naples is taken by Fifth Army. Eighth Army begins to advance its main forces once again. For the moment only two divisions, 78th and 1st Canadian of XIII Corps, are sent forward. V corps is kept back in reserve for the moment.

Owing to the success achieved by the delaying actions so far, Hitler orders Kesselring to hold a line south of Rome during the coming months rather than retire farther north.

1-6 October 1943

Eastern Front The Soviets cross the Dniepr in several places north and, more particularly, south of Kremenchug. Konev is in command here and farther north beyond Kiev Vatutin organizes similar work. Bridges are quickly improvised.

2 October 1943

New Guinea Finschhafen is taken by troops from the Australian 20th Brigade. The 23rd Brigade, which has advanced overland from Lae, also reaches the town.

2-3 October 1943

Italy The US VI Corps takes Benevento on the 2nd at the same time as the advance units of 78th Division on the east coast cross the Biferno. During the night commandos land near Termoli and take the town. The Germans send 16th Panzer Division from positions on the Volturno to meet this attack. The commandos succeed in joining up with 78th Division as the battle continues.

3 October 1943

Aegean The Germans land on Cos. They complete the capture on 4 October and take 1400 British and 3150 Italians prisoner.

4 October 1943

Corsica The liberation of the island is completed when the Free French forces enter Bastia.
New Guinea Australian troops manage to capture Kumpu as they extend their advance into the Ramu Valley from the Markham Valley.
Arctic German shipping off the Norwegian coast near Bodo is attacked by aircraft from the US carrier *Ranger* operating with the British Home Fleet. Four freighters are sunk and seven badly damaged at little cost. The battleships *Duke of York* and *Anson* are in support.
British Command Admiral Pound resigns his post as First Sea Lord because of ill health. He dies on 21 October. His position is taken by Admiral Andrew Cunningham after Admiral Fraser has refused the job.
Solomons The Japanese complete the evacuation of Kolombangara. Despite the attention of American destroyers, 9400 men of General Sasaki's garrison have been got away by Admiral Ijuin's ships.

5 October 1943

Italy Fifth Army takes Aversa and Maddaloni. Forward units of X Corps reach the Volturno. In the battle around Termoli, 16th Panzer comes into action and for a time pushes the British back.

5-6 October 1943

Central Pacific Wake Island is shelled and bombed on both days by ships and planes from Admiral Montgomery's Task Force 14. There are six carriers, seven cruisers and 25 destroyers in this force. The carrier aircraft fly 738 sorties.

6 October 1943

New Britain Small parties of US troops land secretly around Cape Gloucester to spy out the land.
Italy Fifth Army takes Caserta, drives on to the Volturno and captures Capua. On the east coast the British gain the upper hand in the fighting around Termoli.

6-7 October 1943

Solomons The American 25th Division lands unopposed at Vila on Kolombangara on the 6th. The whole island is occupied by the 9th. During the night of 6/7 October two Japanese destroyers are sent to evacuate 600 men from Vella Lavella. Six more destroyers escorting them are engaged by three American ships. In a torpedo action each side loses one destroyer and both the other American vessels are damaged.

7 October 1943

Aegean Two British cruisers and two destroyers intercept a German convoy bound for Cos and sink seven transports and one escort.
Eastern Front In a new offensive in the north the Soviets take Nevel. At the western end of the Kuban Peninsula Taman is captured. Along the Dniepr to the south of Kiev there is something of a lull as the Soviets bring up supplies and build bridges.
Italy The Germans withdraw from contact with the 78th Division around Termoli and pull back behind the Trigno. Montgomery does not feel able to follow them closely at this stage.

8 October 1943

Italy Eighth Army takes Larino and Guglionesi inland from the coast on either side of the Biferno. Fifth Army has now come up to the Volturno line and plans an attack for 12 October.

9 October 1943

Eastern Front Petrov's forces complete the occupation of the Kuban but most of Seventeenth Army have escaped to the Crimea. Seventeenth Army is to be sent to join the right of the German line to the south of Zaporozhye but will in fact be too late to move out of the Crimea when the front around Melitopol is broken in the next few days.

10 October 1943

Eastern Front The Soviets take Dobrush, just to the east of Gomel.
Italy Troops from Fifth Army enter Portelandalfo, north of Benevento.

11 October 1943

Eastern Front The Soviets capture Novobelitsa on the outskirts of Gomel.
Italy Montgomery regroups his forward troops. Both V and XIII Corps are now in the line but there will be a pause while the reorganization is completed.

Above: The five-man crew of a Vickers Wellington bomber walk out to their aircraft, October 1943.

12 October 1943

New Britain In a surprise attack 349 planes of Fifth Air Force drop 350 tons of bombs on Rabaul.

12-13 October 1943

Italy During the night Fifth Army starts its attacks on the Volturno line. On the left are the three divisions, 46th, 56th and 7th Armored, of McCreery's X Corps. Between the coast and Capua 46th and 7th Armored make some progress but are held by German counterattacks. Around Capua 56th Division can make no ground at all. The American VI Corps (General Lucas) does rather better. All three divisions, 3rd, 34th and 45th, make good advances. The German defense is energetically conducted throughout and in any case the river, swollen by recent rain, and the roadless hills would have been formidable obstructions. The combination of bad weather, inadequate roads and German demolitions means that, until the ground hardens in the spring, the Allied advance must hinge around the three or four major roads.

13 October 1943

World Affairs Italy declares war on Germany.

14 October 1943

Eastern Front The Soviets capture Zaporozhye. To the south they begin to assault Melitopol and farther south still they cut the railroad leading to the Crimea from Melitopol.
Europe, Air Operations A force of 291 Flying Fortresses from Eighth Air Force is sent to attack the German ball-bearing works at Schweinfurt. They do considerable damage to the target but lose 60 planes with a further 140 damaged. Most of the losses occur during the 400-mile round trip unescorted from Aachen.

Below: The South African Field Marshal Smuts (center) visits Eisenhower (right) and Alexander (left), the Allied commanders in Italy, October 1943.

Above: The second USAAF raid on ball-bearing factories at Schweinfurt in Bavaria, 14 October 1943 – a costly daylight operation.

The Eighth Air Force has lost a further 88 aircraft in the last week. These losses are intolerable and the USAAF abandons long-range, unescorted daylight attacks for the time being. They are not equipped to attack by night. The theories of the American airmen have been disproved on two counts. Bombers cannot fight their way to the target without prohibitive casualties and even carefully selected targets like Schweinfurt offer no great gains. Production in Germany is quickly switched to other areas, extra supplies are bought from Sweden and in any case an investigation ordered by Speer shows that stocks of ball bearings will last for several months.
Italy The battle on the Volturno goes on. The American V Corps continues to advance, especially on their right. The British 56th Division crosses the river east of its previous position and also pushes forward. In the Eighth Army sector 1st Canadian Division takes Campobasso.

15 October 1943

Southeast Asia, Command The British General Pownall is appointed Chief of Staff to Admiral Mountbatten at SEAC. General Wedemeyer, an American, is to be his deputy Chief of Staff.
New Guinea The Japanese mount an air attack on Allied positions in Oro Bay. The attacking aircraft take heavy losses. The attack is repeated on 17 October with the same results.
Italy The Canadians from Eighth Army take Vinchiaturo. The battle in Fifth Army's sector has now moved north of the Volturno but the Germans are still defending expertly. They intend to fall back to two intermediate defense lines, the Barbara Line and the Reinhard Line, before the principal Gustav Line defenses behind the Garigliano, Rapido and Sangro.

16 October 1943

United States, Command General Brereton takes command of the US Ninth Air Force in the UK.
Italy In the Fifth Army sector the Germans begin to make a fighting withdrawal to the Barbara line according to the schedule that Kesselring has ordered.

16-18 October 1943

New Guinea The Japanese counterattack from the few remaining outposts around Finschhafen but the Australians hold them off.

17 October 1943

German Raiders The last operational German auxiliary cruiser, *Michel,* is sunk by the US submarine *Tarpon* off the Japanese coast. *Michel* has sunk 17 ships during its cruise.
Eastern Front The Soviets break the German line around Kremenchug and push forward once more. They also cross the Dniepr south of Gomel and take Loyev.
Italy The Americans take Liberi and Alvignano.

18 October 1943

Italy The US 3rd and 34th Divisions reach Dragoni and prepare to attack it. Gioia is also taken.
Solomons There is a heavy air attack on the Japanese base at Buin on Bougainville.
Eastern Front The fighting for Melitopol continues. The Soviets have now penetrated to the center of the town.

19 October 1943

Italy The Germans pull out of Dragoni just before the attack from 34th Division goes in.
Eastern Front The Soviets attack Pyatikhatki, to the west of Dnepropetrovsk. Konev's forces are storming out of the Kremenchug bridgehead and making for Krivoy Rog. Manstein is desperately bringing up reserves to meet this attack and give the forces holding the bend of the Dniepr time to pull back. In the Kiev sector the Soviet units are busily consolidating their bridgeheads north of the city. They capture Vishgorod as well.

20 October 1943

Pacific The aircraft from the Japanese carriers in Truk are tranferred to Rabaul. The ships concerned are *Zuikaku, Shokaku, Zuiho, Junyo, Hiyo* and *Ryuho.* Although the aircraft are withdrawn from Rabaul in November they take heavy losses in the meantime, further signalling the decline of the Japanese naval air force as the number of experienced pilots dwindles.
Italy The US 45th Division takes Piedimonte d'Alife while on its left 3rd and 34th Divisions advance on either side of the Volturno.
New Guinea The 24th Brigade arrives at Finschhafen to reinforce the Australian troops already there and to help clear the continuing Japanese resistance in the area. As ever, the Japanese hang on doggedly to their positions.

21 October 1943

Mediterranean, Command Admiral Sir John Cunningham succeeds Admiral Sir Andrew Cunningham in command of the RN forces in the Mediterranean.

22 October 1943

British Command General Laycock becomes the British Chief of Combined Operations.
Italy Eighth Army comes into action once more. Near the coast 78th Division seizes a small bridgehead over the Trigno during the night. Fifth Army is still fighting hard to make any sort of advance.

23 October 1943

Eastern Front Melitopol falls to the Soviets after 10 days of fighting. The thrust from Kremenchug toward Krivoy Roy is still making good progress but slows as the opposition stiffens. The Soviets are now within 20 miles of the town.
English Channel A German squadron protecting a blockade runner sinks the British cruiser *Charybdis* and the destroyer *Limbourne*.
Italy In the Fifth Army sector Sparanise is taken by the British 56th Division.

Below: Field Marshal Paul Ewald von Kleist, commander of the German Army Group A in the long retreat through the southern Ukraine, 1943-44.

23-24 October 1943

New Britain Rabaul is raided on both days. One destroyer is sunk in the harbor along with five merchant ships.

24 October 1943

Italy The US 34th Division takes Sant 'Angelo.

25 October 1943

Eastern Front Malinovsky launches a powerful attack across the Dniepr at Dnepropetrovsk and Dneprodzerzhinsk. Both towns are taken comparatively easily because the German forces there have been weakened to meet Konev's attacks and Kleist's forces have not yet been brought into line from the Crimea. Holding a defensive position on the River Dniepr has become a major problem for the Germans.

26 October 1943

New Guinea The Japanese outposts around Finschhafen begin to withdraw toward Sattelberg.

27 October 1943

Italy Eighth Army captures Montefalcone. Nearer the coast a night attack expands 78th Division's bridgehead across the Trigno but the main German defenses still hold out.
Eastern Front The Germans stage limited counterattacks south of Nikopol on the Nogaysk Steppe in an attempt to prevent the Soviets cutting off the Crimea.
Solomons New Zealand troops land on the Treasury Islands. The soldiers are from General Row's 8th Brigade and they meet no opposition on Stirling Island and only a few Japanese on Mono.

28 October-3 November 1943

Solomons In Operation Blissful the 2nd Marine Parachute Battalion is landed by sea at Voza on Choiseul. This is intended to be a diversion from the attack on Bougainville. After a series of sharp actions they are withdrawn from the operation.

Above: A Japanese coastal freighter comes under air attack in the south-western Pacific, 1943, as part of a campaign against merchant trade.

29 October 1943

Eastern Front The German forces between Orsha and Vitebsk come under renewed pressure from the Soviet armies. The brunt of the attacks is borne by General Heinrici's Fourth Army but he expertly organizes the defense to beat them off. His performance in these and later battles earns him the reputation as probably the best defensive tactician in the German army.
Italy Cantalupo is taken by troops from XIII Corps of Eighth Army.

30 October 1943

Eastern Front In their advance across the Nogaysk Steppe, the Soviet forces reach Genichesk cutting one exit from the Crimea.
Italy On the west coast Fifth Army takes Mondragone, having penetrated the Barbara line there. Inland the other units of the army continue their advance over the difficult hilly terrain against tenacious defense.

31 October 1943

Italy In the British X Corps sector Teano is taken in the course of attacks toward Monte Santa Croce. To the left attacks also go in against Monte Massico.
Eastern Front The Soviets capture Chaplinka and have now, therefore, cut all the railroad lines leading out of the Crimea, cutting off German supplies.

November 1943

Europe, Air Operations RAF Bomber Command drops 14,500 tons of bombs in various raids. Berlin is raided on three nights and is hit by more than 4000 tons of bombs. The 'Battle of Berlin' begins on the 18th. Dusseldorf and Frankfurt are other targets. American heavy bombers drop 6300 tons of bombs on a range of objectives in Norway and Germany. Ryukan and Knaben in Norway, and Wilhelmshaven and Munster are all attacked. The raid on Bremen on 26 November is the heaviest yet by the Americans. US medium bombers drop 1300 tons over France and the Low Countries. RAF aircraft also attack communications targets in these areas.

The Mediterranean forces attack a range of communications targets in Italy, especially later in the month to coincide with Eighth Army's attacks across the River Sangro. Strategic targets include Turin, Sofia and Toulon. Aircraft from the Middle East are active against shipping in the Aegean.

Pacific Japanese shipping losses reach a new high this month with the sinking of 265,000 tons, mostly by US submarines. Japan began the war with a merchant fleet of almost 6,000,000 tons capacity (not counting very small vessels). This has now been reduced, despite new construction, to less than 5,000,000 tons.

November-December 1943

Battle of the Atlantic During these months 78 North Atlantic convoys pass across the ocean without loss. Seventeen U-Boats are sunk. During the six months up to November, 12 of the German U-Tanker fleet of 17 boats are sunk. Shipping losses in the two months total 60 ships of 313,000 tons.

1 November 1943

Solomons The US landings on Bougainville begin. The island is defended by General Hyakutake's Seventeenth Army with about 40,000 men and 20,000 naval personnel. Most are concentrated in the south of the island where the Japanese airfields are and where the sea conditions favor a landing. The Americans chose instead to land in Empress Augusta Bay at Cape Tarokina. The landing force is General Turnage's 3rd Marine Division, transported by Admiral Wilkinson's Task Force 31. The local Japanese garrison is only 200 men and is quickly overcome. Offshore a marine battalion lands on Puruata Island and takes it after a fight. By the end of the day 14,000 men are ashore. Admiral Merrill's Task Force 39, with four cruisers and eight destroyers, is in support and also shells Buka Island. Admiral Sherman has the carriers *Saratoga* and *Princeton* of Task Force 38 to the west and they add air attacks against Buka and the airfields at Buna.

After unsuccessful air attacks on the landings the Japanese send Admiral Omori from Rabaul with four cruisers and six destroyers to make attacks.

United States, Home Front President Roosevelt orders Ickes and his Solid Fuels Administration to take over the running of the country's coal mines. There are 530,000 men out on strike. There have been a number of disputes throughout October but from 28 October the strike gains momentum. The problem is resolved, for the moment, on 3 November.

Roosevelt urges Congress to continue food subsidies to encourage production and as a measure against inflation.

Eastern Front The Soviets take Perekop and advance to Armiansk, thus isolating the Crimea. Manstein's forces around Krivoy Rog begin a series of counterattacks which temporarily hold the Soviet advance. Part of the Soviet Fifty-sixth Army is landed in the Crimea near Enikale.

Arctic The first in a new series of Arctic convoys sails from the Kola Inlet to Loch Ewe and arrives without loss on 14 November. Of the next three convoys only one is attacked and the only damage is to an attacking U-Boat. These operations are completed by 9 December.

Italy The British X Corps continues its attacks against the German line between Monte Massico and Monte Santa Croce. Roccamonfina is taken by 56th Division in these attacks. The fighting along the Trigno in Eighth Army's sector continues.

2 November 1943

Solomons Just after midnight Omori's squadron steaming for Bougainville is detected by the radar of the American Task Force 39, led by Admiral Merrill. A confused night action ensues in which the American radar proves crucial. The Japanese lose one cruiser and one destroyer and most of their other ships are damaged. Two cruisers and two destroyers are damaged on the American side but the Japanese are forced to turn away. During the day, air attacks on Merrill's ships fail. On Bougainville itself the Americans extend their beachhead without difficulty, having wiped out the local garrison. Aircraft from Task Force 38 raid Buna and Buka.

Above: General Nikolai Vatutin, commander of the Russian 1st Ukrainian Front (Army Group); he liberated Kiev in January 1944.

New Britain The Japanese base at Rabaul is attacked by about 160 land-based aircraft from Fifth Air Force. Perhaps 20 aircraft on each side are lost. The US sinks three ships in the harbor.

United States Command General Spaatz takes command of all US Air Forces in the Mediterranean.

Italy Eighth Army's operations across the Trigno are stepped up into a full-scale attack. In the main coastal sector the advance of 78th Division is supported by a naval bombardment. On the west coast the Allied forces continue to make ground slowly. The 7th Armored Division from British X Corps reaches the Garigliano.

Eastern Front The Soviets take Kakhovka on the lower Dniepr.

3 November 1943

Italy The British forces attacking near San Salvo meet heavy resistance from 16th Panzer Division (soon to be withdrawn to refit for the Soviet Union) but manage to break into the main defensive positions. In the Fifth Army sector Sessa Aurunca falls to X Corps.

4 November 1943

New Britain A fresh Japanese squadron led by Admiral Kurita with 10 cruisers and as many destroyers arrives in Rabaul. They are sighted en route and Task Force 38 is ordered to attack with its aircraft.

Eastern Front Vatutin's forces begin to break out of their bridgeheads over the Dniepr near Kiev. They find the weak spots in the inevitably thin German defense. In the south the Soviets are also attacking near Kherson.

Below: US Army Air Force enlisted men help to cement Anglo-American relations at a dance on a bomber base, October 1943.

Italy The British X Corps now holds Monte Massico and Monte Santa Croce and sends the 78th Division against Monte Camino. On the American VI Corps' sector Venafro and Rocavirondola are taken as the advance nears the Reinhard line. In the Eighth Army area the Germans are withdrawing to the Sangro. The two Allied armies now have full lateral communications through Isernia.

5 November 1943

New Britain Sherman leads *Saratoga* and *Princeton* to attack Kurita's quadron, newly arrived in Rabaul. Four heavy cruisers and two light cruisers as well as two destroyers from the squadron are damaged by the 107 attacking planes. The Americans only lose 10 planes. A second assault, this time by land based Liberators, adds to the confusion.
Solomons The marines on Bougainville beat off a counterattack by the Japanese 23rd Regiment. Few of the Japanese garrison of the island are being sent to oppose the landings, partly because of the difficult terrain that intervenes between the landing and the main Japanese concentrations but more because the Japanese commander judges that the attack is a feint.
France, Resistance Resistance workers set bombs in the Peugeot factory at Sochaux, destroying equipment used in the manufacture of tank turrets. When the Germans try to bring in new machinery that too is sabotaged. This factory is described by the British Ministry of Economic Warfare as the third most important target in France.
Eastern Front The Soviet threat to encircle Kiev grows as they cut the Kiev-Zhitomir railroad and continue to advance at practically pursuit pace. In the south they completely overrun the area between the lower Dniepr and the Crimea.
Italy Fifth Army begins major attacks against the Reinhard line. The most important efforts are in the center where the British 56th Division assault Monte Camino and the US 3rd Division attacks near Mignano. The tenacious defense made by Hube's XIV Panzer Corps is aided by the extremely difficult terrain and the vile weather. The attacks make little progress but are continued. In the Eighth Army sector Vasto, Palmoli and Torrebruna are taken.

6 November 1943

Eastern Front The Soviet Union's third city, Kiev, is retaken by Vatutin's forces. Stalin issues a special order of the day and makes a broadcast to celebrate the achievement. Only 6000 prisoners have been taken, however. Once more the Germans have managed to slip away.
Italy Fifth Army's attacks are repeated but can gain nothing against stubborn defense.

7 November 1943

Eastern Front The Soviet attacks west of Kiev reach Fastov, 40 miles away, where there is a thin German defense line.
Solomons The carriers *Saratoga* and *Princeton* are attacked by 100 Japanese aircraft when 240 miles southeast of Rabaul but are not hit. Early in the day a Japanese battalion is landed just north of the American beachhead on Bougainville and immediately begins a fierce action.

8 November 1943

Italy The battle in the Fifth Army sector continues with no decisive success as both sides organize attacks and counterattacks. Troops from the left of Eighth Army reach the Sangro high up in the hills.

9 November 1943

France, Politics Generals Giraud, Georges and three others resign from the Committee of National Liberation. Giraud remains as Commander in Chief for the moment.
Solomons As the Americans advance inland on Bougainville to extend their bridgehead they meet up with the main body of the Japanese 23rd Regiment on the jungle tracks and a vicious battle develops. The second wave of the landings begins with the arrival of most of the 37th Infantry Division.
Eastern Front The Soviet forces have overcome the German resistance west of Kiev around Fastov, and are now advancing toward Zhitomir.
Italy Castiglione falls to the 8th Indian Division from Eighth Army.

11 November 1943

Mediterranean An Allied convoy east of Oran is attacked by about 50 German aircraft and loses three transports and one tanker.
Solomons On Bougainville the battle between the marines and the 23rd Regiment ends in defeat for the Japanese infantry, which is pushed back.
New Britain Admirals Sherman and Montgomery lead two separate task forces to attack the Japanese base at Rabaul. Five carriers are in-

Below: Men of the 2/165th US Infantry Regiment wade ashore under Japanese machine-gun fire, Makin Atoll, 20 November 1943.

Below: US Marines push forward under fire on the island of Tarawa in the Gilbert Islands chain during November 1943.

volved and 185 aircraft attack altogether. The Japanese lose almost 70 of the defending Zero fighters to the American planes and one light cruiser and two destroyers in the harbor are put out of action. The strike aircraft sent against the carriers achieve no hits.

Eastern Front The Soviet forces driving west of Kiev take a crossing of the River Teterev and capture Radomyshl and other towns on the approach to Zhitomir.

Italy Montgomery's forces occupy Casalanguida as they push forward to the next German defense line on the Sangro.

12 November 1943

Eastern Front The Soviets capture Korostyshev, west of Kiev, and move on to enter Zhitomir. Zhitomir is a vitally important rail center on the last lateral rail line available to the Germans east of the Pripet marshes.

Aegean German forces from the 22nd Infantry Division under General Muller land on the Dodecanese island of Leros. They complete the capture of the island by 16 November and 3500 British and 5350 Italian troops surrender. In addition the British lose one destroyer offshore.

New Britain The remnants of the Japanese carrier aircraft transferred to Rabaul on 20 October are withdrawn because of their recent heavy losses. Of the 173 planes committed, 121 have been lost, with many irreplaceable pilots.

Italy The Allied attacks are grinding to a half before the Reinhard line. The British 56th Division is forced to retire from some of its positions on Monte Camino.

13 November 1943

Gilbert Islands Flying Fortresses bomb Tarawa Atoll in the first attack in preparation for the coming landings. These attacks are repeated daily for the next week.

Solomons The third wave of the US landing force, the remainder of the 37th Infantry Division and the 21st Marines, begins to disembark on Bougainville. Merrill's Task Force 39 again provides cover with the cruiser *Denver* taking a torpedo hit. There is a further action on the island on the Numa-Numa trail.

Italy Clark tells Alexander that he believes that Fifth Army's attacks should be halted for the present. Eighth Army continues to move forward of the Sangro and captures Atessa.

Eastern Front The Soviets complete the capture of Zhitomir and begin to extend their advance north toward Korosten.

14 November 1943

Eastern Front Manstein orders Manteuffel's 7th Panzer Division to counterattack south of Zhitomir from around Berdichev.

Italy Perano is captured by troops from 8th Indian Division supported by 2nd New Zealand Division. The New Zealanders have only just come into Eighth Army's order of battle and Montgomery now has five divisions and two armored brigades. His oppponents, LXXVI Panzer Corps, have 65th Infantry Division, 1st Parachute Division and part of 26th Panzer Division.

Solomons On Bougainville the Americans continue to push the Japanese back along the jungle tracks, helped now by a few tanks which act as an armored spearhead.

15 November 1943

Italy Alexander calls off Fifth Army's attacks. Casualties have been heavy and the stubborn German defense, backed by rugged terrain and the shocking weather, shows no sign of cracking. In the east small units of Eighth Army succeed in crossing the Sangro but are fighting hard and do not yet have a solid hold.

16 November 1943

Eastern Front The Soviets continue to attack and make gains north of Zhitomir, which is threatened by a German attack from the south. Although the Germans only have a very small force in this attack, by widespread penetrations it gives the appearance of greater strength.

Italy The small British forces on the north bank of the Sangro consolidate their gains.

New Guinea The Australians have brought up tanks to help in their attacks on the Japanese strongholds near Sattelberg. These attacks now begin.

17 November 1943

Eastern Front The Soviets continue to advance toward Korosten and capture Novodichi. Farther north they also make gains near Gomel.

18 November 1943

Eastern Front The Soviets take Korosten and Ovruch, a little farther north in the Kiev sector. West of Gomel they also take Rechitsa and cut the railroad in that direction. The Germans are still applying pressure south of Zhitomir.

Europe, Air Operations RAF Bomber Command begins the 'Battle of Berlin,' the third of Air Marshal Harris' well publicized campaigns. The campaign will include 16 major attacks on the German capital as well as others against different targets. In the attacks against Berlin itself about 9100 sorties are flown and 600 aircraft lost. The battle ends on 24 March.

19 November 1943

Central Pacific US carrier aircraft raid Mili, Tarawa, Makin and Nauru in preparation for the coming landings. Four carrier groups are involved from Admiral Pownall's Task Force 50 which includes 11 carriers, five battleships and six cruisers.

Italy The Germans withdraw the last of their forces north of the Sangro. Although Eighth Army also has troops north of the Sangro they hold only very little ground and a major, formal attack will be necessary to expand their tiny enclaves.

Eastern Front The Germans move in to take Zhitomir as the Soviets realize their danger and retreat.

20 November 1943

Gilbert Islands The American landing operations in the Gilbert Islands begin. There are US landings on Tarawa Atoll. General J C Smith leads 18,600 men from the 2nd Marine Division, escorted by Admiral Hill's Task Force 53 with a bombardment group of three battleships and four cruisers and air support of four escort carriers. The Japanese garrison comprises 4800 men led by Admiral Shibasaki. They have 50 artillery weapons and seven light tanks.

The landings are to be made on Betio Island which is little more than two miles long and is nowhere more than half a mile wide. The highest ground is only nine feet above sea level but the Japanese have added a formidable complex of bunkers and gun emplacements. The preliminary bombardment is massive – the supporting warships fire more than 3000 tons of shells and in addition there are air attacks. There are, however, some difficulties with the timing and coordination of the shelling and air attacks and the bombardment is lifted a little too early. The sandy ground absorbs much of the blast of the explosions and many of the Japanese bunkers remain intact. The reef around the island is also shallower in places than has been expected and many of the landing craft ground, leaving the marines to run through a vicious crossfire to the beach. In many of the Pacific operations a lack of precise topographical information is a problem. With this difficulty and the heavy Japanese fire many of the landing force do not reach the beaches and those who do are mostly pinned down at the water's edge. Of the 5000 who attempt to land, 1500 become casualties. Owing to the state of the tide, another unknown, and confusion in the chain of command, reserves are not sent at first and later cannot be sent. At nightfall the outcome of the battle is still in doubt. During the night the Japanese undertake some infiltrations but because of the bombardment are not able to organize an attack.

There are also US landings on the Makin atoll. The attack force here is drawn from General R C Smith's 27th Infantry Division. Naval support is provided by Admiral Turner's Task Force 52, which includes a bombardment group of four battleships and four cruisers and an air-support group with three escort carriers. The landings on Butaritari are fairly successful despite the energetic defense and the inexperience of the attackers.

The carrier *Independence* from the main carrier Task Force 50 is hit by a submarine torpedo.

Eastern Front In a new attack the Soviets cross the Dniepr near Cherkassy.

Solomons The Americans continue to push inland along the Numa-Numa trail parallel to the Piva River.

Italy Montgomery planned to attack the Sangro line today but heavy rain has swollen the river and made the ground even more difficult, so only a limited effort can be made. Only 36th Brigade is sent across and is quickly involved in a testing action.

Aegean The British evacuate Samos. The Germans move in on the 23rd and disarm 2500 troops on the island. This is the end of the brief campaign in the Dodecanese which has been too quickly improvised by the British with insufficient forces and as a result the British have taken a beating.

21 November 1943

Gilbert Islands The Americans send in new waves of marines to land on Betio Island, Tarawa Atoll. The first group take heavy casualties from Japanese positions established the previous night but at about noon there is a significant change in the tide and the marines begin to flow ashore, both over the original beaches in the north and in the west of the island. Other American units land on Bairiki nearby.

The American forces are firmly ashore on Butaritari Island, Makin and push forward against fierce Japanese resistance.

New Guinea The attacks of the Australian 9th Division around Sattelberg are gradually gaining the upper hand.

Eastern Front Having taken Zhitomir the Germans now extend their attacks toward Korosten. The German attack is gaining momentum.

Above: A US Marine prepares to throw a grenade at a Japanese pillbox on Tarawa.

22 November 1943

Gilbert Islands There is now no question of the outcome of the battle on Tarawa although the Japanese are fighting fiercely for every inch of ground. During the night there are fanatical counterattacks by the Japnese at the east end of the island but they achieve nothing.

The American advance on Makin continues and by nightfall almost all of Butaritari has been

Below: The chaos of the Tarawa beachhead is captured in this photograph.

taken. During the night a Japanese counter-attack is wiped out.

There are US landings on Abimama, another atoll in the Gilbert Islands.

Italy The British forces have now won a fairly substantial bridgehead north of the Sangro about five miles wide and nearly 2000 yards deep. It is very difficult to bridge or cross the river in its present state and supplies and other help to the north bank are tenuous indeed.

22-25 November 1943

Allied Planning Roosevelt, Churchill and Chiang Kai-shek meet in Cairo. The discussions center on plans for Burma and China but no major decisions are reached. Equally there is no attempt, as the British want, to prepare a joint approach for the coming Teheran talks with Stalin.

23 November 1943

Gilbert Islands By noon the battle on Tarawa is over. The Americans have lost 1000 killed and 2000 wounded. The Japanese garrison has been annihilated. The only prisoners are 17 wounded soldiers and 129 Korean laborers. In proportion to the forces engaged it has been the most costly operation in the United States' military history. There have been important lessons for the organization of future attacks, particularly of the need for precise bombardment. Equipment can also be improved. In one respect it has been a successful trial for the new system of the fleet train which provides support and repair for the naval units far from their bases.

The Americans complete the capture of Makin island also. They have about 200 dead and wounded. The Japanese have lost about three times as many, including prisoners. The escort carrier *Liscombe Bay* is sunk offshore by a Japanese submarine with the loss of 600 more lives.

German Planning The prototype of the Me 262 jet airplane is demonstrated before Hitler. He hails it as the ideal light bomber – a decision which is believed to have hindered its development and production for its true role as a fighter. The aircraft first flew in July 1942 and becomes operational in June 1944.

Above: An Australian officer poses aboard the Japanese Light Tank Type 95 he has recently destroyed, Milne Bay, New Guinea, 1943.

24 November 1943

Eastern Front The German attacks around Korosten now have increased strength and the Soviets are forced back.

Solomons The Japanese mount a small attack on the American positions on Bougainville which the marines easily drive off.

Below: Commander Peter Gretton (center), captain of HMS *Duncan* and leader of one of the most successful Atlantic escort groups.

25 November 1943

Eastern Front The Soviets mount a new effort between Mogilev and Gomel. Propaisk is taken.

China, Air Operations Planes from Fourteenth Air Force attack Formosa for the first time, destroying 42 aircraft on the ground at Shinchiku airfield.

New Britain Five Japanese destroyers taking men to Buka in the Solomons are surprised by five US destroyers led by Captain Burke off Cape St George. Three Japanese ships are sunk in a night action. This is the last of the night sea battles which have characterized the Solomons campaign.

New Guinea The Australians at last capture the final Japanese positions at Sattelberg.

26 November 1943

Eastern Front The Soviets take Gomel which has been threatened with encirclement for some time.

Mediterranean A British troop transport is sunk off Bougie by a glider bomb and more than 1000 of the passengers are killed. Eight of the attacking aircraft are shot down.

27 November 1943

Italy The British manage to move a tank brigade across the Sangro to support their troops to the north who are still fighting hard.

28 November 1943

Italy A massive air and artillery bombardment signals the start of Eighth Army's offensive across the Sangro. A new bridgehead is fairly quickly won and by the end of the day 8th Indian Division have penetrated nearly to Mozzogrogna. The defending German 65th Division is badly shaken by the shelling and is in any case

unusually poorly trained and badly equipped. The attack was intended to follow up the initial advance on 20 November but has been delayed by bad weather. This has given the Germans time to assemble reserves behind 65th Division.
Eastern Front The Soviets make important gains northwest of Gomel, near Zhlobin, whereas farther south near Korosten they are in trouble.

28 November-1 December 1943

Allied Planning Churchill, Roosevelt and Stalin and their staffs meet for the first time at Teheran. The decision to invade western Europe in May 1944 is confirmed and a now more definite plan for the invasion of southern France (Anvil) is agreed. This has been an American idea up to now (the British prefer Balkan operations) but Stalin's support gives it increased weight. Churchill accepts it, believing that if there are landing craft in the Mediterranean for Anvil they might be available for other purposes. Perhaps the most important decision to emerge from the conference is Stalin's promise to join the war against Japan when Germany has been defeated.

There were problems of security at the conference and there is reason to believe that the Americans' accommodation was bugged. The Americans were solicitous throughout the proceedings not to appear to be with Britain and against the Soviet Union and in doing so perhaps gave too much ground.

29 November 1943

Italy Eighth Army's battle on the Sangro continues with reasonable progress for the attacks. Mozzogrogna is taken and Fossacesia also falls later in the day.
New Britain Four US destroyers bombard Japanese positions on the south coast, near Gasmata.
New Guinea The Australians capture Gusika and Bonga in their advance from Finschhafen. Sio farther north is shelled by Allied warships.

30 November 1943

Eastern Front The Soviets pull out of Korosten in their second significant setback in this sector.
United States Command General Vandegrift is appointed to become commandant of the US Marine Corps with effect from 1 January 1944.
Italy The attacks of Eighth Army have now cleared the first ridge beyond the Sangro. In the Fifth Army area diversionary attacks begin on the lower reaches of the Garigliano.

December 1943

Europe, Air Operations The heavy bombers of Eighth Air Force and Bomber Command each drop about 12,000 tons of bombs. Bomber Command's targets include Berlin (7000 tons in four raids), Leipzig and Frankfurt. The USAAF attacks Kiel, Emden and Bremen. Both commands hit targets in the Pas de Calais area, especially after 21 December, against launching sites being built for flying bombs.

Bad weather is a problem for the Allied Mediterranean forces throughout the month but there are many sorties against targets including Turin, Innsbruck and Augsburg.

The new variant of the Mustang fighter with the Merlin engine is used operationally for the first time in a fighter sweep over Belgium on 1 December. The first escort mission flown by Mustangs is to Kiel on 13 December. This aircraft will transform the Allied strategic-bombing campaign by its unprecedented combination of range and performance.

1 December 1943

Italy There is growing air and ground activity in Fifth Army's sector as diversionary attacks and other moves are made in preparation for the resumption of the offensive.

2 December 1943

Eastern Front In their attacks south of Kremenchug the Soviets cross the River Ingulets and move on toward Znamenka.
Italy Units of the British X Corps and the newly arrived US II Corps (General Keyes) begin the Fifth Army attack on Monte Camino with massive artillery support. The US VI Corps pushes forward to the right of these attacks. In the east Eighth Army also advances and takes Lanciano and Castelfrentano.
New Guinea On the Huon Peninsula the Australians capture Huanko.

2-3 December 1943

Italy During the night German bombers attack Bari. An ammunition ship in the harbor is hit and explodes, sinking 18 transports of 70,000 tons and destroying 38,000 tons of supplies.

3 December 1943

Eastern Front The Soviets capture Dovsk north of Gomel and make other gains around Rogachev in the same sector. To the south they also push forward west of Cherkassy.
Italy Units from X Corps nearly reach the summit of Monte Camino and to their right units of II Corps capture the slightly lower Monte Maggiore. Eighth Army takes San Vito but does not manage to exploit German weakness around Orsogna where the New Zealand Division is driven back by a desperate counterattack by 26th Panzer Division.

4 December 1943

Marshall Islands Admirals Pownall and Montgomery lead six US carriers and nine cruisers to attack Kwajalein. Six Japanese transports are sunk and two cruisers damaged. Also 55 aircraft are shot down for the loss of five to the attackers. In a subsidiary operation *Yorktown* raids Wotje.
Solomons The marines on Bougainville receive a further reinforcement and are therefore able to extend their perimeter.
Pacific The Japanese escort carrier *Chuyo* is sunk by the US submarine *Sailfish* in Japanese home waters.

5 December 1943

Italy Monte Camino is the scene of more fierce fighting as both sides dispute possession of its summit.

6 December 1943

Italy The British 56th Division captures Monte Camino after a bitter struggle. To the right II Corps now attacks Monte la Difensa, with some success. Eighth Army comes up to the River Moro.

7 December 1943

Italy With the peaks south of the Mignano gap now in Allied hands the second phase of Fifth Army's attack can begin. Operating on a wider front, the US II and VI Corps move against Monte Sammucro and San Pietro but German resistance is strong. Eighth Army attacks Orsogna.
Europe, Air Operations In one of the wilder claims made by the protagonists of strategic bombing, Air Marshal Harris tells his superiors that he believes he can win the war if he is supported in his continuing attacks on Berlin and

Below: General Kurt Student (in peaked cap) inspects German paras, 1943. Student had formed the German airborne arm in the late 1930s.

other targets so that he can send off 15,000 Lancaster missions in the next few months. He will be able to send 14,500 despite arguments about the effectiveness of the bombing, but the war will not be won in this way.

8 December 1943

Marshall Islands Kwajalein is bombarded by five battleships and 12 destroyers led by Admiral Lee. Two carriers give air cover. One Japanese destroyer is damaged.
New Guinea The Australians take Wareo and push on toward Wandokai.
Italy French troops begin to come into the Allied line, first the 2nd Moroccan Infantry Division. Italian troops are also being mobilized. Experienced units are being withdrawn, however, to be moved to Britain to join Operation Overlord. Fifth Army's attacks are making little ground but are continued. Canadian units with Eighth Army begin attacks over the Moro River, a few miles from the east coast.
Eastern Front The Soviets make more progress toward isolating Znamenka by cutting a second rail line out of the town.

9 December 1943

Italy German counterattacks near Monte Sammucro are repelled and to the south the Allied line around Monte Camino is further consolidated.
Solomons The newly built American airfield at Cape Torokina on Bougainville becomes operational.
Eastern Front The Soviets take Mederovo near Znamenka and attack Znamenka itself.

10 December 1943

United States, Home Front The long-running debate on the draft regulations ends when Roosevelt signs a revised bill which puts those who have been fathers since before Pearl Harbor at the bottom of the list.
Eastern Front Znamenka is taken by the Soviets and a little to the north Konev's troops begin a new series of attacks.
Italy Eighth Army is able to cross the Moro River in strength.

Solomons The first American planes arrive at the Cape Torokina airfield. Inland the marines are gradually extending American-held territory.

11 December 1943

Italy The fighting in Fifth Army's sector has continued now for several days. There are as yet no decisive gains for either side and the Allied momentum is being worn down.

12 December 1943

Diplomatic Affairs Dr Beneš visits Moscow to sign a Czech-Soviet treaty of alliance providing for postwar cooperation and mutual assistance for the duration of the war.
Italy The 36th Division of II Corps is now attacking Monte Lungo near its former positions on Monte Maggiore.

14 December 1943

Eastern Front Konev's troops take Cherkassy in the south. Yeremenko's Baltic Front begins a new major offensive just south of Nevel.

15 December 1943

Italy A new phase of Fifth Army attacks begins. The II Corps renews the drive toward San Pietro and Monte Lungo. To the right VI Corps and the Moroccan Division also push forward with the Moroccans doing especially well.
New Britain General Cunningham's 112th Cavalry Regiment lands at Arawe off New Britain. This is a diversionary operation for the main landings on the island (*see* 26 December). The naval units in support are from Admiral Barbey's Task Force 76. An air attack on the Japanese airfield at Cape Gloucester provides further cover.
New Guinea The Australians take Lakona, 15 miles north of Finschhafen.

17 December 1943

Italy The Germans begin to withdraw some troops from San Pietro and from other positions a little to the north. Monte Sammucro is now in Allied hands.

18 December 1943

Italy Fifth Army takes Monte Lungo, making the German position at San Pietro less secure. There are violent German counterattacks all along Fifth Army's front.

Early on, troops from US 36th Division enter San Pietro. To the north VI Corps is advancing all along its front as the Germans pull back a little way.

19 December 1943

New Britain The US forces at Arawe take the nearby Japanese airstrip and beat off minor Japanese counterattacks.

21 December 1943

Italy There is heavy fighting in the Eighth Army sector on the approaches to Ortona and in the Fifth Army area, especially near Monte Sammucro.
Eastern Front The Soviets eliminate a small German bridgehead east of the Dniepr near Kherson. There is heavy fighting in the north near Zhlobin.

22 December 1943

Italy Eighth Army has now entered Ortona but the fight for the town goes on, from street to street and house to house. The town is defended by a unit of 1st Paratroop Division and the attackers come from 2nd Canadian Brigade.

23 December 1943

Italy The 1st Canadian Division from Eighth Army seizes control of most of Ortona. Inland, other Eighth Army units take Arielli.

24 December 1943

Solomons A Task Force of US cruisers and destroyers bombards Buka Island and the Japanese base at Buin on Bougainville, principally to divert attention from the imminent landings on New Britain.
Eastern Front The Soviets have prepared a major effort to retake the ground recently lost west of Kiev. Vatutin leads the reinforced armies of the 1st Ukraine Front in a massive assault. The lines of the defending Fourth Panzer Army are stretched too thin to hold this off, largely because their small reserve has been dissipated in the recent attacks. Once the Soviets succeed in breaking the front there will be little that the German commanders can do to prevent a deep penetration into their rear areas.

Below: A Nakajima B5N 'Kate' attack bomber goes down in flames, December 1943.

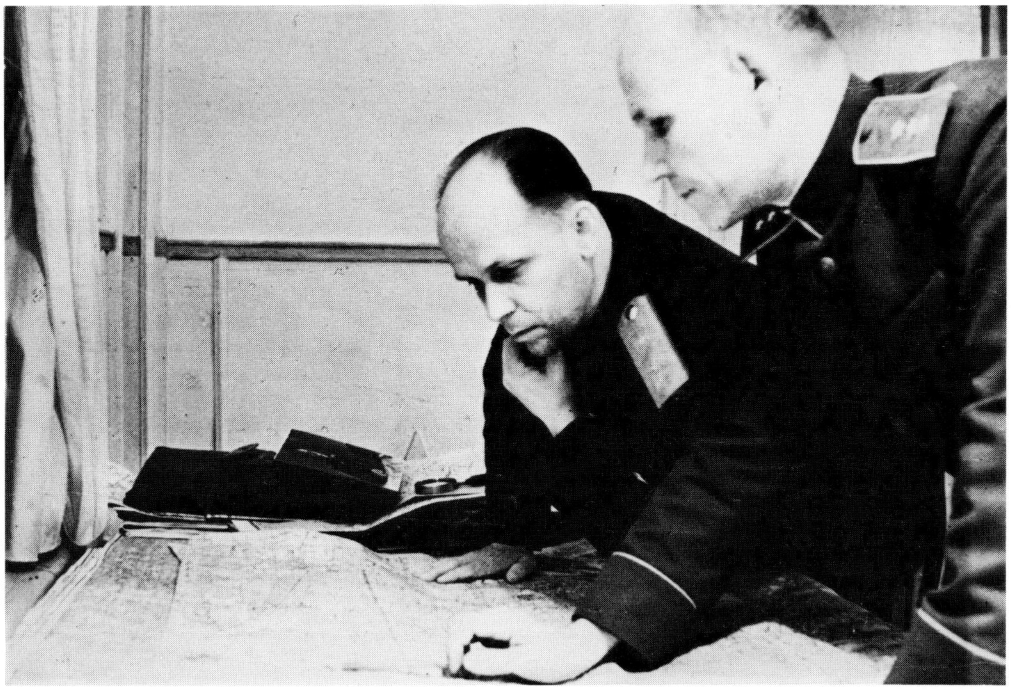

Above: General Ivan Konev (right), commander of the Russian 2nd Ukrainian Front, explains his plans to a member of the Military Council, during the winter of 1943. By now the war had swung the Red Army's way.

24-29 December 1943

Allied Command A series of announcements in London and Washington makes known the leaders for the coming British and American campaigns. General Eisenhower is to be Supreme Allied Commander for the invasion of Europe, with Air Marshal Tedder as his deputy. Admiral Ramsay and Air Marshal Leigh Mallory will lead the naval and air forces respectively. General Montgomery will lead the British group of armies in the operation. General Wilson becomes Supreme Commander for the Mediterranean with General Devers as his deputy. General Alexander commands in Italy. General Eaker commands the Mediterranean Air Forces. General Leese takes over Eighth Army. General Spaatz is appointed to command all the US Strategic Bomber Forces against Germany and General Doolittle will lead Eighth Air Force. General Paget becomes Supreme Commander in the Middle East.

25 December 1943

Eastern Front The Soviet offensive south of Nevel continues and the Vitebsk-Polotsk rail line is cut.
New Ireland Admiral Sherman's Task Group 50.2 raids Kavieng with 86 aircraft. Two carriers and six destroyers are in the attack force and they succeed in sinking only one transport ship.
Arctic The German battlecruiser *Scharnhorst* under Admiral Bey sails from north Norway to attack the convoy JW-55B which has been found by German air and submarine searches. Bey is unaware that the British battleship *Duke of York* is in distant support.

26 December 1943

Arctic In the morning *Scharnhorst* and her destroyers search for the convoy but find instead the three-cruiser covering force led by Admiral Burnett. Visibility is extremely poor and early on *Scharnhorst*'s forward radar set is put out of action. Bey therefore breaks off the engagement and circles north to try to find the convoy. At midday *Scharnhorst* and the cruisers again fight but in better visibility which, combined with the disadvantage of the heavy seas for the smaller ships, should have made things easier for the Germans. If the attack had been pressed home Bey would almost certainly have got among the convoy which was only escorted by small ships with little torpedo armament. Instead the action is broken off. As *Scharnhorst* retreats, *Duke of York*, with Admiral Fraser aboard, comes up and a gun duel begins, surprising the Germans. The British battleship gains the upper hand and eventually the prolonged bombardment and torpedo attacks reduce the *Scharnhorst* to a wreck and she sinks. Only 36 out of her crew of almost 2000 are saved. The Germans now have no large surface ships operational to threaten the Arctic convoys and an important restraint on British dispositions is removed for the rest of the war.
Eastern Front In their offensive in the Kiev sector the Soviets capture Radomyshl.
New Britain After the usual preliminary bombardment, General Rupertus' 1st Marine Division begins landings near Cape Gloucester in three places. Admiral Barbey's Task Force 76 provides the transport and two other groups of cruisers and destroyers are in support. One of these destroyers is sunk by a Japanese air attack. The landing forces get ashore without incident although the terrain is extremely difficult. There are a few small Japanese attacks during the first night but they are driven off.
Italy Monte Sammucro and the surrounding hills are cleared of German defenders.

27 December 1943

New Britain The US beachhead near Cape Gloucester is extended with little resistance from the Japanese. The weather and the ground prove more of a problem. The American forces at Arawe receive reinforcements which make them fairly secure against counterattacks.

27-28 December 1943

Bay of Biscay The German blockade runner *Alsterufer* is sunk in the Bay of Biscay by Allied aircraft on the 27th. On the 28th the 11 German destroyers and torpedo boats which had been sent to escort her are met by two British cruisers, *Enterprise* and *Glasgow*. Three German ships are sunk and the rest break off the engagement. This is a notable achievement by the British against a superior force.

28 December 1943

Eastern Front Vatutin's attacks west of Kiev are making good ground. Korostyshev and Kateyvka near Zhitomir are recaptured.
Italy The Canadians complete the capture of Ortona.
New Britain The marines begin to advance to attack the Japanese airfield at Cape Gloucester.

29 December 1943

Eastern Front The Soviets retake Korosten and Chernakov northwest of Kiev, and Skvira to the southwest.

30 December 1943

New Britain The US Marines complete the capture of the Japanese airfield at Cape Gloucester. It has been a surprisingly easy operation so far.
Eastern Front In the Kiev sector the Soviets take Kazatin near Berdichev.

31 December 1943

Eastern Front The Soviets recapture Zhitomir. Farther north there is increased activity west of Nevel and south of Vitebsk where the road to Orsha is cut. Vitebsk is now almost surrounded.
Italy As the year ends both Fifth and Eighth Armies are battering wearily and almost fruitlessly against the German defenses.

Below: Admiral Sir Bertram Ramsay, appointed Naval Commander for the forthcoming Allied invasion.

US
US
US
US

1944

January 1944

Europe, Air Operations RAF Bomber Command drops 18,000 tons of bombs this month, more than half on Berlin which is attacked by large forces on six nights. Brunswick and Magdeburg are also heavily hit. The American heavy bombers of Eighth and Fifteenth Air Forces drop 22,000 tons as well as destroying many Geman planes in the air. Aircraft factories are among the main targets, especially at Brunswick, Halberstadt and Frankfurt. Both British and American heavy bombers are sent against the V-weapon sites in the Pas de Calais. Although the US Eighth Air Force now has Mustang fighters flying as escorts on its daylight raids, losses can be heavy. On 11 January a quarter of a force of 238 bombers is lost on a mission to Oschersleben. These losses do not reflect, however, the effects of attrition on the German fighter force. For night operations the Germans have now developed an airborne version of the radar-search receiver Naxos fitted to U-Boats to enable them to detect centimetric radar. This is fitted to night fighters using H2S transmissions to help them home into the bomber stream. It is not sufficiently precise for actual interception.

A whole range of communications targets in Italy and southern Europe is attacked by the Allied theater forces. After 22 January 11,000 tons of bombs are dropped in support of the Anzio operation.

Pacific, Air Operations The tempo of the Allied effort quickens here, as elsewhere. Rabaul is attacked on 13 occasions, the Marshall Islands on 11 and other targets also suffer heavy blows.

January-March 1944

Battle of the Atlantic The efforts of the German U-Boats continue but with diminishing success. Altogether 54 Allied ships are lost to submarine attack during these months and 60 U-Boats are sunk. Some U-Boats try to operate in the Western Approaches close to the British Isles, relying on new radar receivers to give warning of aircraft but this does not prove successful. On 22 March Doenitz orders all U-Boats to disperse from groups and work singly. This is the final triumph for the Allied escort forces. The Germans decide to give up convoy attacks until the new experimental types of U-Boat are available.

Previous page: American landing ships disgorge men and supplies onto Utah Beach, 6 June 1944.
Below: Russian T-34/76 tanks move forward.

1 January 1944

New Ireland Aircraft from Admiral Sherman's carrier task group attack a Japanese convoy off Kavieng.

2 January 1944

Eastern Front The Soviets capture Radovel, west of Korosten, just 18 miles from the 1939 Polish border.

New Guinea Admiral Barbey's Task Force 38 lands 2400 men of General Martin's 126th Regiment of 32nd Division at Saidor. The airfield and the harbor are quickly captured. There is little direct air support because of bad weather but other targets are attacked. Admiral Crutchley leads an Allied cruiser and destroyer force as further cover. To the east the Australian advance reaches Sialum.

New Britain The US 7th Marine Regiment mounts an attack to expand the bridgehead near Cape Gloucester but it meets strong resistance and does not reach its objectives.

3 January 1944

Eastern Front The Soviets capture Olevsk and Novograd-Volynskiy, west and southwest of Korosten.

New Britain The fighting in the Borgen Bay area continues but the US forces are not yet able to bring up armor.

4 January 1944

Eastern Front The Soviet offensive in the Ukraine continues with the capture of Belaya Tserkov, south of Kiev.

New Ireland Sherman's carrier group attacks Kavieng yet again. The Japanese destroyer *Fumitsuki* is damaged.

4-5 January 1944

Italy Units of Fifth Army, particularly the British 46th Division, launch attacks on a 10-mile front toward the south end of the Gustav line.

5 January 1944

Eastern Front Before dawn Konev's Second Ukraine Front begins a new series of attacks toward Kirovgrad. Vatutin's First Ukraine Front captures Berdichev and Tarascha, southwest and south of Kiev.

New Guinea The American forces at Saidor meet their Japanese opponents in patrols to the west. The Australians advancing west along the north coast of the Huon Peninsula capture Kelanoa.

6 January 1944

Eastern Front The Soviets capture Rakitino, a few miles over the former Polish frontier.

New Britain The US forces manage to extend their bridgehead at Cape Gloucester southward to the Aogiri River.

7 January 1944

Eastern Front The attacks of both Ukraine Fronts make good progress around Kirovgrad and toward the former Polish town of Rovno.

Italy British and US units of Fifth Army take Monte Chiaia and Monte Porchia in their continuing attacks. San Vittore is also captured.

8 January 1944

Eastern Front The Soviets retake Kirovgrad – another major gain.

8-11 January 1944

Italy, Politics Mussolini's Italian Socialist Republic puts the members of the Fascist Grand Council who overthrew him on trial at Verona. Several are convicted in their absence. Those tried and executed include Ciano and de Bono.

9 January 1944

Italy Two divisions from US II Corps attack Cervaro and Monte Trochio, just east of the Cassino position.

Solomons On Bougainville US engineers complete a second airfield at Piva, inland from the coast.

Eastern Front Vatutin's forces take Polonnoye, midway between Berdichev and Rovno, and farther south Konev's troops take Aleksandrovka.

10 January 1944

New Britain The Americans send reinforcements to their troops at Arawe. In the northern sector they make a small advance along the Aogiri Ridge despite considerable resistance.

11 January 1944

Eastern Front There are new Soviet attacks at Mozyr.

United States, Home Front Roosevelt appeals to Congress for a new national service law to prevent damaging strikes and to mobilize the whole of the adult work force for war work.

New Guinea The American forces at Saidor repair the airfield and it becomes operational.

12 January 1944

Eastern Front The Soviets capture Sarny, well inside former-Polish territory.

Italy The US 34th Division completes the cap-

ture of Cervaro and pushes forward toward Cassino. Farther north troops from the French Corps begin attacks toward Sant 'Elia.

13 January 1944

Eastern Front Vatutin's troops take Korets between Novograd-Volynskiy and Rovno.

14 January 1944

New Britain The fighting around the Cape Gloucester bridgehead continues. While the Japanese can score no positive success they do manage to hold up the US advance.

United States, Home Front The major rail unions accept terms suggested by the president, avoiding a threatened strike. The railroads have in fact been run under the authority of Secretary Stimson since 27 December but they are returned to private ownership and operation on 18 January.

Eastern Front The Soviets recapture Mozyr and Kalinkovichi. In the north the troops of the Leningrad, Volkhov and Second Baltic Fronts begin a major offensive to relieve Leningrad.

Left: Russian troops on the Leningrad Front.
Below: Map showing the Russian liberation of the Ukraine and advance into Rumania.

15 January 1944

Eastern Front There is heavy fighting in the northern sector, especially just north of Lake Ilmen and just south of Leningrad itself.

Italy Troops of General Keyes' II Corps capture Monte Trocchio, the last important bastion before the defenses of the Rapido valley and the formidable Cassino position itself. Fifth Army has now closed up to the Gustav Line all along its front and despite the heavy fighting of the past weeks it must continue to attack to play its part in drawing off German reserves before the Anzio operation.

New Guinea The Australian troops on the north coast of the Huon Peninsula attack and capture Sio, but not before it has been evacuated by the Japanese.

16 January 1944

Allied Command General Eisenhower formally assumes his duties as Commander in Chief of the Allied Expeditionary Forces – one of the key commands of the war.

Eastern Front The Soviets break through in their attacks just north of Velikiye Luki.

New Britain There are considerable Japanese counterattacks toward Cape Gloucester but these are beaten off with heavy loss.

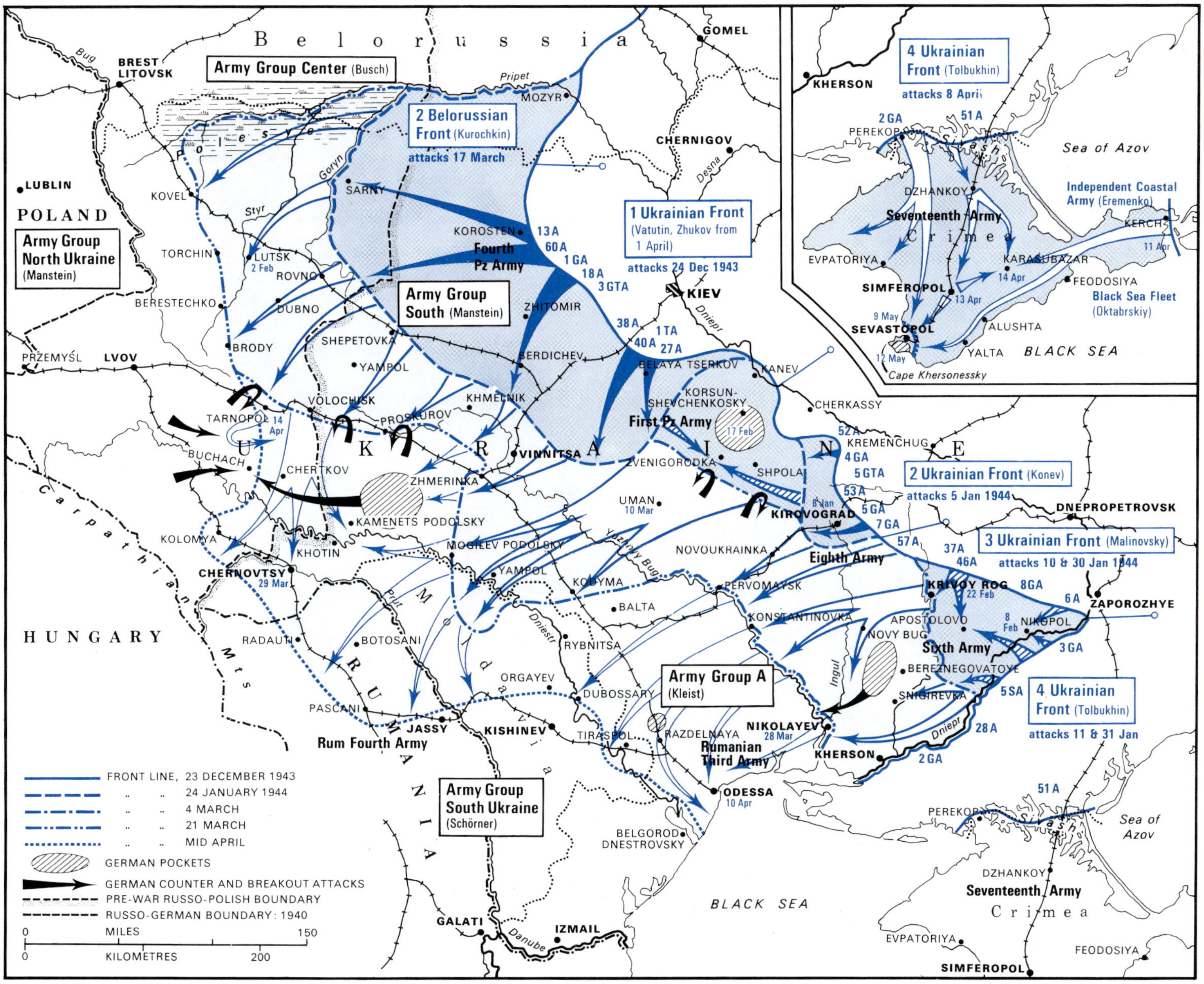

Above: American sailors douse fires started by a German air attack on their ship off the coast of Italy, early 1944.

17 January 1944

Australia, Home Front Meat rationing introduced.

Italy Late in the day the British X Corps from Fifth Army begins formal attacks on the German positions along the Garigliano. Three divisions make the assault. On the left 5th Division, aided by a small seaborne left hook, get successfully across the river as do 56th Division on their right. On the right flank of the attack, however, the efforts of 46th Division at Sant 'Ambrogio and to the south are frustrated by the German defense. The defenders are from the 94th Infantry Division of Senger's XIV Panzer Corps.

Eastern Front Vatutin's troops take Slavuta, continuing the advance toward Rovno.

18 January 1944

Italy By daybreak both 5th and 56th Divisions have crossed the Garigliano, are soundly established on the north bank and are pushing forward. General Vietinghoff commanding the German Tenth Army gets permission from Kesselring, Supreme Commander in Italy, to start to move some of the reserve from the Anzio area to meet this attack.

19 January 1944

Eastern Front The troops of the Leningrad Front take Krasnoye Selo, Popsha and Peterhof, linking the sectors of Forty-second Army and Second Shock Army. A hundred miles farther south the troops of the Volkhov Front make further encircling advances near Novgorod.

Italy Minturno is taken by the British 5th Division in the continuing attacks by X Corps.

20 January 1944

Eastern Front The Soviet Fifty-ninth Army takes Novgorod in a brutal storming attack.

Italy The US II Corps begins attacks across the Rapido toward the Liri valley and Monte Cassino. The main effort near Sant 'Angelo in Theodice is beaten off by the Germans with little difficulty. Farther south the attacks of the British X Corps are still making progress and capture Tufo.

21 January 1944

Eastern Front The Soviet attacks near Leningrad continue. In a new effort Mga is taken and the advance goes on toward Tosno.

Italy The attacks of US II Corps continue but only very small holdings across the Rapido can be gained and these are quickly attacked and eliminated by the Germans. The US 36th Division loses very heavily. The forces for the Anzio landing sail from Naples.

22 January 1944

Italy The Allied landings at Anzio begin. The landing forces are from General Lucas' VI Corps with the US 3rd Division and the British 1st Division providing the bulk of the assault troops. British commando and US ranger units are also involved. The Allied attacks on the Gustav Line, particularly those of X Corps, have been successful in drawing in some of the German reserves so that only light forces are in the Anzio area. Other units are quickly improvised, however, and sent to join the defense. Kesselring calls for reserves from far afield. The landings against the initial light opposition are an exemplary success – of the 36,000 men landed by the end of the first day only 13 are killed and the port of Anzio is taken virtually intact. The naval forces involved include the usual selection of landing craft, cruisers, destroyers, minesweepers and other small vessels. Admiral Troubridge commands the British landing north of the town and Admiral Lowry the US landing to the south.

23 January 1944

Italy By the end of the day the Allies have 50,000 men ashore at Anzio but are only pushing forward very cautiously, inhibited more by the lack of drive from General Lucas than by the Germans. Kesselring insists that the Gustav Line and Anzio can both be held despite Vietinghoff's views to the contrary. Hitler allows reserve forces to be assembled from north Italy, France and the Balkans in the hope of dissuading the British and Americans from future amphibious operations elsewhere in Europe. Within a week eight divisions are in place. Fourteenth Army's headquarters arrives from north Italy to organize and lead them. In view of the scale of this rapid German reaction, criticism of Lucas for failing to push forward to Rome immediately is probably unfounded but a little more vigor could probably have secured better defensive positions before the Germans arrived in strength.

New Guinea The Australian forces in the Ramu valley advance up the slopes of the Finisterre Range toward Shaggy Ridge, capturing Maukiryo. Allied air superiority is an important factor here and in the rest of the campaign in New Guinea.

24 January 1944

Eastern Front In the Leningrad sector Pushkin and Pashovsk are captured and the rail line between Narva and Krasnogvardeisk cut. In the south the First and Second Ukraine Fronts being a major offensive to encircle and eliminate the German salient around Korsun-Sevchenovsky. Five Soviet armies, three of them with large tank units, move in against little more than a corps from First Panzer Army. The attacking pincers are designed to meet at Zvenigorodka.

Italy The slow expansion of the Anzio beachhead continues. On the Gustav Line the French Corps attacks Monte Santa Croce while units of II US Corps attack over the Rapido toward Caira, a little to the south.

25 January 1944

Eastern Front The Soviet attacks around Korsun are driven forward ruthlessly. The south wing of the drive with the Fourth Guards Army and the Fifth Guards Tank Army makes good progress. In the north, Sixth Tank Army, led by an armor expert, General Kravchenko, does scarcely less well. Later in the day the Soviets begin an all-out assault in the Leningrad sector against Krasnogvardeisk. The town is carried early next morning.

New Guinea The Australians complete the capture of Shaggy Ridge, overlooking the Ramu valley.

Italy The fruitless attacks on the Gustav Line continue, especially by the US II Corps, 34th Division. The French Corps to the right makes some gains on Colle Belvedere. At Anzio the Allied forces attempt to extend their perimeter inland but only make a little progress.

26 January 1944

Italy The French Corps move on from Colle Belvedere toward Monte Abate. On their left the US II Corps at last manages to establish a small bridgehead over the Rapido.

Above: American fighter pilots gather for a pre-mission briefing on board the carrier USS *Intrepid*, January 1944.

New Britain There is a particularly heavy US air attack on Rabaul. Many Japanese planes are shot down and the base is gradually becoming worthless.

27 January 1944

Eastern Front General Govorov, commanding the Leningrad Front, issues a special order of the day announcing that the blockade of Leningrad has been completely lifted. Nearby, Tosno and Valosovo are taken. In the south Shpola is captured by Konev's forces as the encircling attacks proceed.

Italy The British X Corps renews its attacks near Santa Maria Infante. The 34th Division of II Corps takes Monte Maiola and Caira, just north of Cassino. The French around Monte Abate are driven back by German counter-attacks.

New Britain The Cape Gloucester bridgehead is further expanded by the marines' capture of Natamo in the northwest.

27-31 January 1944

War Crimes Britain, the United States and Australia formally protest about the ill-treatment of prisoners of war by the Japanese, as more information comes to light. All three nations promise that there will be tribunals to investigate and punish those responsible.

28 January 1944

Eastern Front In the Leningrad sector the troops of the Volkhov Front take Lyuban and several other small towns to the south. South of Kiev Manstein is assembling tank forces from both First Panzer and Eighth Armies to relieve the Korsun pocket. The movement of both sides is becoming difficult in this sector because occasional warm days turn the ground into a sea of mud. This freezes solid each night, trapping vehicles. The Soviet tanks are better suited for such conditions.

29 January 1944

Marshall Islands In preparation for the coming landings, Admiral Mitscher's TF 58 bombs and shells targets on Roi, Namur, Maloelap and Wotje. Land-based aircraft also attack Jaluit and Mille.

Italy At Anzio the Allies now have 69,000 men, 508 guns and 237 tanks ashore. Lucas is at last ready to attack but in fact faces eight German divisions. There have been intermittent German air attacks on the beachhead and shipping offshore. A token of the growing German strength is that on this one day a cruiser and a transport are sunk.

On the Gustav Line the US 34th Division is still pushing slowly but determinedly forward.

Eastern Front Hitler appoints Model to command Army Group North in place of Kuchler. The Soviet attacks continue. Chudovo is taken by Meretskov's men and Novosokolniki by Popov's.

30 January 1944

Indian Ocean The battleships *Queen Elizabeth* and *Valiant,* and the battlecruiser *Renown* with the carriers *Illustrious* and *Unicorn* arrive in Colombo from European waters. A battleship and a small carrier are already on the station and an increasing number of submarines are in operation in the area.

Marshalls Task Force 58 continues its operations against Kwajalein, Roi, Namur and Eniwetok. Seven battleships are involved in bombardment missions and 400 bombing sorties are flown.

Italy At the south end of the Gustav Line the British 5th Division breaks through and captures Monte Natale. Nearer the main focus of action opposite Monte Cassino, the US 34th Division manages to maintain its holding on the west bank of the Rapido. At Anzio the planned Allied attacks begin. The British 1st Division pushes forward a little but takes heavy punishment. In the American sector, a Ranger battalion leading the attack has all but six men killed or captured. The attacks continue with further heavy loss and no worthwhile gains for the next three days.

31 January 1944

Eastern Front Soviet troops reach the outskirts of Kingisepp in their drive west from Leningrad.

Marshalls The landing operations against Kwajalein Atoll begin. Admiral Spruance is in overall command with General Holland Smith in charge of the various landing forces. The first landings are on Roi, Namur and some nearby islets. Admiral Connolly's TF 53 transports General Smith's 4th Marine Division and provides the naval support.

Below: American Generals Holland 'Howling Mad' Smith (left) and Julian C Smith (right) inspect Japanese positions, Betio, February 1944.

Fairly rapid progress is made on Roi but on Namur the Japanese resitance is more substantial. The Japanese counterattack on both islands during the night. Several neighboring islets have been seized and artillery landed to support the main attacks. There are also landings on Majuro Atoll by troops from 27th Infantry Regiment supported by Admiral Hill's Task Force.

Majuro is quickly made ready to become a major American base. It becomes operational on 2 February. The main carrier forces of TF 58 continue their attacks on these objectives and against Eniwetok and Maleolap.

Italy Caira is taken by II US Corps and on their right the French Corps retakes Monte Abate.

February 1944

Europe, Air Operations RAF Bomber Command drops 11,700 tons of bombs with the main efforts being against Berlin particularly, and Leipzig, Stuttgart and Schweinfurt. The US Eighth Air Force based in Britain drops 18,000 tons and the Fifteenth Air Force from Italy drops 5900 tons both aiming at a range of targets connected with the German aircraft industry including Gotha, Leipzig and Oschersleben (*see* 20-27 February 1944). US medium bombers and aircraft of the RAF's 2nd TAF drop 4800 tons, mostly on V-weapon sites in France and Belgium.

In response to the growing Allied attacks the Germans revive their attacks on London but on a much less significant scale. These attacks are known as the 'Little Blitz' and are most intense between 18-25 February.

Below: A US Marine medic gives blood plasma to a wounded comrade on the beach at Namur, Kwajalein Atoll, February 1944.

1 February 1944

Marshalls The US carrier operations continue. The land battle for Roi is virtually over but there is still heavy fighting on Namur. Admiral Turner's TF 52 with the usual complement of battleships and escort carriers lands troops from General Corlett's 7th Infantry Division on Kwajalein itself. The Japanese resistance is stubborn but the US forces are exceptionally well organized and by nightfall have overrun a third of the island. After their experiences at Torawa, the US amphibious forces have devoted much effort and material to improving their landing tactics.

Eastern Front In the north the Soviets take Kingisepp and push on to within one mile of the Estonian border. A little to the south between Luga and Utorgosh German counterattacks score local success.

Italy The US 34th Division continues to batter at the German positions north of Cassino around Monte Maiola. A little more ground is gained.

2 February 1944

Marshalls The American occupation of Roi and Namur is complete. The Japanese have lost virtually every man of the 3700 defenders. The American casualties number 740 killed and wounded. The battle for Kwajalein continues.

Eastern Front In the south, Third and Fourth Ukraine Fronts are pressing strongly against Sixth Army's salient around Nikopol. In the north Soviet troops penetrate into Estonia, capturing Vanakula.

Italy The Allied attacks around Anzio are brought to a halt. Although they have achieved no positive success and taken heavy losses the Germans have been forced to postpone their general attack planned to start now.

3 February 1944

Marshalls Admiral Ginder's TG 58.4 attacks Eniwetok with its carrier planes. Landings are made on Burton Island, one of the smaller islands of the Kwajalein group.

Eastern Front The encirclement of the Korsun pocket is announced and celebrated in Moscow. Hitler has, as usual, ordered no retreat and Manstein is trying to assemble sufficient panzer forces to break through in relief.

Italy Mackensen's troops begin limited attacks against the British 1st Division's salient around Campoleone in the Anzio bridgehead. General Freyberg's New Zealand Corps joins the order of battle of Fifth Army and prepares to join the fighting in the Cassino sector.

4 February 1944

Marshalls All organized Japanese resistance in the Kwajalein Atoll is over. Almost all of Admiral Akiyama's 8700-strong garrison are dead, only 265 have been captured, many of them Korean laborers or wounded. Altogether the Americans have landed 41,000 men, of whom 370 have been killed and 1500 wounded.

Eastern Front The Soviets reach the mouth of the Narva in the north and on the east side of Lake Peipus they occupy Gdov. In the southern sector Hitler alters Manstein's dispositions, sending 24th Panzer Division back toward Nikopol rather than letting it join the counterattack toward Korsun which has now started. It returns to Nikopol too late to affect that battle.

Italy Just north of Cassino the US 34th Division takes ground near Point 593 and Point 445 as well as attacking Colle Sant'Angelo. In the Anzio sector the German attacks continue and the British 1st Division is forced to give ground.

5 February 1944

Eastern Front The Soviets of First Ukraine Front occupy Rovno and Lutsk, pushing Fourth Panzer Army back once more. Inside the Korsun pocket General Stemmermann withdraws his forces slightly into a tighter perimeter. Air activity in this sector is very intense, with the Germans flying supplies fairly successfully to the trapped force from their airfields around Uman. The Soviets mount a considerable ground-attack effort as well as trying to cut off German supplies.

6 February 1944

Eastern Front The Third Ukraine Front captures Manganets, east of Nikopol. More significantly, the area west of the town Apostolovo also falls, threatening a further encirclement.

Italy The fighting in the hills just north of Cassino continues, with the American forces striving to recapture recently lost ground.

7 February 1944

Marshalls The US forces complete the mopping up of the last pockets of Japanese resistance on the Kwajalein Atoll. Various small groups have been found and wiped out.

Eastern Front Hitler has agreed to allow the troops in the Korsun pocket to try and break out. Stemmermann therefore pulls out of Gorodische and Yanovka to concentrate his forces.

Italy At Anzio, the German attacks against the British 1st Division are renewed. The objective is now Aprilia village and 'The Factory' nearby. The battle continues on 8 February. The British 56th Division and the US 45th Division have now arrived at Anzio.

Above: New Zealand gunners fire a captured German 7.5cm Pak 40 anti-tank gun against enemy positions on Monastery Hill, Cassino.

8 February 1944

Eastern Front Troops of the Third Ukraine Front take Nikopol but most of the German defenders have managed to retreat. The area around Nikopol is important in the production of manganese.

9 February 1944

Eastern Front The Germans make renewed efforts to supply the Korsun pocket by flying large quantities of fuel and ammunition. They evacuate some of the wounded.
Italy The British 1st Division is driven out of Aprilia but manages to keep control of 'The Factory.'

10 February 1944

New Guinea The Australian forces advancing from Sio link up with the Americans near Saidor. The occupation of the Huon Peninsula is now virtually complete.
Eastern Front Vatutin's troops take Shepetovka.

11 February 1944

Italy The fighting at Anzio continues. 'The Factory' finally falls to the Germans after changing hands three times in the last two days. Around Cassino the US 34th Division makes a final, unsuccessful attempt to move forward the last few hundred yards to the Cassino monastery from the north.
Eastern Front Third Panzer Corps under General Vormann renews its attacks to relieve the Korsun pocket in the morning. It manages to capture a vital bridge over the Gniloy Tikich. The Germans inside the pocket begin their attempt to break out late in the day.

12 February 1944

Bismarcks The marines on New Britain take Gorissi, 25 miles east of Cape Gloucester. The Allies land on Rooke Island in the Dampier Strait, Bismarck Sea.
Marshalls There are US landings on Arno Atoll.
Eastern Front The battle for the Korsun pocket grows in intensity. In the north the Soviet attacks also push forward and reach Luga.
Italy The New Zealand Corps replaces the exhausted US II Corps opposite Cassino. In the Anzio sector there is a comparative lull. The British 1st Division is taken out of the line because of its heavy losses and Lucas is busy organizing an inner defensive perimeter.
United States, Politics Wendell Willkie formally announces his candidacy for the Republican nomination for president. General MacArthur has also been suggested as a Republican candidate. Roosevelt's name has been put forward for several of the Democratic primaries but he has made no formal announcement himself.

13 February 1944

Eastern Front In the north the Soviet offensive drives on. Luga, Polna, and Lyady are recaptured. In the south the battles around Korsun-Sevchenkosky continue. The Germans in fact pull out of the town late in the day but do not make very much more progress in the break out attempt.

14 February 1944

Eastern Front The Soviets enter Korsun but can do no more to break down the resistance of the German pocket. A Belgian SS Brigade is especially prominent in the defense. III Panzer Corps is unable to break through the Soviet lines in relief.

15 February 1944

Solomons Part of General Barrowclough's 3rd New Zealand Division is landed by Admiral Wilkinson's III Amphibious Force on the Green Islands, north of Bougainville. Admiral Merrill's TF 39 provides the escort. All the Japanese defenders have been overcome by 21 February.
Italy The monastery on the crest of Monte Cassino is heavily bombed at the request of the New Zealand Corps. The historic buildings are completely wrecked. Despite the reports by US

Below: German troops, laden with kit and weapons, wait to board a Junkers Ju-52 transport in southern Russia, 1944.

Above: General von Senger und Etterlin helps the Abbot of Cassino to leave the area. *Below:* US airmen at a base in England.

troops formerly in the sector that no fire has come from the monastery, more recent reconnaissance has suggested a German presence. Freyberg and Tuker of 4th Indian Division, who have the responsibility of ordering their men to attack the position, decide that they must bomb. Freyberg's responsibility is heightened by his awareness that he leads a large proportion of New Zealand's military manpower. In fact the Germans have been scrupulous not to enter the monastery and have taken the trouble to transport some of its treasures to the safety of the Vatican. Once the abbey has been bombed, however, the Germans move in and find that the ruins and the cellars provide an excellent position – better than the undamaged buildings would have been. The bombers go in on the 15th to take advantage of good weather and so the follow-up attacks by the New Zealand Corps, designed to follow the bombardment, are badly coordinated. They achieve little because the preparations have not been completed.

16 February 1944

Marshalls The carriers of Admiral Ginder's TG 58.4 attack Eniwetok once more. The Japanese airfield on Engebi is virtually put out of action.

Eastern Front The final German attempt to escape from the Korsun pocket through the Soviet lines begins shortly before midnight.

Italy The Germans begin a major attack on the Anzio beachhead. Units of five divisions attack the relatively fresh 45th US and 56th British Divisions. The Luftwaffe has gathered its strength as well, operating in support of the attack and against the shipping offshore. The ammunition ship *Elihu Yale* blows up after one such attack. There is no decisive breakthrough on land but the Allied forces are pushed back. In the Cassino sector the attacks by the New Zealand Corps continue.

Diplomatic Affairs A Finnish diplomat arrives in Stockholm to receive terms for an armistice from the Soviet ambassador.

17 February 1944

Eastern Front The battle of the Korsun pocket comes to an end when the bulk of the surviving German forces reach their own lines. Of General Stemmermann's original force of 56,000, 35,000 have escaped but with little equipment. Stemmermann is himself killed. All of the six divisions involved are totally unfit for further operations for the moment, leaving Manstein even more desperately short of manpower.

Italy The German attacks on the Anzio beachhead continue, with infantry divisions still leading the battle. The Germans almost achieve a breakthrough on the front of US 45th Division. There are heavy losses on both sides. In the Cassino sector Point 593 remains in German hands after being held briefly by 4th Indian Division.

Marshalls The first US landings on Eniwetok Atoll are carried out. Admiral Hill's TF 51.11 lands small parties on islets near Engebi with artillery to cover later operations. There are three battleships and three escort carriers in the supporting force. The total Japanese garrison of the islands is about 3400 men, led by General Mushida.

17-18 February 1944

Bismarcks American destroyers bombard Rabaul and Kavieng. Each of these ports is shelled twice more later in the month on nights chosen to coincide with other operations, particularly the landings on Los Negros.

Carolines The Japanese base at Truk is attacked by three groups of Admiral Mitscher's TF 58 and a group of TF 50 led by Admiral Spruance, who is in overall command. Nine carriers (five fleet carriers and four light carriers) and six battleships are involved as well as cruisers and destroyers. Air attacks are mounted against Truk on both days (1250 sorties in all) and nearby shipping is also sought out. The Japanese lose a cruiser, two destroyers and several other warships to the air attacks, as well as 140,000 tons of shipping. Another cruiser and two destroyers are sunk by the battleships *Iowa* and *New Jersey*. In the air the Japanese lose 250 machines. US submarines in supporting operations sink several more vessels. The Americans lose less than 30 planes and the carrier *Intrepid* is damaged.

18 February 1944

Marshalls With land-based artillery support as well as naval and air bombardment the American forces land on Engebi. The attacking force gets solidly established ashore and Japanese counterattacks are driven off.

Eastern Front In the north Popov's forces take the important town of Staraya-Russa. Meretskov's forces take Shimsk.

Italy The Germans commit 26th Panzer and 29th Panzergrenadier Divisions (their main tank reserve) to the attack at Anzio. The focus of the action is the 'Flyover' on the Anzio-Campoleone road and although some gains are made the strong Allied artillery holds off and blunts the attacks. Kesselring and Mackensen realize that the Allied beachhead cannot be wiped out. Offshore, the cruiser *Penelope,* damaged on 17 February by a torpedo attack, is hit again and sinks.

There are further attacks by Indian and New Zealand troops in the hills north of Cassino monastery and over the Rapido against Cassino town. Some gains are made but cannot be held in face of fire from dominating German positions.

United States, Home Front President Roosevelt vetoes the Bankhead Bill which had proposed to end food subsidies.

19 February 1944

Marshalls The fighting continues on Engebi. The US forces now land at regimental strength on Eniwetok itself. Despite the usual heavy preparations, the Japanese resistance is strong.
Italy The front at Anzio becomes stable, with no further major effort planned by either side for some time. The fighting on the Gustav Line also dies down.

20 February 1944

Marshalls Aircraft from Admiral Reeves' TG 58.1 attack targets on Jaluit Atoll. The fighting on Eniwetok continues with the American forces gaining the upper hand. Parry, close to Eniwetok, is shelled.
Eastern Front Popov's Second Baltic Front sends Twenty-second Army on a new attack toward Kholm which is quickly successful.
Norway, Resistance A ferry carrying a stock of heavy water on the first stage of the journey from the Ryukan hydroelectric plant to laboratories in Germany is sunk and the cargo lost in an attack by resistance fighters acting on instructions from the British and Norwegian governments. Heavy water is used in atomic research.

20-27 February 1944

Europe, Air Operations During this period the US Strategic Air Forces launch a series of massive attacks against the German aircraft industry. Brunswick, Leipzig and Regensburg are among the targets. In the operations on the 20th, 940 bombers and 700 fighters are sent on attacks and 21 bombers are lost. Operations on the 25th are less successful, with 65 of a force of 800 bombers being lost. The series of attacks becomes known as 'Big Week.' The losses on the 25th are not typical of the present US operations and the continuing high German losses in the fighting are beginning to tell in the strength and quality of their forces. In effect, the Luftwaffe is being shot out of the skies.

21 February 1944

Eastern Front The Soviets in the northern sector take Soltsy, southwest of Shimsk, and Kholm, 60 miles farther south. In the Ukraine the Soviet advances around Krivoy Rog proceed apace.
Japan, Politics Prime Minister General Tojo takes on the office of Chief of the Army General Staff in place of Field Marshal Sugiyama. The navy minister, Admiral Shimada also takes on an additional office, replacing Admiral Nagano as Chief of Staff.

22 February 1944

Eastern Front Faced by another massive encircling threat the Germans pull out of Krivoy Rog.
Marshalls After another long bombardment the US forces land on Parry in the Eniwetok Atoll. The Japanese resistance is fierce.

23 February 1944

Eastern Front In the north the Red Army takes Strugi Krasnyye, midway between Luga and Pskov. It also begins to attack Dno.
Marianas The carriers of Sherman's TG 58.3 and Montgomery's TG 58.2 attack Rota, Tinian and Saipan. They sink 20,000 tons of Japanese shipping.
Marshalls The fighting for Parry comes to an end and with it the battle for the whole Eniwetok Atoll. The US losses are 300 dead and 750 wounded. Typically, the Japanese garrison has fought practically to the last man. There are 66 prisoners out of a force of 3400.
Italy General Truscott, for some time deputy, takes full command of VI Corps at Anzio, replacing General Lucas. Somewhat ironically the battle has now settled down to the sort of careful position warfare that Lucas is probably well fitted to control.

24 February 1944

Eastern Front In the north the Soviets take Dno and in the central sector Rogachev falls to the troops of the Second Belorussian Front.
New Guinea The US advance reaches Biliau near Cape Iris.

Below: The remains of the town of Cassino after weeks of fighting. Mud and rubble did much to hamper Allied operations, especially during March 1944.

Above: The crew of a German 2cm anti-aircraft gun prepare for further action, Italy 1944. The symbols on the shield denote 'kills.'

26 February 1944

Eastern Front In the north the Soviets take Porkhov, east of Dno.

27 February 1944

Admiralty Islands There are US air attacks on Momote and Lorengau in preparation for the planned reconnaissance in force shortly to be executed. The troops for this operation are now embarking in Oro Bay.

28 February 1944

Italy The Germans begin a second offensive at Anzio. The main weight of the attack falls on the 3rd US Division on either side of the Cisterna-Anzio road. The four attacking divisions fail to break through.

29 February 1944

British Planning RAF Fighter Command is reorganized and renamed Air Defence of Great Britain.

Admiralty Islands One thousand men of General Chase's 5th Cavalry Regiment are landed at Hyane Harbor on Los Negros. General MacArthur and Admiral Kinkaid, commanding Seventh Fleet, are present offshore and decide to convert the landings into a full-scale occupation. Japanese counterattacks during the night are beaten off.

Italy The Germans make a further limited effort against the Anzio defenses but it cannot be driven home in the dreadful weather.

March 1944

Europe, Air Operations American heavy bombers drop 30,000 tons of bombs on a selection of targets including Berlin (*see* 6-8 March), Brunswick, Friedrichshafen, French airfields and V-weapon sites. RAF Bomber Command makes over 8000 sorties, including four 1000-bomber raids during which 27,000 tons of bombs are dropped. Objectives include Frankfurt, Stuttgart, Berlin, Essen, Nuremberg (*see* 30-31 March) and rail targets in France for Overlord. US and British medium and fighter bombers attack targets in occupied territory. The Mediterranean air forces also hit rail targets in north Italy.

1 March 1944

Admiralty Islands On Los Negros the US forces eliminate some small Japanese units that have infiltrated their lines during the night.

Eastern Front The Soviets capture Russaki, near Pskov.

2 March 1944

Diplomatic Affairs Owing to Turkey's reluctance to join the war or to make any other contribution to the Allied effort, Lend-Lease aid is cut off.

Admiralty Islands A second wave of 1000 men from the US 5th Cavalry Regiment arrives at Los Negros. The forces already established on the island take Momote airfield with the help of fire support from destroyers offshore.

3 March 1944

Italy There is another flurry of activity in the Anzio sector where the American 3rd Division meets and holds an attack near Ponte Rocco. After this failure the German Fourteenth Army goes over to the defensive.

Admiralty Islands The Japanese send in a strong night attack against the American force on Los Negros. The attackers take heavy losses however, and much of the Japanese strength on the island is thereby dissipated.

4 March 1944

Eastern Front The Soviets begin another series of massive attacks in the Ukraine with advances by Vatutin's forces in the area to the north and east of Tarnopol.

Admiralty Islands Admiral Crutchley's cruiser TF 74 shells Japanese batteries on Hauwei and Ndrilo which have been hampering access to Seeadler Bay.

5 March 1944

Eastern Front The First Ukraine Front's attacks make rapid progress, fracturing Manstein's attenuated lines. Izyaslav, Yampol and Ostropol in the Shepetovka sector are all taken.

New Guinea Two battalions of the US 126th Infantry Regiment land at Yalau Plantation, 30 miles west of Saidor.

Admiralty Islands The US forces move into the northern half of Los Negros. A third wave of 1400 troops arrives with destroyers which also give fire support.

Burma The 77th Long Range Penetration Brigade (LRP) is flown in to the landing area named 'Broadway,' 50 miles southwest of Myitkyina. A second Chindit Brigade, 16th LRP, has been on the march south from Ledo since 5 February heading for the 'Aberdeen' area.

6 March 1944

Eastern Front The Third Ukraine Front begins a new offensive. Vatutin's attacks continue to make good advances, cutting the Odessa-Lvov rail line and capturing Volochisk.

New Britain The US 1st Marine Division is sent to land on the east side of Willaumez Peninsula with the aim of taking Talasea. The Japanese defense is not particularly formidable but the terrain is difficult and the advance inland is not very rapid.

6-8 March 1944

Europe, Air Operations On 6 March US heavy bombers raid Berlin for the first time. A force of 660 bombers is sent and 69 are lost. The raid is repeated on the 8th when the 580 bomber force again loses about 10 percent of its number despite an escort of 800 fighters.

7 March 1944

Solomons The Japanese have at last assembled large forces around the US beachhead on Bougainville and are preparing a major attack. On the Green Islands the Allied forces have now completed the construction of an airfield.

Admiralty Islands The Japanese batteries at the entrance to Seeadler Bay are bombarded once again by Admiral Crutchley's three cruisers and four destroyers.

8 March 1944

Diplomatic Affairs The Finns reply to the Russian armistice terms asking for further guarantees. The principal difficulty is the Russian demand for the internment of German military personnel. This reply is rejected by the Russians on 10 March.

Solomons The Japanese begin attacks on the American positions on Bougainville. The airfields at Piva are shelled causing the Americans to withdraw some of their bombers. American artillery and naval vessels return the fire. Japanese infantry infiltrate the positions of 37th Division. The attacking troops are mostly from General Hyakutake's 6th Division.
New Britain The attacks of 1st Marine Division make good progress toward Talasea as does the other American advance along the coast from Cape Gloucester.
Burma The Japanese offensive *U-Go* begins. The aim is to destroy the British forces around Imphal and Kohima and then push on through the passes to Dimapur, cutting off the Chinese and Americans in the north, and with the road to India ahead. Three divisions of General Mutaguchi's Fifteenth Army are to be employed in the initial operations. The offensive begins with advances by General Yamagida's 33rd Division against the positions of General Cowan's 17th Indian Division around Tiddim. These attacks are meant to commit the British reserves so that when the main attack goes in its task will be easier. The British are well aware that the Japanese plan to attack, but they under-estimate the strength of the force to be used. The plan is for 17th and 20th Indian Divisions, both in fairly advanced positions, to fall back to around Imphal and protect and live off the large base organization there. The British forces at this stage are all from General Scoones' IV Corps. It is an essential part of the Japanese plan to capture large quantities of British supplies because most of their advances are to be made over jungle tracks impassable to supply vehicles. Food is the crucial element of the problem. It is precisely because of these difficulties that the British expect a smaller attack.

9 March 1944

Eastern Front Vatutin's First Ukraine Front takes Starokonstantinov south of Shepetovka and reaches the outskirts of Tarnopol where there is bitter fighting.

Above: A B-17 Flying Fortress bomber goes down in flames during the raid on Berlin by the Eighth USAAF, 6 March 1944.

Solomons On Bougainville the Japanese attacks on 37th Division make a few gains. The airfields at Piva and Torokina are shelled.
Admiralty Islands The first US planes begin operations from Momote airfield.
Burma News of the advance of 33rd Division reaches General Cowan's headquarters, but is not at first believed.

10 March 1944

New Britain The American forces take Talasea.
Eastern Front The attacks of Konev's troops push forward up to 40 miles on a 100-mile front. Uman is taken.
Solomons On Bougainville the Japanese gain Hill 260 but lose ground to American counterattacks in other areas.
Burma The Japanese attack the rear of 17th Division's positions at Tongzang. It is becoming clear to the British command that the Japanese offensive is under way.

Below: Orde Wingate briefs American pilots of the 1st Air Commando, March 1944.

11 March 1944

Eastern Front Troops of Third Ukraine Front take Berislav north of the Dniepr east of Kherson.
Admiralty Islands Advance guards are sent to scout landing places on Manus Island. One unit lands on Butjo Luo offshore and takes heavy punishment from the Japanese defenders.
Burma The Japanese 33rd Division as well as attacking 17th Division is infiltrating behind 20th Division but their advances in this sector are held near Witok. More Chindit forces are flying in to central Burma and are already disrupting Japanese communications with the forces facing Stilwell's Chinese and American troops. In the Arakan Buthidaung falls to the British.

12 March 1944

Solomons On Bougainville the American forces begin to gain the upper hand over the attacking Japanese.
Admiralty Islands A small American force lands on Hauwei Island. There is strong Japanese resistance under the command of Colonel Ezaki.
Marshalls US forces occupy Wotho Atoll. There is no opposition.
Eastern Front Konev's forces reach the River Bug at Gayvoron. Other attacks capture Dolinskaya.

13 March 1944

Eastern Front Kherson is taken by Third Ukraine Front after a hard struggle.
Solomons On Bougainville powerful American counterattacks with tank and air support retake almost all the gains made by the Japanese in the last few days.
Admiralty Islands Hauwei is completely overrun by the American landing force. Artillery is landed to support the coming operations on Manus.
Burma General Scoones authorizes 17th and 20th Divisions to withdraw from their advanced

Above: Spearheaded by an M4 Sherman tank, US soldiers close with the Japanese on the island of Bougainville, March 1944.

positions to Imphal. General Gracey with 20th Division has made better preparations for this move than Cowan with 17th. Scoones and his superiors Slim and Giffard agree that reinforcements are needed and Mountbatten therefore sends requests to the highest level for the use of American aircraft (those normally used for ferrying supplies to the Chinese) to move 5th Division from the Arakan. The Japanese begin air attacks against the Chindits' Broadway airfield.

14 March 1944

United States, Politics Willkie and Roosevelt top the polls in their parties' respective primary elections in New Hampshire.
Eastern Front The Russians have isolated a few German units North of Kherson. Eventually 4000 men are captured.
Burma The 17th Indian Division starts its withdrawal a crucial 24 hours late. The Japanese have created four roadblocks on the route it must take to Imphal. To the north 20th Division is pulling back in a more controlled manner.

15 March 1944

Eastern Front Konev's forces have quickly crossed the Bug and now capture Vapnyarka cutting the Odessa-Zhmerinka rail line. Farther north near Vinnitsa Kalinkova falls to the Russians.
Italy Once more the Allied forces attack Cassino. The massive preliminary bombardment, 1400 tons of bombs and 190,000 shells, is mostly directed against Cassino town. The New Zealand Division moves in to attack the town with 4th Indian Division ready to follow up against the monastery. The advance of the Allied tanks is hampered by the mass of rubble created by the bombardment. The German resistance by a regiment of 1st Paratroop Division is very tenacious and well directed, but nevertheless some gains are made by the attacks in the town and on the lower slopes of the mountain at Castle Hill and Hangman's Hill.
Solomons The Japanese make another abortive effort against the American positions on Bougainville.
Admiralty Islands Units of 7th and 8th Cavalry Divisions are landed on the north coast of Manus Island near Lugos Mission. Once ashore they advance toward Lorengau by two routes.
Burma The main effort of the Japanese offensive begins with crossings of the Chindwin by 15th and 31st Divisions in several places north and south of Homalin.

16 March 1944

Italy The heavy fighting around Cassino continues but the Allied forces can make no progress either in the town or on the slopes leading up to the monastery against the determined defense of the German 1st Paratroop Division.
Admiralty Islands The American advances on Los Negros and Manus proceed although the Japanese resistance on Manus is stiffening.
New Guinea American planes attack a Japanese convoy off Wewak. During the next few days it is almost completely destroyed.

17 March 1944

Eastern Front Dubno is taken by the First Ukraine Front.
Admiralty Islands The US forces on Manus capture Lorengau airfield, their main objective.
Burma There are heavy Japanese air attacks on the Chindit's landing ground at Broadway. Several of the supporting Spitfires are destroyed on the ground.

17-19 March 1944

Italy The battle for Cassino continues to be very fierce. The New Zealand and Indian troops mount unsuccessful attacks toward the southwest of the town and along Snake's Head Ridge to Point 593. The Germans similarly fail in their efforts against the Allied positions on Castle Hill and Hangman's Hill.

18 March 1944

Admiralty Islands The village of Lorengau on Manus is taken by the US forces. On Los Negros there is a brisk engagement near Papitalai Mission.
Eastern Front Zhmerinka falls to the attacks of First Ukraine Front.
Marshalls Admiral Lee's TG 50.10 with two battleships and the carrier *Lexington* bombards the Mili atoll. The battleship *Iowa* is hit by return fire.
Diplomatic Affairs Admiral Horthy, the Regent of Hungary, is summoned to visit Hitler and is arrested.

18-19 March 1944

New Guinea An Allied destroyer group bombards the Japanese base at Wewak.

19 March 1944

Eastern Front Konev's forces have reached and crossed the Dniepr near Yampol capturing Soroki a little to the south. Near Dubno the Russians also take the town of Krzemienic.
Hungary The Germans move into Hungary (Operation Margaret) to prevent a collapse and ensure a line of retreat for their forces and continued access to the oil resources.

20 March 1944

Eastern Front The Russians capture Mogilev Podolsky and Vinnitsa both important communications centers. The Russian advance in all sectors of the Ukraine is in considerable strength on a very wide front giving the Germans little opportunity for concentrated resistance.
Burma The first brigade of 5th Division has arrived at Imphal by air. A battalion is sent to Kohima.
Italy General Alexander agrees with General Freyberg that the losses in the battle for Cassino are growing too heavy and that it must be halted unless there are good gains in the next two days. The Germans are managing to bring their reserves into the battle while the Allies must move theirs over difficult ground under German artillery fire.
Bismarcks General Noble's 4th Marines are landed on Emirau Island in the Matthias group. There is no Japanese resistance. Admiral Griffin leads four battleships and two carriers in attacks on Kavieng as a covering operation. Four more carriers and seven cruisers are in direct support of the landings.

Above: German paratroops, armed with an MG42 machine gun, take full advantage of the rubble left in Cassino after the Allied bombing.

21 March 1944

New Guinea The US forces moving west from Yalau Plantation make contact with the Australian units advancing north from inland on the Huon Peninsula.

Burma The 20th Indian Division has completed its withdrawal most successfully. It now holds positions on the Shenan Hills and between Palel and Wangjing. The 17th Division is still fighting its way back north through the Japanese roadblocks inflicting heavy casualties on 33rd Division as it does so.

22 March 1944

Eastern Front Pervomaysk, southeast of Uman is taken by Konev's troops.

Axis Politics The Germans announce from Berlin that a new Hungarian Government has been formed and will be led by Field Marshal Szotjay.

22-23 March 1944

Italy The New Zealand Corps makes a final effort against Cassino but to no effect. Afterward Freyberg calls off the attack. Some troops are withdrawn from the most advanced positions below the monastery and the remainder of the recent Allied gains consolidated.

23 March 1944

Eastern Front In a new series of attacks First Ukraine Front drives south from between Proskurov and Tarnapol threatening to divide First and Fourth Panzer Armies from each other. Kapychintsy is taken.

Solomons The Japanese try another attack on the American positions on Bougainville but can still make no progress and again lose heavily.

St Matthias Islands US destroyers shell the Japanese seaplane base on Elouae.

24 March 1944

Solomons The last significant Japanese effort on Bougainville comes to an end. There are various small skirmishes for a few months but the Japanese are worn out and the Americans are content merely to watch the Japanese weakness. In the past couple of weeks the Japanese have lost about 8000 casualties, the Americans only 300.

Burma General Wingate is killed in an air crash. The Senior Chindit brigade commander, Lentaigne, replaces him.

Eastern Front The advance of First Ukraine Front continues at speed. Chertkov and Zaleschik are taken in the drive southeast of Tarnopol. Third Ukraine Front takes Voznesensk northeast of Nikolayev.

25 March 1944

Eastern Front Forces of First Ukraine Front take Proskurov. General Hube, commanding First Panzer Army is not obeying Manstein's orders to attack west to prevent encirclement resulting from the Soviet gains at Proskurov and to the southwest.

Admiralty Islands A final elaborate US attack on Manus crushes most of the remaining Japanese forces. On Los Negros too only scattered groups and individuals fight on.

26 March 1944

Eastern Front A large part of First Panzer Army has been cut off around Kamenets-Podolski by the advances to the River Prut by First and Second Ukraine Fronts. Other units of Second Ukraine Front take Balta.

Italy There is a major regrouping of the Allied forces. The New Zealand Corps is taken out of the line and broken up. Units of Eighth Army are brought from the east side to replace it and the French Corps which has also taken heavy losses. The next Allied offensive will be in May when this regrouping and other preparations are complete.

27 March 1944

Italy A small German coastal convoy is destroyed off Vado by a British torpedo boat squadron.

Eastern Front Kamenets-Podolski is taken by First Ukraine Front. Gorodenka is also taken by other units of this formation.

Burma General Stopford's XXXIII Corps is put under Slim's control and ordered to concentrate at Dimapur before advancing to Kohima. A second brigade of 5th Division arrives at Imphal by air and the third brigade is being sent to Dimapur also for Kohima.

27 March-5 April 1944

Arctic The convoy JW-58 sails from Iceland to Murmansk without loss. One feature of the battle is the number of German scout and bomber aircraft shot down by the planes of the escort carriers. In addition three U-Boats are sunk.

28 March 1944

Eastern Front After a vicious struggle Nikolayev falls to Malinovsky's men.

Below: British, West African and Gurkha troops wait to board their C-47 transport aircraft, Burma.

29 March 1944

Eastern Front Troops of the First Ukraine Front have crossed the Prut and taken Kolomya in Rumania (now part of the USSR) in the foothills of the Carpathians.

Burma The road between Imphal and Kohima is cut by Sato's 31st Division at Maram. Slim sticks to his plan to supply the garrison of Imphal by air.

30 March 1944

Eastern Front Russian troops take Chernovtsy. Hitler is furious with his generals and dismisses Manstein and Kleist from their commands of Army Groups North and South Ukraine. Model takes over from Manstein and Schoerner from Kleist. Lindemann takes Model's place at Army Group North.

Admiralty Islands US forces occupy Pityilu Island north of Manus. There is almost no opposition.

30-31 March 1944

Carolines Spruance leads three groups of TF 58, including 11 carriers, in attacks on Palau Island. The Japanese have sighted the approaching Americans on 25 and 26 March and have therefore dispersed their warships. The battleship *Musashi* is hit by a submarine torpedo while moving away on 28 March however. Despite these precautions much ordinary shipping is hit. The operation continues on 1 April.

Europe, Air Operations The RAF raid Nuremberg and lose 96 planes from an attacking force of 795 – the worst losses for the RAF during the whole war. A combination of many factors accounts for this. Nuremberg is a rather more distant target than some of the usual ones and on a clear night the growing technical skill of the German night-fighter controllers and the new *Lichtenstein* airborne radar sets combine with German ability to track the RAF H2S and IFF transmissions in inflicting unacceptable punishment on the attacking force.

Below: General William Slim (center), commander of the British Fourteenth Army in Burma.

31 March 1944

Eastern Front Malinovsky's troops take Ochakov southwest of Nikolayev.

Japanese Command Admiral Koga, Commander in Chief of the Japanese Combined Fleets, is killed in an air crash. Because of political differences no successor is appointed immediately. (*See* 3 May 1944.)

April 1944

Europe, Air Operations The US heavy bomber force drops 43,500 tons of bombs especially on aircraft factories throughout Europe. Steyr, Augsburg, Poznan, Duna and Oschersleben and many others are all attacked. The RAF heavy bomber force's main efforts are switched from German targets to transport centers in France and Belgium. Some attacks are still made on Germany including raids on Cologne and Essen. The rail targets include Laon, Tours, Rouen, Juvisy and Lille. This respite from all-out attacks on Germany is welcome to the crews if not to Air Marshal Harris because of the growing efficiency of the German night fighters. During the month 33,000 tons are dropped. USAAF Marauders add 8800 tons in attacks on French and Belgian rail targets.

Aircraft from the Mediterranean Air Forces attack oil and communications targets in southeast Europe including Ploesti, Sofia and Belgrade. These attacks are some help to the Russian forces advancing toward the Carpathians because they disrupt the rail network.

Indian Ocean During the month the British Eastern Fleet is reinforced by three more escort carriers and the French battleship *Richelieu.*

1 April 1944

Carolines The carriers of TF 58 attack Woleai. In the three days of attacks 130,000 tons of Japanese shipping have been sunk as well as seven small warships. The Americans have lost 26 planes but have shot down 150.

Eastern Front A considerable German force has been surrounded near Skala between the advancing wings of First and Second Ukraine Fronts.

Admiralty Islands The US forces extend their hold occupying Ndrilo and Koniniat.

2 April 1944

Eastern Front The Soviets enter Rumania, crossing the Prut east of Chernovtsy.

Burma Mutaguchi's troops continue their advance. They now cut the road between Kohima and Imphal. South of Imphal 17th Indian Division has nearly completed its retirement to the main position.

3 April 1944

Arctic The *Tirpitz* is attacked and damaged by Barracuda bombers from the carriers of the British Home Fleet. Four aircraft are lost but the *Tirpitz* is put out of action for a further three months. The *Victorious* and *Furious* and four escort carriers are involved.

4 April 1944

Eastern Front There are local German counterattacks near Kovel and farther south where the Soviets are prevented from gaining routes through the Carpathians near Kolomya.

Burma The Japanese 31st Division begins to put real pressure on the British position at Kohima, cutting both routes out of the town toward the rear. It is vital for the Japanese to capture this British supply center as they are relying on its resources for their own replenishment.

France, Politics De Gaulle announces changes in the Committee of National Liberation. Two communists are appointed and de Gaulle himself becomes head of the armed forces. General Giraud is being sidelined. On 9 April he becomes Inspector General of the Army and on 14 April he is placed on the retired list.

5 April 1944

Eastern Front Malinovsky's forces reach Razdelnaya, cutting the rail route from Odessa.

6-8 April 1944

Eastern Front There is heavy fighting north of Razdelnaya as a small German pocket is wiped out.

7 April 1944

Burma Near Kohima the Japanese encircle the 161st Brigade from Stopford's XXXIII Corps at Jotsoma and block the main road to the west near Zubza.

8 April 1944

Eastern Front The Russian forces move to the attack in the Crimea. The defenders from General Jaenicke's Seventeenth Army are attacked by a considerably superior force from Tolbukhin's Fourth Ukraine Front. Farther west the troops of Zhukov's and Konev's Armies penetrate well into Rumania taking Botosani and Dorohoi and Siret to the north. Konev's forces reach the River Siret on a 60-mile front. Patrols from Zhukov's armies reach as far as the Slovakian border.

10 April 1944

Burma Slim now feels that he has a complete picture of the situation and that an offensive is practical and necessary. The troops surrounded at Imphal and Kohima are to continue to be supplied by air and particularly in the case of the Imphal garrison are to operate as offensively as possible. Stopford's XXXIII Corps are to break through and relieve Kohima.

Eastern Front The Russians take Odessa after a vicious battle. The Germans have managed to evacuate by sea 24,000 men, many wounded, as well as 55,000 tons of supplies. In the Crimea the initial German defense lines are being worn down. Armyansk is taken. The Rumanian troops holding the right of the line are in severe trouble. In Rumania itself Second Ukraine Front crosses the Siret. Rumania's position begins to look increasingly vulnerable.

11 April 1944

Eastern Front In the Crimea the Russians make good progress capturing Dzhankoy and, in a new series of attacks in the east by Yeremenko's troops, Kerch is also taken.

12 April 1944

Eastern Front Troops from Malinovsky's forces occupy Tiraspol. The Germans begin a further series of evacuations from the Crimea. In the next four days 67,000 men, Germans and their allies, are taken out with little loss from Russian air and naval attacks.

13 April 1944

New Guinea The Australians take Bogadjim.
Eastern Front In the Crimea Tolbukhin's and Yeremenko's tank forces advance rapidly, capturing Feodosia, Evpatoriya, and Simferopol. The Germans and Rumanians are retreating in some disorder toward Sevastopol. Farther west Malinovsky's men take Ovidiopol at the mouth of the Dniestr.

14 April 1944

Burma The Japanese road block at Zubza is broken and the 161st Brigade at Jotsoma relieved by the attacks of other units of the 2nd Indian Division.

15 April 1944

Eastern Front After fighting for several weeks the Russians take Tarnopol.

16 April 1944

Eastern Front The Russians take Yalta. To the west Malinovsky's troops cross the Dniestr north and south of Tiraspol.

18 April 1944

Eastern Front There are important German attacks around Buchach which are designed to help free units trapped farther east. In the Crimea the Russians take Balaklava and begin operations in the outskirts of Sevastopol.
Operation Overlord The British Government bans all coded radio and telegraph transmissions from London and elsewhere in the British Isles. Diplomatic bags are to be censored and diplomats are to be forbidden to leave the country. The only exemptions are for the USA and USSR and, a tribute to their excellent security, the London Poles. The telephone service to Southern Ireland and the distribution of newspapers to there and to Gibraltar have already been stopped on 5 April. These measures are designed to help with the security of the preparations for D-Day.

Above: The reality of war on the Eastern Front: Russian civilians search for their loved ones in the aftermath of the German retreat.

Burma The advance guard of 5th Brigade makes contact with the Kohima garrison restoring its communications.

19 April 1944

Indian Ocean Admiral Somerville's Eastern Fleet, reinforced for the occasion by the USS *Saratoga,* sends the carrier aircraft to attack Sabang and the nearby airfields. Only one of the attacking planes is lost and 27 Japanese are shot down.
Eastern Front Although the battle for Sevastopol continues, elsewhere on the front activity begins to die down. The recent Russian advances have stretched their supply lines and they need time to prepare their next moves. For their part the Germans and their allies have been so weakened as to welcome the respite.

20 April 1944

Diplomatic Affairs In response to Allied pressure Turkey stops chrome exports to Germany.

21 April 1944

New Guinea In preparation for the Hollandia landings Admiral Mitscher leads TF 58 including 12 carriers in attacks on Wakde Island, Sawar, Sarmi and Hollandia itself. The carrier planes attack during the day and there are cruiser bombardments during the night.

Above: A bombardment group of US B-17 Flying Fortresses engages in a high-altitude bombing mission over a German city.

22 April 1944

New Guinea The US operations against the Japanese positions at Hollandia and nearby begin. The landing forces are carried by the ships of Admiral Barbey's TF 77. Admirals Crutchley and Berkey lead cruiser forces in the covering group in which there are also two escort-carrier squadrons. Admiral Mitscher's carriers which made several of the preparatory raids remain in support. The landing force, I US Corps, is under the overall command of General Eichelberger and totals 84,000 men. The defenders are commanded by General Adachi and number 11,000. Initially there are three landings. One regiment is put ashore at Aitape; General Irving's 24th Infantry Division at Tanahmerah Bay; and General Fuller's 41st Division at Humboldt Bay. There is comparatively little resistance at first. The Japanese are taken somewhat by surprise and retire inland leaving for the moment only harassing forces. All the landings get well established ashore advancing in some sectors as much as eight miles.
Marshalls US forces occupy Ungelap Island completing the campaign for the group.

23 April 1944

New Guinea The US forces take Hollandia without a fight. The advance inland continues meeting its first check near the village of Sabron. The only other problem is with the beach organization as there is some congestion. The subsidiary landing at Aitape is also going well. Tadji airfield is taken.

24 April 1944

New Guinea The Hollandia operation continues to go well. Near Hollandia itself Lake Sentani is reached and there is also good progress at Aitape. Farther east the Australians advancing from the Huon Peninsula reach and capture Madang.

25 April 1944

New Guinea The Allied forces, strengthened by further landings in Humboldt Bay, push forward.

26 April 1944

Arctic The British Home Fleet in which Admiral Moore leads the battleship *Anson* and six carriers, tries again to attack *Tirpitz* but bad weather intervenes and instead a coastal convoy is found near Bodo and three ships sunk.
New Guinea The beachheads at Tanahmerah Bay and Humboldt Bay are linked up. The Australian forces to the east take Alexishafen.

28 April 1944

New Guinea There is fighting near Aitape between the US forces and Japanese units moved west from Wewak.
United States, Politics The Secretary to the United States Navy, Frank Knox, dies. He has played a large part in the revival of the navy since Pearl Harbor.

29 April 1944

New Guinea The captured Japanese airfields at Hollandia and Aitape are reopened.

29-30 April 1944

Carolines On both days Admiral Mitscher's TF 58 sends heavy strikes against the Japanese base at Truk. Of the establishment of 104 aircraft 93 are shot down for the loss of 35 of the carriers' machines many of whose pilots are saved. On 30 April Admiral Oldendorf leads nine cruisers and eight destroyers to shell targets in the Sawatan Islands, southeast of the main Truk base.

30 April 1944

Burma In the continuing battle for Imphal the Japanese attacks are being gradually worn down, especially as the food shortage becomes serious. The defense of 20th Division on the Shenam Ridge is particularly stout.

May 1944

Europe, Air Operations The principal efforts of the Allied air forces based in Britain is directed to preparations for the Normandy landings. RAF Bomber Command only drops 8500 tons on targets in Germany with the major raids being on Duisburg and Aachen. Another 28,500 sorties are devoted to a range of small targets in France including stores dumps and rail and training centers. Mailly, Bourg Leopold and Boulogne are all hit with many others. The American heavy bombers drop 63,000 tons on three types of objective: rail centers, oil production areas and the more usual manufacturing towns. Among the oil targets are Bohlen and Poolitz; the aircraft manufacturing towns are Strasbourg and Poser; and the rail centers hit include Metz, Belfort, Mulhouse and Hamm. To round off the program Berlin and Brunswick are raided. The medium and fighter-bombers of the US Ninth Air Force drop 20,000 tons on targets in France mostly connected with communications. They hit 13 of the Seine bridges as well as road, rail and canal targets. The activities of the

British light and medium forces follow the same pattern with redoubled strength this month. Planes of British Bomber and Coastal Commands step up mining operations in the Channel as well as their other tasks in preparation for D-Day. There is increased air activity here and off Norway to prevent U-Boats being on station in early June. The Mediterranean Air Forces contribute attacks on oil and communications systems in southeast Europe. Bucharest, Brasov and Ploesti are all struck.

English Channel During the month there is intense naval activity as both sides prepare for the coming operations. There are numerous small battles as patrols, coastal convoys and minelaying vessels meet.

1 May 1944

Carolines Admiral Lee leads seven battleships and 11 destroyers to bombard Ponape. The operation is covered by the carriers of Admiral Clark's TG 58.1.

3 May 1944

Japanese Command Admiral Toyoda is named Commander in Chief of the Japanese Combined Fleets. There has been a long delay in choosing a successor to Koga who was killed in an air crash on 31 March.

4 May 1944

United States, Home Front All meats are taken off the ration with the exception of steaks and certain choice cuts of beef for roasting.

6 May 1944

Eastern Front During the night the final Soviet assault on Sevastopol opens, preceded by the customary devastating bombardment. The southeast sector is most heavily attacked. In the last three weeks there have been intensive convoy operations in the Black Sea. Generally the Germans have managed to get sufficient supplies through as well as evacuate 40,000 men.

Above: British 4.2in mortars lay down supporting fire for an infantry assault in the Cassino sector, Italy, May 1944.

6 May-1 June 1944

Arctic There is a series of six operations by the British Home Fleet off the Norwegian coast. Various air attacks on the *Tirpitz* are planned but are prevented by bad weather. As well as the inherent value of these raids they are designed to support one of the deception plans for D-Day, *Fortitude North.* This scheme principally involves false radio activity designed to suggest a coming landing in Norway.

7 May 1944

New Britain Units of the US 46th Division occupy Cape Hopkins Airfield without meeting any resistance.

Below: German paratroops wait in the shelter of farm buildings for orders to attack, Cassino sector, April 1944.

8 May 1944

Eastern Front After refusing several earlier, timely requests, Hitler now gives his permission for full-scale withdrawals from the Crimea. During the next few days 37,500 men will be taken off but a further 8000 will be drowned in ships sunk by the fierce Soviet attacks from the air and submarines and surface naval units.

9 May 1944

Eastern Front Sevastopol falls to the Red Army. The remainder of the German garrison retreats toward Cape Kersonessky where evacuations are still being carried out.

9-13 May 1944

New Guinea There is constant skirmishing with occasional fierce engagements around the US beachheads at Hollandia, but the Japanese forces are ill supplied and weak and achieve little.

10 May 1944

United States, Politics J V Forrestal becomes Secretary to the US Navy.

11 May 1944

Italy Just before midnight the preparatory bombardment for the new Allied attacks, code named Diadem, begins and is quickly followed by the first infantry advances. Four Allied Corps are in the attack: II US, II Polish, XIII British and the French Expeditionary Corps. In the long lull since the last major operations the Germans have done much to strengthen their lines and provide other positions in the rear if a retirement is necessary. At first the Germans will be hampered by the temporary absence of Senger and Vietinghoff, their Corps and Army commanders. The Allies have 12 divisions in the attack as well as ample reserves. The Germans are at a serious disadvantage, with only six divisions including reserves.

11-16 May 1944

Pacific In preparation for the attack on the Marianas which is imminent, the Japanese assemble practically all the heavy units of their Fleet in the Sulu Sea at Tawitawi. Their plan to defend the Marianas' line is code named *A-Go.* Admiral Ozawa is in command of the various squadrons.

12 May 1944

Italy Although the Allied attack is only one hour old at the beginning of the day even before dawn some gains have been recorded. The French Corps (General Juin) finds only the 71st German Division opposite its four and quickly seizes Monte Faito. Elsewhere the defense is more successful. The Poles are beaten back with heavy losses in their attack north of Cassino. To their left the British XIII Corps takes two small bridgeheads over the Rapido opposite Cassino. The two US divisions on the coastal flank to the left of the French can only make a little ground.

Below: Field Marshal Erwin Rommel (left) and his Chief of Engineers, Dr Wilhelm Meise, inspect beach defenses in northern France, early 1944.

13 May 1944

Italy The US and British forces continue to push forward doggedly. Santa Maria Infante is taken by the Americans and Sant'Angelo by the British. The Poles are again bloodily repulsed by the parachutists defending Cassino. The French, however, are still doing well. On their left they take Castelforte and push on. In the center Monte Maio is captured and on their right they reach north to the Liri at Sant'Appollinaire.
Eastern Front The campaign in the Crimea is over. Altogether 130,000 Germans and Rumanians have been evacuated by sea and another 21,500 by air since 12 April but a further 78,000 have been killed or captured and many of those evacuated have been wounded.

14 May 1944

Italy The French break into the Ausente Valley, take Ausonia and push on over the Aurunci Mountains toward the next German line, hoping to break into it before the Germans can occupy it in strength. Their advance helps the American forces on their left to speed their own move forward against the German 94th Division.

15 May 1944

Italy The German position on the Gustav line is beginning to collapse. The French push on once more to take San Giorgio and farther north in the Liri Valley the British reach Pignaturo. The Canadian Corps is put in to the line to try to exploit this advance.

16 May 1944

Italy Of the five attacking Allied Corps only the Poles are still meeting really stubborn defense at Cassino. In the Liri Valley the British and Canadians are pushing toward Pontecorvo and Piumarola aiming later to reach Highway 6. The Americans on the coast are still doing well but the best gains are being made by the French who take Monte Petrella and advance on Monte Revole.
New Guinea American units move on from Hollandia toward Wadke Island. The Hollandia operation has been a notable success. The local Japanese garrison has been quickly and cheaply neutralized and many more Japanese have been cut off to the east. There is hard fighting to come, however.

17 May 1944

Italy Although Kesselring, commanding Army Group C, has given Vietinghoff three more divisions they have been unable to halt the continued Allied progress in the Liri Valley and to the south. This continues with the capture of Piumarolo, Monte Faggeta, Esperia and Formia. Even near Cassino there are renewed Polish attacks which manage to take Colle Sant'Angelo. Although the French advance, the most threatening, is held up beyond Esperia especially near Monte d'Oro, the Germans decide on a general retreat.
Burma Merrill's Marauders help the Chinese forces to capture Myitkyina airfield.
New Guinea US forces are landed on Insumarai Island and on the mainland at Arare nearby. Artillery is quickly sent ashore to provide fire support for the next landings on 18 May. Admirals Crutchley and Berkey lead the cruisers and destroyers which give cover.
Indian Ocean The oil installations at Surabaya on Java are attacked by aircraft from the carriers *Illustrious* and *Saratoga*. The carriers are escorted by the battleships of Admiral Sommerville's Eastern Fleet, designated TF 65 for the occasion (the carriers are TF 66). The damage inflicted is not in fact as great as the attackers believe. One Japanese freighter is sunk and 12 aircraft are destroyed on the ground. Of the 85 attacking planes only one is lost. During the night there is a further attack by land based Liberator bombers.

18 May 1944

Mediterranean In sinking a ship from the convoy HA-43, *U.453* records the last success by a German submarine in the Mediterranean.
German Command Berlin announces that Field Marshal von Rundstedt is to be Commander in Chief West with Field Marshals Rommel and Blaskowitz his subordinates at Army Groups B and G in the north and south respectively. This arrangement is by no means ideal as Rommel and Rundstedt quickly develop diverging views on the necessary strategy and

both put them to Hitler, who establishes a poor compromise.
Italy The Monte Cassino abbey is finally occupied by Allied forces as the Germans withdraw. In the Liri Valley the Canadian I Corps is now up to the Senger line before Pontecorvo. On their left the French, and on the coast the Americans, are meeting equally solid opposition.
New Guinea The main body of the 163rd Infantry Regiment (General Doe) is landed on Insoemar Island and quickly advances to take Wadke airfield.
Admiralty Islands The Sixth Army announces that the campaign is over. The Americans have lost 1400 dead and wounded, the Japanese 3820 dead and 75 prisoners.

19 May 1944

New Guinea On Insoemar the remnants of the Japanese forces retire to the northeast corner.
Italy The US forces take Gasta Itri and Monte Grande nearby while on their right the French push foward almost to Pico and begin fighting for Campodimele.

19-20 May 1944

Marcus Island On both days heavy air attacks are put in by the carriers *Essex, Wasp* and *San Jacinto* of Admiral Montgomery's TG 58.2.

20 May 1944

Poland, Resistance A V2 on test lands near the River Bug about 80 miles east of Warsaw. Polish resistance workers get to it before the Germans and hide and dismantle it. On the night of 25 July parts are flown out by Dakota and are in London seven weeks before the first V2 lands. Nothing effective can be done with this knowledge but it is an astonishing resistance achievement nonetheless.
Italy The French, Canadians and Poles assault the Senger line at Pico, Pontecorvo and Piedimonte San Germano respectively.
New Guinea The battle for Wadke is over with the small Japanese garrison being wiped out. There is a minor Japanese attack near Arare on the mainland.

Above: A view of Cassino, looking towards Monastery Hill, after the eventual capture of the area by the Allies, May 1944.

21 May 1944

Italy A small force is sent by sea from Gaeta to Sperlonga and lands without difficulty. The US forces also take Fondi and the French Campodi-

Below: General Sir Henry Maitland Wilson (right) with Lt General Sir Oliver Leese.

Above: British troops use Bren-gun carriers to open up the Imphal-Kohima road after the Japanese attacks of May 1944.

mele. In the Liri Valley and around Pico, the German opposition is stronger but the Allies are bringing forces forward for another blow.

New Guinea The beachhead at Arare is reinforced and offshore at Wadke the airfield is repaired and reopened by US engineers.

22 May 1944

Italy Keyes' II US Corps continues to push north along the coast and by Route 7. The French forces take Pico.

Sulu Sea A US submarine reports the concentration of the Japanese Fleet around Tawitawi and in operations over the next two or three weeks various destroyers and tankers are sunk. In contrast to the Japanese, who have shown little interest in underwater warfare, the Americans have used their submarines with great skill.

New Guinea The American positions around Aitape come under new and unexpected attacks and some withdrawals are made.

Wake Ialand A strong US destroyer force bombards the island. The same units are in action against Mili in the Marshalls on 26 May.

23 May 1944

Italy The Anzio beachhead bursts into new activity with a fierce bombardment followed by an attack on Cisterna by three divisions of US VI Corps. The German defense is strong and casualties are heavy but some gains are made. Advance guards of US II Corps reach Terracina while inland both the French and Canadians break into the Senger Line. The Canadian attack has been well prepared and by the end of the day they have broken through.

New Guinea The US forces meet heavy resistance on trying to advance west from Arare toward Sarmi. At Aitape the Japanese continue to force slight withdrawals.

Wake Island The destroyer bombardment of the previous day is followed up by heavy air attacks from the carriers of Montgomery's TG 58.2.

24 May 1944

Italy The attacks of Fifth and Eighth Armies continue. The Canadians take Pontecorvo and to the north their 5th Armored Division reaches the River Melfa. Terracina is occupied by II US Corps despite resistance from 29th Panzer Grenadier Division. At Anzio the attacks also continue. Cisterna is still held by the Germans but a little to the south Route 7 is reached near Latina. Hitler authorizes Kesselring to withdraw to the Caesar Line.

Burma There are strong counterattacks by units of the Japanese 18th Division south of Myitkyina.

25 May 1944

Italy Patrols of the II US Corps link up with units of VI Corps from Anzio. The main advance of VI Corps takes Cisterna and Cori. The obvious next move from here is toward Velletri and Valmontone and if this is executed quickly most of the German Tenth Army may be cut off. Kesselring therefore sends his only remaining reserve, the Hermann Goering Division, to join the forces in this sector. General Clark, commanding Fifth Army, only keeps one division moving forward in this sector and despite direct orders from Alexander puts his principal effort into capturing the glory of freeing Rome. In the Liri Valley the battle is still going well for the Allies with Monte Cairo, Piedimonte and Aquino all being taken. Because of Clark's errors however, Senger is able to prepare a strong resistance around Arce and Ceprano which will enable his forces to pull back to the Caesar Line and even for a time look like making a stand.

New Guinea The US forces advancing from Arare cross the Tirfoam River after a brisk engagement.

Yugoslavia, Resistance A small German paratroop force is dropped at Tito's headquarters at Drvar in Bosnia. Tito and Major Randolph Churchill who is with him as a liaison officer both have a narrow escape.

26 May 1944

Italy The Allied advance continues despite stiffer German resistance. McCreery's X Corps takes Roccasecca, the Canadians take San Giovanni, and on their left the US II Corps reaches Priverno. At Anzio the main thrust of VI Corps makes some progress toward Lanuvio but 1st Armored Division cannot make much toward Velletri. The 3rd Division is held after taking Artena and is unable to reach Valmontono.

27 May 1944

Italy Artena is held by 3rd Division despite German counterattacks. In the Liri Valley Canadian units attack Ceprano and the British 6th Armored Division moves toward Arce.

New Guinea US Forces land on Biak Island. There is the usual preliminary bombardment before the men of 41st Infantry Division (General Fuller) land near Bosnek. At first there is little resistance but this is misleading, for the Japanese garrison at 11,000 men (Colonel Kuzume) is little weaker than the attack force. The close escort for the landing ships is provided by cruisers and destroyers led by Admiral Fechteler and as in the other landings on the north coast Crutchley and Berkey are in support. Elsewhere on the island the US troops make a little ground in their advance toward Sarmi.

28 May 1944

Italy Ceprano is taken by the Canadians. Here and on all the other sectors the fighting remains fierce with the Allies everywhere attempting to push forward but in fact making few gains. Apart from rearguards the German XIV Panzer and LI Mountain Corps are falling back to the Caesar Line because of the threat to their rear posed by the Anzio forces.

New Guinea On Biak the Americans begin to extend their perimeter but one battalion is surprised by a fierce Japanese attack near Mokmer village and takes heavy losses. The US forces in that sector pull back. Similarly Japanese attacks cause retreats near Arare. General MacArthur is confident enough, however, to announce that strategically the campaign in New Guinea is over although some hard fighting is still to be done.

29 May 1944

Atlantic The US escort carrier *Block Island* is sunk by *U.549* which also sinks a destroyer in the same engagement before being hunted down.

Italy At Anzio Allied attacks by British and American units take Campoleone and Carroceto but here and near Lanuvio they are later held. The Canadians begin to advance up Route 6 from Caprano toward Frosinone.

New Guinea Both at Biak and at Arare the American beachheads come under heavy pressure. At Biak Japanese tanks are used to force back the 162nd Regiment almost to its landing ground.

30 May 1944

Italy Arce is taken by British troops of Eighth Army after a stubborn battle. In the Anzio sector the US forces are nearing the important position at Velletri.

Eastern Front In the first flurry of summer activity the Germans throw in powerful attacks against Konev's forces near Jassy.

31 May 1944

Italy The Canadians take Frosinone and X Corps takes Sora. In the Anzio sector Velletri and Monte Artemiso nearby fall to the US 36th Division while other units of VI Corps are

attacking round Albano. By the capture of Velletri a gap is torn in the Caesar Line.
New Guinea The Americans narrow down their holdings near Arare. At all their beachheads on the north coast there is considerable skirmishing. To the east Australian troops take Bunabum.

June 1944

Europe, Air Operations The Allied effort is directed mostly at tactical targets in very many fairly small raids. RAF Bomber Command drops 56,000 tons and the 25,600 sorties flown by Eighth Air Force add nearly as much. Light and medium forces contribute another 25,000 tons. A proportion of the heavy bomber raids are against strategic targets mostly connected with oil production. Objectives include Gelsenkirchen, Bohlen, Poolitz and others in Hungary and Yugoslavia. The Fifteenth Air Force from Italy joins these raids as well as attacking communications targets in southeastern Europe like Nish, Giurgiu and Brod. Railways in north Italy are also hit. German production of avaiation fuel falls to one-third of the May figure as a consequence of the raids on oil producing centers. The first Me 262 jet fighters enter operational service with the Luftwaffe. Although these are vastly superior to all the Allied designs there will never be enough of them to cause any significant damage. They will be hindered by the continuing fall in fuel production and by attacks on the bases from which they operate.
Pacific, Air Operations The main targets are in the Marianas and Carolines. The first Superfortress raid on the Japanese mainland is on 15 June.

1 June 1944

Italy Exploiting the success of 36th Division the US II and VI Corps begin to drive toward Rome at full strength attacking through the Alban Hills and toward Albano and Valmonte on either side. Since the Caesar Line has now been breached by these advances, Kesselring orders a fighting withdrawal north of Rome. The German forces still fight skillfully to delay the Americans, however.

Below: American troops liberate Rome, 4 June 1944. Their half-track is armed with a 0.5in Browning heavy machine gun.

Eastern Front Although the German pressure near Jassy is maintained Russian counterattacks are now succeeding in retaking and holding the disputed ground.
Mediterranean A German supply convoy bound for Crete from the Greek mainland is heavily attacked by RAF planes and several ships sunk. After this the Germans only sail occasional ships to the island.
Overlord The first code message, giving a general warning to the French resistance that invasion is imminent, is transmitted by the BBC in the evening. The Germans understand the rough significance of this verse (part of a poem by Verlaine) and alert some of their units.
New Guinea On Biak the American forces resume the offensive. They mount a strong tank and infantry attack and succeed in advancing despite sharp Japanese counterattacks.

2 June 1944

France, Politics The French Committee of National Liberation restyles itself the Provisional Government of the French Republic.
Italy As Kesselring's forces gradually pull back the Allies are able to advance all along the front. The US forces reach Route 6 at Valmontone, which they take, and also in other sectors. They also make good progress in the Alban Hills.
New Guinea The fighting on Biak continues. The US 186th Infantry Regiment is doing the bulk of attacking supported by the 162nd. The objective is to reach and capture the airfields in the center of the island plateau. These airfields have been used as the base for attacks on Wadke.
Burma The final siege of Myitkyina begins.

3 June 1944

New Guinea There are various Japanese attempts to bring reinforcements to Biak between now and June 12 but all are abortive. On Biak the US forces again advance. The 162nd Regiment meets heavy resistance.
Italy The US forces advancing on Rome take Albano and Frascati. Other American and French units move forward along Route 6. The Canadians to the southeast take Anagni. The German forces have already largely abandoned Rome, respecting its status as an 'open city' in return for a temporary truce with local resistance fighters.

4 June 1944

Italy In the evening units of the US 88th Division enter Rome.
Overlord The convoys for the invasion are already at sea but because of bad weather expected on 5 June they turn back to wait. Late in the evening Eisenhower decides, after consulting with the meteorological staff, that the invasion can take place on 6 June when a break in the weather is expected. It has long been decided that the first landings must be at dawn when there is a low tide. This should allow the engineering teams to work their way up the beach to the high-water mark clearing visible obstacles. These tidal conditions only occur on about three days every fortnight. Also desirable is for the moon to rise late to aid the airborne troops. These conditions pertain on 5 and 6 June and less ideally 7 June. If the invasion does not take place then the tides will be right about 20 June but the combination of moon and tides not until July. Eisenhower, therefore, has had to take a very difficult decision because any postponement would be bound to affect the troops' morale; to give the Germans more time to improve their defenses; to upset relations with the Russians; and almost certainly jeopardize the security of the plan (for one thing the deception operation has been scheduled in line with the 5 June date).

The bad weather has helped in putting the Germans off their guard. Rommel has decided to take the opportunity to go to Germany for his wife's birthday on 6 June and to try to persuade Hitler to adopt his strategic ideas which include, among other things, strengthening the Normandy defenses. Other more junior commanders are also away from their posts – many at a training exercise in Brittany.

5 June 1944

Italy The Allied forces make their triumphal entry into Rome and push on beyond in pursuit of the retreating Germans. There are problems of traffic congestion on the few good roads which prevent the Allied forces using their full strength. As usual the German retreat is accompanied by skillful rearguard actions and demolitions.
New Guinea On Biak the 162nd Regiment and 186th Regiment both continue to advance breaking down pockets of Japanese resistance. Near Aitape the Americans evacuate one of their outlying beachheads because of the Japanese attacks. Although the Japanese seem to be doing well here, they are taking dreadful losses.
Overlord The second message warning that the invasion is imminent is sent to the French Resistance. Again the Germans note its significance but in a glaring omission the Seventh Army in Normandy is not alerted. Just before midnight the airborne troops are sent on their way from their various airfields in southern England. The landing ships are already nearing France.
Burma At Kohima an outflanking attack at last forces the Japanese off the Aradura Spur and into retreat. It still remains to clear the road to Imphal.

6 June 1944

D-DAY

The Allied Plans and Preparations
Briefly the Allies intend to land units of four army corps and three airborne divisions on the beaches of Normandy between Caen and

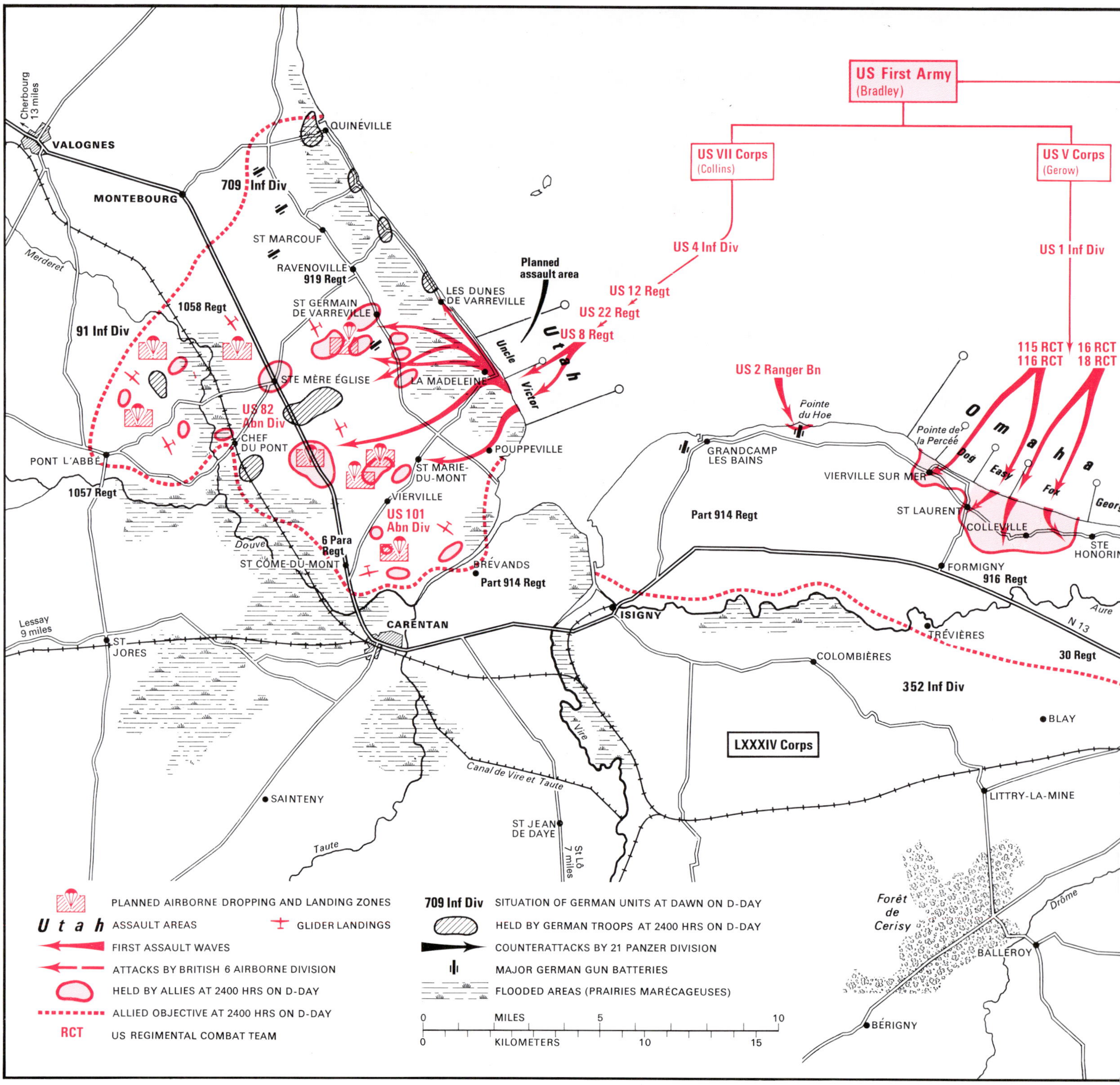
US First Army
(Bradley)
US VII Corps
(Collins)
US V Corps
(Gerow)
US 4 Inf Div
US 12 Regt
US 22 Regt
US 8 Regt
US 1 Inf Div
115 RCT
116 RCT
16 RCT
18 RCT
US 2 Ranger Bn
Cherbourg 13 miles
VALOGNES
QUINÉVILLE
MONTEBOURG
709 Inf Div
ST MARCOUF
RAVENOVILLE
919 Regt
Merderet
Planned assault area
LES DUNES DE VARREVILLE
ST GERMAIN DE VARREVILLE
1058 Regt
91 Inf Div
Uncle
Utah
Victor
STE MÈRE ÉGLISE
LA MADELEINE
US 82 Abn Div
CHEF DU PONT
PONT L'ABBÉ
1057 Regt
POUPPEVILLE
ST MARIE-DU-MONT
VIERVILLE
US 101 Abn Div
6 Para Regt
Douve
ST CÔME-DU-MONT
BRÉVANDS
Part 914 Regt
CARENTAN
Lessay 9 miles
ST JORES
ISIGNY
Pointe du Hoe
GRANDCAMP LES BAINS
Pointe de la Percée
Omaha
Dog
Easy
Fox
George
VIERVILLE SUR MER
ST LAURENT
COLLEVILLE
STE HONORINE
Part 914 Regt
FORMIGNY
916 Regt
Aure
N 13
TRÉVIÈRES
30 Regt
COLOMBIÈRES
352 Inf Div
BLAY
LXXXIV Corps
Vire
Canal de Vire et Taute
LITTRY-LA-MINE
SAINTENY
ST JEAN DE DAYE
St Lô 7 miles
Taute
Forêt de Cerisy
Drôme
BALLEROY
BÉRIGNY
PLANNED AIRBORNE DROPPING AND LANDING ZONES
Utah ASSAULT AREAS
GLIDER LANDINGS
FIRST ASSAULT WAVES
ATTACKS BY BRITISH 6 AIRBORNE DIVISION
HELD BY ALLIES AT 2400 HRS ON D-DAY
ALLIED OBJECTIVE AT 2400 HRS ON D-DAY
RCT US REGIMENTAL COMBAT TEAM
709 Inf Div SITUATION OF GERMAN UNITS AT DAWN ON D-DAY
HELD BY GERMAN TROOPS AT 2400 HRS ON D-DAY
COUNTERATTACKS BY 21 PANZER DIVISION
MAJOR GERMAN GUN BATTERIES
FLOODED AREAS (PRAIRIES MARÉCAGEUSES)
0 MILES 5 10
0 KILOMETERS 10 15

Far left: Newly appointed Supreme Allied Commander in Europe, General Dwight D Eisenhower (second from right) visits the Eighth USAAF HQ. *Left:* US soldiers wait for the orders to go ashore in Normandy, 6 June 1944. The man in the center is carrying a Bazooka anti-tank weapon, a means of providing the infantryman with some degree of protection from enemy armor. *Below:* Map showing the Allied landings on the coast of Normandy, 6 June 1944 – D-Day for Operation Overlord, the liberation of western Europe. *Right:* Supplies are brought ashore from landing ships at Biak, in New Guinea, June 1944. The Allies' extensive material resources allowed them to conduct simultaneous large-scale amphibious operations.

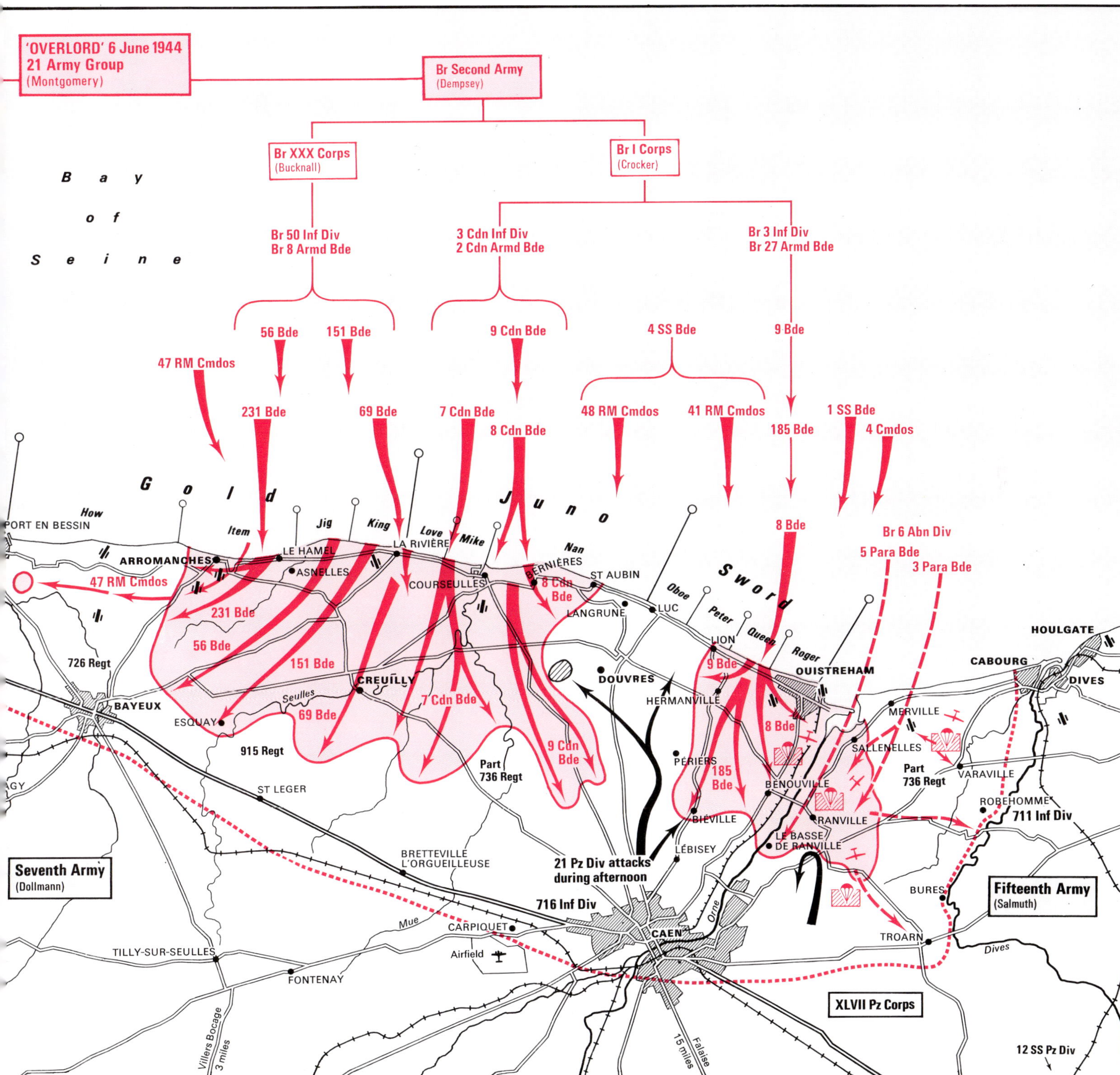

Above: General Eisenhower chats to men of the US 101st Ariborne Division – the 'Screaming Eagles' – as they prepare for the D-Day landings.

Above: Air Chief Marshal Sir Trafford Leigh-Mallory, Allied Air C in C for Overlord.

Valognes. Normandy has been selected for a number of reasons. The topography of the beaches and the area just inland is favorable. Normandy is within fighter range of southern England and is convenient for all the ports on the south coast. It is a less obvious choice than the Pas de Calais and is, therefore, less well defended.

The preparations have been enormous in scale and elaboration. There are nearly 3,000,000 men under Eisenhower's command and a mass of vehicles and stores have been accumulated. Not the least important items of equipment are the various parts of the *Mulberry* Harbors. There are old ships, assorted huge blocks of concrete and steel and all the metal roadways necessary to turn these into great artificial ports as soon as they are sunk off the beaches. This obviates the need to plan to seize a port as a first priority. All the ports are of course heavily defended, as the Dieppe experience has proved. The undertaking for the construction of the parts of the Mulberries (there are two – one British and one American) is so vast that it has absorbed a considerable proportion of the British war-production effort for several months. All the parts have been made in Britain because of their size and unwieldiness. The British have also produced a range of specially modified tanks and other armored vehicles mainly to help their engineers clear beach obstacles under fire. These 'Funnies' are organized as part of the 79th Armored Division which has been led and trained by General Hobart, one of the pioneers of tank warfare. All these devices are offered to the Americans, but they have chosen to accept only the amphibious tanks. This is a serious error.

As well as the preparations for the actual attack, a considerable effort has been put in to misleading the Germans as to the location of the landings. The main section of the deception plan has been designed to suggest a landing in the Pas de Calais by a fictional First United States Army Group (FUSAG) based in Kent and supposedly commanded by General Patton. At first real formations are based in Kent supposedly as part of this army, and when these transfer to France they are replaced by fictional units behind a screen of false radio traffic and reports from double agents. Some dummy installations, airfields and landing craft are also erected. A similar scheme is run to simulate the presence of a British Fourth Army in Scotland preparing for a descent on Norway. Again a real personality is chosen to command, a British General Thorne. It is essential for these schemes to have real commanders of sufficient stature reported to be in charge. After Patton goes to France he is succeeded by another senior American General. The FUSAG scheme is a notable success in drawing attention away from Normandy and keeping alive the idea that the real landings might in fact be a feint.

The enormous number of air attacks on targets in France have been carefully orchestrated to avoid giving away the real location of the landings. Thus, destroying the Seine bridges, which has been done, will seem to the Germans to be just as necessary to prevent troops moving from Normandy to the Pas de Calais as the reverse. These and other air attacks have been a considerable success, but the real effect of the air operations is to come after the landing in the prevention of German reinforcements reaching Normandy in full strength or as quickly as might otherwise have been the case. Lorries and other types of 'soft' vehicles are particularly vulnerable.

The German Dispositions

Altogether in France, Belgium and Holland the Germans have 60 divisions including 11 armored. These figures are somewhat misleading, however. About half of the infantry divisions are not equipped for mobile warfare and all are understrength. Some are in France simply to refit after heavy losses on the Eastern Front and are hardly fit for action. To lead them they have, in Supreme Command, Field Marshal Rundstedt and commanding Army Group B in the northern half of the country, Field Marshal Rommel. Blaskowitz commands in the south. The landings will initially be opposed mostly by units of Dollmann's Seventh Army except on the British left flank where part of Salmuth's Fifteenth Army is stationed. However, this chain of command is made almost totally useless by Hitler's interference. As usual he insists on involving himself in even the most immediate tactical decisions. This difficulty is compounded by real doubts about the correct strategy both as to where the attack is going to fall, and how it ought to be met. As to the location both Hitler and Rommel have nursed a belief that Normandy might well be the target. Interestingly once the invasion has come where he predicted Hitler convinces himself that it is a feint. In the work Rommel has done to make the Atlantic Wall defenses a reality the Normandy area has received at least its fair share. The more important problem concerns how the armor reserve should be handled. Rundstedt wishes, in the classic style, to create a strong central reserve which can be used for a grand counterstroke once the focus of the Allied operation has been discerned. Rommel, on the other hand, believes that the invasion must be defeated as near to the beaches as possible and that the reserves should therefore be spread all along the front. He fears that Allied air power will prevent the sort of counterstroke that Rundstedt desires happening sufficiently promptly or in adequate strength. He realizes also that once solidly ashore the Allied material, quantitatively superior, is bound to tell. This belief can only be reinforced by the German intelligence appreciation that the Allies have 87 divisions in Britain, when in fact the total is 52.

Both Rommel and Rundstedt put their views to Hitler and his decision gives a compromise result fatal to both schemes. He allows Rommel some of his way by releasing a few divisions from the reserve but not the three Panzer Divisions for Normandy that Rommel wants among his other plans. Rundstedt is left with an inadequate force for his strategic reserve, and to make matters worse he cannot call on it without permission from Hitler at OKW.

The Forces Deployed

On the ground in Normandy the Germans have six infantry divisions. Two, 322nd and 716th, are wholly deployed on the beaches concerned along with parts of two more, 709th and 711th (from Fifteenth Army). In reserve on the left there is 91st Division and a parachute regiment and on the right, around Caen, 21st Panzer Division. Three more panzer divisions are within range farther inland but they are part of the OKW reserve and cannot be called in without permission. The fixed defenses are nowhere as formidable as has been planned because of shortages of transport, materials, especially concrete, labor, mines and other explosives. Partly because of these shortages and partly because of his belief that the invasion must be beaten on the beaches, Rommel has largely demolished what there was of a second defense line a little inland to use the materials for the beach defenses. This can only make the initial landings more crucial. The Allied air attacks have contributed to the difficulties with materials and construction.

At sea, the German Commander in Chief West, Admiral Krancke, is dreadfully overmatched. When in port his ships come under constant air attack and at sea are harried equally continuously. He has two large and two small destroyers, 31 motor torpedo boats and about 200 smaller vessels in the Channel. He has about 15 submarines under his direct command. In the air the situation is at least as bad. Sperrle's Third Air Fleet has less than 200 operational aircraft from a paper strength of only perhaps twice that. Many of the pilots are almost complete novices. The Luftwaffe still absorbs a disproportionate fraction of the German manpower and by edict of Goering has only rarely been used to help in, for example, the construction of defenses. The Luftwaffe troops, several divisions, are not fully integrated in the army command structure. An indication of the German weakness in the air is that only one Allied aircraft is shot down by an enemy plane on 6 June.

When the Allied plan is in turn examined, the list of participating units is massive. The naval forces include two battleships, two monitors, 23 cruisers, 105 destroyers and 1076 other warships (minesweepers and antisubmarine vessels especially) as well as 2700 merchant ships and 2500 landing craft. In the air 3500 heavy bombers, 1700 medium and light bombers, 5500 fighters and 2400 transport aircraft are employed. Despite this massive air and naval contribution the actual landing forces are by no means overwhelming in strength when compared to the German garrison in Normandy. There are three airborne divisions and five infantry divisions landed in the first waves as well as various independent Commando and Ranger units and, in the British and Canadian sector, three armored brigades. The principal limiting factor is the number of landing craft available. Partly because of the British commitment to produce *Mulberry*, almost all of the recent production of landing craft has been in the United States under the control of the US Navy. Admiral King has been most reluctant to release landing craft to the European theater and he still has a many times greater number in the Pacific. Altogether there are 59 convoys.

Above: The forward 14in guns of the battleship USS *Nevada* fire towards the American beach known as Utah on D-Day, 6 June 1944.

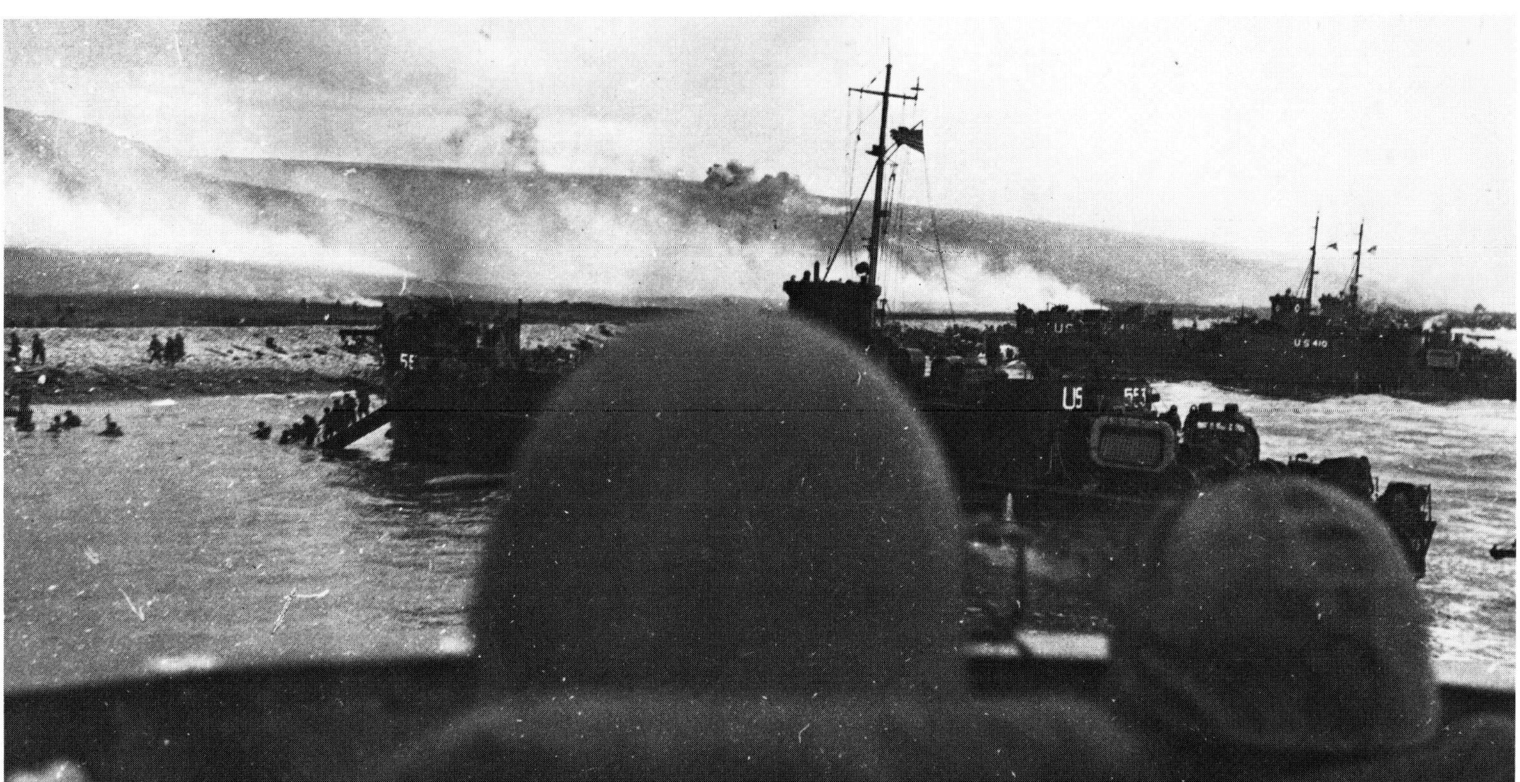

Below: American landing craft approach Omaha Beach on 6 June 1944. The landing here was strongly opposed and US casualties were heavy.

The Airborne Landings

The two US airborne divisions, 101st and 82nd, begin to land shortly after midnight inland from the western flank beach, *Utah*. Just inland from *Utah* the ground is marshy and 101st Division therefore has the task of taking the exits on the various causeways through this area. The 82nd are to land somewhat farther inland and clear ground on either side of the Merderet between St Mère Eglise and Pont l'Abbé. Largely because of the inexperience of many of the pilots the men of both divisions are dropped in widely scattered groups. At dawn, for example, 101st Division only has 1100 men under command out of 6600. Groups of perhaps 50 men are attempting tasks planned for battalions. However, this scattering proves extremely confusing for the German defenders. By a stroke of luck the commander of the 91st Division is ambushed and killed by one such group. This Division, left leaderless, is intended by the Germans to deal with an airborne attack and has been specially trained. In a multitude of small gallant and successful actions the capture of St Mère Eglise stands out.

On the left, eastern, flank of the attack only one division, the British 6th Airborne, can be committed because of lack of aircraft. They have three main tasks. They are to take positions holding various crossings of the Orne and the Caen Canal between that town and Ouistreham. The large battery at Merville is to be stormed and finally various bridges over the Dives are to be blown up to protect the flank. Although, as on the opposite flank, many of the troops are not landed in the correct place, the drops are fairly good and all the objectives are achieved and where necessary held until reinforcements fight their way off the beaches. Even better, a large part of 21st Panzer Division is first attracted by the parachute landings and then held by the threat of a major break out from the beaches. They are unable to follow orders to move against the Americans on *Omaha*.

Utah

The west flank landing beach is allocated to General Collins' VII US Corps. The naval force is commanded by Admiral Moon and includes eight attack convoys and, for bombardment, a battleship, a monitor, five cruisers, and a dozen destroyers. The assault is carried out by the US 4th Infantry Division (General Barton). There are some problems with rough seas which are to some extent offset by a commander of tank landing craft in launching his amphibious cargo closer inshore than the normal American practice. (The British operate differently.) The landings almost all take place by mistake on the southern sector of the beach and there is little resistance. The troops are quickly advancing inland held up mostly by the marshy ground. By the end of the day 23,250 men have gone ashore at *Utah* – an almost unqualified success. Less than 200 have died.

Omaha

The *Omaha* beach runs from Pointe de la Percée to St Honorine and has been allocated to General Gerow's US V Corps, like VII Corps from Bradley's First Army. The naval force is led by Admiral Hall with troops from 1st and 29th Infantry Divisions in the eight initial convoys. There are also two battleships, three cruisers and 11 destroyers to provide a preliminary bombardment which will be amplified by air attacks and rocket and gun fire from the landing craft. The terrain is not at all easy, with low hills just inland from the beaches interspersed with heavily defended gullies. The assault gets off to a poor start. The infantry, engineers and artillery are loaded into the landing craft and DUKWs fully 10 miles offshore in rough seas again contrary to British advice and practice. Some of the amphibious tanks are launched nearly four miles offshore and are swamped. Of the 446 Liberator bombers sent to attack only 329 arrive and most release their bombs too far inland. The rocket craft, designed to provide a final curtain of fire, are largely aiming short. As soon as the various barrages lift the return fire begins to come in and immediately there are heavy casualties. When the first wave reaches the beach they are totally disorganized. Many of the troops are in the wrong sectors. The engineers have suffered as heavily as any in the run in and lack the specialized armor used by the British to get protection from the defensive fire while clearing the obstacles. At first the assault is held almost exactly at the water's edge, but as the tide comes in and with it subsequent waves of troops, the slow advance begins with certain individual leaders gradually inspiring forward momentum. This, combined with a renewed bombardment by destroyers at very short range against individual strongpoints, is the story for the rest of the day. By nightfall thee are 34,250 Americans ashore at *Omaha* but none are as far as one mile off the beach. More than 1000 are dead and many more wounded but, although it is not clear at the time, they have broken the hard crust and there is for the moment easier going ahead.

Gold

This beach, from Arromanches to La Rivière, is the landing ground for the British 50th Infantry Division and the 8th Armored Brigade of Bucknall's XXX Corps. The transports and warships – 13 convoys and four cruisers and 13 destroyers – are led by Commodore Douglas-Pennant. Because of the tide the British landings here and to the east take place later than the Americans and there is therefore no possibility of meeting a startled enemy. Arromanches, La Rivière and Le Hamel especially are all heavily defended and fortified and many of the defending guns in these and other strongpoints survive the preliminary bombardment. The landings west of Le Hamel suffer most seriously, but even here the beaches are quickly cleared with the help of Hobart's armor. Because of the sea conditions the amphibious tanks are held back and landed a little later than planned directly on to solid ground. The advance inland is fairly rapid but the designated objectives of Bayeux and the road to Caen are not reached. Altogether 25,000 men are landed and about 500 are killed, relatively few casualties for what is a stiff fight.

Juno

This beach runs from La Rivière to St Aubin. The landing force is 3rd Canadian Infantry Division and 2nd Canadian Armored Brigade which, like the *Sword* forces, are from General Crocker's I Corps. The naval group is led by Commodore Oliver including 13 convoys, 2 cruisers and 12 destroyers. The landings here are a little later than planned and partly because the tide has therefore come in somewhat the underwater obstacles are particularly troublesome. Here the amphibious tanks are launched sensibly within 1000 yards of the shore and as elsewhere play an important part in silencing strongpoints. The specialized armor is also prominent. Once off the beach tanks and infantry quickly push inland reaching for Breteville and Caen. Here also there are traffic jams on the beaches. On the first day 21,400 go ashore.

Sword

The first landings on *Sword* are by the British 3rd Infantry Division, 27th Armored Brigade and several Marine and Commando units all under General Crocker's I Corps. The beach runs from Lion sur Mer to the Orne estuary.

Below: German soldiers man a machine-gun position overlooking the coast in northern France in 1944. They have a good field of fire.

The naval force is led by Admiral Talbot and as well as the eight assault convoys there are two battleships, one monitor, five cruisers and 13 destroyers. Much of this strength would have been directed at the Merville battery if the paratroops had not succeeded in their mission. Again the amphibious tanks are launched rather too far out but they are well handled and most reach the shore. The 'Funnies' are put ashore safely also. Before 1000 hours most of the exits from the beach have been cleared after a sharp struggle. Commando units hurry inland to aid the paratroops along the Orne but the regular infantry are more cautious against the German resistance at Hermanville and along the Périers Ridge. This problem is compounded by the growing congestion on the beach with the supporting tanks unable to move forward. By late afternoon, however, Biéville has been reached when the counterattack of 21st Panzer comes in. It is beaten off here but there is nothing to stop it driving to the sea between *Sword* and *Juno*. It is

Left: British paratroops wait for the order to jump as they approach their target. *Below:* British Commandos wade ashore on Sword Beach, 6 June 1944. Sherman tanks are already ashore, helping to carve out a lodgement area as a defense against the inevitable German counterattack.

Above: Not everyone walked ashore on D-Day: these men are helped onto Utah Beach.

too weak to achieve much there, however. By nightfall the British have 28,850 men ashore here and although the first day's objectives have not been reached the Orne bridges have been seized. It will take several weeks to take Caen and attain these first day objectives but there is no question of the solidity of this beachhead.

Overall the first day of the Overlord Operation has been a qualified success for the Allies. They have almost 150,000 men ashore and their aircraft are preventing the Germans having any chance of outstripping them in the buildup of forces in Normandy. If this can be maintained there can be only one result later if not sooner.

Italy French troops complete the capture of Tivoli. General Lemelsen becomes commander of the German Fourteenth Army in place of Mackensen. The recent Allied attacks have practically destroyed four German infantry divisions and the six mobile units have also been hard hit.

New Guinea On Biak the 186th Infantry prepares for an attack to take Mokmer Airfield while the 162nd Regiment is engaged near Ibdi.

Below: A German Panzer Mark IV (left) and a Mark VI Tiger lie abandoned in the street of a French village, victims of Allied air attack.

7 June 1944

Italy The Americans take Bracciano and Civitavecchia. The docks there are sufficiently serviceable to be put into use immediately. The South African 6th Armored Division takes Civita Castellana and pushes on up the road to Orvieto. Other units of Eighth Army enter Subiaco.

Western Front Although the Allies have not reached the objectives set for the first day they are everywhere solidly established ashore. The priority is obviously to link up the four beachheads (*Gold* and *Juno* are joined already) and to expand inland to create room for the reinforcements now beginning to arrive. The *Utah* force, VII Corps, tries to link up with the scattered paratroop contingents and to advance toward Carentan and Montebourg. The V Corps from *Omaha* makes a general advance hoping to reach Isigny and Bayeux. They get as far as attacking Formigny. From *Gold* the British 50th Infantry Division takes Bayeux and other units cut the Caen-Bayeux road. Already the pattern for the battle is being established for the weeks to come.

The German reserves are being drawn and held committed by the British advance toward and on either side of Caen. This gives the Americans at *Omaha* especially a welcome respite to consolidate and expand. This is the plan that the Allied Commanders and particularly Montgomery had hoped to work to.

New Guinea The American forces on Biak capture the Mokmer Airfield. Elsewhere on the island the fighting is also fierce with various small groups of Japanese resisting strongly.

8 June 1944

Western Front The second wave of Allied troops is now largely ashore. The US 4th Division (VII Corps) begins the advance toward Cherbourg and there is fierce fighting near Azeville. Units of V Corps take Isigny but cannot yet link with the *Utah* landings. With the capture of Port-en-Bessin by British Marines the link between *Omaha* and *Gold* is completed.

Italy The Allied advance continues in all sectors, but is gradually being slowed down by the German rearguards.

New Guinea On Biak the fighting around Mokmer continues in typical style with the Americans striving with the aid of heavy weapons to winkle the Japanese out of cave positions. On the mainland at Aitape the Americans push forward once more. A Japanese attempt to bring reinforcements to Biak is intercepted and turned back after a sharp action with Admiral Crutchley's cruiser squadron.

9 June 1944

Italy, Politics Marshal Badoglio resigns and Ivanoe Bonomi is invited to form a new government. The Cabinet now includes Count Sforza, Professor Croce and the Communist leader, Togliatti.

France In US VII Corps' advance toward Cherbourg the German strongpoint at Azeville is taken. Other VII Corps attacks move west and toward Carentan. The troops from *Omaha* take Trévières and to the east around Caen the British and Canadian forces are in heavy action with the growing German reserves. Allied aircraft are now operating from landing grounds in France.

Italy US forces take Tarquinia, Viterbo and Vetrella. British units are advancing toward Terni and Orvieto. A small amphibious force lands at Santo Stefano. There are important reorganizations of the Allied forces. The divisions of the British X and XIII Corps are switched around and various American units, mostly of VI Corps, are pulled out of the line entirely in preparation for the invasion of the south of France.

10 June 1944

Western Front The Utah and Omaha beachheads are linked up by the advance of the US 2nd Armored Division. The 101st Airborne Division is still fighting around Carentan. In the British sector the 7th Armored Division and the German *Panzerlehr* Division are heavily engaged near Tilly-sur-Seulles. General Montgomery establishes his headquarters in France.

Italy On the Adriatic coast Pescara and Chieti are taken by units of Keightley's V Corps. Inland the New Zealand Division enters Avezzano but fighting there continues.

10-13 June 1944

Indian Ocean In a diversionary operation for the coming American attacks on the Marianas the British fleet carrier *Illustrious* and the escort carrier *Atheling* raid Sabang.

Eastern Front Cherepanov's Twenty-third Army begins attacks against the Finnish positions on the Karelian Isthmus. As always now in any Soviet operation the artillery support is massive. Terijoki and Yalkena are quickly taken.

11 June 1944

Marianas Admiral Mitscher's TF 58 with nine fleet and six light carriers sends fighter strikes against Saipan, Tinian and the other islands in the group. Thirty-six Japanese planes are shot down. The seven battleships of Admiral Lee's TG 58.7 provide close escort. Japanese shipping also comes under attack from TG 58.4. Three minor warships and 30,000 tons of merchant shipping are sunk by the aircraft. The operations continue. Admiral Spruance, in overall command of the Marianas campaign, is present on board the cruiser *Indianapolis.*

Western Front The main engagements are again at Carentan and Tilly. Carentan is taken by the US forces. At Tilly and elsewhere in the British sector the German resistance is becoming particularly strong. The US forces also take Lison.

Italy French troops capture Montefiascone, west of Viterbo. Farther inland British units are engaged near Cantalupo and Bagnoregio.

Europe, Air Operations The Rumanian airfield at Focsani is raided by planes from Fifteenth Air Force from Italy. After bombing the planes fly on to Russia. This is the first 'shuttle' raid on this pattern. Rumania is now heavily targeted by the USAAF, a particular site being the famous oilfields at Ploesti.

12 June 1944

Western Front The US 4th Division is involved in a series of actions against German strongpoints at Montebourg, Crisbecq and near Azeville. The Germans only hold at Montebourg. Other units of VII Corps are fighting their way across the Cotentin Peninsula and southwest from Carentan. V Corps is helping in these attacks as well as advancing toward St Lô. In this sector Caumont is taken and the Foret de Cerisy and the Bayeux road reached.

The third wave of divisions is now largely ashore. At this stage there are 326,000 men, 104,000 tons of supplies and 54,000 vehicles from the Allied armies in France.

Italy In the Adriatic sector Popoli is reached by the British advance.

12-13 June 1944

Marianas The operations of the US carriers go on. Three groups continue to attack Tinian and Saipan while the other concentrates on Guam. In response to these assaults the Japanese Fleets sail from Tawitawi and Batjan. The main force from Tawitawi is quickly sighted and reported by an American submarine. Altogether there are five fleet carriers, two light carriers and two seaplane carriers. In support there are five battleships and numerous cruisers and destroyers. In every department, therefore, they are outmatched by TF 58. Admiral Kurita leads the Van Force which includes the two seaplane carriers, one light carrier and four of the battleships. Admiral Ozawa leads the main force with the remainder of the ships. The plan for their operation, devised by the Commander in Chief, Admiral Toyoda, intends to cope with their inferiority by relying on the help of land based aircraft from the Marianas and other nearby groups. Unfortunately from the Japanese point of view, the recent and present operations of the American carriers have drastically reduced these land based forces but the local commanders have left their superiors in ignorance of this when such knowledge will in fact prove vital in the coming battle.

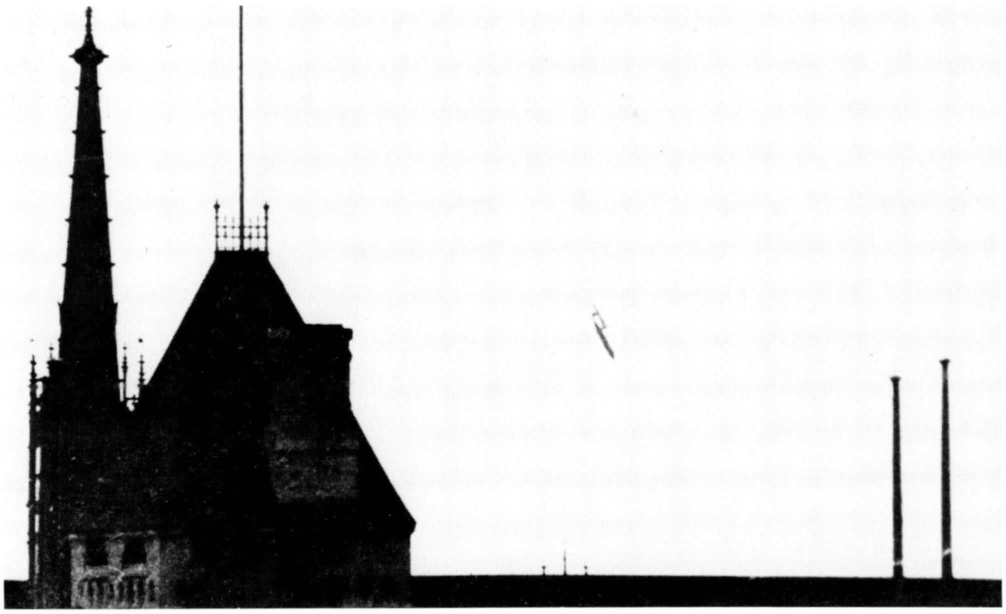

Above: A V-1 flying-bomb, fired from northern France, falls onto central London, 13 June 1944.

13 June 1944

V-Weapons The first V1 Flying Bomb lands in England. In the initial salvo 10 are fired of which four cross the Channel successfully. Only one lands in London, killing six civilians.

Kuriles Admiral Small leads a cruiser and destroyer group to bombard the Japanese on Matsuwa. The sortie is repeated on 26 June this time against Paramushiro.

Western Front After being switched to the far right of XXX Corps 7th Armored Division makes a rapid advance to Villers Bocage but a German counterattack quickly throws them back. There is also a fierce attack by 17th Panzer to retake Carentan which is only held off with difficulty. Elsewhere the US forces make some progress toward St Lô and in the Cotentin they take Pont l'Abbé.

Italy South African troops from Eighth Army take Bagnoregio just east of Lake Bolsena and other units take Narni between Orte and Terni.

New Guinea On Biak the Japanese cave positions in the east of the island are being gradually worn down. American aircraft are now operating from Mokmer Airfield.

14 June 1944

Western Front A third US Corps, XIX, becomes operational in the sector between V and VII Corps. General de Gaulle visits the beachhead and takes measures to prepare for the restoration of French civil government in the captured territory.

Italy Orvieto, Terni and Todi all fall to units of Eighth Army. The US IV Corps on the west coast also pushes forward.

British Command The appointment is announced in London of Admiral Moore to be Commander of the British Home Fleet.

Marianas The preliminary bombardments for the invasion of Saipan and Tinian are made. The two bombardment groups are commanded by Admirals Ainsworth and Oldendorf and their squadrons include seven battleships and 11 cruisers. There are eight escort carriers in support. The battleship *California* is hit by defensive fire. There are also intensive minesweeping operations.

14-15 June 1944

Western Front During the night 325 RAF Lancaster bombers attack Le Havre. They sink 35 small naval vessels, a considerable proportion of the remaining German Channel forces.

14-17 June 1944

Battle of the Philippine Sea The main US carrier forces which have been operating against the Marianas spend this period mostly replenishing. Two groups led by Admiral Clark do, however, attack Iwo Jima, Chichi Jima and Haha Jima on 15 and 16 June. By 17 all are on their way to rendezvous to the west of the Marianas. The Japanese carriers are sighted on 15 June on their way through the San Bernardino Strait while some of their battleships are also seen east of Mindanao. On 16-17 June the Japanese also link up and refuel and are sighted twice more. The Americans are therefore well informed as to the general Japanese intentions.

15 June 1944

Western Front In the Cotentin the US VIII Corps becomes operational. Units of VII Corps take Quineville.

New Guinea On Biak there is a considerable but unsuccessful Japanese counterattack and on the mainland farther east, Australian troops occupy Hansa Bay.

Eastern Front The Finnish IV Corps withdraws, under pressure from the Soviet Twenty-first and Fifty-ninth Armies, to positions before Viipuri.

Far East, Air Operations Superfortress bombers from Twentieth Air Force in China are sent to bomb the Japanese homeland. Yawatta on Kyushu is attacked. This is the first such raid.

Marianas While the heavy ships of TF 52 keep shelling the main phase of the Saipan landings, Operation *Forager* gets under way. Admiral Turner is in command of the support ship as well as the landing vessels and General H M Smith leads the V Amphibious Corps. Altogether there are 67,500 men in the land force mostly from the 2nd and 4th Marine Divisions (Watson and Schmidt). The defending forces come from both the Japanese Army and Navy. General Saito commands the reinforced 43rd Infantry Division and Admiral Nagumo leads the naval contingents.

After three hours of air and naval bombardment the attacks go in north and south of Afetna Point. The landings are farther apart than has been intended and the fierce Japanese resistance prevents the beachheads being linked up. The Japanese artillery is especially destructive of the landing craft. The Marines do get well ashore during the day and by night they beat off the usual counterattacks.

15-16 June 1944

Europe, Air Operations Bomber Command is again active over the Channel ports. This time 300 Lancasters attack Boulogne, sinking 14 small warships as well as other craft.

16 June 1944

Western Front In the Cotentin the US forces advancing toward the west coast fight their way across the River Douvre and capture St Saveur after a fierce struggle. In other sectors all the Allied forces continue to press forward. King George VI visits the forces.
Italy Troops from the British X Corps take Spoleto and push on to enter Spoligno as well. On the west side American units take Grosseto.
Marianas Admiral Ainsworth's battleship squadron shells Guam but the Guam invasion is deferred because of the advent of the Japanese Fleet. On Saipan the two Marine Divisions succeed in linking their positions by taking Charan Karoa and Point Afetna. There is much artillery counterbattery work as well as the fighting on the ground.

17 June 1944

Western Front Rommel, Rundstedt and Hitler meet at Soissons. Both Generals want to order withdrawals to better positions but Hitler overrules them and going into a rage accuses the German army in France of cowardice and says that the V1s will force Britain out of the war.

In the fighting the 9th Division of the US VII Corps reaches the west coast of Cotentin north and south of Barneville. The German divisions cut off to the north are refused permission to attempt a break-out.
Italy The French 9th Colonial Division (Senegalese), led by General de Lattre lands on Elba. They complete the occupation of the island on 19 June. On the main front the Polish II Corps replaces the British X Corps on the Adriatic sector. The advance here is now beyond the River Chieti in some places.
Marianas The US 27th Infantry Division is landed on Saipan.

18 June 1944

Italy In the advance on Perugia units from Eighth Army take Assisi and to the west a French formation enters Radicofani.
Marianas The advance of the 4th Marine Division reaches the west side of Saipan at Magicienne Bay. The Japanese forces are thus separated into two. Part of the 27th Division, on the right of 4th Marines, captures Aslito airfield. Japanese air strikes sink one destroyer and two tankers offshore as well as damaging the escort carrier *Fanshaw Bay*. Much of the air cover and close support has been withdrawn to prepare to take part in the imminent fleet battle.
Battle of the Philippine Sea The US forces make their rendezvous west of the Marianas while the Japanese continue to approach. Late in the evening the Japanese scout planes sight the American fleet. This is the only advantage that the Japanese have and comes about principally because their scout planes have a longer range. The Japanese plan to launch their strike planes early the next day while still at very long range and, after attacking to have them fly on to Guam where the local forces can protect them while they refuel and rearm. Once this is done they can attack again on the return journey. The glaring weakness in this plan is that the air forces on Guam have suffered seriously from American attacks recently and have failed to inform the fleet of this. In fact this shortcoming is less significant than might have been the case as the American ships exact such a heavy price from the first attacks.
Eastern Front The Soviet attacks break through the main Finnish positions on the Mannerheim line and advance toward Viipuri.

19 June 1944

New Guinea Reinforced American attacks go in against Japanese strongpoints in Biak.
Indian Ocean Port Blair in the Nicobars is attacked by aircraft from the carrier *Illustrious*. Admiral Power is in command and among the supporting heavy units are the *Renown* and the *Richelieu*.
Battle of the Philippine Sea Early in the morning the Japanese search finds TF 58, at the same time reamining unsighted themselves. At once the Japanese carriers launch four waves of attack aircraft numbering altogether 372. In numbers of planes the comparison is overwhelmingly in favor of the Americans – about 950 to 550 (including, for the Japanese, land-based aircraft). The American fleet is well disposed to meet air attack. The battleships are sailing slightly to the west to provide a large AA barrier and with the help of radar there is no question of surprise. Early on the Americans have time to send a strike against Guam further reducing the air force there. When the Japanese attacks are detected coming in fighters are sent out to meet them and the bombers are flown off to clear the carrier decks. The fighters make interceptions up to 50 miles out and shoot down many of the attackers. Still more are shot down by the ships' gunfire and only a handful actually make attacks. The battleship *South Dakota* receives the only damage – one bomb hit. The Japanese lose 240 aircraft and the Americans only 29. More Japanese planes are destroyed before landing on Guam and most of those that survive are hit on the ground – 50 machines in all. The list of Japanese misfortune is completed when, soon after launching their aircraft, the carriers *Taiho* and *Shokaku* are sunk by the US

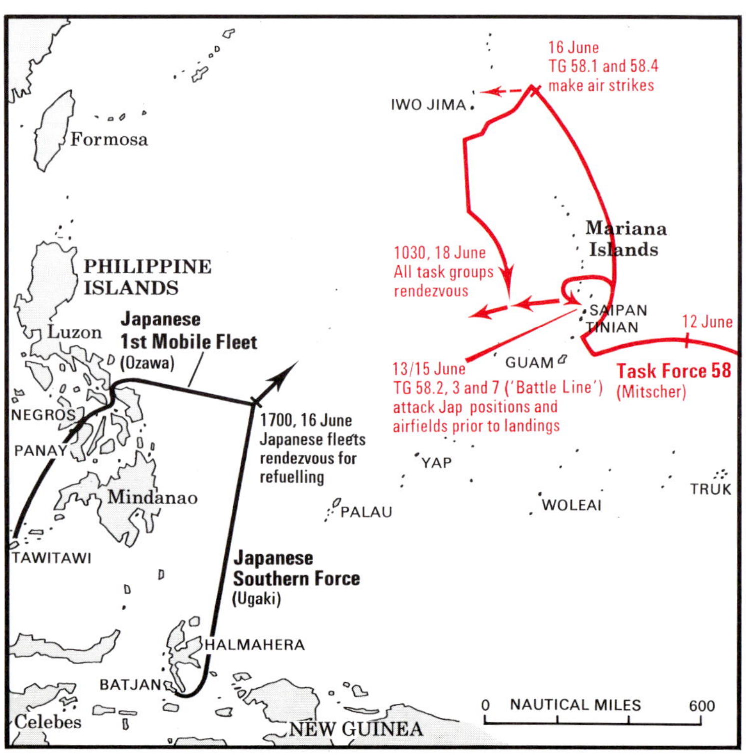

Below: Map of the Battle of the Philippine Sea, 16-20 June 1944.

Below: A Japanese bomber goes down in flames, shot down by anti-aircraft fire, from the American carriers during the Battle of the Philippine Sea, June 1944.

submarines *Cavalla* and *Albacore*. These have been two of the largest and most effective Japanese ships. The Japanese have succumbed so easily that the day is described by the American airmen and gunners as 'The Great Marianas Turkey Shoot.'

Italy British units reach the south and east side of Lake Trasimeno. The next German defense line, the Albert line, is just ahead.

Western Front Various American units complete the clearance of Montebourg and Valognes. From now until 22 June there are gales in the Channel which damage both the Mulberry harbors. The American one at Omaha is irreparable but with the help of sections from it the British harbor at Arromanches is made operable. Many landing craft are also sunk or damaged, especially DUKWs.

20 June 1944

Western Front The American advance is about five miles from Cherbourg and is becoming embroiled in the outer defenses of the town.

Italy Perugia falls to the British 6th Armored Division.

Eastern Front Viipuri falls to the Red Army.

Battle of the Philippine Sea The Japanese do not realize the extent of their losses and begin to withdraw temporarily to refuel. They believe that most of their aircraft have landed safely on Guam. Mitscher, of course, pursues and in the late afternoon sends 216 planes to attack. They meet only 35 defending fighters and break through to sink the carrier *Hiyo* and damage two others, a battleship and a cruiser. In the action 20 American planes are lost. A further 72 crash in attempting to land back on their carriers in darkness despite the flight decks being lit. A feature of the US operation in this and other engagements is the care taken of the pilots – only 16 flyers and 33 aircrew are not picked up and the story in the rest of the battle is similar. By contrast the Japanese have saved almost none of their pilots and although they still have a significant force of ships they cannot possibly train enough men to fly their aircraft. The pattern of all the previous fleet encounters in the Pacific is thus confirmed.

During the night the Japanese withdraw and are not followed.

Above: The Japanese carrier *Zuikaku* and escorting destroyers try to avoid American air attack, 20 June 1944.

New Guinea On Biak there is more heavy fighting in the western caves area. The airfields and the villages at Borokoe and Sorido are also overrun.

Marianas On Saipan 27th Division has been given the task of clearing the south of the island while 2nd and 4th Marines continue their advance to the north.

21 June 1944

Italy The Eighth Army advance comes up to the Albert line at Chiusi to the west of Lake Trasimeno.

Eastern Front General Krutikov's Seventh Army begins a new phase of the Russian attacks against Finland. The advance is now against the Finnish VI Corps between Lake Ladoga and Lake Onega. The Russians also begin to occupy the islands off the Karelian Isthmus. This operation is complete in three or four days.

22 June 1944

Western Front The final battle for Cherbourg begins with a two-hour raid in which more than 1000 tons of bombs are dropped. Despite this preparation the three attacking divisions of VII Corps still meet fierce resistance.

United States, Home Front President Roosevelt signs the 'GI Bill' which introduces a range of benefits to give returned veterans a start in civilian life.

Denmark, Resistance An important rifle manufacturing plant is wrecked by saboteurs in Copenhagen.

Below: US Marines race towards the landing beach at Saipan in the Marianas, June 1944.

New Guinea After a further series of attacks during the day the Americans believe that they have cleared the Japanese positions in the west of Biak, but during the night there is renewed Japanese activity. On the mainland fighting goes on near Aitape and Sarmi.
Marianas On Saipan 2nd Marines take Mount Tipo Pale and are engaged on Mount Tapotchau. The 4th Marines are making good progress farther east on the Kagman Peninsula.
Burma The siege of Imphal is raised when advance units of 2nd Indian Division link with 5th Indian at Milestone 107 on the Imphal-Kohima road. The Japanese are taking ever heavier losses both in combat and, more seriously, because of food shortages and illness as their supply system collapses.

22-23 June 1944

Eastern Front During the night the bombardment for the first major Russian offensive of the summer begins. There are four fronts, First, Second and Third Belorussian and First Baltic, in the attack under the overall command of Marshal Zhukov. Among the massive concentration of force Zhukov has amassed a huge quantity of artillery. The German defenders are from Busch's Army Group Center.

23 June 1944

Western Front The outer defenses of Cherbourg are penetrated slightly in some sections but the battle continues to be intense. In the British sector of the Normandy front, 5th Division takes St Honorina to the northwest of Caen.
Eastern Front After the bombardment lifts the Russians begin their attacks in Belorussia. The front stretches from just north of Vitebsk in a long curve past Mogilev to the Pripet River. Advances of up to 11 miles are claimed in the first day. As well as their massive artillery superiority the Russians have almost complete dominance in the air to speed them on their way. They have been building such strength for some time but in recent weeks many Luftwaffe units have been transferred to fight the British and American bomber offensive.

In the Finnish sector Krutikov's troops manage to cross the Svir.
Marianas The battle for Mount Tapotchau continues with attacks and counterattacks being sent in by both sides.

24 June 1944

Western Front The American attack on Cherbourg continues to grind forward slowly but surely. The German commander, General Schlieben, still refuses to surrender although he does not believe that he can hold out much longer.
Eastern Front Already, on the second day of the Soviet offensive, the strain on the German defenders in Army Group Center is considerable. The advance is as much as 25 miles deep in some places and the Orsha-Vitebsk rail line has been cut.
Marianas The 27th Division has completed the clearance of the southern part of the island and most of the component parts of the division join the main advance of the Marines to the north. The fighting here is fiercest, still, on Mount Tapotchau.
Bonin Islands The Japanese bases on Iwo Jima and Chichi Jima are attacked by American carrier aircraft. The Japanese lose 66 planes. The carriers involved are *Hornet, Yorktown, Bataan* and *Belleau Wood.*

25 June 1944

Western Front Units of the three attacking divisions have penetrated into the suburbs of Cherbourg. They have massive support from naval gunfire including three battleships, four cruisers and 11 destroyers. In the British XXX Corps sector 49th Division mounts an attack toward Rauray.
Italy The US 36th Division takes Piombino before it, like other units is taken out of the line to prepare for the Anvil landings in the south of France. Inland there are fairly successful British and French attacks against the Albert line west of Lake Trasimeno, especially at Chiusi.
Eastern Front The Russian advances in Belorussia continue, particularly near Vitebsk where five German divisions are now trapped. In this sector the troops of Third Belorussian Front have crossed the Bvina, and in the other sectors the fighting is nearing Mogilev and Bobruysk.
Marianas On Saipan the Marines fight their way to the top of Mount Tapotchau. There is also fierce fighting in the Hagman Peninsula and near the southwest tip of the island.

26 June 1944

Western Front Most of Cherbourg, except the docks area, is taken by the US VII Corps. The garrison commander, General Schlieben and the local naval chief, Admiral Hennecke, are captured. The battleship *Rodney* and the monitor *Roberts* along with three cruisers give heavy gunfire support to the British forces attacking near Caen.
Italy The French troops are able to push forward north of Radicofani and on their right South African armored units are able to take Chiusi.
Eastern Front The Russian forces burst into Vitebsk after a heavy bombing raid. To the south near Rogachev they take the railroad town of Zhlobin.
Marianas A small Japanese reinforcement convoy for Saipan is met and turned away by US forces. On the island the American attacks grind forward a little more.

27 June 1944

Western Front The capture of Cherbourg is completed and at last the Allies have access to a major port. It will, however, be some time before the port can be made operational because of booby traps and demolitions. Near Caen Rauray is captured by the British and slightly farther east there are new attacks by the British VIII Corps.
Eastern Front The Soviet advance goes on. Near Vitebsk the German pocket is whittled down still more. In the center of the offensive Orsha is taken. To the left the Dniepr is crossed north and south of Mogilev and near Bobruysk another pocket is surrounded.
Axis Diplomacy The Germans announce that they have concluded successful talks with the Finns and promised them help against the Russians. On 28 June Keitel arrives in Finland to organize this.

28 June 1944

United States, Politics At the Republican Party convention in Chicago Governor Thomas Dewey and Governor John Bricker win the nominations for president and vice-president respectively.
France, Resistance The Vichy Minister for Propaganda, Philippe Henriot, is assassinated in Paris.
Western Front In the Cotentin the US 9th Division is preparing for final attacks to eliminate the German resistance in the direction of Cap de la Hague. Just west of Caen advancing British troops cross the Odon on a two-mile front near Mondrainville.
Eastern Front In Finland the northern wings of the Russian advance reach Petrozavodsk and also cross the Murmansk rail line farther north. In the main battles in Belorussia Zakharov's troops take Mogilev and are now across the Dniepr nearby on a 70-mile front. Hitler dismisses Busch from command of Army Group

Below: US Marines use special satchel-charges against a Japanese dug-out on Saipan, June 1944 – scene of desperate hand-to-hand fighting.

Center. Field Marshal Model is appointed as his replacement.
New Guinea On Biak the US forces, now commanded by General Doe, have finally cleared the caves in the west of the island. The Japanese strength has now largely been dissipated and the main task for the Americans is mopping up.

29 June 1944

Eastern Front Rokossovsky's forces take Bobruysk. To the west they also capture Slutsk and Lyuban and a little to the north they are across the Berezina.
New Guinea The Australian forces advancing from Wewak reach the River Sepik, 70 miles to the west.

30 June 1944

Diplomatic Affairs The United States breaks diplomatic relations with Finland.
Denmark, Resistance A general strike begins in Copenhagen. On 1 July the Germans proclaim a state of emergency, but are forced to concede on some points on 4 July when the strike ends.
Western Front The last German forces in the Cotentin either surrender or are wiped out. The major British and American units are still battling on the approaches to Caen and St Lô respectively. Since D-Day the Allies have landed 630,000 men, 600,000 tons of supplies and 177,000 vehicles in Normandy. They have lost 62,000 dead and wounded.
Marianas On Saipan the US forces make ground north of Mount Tipo Pale and Mount Tapotchau. Other units clear the area known as Death Valley and the nearby Purple Heart Ridge. More than half of the island has now been taken.
Italy On the Tyrrhenian coast the US 34th Division is heavily engaged just south of Cecina, while inland the main Allied advance is being slowed by a new German defense line south of Siena and Arezzo.

July 1944

Europe, Air Operations The US Eighth and Fifteenth Air Forces drop 73,000 tons of bombs and RAF Bomber Command adds 57,000 tons more. Among the targets are, for the Americans, Munich, Friedrichshafen, Metz and Belfort and, for the British, Stuttgart and Hamburg. The German oil industry is heavily hit by both British and Americans especially at Wesseling, Bohlen, Merseburg, Vienna and Ploesti.
English Channel Throughout the month there are many sharp engagements, usually at night between German and Allied, mostly British, naval units. Both sides take some losses but the Allied preponderence of strength is normally decisive. The German submarine force suffers especially heavily.

1 July 1944

World Affairs An international monetary conference begins at Bretton Woods, New Hampshire, with an opening speech by the US Treasury Secretary, Morgenthau. The conference lasts until 22 July. Forty-four countries are represented. Agreement is reached on the establishment of an International Monetary Fund and an International Bank for Reconstruction and Development.
Western Front The German I SS Panzer Corps mounts an armored attack around Grainville, but the British defense is very strong and little progress is made.
Italy Troops from Fifth Army take Cecina on the west coast and inland, in the advance to Volterra, Pomerance also falls. Farther inland still the German units opposite the British X and XIII Corps begin to pull back.

Above: Russian truck-borne *Katyusha* rockets are fired in salvo toward German positions in the Carpathian mountains.

2 July 1944

Eastern Front The Russian forces cut several of the rail lines leading west from Minsk.
Marianas On Saipan the American forces manage a general advance. The remains of Garapan village are overrun.
New Guinea There are Allied landings on Numfoor Island. General Patrick commands 7100 men of the US 168th Infantry and some Australian units. Admiral Fechteler leads the naval force and TF 74 and TF 75 provide the escort and a preliminary bombardment. The landings are on the north coast of the island near Kamiri Airfield. There is no resistance on the beaches. At Biak the skirmishing goes on.
Italy The Allied advance proceeds in the center and west. Foiano falls to the British 4th Infantry Division.

Below: RAF bomber crews celebrate the 100th operation completed by veteran Avro Lancaster S-Sugar. The aircraft survived the war and is now at the RAF Museum, Hendon.

Above: The ruins of Caen, heavily bombed by the Allies in June and July 1944 as part of the breakout from the Normandy beachhead.

3 July 1944

Western Front The US forces begin a major drive south from the Cotentin Peninsula aiming to reach a line from Coutances to St Lô. The terrain here is very difficult with narrow lanes and high hedges canalizing the advance. The weather too is poor and at the start only a little ground is made toward St Jean de Daye and La Haye du Puits.

Italy French troops capture Siena. To their right in the advance toward Arezzo the British 78th Division takes Cortona, and on the left on the Tyrhennian coast the US forces reach Rosignano.

Eastern Front Troops of First and Third Belorussian Fronts complete the capture of Minsk. Many German units, particularly from Fourth Army are now isolated to the east and casualties and losses of equipment have been enormous. Already after less than two weeks of the Soviet offensive, Army Group Center is in total disarray and before long it will have practically ceased to be a coherent fighting formation. General Freissner replaces General Lindemann in command of Army Group North.

New Guinea On Numfoor the beachhead is expanded and a parachute battalion is dropped at the Kamiriz airfield and despite many casualties the area is occupied.

4 July 1944

Marianas and Bonin Islands Two groups of TF 58 send their carrier aircraft against the Japanese bases on Iwo Jima and Chichi Jima. The other two groups of the task force similarly attack Guam. The Guam attacks continue on 5 July.

Western Front The Canadian 3rd Division takes Carpiquet village just west of Caen but cannot yet capture the nearby airfield. The attacks of the US VII and VIII Corps continue.

Eastern Front There is a new series of attacks by First Baltic Front against the positions of Army Group North. The German armies here are in a very dangerous situation because of the Soviet advances to the south toward their right flank and rear. Polotsk is very quickly taken.

New Guinea On Numfoor the Kornasoren airfield is captured. A second parachute battalion is flown in and loses heavily because of inexperience.

5 July 1944

Western Front The US forces take La Haye du Puits.

New Guinea The Japanese garrison on Numfoor tries a counterattack but they are soon beaten off. The US forces are preparing to move against the island's third airfield at Namber.

6 July 1944

German Command Berlin announces that Field Marshal Kluge has replaced Field Marshal Rundstedt as Commander in Chief West.

Italy The Polish 3rd Division takes Osemo just south of Ancona on the Adriatic flank. Throughout the rest of July the German forces will fall back gradually from river to river, a few miles at a time. The next major delay will be on the Arno.

Eastern Front Troops of First Belorussian Front take Kovel, 70 miles east of Lublin. The Germans have pulled back in this sector. Svir, southwest of Minsk, is also taken.

New Guinea On Numfoor the Americans take the Namber airstrip after a short amphibious operation. Fighters are quickly flown in.

Marianas On Saipan the Americans continue to push forward toward the north end of the island. The senior Japanese commanders, Admiral Nagumo and General Saito both commit suicide while their remaining subordinates plan a final fanatical attack.

6-11 July 1944

Allied Diplomacy De Gaulle visits Washington for talks on the status of his administration and aid for the fighting French.

7 July 1944

France, Politics The former Cabinet Minister and anticollaborationist, Georges Mandel, is executed at Fontainebleau on the orders of the Vichy police chief, Darnand.

Western Front The US VIII, VII and XIX Corps are still attacking along a line from La Haye du Puits to just east of the Vire. The German opposition is still formidable. The British battleship *Rodney* shells German positions around Caen in preparation for the imminent British attack.

Italy Units of the US 34th Division take Pignano in their advance up the Tyrrhenian coast.

Marianas On Saipan practically the whole of the Japanese garrison, now reduced to about 3000 men, mount a wild attack on the American lines south of Makunsha Village. They succeed in coming to close quarters but by about midday they are driven off by the well-armed American forces with terrible losses.

8 July 1944

Western Front Early in the morning a major British and Canadian attack goes in around Caen. The preliminary bombardment includes 2500 tons dropped by 450 RAF heavy bombers. The advance enters the outskirts of the city. To the west the US forces' attack is reinforced by two more divisions newly arrived from Britain. The heaviest fighting in the American sector is along the line of the road from Carentan to Periers.
Eastern Front Rokossovsky's men take Baranovichi, midway between Minsk and Brest-Litovsk.

8-19 July 1944

Marianas Ainsworth's three battleships several times shell targets on Guam in preparation for the coming landings. There are also carrier attacks.

9 July 1944

Western Front Troops from 3rd Canadian Division and 1st British Division enter Caen and take most of the city north of the Orne. The Canadians also take Carpiquet Airfield. The American advance toward St Lô and farther west continues.
Italy The US 88th Division takes Volterra while on their right French units are advancing on Poggibonsi.
Eastern Front Troops from the Third Belorussian Front take Lida, 50 miles east of Grodno. Farther north other units reach the outskirts of Vilna.
Marianas The US forces reach Point Marpi and the final organized Japanese resistance is overcome. The Japanese have lost an estimated 27,000 dead as well as 1780 prisoners, both figures including a number of civilians. The US forces have a casualty list of 3400 dead and 13,000 hurt.

10 July 1944

Western Front The British VIII Corps begins new attacks toward Evrecy.
Eastern Front Model, commanding Army Group Center, asks for Army Group North to be moved south behind the Dvina to bolster his front and to prevent them being cut off by the Russian drive to the Baltic. Hitler refuses to allow this sensible step. In the middle of Model's sector Slonim is taken.
New Guinea In the Aitape sector a series of Japanese attacks starts along the line of the Driniumor River.

11 July 1944

Western Front A counterattack by the German *Panzerlehr* Division makes some progress against the US 9th Division southwest of St Jean de Daye but later the Germans are pushed back. In the British sector the slow advance continues. VIII Corps take the important Hill 112, southwest of Caen. The British around Caen are again supported by heavy naval gunfire.
United States, Politics President Roosevelt tells a Press Conference that he will run if nominated. He says, 'If the people command me to continue in office . . . I have as little right as a soldier to leave his position in the line.'
Allied Diplomacy Roosevelt announces that the US will recognize de Gaulle's French Provisional Government as the *de facto* authority for the civil administration of the liberated territory in France.
New Guinea In the Aitape sector the US forces pull back from the Driniumor River under pressure but are planning a counterstroke.

Above: Admiral Raymond Spruance (left), commander of the US Fifth Fleet, and General Holland Smith.

Below: A German U-Boat is caught on the surface by a Sunderland flying boat, July 1944.

Eastern Front Second Baltic Front (Yeremenko) starts a new program of attacks on a 90-mile front east of Idritsa. Elsewhere the German pocket east of Minsk is wiped out.

12 July 1944

Western Front The US attack toward St Lô has now reached to within two miles of the town but is being slowed down by stubborn defense. A little east of the town Hill 192 is taken.
Italy A major sequence of Allied air attacks against the Po bridges begins. At the front the US 88th Division takes Lajatico.
Eastern Front Yeremenko's troops take Idritsa.

13 July 1944

Western Front The advance of the US First Army toward St Lô is practically brought to a halt. Plans are in preparation for a formal assault on the German lines east of the town. This is to be Operation Cobra.
Italy The French Corps is attacking around Poggibonsi and Castellina about 20 miles south of Florence.
Eastern Front After several days of vicious street fighting Vilna falls to the Russians.
New Guinea In the Aitape sector the US 128th Regiment pushes back to the Driniumor River. On Numfoor the final Japanese pocket comes under attack.

14 July 1944

Italy The French troops take Poggibonsi.
Eastern Front Konev's First Ukraine Front joins the attacks of the Belorussian Fronts to the north. Troops from First Belorussian Front take Pinsk.

14-26 July 1944

New Guinea The Japanese positions near Aitape between Yakamul and But are bombarded on many occasions by the ships of Commodore Collins' TF 74. There are two cruisers and six destroyers involved in these operations, mostly Australian ships.

Below: Hitler shows Mussolini the remains of the briefing hut after the Bomb Plot of 20 July 1944.

15 July 1944

Western Front The outskirts of Lessay are reached by the US forces. From here east to the River Taute the advance is halted while regrouping takes place. Nearer St Lô the fighting is heavy.
Italy Two divisions of Eighth Army begin a formal attack on the German positions at Arezzo. Nearer the west coast the Americans push forward toward Leghorn and the French take Castellina.
Eastern Front Second Baltic Front take Opochka, 30 miles north of Idritsa. Other Russian formations cross the Niemen in several places west and southwest of Vilna.

16 July 1944

Western Front The US forces continue their attacks near St Lô. In the British sector there are advances toward Hottot-les-Bagues and in the direction of Evrecy.
Allied Diplomacy The London Polish government publish a paper claiming territory in East Prussia, Danzig and the Polish Corridor for postwar Poland.
Italy Arezzo falls to the Eighth Army. Other British units from XIII Corps cross the Arno as the Germans fall back.
Eastern Front Russian tank units storm Grodno, southwest of Vilna. Farther south First Ukraine Front begin a new offensive toward Lvov on a 300-mile front.
New Guinea On Aitape the Japanese forces along the Driniumor River are losing ground.

17 July 1944

Western Front Field Marshal Rommel is severely wounded by the attack of an Allied aircraft on his car while he is returning to his Headquarters after an inspection trip. Field Marshal Kluge assumes Rommel's duties as well as his own as Commander in Chief. In the battle for St Lô the US forces have entered the town.
Arctic The British carriers *Formidable*, *Indefatigable* and *Furious* escorted by the battleship *Duke of York* send attacks against the *Tirpitz* in the anchorage at Kaafiord. The attacks are detected on the way in and the Germans successfully conceal the target with smoke.
Japan, Politics A new Navy Minister, Admiral Nomura, replaces Shimada. On 18 July Tojo resigns his posts as prime minister and Chief of Staff. General Kuniaki Koiso and Admiral Yonai are chosen to form the new Cabinet. General Umezu becomes Chief of Staff. These changes are in fact manifestations of a growing desire on the part of many Japanese statesmen to end the war. They worry about an unfavorable peace, however, and wish to maintain the appearance of a strong front. The Allies are unable to recognize or correctly interpret these indications and the war therefore con-
United States, Politics President Roosevelt announces that he will leave the choice of his running mate to the Democratic Party convention.

18 July 1944

Western Front St Lô is almost completely taken by units of the US XIX Corps. The British and Canadians begin a major push from east of the Orne southward in the direction of the high ground beyond Caen. This operation code named Goodwood is to become very controversial. Montgomery hopes that it will lead to a break out from Normandy, but even if this difficult aim is not achieved he believes the attack necessary to maintain the established pattern of drawing the German reserves to the British rather than the American sector. Montgomery has made some unfortunate, extravagant comments on the prospects for Goodwood (notably in arguing for heavy bomber support) which will backfire when in fact there is no breakthrough.

More than 2200 planes are involved in the massive bombardment which precedes the operation, including 1000 RAF heavy bombers which drop more than 7000 tons of bombs. The scale of the preparation does much to disorganize and demoralize the defense, and at first the attack goes well. Gradually severe traffic congestion problems develop in the rear. There are only four bridges available over the Orne and the Caen canal and in the dust raised by the bombardment and the advance the vehicles of the attacking and following divisions quickly become mixed and misdirected.
Italy Part of the US IV Corps begins to attack Leghorn on the west coast while a little inland other units reach the Arno at Pontedera which is taken. On the east coast the Poles also advance taking Ancona. The capture of Leghorn and Ancona will ease Allied supply difficulties.
Eastern Front There are new Russian offensives by First Belorussian Front around Kovel and by Third Baltic Front toward Ostrov and Pskov. First Ukraine Front is beginning to make progress toward Lvov after two days of attacks.

19 July 1944

Western Front East of Caen the Goodwood battles continue with large numbers of tanks being engaged from both sides. The Germans usually have the advantage of better positions and this, combined with their armament, tips the balance in their favor despite the disparity of numbers. The Caen suburb of Vaucelles, however, is cleared by Canadian units who also take Louvigny and Fleury-sur-Orne.
Italy The US 34th Division takes the Italian port of Leghorn.
Eastern Front In their advance to Lvov First Ukraine Front surround five German divisions. Farther north, just east of Dvinsk, Russian units enter Latvia.

Above: General Sir Bernard Montgomery, commander of Allied Land Forces in Normandy, addresses men of the 50th Division, July 1944.

19-21 July 1944

United States, Politics In the Democratic Party convention at Chicago Roosevelt is selected by an overwhelming majority as the presidential candidate. He receives 1086 votes, Senator Byrd 89 and James Farley 1. Harry Truman is chosen as running mate by 1031 votes to Wallace's 105.

20 July 1944

Western Front The British attacks south and east of Caen continue, but the tenacious German antitank defense has worn down the advance units and cut their momentum.

Germany, Resistance Shortly after midday a bomb explodes in the conference room at Hitler's Headquarters at Rastenburg in East Prussia. Hitler, although badly shaken, is only slightly hurt. The bomb has been planted by Colonel Count von Stauffenberg who represents in this a wide-ranging conspiracy of senior officers and a few politicians. Immediately after the bomb goes off the conspirators act on the assumption that Hitler is dead. In fact the bomb, disguised in a briefcase has been moved slightly by accident by another officer and Hitler, shielded from the blast by the heavy leg of the map table, thus survives. Not all the elements of the conspirators' plan are carried out with sufficient ruthlessness to achieve much success, and once it is clear that Hitler has survived the plot falls apart. On the first day several of the leading participants, including Stauffenberg, are shot in Berlin, and eventually the Nazi vengeance will encompass several thousand executions. Hitler later delights in watching film of these. Among those actively involved in the plot are General Beck, Carl Gördeler (formerly mayor of Leipzig), Field Marshal Witzleben, General Halder and others taken from aristocratic and Roman Catholic groups. Many others know of the plot including Rommel, Kluge and Canaris but have done nothing to help or hinder it. The security of the plot is easily penetrated and many of the conspirators are quickly rounded up. The effect of the incident on Hitler is first to increase his pathological distrust of the generals and second, when combined with the physical deterioration caused by the dubious combination of medicines he takes, the shock of the explosion further weakens his ability to concentrate and to remain stable in the face of reverses. He becomes less interested in his work and more prone to wild outbursts.

Marianas The bombardment of Tinian is stepped up a stage when army artillery based on Saipan adds its weight to the attacks from the air and by naval shelling.

21 July 1944

Italy The French Expeditionary Corps is taken out of line to prepare for the Anvil/Dragoon operation, which is to invade the south of France on 15 August 1944.

Marianas Troops of Geiger's III Amphibious Corps land on Guam. The naval force is commanded by Admiral Connolly and among the vessels in his TF 53 are six battleships and five escort carriers. Three groups of TF 58 also send their carrier aircraft to attack on 21 and 22 July. General Turnage's 3rd Marine Divsion is landed west of Agana at Asan and the 1st Marine (Shepherd) lands near Agat. Eventually in the campaign 54,900 American troops are landed. The Japanese defense is 19,000 strong under the command of 29th Infantry Division (Takashima). General Obata who commands the Thirty-first Army is also on the island.

When the landings go in there is only moderate resistance on the beaches.

New Guinea The Japanese send in another attack over the Driniumor River near Aitape. To begin with they achieve some success but later are held.

Eastern Front Troops from Maslennikov's Third Baltic Front take Ostrov in their continuing attacks.

German Command General Zeitzler resigns his post as Chief of Staff at OKH (the Army High Command with responsibility for the Eastern Front) and is replaced by Guderian.

22 July 1944

Eastern Front Rokossovsky's First Belorussian Front take Chelm in their advance on Lublin.

Marianas On Guam the Marines from both beachheads launch converging attacks in an attempt to link up. Both advance for about a mile despite heavy resistance.

23 July 1944

Eastern Front The Soviet forces capture Pskov – the last major town of the prewar Soviet Union in German hands. Farther south troops from First Ukraine Front enter Lublin.

In the German command Field Marshal Schoerner replaces General Friessner at Army Group North.

Poland, Politics The formation of a Polish Committee of National Liberation is announced from Moscow. The London-based Polish government call it 'the creation of a handful of unknown communists.'

Italy Units of the US IV Corps enter the out-

Below: General Eduard Dietl (center), commander of mountain troops in Finland, makes a point to General Ferdinand Schörner of Army Group North.

skirts of Pisa but are only able to occupy the districts south of the Arno.
Marianas The Marines succeed in extending the northern beachhead on Guam to Point Adelup. Other units from the southern landing cross the neck of the Orote Peninsula cutting off the main Japanese airfield on the island.
Western Front General Crerar's First Canadian Army becomes operational.

24 July 1944

Marianas Admiral Hill's TF 52 lands General Schmidt's V Amphibious Corps on Tinian. Fire support is provided by the battleship groups led by Oldendorf and Ainsworth as in the earlier Marianas operations. The landing force is composed of the 2nd and 4th Marine Divisions and numbers 15,600 men. Colonel Ogata and Admiral Kakuta are the Japanese commanders and their force is approximately 6200 strong. The 2nd Marines are first involved in a feint landing on the southwest of the island while the 4th Marines in fact land in the northwest. The assault forces succeed in establishing a solid beachhead and heavy Japanese attacks are beaten off with great loss. Napalm is used in these engagements for the first time in the Pacific. It is also being introduced in Europe at this time.
Western Front The US Cobra attack just west of St Lô is scheduled to begin now but bad weather, hampering the air support, causes a postponement.
Eastern Front Lublin falls to Rokossovsky's troops. Other units of First Ukraine Front overrun the site of Majdanek Concentration Camp.

25 July 1944

Western Front Operation Cobra begins. The main attack just west of St Lô is made by General Collins' US VII Corps with VIII Corps on their right and XIII Corps to the left. There is a massive preparation, especially from the air. More than 3000 planes are involved including 1500 heavy bombers from Eighth Air Force. Some of the bombers aim short and cause many casualties including a general from HQ up to observe the operation. Despite this both VII and VIII Corps make good progress. The British attacks around Caen have contributed to draw away the German tank forces and reserves. South of Caen the Canadian troops are attacking along the road to Falaise but are meeting heavy resistance.
Eastern Front Russian units enter Lvov which is now also partially surrounded.
Germany, Home Front Goebbels is appointed Reich Plenipotentiary for Total War and new decrees are issued cancelling vacations for women involved in war work.
Allied Diplomacy Talks begin in Washington between British and United States representatives on arrangements for the control of oil production and trade in the postwar world.
Indian Ocean Admiral Somerville's British Eastern Fleet attacks Sabang. First planes from the carriers *Victorious* and *Illustrious* are sent against the airfield, then four battleships along with cruisers and destroyers move in close to shell the harbor and oil installations.
Marianas The Americans are still unable to join their beachheads on Guam. Units from the southern landing force are also fighting on the Orote Peninsula.

After repulsing Japanese counterattacks during the early hours, 2nd and 4th Marines advance carefully to the south on Tinian.

Above: Nazi propaganda chief Joseph Goebbels speaks to the German people in Berlin during the summer of 1944.

25-28 July 1944

Carolines Two carrier groups from TF 58 attack Palau while a third sends its planes against Yap, Ulithi, Ngulu, Tais and Sorol. Mitscher is in command.

26 July 1944

Western Front The US attacks continue. Marigny and St Gilles are both taken by VII Corps and to the west VIII Corps is across the Lessay-Périers road.
Eastern Front Units of First Ukraine Front reach the Vistula west of Lublin and capture Deblin. Farther north Narva is taken by troops of the Leningrad Front.
New Guinea The fighting in the Aitape sector continues. On Biak and Numfoor also the Japanese resistance still goes on.
United States, Planning Roosevelt meets MacArthur and Nimitz in Honolulu. MacArthur argues for an attack on the Philippines, but the navy suggests that they can be passed by and instead advocate Formosa as the next major strategic target. This debate is to become very heated and controversial.

27 July 1944

Western Front In the continuing American attacks VIII Corps makes an important breakthrough between Lessay and Périers.
Eastern Front The Soviets make good ground in several sectors. First Ukraine Front (Konev) takes Lvov and Stanislav 70 miles to the south; Second Belorussian Front (Zakharov) captures Bialystok after a harsh struggle; First Baltic Front (Bagramyan) takes Siauliai; and on their right Second Baltic Front (Yeremenko) takes Daugavpils and Rezekne.
Marianas On Guam the 77th Division is preparing to attack Mount Tenjo.

Work begins on the newly taken airfield at Ushi Point on Tinian.

28 July 1944

Western Front The US 4th Armored Division enters Coutances. This is the first objective for Operation Cobra.
Eastern Front The Russians take Brest-Litovsk and Przemysl.
Marianas Much of the Orote Peninsula of Guam is now occupied by the Marines. Inland a little the US forces take Mount Chachao and Mount Alutom in the continuing fight to join the beachheads.

29 July 1944

Eastern Front In a new offensive by Third Belorussian Front the Niemen is crossed.
Western Front The XIX Corps on the left of the US attack is advancing on Torigny and Tessy. In the center VII Corps reaches Percy and on the right VIII Corps is across the Sienne and moving toward Granville.
Marianas The Marines have now occupied rather more than the northern half of Tinian but the Japanese resistance is increasing again after a slight lull.
New Guinea On Biak the Americans complete the destruction of the Japanese pocket around Ibdi. There is no more organized fighting. On the mainland near Aitape the US forces retire slightly at Afua.

30 July 1944

Western Front The advancing US forces take Granville and enter Avranches seizing the important bridges over the Sée. The left flank of the advance is, however, strongly counterattacked by German forces from II Parachute Corps especially at Percy and Villedieu. Farther east there are successful British attacks near Caumont.
Marianas The main town on Tinian, also known as Tinian, is taken by the American forces. The Americans have now largely cleared the southern half of Guam.
Philippine Sea The American heavy cruiser *Indianapolis* is sunk by a Japanese submarine.
New Guinea General Sibert's 6th Division lands unopposed on the small islands of Amsterdam and Middleburg off Cape Sansapor. Admiral Berkey's TF 78 is in support.

31 July 1944

Western Front The US 4th Armored Division pushes on from Avranches and succeeds in taking crossings of the Sélune near Pontaubault. On the left of the advance the German counterattacks continue around Tessy and Percy.
New Guinea One American battalion is moved from the offshore islands to land just west of Cape Sansapor. At Aitape the American forces go over to the attack along the Driniumor River.
Eastern Front In its advance from Vilna Third Belorussian Front now enters Kaunas. Farther south the First Belorussian Front is driving toward Warsaw. It takes Siedlice and Otwock only 12 miles southeast of the city.
British Command Admiral Fraser takes command of the British Eastern Fleet in succession to Admiral Somerville.
Marianas The Marines begin attacks on the last organized Japanese defenses in the south of Tinian.

August 1944

Europe, Air Operations The Allied bombing effort this month can be divided into four categories. First, general strategic bombing, area bombing, carried out solely by the heavy bombers of the RAF. Targets include Kiel, Bremen and Brunswick. Second, the attacks on particular target systems including oil, rail transport and aircraft manufacturing. Oil targets are attacked by both British and Americans and include Zeitz, Bohlen, Freital, Kolin, Poolitz and Hamburg-Meerbeck. Rail centers hit are Saarbrucken, Mulhouse and Strasbourg and others. Aircraft works bombed are Anklam, Neustadt and Rakmel. The third type of operation is in direct support of the ground forces. British light and medium forces fly 33,000 sorties in this work. The American fighter-bombers fly 24,000 missions and their medium bombers a further 8500 in which they drop 10,500 tons of bombs. The lighter forces are in action everywhere and claim to destroy 12,000 vehicles, 850 tanks and much more. The heavy bomber forces are also involved in such attacks from time to time. The efforts of the RAF on 7-8 and 14 August are especially large. The final category of attacks is against the V-weapon sites. Most of these are carried out by British forces. The most notable raid is the 2000 tons dropped on the depot at Trossy St Maximin.

Developments during the month include shuttle raids by the Eighth Air Force in which planes fly to Russia and then Italy, attacking on each trip. Also large forces from Bomber Command are sent over Germany during daylight for the first time since the early months of the war. In all the US Eighth and Fifteenth Air Forces drop 75,000 tons and Bomber Command 65,000 tons. The German V-weapon effort also continues, causing 4000 casualties this month.
Far East, Air Operations There are Superfortress raids on Nagasaki and Yawata. There are in addition the by now usual range of attacks on targets in New Guinea and the Marianas. Davao on Mindanao is also hit.

1 August 1944

Western Front General Patton's Third Army becomes operational and takes positions on the Allied right flank. The US forces are now organized as 12 Army Group (Bradley), First Army (Hodges) and Third Army. Dempsey's British Second Army and Crerar's First Canadian Army form 21 Army Group which Montgomery commands. As well as this post he still retains overall direction of the ground forces.

Patton's main task initially is to overrun Brittany, but some of his troops will head for Le Mans from the beginning. US First Army will advance on Mortain. The British and Canadians will continue to attack between Caumont and Caen. In this sector the British XXX Corps is at the moment advancing on Villers Bocage.
Finland, Politics President Ryti resigns. Marshal Mannerheim is chosen to replace him.
Eastern Front Troops from Chernyakhovsky's Third Belorussian Front take Kaunas, capital of Lithuania. Many of the routes leading to East Prussia from the Baltic States (described by the Germans as Ostland) are cut. In Poland the patriots of the Home Army (AK) begin open operations in Warsaw. This army is aligned politically with the exile government in London and, although by no means of one mind in political affairs, is generally anticommunist. The rising is timed so that when the Russians arrive in Warsaw, as they seem certain to do very shortly, they will find an established Polish government with the prestige of having liberated the national capital. However, the Russian advance almost immediately comes to a halt. This has since caused controversy. The Russian accounts claim that because of the long rapid advance they have made during July, they are unable, for the moment, to move further. The western position is that the Russians have stopped so that the Germans would do the job of wiping out the anti-Soviet forces in Poland. The most telling point on the western side is the reluctance of the Russians to lend any help to British and American plans and, after much negotiation, attempts to drop supplies to the Poles.

Below: General Montgomery (right) talks to US Generals Bradley (center) of 12th Army Group and Patton of US Third Army (left).

Above: A British Churchill tank of 51st Royal Tank Regiment is given a final check before going into battle in Italy, July 1944.

Marianas On Tinian the last organized resistance from the Japanese forces comes to an end. As usual the garrison has all but been wiped out. There are over 6000 Japanese dead and 250 prisoners, an unusually large proportion. The Americans have lost 390 killed and 1800 wounded.

2 August 1944

Western Front The VIII Corps of Patton's Third Army advances into Brittany, reaching Dinan and the outskirts of Rennes. On their left First Army units attack around Tessy and toward Mortain, taking Villedieu.

Marianas The American forces again attack on Guam. They make good ground on the west side of the island but are repulsed in the east.

3 August 1944

Western Front Part of Middleton's VIII Corps begins the attack on Rennes while other units by-pass the city. Mortain falls to First Army units.

Eastern Front Konev's troops seize crossings over the Vistula just south of Sandomierz itself 110 miles south of Warsaw.

Marianas The 77th Division renews its advance on the east side of Guam where the Japanese have pulled back. Defensive positions are being prepared on Mount Santa Rosa and these are shelled by US warships.

Burma Myitkyina is finally taken by the Chinese and American attack after the bulk of the Japanese garrison have managed to slip away.

4 August 1944

Western Front In Brittany the German forces, General Farmbacher's XXV Corps, pull back to the major ports, St Malo, Brest, Lorient and St Nazaire (these last two will hold out until May 1945). Middleton's troops complete the liberaton of Rennes and advance on toward Vannes. From First Army V and XIV Corps also push forward while in the British sector Evrecy and Villers Bocage are taken.

Italy South African units of the British XII Corps enter Florence and take the districts of the river south of the Arno River. The Allied plans are revised according to proposals from General Leese that the next major offensive should be mounted by Eighth Army in the sector near the east coast.

Eastern Front In the north there are German counterattacks between Riga and Jelgava which reopen communication between Riga and the German forces in Lithuania.

Burma The British 2nd Division from XXXIII Corps takes Tamu.

4-5 August 1944

Volcano Islands Admiral Clark leads two groups of TF 38 in attacks on Iwo Jima and Chichi Jima. One Japanese destroyer is sunk and considerable damage done.

5 August 1944

Western Front In Brittany Vannes is liberated. Other VIII Corps units attack near St Malo and reach the outskirts of Brest. General Haislip's XV Corps, also from Third Army, is advancing rapidly to the southeast from the Sélune and reaches Mayenne and Laval. On their left VII Corps is also hurrying forward beyond Mortain.

Eastern Front The Russians bring a new army group, Petrov's Fourth Ukraine Front into their line in southern Poland and northern Hungary.

6 August 1944

Western Front The US VIII Corps extends its hold on Brittany. The 4th Armored Division reaches nearly to Lorient. Haislip's XV Corps takes Laval and advances on Le Mans. In the US First Army sector Vire is taken by 29th Division.

Marianas On Guam one regiment of 77th Division takes heavy casualties in a brief, fierce Japanese counterattack.

Italy The Allied forces in Florence begin to cross the Arno into the northern half of the city.

7 August 1944

Western Front The Germans begin an important counterattack just east of Mortain. The blow falls between VII and XIV Corps. The attackers are from 2nd and 116th Panzer Divisions. Mortain is retaken by the Germans but heavy Allied air attacks help to prevent any more serious loss. In Brittany VIII Corps is now attacking Brest, St Malo and Lorient.

During the night there are attacks southwest of Caen by Canadian forces after more than 1000 RAF heavy bombers have dropped in excess of 3000 tons of bombs on the German positions.

Eastern Front The Russian forces advance in the Carpathian foothills to take Sambor southwest of Lvov.

Marianas There are US attacks and fierce fighting all along the front on Guam. The difficult jungle terrain helps the Japanese defenders to concede only a little ground.

Below: B-17 Flying Fortress bombers of the 381st Bombardment Group, Eighth USAAF, fly over England, 1944. The B-17 was the best heavy bomber available to the Eighth Air Force.

8 August 1944

Western Front The battles around Mortain continue with the Germans still trying to press their offensive home to Arromanches. Despite this threat Third Army goes on with its attacks to the south and southwest. The 79th Division from XV Corps enters Le Mans while on its right XX Corps newly in the line advances toward Nantes and Angers. The fighting around the Brittany ports goes on. The commanders of these German-occupied ports have been ordered to hang on, regardless.

Marianas The remaining Japanese forces are compelled to retire toward the north end of Guam when the US troops manage to overrun Mount Santa Rosa.

Eastern Front The AK forces have now managed to seize control of most of Warsaw and have expanded their strength with much captured German equipment. SS General Bach-Zelewski is appointed to lead the German forces charged with defeating the Poles. The units employed by the Germans are mostly SS, police and punishment battalions, all alike in their liking for cruel and violent methods. After complaints from Guderian and others the worst offenders will be taken out of the fight and some of their leaders executed.

9 August 1944

Western Front The Canadian II Corps continues to attack along the Caen-Falaise road. The German attacks around Mortain are gradually being worn down. The XV Corps turns north from Le Mans heading for Argentan and eventually a junction with the Canadians between Argentan and Falaise. Allied fighter-bombers are very active.

10 August 1944

Western Front British troops operating as part of Canadian First Army take Vimont in the attack south of Caen. In the US Third Army sector all three corps are involved in vigorous fighting. In Brittany Middleton's troops have cleared most of St Malo and Dinard. In the main operations XX Corps takes Nantes and also reaches the Loire near Nantes and to the north XV Corps continues to advance on Alençon from Le Mans. Around Mortain the Germans pull back slightly, principally because of direct American pressure but also because of the growing threat to their rear.

Marianas The Americans wipe out the last serious opposition in the north of Guam. There are various small groups of Japanese holding out in jungle hideouts (one survivor at least will stay in the jungle until 1972). The Americans have taken 7000 casualties including 1300 dead. There are less than 100 Japanese prisoners out of a total garrison of at least 10,000.

Italy The advance of the Polish II corps reaches the Cesano River.

11 August 1944

Western Front The German Commander in Chief, Field Marshal Kluge wishes to pull back from Mortain but Hitler will only allow a partial retreat. Farther south the US forces cross the Loire.

Eastern Front Third Baltic Front begins a new offensive south of Lake Peipus. The German line is fractured and advances of up to 15 miles are made to the west and northwest.

12 August 1944

Western Front The US XV Corps takes Alençon and advances to the outskirts of Argentan where the German 116th Division is in position.

The first PLUTO (Pipe Line Under The Ocean) is in operation carrying fuel from the Isle of Wight to Cherbourg.

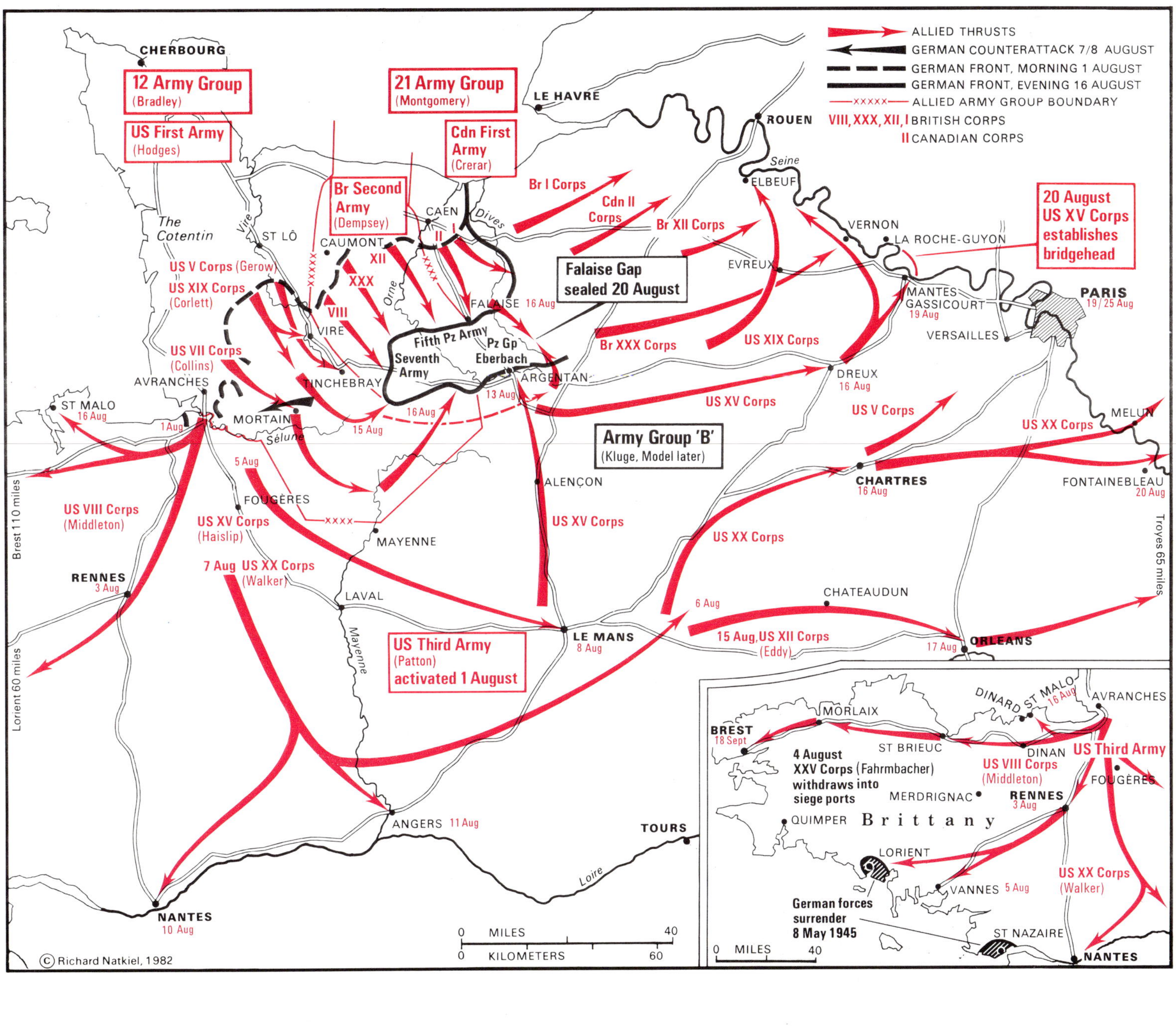

Below: The breakout from Normandy and liberation of Brittany, August 1944.

Above: Destruction in the Falaise Pocket, August 1944. Although many German troops escaped, they lost much of their equipment to air attack.

Italy The Allied forces complete the capture of Florence.

13 August 1944

Western Front Argentan is largely cleared by XV Corps attacks but General Bradley, commanding 12 Army Group, orders a halt here. To the south units of XII and XX Corps are advancing on Orleans and Chartres from around Le Mans.

14 August 1944

Western Front The Canadian advance has reached to within about five miles of Falaise from the north. RAF heavy bombers drop 4000 tons of bombs in supporting attacks as the Canadian drive continues. The US XV Corps begins to move east from around Argentan toward Dreux. Other units are taking post at Argentan. In Brittany all of St Malo has been cleared except for the ancient citadel in the port area.

15 August 1944

Western Front In northern France the British VIII Corps enters Tinchebray from the north. Other British and Canadian units are attacking fiercely along a line from here to east of Falaise. From just south of Tinchebray to Argentan the US VII Corps and V Corps are attacking northward and trapped as meat in the sandwich are the divisions of the German Seventh Army and units of Fifth Panzer Army and Panzer Group Eberbach. These forces are now beginning a desperate retreat to the east. Field Marshal Kluge is forced to take cover from Allied air attacks for most of the day while attempting to visit the front. His long absence from HQ increases Hitler's suspicions that Kluge is disloyal and attempting to defect to the Allied side.
Southern France Allied forces land in southern France between Toulon and Cannes. This is operation Dragoon, originally and for most of the planning stage, known as Anvil. The code name has been changed because it is believed that the Germans have discovered it and its significance. The landing forces are from General Patch's US Seventh Army. Truscott's VI Corps provides the three divisions that make up the bulk of the assault force. The follow-up formation is General de Lattre's II French Corps. French commando units also land from the sea in the first wave and there is also an airborne attack. This involves 5000 men from a composite parachute group and they drop inland near Le Muy. Before these or the seaborne forces go in there are attacks by 1300 land-based aircraft and naval shelling. Admiral Hewitt is in command of the naval forces.

The largest group of special troops lands on the island of Levante with cover from the battleship *Lorraine* and other vessels. General Daniels' 3rd Infantry Division lands in the Baie de Cavalaire and among the bombardment group here is the battleship *Ramillies*. The fire support for General Eagle's 45th Infantry is provided by the battleships *Texas* and *Nevada*. This landing is in the Baie de Bugnon. The left flank division is the 36th Infantry, General Dahlquist, with support from the *Arkansas*. As well as the land-based air cover, five British and two American escort carriers add fighter support (216 aircraft). In addition to the battleships mentioned fire support is also provided by 20 cruisers and 31 destroyers. A further four cruisers and 60 destroyers perform escort duties. There is almost no resistance to the landings and only 183 casualties are taken. Churchill has come to observe the operation from aboard a destroyer and, from his account in his memoirs, seems to have been bored by the lack of action. The German force in the south of France is General Weise's Nineteenth Army. This formation has only seven poor quality infantry divisions and the better trained and equipped 11 Panzer Division to cover the whole of the south and southeast of the country. Clearly, this is an inadequate force.

16 August 1944

Eastern Front The Russian attacks reach Ossow only seven miles northeast of Warsaw but they are pushed back by a German counterattack.
Northern France Canadian troops from II Corps enter the ruins of Falaise and a bitter battle develops. To their right Polish units of British I Corps begin to move west over the River Dives. To the south Chartres falls to the advance of US XX Corps.
Southern France The French II Corps (de Lattre) lands and passes forward through the US forces which are consolidating the beachhead.

17 August 1944

Eastern Front In Lithuania Army Group North sends in counterattacks all along the line but especially against Siauliai. The aim is to prevent Riga being cut off.
Northern France The capture of Falaise is completed by the Canadian 2nd Division. The damage to the town in the bombing and bitter fighting of the past few days has been so severe that in many places it is impossible to tell where the streets once were. The gap between the Canadian front to the north and the US V Corps to the south is now only a handful of miles.

To the south and west of these battles the American advance into the heart of France continues. Dreux, Chateaudun and Orleans are taken. In Brittany the defenders of the citadel at St Malo surrender.

Hitler dismisses Field Marshal Kluge. Model is appointed in his place. Kluge commits suicide on 18 August rather than face a treason trial.
Southern France Among the towns taken in the Allied advance are St Raphael, St Tropez, Fréjus, Le Luq and St Maxime. There is little German resistance.
New Guinea The American holdings near Aitape are extended by a general advance. Japanese interference is negligible. On Numfoor the last significant Japanese force is brought to battle after several days maneuvering and is largely destroyed.

18 August 1944

Northern France The Falaise gap is closed by the junction of the Poles and Americans at Chambois. A considerable German force is still to the west. The German retreat through the Falaise gap in the past few days has provided unrivalled opportunities for the Allied fighter-bombers since there has been an enormous amount of vulnerable traffic compelled to travel by day on virtually one road.

In Third Army's advance toward the Seine forward patrols reach Versailles.
Southern France The US VI Corps is now moving toward Aix-en-Provence while on their left the French forces are attacking nearer the coast toward Toulon and eventually Marseilles. There is also a US advance north toward Gap.
Eastern Front In the north troops of Third Baltic and Leningrad Fronts advance north and south of Lake Peipus. In southern Poland Sandomierz, on the west bank of the Vistula, is taken by First Ukraine Front.

19 August 1944

Northern France The XV Corps from Third Army reaches the Seine at Mantes Grassicourt. The fighting between Falaise and Argentan is still very fierce and continues to go badly for the Germans. In Paris the resistance begin open operations against the Germans.

20 August 1944

Northern France The last units of the German Fifth Panzer and Seventh Armies which are to escape the Falaise pocket do so during the

night by passing through the Allied lines around Chambois and St Lambert. Seventy or eighty miles to the east Patton's troops take crossings of the Seine at Mantes Grassicourt, thirty miles west of Paris. Farther up the river beyond Paris, XX Corps units enter Fontainebleau.
France, Politics Pétain is arrested by the Germans in Vichy for refusing to go to an area safe from the Allied advance. General de Gaulle is in France and the FFI (resistance) forces claim to control eight departments.
New Guinea The Americans announce that the fighting on Biak has come to an end. The Japanese have lost 4700 dead and 220 prisoners. The Americans have had 2550 casualties.
Eastern Front After a fierce artillery preparation during the night a major Soviet offensive begins in the south with two main attacks near Jassy and Tiraspol. Malinovsky's Second Ukraine Front advance south around Jassy and Tolbukhin's Third Ukraine Front southwest from Tiraspol. Their attacks fall on Third and Fourth Rumanian Armies and the German Sixth Army which in fact contains many Rumanian troops. These forces are all part of General Freissner's Army Group South Ukraine. In the north in Latvia the Russian attacks also continue fiercely. The fire of the German heavy cruiser *Prinz Eugen* helps beat off one important Russian advance near Riga.

21 August 1944

Northern France All the Allied armies begin a rapid advance to the northeast in pursuit of the broken and retreating German forces. Although at this stage, the invasion of France is behind the schedule set out in the Overlord plan, this will be corrected by the speed of the advance in the next few weeks. Third Army improves its bridgeheads over the Seine. On the right flank the advance reaches Sens.
Southern France Aix-en-Provence is taken by units of General Truscott's US VI Corps.

21-29 August 1944

World Affairs Senior Allied representatives meet at Dumbarton Oaks to discuss plans for maintaining postwar security. They agree that there should be an assembly of all nations backed up by a council of leading states. There should also be an International Court of Justice. The leader of the American delegation is Edward Stettinius, of the British team Sir Alexander Cadogan and for Russia Andrei Gromyko.

22 August 1944

Japan, Home Front The government introduces measures to conscript all women between the ages of 12 and 40 to do war work.
Arctic Admiral Moore leads three fleet carriers and two escort carriers of the British Home Fleet to attack the battleship *Tirpitz* in Kaafiord. The battleship *Duke of York* is in support. The attack is detected on the way in and loses heavily to the German barrage and to the defending fighters. No hits are achieved because of the smoke defenses. The attacks are repeated without result on 24 and 29 August.
Eastern Front Jassy is taken by Malinovsky's troops. Third Ukraine Front is extending its attacks northward toward Kishinev and has advanced up to 50 miles in the past two days.

Above: An American M-10 tank destroyer moves through the rubble of a town in southern France, August 1944.

23 August 1944

Northern France The resistance forces have, for the moment, largely freed Paris after a bitter struggle. To the east of the capital Melun falls to the American advance and to the south of the city French troops fighting with the US V Corps are brought forward to join the liberating advance. Montgomery's 21 Army Group and US First Army are hurrying forward to the Seine. Evreux is taken by units of US XIX Corps. Small Allied forces on the Atlantic coast link with resistance units near Bordeaux.
Southern France French troops reach the outskirts of both Marseilles and Toulon.
Rumania, Politics King Michael dismisses

Below: French Resistance fighters gather in Chartres after the liberation. The role of the Resistance was important to Allied success.

Marshal Antonescu and the new prime minister is General Senatescu. Rumania accepts the Russian armistice terms. On 25 August Rumania declares war on Germany. There is fighting near Bucharest.

Eastern Front The attacks of Second and Third Ukraine Fronts link up cutting off a large part, about 12 divisions, of the German Sixth Army. Second Ukraine Front also takes Vaslui, 35 miles south of Jassy. Many of the Rumanian troops formerly allied with the Germans have either simply deserted.

New Guinea The battle for Numfoor is over and most of the victorious American force is withdrawn to other sectors.

24 August 1944

Northern France The fighting in Paris flares up again as the Germans make a final effort. General Leclerc leads the French 4th Armored Division to the outskirts of the city.

Southern France An American force advancing east from the landing areas takes Cannes. Inland, in the drive north, Grenoble is taken and in the main advance west Arles is taken, on the Rhône south of Avignon, by the US 3rd Division.

Indian Ocean Admiral Moody leads the carriers *Victorious* and *Indomitable* in an attack on Padang in the southwest of Sumatra. The battleship *Howe* is one of the escorting ships. On 23 August Admiral Fraser has taken over command of the British Eastern Fleet from Admiral Somerville. In addition to the forces sent against Padang there are three battleships and two fleet carriers.

Eastern Front The Russian forces in the south advance at great speed. Freissner's Army Group South Ukraine has been shattered by the Russian attacks and the defection of the Rumanians. Kishinev is taken.

25 August 1944

Northern France General Leclerc's 4th Armored Division enters Paris. The German commander General Choltitz disobeys orders to fight fiercely for the city and instead of causing such damage for nothing he surrenders. The British XXX Corps takes Vernon on the Seine and seizes river crossings nearby. On their left XII Corps is preparing to cross the river at Louviers and the Canadians take Elbeuf. In Brittany

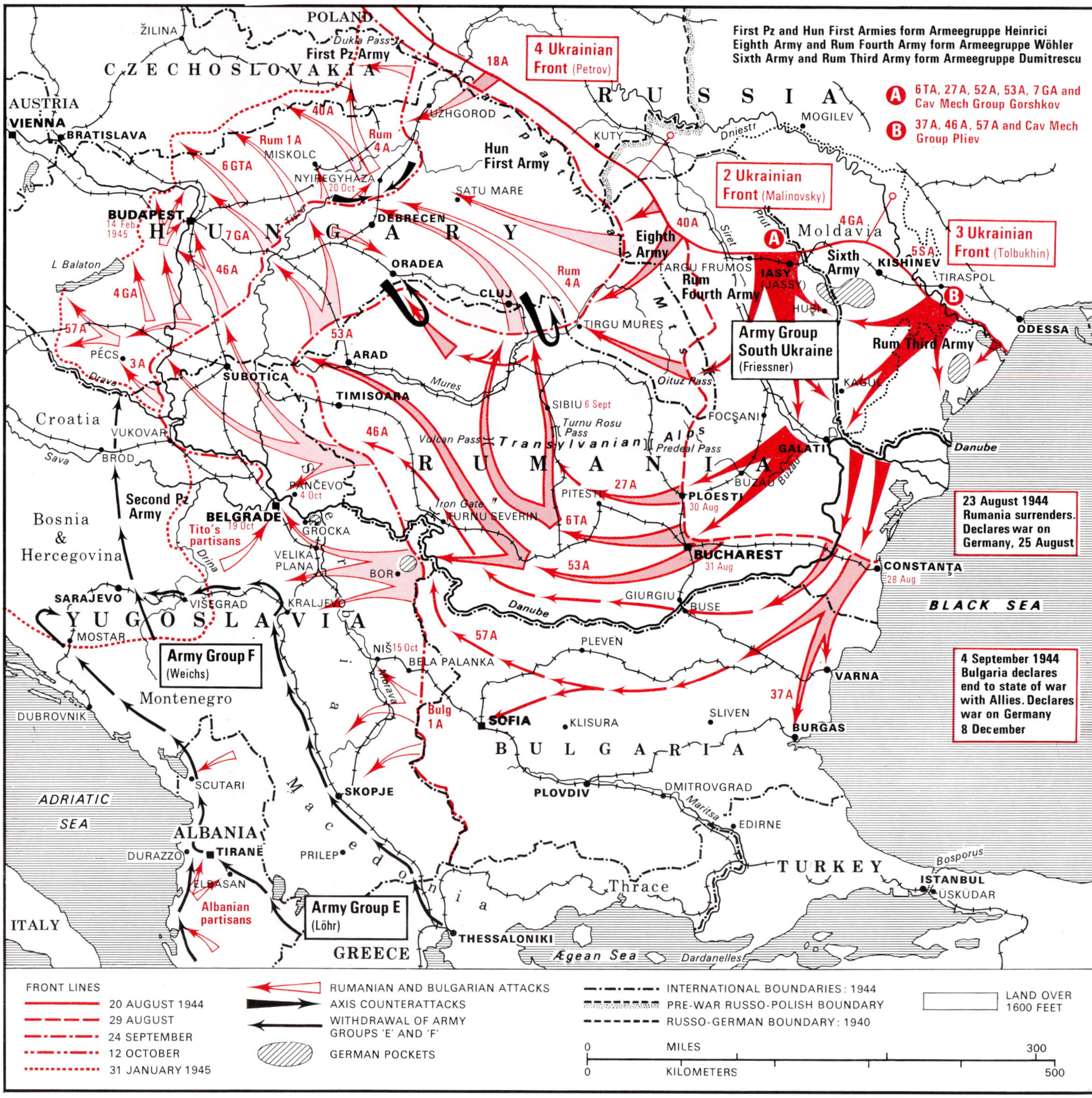

Below: The Russian advance into the Balkans, August 1944-January 1945.

the US VIII Corps begins major attacks on Brest where the German garrison still resists stubbornly. The battleship *Warspite* shells targets in the town.

Southern France Avignon is taken by the US forces. The majority of General Weise's Nineteenth Army is now withdrawing rapidly northward up the Rhône valley. The fighting in Marseilles and Toulon continues, however.

Italy Eighth Army begins a new offensive over the River Metauro on the Adriatic sector. The German defenders are caught by surprise and good progress is made by the offensive. The V British Corps, the Polish Corps and I Canadian Corps provide the attacking units.

Eastern Front In Estonia Maslennikov's forces take Tartu, an important position in the German defense lines.

26 August 1944

Northern France Most of the Allied Armies now have units over the Seine and advancing to the northeast. General de Gaulle returns to Paris and joins a ceremonial parade despite the danger from a few remaining German snipers.

Italy Eighth Army establishes solid bridgeheads over the Metauro. The German 71st Division is pushed back rapidly by V Corps.

Eastern Front In the south the Russian advance reaches the Danube east of Galati. The main attacks are, however, west of the town between it and Focsani.

Bulgaria The Bulgarian government announces that it has withdrawn from the war and that German troops will be disarmed. On 29 August the Soviet Union announces that it cannot accept or recognize Bulgarian neutrality.

27 August 1944

Northern France The Allied attacks over the Seine continue. The advance of US First Army and the British and Canadian forces has not yet gone far beyond the river, but the US Third Army on the right takes Chateau Thierry on the Marne as well as reaching the Seine farther inland at Troyes.

Eastern Front In Rumania Focsani and Galati are captured along with a large part of their garrisons. The advance continues in the direction of Ploesti and Bucharest.

Europe, Air Operations The RAF raid on the Hamburg-Meerbeck oil plant is the first large-scale daylight operation by Bomber Command over Germany since the early months of the war. Although Mosquito bombers have often made daylight attacks before this, the employment of the slower, more vulnerable heavy bombers shows the extent of the air superiority which has been established by the long-range fighters.

28 August 1944

Northern France US First Army units cross the Marne at Meaux. Third Army is moving toward Reims and west of Paris the Allied advance is also continuing.

Southern France The last German forces in Toulon and Marseilles surrender. In the Rhône valley some German units, particularly 11th Panzer Division, have been cut off south of Montélimar but in attacks northward they mostly succeed in breaking through, although they take heavy losses from Allied artillery and air power.

Eastern Front Some of Second Ukraine Front's attacking units swing west and move through the Oituz Pass over the Carpathians toward Transylvania. On the Danube Third Ukraine Front takes Braila.

Above: British Bren-gun carriers of the 43rd Wessex Division cross a pontoon bridge over the River Seine, August 1944.

Hungary, Politics A new government, led by General Lakatos, takes office. They announce that they are ready to negotiate with the Russians.

29 August 1944

War Crimes The Russians and the Polish communists jointly announce that they have discovered evidence that the Germans have murdered around 1,500,000 people in the former Majdanek concentration camp. This is the first of a series of such dreadful discoveries.

Northern France The Allied advance continues apace. The US VII Corps takes Soissons and crosses the Aisne. To the east Third Army units take Reims and Chalons-sur-Marne.

Italy The advance of Eighth Army reaches the River Foglia. The next obstacle is the German Gothic Line which lies immediately to the north.

Eastern Front The Russians take the important Black Sea port of Constanta. Buzau, east of Ploesti also falls.

Poland, Resistance The British and United States' governments declare that they recognize the Home Army (AK) as a responsible belligerent force and that it should be treated as such. The Germans officially reject this procedure. In Warsaw the fighting continues to be very fierce and brutal.

30 August 1944

France, Politics The Provisional Government of General de Gaulle is established in Paris and begins work.

Northern France The British XXX Corps takes Beauvais in its continuing and accelerating advance.

Italy The Eighth Army begins its offensive against the Gothic Line. The main attacks are by V Corps units with support from part of the Canadian I Corps. The Polish Corps is fighting on the coast at Pesaro.

Eastern Front The Russians take Ploesti. Most of the Rumanian oilfields are now in Russian hands further increasing the shortages which have been imposed on the Germans by the American and British air offensive. Although Germany has attempted to build up oil reserves they have proved totally inadequate.

31 August 1944

Italy In the east Eighth Army continues to attack in some places breaking in to the Gothic Line. In the west the US IV Corps pushes forward following a German withdrawal from some positions along the Arno.

Eastern Front The troops of Second Ukraine Front take Bucharest.

31 August- 2 September 1944

Volcano Islands As part of the preparation for the coming operation against the Palau Islands TG 38.4 attacks Iwo Jima and Chichi Jima. Admiral Davison commands the three carriers. On 1 and 2 September, in addition to the air attacks, the supporting cruisers and destroyers go in to shell the islands.

September 1944

Europe, Air Operations The Allied Air Offensive continues to be very destructive. Altogether 112,400 tons of bombs are dropped by the heavy bombers this month. RAF Bomber Command drops just under half with targets including Frankfurt, Bremerhaven and Karlsruhe. The Channel ports Calais, Boulogne and Le Havre are also strongly hit with Calais being the target for 6500 tons on two occasions. The US Eighth and Fifteenth Air Forces drop 60,000 tons in their attacks and strike at Mainz, Hamm and Ludwigshafen among the general targets and in the more specialized oil offensive they hit Sterkrade, Merseburg, Bratislava and Lutzkendorf among others. The lighter forces of both Allies continue to be very active in their tactical role. Their attacks are particularly heavy in support of the airborne Operation Market Garden.

Atomic Research Work on the atomic program at Los Alamos has now proceeded so far that a special bomber unit is established to begin training to drop a bomb when one can be made. Some of the scientists working on the project are now beginning to have doubts about the morality of continuing their work when the war seems to be well on the way to being won and when intelligence information suggests that there is little danger of any of the Axis powers making a bomb. There are also some suggestions that the knowledge that is being gained should not remain secret after the war but should be shared throughout the scientific world. Despite these doubts the work continues.

Far East, Air Operations The Superfortresses from China bomb targets in Manchuria on several occasions including Anshan and Penhsiku. There are also attacks on various Japanese-held islands in the Pacific.

1 September 1944

Western Front Dieppe is liberated fittingly by Canadian units. Inland British forces take Arras in their advance north of the Somme. The attacks of US First Army come near St Quentin and Cambrai. On the right Third Army take Verdun and Commercy. Eisenhower officially establishes his HQ in France and takes over direction of the Allied land forces.

During the past few days there has been an increasingly acrimonious strategic debate among the Allied generals as to how to exploit the serious German collapse. Eisenhower believes in a 'broad front' advance with all the Allied armies having an approximately equal share of the supplies and other support. This is entirely safe because no part of the force will ever get far enough ahead to be in any danger of isolation. The alternative is for the majority of resources, especially in logistical support, to be placed behind a portion of the allied force and for this group to push forward at speed and, it is hoped, quickly cross the Rhine and win the war. The most forceful version of this argument is put forward by General Montgomery. He proposes a thrust by a force of about 20 divisions drawn from both his and Bradley's armies which should aim to cross Belgium and encircle the Ruhr. Of course, he wishes to command himself but he is prepared to work under Bradley. Eisenhower recognizes the risks inherent in this plan and the political difficulties which would arise if a large part of the US forces was compelled to halt to allow the narrow front attack. He argues too that there are simply too few lorries to carry the supplies needed for such a scheme. In fact there are probably just enough. This debate on strategy is to continue in various forms for several months. It is clear that many of the Allied supply problems which are making a strategic choice pressing stem from the lack of a major port near the advance. None of the French Channel ports are really large enough to fill the gap and they are in any case still in German hands. Antwerp is the obvious choice and will be the focus of much of the Allied efforts for the next two months once the excitement of the Market Garden parachute operation is over. In practice it may have proved impossible to have brought Patton's Army to a halt because his supply officers are already in the habit of commandeering any supply columns which fill their needs whether they have priority or not. They have also been less able to put captured railroad equipment into service than the other armies largely because of the troops' habit of wildly shooting up any such captures.

The advance in southern France continues.

Above: Black American soldiers of the 92nd Infantry Division cross the Arno river in Italy, September 1944.

Below: A Cromwell tank of the British Guards Armoured Division enters Brussels, to the wild appreciation of the population.

Italy Eighth Army continues its attacks on the Gothic line in the Adriatic sector. The advance of the Canadian I Corps around Tomba di Pesaro is particularly successful.

Eastern Front The Russian advance reaches the Bulgarian frontier at Giurgiu on the Danube. Calarasi is also taken.

Bulgaria, Politics Prime Minister Bagrianov resigns and is replaced by Constantine Muraviev.

2 September 1944

Western Front In southern France the Allied landings have now put ashore 190,000 men with 41,000 vehicles and 220,000 tons of supplies. The American advance has reached almost to Lyons. French units are being brought up to be the first into the city. In northern France the Allied advance continues rapidly, but supply problems and shortages are beginning to cause difficulty for US First and Third Armies. British troops enter Belgium. Among the towns liberated by various Allied forces are Douai, St Valery and Lens.

Finland The Finnish Prime Minister Antii Hackzell announces that Finland is breaking diplomatic relations with Germany and demands that all German troops are withdrawn.

Italy The Canadian forces in Eighth Army make a partial breakthrough and advance several miles to the Conca River west of Cattolica. San Giovanni is taken. The Polish forces fighting in Pesaro have nearly completed the capture of the city. The eastern end of the Gothic Line has been overrun despite the arrival of some German reserves.

3 September 1944

Western Europe Brussels is entered by the British Guards Armored Division. Other towns taken by 21 Army Group are Tournai and Abbeville. The US Third Army has advance units across the Moselle. Mons is taken by US First Army. In the advance in southern France Lyons falls to the French 1st Infantry Division.

Wake Island Admiral Smith leads three heavy cruisers and three destroyers to bombard the Japanese positions on the island. The light carrier *Monterey* provides air cover.

Italy Canadian units cross the Conca and continue their advance.

4 September 1944

Western Front The British 11th Armored Division enters Antwerp but fails to push forward to take the important canal crossings which lead to ground dominating the approaches to this large and enormously valuable port. Other towns freed by the Allied advance are Lille, Louvain, Malines and Etaples.

Finland A cease-fire is agreed between the Russians and the Finns and comes into effect immediately. The armistice is signed on 10 September and provides for the restoration of the 1940 frontiers and for Finland to pay reparations. The Germans begin to pull out of Finland by land and sea. The bulk of their force will go to Norway, but about 7000 men will be taken off through the Baltic ports.

Eastern Front In their attacks through the Carpathians the Russians take Brasnov. Senaia is also taken.

5 September 1944

Western Europe The US First Army takes Namur and Charleroi. Hitler brings Field Marshal Rundstedt back to command in chief the armies in the west.

Italy Eighth Army's attacks continue but they are now up against the strong German positions on the Coriano and Gemmano ridges. Tank units have been brought forward but cannot break through. On the western side of the country units of US IV Corps take Lucca.

Bulgaria The Bulgarian attempts to stay out of the war prove unsuccessful. The Soviet Union today declares war. The Bulgarian prime minister broadcasts and declares war in turn on Germany on 8 September.

Diplomatic Affairs The Benelux Customs Union (between Belgium, Netherlands and Luxembourg) is established by agreement of the exile governments. This is one of the first moves which will lead eventually to the establishment of the European Economic Community.

6 September 1944

Western Front The Canadian forces reach the Channel north of Calais and just south of Boulogne. The US First Army crosses the Meuse at several points south of Namur. Ghent, Courtrai and Armentières all fall to 21 Army Group. In southern France Chalons-sur-Saone is taken by the French II Corps.

Eastern Front The Russian advance through Rumania reaches the Yugoslavian border on the Danube at Turnu-Severin. Nearer the opposite end of the Russian front Ostroleka is taken only 25 miles from the East Prussian border.

United States, Home Front The army is able to announce that it will demobilize 1,000,000 men when the war with Germany is over.

Britain, Home Front The Minister for Home Security, Herbert Morrison relaxes blackout and other civil defense regulations. The War Office ends compulsory training and drills for Home Guard units.

6-8 September 1944

Carolines All four groups, 16 carriers in all, of Admiral Mitscher's TF 38 attack Palau. Admiral Halsey, commanding Third Fleet, is present aboard the battleship *New Jersey*. By now US power is overwhelming.

7 September 1944

Western Front In Belgium British and American units cross the Albert canal east of Antwerp. Other American formations from First Army have nearly reached Liège.

Below: The Allied advance through northern France and Belgium in August-September 1944. The Ruhr industrial area was a key objective.

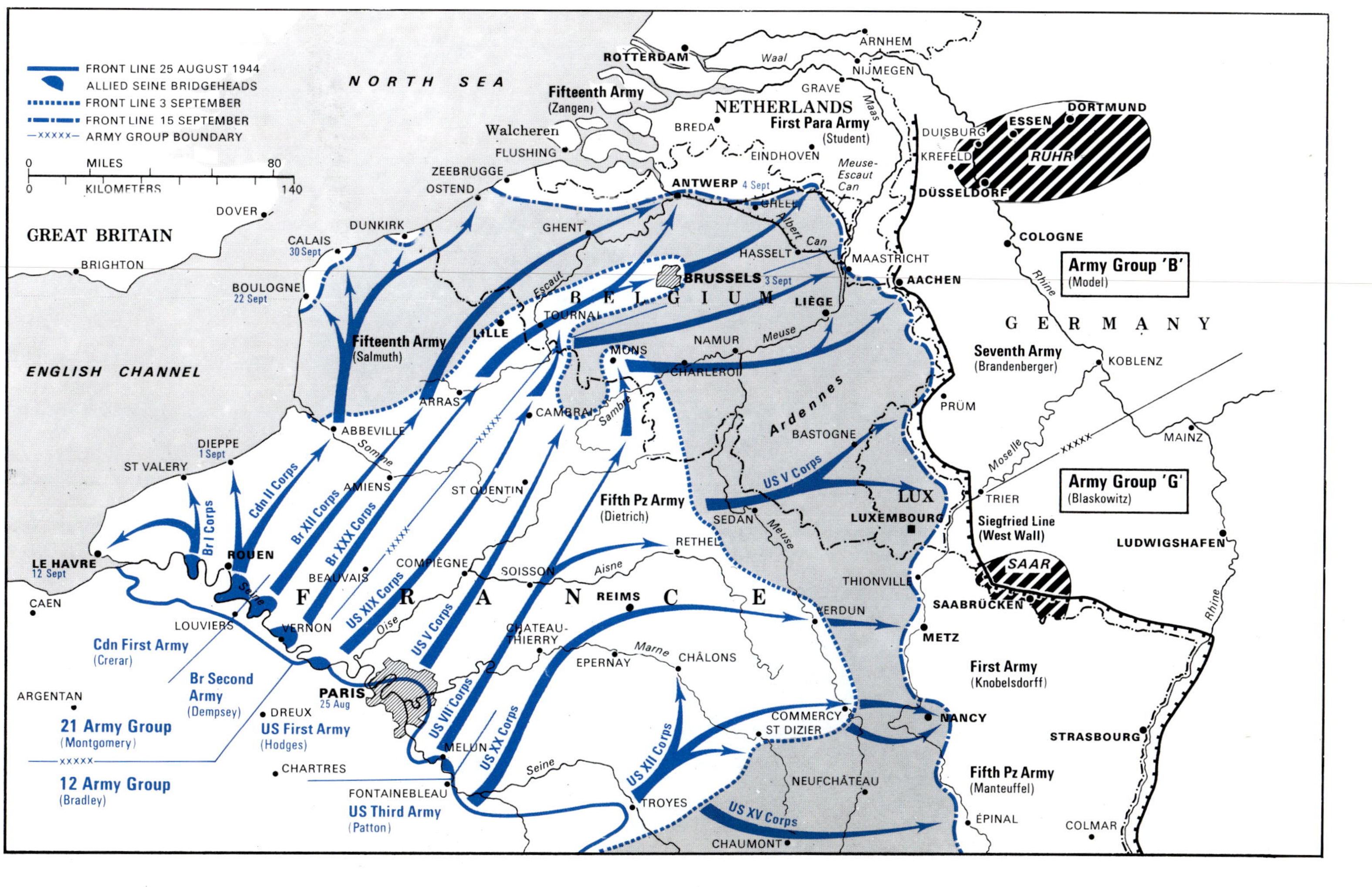

Above: Lt General Miles Dempsey (center), commander of the British Second Army in Normandy, with his corps commanders, Crocker (left) and Bucknall.

8 September 1944

V-Weapons The first German V2 rocket weapon lands in the Chiswick area of London.
Western Front The VII Corps from the US First Army takes Liège. Troops from Canadian First Army capture Nieuport and Ostend. In southern France Besançon falls to US VI Corps.
Italy After two days of rain Eighth Army continues its attacks on the Gemmano and Coriano ridges without success.

9 September 1944

Western Front In Belgium the Canadians take Bruges while in southern France Beaune, Le Creusot and Autun all fall to French units.
France, Politics General de Gaulle appoints a new Cabinet. The principal change is the appointment of Georges Bidault as Foreign Minister.

9-10 September 1944

Philippines Three groups, 12 carriers in all, from TF 38 attack airfields on Mindanao.

10 September 1944

Western Front Troops from US First Army enter Luxembourg. On the Channel coast Le Havre is shelled by the battleship *Warspite* and the monitor *Erebus*, in preparation for an Allied assault. Farther north the Canadians are attacking near Zeebrugge. Eisenhower accepts Montgomery's proposal that an airborne operation should be mounted to take the bridges over a series of canals and rivers in Holland. This operation will be known as Market Garden and is designed to allow a rapid advance into Germany. It is based on the assumption that the Germans have only light forces in the relevant areas and will not be able to prevent the advance of ground forces to link up with the paratroops. The operation will begin on 17 September.
Italy Fifth Army steps up its attacks with efforts by II US Corps toward the Futa and Il Giogo Passes north of Florence.

11 September 1944

Western Front The attack on Le Havre by British I Corps goes in after a heavy RAF raid. US First Army units actually reach German soil north of Trier but they have little strength here. Malmédy is taken in this sector. The British Second Army enters Holland near Bourg Leopold and takes an important bridgehead over the Meuse-Escaut canal. The forces moving up from the south of France take Dijon and link with the French 2nd Armored Division of US Third Army near Sombernon.
Italy Fifth Army's advance continues. Pistoia is taken by South African units of British XIII Corps.

11-16 September 1944

Allied Planning Churchill and Roosevelt and their staffs meet in Quebec for the Octagon Conference. There is little change made to the overall strategy. It is agreed to continue with the campaigns in northwest Europe and Italy along the established lines. Unusually there is no opposition even from the US Navy representatives to a vigorous policy in Italy. A program of attacks for Burma is agreed. Also after Churchill and Roosevelt have talked the matter over the US Navy concede that British forces should join their own for the final campaigns against Japan.

12 September 1944

Western Front The 12,000-strong German garrison of Le Havre surrenders to the attacks of British I Corps. More units of the US First Army reach the German border between Aachen and Trier.
Aegean The Germans evacuate Mytilene.

The exiled Greek government moves from Cairo to Caserta in southern Italy to be nearer to home when the time comes for the return.

12-14 September 1944

Philippines The three groups of TF 38 which attacked Mindanao on 9 and 10 September shift their attention to the Visayas or Central Philippine Islands. On 14 September one group again hits targets on Mindanao. More than 200 Japanese planes are destroyed in the 2400 missions flown.

13 September 1944

Rumania The armistice between the Allies and Rumania is signed. The terms have been dictated by the Soviets and include reparations of $300,000,000 and the cession of territory to the USSR.
Western Front The US Third Army continues its attacks taking Neufchateau.
Eastern Front Second Belorussian Front take Lomza on the Narew west of Bialystok. The Soviets respond to British and American pressure and begin supply drops to the Polish Home Army (AK) forces fighting in Warsaw.
Italy Eighth Army has succeeded in clearing the Germans entirely from the Coriano Ridge and almost completely from the Gemmano positions.

13-14 September 1944

Palau Islands The American forces begin their preliminary bombardment of Peleliu and Angaur. Admiral Oldendorf leads five battleships, nine cruisers and numerous destroyers in this operation. Also in support is an escort carrier force which varies in strength at different times from seven to 11 ships. Minesweeping operations also begin to clear the approach to the islands.

14 September 1944

Italy With the capture of Zollara the Gemmano Ridge is finally cleared of German forces and the Eighth Army is able to push forward to the Marano River.
Eastern Front The Warsaw suburb of Praga is taken by Soviet troops of First Belorussian Front.

15 September 1944

Arctic A force of 28 British Lancaster bombers from a Russian base is sent to attack *Tirpitz* in the anchorage at Altafiord. Special 12,000-pound bombs are used but only one hit is obtained on the *Tirpitz*'s bows because of effective smoke screens shielding the target.
France, Politics François de Menthon, the Justice Commissioner, orders the arrest of Marshal Pétain and all the members of the Vichy Cabinet because of their alleged collaboration with the Germans.
Moluccan Islands American forces land on the southwest of Morotai at the Gila Peninsula. There is no Japanese resistance. The landing force is from Hall's XI Corps and includes the 31st Division and an additional regiment. The naval support is commanded by Admiral Barbey and includes six escort carriers as well as cruisers and destroyers. General MacArthur is present. On the first day 19,960 men go ashore and by the start of October the force has been built up by 26,000 combat troops and 12,200 in the construction units. Airfields are quickly built and until they become operational Fifth Air Force gives cover.
Palaus There are US landings on the southwest coast of Peleliu. The Japanese garrison of the island is made up of a regiment of the 14th Division commanded by Colonel Nakagawa. The main Japanese force in the area is on Babelthaup. The landing force is General Rupertus' 1st Marine Division from Geiger's III Amphibious Corps. The naval forces which carried out the preliminary bombardment remain in support.

The landings meet fairly moderate resistance on the beaches but as soon as they move inland the fighting becomes very fierce. The Japanese have constructed a formidable defense system based principally on the complex of caves with which the island is riddled. At the end of the day the beachhead is only a few hundred yards wide at the most.

Western Front The British Second Army takes a second crossing point over the Meuse-Escaut canal. This move is undertaken as a preparation for Operation Market Garden. Maastricht and Eisden are both taken by US First Army and Nancy and Epinal by US Third Army. The forces moving up from the south of France, General Patch's US Seventh Army and General de Lattre's French First Army come under General Eisenhower's command.

Italy Eighth Army creates a bridgehead over the Marano.

16 September 1944

Eastern Front There is a new large-scale Soviet offensive in the Baltic States involving principally attacks toward Riga and Tallinn. In the south in Bulgaria, Sofia is taken by that proportion of Third Ukraine Front which has crossed the Danube before turning west to threaten the retreat of the German forces in Greece.

Palaus The Marines consolidate and extend their beachhead on Peleliu. The island's airfield is partly captured.

16-20 September 1944

Indian Ocean The British Eastern Fleet sends two carriers and one battleship to raid Sigli in northern Sumatra.

16-21 September 1944

Denmark, Resistance There is a general strike in Denmark as a protest against recent deportations carried out by the Germans.

17 September 1944

Western Front Operation Market Garden is begun. The Allied plan has as its chief proponent General Montgomery and is for airborne troops to seize a series of bridges over river and canal lines in Holland allowing the main Allied forces , or part of them, to continue their advance into Germany unimpeded by such natural barriers. The belief is that the German armies in the west have been so decisively weakened by the battles since D-Day that they will collapse if momentum can be sustained. In fact the German forces in Holland generally and especially around the Arnhem area in particular are not as weak as has been believed. It is indeed arguable that the effort put into Market Garden would have been better spent in clearing the Scheldt estuary and getting Antwerp working to create a solid basis for the future Allied campaigns.

In detail the plan provides for three airborne division to be dropped and five main bridges to be captured while the British XXX Corps attacks north to link up with each division in turn. The nearest bridges, over canals north of Eindhoven at Veghel and Zon, are the objectives of the US 82nd Airborne Division. These objectives are taken on the first day. The US 101st Airborne Division is dropped around Grave south of Nijmegen with the task of taking the bridges over the Maas as Grave and the Waal at Nijmegen. The first of these is taken on the first day. The farthest bridge is at Arnhem over the lower Rhine. This is the objective of the British 1st Airborne Division. They are dropped deliberately a little distance away from the town to allow some organization before going into battle and on balance this proves to have been a mistaken tactic because of the time it gives the German forces to react. It is unfortunate that two SS Panzer division are refitting in the Arnhem area and are formidable opponents. The airborne troops, of course, have only weapons light enough to be carried in gliders. One battalion manages to reach the bridge but is there cut off from the remainder of the force which is in itself fighting for its life. The Germans retain control of one end of the bridge while the paratroops

Below: Men of the US 82nd Airborne Division drop from their C-47 transport planes over Holland, Operation Market Garden.

hold the other. Overall the first day of the operation has been fairly successful. All the bridges are still intact but the deciding factor will be whether XXX Corps can advance fast enough to aid the paratroops in the various landing grounds.

As well as the air support for this operation there is a heavy, 3500 tons, RAF attack on Boulogne before an assault by Canadian forces goes in.

Palaus General Mueller's US 8th Infantry Division lands on Angaur. The Japanese garrison is about 1600 strong. Resistance to the landings immediately and later during the first night is energetic but neither very powerful nor effective.

There are Japanese attacks by night but by day the Americans still hold most of the south side of Peleliu comfortably enough. They begin attacks on the Japanese positions on Mount Umurbrogol. Only a little progress is made here despite the support from heavy naval guns because of the strength and elaboration of the Japanese defenses.

18 September 1944

Palaus On Peleliu the Marines try to extend their attacks on Mount Umurbrogol but they are thrown back by the Japanese and suffer heavy losses.

The American force makes a confident advance toward the center of Angaur. Although the Japanese infiltrations cause some problems, they are too heavily outnumbered to do much more.

Western Front The British XXX Corps links up with the 101st Airborne Division at Eindhoven and Veghel. These attacks continue, meeting gradually increasing resistance. To the north both the other airborne divisions in the Market Garden operation are fighting fiercely to maintain their position.

Below: Arnhem, 17 September 1944: British gliders land to the west of the town and a signals jeep is prepared for the advance.

Warsaw In the only major attempt to drop supplies allowed by the Soviets 1284 containers are dropped to the AK by a force of B-17 bombers, but only 228 fall in Polish-held territory.

19 September 1944

Western Front In the morning the continuing XXX Corps attacks link up with the 82nd Airborne Division at Grave. Together these formations move toward Nijmegen. At Arnhem the main body of the British paratroops still cannot reach the battalion which continues to hold its position at the north end of the bridge.

Back in Brittany the last resistance of the German garrison in Brest comes to an end.

Eastern Front In Estonia Valga falls to Maslennikov's troops. The Russian offensive here and throughout the Baltic States continues.

Palaus The heavy fighting on Peleliu around Mount Umurbrogol goes on. The American advance is being held fairly comfortably by the Japanese.

On Angaur the fighting is also intense.

20 September 1944

Western Front A joint attack by the British Guards Armored Division and the US 82nd Airborne Division takes Nijmegen and the vital bridge over the Waal before it can be destroyed by the Germans. At Arnhem the British paratroops are driven away from the north end of the bridge despite a desperate fight.

In other attacks Polish troops of Canadian First Army make gains along the Scheldt estuary and US Third Army takes Châtel and Lunéville.

Italy The advance of British V Corps, Eighth Army, enters the Republic of San Marino.

Palaus On Angaur the main Japanese forces have been wiped out but a few units will hold out for sometime in the northwest of the island.

21 September 1944

Italy Eighth Army's advance reaches Rimini. The town is taken by a combination of Canadian and Greek units.

Western Front The British XXX Corps continues to attack northward from Nijmegen but can only make very slow progress because the advance must go along or very near to the roads and rail lines which are raised above the marshy surrounding ground and consequently exposed. It is, therefore, comparatively simple to meet these attacks. The British paratroops have been driven out of Arnhem and are now holding a perimeter west of the town but still north of the Rhine. The Polish Parachute Brigade is dropped two miles south of this position on the opposite side of the river. Although well placed they have been dropped too late.

21-24 September 1944

Philippines Twelve carriers from TF 38 attack targets on Luzon, especially near Manila and in Manila Bay on 21 and 22 September. On the 23rd there are no attacks, but on 24 September the Visayan islands are hit once again. In the operations since 31 August TF 38 has destroyed at least 1000 Japanese aircraft and sunk 150 ships of all types. The Americans have lost 72 aircraft including 18 accidents.

22 September 1944

Western Front The Polish paratroops joined later by British 43rd Division try to reach the Rhine to help the British airborne troops still cut off on the north bank. Other XXX Corps forces continue to meet heavy resistance in their advance toward Arnhem. Elst five miles north of Nijmegen is taken. In other Allied attacks Boulogne falls to the Canadian 3rd Division.

Eastern Front Troops from Govorov's Leningrad Front take Tallinn the capital of Estonia. In Rumania the Russian advance reaches Arad.

Palaus General Geiger decides to bring in a regiment of 81st Infantry Division to replace some of the Marine units which have taken heavy losses in the attacks on Mount Umurbrogol. Later a second regiment of this division is committed.

23 September 1944

pacific Ulithi atoll, just north of the Palaus, is occupied by a part of the US 81st Division after a naval reconnaissance has suggested that it is not used by the Japanese. By the end of the war it will have become one of the main bases for the American fleets.

Eastern Front In Estonia the Russian advance reaches the Baltic at Pärnu. The Russian force in Rumania pushes on beyond Arad to the Hungarian frontier.

Western Front The battles in the Arnhem area continue with no real change in fortune for either side. To the west of the British XXX Corps advance, Canadian units cross the Escaut canal in the beginning of their offensive to clear the north bank of the Scheldt.

Italy Fifth Army's attacks north of Florence clear the Futa Pass through the Apennines.

24 September 1944

Western Front XXX Corps' advance reaches the south bank of the Rhine west of Arnhem. North of the river the paratroops are still holding out despite many casualties from fierce attacks and shortages of food and ammunition. Other XXX Corps units enter Germany southwest of Nijmegen.

Palaus On Peleliu heavy naval and air bombardments herald new American attacks, but these too are thrown back.

Above: The road bridge at Arnhem in the aftermath of the epic battle fought by the 2nd Battalion, Parachute Regiment, September 1944.

25 September 1944

Western Front Troops from British Second Army take Helmond and Deurne only a few miles east of Eindhoven. It is decided to evacuate as many as possible of the surviving Arnhem paratroops across the Rhine in small boats. During the night 2400 of the 10,000 who landed get away. About 1100 have been killed and 6400 taken prisoner. Some few more are sheltered by Dutch families despite dreadful food shortages and the terrible danger of discovery.

On the Channel coast the Canadian 3rd Division attacks Calais where the German garrison still holds out.

The Allied landings in the south of France which are still continuing have now contributed 324,000 men to the AEF along with 68,000 vehicles and 490,000 tons of supplies. Much of the supplies for the southern armies along the German border are still coming through Marseilles.
Eastern Front In Estonia the Baltic port of Haapsalu falls to the Russians. In Yugoslavia the Partisan forces take Banja Luka.
Palaus The Americans make some gains in the north of Peleliu on Mount Amiangal after attacks employing tanks and flame throwers.

The fighting continues around Japanese pockets near Lake Salome on Angaur.

26 September 1944

Greece, Politics At Caserta in Italy an agreement is concluded between the exile Greek government and the various guerrilla leaders in which the guerrillas undertake to obey the orders of the government. The government delegates military authority to the British General Scobie who has been appointed by General Wilson who has supervised the talks.
Italy Eighth Army units cross the Rubicon River as their advance goes on.
Western Front The Allied attacks in Belgium and Holland continue. Turnhout, in north Belgium midway between Antwerp and Eindhoven, and Oss, west of Grave, are both taken as the advance of XXX Corps to the Rhine is consolidated. This has been a considerable achievement even though the prize of the bridge at Arnhem has not been won.

27 September 1944

Western Front The US XX Corps, Third Army, begins to attack the outer defenses of Metz. Much of Third Army's efforts will be devoted, perhaps wastefully, to this sector for some time to come.
Eastern Front German resistance on the Estonian mainland is largely over. The Soviets land on Vormsi Island west of Haapsalu. In Hungary there has been heavy fighting around Cluj for several days because of German counterattacks. These battles continue.

28 September 1944

Palaus US forces from Peleliu land on Negesbus and Kongauru, other small islands in the group. There is little fighting on either.

On Peleliu itself the full-scale US attacks come to an end but bitter fighting continues all around Mount Umurbrogol as the Americans keep trying to eliminate individual Japanese positions.

29 September 1944

Western Front In their continuing attacks at Calais the Canadian 3rd Division begins to make real progress against stubborn German defense.
Palaus The US forces tighten their hold on the remaining Japanese pockets, still further confining them to a very small area in the northwest of Angaur.
Eastern Front Troops of the Russian Eighth Army land on Muhu Island in the Baltic. The German forces withdraw from this position to the nearby Saaremaa.

30 September 1944

Western Front The attacks of First Canadian Army north and west of Antwerp continue. Calais surrenders to the Canadian 3rd Division. There are brief German attacks against the US XII Corps, Third Army, but these are held.
Palaus Admiral Fort takes over command of the American operations in this group and announces that Peleliu, Angaur, Negesbus and Kongauru have all been completely occupied. The fighting is not over yet, despite this announcement.

Below: Brigadier P H W Hicks, commander of the British 1st Airlanding (gliderborne) Brigade at Arnhem, September 1944.

Above: The American destroyer USS *Downes* fires against Japanese positions on Marcus Island, October 1944.

October 1944

Europe, Air Operations The American heavy bomber forces drop 57,000 tons, most of it by Eighth Air Force. Among the targets are Kassel, Cologne, Hamm and Munster and in the oil offensive Buer, Sterkrade, Bohlen, Homberg and Regensburg. Synthetic manufacturing plants, refineries and stores are all hit. RAF Bomber Command drops 50,000 tons on German targets including Duisburg, 10,000 tons in two raids, Essen and Cologne. There are also heavy attacks in support of the armies and in these the RAF drops 10,000 tons mainly in the Walcheren area.

Far East, Air Operations Among the targets for the USAAF heavy bomber forces are the aircraft plants at Omura, military installations in many areas of Formosa and above all a range of objectives in the Philippines.

1 October 1944

Italy General McCreery takes over command of Eighth Army from General Leese who is being sent to command Allied Land Forces, Southeast Asia. The US II Corps, Fifth Army, begins a new drive toward Bologna.

Greece British commando units land at Poros. Greek troops land at Mitilini, Lemnos and Levita.

2 October 1944

Western Front US First Army begins a new offensive against the Siegfried Line between Aachen and Geilenkirchen to the north.

Eastern Front The brave resistance of the patriot forces in Warsaw comes to an end. At least 200,000 Poles have died in the brutal fighting. Much of the central part of Warsaw has already been destroyed and much more will be razed to the ground at Hitler's order.

Palaus On Peleliu the Japanese pockets on Mount Amiangal are mopped up. Resistance continues to be very fierce around Mount Umurbrogol.

3 October 1944

Western Front The US First Army goes on with its attacks north of Aachen and succeeds in breaking through the Siegfried Line defenses in some areas.

The dikes around Walcheren Island are breached near Westkapelle by a heavy attack by RAF bombers. This causes much of the island to be flooded and is meant to hamper the German defense.

Eastern Front The Russians land on Hiiuma Island off the Estonian coast and practically overrun it.

4 October 1944

Western Front There is a German counterattack against the forces of US First Army which have broken through the Siegfried Line north of Aachen. The Americans hold their ground, however, and the attack comes to a halt.

Eastern Front Pančevo on the north bank of the Danube just east of Belgrade is taken by troops of Third Ukraine Front. The Russian forces also reach Vladimirovac and link with Partisan units near there.

Greece Allied forces land on the Peloponnese near Patras. There are other landings on the Aegean islands. Patras is occupied by the Allies on 5 October.

5 October 1944

Eastern Front Soviet forces land on Saaremaa Island in the Baltic. The German forces on the island make a fighting withdrawal toward the Syrve peninsula. The Russian offensive in the Baltic States proper is continuing. Army Group North is hard pressed on the approaches to the Estonian capital of Riga.

6 October 1944

Western Front The Canadian II Corps begins attacks to eliminate the German forces holding out south of the Scheldt between the Leopold canal and the south bank of the river around Breskens. The ground conditions are very difficult with many wet and flooded areas. The attack makes a little progress.

7 October 1944

Western Front The Canadians have managed to get some of their attacking forces across the Leopold canal into two small bridgeheads, but they are halted there by fierce German resistance. There is also heavy fighting in the US Third Army sector. The Americans gain some ground in Luxembourg and near Metz but between these areas there are effective German counterattacks.

Below: Japanese soldiers sing a patriotic song to the sea, 1944. Despite setbacks, Japanese morale remained remarkably high.

8 October 1944

Western Front All along the front the attacking Allied troops are held by fierce resistance. The heaviest fighting is in the sectors of the Canadian II Corps and the US XII and XIX Corps.

Eastern Front Finnish troops retake Kemi at the head of the Gulf of Bothnia. This is the last port in Finland that has been held by the Germans.

Greece Corinth and Samos are taken by British forces. Part of the British 9th Commando also lands at Nauplion.

9 October 1944

Western Front Troops from the Canadian 3rd Division land at Breskens on the south bank of the Scheldt opposite Flushing. The fighting in the Aachen and Metz areas continues to be quite fierce.

Marcus Island A US Task Force of cruisers and destroyers is led to shell the island by Admiral Smith.

9-20 October 1943

Allied Diplomacy Churchill and Eden visit Moscow for talks with the Russians on arrangements for the political future of eastern Europe. For some of the discussion there are representatives of the exile, London Polish government present. They achieve no real concessions from the Soviets. Similarly Stalin insists that Bulgaria and Rumania are to remain a Soviet sphere of influence entirely. Greece is to come under British sway and in Hungary and in Yugoslavia influence is to be divided. The western powers do not feel able to press Stalin any harder than this because they value his promise to join the war against Japan as well as his continuing help against a still undefeated Germany. Stalin will in fact scrupulously stick to his word about keeping out of Greece.

10 October 1944

Ryukyu Islands The main American carrier force, TF 38 begins a series of operations with attacks by one of its four groups on Onami-Oshima, two on Okinawa and the fourth against Sakashima. Many Japanese aircraft are destroyed over the islands but the Japanese fail to find the American ships with their strikes. Ten Japanese merchant vessels are sunk around Okinawa.

TF 38 is led by Admiral Mitscher and includes 11 fleet carriers, six light carriers, six battleships as well as cruisers and destroyers. Admiral Halsey commands Third Fleet of which TF 38 is part.

Western Front The attacks of US First Army around Aachen continue to press forward. The German garrison of the city is summoned to surrender.

Italy The US II Corps is still continuing its attack in the direction of Bologna, but the rugged terrain and the worsening weather help the vigorous German defense. To the east the British attacks are over the Rubicon.

Eastern Front The advance of First Baltic Front reaches the sea north of Memel. In the south Third Ukraine Front continues to attack south of Belgrade. The rail line from there to Niš is cut around Velika Plana.

11 October 1944

Philippines Two groups of TF 38 led by Admirals Cain and Davison carry out a small attack on airfields in the north of Luzon while the remainder of the force is refuelling.

Western Front Bardenburg is taken by units of XIX Corps (US First Army). Third Army take Parroy, having cleared the Forêt de Parroy nearby. In the Scheldt estuary the Canadians cut the causeway between the mainland and Beveland and Walcheren.

Italy The 91st Division of US II Corps is heavily engaged at Livergnano. Troops of Eighth Army take Lorenzo.

Eastern Front In Hungary troops from Second Ukraine Front (Malinovsky) cross the Tisza around Szeged which is taken. To the east there is fighting at Debrecen and Cluj, which falls after a long struggle.

12 October 1944

Greece Allied paratroops land at Athens airfield. The Germans evacuate the Piraeus. There are other British landings on Corfu.

Eastern Front In Hungary Oradea is taken by Second Ukraine Front while a little to the north the battle for Debrecen goes on. Subotica, just west of Szeged, is taken by combined attacks by Tito's Partisans and the Russian forces.

Palaus On Peleliu the fighting here goes on, with 1st Marines heavily engaged with the Japanese defenses on Mount Umurbrogol.

12-14 October 1944

Formosa On 12 and 13 October all four groups of TF 38 send attacks against targets on Formosa. Altogether 2350 missions are flown by the carrier planes and in return the Japanese can only organize 190. Most of the Japanese attacks are intercepted and many more of their planes are destroyed over the island and on the ground. The Americans lose 48 aircraft. The carrier *Franklin* is slightly damaged and the Australian cruiser *Canberra* seriously hit. On 14 October one group continues the attack on Formosa, losing 23 planes from 246. The cruiser *Houston* is crippled in a torpedo attack.

13 October 1944

Western Front Units of British VIII Corps begin an attack from south of Nÿmegen toward Venlo. Troops from the US 1st Division enter Aachen from the east and vicious street fighting begins.

The first V1s and V2s in what is to be a major part of the rocket campaign land on Antwerp.

Italy The British 46th Division (V Corps) takes Carpineta. Inland the fighting south of Bologna continues.

Eastern Front Troops from Second and Third Baltic Fronts break the German defense ring around Riga and reach nearly to the outskirts of the city.

Greece Advance guards of a major British and Greek force land at the Piraeus.

14 October 1944

Western Front The advance of Canadian II Corps links up with the landing force at Breskens.

Greece Athens and the Piraeus are completely liberated. There are further British landings on Corfu. The main body of the British III Corps is about to land at Piraeus.

German Command Suspected of complicity in the 20th July plot against Hitler, Rommel is visited at home by two of Hitler's staff and given the choice of a humiliating public trial or a suicide by poison with a state funeral and a guarantee of immunity from persecution for his wife and family. Rommel decides to commit suicide and it is announced in Germany that he has died of wounds.

Palaus The 81st Infantry Division replaces the Marines at the front on Peleliu where the fighting is still fierce.

The American authorities announce that the occupation of Angaur is complete although skirmishing continues on the north side of the island.

14-15 October 1944

Philippines On Luzon the carrier forces of TG 38.4 send attacks on Aparri Airfield on 14 October and against other targets north of

Below: The bulk of a Panzer Mark VI King Tiger, armed with an 8.8cm main gun. The turret is covered in *Zimmerit* anti-magnetic paste.

Above: American landing craft move toward the shore of the island of Leyte in the Philippines, 20 October 1944.

Manila on 15 October. In the operations of the whole of TF 38 between 10 and 15 October the Japanese have lost about 370 planes and the Americans less than 100.

15 October 1944

Western Front The US VI Corps (Seventh Army) begins an offensive to the west of Epinal. The battles for Aachen and in the Scheldt estuary go on.
Italy The Polish 2nd Division takes Gambettola. American and South African units make some ground near Livergnano and Grizzana.
Eastern Front The Russian Fourteenth Army takes Petsamo in the far north of Finland. In Latvia Riga falls to Second and Third Baltic Fronts.

15-16 October 1944

Hungary Budapest radio transmits a broadcast by Admiral Horthy, the prime minister and regent asking for an armistice from Russia. On 16 October it is announced on the radio that the request is void. Horthy resigns and is taken off to Germany. Ferenc Szalasy becomes regent and prime minister.

16 October 1944

Western Front While the fighting inside Aachen continues, troops from US XIX and VIII Corps link up to the east, completing the isolation of the city.

The US VI Corps meets heavy resistance on the Moselle around Bruyères. On its right the French First Army begins a new drive.
Eastern Front In Yugoslavia the Russians take Niš recently evacuated by the Germans. In this sector Russian, Bulgarian and Yugoslav forces are all working together.
Greece British forces land on Lemnos.

16-19 October 1944

Philippines The preliminary air attacks and fleet movements for the US landing on Leyte take place. On 16 October there are attacks by land-based aircraft of Thirteenth and Fifth Air Forces from Biak, Sansapor and Morotai against targets on Mindanao. The 18 escort carriers of Admiral T F Sprague's TG 77.4 also begin operations with attacks on Leyte, Cebu and Mindanao. These attacks continue on 17 October and are reinforced by the four carriers of Davison's TG 38.4 who attack Luzon. Also on 17 October minesweeping begins in Leyte Gulf. The small islands of Suluan and Dinagat at the entrance to the Gulf are occupied by minor US Ranger units. On 18 October the escort carriers concentrate their efforts on Leyte while the large carriers, now 12 in three groups, still strike at Luzon. On 19 October the escort carriers maintain their attacks on Leyte. Fifth Air Force strikes at Mindanao.

The Japanese air forces lose heavily in these operations and in their own, unsuccessful attacks on the American naval squadrons. On 19 October the remaining units are concentrated in First Air Fleet under Admiral Onishi's command on Luzon.

17 October 1944

Western Front Troops from the British Second Army take Venray in their drive toward Venlo. The US Seventh Army continues its battle around Lunéville and Bruyères.
Italy The Polish II Corps begins attacks just south of Forlí while farther inland the offensive of US II Corps toward Bologna still grinds forward but only very slowly.
France, Politics The French War Ministry and the National Council for the Resistance reach agreement on the process for the integration of the resistance forces, FFI, into the regular army. This negotiation has not been easy because of the various political loyalties of the resistance groups.

17-19 October 1944

Indian Ocean TF 63 from the British Eastern Fleet sends two carriers, one battlecruiser and lighter forces to attack the Nicobar Islands as a diversion for the US attack on Leyte. The carrier aircraft attack on 17 and 19 October and the islands are shelled on 17 and 18 October. Although considerable damage is done, as a diversion the operation fails.

18 October 1944

Greece The Greek exile government returns home. Santorini and Scarpanto are occupied by British forces and the port of Patras is opened to shipping.
Germany, Home Front From now on all able-bodied males between the ages of 16 and 60 are to be liable for conscription into the home defense force, the Volkssturm.
Western Europe General McClain replaces General Corlett in command of the US First Army.
Eastern Front Moscow announces that Red Army units from Petrov's Fourth Ukraine Front have entered Czechoslovakia. The Germans are rapidly retreating north from Greece and southern Yugoslavia, fearful of being isolated.

Below: The American carrier USS *Gambier Bay* is straddled by fire from the Japanese heavy cruiser *Chikuma*, Battle of Leyte Gulf.

19 October 1944

Western Front The attacks on Aachen are proceeding and the German resistance is being worn down. Farther south, in the Seventh Army sector, Bruyères falls to the US 36th Division. Nearby other units are preparing to assault St Dié.

Italy Troops from the 10th Indian Division are attacking over the Savio River.

20 October 1944

Philippines There are US landings on the east coast of Leyte. All the escort and fleet carriers involved in the preparatory attacks and Fifth Air Force provide air support. The landing ships and the bombardment and escort groups are from Kinkaid's Seventh Fleet and the troops landed are from Krueger's Sixth Army. Four divisions from two corps are landed. Sibert's X Corps, 1st Cavalry and 24th Infantry Divisions, land slightly to the south of Tacloban and Hodge's XXIV Corps, 96th and 7th Divisions, around Dulag. Each corps has fire support from three battleships as well as cruisers and destroyers. The cruiser *Honolulu* is badly damaged by aerial torpedo in these operations. There is little fighting on the beaches as the defending Japanese 16th Division soon retires to prepared positions inland to await reinforcements. The Americans are, therefore, able to take Tacloban Airfield but cannot link the beachheads of the two corps. By nightfall 132,000 men are ashore.

General MacArthur, who is in Supreme Command, lands a few hours after the assault troops and broadcasts to the Philippine people recalling his famous promise, 'I shall return.'

The Japanese have set in train a massive fleet operation, Sho-go, to counter the American landings. A carrier force commanded by Admiral Ozawa leaves Japan while other units are assembling at Brunei in North Borneo. (*See* 22 October for the Japanese plan and the composition of forces.)

Western Front The British I Corps, First Canadian Army, begins an offensive driving north from northeast of Antwerp. In the area opposite Patton's Third Army there is extensive flooding in the German rear after the 19th TAF have breached the dam at Dieuze.

Italy The 4th and 46th Divisions, British V Corps, enter Cesena. In the central sector, south of Bologna, the South African 6th Armored Division, serving with Fifth Army, repulses a German counterattack.

Eastern Front A combined attack by Tito's Partisans and Russian units completes the liberation of Belgrade. The Partisans also take Dubrovnik on the Adriatic coast while in Hungary Debrecen is taken by the Russians.

21 October 1944

Philippines After a successful battle with Japanese night attacks, the US forces take Dulag Airfield and Tacloban village but they are still unable to link their bridgeheads. The ships of Seventh Fleet and one group of TF 38 give gunfire and air support. Two groups of TF 38 attack targets on Panay, Cebu, Negros and Masbate.

Western Front At midday Aachen is surrendered to the American forces. Much of the city has been ruined in the battle.

Italy The British V and Canadian I Corps continue to push troops over the Savio despite the river being in spate because of recent heavy rain.

Palaus The Japanese resistance on Angaur comes to an end. The Japanese have lost 1300 dead and 45 prisoners and the Americans 265 dead and 1335 wounded.

The larger islands in the group are left with their Japanese garrisons isolated and impotent. Already US heavy bombers are operating from Angaur.

22 October 1944

Philippines On Leyte all the US forces push forward. The most notable gains are by the 7th Division on the right flank who advance toward Abuyog.

Battle of Leyte Gulf The main units of the Japanese fleet sail from Brunei. The other two squadrons which are to take part in the operation are already at sea and approaching the Philippines from the north. The plan is for Ozawa's carriers to draw off the main American forces to the northeast while the battleships and cruisers pass through the San Bernardino and Surigao Straits to get among the invasion transports and their comparatively vulnerable escorts. Ozawa has one large and one small carrier, two seaplane carriers and two hybrid carrier-battleships as well as smaller vessels. They have only 100 aircraft, with inexperienced pilots. The Center Force which is intended to pass through the San Bernardino Strait is led by Admiral Kurita from Brunei and includes five battleships, with the giant *Yamato* and *Musashi* among them, 12 cruisers, almost all heavy, and 15 destroyers. The Southern Force (Nishimura) also sails from Brunei with two battleships, a cruiser and four destroyers. They are to be joined in the Surigao Strait by Shima's Second Striking Force now approaching the Philippines from the northwest. This group is composed of three cruisers and seven destroyers. Although one group of TF 38 has left to replenish, Halsey still has 12 carriers and six battleships and Kinkaid has 18 escort carriers and the six older battleships which have been supporting the landings. Only in cruisers is there anything like an equality in numbers. In destroyers the Americans have three times the Japanese force.

Western Front The Canadians complete the capture of Breskens on the south bank of the Scheldt estuary. In southern Holland the British XII Corps is attacking toward Tilburg.

Italy Canadian troops from Eighth Army take Cervia.

Eastern Front In the far north advance units of the Russian Fourteenth Army from the Karelia Front reach the Norwegian border. In Hungary Malinovsky's forces reach Baja on the Danube south of Budapest.

France, Politics General de Gaulle's administration is recognized by the Allies as the *de jure* Provisional Government of France.

Below: Map showing the various fleet movements during the Battle of Leyte Gulf, October 1944.

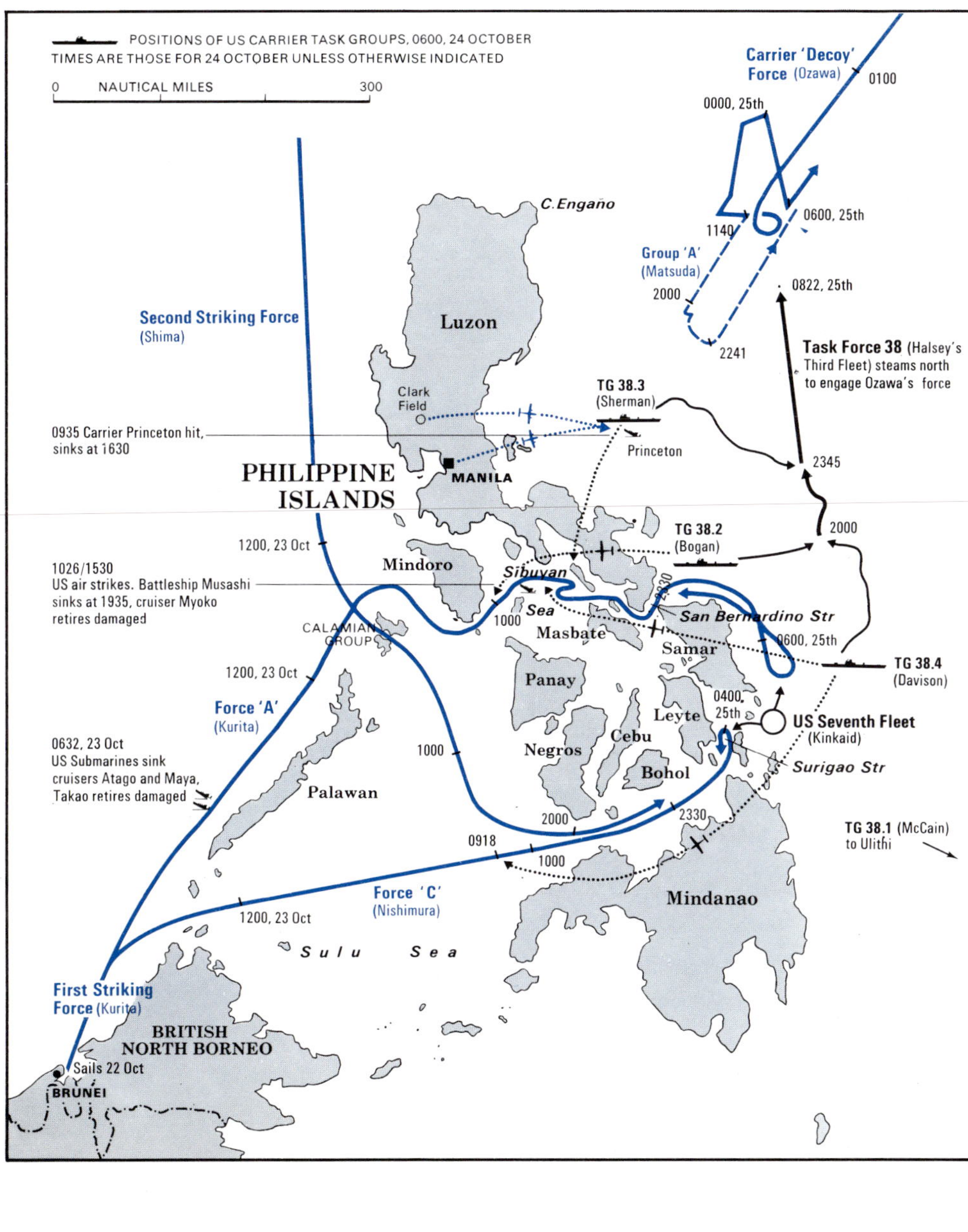

Above: American PT boats are witness to a Japanese air attack on shipping off the coast of Leyte, October 1944.

23 October 1944

Western Front There are attacks by the British 4th Armored Division at the east end of the Beveland Isthmus. The US Seventh Army is still engaged around Bruyères and St Dié.

Eastern Front In the far north the Russians complete the clearance of the Petsamo region.

Philippines The battles on Leyte continue. The 1st Cavalry Division attacks northwest from Tacloban. In the XXIV Corps sector a tank unit accompanying 7th Division takes Burauen.

Battle of Leyte Gulf Kurita's Center Force is sighted off Palawan in the early hours by two US submarines. Two heavy cruisers are sunk in the subsequent attacks and one more damaged and forced to retire. One of the submarines is lost but because of their reports the three remaining groups of TF 38 east of the Philippines prepare to attack when the Japanese squadron is in range.

24 October 1944

Western Front The Canadian 2nd Division begins to advance along the Beveland Isthmus. Inland the attacks of the British XII Corps penetrate to Hertogenbosch.

Greece British troops enter Lamia.

Philippines A small force from 1st Cavalry Division crosses the San Juanico Strait from Tacloban to land on Samar. Other units from the division advance along the south side of the Strait to Guintiguian.

Battle of Leyte Gulf Land-based aircraft from Luzon attack Sherman's TG 38.3 fatally damaging the carrier *Princeton*. Kurita's Center Force, now in the Sibuyan Sea, is found by scout planes from TG 38.2 and attacked throughout the day by strike aircraft from the three US carrier groups. The battleship *Musashi* sinks in the early afternoon after taking at least six torpedo and 10 bomb hits. One cruiser is also forced to return to base. Kurita turns away because of the weight of the attacks, convincing Halsey that his withdrawal will be permanent. During the evening Kurita again reverses course. Nishimura's Southern Force is also sighted in the approach but takes only negligible damage from the resulting air attacks. Admiral Oldendorf who has been leading one of the bombarding squadrons assembles a considerable force in the Surigao Strait to intercept Nishimura. Ozawa's carriers locate Sherman's group and send the majority of their aircraft to attack. They do not find their targets and are forced to land on Luzon. Ozawa has only 25 planes after this. Late in the day Halsey orders his carriers and modern battleships to assemble before moving to attack Ozawa, believing that Oldendorf will handle Nishimura and that Kurita has withdrawn.

25 October 1944

Philippines In the northeast of Leyte 1st Cavalry Division continues its advance. To the south, however, some US units are forced to be inactive because of lack of supplies.

Eastern Front In the far north Soviet troops enter Norway and take the port of Kirkenes. The advance in this region is supported by naval units who provide fire missions and transport for several small amphibious operations. In the south the Soviet and allied attacks have completely cleared Transylvania.

Italy The British V Corps advance reaches and in one sector crosses the River Ronco.

25-26 October 1944

Battle of Leyte Gulf Between midnight and 0430 there is a running battle as Nishimura's and then Shima's forces try to pass through Surigao Strait. Oldendorf first sends PT Boats and then destroyers to attack with torpedoes while waiting with his six battleships and eight cruisers at the north end of the Strait. The PT Boats sink one cruiser and the destroyers twice hit the battleship *Fuso*, sinking it and three destroyers. The other battleship, *Yamashiro*, is damaged and, steaming on, is sunk by Oldendorf's heavy ships. In the gun action the cruiser *Mogami* is nearly wrecked and will be abandoned later after a collision with the *Nachi*. The surviving Japanese forces withdraw.

Battle of Samar Kurita's force, now four battleships, six heavy and two light cruisers and 11 destroyers, passes the San Bernardino Strait in the early hours and in the morning off Samar finds Admiral C A F Sprague's TF 77.4.3 which consists of six escort carriers and seven destroyers. The aircraft of this group have been used to support land operations and are not, therefore, provided with the torpedoes or armor-piercing bombs needed for attacks on heavily protected ships. The American force is immediately compelled to flee with some cover from smokescreens and rain squalls. The destroyers attempt torpedo attacks and Sprague's planes are reinforced by those of a second escort-carrier group, TF 77.4.2. For two hours between 0700 and just after 0900 the Japanese ships gradually close in despite being repeatedly forced to alter course to avoid torpedo attacks. In these attacks one of the Japanese cruisers is sunk but as the range shortens the American squadron begins to take punishment. Three destroyers and one escort carrier are sunk from Sprague's force. The second carrier group is sighted and engaged also at the same time as three more of the Japanese cruisers fall to air attacks. At this stage some of the Japanese cruisers are within 10,000 yards of the escort carriers and are beginning to hit their targets regularly. Kurita, however, believes that the attacking aircraft may be from the much more powerful TF 38 and he decides that he must withdraw. This decision is probably an error since there is little doubt that Sprague's force, with all its destroyers damaged, could not have held out much longer. It is probable also that once this battle was completed, the Japanese could have reached and destroyed much of the transport fleet off Leyte. While Kurita is turning away there are Japanese Kamikaze air attacks on TF 77.4.3 in which four escort carriers are sunk (some are already damaged). At about the same time the third US escort-carrier group, not previously engaged, faces a similar attack in which three carriers are damaged. These are the first significant, premeditated suicide attacks. Kurita continues to retire toward the San Bernardino Strait and is attacked by more US aircraft on the way.

The Carrier Battle While other actions are going on, Halsey is leading the modern battleships and the main carrier force north to intercept Ozawa who has therefore exactly performed his decoy mission. In the morning the first American strikes go in. There are two waves of attacks in the morning in which two of the Japanese carriers are sunk. Before midday Halsey hears news from the south and turns south with the battleships and one carrier group. The other two carrier groups continue the pursuit, sinking the remaining carriers *Zuiho* and *Zuikaku*. Two destroyers and a cruiser are also sunk. The only major units to escape are the carrier-battleships *Ise* and *Hyuga*. Halsey's return south is too late to catch Kurita.

On 26 October American air attacks sink three more cruisers from the various retiring Japanese squadrons. Overall the Leyte Gulf battle has been a shattering defeat for the Japanese as well as, in part, a tale of missed opportunities. The only important American units sunk have been the escort carriers of which there are many more in service. After Leyte the Japanese have few of their purpose-built carriers remaining, but this loss is of less consequence than the serious damage done to their battleship and cruiser force because of the already existing shortage of trained pilots. Three battleships and 10 cruisers have been lost, others have been damaged and all the survivors have been forced to retire without coming to grips properly with the American forces. In the action in the Surigao Strait there is none of the former night-fighting expertise. Clearly, in the future, the operations of the Japanese Fleet will be even more circumscribed and their only hope now is in the new suicide attacks which have been very successful in their way so far.

26 October 1944

Philippines On Leyte the Japanese positions on Catmon Hill just north of Dulag, are fiercely attacked by the US forces. The attacks are repulsed but the defenders later retire. The Japanese garrison on the island receives reinforcements at their base at Ormoc.

Western Front The British 52nd Division lands on the south side of Beveland near Baarland against heavy German resistance. The Canadian forces are still fighting along the Beveland Isthmus. To the south in the Seventh Army sector the battle for St Dié continues.

Eastern Front The pincers of Second and Fourth Ukraine Fronts link up at Mukachevo in the southern Carpathian foothills near Uzhgorod.

27 October 1944

Philippines On Leyte the US 7th Division takes Buri Airfield.

Western Front The Canadian drive against Beveland goes on. The German positions just inland from here are also attacked. Bergen-op-Zoom is taken. Near Venlo, in the British Second Army sector, there is a sharp German counterattack.

Italy The Allied advance is gradually becoming bogged down as the winter weather sets in.

Eastern Front Fourth Ukraine Front takes Uzhgorod in northeast Hungary. In the northern sector there is a new Soviet drive in Latvia.

27-30 October 1944

Philippines On 27 October one group of three carriers commanded by Admiral Sherman attacks Japanese shipping around Luzon, sinking two destroyers. They also send attacks against Luzon Island. The battleship *California* is damaged by the Japanese. On 28 October Davison and Bogan take over and in air operations and ground-attack missions on 28 and 29 October they destroy almost 100 Japanese aircraft for the loss of just 15. The carrier *Intrepid* is slightly damaged by a Kamikaze attack. On 30 October two more carriers are badly hit by suicide attacks as the ships of TF 38 begin to withdraw to Ulithi.

28 October 1944

Western Front Tilburg is taken by troops from Dempsey's Second Army while west of Venlo there is an Allied attack against the German paratroops who advanced the previous day.

Eastern Front The USSR-Bulgaria armistice is signed. Bulgarian troops now come officially under Soviet command. Such arrangements have already been operating.

Philippines Around Dagami the US attacks only make slow progress and there are heavy losses. In the north of the island there is a fierce engagement near Carigara where the advance of 1st Cavalry Division is held up.

29 October 1944

Western Front On Beveland the 52nd Division reaches Goes. Inland Breda falls to Polish 1st Armored Division.

Philippines On Leyte Abuyag, south of Dulag, falls to the US forces. Elsewhere Catmon Hill is cleared of one or two final pockets of resistance and the advance to Dagami continues.

30 October 1944

Western Front The Canadian forces succeed in fighting their way across south Beveland to reach the Walcheren Channel.

Philippines Dagami on Leyte is taken by an attacking regiment from 7th Infantry Division.

31 October 1944

Denmark The Gestapo Headquarters in Aarhus is destroyed by the RAF in a precision attack designed to aid the resistance forces by wiping out many of the Gestapo records.

Greece The Germans evacuate Salonika. This means that the remaining island garrisons cannot be evacuated. In recent weeks many of the German Aegean forces have been taken off in small vessels despite Allied patrols.

November 1944

Europe, Air Operations The USAAF heavy forces drop 55,700 tons of bombs this month. Many German planes are destroyed in the air and on the ground especially on 2 and 27 November. The German railroad system also comes in for heavy punishment, Hamm, Coblenz and Saarbrucken being among the centers hit. The attack on oil production also continues. Leuna, Merseburg, Misburg and Gelsenkirchen are all targets for major raids. The British Bomber Command effort includes area attacks on Berlin, Hanover, Cologne, Essen and others as well as one particularly large attack on 16 November on Julich, Düren and Heinsburg which are almost obliterated in support of the American advance on the ground. The oil offensive is also part of the British operations with Homberg and Castrop-Rauxel being among the targets. Altogether Bomber Command drops 53,000 tons. The lighter forces of both allies provide copious escorts for the main bomber forces as well as performing tactical support missions and striking at V-weapon bases. Special RAF attacks breach the Dortmund-Ems and Mitteland canals which are important for the transport of industrial materials within Ger-

General Douglas MacArthur (third from right) accompanies the Philippine President Sergio Osmena (center) on his journey home.

many. This also hits at the continuing German efforts to build U-Boats because the prefabricated sections that are now being used have been transported on these canals. RAF mining operations in the Baltic are also hindering U-Boat training.
Pacific, Air Operations American Superfortress bombers hit Tokyo and Omura each three times. Although these attacks do not yet compare in scale to those being undertaken in Europe, they are still causing considerable damage. Other targets for the bombers are Singapore, Nanking, Shanghai and Bangkok.

1 November 1944

Western Front The battle for Walcheren begins. There are landings by a brigade of British 52nd Division and three commando groups. Flushing is partly taken by one landing force while the other is fighting near Westkapelle. Much of the planned air support has to be cancelled because of the bad weather. The landings receive gunfire support from the battleship *Warspite* and two monitors as well as other vessels. Many landing craft are lost on the approach, including gun-armed ships which have been intended to give close support. The German garrison of the island is the 70th Infantry Division commanded by General Daser.
Italy The fighting continues in some sectors and there is a small advance by British V Corps units near Forli.
Eastern Front Kecskemet, 50 miles southeast of Budapest is taken by the Soviets.
Greece Distribution of food begins in and around Athens. Because of the war food imports to Greece have of course been drastically reduced and much damage has been done to the indigenous agriculture. Famine-relief measures are therefore highly necessary. The Germans evacuate Florina. All of their troops except isolated pockets and island garrisons will be gone by the middle of the month.
Yugoslavia Tito and the prime minister of the exile government sign agreements on the future constitution of the country.
Philippines The Japanese forces receive 2000 reinforcements at their base at Ormoc on Leyte. General Suzuki now commands the Thirty-fifth Army which includes the original 16th Division and the newly arrived 30th and 102nd. In the American advance 7th Division takes Baybay. Offshore one US destroyer is sunk and five badly hit in suicide and conventional bombing attacks.

2 November 1944

Western Front The fighting on Walcheren continues to be most intense. Flushing falls to the attacking troops of 52nd Division. The British 7th Armored Division from Second Army renews the activity on that front with a short advance. There is also an attack on the US Third Army front and on the Channel coast in the rear of the main attacks Zeebrugge and Heyst are cleared.
Eastern Front Partisans take Zadar.
Italy Casseta south of Bologna is taken in the Allied advance.

3 November 1944

Western Front The fighting at Breskens comes to an end. Over the river at Walcheren the battle is still very fierce but the British and Canadian assault forces manage to advance a little more. The Polish 1st Division and the Canadian 4th Armored Division are also pushing forward with some success.
Italy General McCreery is appointed to command Eighth Army.

4 November 1944

British Command General Dill, head of the British Chiefs of Staff Mission in Washington, dies.
Western Front The British 1 Corps continues to advance to the Maas estuary, capturing Geertruidenberg. The fighting on Walcheren continues. British minesweepers reach up to Antwerp as the work of clearing the port and approaches continues. Even at this stage many of the supplies for the Allied armies are still being landed in Normandy, many miles to the rear of the main armies.
Eastern Front Southeast of Budapest Szolnok falls to the Soviets. They then push on to Cegled only 40 miles from the capital. In Dalmatia Sebenico is taken by the Partisans.
Burma In Fourteenth Army's advance 5th Indian Division takes Kennedy Peak.
Philippines On Leyte there are American advances west of Dagami around the feature known as 'Bloody Ridge.'

5 November 1944

Middle East Lord Moyne, British Resident Minister in the Middle East, is assassinated in Cairo by two members of the Zionist Stern Gang.
Greece British forces land at Salonika.

5-6 November 1944

Philippines Admiral McCain, who has replaced Mitscher in command of TF 38, leads three groups of the force in attacks on targets on Luzon and the waters nearby. Among the carriers involved is the new *Ticonderoga*. The Americans lose 25 planes and manage to destroy about 400 of the Japanese force. One Japanese cruiser is sunk by submarine attack and a second badly damaged and forced to beach. The US carrier *Lexington* is badly damaged by a concerted attacks of Kamikazes.

6 November 1944

Western Front On Walcheren Middleburg, the largest settlement on the island, falls to II Corps attacks.
Yugoslavia Tito's forces enter Monastir. They now control almost the whole of the Greece-Yugoslavia border.
United States, Politics In the presidential election Roosevelt is voted in for an unprecedented fourth term. He beats Dewey by winning 36 states with 53 percent of the vote. In the elections for the House of Representatives the results give 243 Democrats, 190 Republicans and 2 others.

7 November 1944

Philippines On Leyte the US 96th Division completes the capture of Bloody Ridge wiping out the last Japanese pockets. Near the north coast at Carigara the American advance is held for the moment.

8 November 1944

Western Front The last German resistance on Walcheren is overcome and the remainder of the garrison surrender. The US Third Army begins an offensive around Metz and to the south. The eventual objective is the Saar. South of Metz the Seille is crossed and Nomony taken.
Italy There are new British attacks south of Forli by the VIII Corps of Eighth Army.
Burma Fort White, just south of Tiddim, is taken by the British advance.

9 November 1944

Western Front In the continuing Third Army offensive various units cross the Moselle around Metz while farther south XII Corps maintains its advance beyond the Seille taking Chateau Salins.
Italy The town of Forli is taken by the British 4th Division.
Philippines Further Japanese reinforcements, 2000 men of 26th Division land at Ormoc on Leyte but the transporting warships are forced to retire before all the supplies are ashore.

Below: Josip Broz (Tito), leader of the communist partisans, seizes power in Yugoslavia as the Axis occupiers withdraw.

10 November 1944

Western Front Third Army's attacks go on. Good progress is made over the Moselle just south of Thionville and farther south beyond Metz the advance is even more rapid.
Philippines The fighting near Carigara is still fierce. There is a small amphibious move by units of 24th Division west along the north coast from Carigara toward Belen.

11 November 1944

Philippines A Japanese convoy is attacked off Ormoc by planes from eight carriers from TF 38. Four destroyers and one minesweeper are sunk as well as five transports with nearly 10,000 troops.

11-12 November 1944

Bonin Islands Iwo Jima is shelled during the night by a US destroyer and cruiser task force led by Admiral Smith.

12 November 1944

Norway The German battleship *Tirpitz* is attacked at anchor in Tromsofiord by 21 Lancasters carrying 12,000-pound bombs. There are several direct hits and other near misses and the *Tirpitz* capsizes.
Offshore a German coastal convoy is attacked by Royal Navy cruisers and destroyers.

13 November 1944

Western Front Third Army has now crossed the Moselle north of Thionville and built a bridge at Cattenom. South of Metz other Third Army units from XII Corps are attacking toward Morhange and Falquemont. Farther south still the Germans pull out of St Dié because of Seventh Army pressure there.
Eastern Front The Germans evacuate Skopje in southern Yugoslavia. The Bulgarian First Army is advancing in this sector.

13-14 November 1944

Philippines McCain's carriers once more attack shipping and targets on Luzon especially near Manila. One cruiser and four destroyers are sunk by the carrier planes.

14 November 1944

Western Front The British XII Corps begins attacks to eliminate the German holdings west of the Maas around Nederweert near Venlo. In the far south of the front the French First Army starts its Operation Independence to free Belfort.
Norway The Norwegian government in exile announces that Norwegian troops are operating alongside the Soviets in the far north.

15 November 1944

Western Front The attacks of Third Army around Metz press forward once more. South of the city the rail line to Saarebourg is cut and from here into the Seventh Army sector north of St Dié ground is gained all along the front. The French drive toward Belfort continues.
Eastern Front Jasberény, 30 miles east of Budapest, is taken by the Russians.
Mapia Island This small island 160 miles north of the west end of New Guinea is occupied by a regiment of the US 31st Division. The small Japanese garrison is overcome with little difficulty. The transport and covering squadron is made up of British and American ships and is commanded by Admiral Lord Ashbourne.

Above: A Japanese supply train comes under air attack from British bombers in Burma. Air superiority was crucial to British victory.

16 November 1944

Western Front There are heavy Allied air attacks in preparation for offensives by US Ninth and First Armies. Ninth Army attacks toward Geilenkirchen and Eschweiler with the intention of reaching the Rür. On their right First Army is moving toward Düren east of Aachen.

16-20 November 1944

Belgium, Politics There are political quarrels between the Belgian government and representatives of the resistance movement. On 16 November three ministers resign because of these problems. On the 17th there are meetings between Allied representatives and the ministers in which it is agreed to try and have the resistance surrender their arms. On the 18th the resistance agree to this and it is announced on the 20th.

17 November 1944

Western Front On the right of the Allied front the French offensive in the Belfort area reaches Montbéliard. To the north both Third and Seventh Armies advance following German withdrawals. Around Aachen First and Ninth Armies also push forward.
China Sea The Japanese fleet carrier *Junyo* is sunk by an American submarine.

18 November 1944

Western Front The Third Army advance reaches close to the German border. Bouzonville on the River Nied is taken. Metz is entered from both north and south. Around Aachen the British XXX Corps joins the attacks of First and Ninth Armies. Jülich and Düren are entered.
Eastern Front The Eighth Army from Govorov's Leningrad Front renews its attacks on Saaremaa Island in the north of the Gulf of Riga.

19 November 1944

Western Front There are Allied attacks and advances all along the front. The British XII and VII Corps make ground near Venlo. In the Ninth Army sector a counterattack is beaten off and Geilenkirchen occupied. To the south Third Army completes the isolation of Metz. Farther south still the French attacks reach the outskirts of Belfort while on their right flank the advance has penetrated to the Swiss border north of Basle.
Philippines McCain's carriers carry out further attacks on Luzon and shipping targets in Manila Bay. They sink one cruiser and three other vessels.

20 November 1944

Western Front The fighting east of Aachen continues with units of US XIX Corps attacking near Jülich. In the Third Army sector the battle in Metz continues as other formations of the Army advance east taking Dieuze. To the south the French are still fighting in Belfort and advance patrols, passing the city on the right, reach Mulhouse and the Rhine.
Indian Ocean Two carriers from the British Eastern Fleet send two waves of attacks against airfields at Sabang and oil installations at Belawan Deli on Sumatra.
Greece The British General Scobie is placed in charge of measures for disbanding the guerrilla armies in Greece.

21 November 1944

Western Front In Holland Second Army attacks near Venlo. The efforts of US First and Ninth Armies can make little ground against the

Above: German civilians join the *Volkssturm* (Home Guard), 1944. Most are carrying *Panzerfaust* anti-tank weapons.

German resistance west of the Rür. The Third Army is still moving forward near Saarebourg.
Philippines On Leyte the US advance by 32nd Division from the north coast is strongly held in the Ormoc Valley. The 7th Division also begins to try to move toward Ormoc, attacking north from around Baybay.
China Sea The US submarine *Sealion* sinks the Japanese battleship *Kongo* as well as a destroyer in waters to the northeast of Formosa.
Eastern Front Tirana is occupied by Albanian resistance fighters. The Germans have pulled out on 20 November. Durazzo is also taken.

22 November 1944

Western Front In the southern sector of the front the French forces take Mulhouse after beating off a German counterattack in that area. The US Seventh Army, in line on the left flank of the French, advances at several points along its front. St Dié is taken and other units move toward Saverne. Farther north Third Army completes the capture of Metz.

23 November 1944

Western Front At the north end of the front the German Fifteenth Army pulls back a little deeper into Holland. By contrast the German Seventh Army begins a series of sharp attacks against US Ninth Army. In the advance of US Seventh Army French troops with the army reach Strasbourg.
Eastern Front In northern Hungary the Russians take Tokay. In the far north they are able to announce that, with Finnish help as the recent treaty has provided they have cleared Finnish Lapland of German troops.

24 November 1944

Western Front Patton's troops take crossings over the Saar about 25 miles north of Saarbrucken. Farther south the French 2nd Division completes the capture of Strasbourg.
Eastern Front The Russians expell the last German troops from Saaremo Island in the Gulf of Riga. The remaining heavy units of the German Navy, *Lützow*, *Admiral Scheer* and *Prinz Eugen*, have covered the evacuation of the 5000 troops that were on the island and given gunfire support to the land battle nearby in the past few days.

25 November 1944

Philippines The US advance is being held in most sectors of Leyte. One US paratroop unit is advancing in difficult terrain west of Burauen.

TG 38.2 and TG 38.3 again attack Luzon and the waters nearby. Seven American carriers are involved and they sink the cruisers *Kumano* and *Yasoshima*. In return Kamikaze attacks damage four of the carriers.
Western Front To the southeast of Aachen US forces from First Army advance beyond Hurtgen.

26 November 1944

Eastern Front Russian troops take Michaloyce in eastern Slovakia.
Philippines The Japanese start a sequence of fierce night attacks in several parts of Leyte, but especially west of Burauen.

27 November 1944

Philippines The battleship *Colorado* and two light cruisers are damaged in suicide attacks in Leyte Gulf. On Leyte the Japanese attacks around Burauen continue and are reinforced by a small parachute unit. They come close to taking the Burauen airfield.
United States, Politics Cordell Hull resigns his post as Secretary of State. Edward Stettinius is appointed his successor.

28 November 1944

Western Front The first Allied convoy reaches Antwerp. During the time the German troops and mines have been being cleared from the estuary much work has been done to put the quays and dock machinery in good order. There is still a problem, however,with transport for the stores once they have arrived. Nevertheless the opening of the port does totally alter the supply position of most of the Allied armies. There will be no more real shortages like those which limited the advance in the late summer. The German rocket attacks on the port do little to limit its capacity.
Philippines On Leyte there are more Japanese night attacks in all sectors. The heaviest pressure is at Kilay Ridge in the north and around Buri and Burauen.
Eastern Front The Soviet force on the Danube is just north of the confluence of the Drava. Mohacs is quickly taken on the west bank and the advance reaches Pécs.

29 November 1944

Philippines The Japanese attacks continue on Kilay Ridge on Leyte but in fact they lose ground to later US counterattacks.

The battleship *Maryland* and two destroyers are seriously hit in Kamikaze attacks in Leyte Gulf.
Pacific The US submarine *Archerfish* sinks the carrier *Shinano* in waters off Honshu. *Shinano* was originally designed as a sister vessel of the giant battleships *Yamato* and *Musashi*.
Western Front There is considerable activity in the US First, Third and Ninth Army sectors but little change in the position of the troops.
Eastern Front In Albania the last German forces leave Scutari. Lohr's Army Group E are now attempting to form a line along the Drina and then the Drava Rivers.

30 November 1944

Western Front There is a small advance in the Second Army sector west of the Maas near Venlo. North and south of Aachen Ninth and First US Armies continue their attack. In the Third Army sector units on the right of the advance have reached the Saar but on the left they are still some miles away from the river.
Eastern Front The Second Ukraine Front has begun a new offensive northwest of Debrecen in north Hungary.

December 1944

Europe, Air Operations The US heavy-bomber forces concentrate on two target systems

Below: A Japanese naval pilot prepares for a *kamikaze* (suicide) mission, in a desperate attempt to disable an American ship.

this month. Communications centers are attacked including Coblenz and Bingen. The effort on 11 December is particularly great with the targets being Giessen, Hanau and Frankfurt. The other range of targets is in the oil industry. Plants in Silesia and near Vienna are hit as are Harburg and Meiderich. On 24 December Eighth Air Force sends 2000 bombers on missions. The Allied Air Forces based in Italy contribute to these attacks as well as hitting targets on their own front and harrying the German retreat in Yugoslavia with bombing and arms drops to resistance forces. RAF Bomber Command drops 48,700 tons during the month. One third of the operations are made during the days and the targets are throughout Germany. Transport and oil systems are again favored targets. Hagen, Essen, Trier, Leuna and Poolitz are all hit.

Light and heavy forces of both British and American Air Forces also attack transport centers and troop concentrations during the German Ardennes attacks when weather permits. Altogether 35,500 tons are dropped in these operations.

Pacific, Air Operations US Superfortress bombers continue and extend their strategic bombing campaign from their bases in China and Saipan. Tokyo is attacked on four occasions during the month, Nagoya three times and Omura, Yokohama and Yokosuka once. Outside Japan targets include Mukden, Shanghai and Nanking.

Pacific, Naval War The American submarine fleet and mining campaign has now reduced the carrying capacity of the Japanese merchant fleet. The carrying capacity is now less than half the total possible at the beginning of the war. Food and oil imports from the East Indies are now down to a trickle.

1 December 1944

Western Front In the Ninth Army area the advance northeast of Aachen reaches Linnich which is taken by 102nd Division. The attacks by Third and Seventh Armies farther south are still proceeding but the advance here is, as in the north, very slow indeed.

Eastern Front In the attacks south of Budapest most of the Russian forces are held except around Pécs where Fifty-seventh Army is operating. Northeast of Budapest Fourth Ukraine Front attack the positions of First Panzer Army along the Ondava River.

2 December 1944

Western Front Several Divisions of Patton's Third Army seize new crossings over the Saar. Saarlautern is entered by patrols of one unit.

Eastern Front In northern Hungary troops from Malinovsky's armies attack the well-defended German positions around Miskolc.

3 December 1944

Greece Police open fire on demonstrations in Athens sponsored by the communist EAM party and the situation degenerates into open fighting. On 4 December martial law is declared as the fighting continues. During 5 December British tanks are used in the fighting and British warships shell EAM positions near Piraeus. The fighting goes on for most of the month but the former guerrillas are no match for the British troops in an open battle. Stalin keeps his agreement with Churchill and does not send any help to the communists.

Italy Eighth Army begins a new offensive on a three corps frontage with the right flank of the advance resting on the Adriatic coast. British, Polish and Canadian units are all involved.

Western Front The River Rür is reached by the advance of XIII Corps from Ninth Army.

Eastern Front Miskolc is taken by troops from Second Ukraine Front.

Britain, Home Front The volunteer defense force, the Home Guard, is 'stood down' from service since it is not now needed to watch for a German invasion.

4 December 1944

Western Front The British Second Army clears out the last German pocket west of the Maas. To the right of the British forces the US Ninth Army ends its offensive toward the Rür. In the Third Army area units of XX Corps rush troops toward Saarlautern where a bridge over the river has been discovered intact.

5 December 1944

Eastern Front The Russians take Vukovar on the Danube and to the northwest they also capture Szigetvar.

Italy Troops from I Canadian Corps take Ravenna as Eighth Army's attacks go on.

6 December 1944

Western Front In the Third Army sector a division of XX Corps uses assault boats to cross the Saar near Patchen.

7 December 1944

Eastern Front The Russian attacks in southern Hungary reach Lake Balatan. To the south Baros on the Drava is taken.

Rumania, Politics A new government takes office. Led by General Badescu they are pledged to implement fully the terms of the armistice, to help the Allies and to purge all pro-Nazis.

Philippines Early in the day the US 77th Division (General Bruce) land about a mile south of Ormoc on Leyte. The Japanese resistance is not particularly fierce. The escorting naval forces include 12 destroyers, one of which is sunk by a suicide attack. The US 7th Division which is already attacking north toward Ormoc along the coast, makes good progress in its advance.

8 December 1944

Volcano Islands Three American heavy cruisers and their destroyer escorts bombard Iwo Jima. Admiral Smith commands. The operation is repeated twice more during December.

Eastern Front In Hungary the Russian troops of Third Ukraine Front attack near Szekesfehervar only 40 miles southwest of Budapest, the capital.

Philippines The newly landed 77th Division makes an important advance to within a mile of Ormoc. In the center of Leyte part of the Japanese 26th Division attacks near Buri but is beaten off.

Italy Eighth Army troops cross the Lamone River south of Faenza.

9 December 1944

Western Front The northern half of the front is largely at rest. In the Third Army sector there is fighting around the various bridgeheads over the Saar. To the south of these battles both Seventh Army and French First Army are still pushing forward.

Eastern Front The Second Ukraine Front reaches the Danube north of Budapest at Vac. On the right of these attacks Balassagyarmat on the Slovak border is taken. The attacks southwest of Budapest also make progress.

Philippines The Japanese succeed in landing a small group of reinforcements at Palompon on the west coast of Leyte northwest of Ormoc. South of Ormoc the US 77th Division increases the extent of its holdings.

Britain, Home Front The black-out regulations are relaxed. There is as yet no question of restoring street lights but the rules for houses and other premises are not now so strict.

10 December 1944

Philippines Ormoc is taken by the US 77th Division. Ormoc has been the major Japanese base on the island of Leyte. The main Japanese forces are now northwest of Ormoc, especially at and near Palompon.

Western Front The VII Corps from First

Below: American bombs, dropped by B-25 Mitchell bombers, crash into a Japanese destroyer at Ormoc Bay, late 1944.

Army starts a powerful attack west of Aachen in an attempt to take Düren. Third Army's battles on the Saar continue.

Diplomatic Affairs Following the recent visit of General de Gaulle, Bidault, the Foreign Minister and General Juin to Moscow a treaty of alliance is signed by French and Soviet representatives.

12 December 1944

Greece After taking heavy setbacks in the recent fighting the Greek communists ask for terms for a cease fire. It is demanded that the communists surrender their arms. On 16 December General Scobie publishes the text of the Caserta agreement in which the guerrillas had promised to work with the established government (then in exile). (*See* 26 September 1944.) On 20 December Scobie warns civilians to stay away from areas occupied by the ELAS troops because he may find it necessary to bomb them. On 25 December, as the fighting begins to die down with the British very much in control, Churchill and Eden arrive for talks with the Greek leaders.

Burma A British offensive begins in the Arakan. The attacking unit is XV Corps. The objective is Akyab. Three divisions are allocated to make the attack.

Western Europe First Army takes Düren.

13 December 1944

Sulu Sea The American heavy cruiser *Nashville* and a destroyer, part of the force on the way to make landings on Mindoro, are both heavily damaged in Kamikaze attacks. *Nashville* is the flagship of the force and there are many casualties among the senior officers.

Italy In the Fifth Army sector units of British XIII Corps make strong attacks on Tossignano.

14 December 1944

Italy Eighth Army is attacking to widen the bridgehead already established over the Lamone.

14-16 December 1944

Philippines To cover the landings on Mindoro there are intensive attacks on airfields throughout Luzon by planes of TF 38. Admiral McCain now commands this force and it includes 13 carriers and eight battleships as well as the usual complement of cruisers and destroyers. Of the 1670 missions flown all but 250 are by fighters. The Americans lose 65 planes, the Japanese 170.

15 December 1944

Philippines There are US landings at San Augustin on Mindoro. There is almost no resistance and the forces advance inland up to eight miles. General Dunckel is in command and his troops include part of the 24th Division and a parachute regiment. The naval cover includes three battleships and six escort carriers. One of the carriers and two destroyers are hit by Kamikazes.

16 December 1944

Western Front The Germans begin a major offensive in the Ardennes. The attack begins with a short, sharp artillery barrage along the chosen front between Monschau and Trier. Almost complete surprise is achieved. Allied intelligence has received some indications of the attack despite elaborate security on the German side but these signs have not been interpreted properly. Partly because of the enforced shortening of their front the Germans have been able to assemble a considerable reserve of armored divisions. They have chosen to strike here with the immediate aim of retaking Ant-

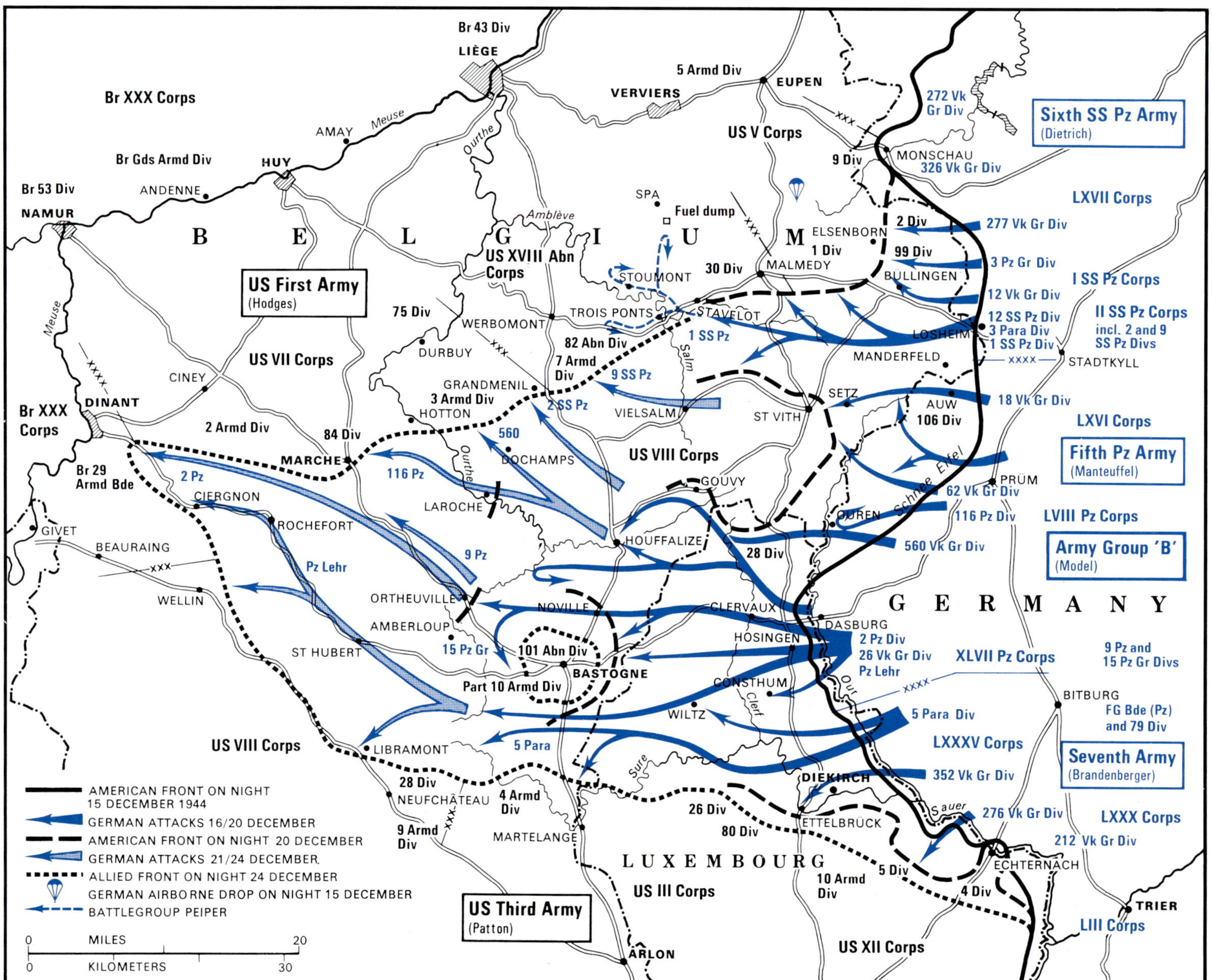

Below: The Battle of the Bulge, Hitler's last desperate offensive in the west, December 1944.

Above: American carriers and battleships of Task Force 38 enter Ulithi anchorage after strikes against Japanese positions in the Philippines.

werp and splitting the British and American armies in two. In the longer term Hitler hopes to discourage and divide the British and Americans politically so that forces can be switched to the Eastern Front, perhaps even with help from anticommunist leaders who may emerge in Britain and America. Altogether the Germans have assembled 24 divisions, including 10 armored. These forces are distributed largely between Dietrich's Sixth SS Panzer Army and Manteuffel's Fifth Panzer Army. On the flanks of the attack are Fifteenth and Seventh Armies. All these forces are part of Model's Army Group B. Rundstedt has been brought back to have overall charge of the operation. To oppose the German forces are about six American divisions from V and VIII Corps consisting partly of inexperienced troops and partly of resting veterans. The terrain here in the same Ardennes area as was chosen for the start of the attack in 1940, is fairly rugged with many defiles and much heavily wooded country. Most of whatever movement is attempted must take place on the few major roads so, as will emerge, it is vital to seize the various junctions. The Germans hope to spread confusion in the American rear areas by infiltrating small groups of specially trained English-speaking troops with captured uniforms and equipment to perform sabotage and intelligence missions. This move is very successful at least in causing an atmosphere of suspicion and uncertainty. Many road-blocks and checkpoints are set in the American rear areas and they do something to hinder the movement of reserves.

The Germans are relying on bad weather to keep the Allied air forces grounded and for the moment this hope is fulfilled.

In the first day of the attack the Germans succeed in disrupting the Allied front and make good ground in many sectors.

In other areas US Third Army units are still attacking along the Saar but these operations are suspended when news of the Ardennes battle is received. The Ardennes battle is often popularly styled the Battle of the Bulge.

Italy Faenza is taken by units of the British V Corps.

Philippines There is considerable air activity with the Japanese attacking American shipping and the Americans replying with strikes against the Japanese air bases. On Mindoro the landing force does not attempt an advance but confines itself to construction work on an airstrip and to consolidating its perimeter.

Below: A Panzer Mark VI King Tiger, with paratroops hitching a ride, moves through the snow-covered forests of the Ardennes.

17 December 1944

Western Front The US 82nd and 101st Airborne Divisions are sent to reinforce the Allied troops in the Ardennes although these paratroops are officially still resting after the Arnhem operation. Various other armored and infantry units from several of the Allied armies are being rushed to the threatened sectors.

Indian Ocean The oil and harbor installations at Belawan-Deli in northern Sumatra are attacked by planes from the British carriers *Indomitable* and *Illustrious*. Admiral Vian is in command.

Italy Near Faenza 10th Indian Division manages to capture crossings over the Senio River.

Philippines On Mindoro the US forces take San Jose Airfield. There are advances by units of both X and XXIV Corps on Leyte.

18 December 1944

Philippine Sea TF 38, retiring to refuel and replenish after the recent attacks on Luzon, is caught in a violent typhoon along with the units

Above: Supplies are air-dropped to US forces besieged in Bastogne, late December 1944. Once again, Allied air superiority was vital.

of the fleet train. Three destroyers are sunk and the damaged ships include three fleet carriers, four escort carriers and 11 destroyers.

19 December 1944

Western Front At a meeting of the senior Allied commanders Eisenhower decides to appoint a single leader for each for the areas north and south of the Bulge which is being created. Montgomery is appointed for the northern units and Bradley for the southern. This arrangement will not be made public until 5 January 1945.

On the ground the Germans have reached the Stavelot and Houffalize areas but between these advances some of the US forces are holding their ground around Gouvy and St Vith. Houffalize itself will be defended a little longer by 82nd Airborne Division while 10 miles to the south 101st Airborne is among the American forces which are preparing to hold the important road junction at Bastogne.

Philippines The Japanese decide that they can do no more to send reinforcements or supplies to Thirty-fifth Army on Leyte. The fighting continues north of Ormoc and throughout the northwest of the island.

20 December 1944

Western Front On the northern flank of their Ardennes offensive the German forces attack northward from around Stavelot but, although they quickly make some gains, they are soon forced to retire. The units on the right of these in the German drive have not made much ground toward their objectives around Malmedy and to the north. The two vital junctions at St Vith and Bastogne are still being held despite deeper penetrations all around these towns. If the Germans are to develop their offensive much farther they must do so quickly before the weather clears and before the Allied reserves arrive in force. To maintain the momentum of the attack they must take the road junctions so they can easily speed their main forces and their supports forward.

21 December 1944

Philippines The advances of the US X Corps and XXIV Corps meet in the center of the Ormoc Valley on Leyte. There are still various groups of Japanese holding isolated positions in this area.

Western Front Bastogne is now almost completely surrounded. The 82nd Airborne Division has been driven out of Houffalize in the continuing German advance between and behind Bastogne and St Vith. On the north flank of the advance American forces retake Stavelot and from here to Monschau the German LXVII Corps has been brought to a halt.

22 December 1944

Western Front The American forces in Bastogne contemptuously reject a German demand that they surrender. It is said that General McAuliffe's reply to the demand consists of a single word 'Nuts.' The weather is beginning to change and all the German generals involved in the attack, Rundstedt, Model and Guderian the Army Chief of Staff, recommend that the offensive be brought to an end because of the delays that have been imposed by the Allied resistance and the imminent arrival of the mass of the Allied reserves. To the generals it is clear that there is no question of reaching the grand objective of Antwerp. Although St Vith is taken late in the day this does not come close to curing the problems of delay that have been created.

Philippines On Leyte the main Japanese forces are now near Palompon, and this will be the main American objective for the next few days.

23 December 1945

Western Front Although Bastogne still holds out against repeated German attacks they have been able to send forces past the town to advance to the west and northwest. These attacks are now beyond Rochefort and Laroche but have neither the necessary strength nor the logistical backing because of the blocks behind them and the growing effectiveness of the Allied air interdiction.

24 December 1944

Western Front The German offensive in the Ardennes is brought to a halt by the end of the day. The longest advance is by 2nd Panzer Division to just outside Dinant. They form the point of the German wedge and on their flanks they have 116th Panzer to the north near Hotten and to the south Panzer *Lehr* Division west of St Hubert. Opposing the German units, now much weakened when compared with 16 December, are the main forces of US First and Third Armies, the British XXX Corps and, of course, the Bastogne defenders.
Eastern Front The Russians are now fighting in the outskirts of Budapest on the east side while other units advancing beyond the city have almost cut it off. The corridor from the city to the west is only about 25 miles wide.
United States, Home Front All beef products are rationed once more. New quotas are introduced for most other commodities also.

25 December 1944

Western Front The Allies begin their counteroffensive against the German forces in the Ardennes. In this advance the attack of US 4th Armored Division from around Mortelange is to be designed to relieve Bastogne.
Philippines Part of the US 77th Division is moved by sea from Ormoc to San Juan on the west coast of Leyte north of Palompon. There is no opposition to the landing.

26 December 1944

Western Front Bastogne is relieved by units of 4th Armored Division. Elsewhere in the Ardennes sector the Allied attacks have not yet really begun to have real effect.
Philippines A Japanese naval force which has come from Indochina bombards the American beachhead on Mindoro. There are two cruisers and six destroyers in the attack. One destroyer is sunk by an American PT-Boat. This is the last sortie by a Japanese naval force in the Philippines area.
Eastern Front Budapest is now almost completely encircled by Tolbukhin's Third Ukraine Front.

Above: American soldiers dig in among the forests of the Ardennes, December 1944. The enemy is close by, as the dead body implies.

Below: Brigadier General Anthony McAuliffe, temporary commander of the US 101st Airborne Division in Bastogne, December 1944.

27 December 1944

Western Front The German 2nd Panzer Division is driven out of Celles by the attacks of British XXX Corps. This division has pushed so far forward and is so isolated that it is bound to suffer severely in the Allied counterstroke.

29 December 1944

Western Front There is something of a lull in the Ardennes battle. The Allies are busy preparing to extend their counterattacks.
Eastern Front There is fighting in Budapest. The Russians attempt to start negotiations with the garrison but there is a misunderstanding and some of the Russian emissaries are killed in the course of their mission.
Greece It is announced that a regency is to be established and that Prime Minister Papandreou will resign when a regent has been chosen. On 31 December Archbishop Damaskinos of Athens is sworn in and Papendreou resigns.

30 December 1944

Western Front The VIII Corps from Patton's Third Army begins a new attack northward from a line between Bastogne and St Hubert. Houffalize is the objective.
Eastern Front The fighting in and around Budapest continues. Russian units from both Second and Third Ukraine Fronts are involved.

31 December 1944

Philippines There are vicious Japanese counterattacks in several parts of the northwest of Leyte, but the American forces beat them off with heavy losses. Elsewhere on the island the Japanese resistance is all but over. In the battle for Leyte Japanese casualties have been around 70,000, almost all killed. The American casualties have been 15,000 dead and wounded. The US Sixth Army which has fought the battle is now being prepared to move on Luzon and the Eighth Army is taking its place on Leyte.
Poland, Politics The Lublin-based Committee of National Liberation assumes the title of Provisional Government. The London exile government protests unavailingly.
World Affairs Hungary declares war on Germany.
Western Front The British XXX Corps takes Rochefort at the western end of the Ardennes salient.

1945

January 1945

Europe, Air Operations Both the British and American heavy-bomber forces continue their operations. The Eighth Air Force drops 39,000 tons and Fifteenth Air Force 6,000 tons in various attacks. As well as tactical support missions, especially early in the month against targets in the Ardennes, there are mostly attacks on oil and communications targets. Berlin, Cologne and Hamm are all hit. The British heavy-bomber force attacks oil targets at Bochum and Leuna, some rail centers and general area targets at Hanau, Munich and Stuttgart. Bomber Command drops 36,000 tons in all operations. The Ninth Air Force, Second Tactical Air Force and RAF Fighter Command all send many attacks against targets in the Ardennes and against V-weapon sites. A further 11,500 tons is dropped in these operations.
Far East, Air Operations US heavy bomber forces continue to attack targets in Japan. Nagoya is bombed three times, and Omura and Tokyo are also hit. In China there are attacks on Japanese communications and airfields. Singapore and Saigon are also hit by heavy bombers. There are, of course, many attacks against Japanese-held islands and shipping.

1 January 1945

Europe, Air Operations The Luftwaffe makes a series of heavy attacks on Allied airfields in Belgium, Holland and northern France. They have assembled around 800 planes of all types for this effort by scraping together every available machine and pilot. Many of the pilots have had so little training they they must fly in special formations with an experienced pilot in the lead providing the navigation for the whole force. The Allies are largely taken by surprise and lose many aircraft on the ground. Among the German losses for the day are a considerable number of planes shot down by 'friendly' antiaircraft fire. Although the Allied losses of 300 planes are 100 greater than the German, the Luftwaffe comes off relatively worse. The Allied planes can be replaced immediately, but for the Germans neither the planes nor the pilots can be.
Western Front The land battle in the Ardennes continues with the Allied counter-attacks gathering force. The most notable gains are in the US VIII Corps sector. Farther south in Alsace the German Army Group G begins an offensive in the Sarreguemines area. The US Seventh Army retires before this attack, on orders from Eisenhower.

2 January 1945

Western Front In the Ardennes Third Army troops take Bonnerue, Hubertmont and Remagne. Hitler turns down requests from Model and Manteuffel for withdrawals from the area west of Houffalize. In Alsace the German pressure and the Seventh Army withdrawals continue.
Eastern Front There are German counter-attacks northwest of Budapest which aim to relieve the siege of the city. The main forces involved in this offensive are two SS Panzer Divisions which have been withdrawn from the reserve in the more important Warsaw sector without the consent or knowledge of Guderian, the Army Chief of Staff.
Allied Command Admiral Ramsay, Naval Commander in Chief of Allied forces in Europe, is killed in an air accident while on his way to meet Montgomery.

2-8 January 1945

Philippines From 2nd to 5th January the various transport, bombardment and escort carrier groups for the US landings on Luzon leave their bases on Leyte. There are six battleships, 16 escort carriers, 10 cruisers and many destroyers, landing craft and transports of all kinds. Several of the cruisers and destroyers are Australian. From 3 January the American movements are detected by the Japanese and attacks by midget submarines, Kamikaze planes and small surface ships begin. On 4 January the escort carrier *Ommaney Bay* is badly damaged by a Kamikaze and has to be abandoned. On the 5th two escort carriers, two cruisers and several smaller ships are damaged. The cruiser *Boise*, with General MacArthur aboard, has a narrow escape from a torpedo attack. One Japanese destroyer is sunk by US planes. On 6 January Admiral Oldendorf's battleship groups enter Lingayen Gulf to begin the preliminary bombardment and come under heavy attack. One minesweeper is sunk and two battleships, four cruisers and six destroyers are damaged. There are more attacks on the 7th and 8th, but these are less effective, hitting two escort carriers and the cruiser *Australia* for the second time. In the night of 7/8 January there is the last surface engagement of the Pacific campaign in which a single attacking Japanese destroyer is sunk by four US ships.

Previous page: Cheering US Marines pose for the newsmen, Iwo Jima, 23 February 1945. *Below:* Battle-weary GIs on the streets of Bastogne after the siege has been lifted.

3 January 1945

Western Front In the Ardennes the fighting continues. There are desperate German attacks on the narrow corridor leading to Bastogne which manage to upset the timetable of the US attacks a little but achieve nothing else. Forces from US Third and now also First Armies are attacking toward Houffalize from the south and north.

In Alsace the German attacks and the American retreat continue. The US VI Corps is being pressed particularly hard in the area around Bitche. Farther south there is also fighting near Strasbourg.
Burma There are British landings at the northwest tip of Akyab Island in the Arakan area. A Commando and an Indian brigade are involved, but there is little resistance from the Japanese. Inland troops of XXXIII Corps take Yeu in their advance to the Irrawaddy.

3-4 January 1945

Formosa and Ryukyus There are attacks by three of the fleet carrier groups of the US Third Fleet against targets throughout Formosa and the southern Ryukyu Islands and the Pescadores. Bad weather prevents the operations from being fully effective, but about 100 Japanese planes are destroyed for the loss of just over 20.

4 January 1945

Western Front The fighting in the Ardennes continues. There are attacks by US VIII and III Corps and by the British XXX Corps. Some of the units of Dietrich's Sixth SS Panzer Army are withdrawn and sent to the Eastern Front. In Alsace the German attacks in the Bitche area continue.
Indian Ocean Three British carriers of Admiral Vian's TF63 attack the oil refineries at Pankalan Brandan on Sumatra.
Burma Akyab Island is completely occupied by the British forces.

5 January 1945

Western Front In the Ardennes there is less activity on the Third Army sector, but First Army maintains its attacks. There are German attacks just north of Strasbourg.

Italy There are some limited operations by Eighth Army to complete the Allied hold on the south bank of the Senio. Apart from these the wet weather and a lack of reinforcements and extra supplies means that the Allied armies are unable to go over to the offensive on any large scale. There will be some comparatively minor efforts in February and March but no big attack until April.

8 January 1945

Western Front The battles north and south of Strasbourg continue. The US Seventh Army is under considerable pressure near Rimling and Gambsheim.

9 January 1945

Philippines Operation Mike 1, the US landings on Luzon at Lingayen Gulf, is begun. General Swift's I Corps lands from the ships of TF 78 around San Fabian. The assault units are from 43rd and 6th Infantry Divisions. General Griswold's XIV Corps lands from TF 79 near

Left: The reality of the Ardennes in winter: men of the US 82nd Airborne Division follow a snow-covered Sherman tank along a forest track.
Below: The liberation of Luzon, the main island of the Philippines, 1945.

Bonins Admiral Smith leads a force of cruisers and destroyers to shell Iwo Jima, Haha Jima and Chichi Jima. There is a simultaneous attack by Superfortress bombers.
Burma Shwebo is taken by the British 2nd Division of Stopford's XXXIII Corps, as the advance of the corps to the Irrawaddy continues.
Kuriles Admiral McCrea leads three cruisers and nine destroyers to bombard Suribachi Wan.
Diplomatic Affairs The Soviets recognize the Lublin Committee as the Provisional Government of Poland. The USA and Britain announce that they continue to recognize the exile government in London.
Greece The fighting between the British and the Greek Communists come to an end in the Athens area. General Alexander and British political representatives arrive in Athens for talks with the Communist leaders and the Greek government.

6 January 1945

Western Front There are various local actions all along the Ardennes front. Rundstedt again requests that the German forces be allowed to withdraw because of the Allied pressure. Hitler again orders no retreat.
Allied Planning Churchill asks Stalin if the Soviet forces can go over to the offensive in Poland to take some of the pressure off the Allied armies in the Bulge. Stalin agrees to bring forward the plans for the next Red Army offensive.

6-7 January 1945

Philippines The American fleet carrier groups of TF 38 join in the operations by the escort carrier and land-based forces against the Kamikaze airfields on Luzon.

7 January 1945

Western Front The attacks of VIII Corps of First Army along the line of the Ourthe west of Houffalize make good progress around Laroche.

The German attacks in Alsace also continue with some success south of Strasbourg in the area around Erstein.

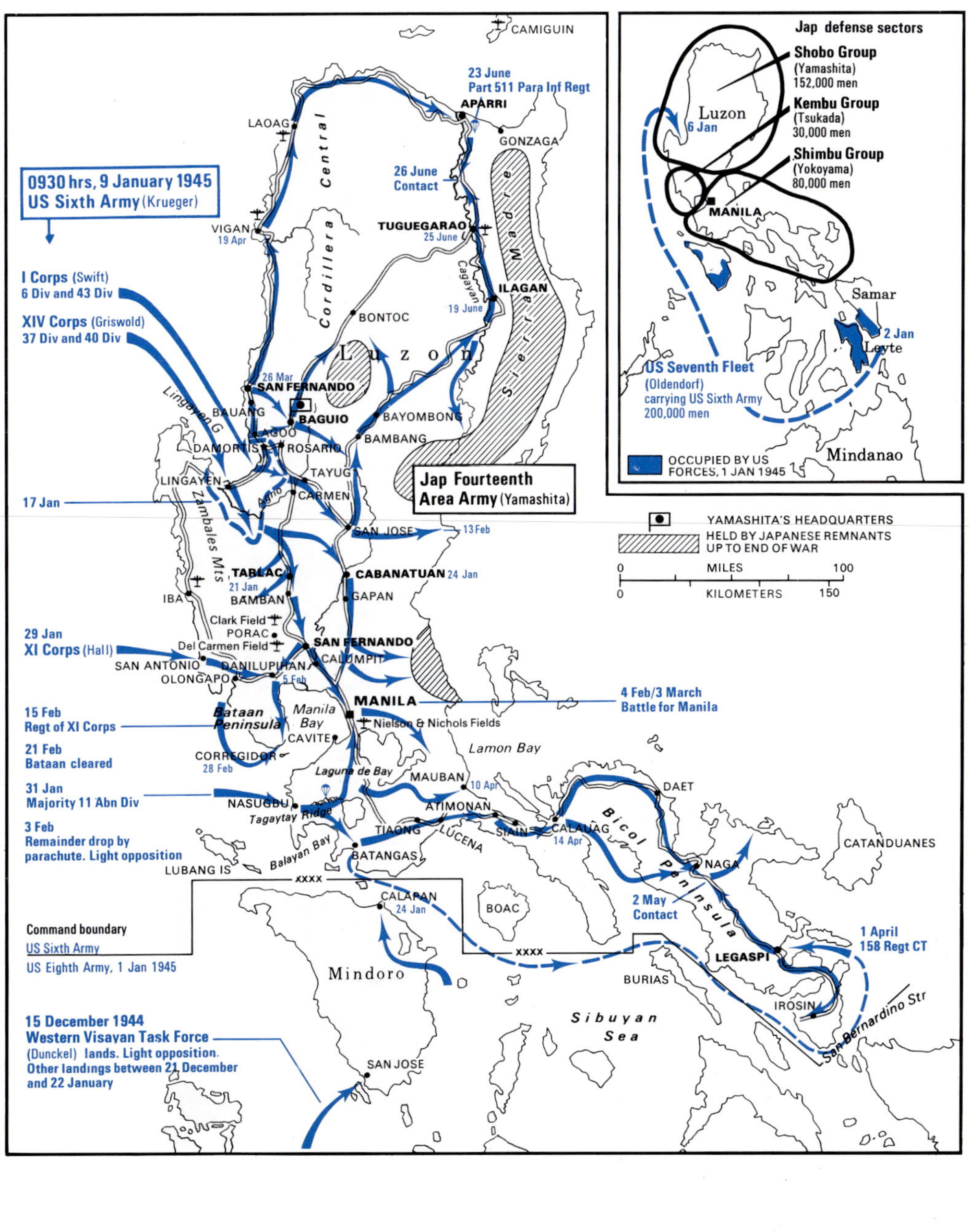

Lingayen village. The assault units are from 37th and 40th Divisions. The Japanese commander in north Luzon is General Yamashita and he has decided not to contest the landing grounds. The nearest Japanese forces are from 23rd Division but they will not intervene in strength in the first two days. There are, however, continued Japanese air attacks in which the battleship *Mississippi* and two cruisers are hit. In a night attack by explosive boats several landing craft and transports are damaged. The American units are from Krueger's Sixth Army and the naval support is commanded by Admiral Kinkaid. As well as 150,000 men under his direct leadership in the north of the island Yamashita commands the additional 110,000 men around Manila to the south.

Formosa and Okinawa The fleet carriers of TF 38 attack targets on Okinawa and Formosa in conjunction with Superfortress bombers from bases in China. This is intended to give cover to the landings on Luzon. One Japanese destroyer is sunk along with seven other ships.

Western Front The US Third Army increases the force of its attacks northeast and southeast of Bastogne.

10 January 1945

Western Front In the Ardennes battle there is fighting near Laroche in an attack by the British XXX Corps. US First and Third Armies are also continuing to advance.

Philippines The US forces stream ashore on Luzon. Their beachhead is now several miles wide and deep.

Burma While the advance of XXXIII Corps to the Irrawaddy is attracting the Japanese attention, IV Corps is moving southward to the west of the Chindwin with the intention of crossing the Irrawaddy near Meiktila. Gangaw is taken in this advance.

11 January 1945

Western Front Units of the Third Army and the British XXX Corps join up near St Hubert as the German salient in the Ardennes is further reduced. To the south the fighting in the Seventh Army area around Bitche is also continuing, but the Germans attacks are being held.

Philippines The US 25th Division and an armored group are landed at Lingayen to reinforce the US bridgehead. The first serious fighting begins ashore. There are more Kamikaze attacks on the American shipping. Many smaller craft are damaged.

12 January 1945

Eastern Front A major Soviet offensive begins all along the front from the Baltic to the Carpathians. The principal attacks are by Rokossovsky's Second Belorussian Front with nine armies immediately north of Warsaw; by Zhukov's First Belorussian Front opposite Warsaw and to the south with seven armies initially; and by Konev's First Ukraine Front from the salient west of Sandomierz also with seven armies in the front line. There are additional efforts by Third Belorussian and both Baltic Fronts against the German forces in East Prussia and those cut off in Latvia. The defending German forces are mostly from Army Group Center and Army Group A. Second Army will bear the brunt of Rokossovsky's attack; Ninth Army faces Zhukov; and Fourth Panzer Army faces Konev. These German troops are outnumbered by at least four or five to one in all classes of equipment, and despite brave resistance they will have no answer to the Red Army's power.

Burma The 19th Indian Division takes bridgeheads over the Irrawaddy north of Mandalay at Kyaukmyaung and Thabeikkyin. Fierce Japanese attacks in these areas immediately begin. In the Arakan there are landings of British Commando troops near Myebon on the mainland between Akyab and Ramree.

Indochina There are air attacks from the planes of the carriers of TF 38 against Japanese installations at the naval base at Camranh Bay and other areas in Indochina. TG 38.5 continues the attacks from its specially trained carriers. Japanese shipping losses to the attacks amount to 29 ships of 116,000 tons. Eleven small warships are also sunk.

Western Front There are new attacks on the north flank of the Ardennes salient by VII and XVIII Corps of the US First Army.

13 January 1945

Eastern Front The German defense lines all along the front in Poland are shattered by the Soviet attacks.

Philippines The escort carrier *Salamaua* is badly damaged in a Kamikaze attack. These are now becoming rare, however, because most of the Kamikaze aircraft have been lost and the rest withdrawn. Ashore the US bridgehead is steadily being extended. Damortis is taken.

Western Front In the Ardennes units of US First Army from the north and of the British XXX Corps from the west, reach the Ourthe between Laroche and Houffalize. Third Army forces are also moving toward Houffalize.

14 January 1945

Eastern Front The Soviet offensives in Poland begin to achieve important successes. Konev's forces cut the rail line to Krakow south of Kielce. Farther south in Hungary the Soviets resist German attempts to relieve Budapest and in eastern Czechoslovakia they take Lucenec.

Greece A cease-fire is agreed between the British and the Communist ELAS organization. ELAS agrees to release all hostages it has taken except for those accused of collaboration.

15 January 1945

Eastern Front Kielce falls to the First Ukraine Front. To the south of Konev's forces Petrov's Fourth Ukraine Front also goes over to the offensive.

Philippines On Luzon the US XIV Corps continues to advance south from the beachhead and has now crossed the River Agno. The I Corps is attacking north and east but cannot takes its objective of Rosario.

15-16 January 1945

Formosa The American fleet carrier groups attack targets mainly in Formosa but also in the Pescadores and along the south China coast. The weather is poor but some success is achieved and two Japanese destroyers are sunk.

16 January 1945

Eastern Front Zhukov's forces take Radom while to the north some of his other units have encircled Warsaw and are fighting their way through the city. Most of the defending German troops have escaped to the west however. Konev's troops to the south are making even better progress than Zhukov's and have reached Czestochow.

Above: Marshal Georgi Zhukov, commander of the Russian forces which liberated the Ukraine and drove into Germany as far as Berlin.

Western Front There are attacks by the British XIII Corps near Roermond aimed at eliminating the small German salient west of the Maas. In the Ardennes the First and Third Armies link up at Houffalize.

Burma Namhkam is taken by Chinese units which had advanced from Myitkyina along the Ledo Road. The road northeast from Namhkam into China is not yet clear.

17 January 1945

Eastern Front The totally devastated city of Warsaw is cleared of German resistance by Zhukov's forces. A Polish unit fighting with the Red Army is involved in the final attacks. To the north Rokossovsky's troops take Modlin.

Western Front The US Third Army captures Diekirch.

19 January 1945

Philippines On Luzon the US attacks are now being concentrated to the south of the beachhead with the aim of striking to Manila. Carmen is taken.

On Mindoro there is a brief flurry of activity as the Japanese try to slow the advance toward Calapan of the US 21st Infantry. Filipino guerrillas are active throughout the island in support of the US forces.

Eastern Front Konev's troops take Tarnow and Krakow. To the south of these attacks Nowy Sacz is taken by Fourth Ukraine Front while Zhukov's forces take Lodz. Wloclawek on the Vistula also falls.

20 January 1945

Eastern Front The Soviet offensive against the German forces in East Prussia achieves an important breakthrough in the attacks from the northeast. Tilsit is taken. All the Soviet fronts in Poland are moving forward despite German resistance. In Hungary the fighting in Budapest continues, but the Soviets now control the Pest half of the town.

Above: M-10 tank destroyers, attached to the US 77th Division, probe Japanese positions in the north-west of Leyte Island, January 1945.

Western Front General de Lattre's French First Army begins an offensive in the Vosges area near Colmar. Bad weather hinders the advance and the defense by the German Nineteenth Army is strong. Progress is gradually made, however. In the Ardennes the advance of Patton's Third Army goes on. Brandenburg is taken.
Burma On the Ledo Road the Chinese forces have only a few more miles to clear. The advance from Yunnan has reached Wanting on the border and from the other direction Mu-se is taken only ten miles away.
United States, Politics President Roosevelt is inaugurated for a fourth term. Vice President Truman is also sworn in. In his speech Roosevelt promises to continue to work for the Allied victory and for the establishment of peace and security for the postwar world.
Hungary, Politics The Hungarian Provisional Government concludes an armistice with the USSR, the USA and the UK. The Hungarians agree to pay reparations and to join the war against Germany.

21 January 1945

Eastern Front In East Prussia the Soviet attack pushes forward once more. Gumbinnen is taken.
Burma There are British landings at the northern tip of Ramree Island. The 4th British and 71st Indian Brigades are put ashore. The battleship *Queen Elizabeth* and an escort carrier are in support but there is little resistance. In the XXXIII Corps sector on the mainland Monywa on the Chindwin is taken by 20th Indian Division.
Philippines On Luzon the US 40th Division takes Tarlac and pushes south toward Clark Field.
Western Front Wiltz falls to the US III Corps in the Ardennes.

21-22 January 1945

Formosa and Ryukyus There are more operations by the fleet carriers of TF 38. Over 1150 sorties are flown over Formosa on the 21st, and 104 Japanese aircraft are shot down and 10 ships sunk. The carriers *Langley*, *Ticonderoga* and *Hancock* are all hit in Japanese attacks. On the 22nd Okinawa is the main target. After this operation the carrier groups all return to Ulithi. Since they were last in port on 30 December 1944 the carriers have sunk 300,000 tons of shipping and shot down 615 Japanese planes. They have lost 201 planes and 167 pilots.

22 January 1945

Eastern Front As well as the attacks of First Baltic and Third Belorussian Fronts from the northeast the German position in East Prussia is being threatened by the northwest advance of Second Belorussian Front toward the Elbing and Danzig area. In the attacks from the northeast Insterburg falls while in the other advance Allenstein and Deutsch Eylau are taken. To the south Gneizo is taken in Marshal Zhukov's drive to Poznan.
Western Front The British Second Army is continuing its attacks in the Roermond area and takes St Joost and other towns near Sittard. In the Ardennes US First Army attacks all along the front between Houffalize and St Vith.
Philippines On Luzon there is heavy fighting within the US 1 Corps sector near Carmen and Rosario.
Burma The British IV Corps takes Tilin in its continuing advance toward the Irrawaddy to the south.

Below: Japanese pilots salute the flag before setting out on a mission. By 1945, many pilots were being used on *kamikaze* raids; a reflection of Japan's desperate position.

23 January 1945

Eastern Front As well as the continuing attacks in Poland and East Prussia, there is a new advance from around Miskolc by Malinovsky's Second Ukraine Front with both Soviet and Rumanian troops involved.

Western Front St Vith falls to the attack of tank units from XVIII Corps. The German forces are falling back over the River Our from throughout the Ardennes salient but are losing heavily to Allied air attacks.

Burma Myinmu is taken by 20th Indian Division. This division, and the other XXXIII Corps units which have crossed the Irrawaddy north of Mandalay, are attracting important Japanese counterattacks because of Japanese fears of a threat to Mandalay. This is exactly what General Slim, commanding Fourteenth Army, has hoped for while IV Corps prepares the real advance farther south.

Philippines Units of Griswold's XIV Corps take Bamban in the continuing southward attacks and reach almost to Clark Field.

Below: The Vistula-Oder offensive – the Soviet drive from Warsaw toward Berlin – January-March 1945. The Third Reich was doomed.

24 January 1945

Western Front Units from the French First Army take crossings over the River Ill in Alsace. In the Ardennes there are Allied advances north and south of St Vith.

Eastern Front Konev's troops are attacking near Breslau and Oppeln on the Oder. They take Gleiwitz. SS leader Himmler is appointed by Hitler to lead a new Army Group Vistula to oppose the main Soviet thrusts. Himmler has no experience or aptitude for operational command and his appointment is a further blow and insult to the German Army and General Staff.

Philippines Calapan is taken by the US forces on Mindoro. Japanese resistance on the island has now been totally overcome except for a few stragglers.

Cabanatuan is taken by the US forces on Luzon.

China The Fourteenth Air Force has to abandon its Suichuan airfield because of Japanese advances nearby.

24-29 January 1945

Indian Ocean The British carriers make their last attacks before sailing for Australia on the way to join the main US carrier groups in the Pacific. Admiral Rawlings leads the four carriers in attacks on the oil refineries at Plodjoe north of Palembang on the 24th and against Soengi-Gerong on the 29th. Over 130 Japanese aircraft are shot down and 48 British aircraft lost. The battleship *King George V* and cruisers and destroyers escort the carriers.

25 January 1945

Eastern Front The German forces in East Prussia are now virtually cut off and evacuation operations therefore begin. These evacuations continue into April and involve about 40 large passenger ships and many other transports as well as practically all the remaining surface ships of the German Navy including the cruisers *Emden* and *Hipper*. There are considerable losses to many mines laid in the Baltic by RAF Bomber Command and to the submarines of the Soviet Baltic Fleet. General Reinhardt, who has been in command of the German Army Group Center in East Prussia, is dismissed and General Rendulic is appointed to the renamed Army Group North.

In the fighting on other fronts Ostrow is taken by Konev's left flank units. His troops also take crossings over the Oder near Breslau.

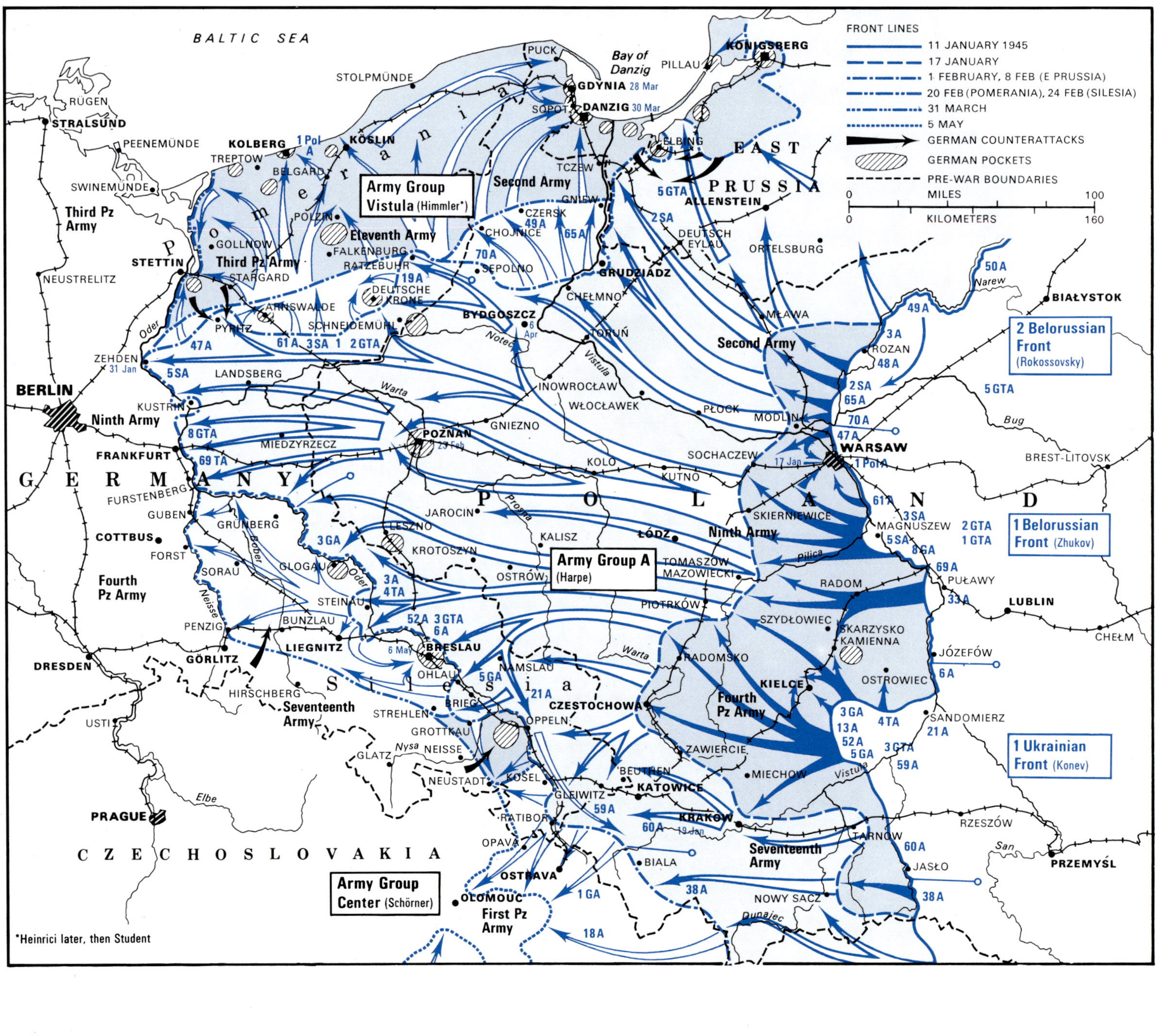

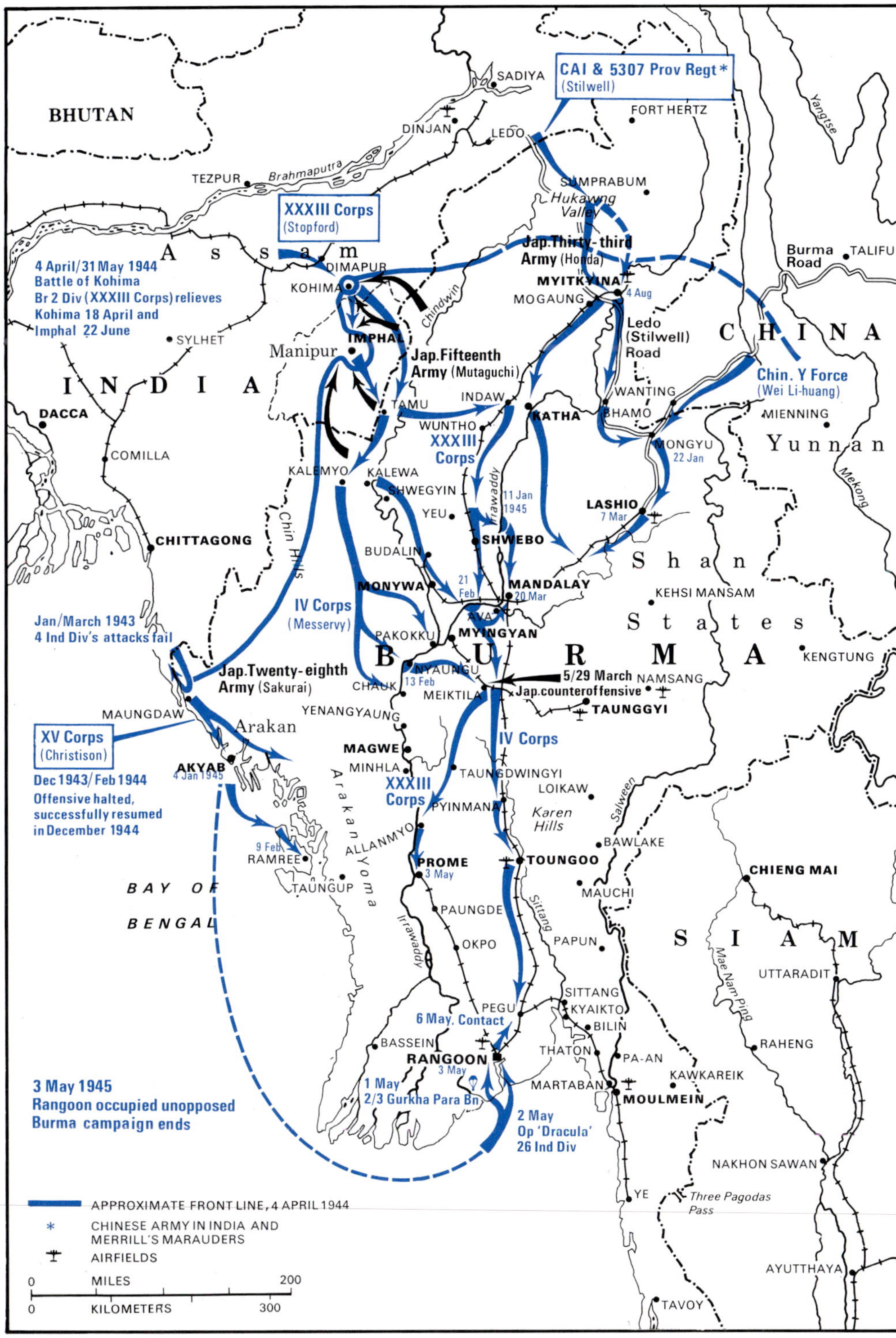

Above: Heinrich Himmler, head of the SS and unsuccessful commander of Army Group Vistula. *Right:* The Japanese offensive against Imphal and Kohima and the British counter-offensive to liberate Burma, 1944-45.

Philippines The 37th Division of Griswold's XIV Corps occupies a large part of the Clark Field air base.

Iwo Jima The island is bombarded by the battleship *Indiana* and a force of cruisers and destroyers. There are also air attacks by B-24 and B-29 bombers. This is the first step in the preparation for the US landings in February.

26 January 1945

Eastern Front Rokossovsky's advance reaches the Baltic north of Elbing, completely cutting off the German forces in East Prussia.

Western Front Units of Third Army in the Ardennes have now crossed the Clerf in several areas and are attacking all along the front of III and XII Corps.

Burma There are British landings on Chedube Island south of Ramree. A small force of Marines goes ashore on the first day and they are later reinforced by the 36th Indian Brigade. On the mainland to the north the 81st African Division takes Myohaung. Inland in the advance of IV Corps to the Irrawaddy, Pauk is taken by 7th Indian Division.

27 January 1947

Burma The Ledo Road into China is finally cleared when Chinese troops from Burma and Yunnan province link up near Mongyu. General Sultan, who leads the British, American and Chinese in this area, has in fact announced the road as open on 22 January. Sultan's forces are now moving south toward Mandalay and Lashio by several routes.

Eastern Front In Poland Zhukov's troops have swept round Poznan where the garrison still holds out and are maintaining their advance to the Vistula. Zhukov's forces are also attacking near Toruń and Bydgoscz. In Lithuania the port of Memel finally falls to the Soviets.

Western Front Troops from Patton's Third Army cross the Our and take Oberhausen. The gains made by the German Ardennes offensive are now almost completely eliminated.

Philippines The US 32nd Infantry Division lands at Lingayen Gulf to reinforce the American troops there.

28 January 1945

Eastern Front The advance of First Belorussian Front enters German Pomerania. Sepolno and Leszno are taken on the flanks of the advance. To the south Konev's troops complete the capture of Katowice.

29 January 1945

Eastern Front There are German counterattacks from East Prussia against Rokossovsky's troops to the west, but toward the south of the German pocket Bischofsburg falls to the forces of the Red Army.

Philippines On Luzon General Hall's XI Corps is landed at San Antonio north of Subic Bay to join the American offensive. About 30,000 men go ashore on the first day of the landing. Their task is to advance across the neck of the Bataan Peninsula and clear it of Japanese.

30 January 1945

Philippines A US battalion is landed to take Gamble Island in Subic Bay. To the north XI Corps begins to advance inland quickly and takes Olongapo on Luzon.

30 January-2 February 1945

Allied Planning Churchill and Roosevelt and their advisors meet in Malta to make preparations for the Yalta meeting with Stalin. They leave for Yalta on the 2nd.

31 January 1945

Eastern Front Zhukov's troops reach the Oder at Zehden and along a wide front to the south to beyond Frankfurt. The Oder here is less than 50 miles from Berlin.

Western Front Units of XVIII Corps from First Army enter Germany east of St Vith as they

Above: Preparing a Handley Page Halifax Mark II heavy bomber for a raid against Germany. This is any early version of the aircraft.

continue their advance from the Ardennes. In Alsace French attacks near Colmar also make some ground.

Philippines On Luzon two regiments of General Swing's 11th Airborne Division are landed by sea near Nasugbu southwest of Manila. Admiral Fechteler leads the naval support with a cruiser and eight destroyers. There is little opposition to the landing. North of Manila the US advance is still making progress. XIV Corps units have nearly reached Calumpit in a converging attack.

Diplomatic Affairs The Czechoslovakian Government in London recognizes the Polish Lublin Government as the Provisional Government of Poland.

February 1945

Europe, Air Operations The Allied strategic bombing effort continues. The US Eighth Air Force and RAF Bomber Command both drop over 50,000 tons of bombs and other US strategic bombers add a further 23,000 tons. Many towns throughout west Germany are hit for both strategic and tactical reasons. Communications targets are among the most common. The Eighth Air Force sends more than 1000 bombers on attacks on 15 days during the month. In Operation Clarion which begins on the 22nd tactical targets throughout Germany are attacked by up to 9000 planes including lighter forces. The US Ninth Air Force drops almost 20,000 tons in all missions and RAF tactical support further increases this figure. The Mediterranean Air Forces also attack communications in that theater as well as dropping supplies to Tito and his Partisans. The attack on Dresden by the strategic forces is particularly controversial (*see* 13-15 February).

Far East, Air Operations Among the major attacks by B-29 forces are those targeted on Kobe, Nagoya and Tokyo. Some of these are made in conjunction with the carrier forces of the Pacific Fleet. Allied heavy bombers and tactical support forces are active on all other Pacific fronts.

Battle of the Atlantic German U-Boat strength remains roughly about 150, but Allied material and technical superiority means that they can achieve very little. There is something of a revival in the campaign, however, in the inshore waters of the Western Approaches. The U-Boats sink 15 ships during the month but 22 of their number are lost.

1 February 1945

Eastern Front Toruń falls to attacks from Zhukov's and Rokossovsky's forces. Zhukov's troops which have reached the Oder opposite Berlin halt there to regroup while the many pockets of German resistance in their rear are being eliminated and while the units on their flanks broaden the advance by attacking into Pomerania in the north and crossing the Oder and moving toward the Neisse in the south.

Philippines The American advance on all fronts is slowed by fierce Japanese resistance. I Corps is heavily engaged near Rosario and San Jose while XI Corps is struggling to make more ground across the neck of the Bataan Peninsula.

Western Front The US VI Corps from Seventh Army crosses the river Moder and advances nearly to Oberhofen.

1-15 February 1945

Iwo Jima The US air attacks on the island are stepped up with B-24s and B-29s over the island every day. In this preparatory phase for the landings later in the month 6800 tons of bombs are dropped.

2 February 1945

Western Front First Army Units are attacking near Remscheid. British forces mount attacks over the Maas, north of Breda and near Nijmegen to put pressure on the Germans.

3 February 1945

Western Front French and American units complete the capture of Colmar. All formations of French First Army are now making good progress in this sector. The other Allied armies keep up the pressure on the Germans all along the front.

Eastern Front In East Prussia the Soviet attacks continue to confine and divide the German forces. Landsberg and Bartenstein are taken.

Philippines On Luzon in the Tagaytay Ridge area the uncommitted regiment of 11th Airborne Division is dropped to help the advance of the other regiments. The fighting north of Manila also continues.

4 February 1945

Philippines On Luzon advance units of 1st Cavalry Division reach the outskirts of Manila from the north while units of 11th Airborne Division approach from the south. Yamashita has not ordered his forces to defend the city, but the 20,000 Japanese troops are prepared to fight to the end.

Below: The 'Big Three' – (left to right, seated) Churchill, Roosevelt and Stalin – meet at Yalta to discuss the post-war world.

Western Front The Allies announce that all German forces have been expelled from Belgium. First and Third Army units are attacking toward the Rür River around Düren.

4-11 February 1945

Diplomatic Affairs Roosevelt, Churchill and Stalin and their senior military and political colleagues meet at Yalta in the Crimea.

It is now clear to all that the war in Europe has been won but both Britain and the US believe that they still have much to do to defeat Japan. Partly because Roosevelt's illness seems to be weakening his negotiating powers and judgement, Stalin is able to obtain the promise of territorial concessions in Sakhalin and the Kurile Islands in return for a promise to declare war on Japan within two months of the end of the war in Europe.

The postwar borders of the countries of eastern Europe are also largely determined at the Yalta meeting. The most notable changes are in the position of Poland, with the whole country being effectively moved westward at the insistence of the Soviets. Stalin gives assurances that elections will be held in eastern Europe and that non-Communist parties will not be forbidden or persecuted: however, the Western powers will not be able to supervise any such elections and they will never take place in a form regarded by the West as free or democratic. The arrangements for the division of Germany into occupation zones for each of the major powers are confirmed and defined. In reality the arrangements for Europe, however distasteful for western opinion, only reflect the predominant share the USSR has played in the defeat of Germany. For the war against Japan the British and American eagerness to bring the Soviets in is also easy to understand, bearing in mind the fanatical resistance of the Japanese garrisons yet fought and the large Japanese forces in Manchuria and China. The establishment of a United Nations Organization is also discussed, and it is agreed that the preliminary meetings to create the organization should be held in April in San Francisco. It is already clear that the Soviets will lead the other great powers in insisting that they be granted veto powers in votes on major issues.

5 February 1945

Western Front The German pocket near Colmar is cut in two by a link between French units and part of the US XXI Corps. Farther north US First Army extends its attacks, led by V Corps, toward the Rür, aiming to take the Schwammenauel Dam.
Eastern Front The Soviet attacks on the surrounded city of Poznan make some progress. Soviet pressure continues in many other sectors.
Philippines The US forces close in tighter around Manila. The XI Corps has completed its attack across the Bataan Peninsula.
South China Sea The Japanese carrier/battleship *Ise* is damaged by a mine off Indochina.
Greece The Greek Communist Party accepts the Greek government's terms for an amnesty. The communists have to surrender their arms. The amnesty comes into force on 12 February.

6 February 1945

Eastern Front Southeast of Breslau the Soviet forces begin to push out of their bridgehead over the Oder.
Italy Units of IV Corps from Fifth Army take Gallicano in a brief offensive designed to improve the Allied positions on either side of the Serchio Valley.

7 February 1945

Eastern Front Zhukov's troops on the Oder seize some small bridgeheads over the river in the Kustrin area and near Furstenberg. There are also attacks in Pomerania where Answalde and Deutsche Krone are among the main centers of German resistance. When trapped these German garrisons fight with the desperation of a cornered animal.
Western Front In the V Corps' advance toward the Rür Schmidt is taken. To the south Third Army units move into Germany east of the Our.

8 February 1945

Western Front A new offensive is begun by the Canadian First Army and British Second Army from between the Maas and the Waal southeast of Nijmegen. There is considerable air support and the advance penetrates the Reichswald area on the first day. In the US Third Army sector the VIII Corps manages to advance beyond the Our.
Eastern Front In East Prussia the German forces have now been virtually split into three groups: the defenders of Königsberg, some forces trapped on the peninsula to the west of the town, and those to the south, the largest group, holding out around Keiligenbeil and inland.
Philippines The 1st Cavalry Division is heavily engaged in the eastern suburbs of Manila. The 37th Division is also fighting in the city.

9 February 1945

Western Front In the British and Canadian offensive near Nijmegen the Rhine is reached at Millingen, which is captured. The US Third Army is attacking near Prüm in the north of its sector while XII Corps to the south is also making gains. Farther south still the resistance of the German forces around Colmar comes to an end.
Philippines As well as the fighting in Manila there is an attack by 11th Airborne Division southeast of the city near Nichols and Nielson Fields.
Burma In the Arakan area 26th Indian Division completes the capture of Ramree Island.

10 February 1945

Western Front In the First Army sector German forces open the Schwammenauel Dam in an attempt, partly successful, to delay the advance of the US forces nearby. To the north there are unsuccessful German attacks on the British and Canadian units which have now advanced almost to Cleve and Materborn.
Eastern Front The last German resistance in Elbing comes to an end and the town is taken by Second Belorussian Front.

11 February 1945

Eastern Front Konev's troops begin to break out of their bridgehead over the Oder near Steinau and attack west and north threatening Glogau. Other units will turn south to help surround Breslau. Leignitz is also attacked.
Western Front British and Canadian units take Cleve in their continuing advance toward the Rhine. In the Third Army sector to the south the important road junction at Prüm is taken by VIII Corps units.

Above: Consolidated B-24 Liberators of the Seventh USAAF drop 55-gallon drum incendiary bombs on Japanese positions on Iwo Jima.

12 February 1945

Burma West of Mandalay XXXIII Corps units begin to take their second series of bridgeheads over the Irrawaddy. The advance here is by 20th Indian Division opposite Myinmu. To the south IV Corps has reached the Irrawaddy at Myitche and Seikpyu and is preparing to cross. British and US units of Sultan's Northern Area Combat Command are advancing south toward Lashio and Kyaukme, but are being held for the moment in heavy fighting near the River Shweli.
Philippines The US XI Corps has now closed the neck of the Bataan Peninsula and is advancing southward to clear the Japanese forces from it.

13 February 1945

Eastern Front After a battle lasting for almost two months the garrison of Budapest surrenders to Malinovsky's forces. Over 100,000 German prisoners have been taken in the city. The Soviet advance from the Oder to the Neisse begins to gain momentum despite desperate German efforts. Bunzlau on the River Bober is captured.
Philippines US Navy forces begin operations in Manila Bay, clearing minefields and shelling landing grounds. Corregidor is bombarded. In the ground fighting the 11th Airborne Division takes Cavite and completes the capture of Nichols Field.
Western Front The British forces clear the last German units from the Reichswald in the northern sector of the front.
Burma The 20th Indian Division has now established a solid bridgehead over the Irrawaddy despite fierce Japanese attacks.

13-15 February 1945

Europe, Air Operations On the night of 13/14 February there is a massive RAF attack on Dresden by 773 Lancaster bombers. This is followed up by daylight attacks by Eighth Air Force on the 14th and 15th involving 600 planes altogether. The greatest damage is done in the RAF attack when the city, crowded with refugees from the Eastern Front, is devastated in a horrific fire storm. Various authorities give different figures for the number of casualties ranging from 30,000 dead to 200,000 dead. The best estimates suggest a figure around 70,000 is most accurate. The raid becomes very controversial because Dresden is not an important military target and has been a city of much historical interest.

14 February 1945

Eastern Front In the Soviet attacks on Pomerania Schneidmühl falls. Deutsche Krone is also taken after being surrounded but Arnswalde holds out against a similar attack. In Konev's drive to the Neisse, Sorau and Grünberg are both captured.
Western Front The British and Canadian offensive reaches the south bank of the Rhine opposite Emmerich. Other British and Canadian units also make advances in this sector. The US forces farther south are mostly regrouping to prepare for the next series of attacks.
Burma The 7th Indian Division from IV Corps begins to cross the Irrawaddy near Myaungu. There is only slight Japanese opposition because most of the Japanese forces have been withdrawn to defend Mandalay. North of Mandalay 19th Indian Division takes Singu despite the efforts of the defenders.

15 February 1945

Philippines A regiment from XI Corps is landed at the southern tip of Bataan on Luzon to help in the operations of the remainder of the corps. The fierce fighting in Manila continues.

Below: US commander, General MacArthur (hands on hips) inspects the recently liberated Bilibid prison in Manila, February 1945, as ex-PoWs look on.

Eastern Front In Konev's attacks west of the Oder Breslau has been surrounded.

16 February 1945

Philippines Two battalions, one seaborne and one dropped by parachute, land on Corregidor Island in Manila Bay. The attacking troops land successfully enough but a bitter struggle soon develops among the tunnels and gun emplacements of the island. The US troops are quickly reinforced. Since the battle for Luzon began 3200 tons of bombs have been dropped on Corregidor.

16-17 February 1945

Japan There are attacks by the 12 fleet carriers and four light carriers of TF 58, now returned to Spruance's command as part of Fifth Fleet, against Tokyo alone on the 16th and against Tokyo and Yokohama on the 17th. Over 2700 sorties are flown and 88 American planes and twice as many Japanese are shot down. The carriers are escorted by eight battleships, 15 cruisers and 83 destroyers as well as many other support ships and their escorts. The force moves off toward Iwo Jima when the strikes have been completed.

16-18 February 1945

Iwo Jima The preliminary bombardment for the American landings begins in earnest. Admiral Rogers leads the six battleships, five cruisers and 16 destroyers of TF 54 in the operation and the 10 escort carriers of TF 52 also make attacks including many with the new napalm bombs. On the 16th the bombardment is comparatively ineffective because of bad weather and poor observation, but on the 17th and 18th more is achieved. On the 17th there are also bombing raids by B-24 bombers. The battleship *Tennessee* is hit on the 17th, and a cruiser and several of the smaller ships charged with minesweeping and obstacle clearing duties are also damaged.
Kuriles On the 16th and 18th an American cruiser and destroyer force shells Kuraba Zaki.

17 February 1945

Western Front There are new attacks by XII and XX Corps of the US Third Army from southern Luxembourg and farther south around Saarlouis. US Seventh Army units are attacking near Saarbrücken while in the north Canadian troops have now reached the Rhine on a 10-mile front.
Burma The British operations in the Arakan continue with successful landings at Ru-Ya, 40 miles southeast of Myebon. Heavy fighting continues in the area of XXXIII Corps bridgeheads over the Irrawaddy and along the Shweli River farther north especially near Myitson.
Europe, Air Operations The Italian battleship *Conte di Cavour,* already damaged, and the unfinished *Impero* are sunk in Trieste harbor by the RAF.

18 February 1945

Western Front All US Third Army units are attacking. The Siegfried Line is broken north of Echternach by VIII Corps while both XII and XX Corps to the south are also gaining ground. In the continuing British and Canadian offensive the British XXX Corps attacks Goch.
Eastern Front Chernyakhovsky, commander of Third Belorussian Front, dies of wounds. His replacement will be Vasilievsky.
Italy There are new attacks by IV Corps of Fifth Army in the area of the front just west of the Bologna-Pistoia road.
Bonin Islands While most of TF 58 is replenishing, one group of four carriers commanded by Admiral Radford attacks Haha Jima and Chichi Jima.

19 February 1945

Iwo Jima Two Marine Divisions of the V Amphibious Corps land on Iwo Jima in Operation Detachment. Before the landing the bombardment groups step up their effort and are joined by the aircraft of two carrier groups and by two battleships, several cruisers and destroyers from TF 58. The assault forces are from 4th and 5th Marine Divisions with 3rd Marines in reserve. They are carried in Admiral Hill's TF 53 and land on the southeast of the island. About 30,000 men go ashore on the first day.

General Kuribayashi commands the Japanese garrison of about 21,000 men, and they have prepared exceptionally elaborate and tough defenses so that the eight square miles of the island is completely fortified. The topography of the island is dominated by the 600-foot high Mount Suribachi at the southern tip. The rest of the island is flat, sloping gradually upward toward the north end.

There is almost no resistance to the landings at first, but after about half an hour the defenders open fire. The increasingly fierce Japanese resistance fails to prevent the Marines consolidating their beachhead and fighting their way across to the other side of the island before the end of the first day.

The Americans are well aware that the island is going to be strongly defended since it is part of metropolitan Japan, but it is strategically important because it is within fighter range of Tokyo, and this means that the B-29 bombers from the Marianas can be escorted. Iwo Jima will also provide an emergency landing field for damaged bombers on their return from missions over Japan. Large numbers of airmen's lives are saved thanks to the construction of this emergency runway on Iwo Jima.

Above: A sniper of the Black Watch uses a hole in a roof as a 'hide', Gennep, Netherlands, February 1945.

19-20 February 1945

Philippines There are US landings in the northwest of the island of Samar and on the small islands offshore of Dalupiri, Capul and Biri. There is some resistance on Biri.

20 February 1945

Eastern Front The Soviet forces are now moving northward into German Pomerania on a 200-mile front. The German forces opposing them are from Himmler's Army Group Vistula, and his incompetence has contributed to their plight.

Western Front The XX Corps of Third Army continues its attacks on the 'Saar-Moselle triangle.'

20-22 February 1945

Iwo Jima The fleet carriers of TF 58 and the bombardment groups continue to give lavish support to the Marines. On the 21st the escort carrier *Bismarck Sea* is sunk and the fleet carrier *Saratoga*, an escort carrier and other ships are all damaged by Kamikaze attacks. In the fighting on the island the US forces are inching their way forward on to Mount Suribachi in the south and taking most of the island's first airfield to the north of the beachhead. Every advance, however small, has to be prepared and accompanied with enormous firepower. There are Japanese attacks and infiltration attempts during each night.

21 February 1945

Burma The 17th Indian Division and supporting tank units begin to break out of IV Corps' bridgehead at Myaungu and advance toward Meiktila. The Japanese know of the presence of British units in this area, but do not realize such strong forces are involved because the advance of IV Corps has been well disguised. Farther north troops of the British XXXIII Corps step up their efforts to attract the main Japanese forces when the British 2nd Division crosses the Irrawaddy near Ngazun to link with 20th Indian Division who already have a bridgehead near there. Farther north still the British 36th Division takes Myitson.

Philippines The US XI Corps completes the capture of the Bataan area of Luzon. Fighting on Corregidor continues, as does the battle for Manila.

Western Front Goch falls to the attacks of 51st Division of the British XXX Corps.

22 February 1945

Western Front The US XX Corps largely completes its battle in the Saar-Moselle triangle with almost complete success.

Italy Fifth Army makes some gains in mountain fighting high up in the Reno Valley.

22-23 February 1945

Burma There are British landings near Kangaw carried out by 6000 men of the 3rd Commando Brigade and other units.

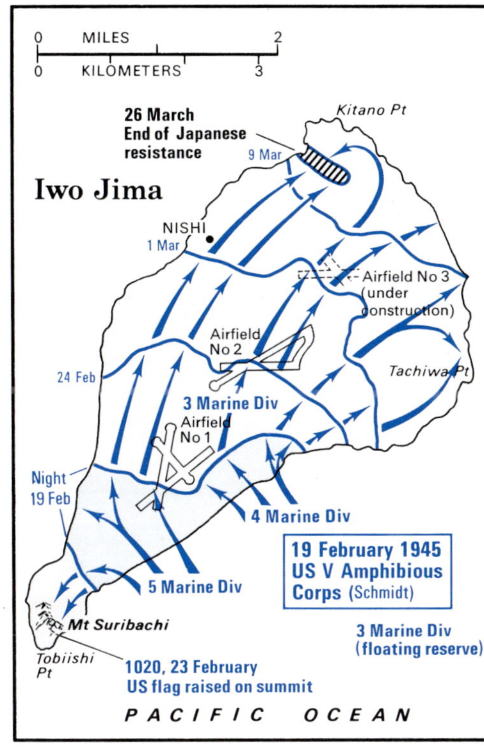

Above: The US invasion and seizure of Iwo Jima, February-March 1945.

23 February 1945

Western Front A major new offensive by US First and Ninth Armies begins with heavy attacks along the Rür, especially in the Jülich and Düren areas. The river is crossed in several sectors. The attacks are opposed by the German Fifth Panzer and Fifteenth Armies which are part of Model's Army Group B. Farther south there are also attacks by units of US Seventh and Third Armies.

Eastern Front Poznan falls to the Red Army after a 28-day battle. In Silesia Konev's troops have largely completed their advance from the Oder north of Breslau to the Neisse. In Breslau the fighting continues. The German garrison of

Below: As the invasion fleet stands offshore, US Marines cling to the volcanic-ash beach on Iwo Jima, 19 February 1945. The battle for Iwo Jima was hard and long.

Above: Perhaps the most famous photograph of the war: a group of US Marines raises the Stars and Stripes on top of Mount Suribachi, Iwo Jima, 23 February 1945.

the city will not surrender until the end of the war, despite repeated Soviet attacks.
Iwo Jima Most of Mount Suribachi is taken by the US forces during the day and the US flag is hoisted on the summit. To the north of the beachhead the pattern of slow US advance after much effort is maintained.
Philippines The US forces attacking in Manila step up their offensive after a fierce bombardment. The Japanese resistance is now largely confined to the old walled section of the town, the Intramuros, but the fighting there is very fierce.
Arctic German Ju 88 bombers sink the SS *Henry Bacon* from the convoy RA-64. This is the last Allied merchant ship to be sunk by German aircraft during the war.

24 February 1945

Western Front Jülich is taken by units of the XIX Corps as the US Ninth Army begins to extend its advance over the Rür. To the north the British and Canadian attacks continue to drive southeast toward Udem and Weeze. The US First and Third Armies also push forward in their sectors.
Iwo Jima The US advance to the north takes part of the island's second airfield.
Burma In their advance on Meiktila 17th Indian Division takes Taungtha.

25 February 1945

Western Front Düren is taken by VII Corps of US First Army. Other bridgeheads over the Rür have been taken north and south of here and they are rapidly being extended. On the right flank of Third Army to the south, crossings over the Saar have also been made near Saarburg.
Iwo Jima The US advance continues but there are heavy losses in the area around the second airfield. As ever, Japanese resistance was fanatically determined.
Eastern Front There is a German counterattack from south of Stettin toward Pyritz, but although some success is achieved its effect is only local and temporary.

25-26 February 1945

Japan The aircraft from the carriers of TF 58 again send attacks against Tokyo. Bad weather hinders their effectiveness.

26 February 1945

Eastern Front In the face of the Soviet attacks into East Pomerania and the Soviets' retention despite counterattacks of positions near Stettin, the Germans begin evacuations of wounded and refugees from Kolberg and other ports along the coast. These operations continue until the ports are taken during March.
Burma The advance of 17th Indian Division toward Meiktila continues to go well. Mahlaing and the Thabuktong airfield are taken. Reinforcements for IV Corps will be flown in to this airfield.
Western Front There are renewed British and Canadian efforts near Udem and Calcar. US First and Ninth Army units are moving rapidly from their bridgeheads over the Our.
Philippines The fighting on Corregidor comes to an end. The US forces find more than 5000 Japanese dead on the tiny island and others have been trapped in collapsed tunnels. There are 19 prisoners. US casualties are around 1000.

27 February 1945

Western Front Udem and Calcar both fall to the British and Canadian attacks. The advance in this sector reaches the Rhine northeast of Calcar. In the US First Army area units of VII Corps cross the Erft at Modrath in their advance toward Cologne. The US Ninth and Third Armies are both moving forward well, two of Third Army's corps converging on Trier.
Burma Units of the 19th Indian Division begin to break out of their bridgehead over the Irrawaddy at Habeikkyin and advance south toward Mandalay against heavy Japanese resistance.
Iwo Jima The carriers of TF 53 again add their support to the ships aiding the Marines' attacks. The main focus of the advance is now the three Japanese positions overlooking the island's second airfield. Despite three days of attacks the Japanese defenders cannot be dislodged.

28 February 1945

Burma The British IV Corps begins to attack Meiktila in strength. The Japanese command has known of the presence of this force but has believed it to be only lightly armed in the Chindit pattern. They have, therefore, left it to the local troops at Meiktila to defend their own base. This is a serious error because Meiktila is a vital communications center, serving all the Japanese forces around Mandalay and to the north.
Philippines There are US landings at Puerto Princesa on Palawan by 8000 men of 41st Infantry Division. Admiral Fechteler leads a bombardment group of cruisers and destroyers and there is also support from land-based aircraft. There is little Japanese resistance to the landings.

March 1945

Europe, Air Operations Both RAF Bomber Command and the US Eighth Air Force step up their efforts, each dropping more than 73,000 tons of bombs. Among the RAF targets are Mannheim, Kassel, Essen and Dortmund. The raid on Dortmund on the 12th sees 4850 tons of bombs dropped – the heaviest attack on any target during the war. In an attack on the Bielfeld viaduct on the 15th the largest bomb dropped during the war is used for the first time, the 22,000-pound Grand Slam. The Eighth Air Force is able to send 1500 heavy bombers out on any one day and among its targets are Chemnitz, Osnabruck and Swinemünde. The German communications system and the synthetic oil industry are attacked by both British and American forces. Tactical targets are also hit by the heavy bombers. Ninth Air Force flies 55,000 missions and drops 33,000 tons of bombs in its

Above: The chaos of war: German civilians flee from the battle-zone, carrying as many possessions as they can.

support tasks. RAF tactical support forces fly 30,000 missions. The Mediterranean Air Forces also contribute to the Allied effort.

Far East, Air Operations This month there is a notable change in the American tactics for their attacks on targets in Japan. General Le May, commanding the bomber forces based in the Marianas, has become dissatisfied with both the weight and accuracy of attack achieved in precision bombing from B-29s at high altitude. The very high winds met at around 30,000 feet, which has been the operational altitude until now, mean that bomb accuracy is very difficult and attaining this altitude overstrains the aircraft and restricts the bomb load. The new tactics involve the attacks being made by night on city targets with the bombs being mostly incendiaries. The first and most horrific attack on this new pattern is aimed at Tokyo (*see* 9-10 March). Other targets hit in Japan include Nagoya, Osaka and Kobe.

Elsewhere there are many Allied air operations in the Philippines, Burma and over China where Fourteenth Air Force is maintaining its efforts.

1 March 1945

Western Front München-Gladbach and Neuss fall to the US Ninth Army which is now advancing rapidly toward the Rhine. The attacks of First Army toward Cologne are continuing as are the efforts of Third Army near the River Kyll and south of Trier.

Eastern Front In Pomerania the northward attacks of Zhukov's forces achieve a breakthrough north of Arnswalde and move on in the Kolberg direction.

Iwo Jima The US forces now hold both the first and second of the island's airfields and have a foothold at the south end of the third. The fighting is still very fierce all along the line.

Philippines The Japanese resistance in Manila is now confined to only a few blocks in the administrative area of the city. Nearer the landing area at Lingayen Gulf there are renewed efforts by I Corps in the direction of Baguio and north along the coast.

Okinawa Part of the TF 58 carrier force attacks targets on Okinawa and shipping nearby. Two small Japanese warships are sunk.

2 March 1945

Western Front Trier is captured by units of XX Corps from Patton's Third Army. First Army to the north is extending its advance beyond the Erft both toward Cologne and to the right also. Ninth Army captures Roermond and Venlo on the Maas on the left of its advance while on the right the Rhine is reached opposite Dusseldorf.

Ryukyu Islands Four cruisers and 15 destroyers commanded by Admiral Whiting and drawn from TF 58 bombard Okino Daito Jima.

Rumania King Michael of Rumania is forced under pressure from the Soviets to dismiss his government and on 6 March to appoint a new government dominated by the Rumanian Communist Party. This is the first token since Yalta that Stalin will not hold to his assurances about doing nothing to hinder the process of democracy in eastern Europe.

3 March 1945

Burma Meiktila is completely occupied by IV Corps units. They immediately dig in. The main route for supplies to the bulk of the Japanese forces in Burma is, therefore, cut and they will be compelled to turn away from the fighting farther north and try to clear their lines of communication. At the same time they must do something to hold off XXXIII Corps to the north.

Western Front Troops of Ninth and First Canadian Armies link up near Geldern. Farther south units of the US XII Corps from Third Army take a crossing over the Kyll. In the Seventh Army sector Forbach is taken.

Iwo Jima The area of the island which has become known as 'the Mincer' is finally cleared by the Marines' attacks after a vicious struggle. The third airfield is now completely in American hands.

Philippines Japanese resistance in Manila comes to an end after a bitter month-long fight. The 20,000 defenders have been wiped out and the town devastated.

Troops from the Americal Division are landed on Ticao and Burias Islands to the west of the San Bernardino Strait.

4 March 1945

Western Front Geldern is taken by the British XXX Corps from First Canadian Army. US First and Ninth Armies continue their advance to the Rhine. VII Corps from First Army reaches the Rhine just north of Cologne.

Eastern Front The Soviet offensive in Pomerania continues to make gains especially toward the west near Stettin. There is also renewed fighting in East Prussia.

5 March 1945

Western Front Units of the US VII Corps enter Cologne from the south and the east. The Allied advance in other sectors continues.

Burma Japanese counterattacks against IV Corps begin. The small town of Taungtha is retaken by the Japanese and 17th Indian Division is almost cut off in Meiktila. Air supply continues, however.

Germany, Home Front Fifteen- and sixteen-

Below: An RAF 12,000lb 'Tallboy' bomb, photographed as it leaves the bomb-bay of an Avro Lancaster over Germany, 1945.

Above: General Sir William Slim, commander of the British Fourteenth Army and architect of victory in Burma.

year-old boys from the class of 1929 are called up to serve in the German army.

6 March 1945

Eastern Front The German forces in Hungary launch a major counteroffensive in the area just north of Lake Balaton. Dietrich's Sixth SS Panzer Army, which was withdrawn from the Ardennes battle early in January, has been moved here to lead the attack. Other units from Wöhler's Army Group South also take part in the offensive. The operation is code named Frühlingserwachen or Spring Awakening. The Soviet Twenty-seventh Army bears the brunt of the attack initially and is forced to give ground but reserve units of Tolbukhin's Third Ukraine Front will soon arrive to slow the advance down. The optimistic German aim is to retake all the territory between Lake Balaton and the Danube.

In the fighting in Poland Second Belorussian Front completes the capture of the fortress town of Grudiadz which has been surrounded for some time.

Western Front The US Ninth Army has now reached the Rhine all along its front. Units of the Canadian First Army to the north are preparing to clear the final German pocket west of the Rhine around Xanten. To the south of Ninth Army First Army is fighting in Cologne and driving toward Remagen farther south. The 9th Armored Division leads the advance here. Farther south still units of Third Army are making a rapid advance in one section of the front toward the Rhine at Koblenz.

Burma In their slow advance down the Burma Road units of the Chinese First Army reach and capture Lashio.

7 March 1945

Eastern Front In Hungary the German offensive continues and more gains are made. As well as the forces north of Lake Balaton there are attacks by units of Second Panzer Army toward Kaposvar to the south and from over the Yugoslav border by units of Löhr's Army Group E. In Poland evacuations begin from around Danzig. These last until the middle of April.

Western Front The leading tanks of III Corps reach the Rhine opposite Remagen and find the Ludendorff Bridge there damaged but still standing. Troops are immediately rushed across and brilliant staff improvisation sends more units hurrying to join them. Hitler is furious and sacks Field Marshal Rundstedt from command of the German armies in the west. Other Allied units complete the capture of Cologne while XII Corps units from Third Army continue to move forward particularly quickly.

Philippines There is fighting in the I Corps sector south of San Fernando. South of Manila the XIV Corps is fighting near Balayan Bay and Batangas against the defense lines of the south Luzon Shimbu Group of the Japanese forces.

Yugoslavia, Politics The two existing governments, Tito's and the royalist government, are merged into a new single government dominated by Tito and his followers.

8 March 1945

Western Front American efforts to pass forces over the Remagen Bridge continue but there is unavoidably some congestion. German bombers, including some jets, begin all-out attacks on the bridge but fail to destroy it. To the north units of the Canadian II Corps take Xanten.

Burma The 2nd British and 20th Indian Divisions begin to break out of their bridgeheads over the Irrawaddy to the west of Mandalay.

Iwo Jima The US forces are still methodically pushing forward to the north of the island with continued heavy fire support. The Japanese forces are now all within one mile of the north end of the island.

8-9 March 1945

France There are still German garrisons in the Channel Islands, and during the night they mount a raid on Granville on the west coast of the Cotentin. One small US warship is sunk and four merchant ships.

9 March 1945

Western Front Bonn and Godesberg are taken by units of US First Army while others continue to expand the bridgehead beyond the Rhine at Remagen. Erpel is taken here. A little farther south toward Koblenz Third Army units reach the Rhine at Andernach.

Burma The southward advance of the 19th Indian Division reaches the outskirts of Mandalay. Other XXXIII Corps units are advancing toward the city from the west. The fighting around Meiktila is still very fierce as the Japanese continue to bring troops from the Mandalay area in a desperate attempt to free their communications.

9-10 March 1945

Iwo Jima On both days the US attacks continue but during the night between there is an unusually fierce Japanese suicide attack. The attack achieves little and almost all those taking part are killed.

Far East, Air Operations There is a devastating attack by 279 Superfortress bombers on Tokyo. Over 1650 tons of incendiaries are dropped on the city in a new form of attack designed specifically to take advantage of the wood and paper construction of many Japanese houses. A massive fire storm is raised and many thousands of homes are completely destroyed. The death toll is at least 80,000 and probably as many as 120,000. It is the most damaging air attack of the war including the atomic attacks on Hiroshima and Nagasaki. This is only the first of many such raids on Japanese cities.

10 March 1945

Western Front The last German forces are withdrawn from the pocket west of the Rhine between Wesel and Xanten. They have lost heavily to the British and Canadian attacks. US First and Third Armies link up near Andernach completing the Allied hold on the west bank of the Rhine everywhere north of Koblenz. Field Marshal Kesselring arrives from Italy to take command of the German armies in the west.

Eastern Front The Germans advance in the Lake Balaton area begins to be slowed by the fierce Soviet ground and air resistance, by the

Below: View from the eastern end of the Ludendorff railway bridge at Remagen on the Rhine, seized intact by US forces, 7 March 1945.

atrocious muddy conditions and by the lack of fuel for the tanks and other vehicles.
Philippines Most of the 41st US Infantry Division is landed at the southwest of Mindanao near Zamboanga. General Doe commands the troops and Admiral Barbey the naval support.

On Luzon fighting continues south of Laguna de Bay where the US forces are still trying to break through to the east.

Organized Japanese resistance on the island of Palawan comes to an end.

11 March 1945

Burma Mongmit is captured by a converging attack by the two brigades of the British 36th Division which have moved south from Myitson and the third brigade of the division which moves in from the west.
Philippines There is more fighting in the Batangas area south of Manila and in the north toward Baguio.
Ulithi Atoll The carrier *Randolph* is damaged in a Kamikaze attack on the Pacific Fleet base at Ulithi.

12 March 1945

Eastern Front Kustrin falls to Zhukov's forces after a bitter struggle. Apart from a small area in the north near Stettin the Soviets now hold the whole of the Oder-Neisse line as far south as Görlitz.

Rokossovsky's forces continue to push forward toward the Gulf of Danzig. In the Polish Corridor they capture Tczew.
Western Front There is heavy fighting in the Remagen bridgehead where units of the German Seventh Army are counterattacking fiercely – but to no avail.
Burma Myotha, southwest of Mandalay, falls to the 20th Indian Division.

14 March 1945

Western Front The XII Corps of Third Army begins an offensive southeast over the Moselle from near Koblenz and XX Corps expands its attacks from between Trier and Saarburg. To the north of these actions fighting around the Remagen bridgehead goes on but it is steadily being expanded despite the German efforts.
Burma Maymo, to the east of Mandalay, is taken by the 62nd Indian Brigade. The last rail line to Mandalay is, therefore, cut. Other units of 19th Indian Division are still fighting in Mandalay but have captured much of the city in a bitter house-to-house engagement.
Eastern Front The Soviets capture Zvolen in western Czechoslovakia.

15 March 1945

Western Front The US Seventh Army goes over to the attack once more especially in the area around Saarbrücken and Bitche. Seventh Army is joining Third Army in the attempt to expel the Germans from the area between the Saar, Moselle and Rhine.
Burma The Japanese step up their efforts against Meiktila but can make no important progress against 17th Indian Division which is receiving supplies, reinforcements and ground attack support from the air.
Iwo Jima The fighting continues but the Japanese forces are now mostly confined in a small area in the northwest of the island.
Kuriles Admiral McCrea leads a squadron of US cruisers and destroyers in a bombardment of Matsuwa.

16 March 1945

Eastern Front The Soviet forces in Hungary have regrouped following the German advance in the Lake Balaton area and now begin an offensive against the northern flank of the recently won German salient. The Third Hungarian Army takes the brunt of the first assaults and is soon in great difficulty.
Philippines Part of the US 41st Division lands on Basilan Island. Here, as on other small islands, the pattern will be for the US forces to subdue the Japanese in the first few days' fighting and then mostly to withdraw, leaving the mopping up to Filipino guerrillas.

Fighting continues along the Shimbu Line southeast of Manila and in the I Corps sector to the north, especially on the Villa Verde track.
Western Front Bitche is taken as Seventh Army continues its effort to break through the Siegfried Line.

17 March 1945

Western Front The Remagen Bridge collapses under the combined strain of bomb damage and heavy use but US Army engineers have built several other bridges nearby and the advance over the Rhine continues. To the south the Third Army offensive over the Moselle takes Koblenz and Boppard on the left flank of the drive while farther forward the Nahe River has been crossed.
Burma Units of the Chinese Sixth Army take Hsipaw on the Burma Road, 50 miles southwest of Lashio. The Chinese First Army is still trying to advance along the road from Lashio to clear it of Japanese blocks.

18 March 1945

Western Front Patton's offensive captures Bingen and Bad Kreuznach as the advance to the southwest continues. To the south Seventh Army is also beginning to accelerate its progress, most of its forward units having now crossed the German border.
Eastern Front Zhukov's troops take Kolberg on the Pomeranian coast. Other Soviet forces are closing in around Gdynia and Danzig to the east and making further inroads into the German positions in East Prussia.
Philippines There are US landings on Panay by 14,000 men of 40th Infantry Division commanded by General Brush in the area near Iloilo. There is little opposition from the Japanese at first.
Burma The British 2nd Division takes Ava on the bend of the Irrawaddy only a few miles south of Mandalay. The heavy fighting in Mandalay and round Meiktila continues.

18-21 March 1945

Japan The carriers of Admiral Mitscher's TF 58 carry out a series of attacks on targets in the Japanese Home Islands. Admiral Spruance, commanding Fifth Fleet is also present. On the 18th airfields on Kyushu are the main targets. There are Kamikaze attacks by about 10 planes on the American ships in which *Intrepid*, *Yorktown* and *Enterprise* are all hit but are not put out of action. On the 19th the carrier strikes are mostly sent against Japanese naval bases in the Inland Sea area. Kure is especially singled out. Six Japanese carriers and three battleships are damaged. The Kamikaze attacks in reply are very effective. The carriers *Franklin* and *Wasp* are both badly damaged and the *Enterprise* and *Essex* less so. The 832 dead on *Franklin* make this the heaviest ever casualty list on any US ship. On the 20th and 21st the carriers are replenishing to prepare for operations around Okinawa, but the Japanese attacks continue. They achieve little success on either day but a feature of the attacks on the 22nd is that many are made by manned rocket bombs.

19 March 1945

Germany, Home Front Hitler orders a total scorched earth policy to be put into operation on all fronts. Industrial plants, buildings and food are to be completely destroyed. Speer, who remains in charge of German industry, does his best to prevent this decree being carried out. He is helped by many army leaders.
Western Front General Patch's Seventh Army completes the capture of Saarlouis. Fighting in Saarbrücken and the towns to the east continues. Third Army keeps up its rapid advance

Below: A specially converted Bren-gun carrier of the British Fourteenth Army crosses the River Mu in Burma, early 1945.

Above: British troops file aboard assault craft to take them over the Rhine, the last great barrier in the west, March 1945.

east and southeast toward the Rhine. Worms is reached, while to the left and right other units are near Mainz and Kaiserslautern.

Eastern Front There are renewed attacks by Third Belorussian Front against the German forces in East Prussia, especially in the area south of Königsberg. The drive lasts for a week until most of the German forces are eliminated or evacuated. About 38,000 are taken off by the many ships involved including large numbers of wounded and refugees.

Philippines In their northward attacks along the west coast I Corps takes Bauang south of San Fernando on Luzon.

Burma Mogok is taken by the British 36th Division.

20 March 1945

Eastern Front Soviet forces in the Stettin area eliminate the German bridgehead over the Oder at Altdamm. In East Prussia Braundsberg is captured. General Heinrici, one of the best defensive tacticians in the German army, is appointed to command Army Group Vistula in succession to Himmler. Heinrici will have the task of building up defenses along the Oder for when the Soviets extend their advance toward Berlin, but Army Group Vistula has already lost a large part of its original force in the fighting in Pomerania. It is perhaps unnecessary to point out that only the small pockets holding out near Danzig are anywhere near the Vistula.

Burma The 19th Indian Division completes the capture of Mandalay. The Fort Dufferin position has been among the most stubbornly defended by the Japanese.

Western Front Patch's forces take Saarbrücken and Zweibrücken a little to the east. In the Third Army sector Ludwigshafen and Kaiserslautern are captured. First Army is still fighting to expand the Remagen bridgehead. It is now almost 30 miles wide and 19 miles deep.

21 March 1945

Western Front The main body of Third Army is now clearing the west bank of the Rhine everywhere north of Mannheim. Other Third and Seventh Army units are cooperating to take Annweiler, Neustadt and Homberg.

22 March 1945

Western Front The US 5th Division from Patton's Third Army crosses the Rhine near Nierstein with none of the elaborate preparations which Montgomery is making in the admittedly more difficult sector farther north. It shows the contrast between their styles of generalship. Other Third Army units are completing the mopping up west of the Rhine and preparing to make crossings of their own.

Eastern Front In Silesia Konev's troops achieve a breakthrough in attacks over the Oder to the south of Oppeln and to the north of the town they extend an already existing bridgehead over the river. In the Polish Corridor the Soviet forces are still fighting to reach the Baltic between Gdynia and Danzig.

23 March 1945

Western Front The British Second and Canadian First Armies mount a carefully prepared operation, code named Plunder, to cross the Rhine in the area from Emmerich to just south of Wesel. There is massive artillery and air support. Two parachute divisions are also to be dropped to aid the crossing. The operation begins at 2100 hours. US First Army and the small part of Third Army which has crossed the Rhine are also extending their hold.

Burma As well as capturing Mandalay, XXXIII Corps units have been striking south. Wundwin is taken by 20th Indian Division on one flank of this advance.

Italy General Vietinghoff takes over command of German forces in Italy replacing Field Marshal Kesselring who has been withdrawn to the Western Front. Throughout March there have been small attacks by both II and IV US Corps of Fifth Army in the area around the Pistoia-Bologna road and to the west.

Philippines On Luzon San Fernando is taken by I Corps with help from Filipino guerrillas.

23-31 March 1945

Ryukyu Islands There are various operations by US forces in preparation for the landings on Okinawa. Between 23 and 25 March the carriers of TF 58, now 14 organized in three groups, attack targets on Okinawa Island. On the 24th scout planes from the carriers find a Japanese convoy south of Kyushu and all eight ships in it are sunk. Also on the 24th Okinawa is bombarded by five battleships and 11 destroyers commanded by Admiral Lee. On 26/27 March the British Pacific Fleet, organized as TF 57 and commanded by Admiral Rawlings, makes attacks on airfields and other targets on Sakashima Gunto. There are four fleet carriers, two battleships, five cruisers and 11 destroyers in the British force. From the 25th, the 17 escort carriers of Admiral Durgin's TF 52 begin attacks on the same targets as the fleet carriers, both supplementing their efforts and giving them opportunities to refuel. On the 25th there is a bombardment of the small island of Kerama Retto just to the west of Okinawa itself. On the 26th General Bruce's 77th Infantry Division lands on Kerama Retto and overruns it against slight Japanese resistance. This landing is necessary to protect the waters that are going to be used for the main landings on Okinawa. Also on 26th March the main bombardment of Okinawa begins. Admiral Deyo leads the 10 battleships, 10 cruisers and 33 destroyers of TF 54 in this task. Also taking part are many rocket craft.

The Japanese reply to these Allied operations includes many unsuccessful submarine attacks in which two submarines are sunk and no torpedo hits achieved. The more deadly Kamikaze attacks start on the 25th. The Kamikaze attacks on the US naval forces are to be one of the dominating features of the Okinawa campaign. The planes are from various Air Fleets in the Japanese Home Islands and on Formosa. Admiral Ugaki commands. On the 25th 26 planes attack making eight hits including one on the battleship *Nevada.* On the 27th attacks by explosive boats are beaten off and on the 30th the cruiser *Indianapolis* is badly damaged by a suicide plane.

24 March 1945

Eastern Front In Hungary Szekesfehervar falls to the attacks of Malinovsky's troops. The front line of the Soviet offensive in this area has already pushed farther to the west, taking Veszprem and Mor. The German and Hungarian forces are retiring in disorder after taking heavy losses. In north Poland the Soviets take Spolot on the coast between Gdynia and Danzig.

Western Front Montgomery's Rhine crossing operation goes well and by the end of the day the bridgehead is more than five miles deep. What remains of the town of Wesel after the preliminary bombardment is captured by British troops. The US Ninth Army, also part of Montgomery's Twenty-first Army Group, begins to cross the Rhine a little to the south of the British and Canadians.

25 March 1945

Eastern Front In East Prussia Keiligenbeil falls to units of the Third Belorussian Front. In Hungary the Soviet offensive continues with the capture of Esztergom on the Danube. Just north of the Danube there are attacks by more of Malinovsky's troops.

Western Front The various crossings of Twenty-first Army Group are consolidated into one bridgehead 30 miles wide. Further south US First Army units, principally from III Corps, begin to break out of the Remagen bridgehead. The VIII Corps from Third Army begins to cross the Rhine near Boppard. To the south Darmstadt is taken by XII Corps units who crossed at Nierstein.

Right: The Anglo-American drive into western Germany, March-May 1945.

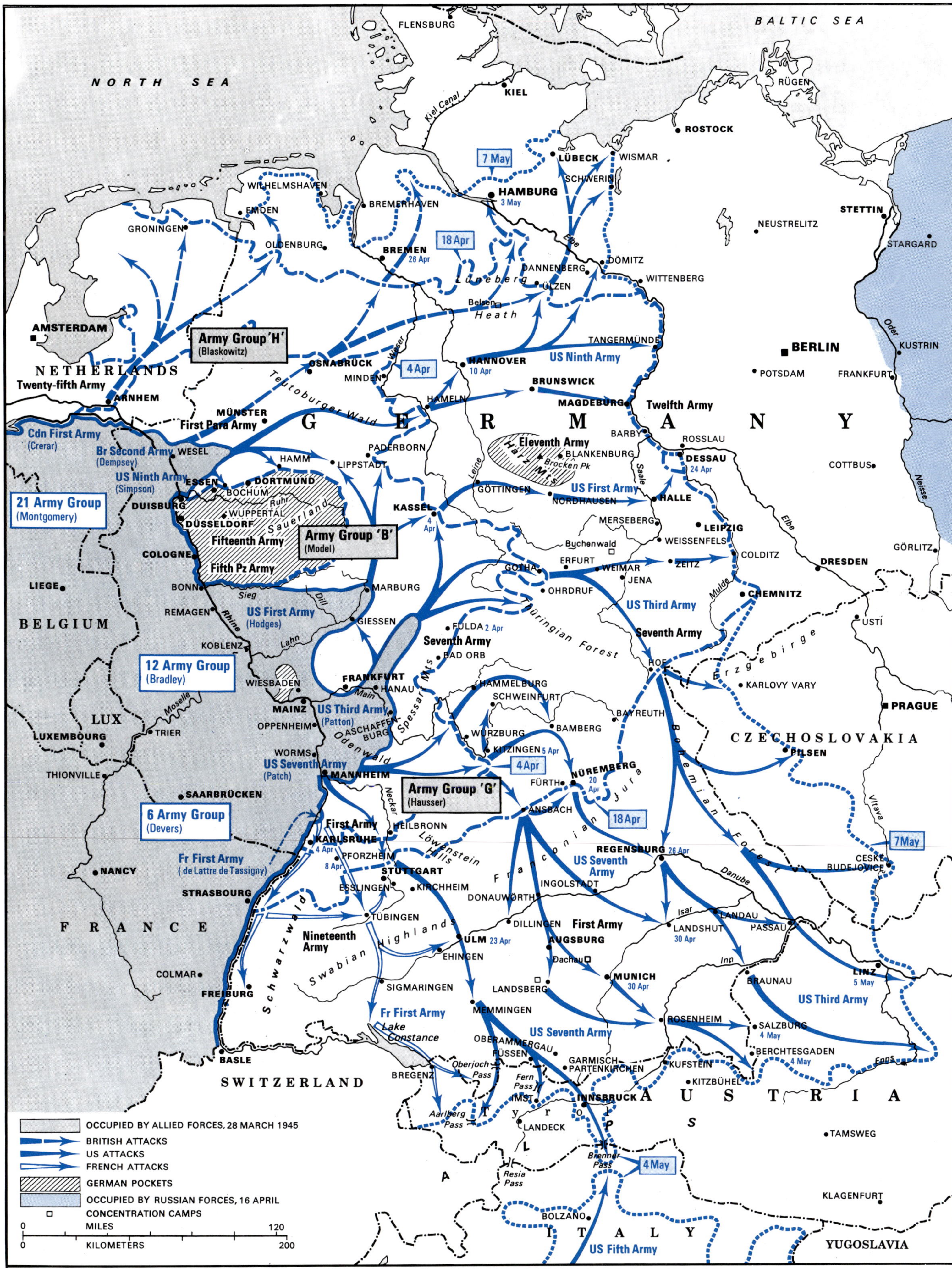
BALTIC SEA
NORTH SEA
FLENSBURG
KIEL
Kiel Canal
RÜGEN
ROSTOCK
LÜBECK
WISMAR
7 May
SCHWERIN
HAMBURG
3 May
WILHELMSHAVEN
EMDEN
BREMERHAVEN
GRONINGEN
OLDENBURG
BREMEN
26 Apr
18 Apr
Elbe
DÖMITZ
WITTENBERG
DANNENBERG
ÜLZEN
Lüneberg
Belsen
Heath
NEUSTRELITZ
STETTIN
STARGARD
Oder
KUSTRIN
BERLIN
POTSDAM
FRANKFURT
AMSTERDAM
Army Group 'H'
(Blaskowitz)
NETHERLANDS
Twenty-fifth Army
ARNHEM
OSNABRÜCK
Weser
MINDEN
4 Apr
HANNOVER
10 Apr
US Ninth Army
TANGERMÜNDE
BRUNSWICK
Teutoburger Wald
MÜNSTER
First Para Army
HAMELN
MAGDEBURG
Twelfth Army
GERMANY
Cdn First Army
(Crerar)
Br Second Army
(Dempsey)
WESEL
HAMM
LIPPSTADT
PADERBORN
BARBY
Eleventh Army
BLANKENBURG
Harz Mts
Brocken Pk
ROSSLAU
DESSAU
24 Apr
COTTBUS
US Ninth Army
(Simpson)
ESSEN
DORTMUND
BOCHUM
Ruhr
21 Army Group
(Montgomery)
DUISBURG
WUPPERTAL
Sauerland
DÜSSELDORF
Fifteenth Army
Fifth Pz Army
KASSEL
4 Apr
Leine
GÖTTINGEN
NORDHAUSEN
US First Army
Saale
HALLE
Neisse
Army Group 'B'
(Model)
MERSEBERG
LEIPZIG
Buchenwald
WEISSENFELS
Elbe
COLDITZ
GÖRLITZ
COLOGNE
BONN
Sieg
MARBURG
GOTHA
ERFURT
WEIMAR
ZEITZ
JENA
OHRDRUF
DRESDEN
LIEGE
REMAGEN
Rhine
US First Army
(Hodges)
Dill
GIESSEN
Mulde
CHEMNITZ
US Third Army
BELGIUM
KOBLENZ
Lahn
FULDA 2 Apr
Seventh Army
Thüringian Forest
Seventh Army
USTI
BAD ORB
12 Army Group
(Bradley)
WIESBADEN
FRANKFURT
Main
HANAU
HOF
Erzgebirge
KARLOVY VARY
HAMMELBURG
SCHWEINFURT
PRAGUE
LUX
Moselle
MAINZ
US Third Army
(Patton)
OPPENHEIM
ASCHAFFENBURG
Spessart Mts
BAYREUTH
LUXEMBOURG
TRIER
WÜRZBURG
BAMBERG
CZECHOSLOVAKIA
WORMS
Odenwald
KITZINGEN 5 Apr
4 Apr
PILSEN
THIONVILLE
US Seventh Army
(Patch)
MANNHEIM
NÜREMBERG
20 Apr
Jura
FÜRTH
Army Group 'G'
(Hausser)
Neckar
SAARBRÜCKEN
ANSBACH
18 Apr
Bohemian Forest
Vltava
6 Army Group
(Devers)
First Army
HEILBRONN
KARLSRUHE
4 Apr
Löwenstein Hills
Franconian
REGENSBURG 26 Apr
7 May
PFORZHEIM
8 Apr
NANCY
Fr First Army
(de Lattre de Tassigny)
STUTTGART
US Seventh Army
CESKE BUDEJOVICE
Danube
STRASBOURG
ESSLINGEN
KIRCHHEIM
INGOLSTADT
DONAUWORTH
Isar
LANDAU
TÜBINGEN
FRANCE
Nineteenth Army
Schwarzwald
DILLINGEN
First Army
LANDSHUT
30 Apr
PASSAU
Swabian Highlands
ULM 23 Apr
AUGSBURG
EHINGEN
Inn
Dachau
COLMAR
SIGMARINGEN
MUNICH
30 Apr
LINZ
5 May
LANDSBERG
BRAUNAU
FREIBURG
US Third Army
Fr First Army
MEMMINGEN
ROSENHEIM
SALZBURG
4 May
Lake Constance
OBERAMMERGAU
US Seventh Army
FÜSSEN
GARMISCH-PARTENKIRCHEN
BERCHTESGADEN
4 May
Enns
BASLE
KUFSTEIN
SWITZERLAND
BREGENZ
Oberjoch Pass
Fern Pass
KITZBÜHEL
IMST
INNSBRUCK
AUSTRIA
Tyrol
Arlberg Pass
LANDECK
ALPS
TAMSWEG
Brenner Pass
4 May
Resia Pass
KLAGENFURT
BOLZANO
ITALY
US Fifth Army
YUGOSLAVIA
OCCUPIED BY ALLIED FORCES, 28 MARCH 1945
BRITISH ATTACKS
US ATTACKS
FRENCH ATTACKS
GERMAN POCKETS
OCCUPIED BY RUSSIAN FORCES, 16 APRIL
CONCENTRATION CAMPS
0 MILES 120
0 KILOMETERS 200

26 March 1945

Iwo Jima The few hundred Japanese troops remaining on the island mount a final suicide attack. They are wiped out by the 5th Marine Division units which have been given the task of finishing off the last pockets. Only just over 200 of the Japanese garrison of 20,700 remain alive as prisoners of the Marines. The American casualties have been almost 600 dead and 17,200 wounded. In addition 90 USN personnel have died.
Western Front The US Seventh Army begins to send units of XV and VI Corps across the Rhine between Worms and Mannheim. To the north all the Allied armies continue to push forward.
Philippines About 14,000 men commanded by General Arnold and drawn from the units of the Americal Division land just south of Cebu City. Admiral Berkey leads a bombardment group in support.

27 March 1945

Eastern Front The Soviets have now penetrated to the final defense lines at both Gdynia and Danzig. The attacks go on. In Hungary and Czechoslovakia Second and Third Ukraine Fronts continue their attacks. The heaviest fighting is along the line of the Rába River where Sixth SS Panzer Army loses heavily in fruitless attempts to stem the Soviet advance.
Western Front In the northern sector Twenty-first Army Group units are advancing along the line of the River Lippe and Ninth Army especially is beginning to penetrate south into the Ruhr area. Third Army has now crossed the Main both west of Frankfurt, where Wiesbaden is attacked, and to the east.
Philippines Cebu City is taken by the US landing force. As on the other islands the Japanese are beginning to withdraw to inland strongholds where they will be confined and worn down by Filipino guerrillas. Only on Luzon, Mindanao and Negros will the prolonged presence of US troops be necessary.

Below: A German V2 (*Vergeltungswaffe* or 'Reprisal Weapon') liquid-fuel rocket is launched against England, early 1945.

Above: US pilots race toward their waiting Grumman F6F Hellcat fighters on board the carrier USS *Hornet*, China Sea, February 1945.

In Manila Bay an American force lands on Caballo Island, better known to the former defenders of the island as Fort Hughes. After struggling to penetrate the Japanese defenses until 5 April, the US forces will pour thousands of gallons of a diesel/gasoline mixture into the fort and set it on fire. Even after this treatment the Japanese resistance is not entirely finished.
Britain, Home Front The last German V2 rocket lands southeast of London at Orpington. The V2 campaign has killed over 2700 British civilians and injured 6500. As well as the 1115 launched at British targets a further 2050 were aimed at Antwerp, Brussels and Liège.

28 March 1945

Western Front Marburg is taken by US III Corps which has made a rapid advance from the Remagen bridgehead.

General Eisenhower sends a controversial signal to Stalin giving details of his order of battle and saying that he intends to send the main weight of his advance across southern Germany and Austria. The main thrust is to be toward Erfurt and Leipzig and a secondary effort is to go for Nüremberg, Regensburg and Linz. The British protest very strongly about this signal suggesting that decisions of such importance should not be taken by Eisenhower alone and that he is also overstepping his authority in communicating directly with the Soviets. The British would prefer the advance to be directed on Berlin as has been the plan up to now for the political value of this move. They believe that this plan is superior to one based on doubtful reports and worries of the preparation of a German National Redoubt in Bavaria. Both Churchill and the British Chiefs of Staff present this case to Washington. President Roosevelt has now become so weakened by his illness that most military decisions are left to General Marshall and the Joint Chiefs of Staff. Marshall has always been inclined to favor military rather than political reasoning in making strategic decisions and, therefore, confirms his support for Eisenhower. With the advantage of knowledge of future Soviet behavior, it is easy to comment that the war was fought for political and not military reasons, and that an advance to Berlin might have left the Western Allies in a stronger position in postwar Europe.
German Command After a blazing row with Hitler, General Guderian is dismissed from his post as Chief of the Army General Staff. His replacement is General Krebs, a less talented officer. Although Guderian has only been able to achieve a fraction of his aims against Hitler's opposition he has managed to preserve some sanity in the actions of the German High Command. He is the last of the famous German leaders from the early war period to be dismissed.
Eastern Front Gdynia falls to Rokossovsky's forces. Just south of the Danube Györ is taken by troops from Second Ukraine Front.
Burma The Japanese have failed in their efforts to retake Meiktila and while they have been involved in this area XXXIII Corps has been making important gains to the north. General Kimura, commanding Japanese forces in Burma, decides that with his main communications cut, he must try to retreat as best he can. Many of the Japanese will manage to escape via Thazi to the east of Meiktila.

29 March 1945

Philippines There are US landings in the northwest of the island of Negros near Bacolod. The landing force is from 185th Regiment. The Japanese on this island will fight very fiercely.

30 March 1945

Eastern Front On the Baltic coast the final German positions in Danzig are overcome by Soviet attacks. In Hungary the attacks of Third Ukraine Front beyond the Raba have made such good progress that the advance units enter Austria north of Köszeg. To the north of these attacks Second Ukraine Front is closing in on Bratislava.
Western Front The US First Army advances north out of its salient around Marburg and reaches and crosses the River Eder. Third Army is attempting to strike east and north toward Gotha and Kassel.
Burma Kyaukse is taken by 20th Indian Division. The British forces now hold most of the important positions on the road between Mandalay

and Meiktila. The Japanese forces in central Burma have been brought to battle and defeated exactly as General Slim has hoped. The Japanese have not been able to slip away largely intact as they intended, and instead have been compelled to fight the main action with improvised forces against the carefully organized British defense around Meiktila.

Europe, Air Operations In US attacks on the north German ports the cruiser *Köln* and 14 U-Boats are sunk.

31 March 1945

Western Front Forces of French First Army begin to cross the Rhine near Speyer. To the north all the Allied armies maintain their advance.

Eastern Front Ratibor on the upper Danube is taken by Konev's troops.

Burma Northeast of Mandalay the British 36th Division and units of the Chinese Sixth Army take Kyaukme. The Burma Road from Mandalay to Lashio is now clear.

April 1945

Europe, Air Operations Despite the progress of the Allied ground forces the efforts of the British and American Strategic Air Forces continue until almost the end of the month. The Eighth Air Force flies 18,900 sorties to drop 46,600 tons of bombs. The targets include jet airfields and communications centers. Nuremberg, Bayreuth, Neumark and Berlin are all hit. RAF Bomber Command drops 38,400 tons particularly against ports and shipping including Hamburg, Kiel, and Bremen. Leipzig is also attacked. Heavy bombers are used to drop food to parts of Holland and to evacuate freed prisoners of war from Germany. Tactical targets are attacked by the heavy bomber forces and other units. On 16 April American and Soviet ground attack forces meet near Dresden when they try to attack the same German train. On 30 April the British and American authorities announce that the strategic bombing offensive is over.

Far East, Air Operations The fire bombing attacks on Japanese cities go on. Tokyo is heavily attacked on six occasions during the month, and after 6 April land based escorts can be provided for the bombers. Kawasaki and Nagoya are among the other city targets. Also attacked are airfields in the Home Islands used by Kamikaze aircraft involved in the Okinawa operation. At the very end of March a major mining campaign in Japanese home waters has been begun by the B-29 forces and this now gets fully under way.

There are many air operations in support of the land forces in Southeast Asia Command and Fourteenth Air Force in China is active against rail targets particularly.

Battle of the Atlantic The German submarine strength still remains high at 166 operational and 278 on trials or in training at the start of the month. They sink 13 ships this month, but 27 are sunk at sea and 15 more destroyed by bombing. Only now does the first of the advanced Type XXI see service.

1 April 1945

Okinawa The US forces begin Operation Iceberg, the invasion of Okinawa. It is the largest naval operation yet in the Pacific. Admiral Turner's TF 51 provides the 1200 transport and landing ships with over 450,000 Army and Marine Corps personnel embarked. The troops landed are from III Amphibious and XXIV Corps of General Buckner's Tenth Army. The landings are in the Hagushi area in the southwest of the island. Geiger's III Corps lands on the left with 6th and 1st Marine Divisions providing the assault units. Hodge's forces on the right are 7th and 96th Infantry Divisions. Hodge is to deal with the south end of the island and Geiger to advance to the north. There is almost no resistance on the first day and a solid beachhead three miles deep and nine miles wide is established. (Okinawa is 70 miles long and a maximum of 10 miles wide.) Kadena and Yontan airfields are taken.

The explanation for the lack of resistance is that the Japanese forces, 130,000 men of General Ushijima's Thirty-second Army, are entrenched in concealed positions and caves mostly to the south of the US landings on the Shuri Line. There are also 450,000 civilians on the island.

Throughout the battle at least two of the carrier groups of TF 58 will normally be available to give air support. The British TF 57 and the escort carrier groups will also be heavily involved. There will be almost daily bombardment by the heavy ships of TF 54. Japanese air operations, both conventional and Kamikaze attacks, will be equally plentiful. On the first day the US battleship *West Virginia* and the British carrier *Indomitable* are hit along with eight other ships.

Western Front The US First and Ninth Armies link up at Lippstadt, cutting off the German forces in the Ruhr which consist of 325,000 men mostly from Fifteenth and Fifth Panzer Armies under Model's command. Other First and Ninth Army units take Hamm and Paderborn. To the north British units have crossed the Mitteland Canal near Münster and are advancing toward Osnabruck.

Eastern Front Tolbukhin's forces capture Sopron in western Hungary south of Vienna. The advance here and by Malinovsky's forces to the north continues. On the Oder the resistance of the German pocket at Glogau is overcome by Konev's forces.

Philippines General MacNider's 158th Regiment lands at Legaspi in the southeast of Luzon and takes the town and airfield nearby. There is no Japanese resistance at first. Elsewhere on Luzon the US forces are beginning to make ground toward the southeast of Manila after much hard fighting against General Yokoyama's Shimbu Group. Yamashita's forces in the north of the island have also been fighting hard against both regular American units and guerrillas.

Italy British Guards and Commando units attack over the River Reno between Lake Comacchio and the sea.

2 April 1945

Western Front The British Second Army continues its advance north of the Ruhr. Münster is taken. The Canadian First Army also begins to move north and east from between Nijmegen and Emmerich.

Eastern Front In southeast Hungary Nagykanizsa falls to the Soviet advance while in Slovakia Kremnica is taken.

Okinawa The US forces on the island advance easily across to the east coast and make some progress to the north and south.

Philippines Part of the US 163rd Regiment is landed on Tawitawi in the Sulu Archipelago.

2-5 April 1945

Okinawa, Air and Naval Operations On the 2nd as well as the normal bombardment and air support missions performed by the US forces there are attacks by the British carriers on Sakashima Gunto Island. In Kamikaze attacks four US transports are badly damaged with many casualties among the troops aboard. On 3 April one escort carrier and other ships are hit and on 5 April the battleship *Nevada* is damaged by fire from a shore battery. Bad weather which sets in from the 4th damages many landing craft.

3 April 1945

Eastern Front In Austria the Soviet forces take Wiener Neustadt. Almost all of Hungary is now clear of Axis troops while in Czechoslovakia Bratislava is besieged.

Below: Type XXI U-Boats, surrendered by the Germans. The Type XXI was a modern ocean-going design, but it appeared too late to be decisive.

Philippines Part of the US 40th Division lands on Masbate to help the Filipino guerrillas who have controlled part of it for several days.

4 April 1945

Western Front British and Canadian units take Osnabruck and move on Minden. US Ninth Army units have reached the River Weser opposite Hameln. Troops from Third Army capture Kassel while other units of Patton's force are advancing near Erfurt after taking Gotha. French units take Karlsruhe.
Okinawa The US forces begin to meet the first real Japanese resistance on the ground. Hodge's troops are brought to a halt on a line just south of Kuba while Geiger's have reached the Ishikawa Isthmus.
Eastern Front Bratislava falls to Malinovsky's forces.

5 April 1945

Philippines South and west of Manila the US forces on either side of Laguna de Bay are beginning to make significant gains in their attacks.
Italy On the west coast US units from Fifth Army begin to attack north near Massa, south of La Spezia.
Western Front Allied forces cross the Weser at several points.
Japan, Politics General Koiso and his cabinet resign. Admiral Suzuki forms the new government. Togo is Foreign Minister and Hiranuma President of the Privy Council. There is less military influence in this Cabinet than in Koiso's and all its members are agreed that no reasonable offer of peace should be turned down. Some even go as far as to think that any offer should be accepted if this is the only way that invasion can be avoided.
Diplomatic Affairs Molotov tells the Japanese ambassador in Moscow that the USSR does not propose to renew the 1941 Nonaggression Pact.
United States Command It is announced that General MacArthur will take control of all army forces in the Pacific and Admiral Nimitz all naval forces in preparation for the invasion of Japan.

6 April 1945

Eastern Front The Soviet forces begin to besiege Vienna. In East Prussia Third Belorussian Front begins its final attacks on Königsberg after several days of preparatory bombardment and air attacks. Yugoslavian forces expel the Germans from Sarajevo.
Okinawa Geiger's Corps continues to advance to the north, but the other US units can make no progress against the first defenses of the Shuri Line.

6-9 April 1945

Okinawa Air and Naval Operations/Battle of the South China Sea On 6 April the giant battleship *Yamato* leaves the Inland Sea accompanied by a cruiser and eight destroyers on a Kamikaze mission to Okinawa. *Yamato* only has enough fuel to reach Okinawa but not to return and the Japanese intention is to beach the giant ship off Okinawa and to fight from that position any US forces nearby. The *Yamato* is sighted several times and reported by US submarines. Also on the 6th there are many suicide plane attacks on shipping around Okinawa. The carriers *San Jacinto* and *Illustrious* are both hit along with 25 other ships. The small warships are put out of action. The British carriers are well served by their armored decks in this and all the actions off Okinawa.

On 7 April the *Yamato* is found by planes from the US carrier groups and in two waves of attacks involving 380 planes the battleship takes 10 torpedo and five heavy bomb hits before going down. Kamikaze attacks on the American shipping damages the carrier *Hancock* and the battleship *Maryland* as well as other units. On the 8th and 9th there are less concentrated attacks in which three destroyers and two other ships are badly hit.

7 April 1945

Western Front Large parts of US First and Ninth Armies are heavily engaged around the Ruhr pocket while among the gains in the advance to the east is Göttingen.

8 April 1945

Burma The British forces have regrouped following their success at Mandalay and Meiktila and are now ready for a rapid armored and motorized advance to finish the campaign in Burma. The British IV Corps is to advance down the Sittang Valley and XXXIII Corps by the Irrawaddy Valley. All units have been specially organized to make them more mobile.

Below: The American invasion of Okinawa, April-June 1945.

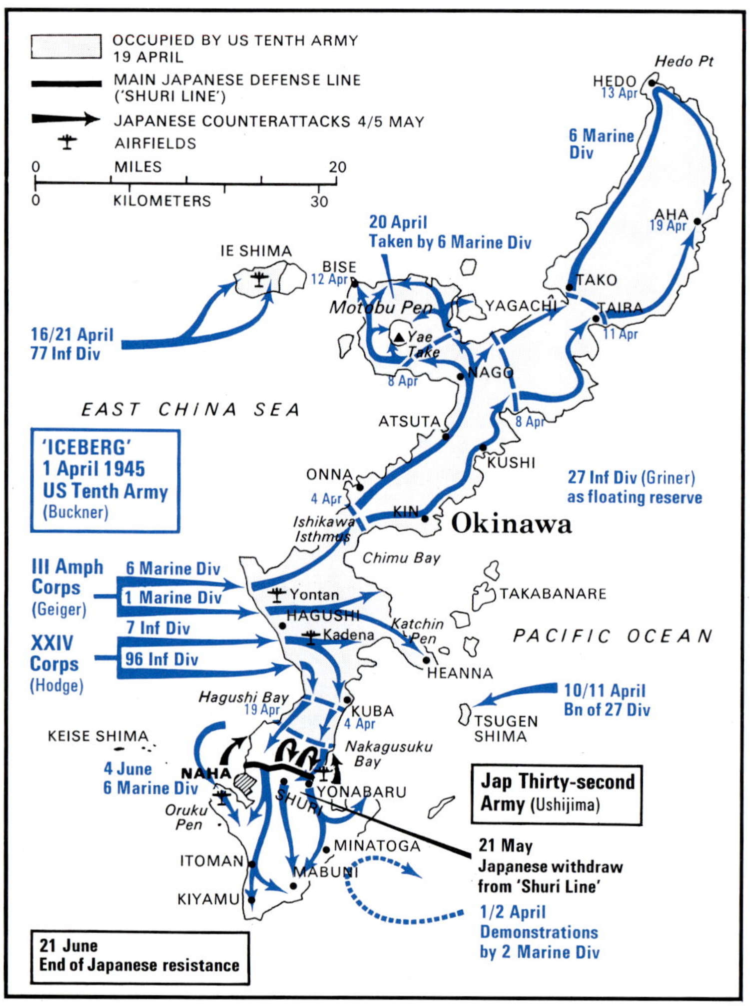

Below: A Japanese *kamikaze* pilot, adorned with various symbols of his impending sacrifice, prepares to fly a mission.

Above: American battleship USS *Idaho* (right) contributes to the bombardment of Okinawa, 1 April 1945.

Eastern Front In Austria the Soviet forces push on west of Vienna despite German counterattacks. There is very fierce streetfighting in the Austrian capital. In East Prussia the Soviet attacks on Königsberg begin to break through the defenses.
Western Front In the southern sector of the front French troops take Pforzheim as they continue their drive to the southeast. To the north US Seventh Army units capture Schweinfurt. Other Allied armies farther north also advance.
Okinawa The III Corps advance has now cut the neck of the Motobu Peninsula and 6th Marine Division begins operations to clear it of Japanese forces.
Philippines The US forces are reinforced by the landing of a second regiment in the northwest of Negros near Bacolod.

9 April 1945

Italy The Allied spring offensive gets under way with attacks by General McCreery's Eighth Army. Fifth Army is also to attack but in order to make best use of the available air support in the assault phases of both attacks Fifth Army will not begin full-scale operations until the 14th. The main units of Eighth Army will be directed toward Ferrara but the left flank will reach to Bologna. Fifth Army is to advance with its right toward Bologna while other units penetrate past Modena to the Po.
Eighth Army's offensive begins with attacks by II Polish Corps along Route 9 toward Imola and by British V and X Corps to the right and left of the Poles.
Eastern Front The surviving defenders of the Königsberg fortress surrender to the Red Army. Some of the German troops in East Prussia fight on in the Samland Peninsula.
Western Front In the attacks against the Ruhr pocket Ninth Army units penetrate into Essen and reach the famous Krupp factories. Other British and US units, including some more from Ninth Army, are advancing near the River Leine to the east.
Okinawa There are unsuccessful XXIV Corps attacks in the Kakazu sector of the Shuri Line.
Philippines The 163rd Regiment of 41st Division lands on Jolo. There is no Japanese resistance. Other 41st Division units land on Busuanga in the Calamian group.
Europe, Air Operations In an RAF attack on Kiel the German navy ships *Scheer, Hipper* and *Emden* are damaged beyond repair.

10 April 1945

Western Front Hanover falls to the US XIII Corps from Ninth Army. Canadian forces are beginning to put pressure on the German positions in Holland. They begin operations to cross the River Ijssel. British Second Army is advancing toward Bremen, US Third Army toward Erfurt and Seventh Army to Nuremberg.
Italy Eighth Army's attacks make some good progress largely because the Germans have expected the main effort to come farther to the west. In the as yet limited efforts of Fifth Army on the west coast Massa is taken.
Philippines On Luzon the advance of XIV Corps reaches Lamon Bay and the coastal town of Mauban is captured.
Burma Thazi, east of Meiktila, is captured by the British IV Corps.

11 April 1945

Eastern Front In Vienna Tolbukhin's attacks continue and have reached the Danube Canal near the city center.
Western Front Advance tank units of Ninth Army reach the Elbe south of Magdeburg. Forces of Third Army take Weimar. The British cross the Leine near Celle.
Italy Carrara is taken by the US 92nd Infantry Division which has advanced on from Massa. Eighth Army's attacks have now pushed the leading units over the Senio to the Santerno and bridging operations there have begun.
Indian Ocean Sabang is shelled by the battleships *Queen Elizabeth* and *Richelieu* of Admiral Walker's British Eastern Fleet. Two escort carriers give air cover and attack installations and shipping at Port Blair and Emmahaven.
Philippines Units of the Americal Division land on Bohol.

11-14 April 1945

Okinawa, Air and Naval Operations All four groups of TF 58 participate in operations against Okinawa and Japanese air bases. From 11 to 13 April the British carriers attack Sakashima Gunto. Japanese attacks score hits on the battleship *Missouri* and the carrier *Enterprise* on the 11th, on several of the radar picket ships on the 12th as well as two battleships and eight other vessels of the main forces. On the 13th only one destroyer is hit and on the 14th the battleship *New York* is damaged. The radar picket system provides for destroyer patrols to be stationed some way from the main forces to give warning of air attacks so that fighters can make interceptions before the attacking aircraft can close. Their advanced position makes the picket destroyers especially vulnerable to the Japanese attacks.

Below: Young German soldiers surrender to an American rifleman in the city of Mannheim, April 1945. The war in the west was almost over.

Above: Major General Lemuel C Shepherd, commander of the US 6th Marine Division on Okinawa, April 1945. His men saw hard fighting.

12 April 1945

United States, Politics President Roosevelt dies of a cerebral haemorrhage at Warm Springs in Georgia. Vice-President Truman becomes President. Truman has so far had little involvement in the work of Roosevelt's administration (he was a surprising choice as running mate in 1944) and among the subjects on which he receives his first briefing in the next few days is the atomic-weapons project.

Roosevelt has been a president of whom strong opinions have been held. Most of the American people have valued his undoubted qualities of leadership both in bringing the United States out of the troubles of the Depression and in leading his country into war against the Axis dictatorships. A considerable number of Americans have held equally forceful opinions opposed to Roosevelt's ideas and methods. In the other Allied countries, especially in Britain, Roosevelt has been almost universally liked and respected.

Western Front US Ninth Army forces cross the Elbe near Magdeburg while in the rear of their advance Brunswick falls. Patton's troops take Erfurt. In the south French units take Baden Baden. The Ruhr pocket has been reduced by the capture of Essen by US attacks.

Italy Eighth Army has three separate bridgeheads over the Santerno. On the right of the attack V Corps is advancing along the north bank of the Reno.

Okinawa Fighting continues on the Motobu Peninsula and in the Kakazu sector of the Shuri Line but the US forces make little ground in these areas.

Burma The IV Corps advance is beginning to make progress in the Sittang Valley. There is fighting at Pyaubwe and Yamethin. To the west of Meiktila 7th Indian Division from XXXIII Corps takes Kyaukpadaung.

13 April 1945

Western Front The full horror of German crimes begins to become clear to the west, with the liberation of Belsen and Buchenwald by British and American forces respectively. Jena is taken by Third Army units. Patch's forces take Bamberg.

Eastern Front Vienna falls to Tolbukhin's Third Ukraine Front after a fierce street battle.

Okinawa The units of 6th Marine Division not engaged on the Motobu Peninsula continue their advance up the west coast and reach the northwest tip of the island at Hedo Point.

Philippines In Manila Bay US forces land on Fort Drum, 'the Concrete Battleship,' and begin to pour 5000 gallons of oil fuel into the fortifications. This is then set on fire and burns for five days eliminating the Japanese garrison. On 16 April a landing on Fort Frank finds it abandoned. This completes the capture of the islands in Manila Bay.

14 April 1945

Italy Fifth Army joins Eighth Army in major offensive operations. The Fifth Army attacks are sent in on either side of the roads to Bologna from Florence and Pistoia. In this latter sector Vergato is taken.

Philippines The US XIV Corps continues its advance onto the Bicol Peninsula in the southwest of Luzon. Calauag is taken. In north Luzon I Corps is still attacking near Baguio, but can only make very slight progress.

14-20 April 1945

France There are attacks by French land, sea and air units on remaining German positions in the southwest at Royan. The battleship *Lorraine* provides bombardment support. The Germans surrender on 20 April.

15 April 1945

Burma In XXXIII Corps' advance Taungdwingyi falls to 20th Indian Division. Other units of XXXIII Corps are still fighting farther up the Irrawaddy than the next objectives for 20th Indian which now moves toward Magwe and Thayetmyo.

Western Front In Holland Canadian troops take Arnhem and attack toward Gronigen. The US First Army takes Leuna, but the units of Ninth Army which have crossed the Elbe near Magdeburg are forced to retreat.

Eastern Front The Soviets begin a final series of attacks against the German positions in Samland.

Okinawa The 6th Marine Division fights hard to capture Yae Take Hill but is driven back by the defense.

Italy Both Fifth and Eighth Armies continue their attacks. In the Eighth Army sector the Polish II Corps has now reached the Sillaro after crossing the Santerno.

15-26 April 1945

Okinawa, Air and Sea Operations The escort carrier groups are active throughout the period while the fleet carriers rotate their duties with one group attacking targets on Okinawa, two attacking airfields on Kyushu and the fourth

Below: US Marine Vought F4U Corsair fighters are silhouetted against a sky woven by AA tracer fire during a Japanese attack, Okinawa.

away replenishing. The British carriers mostly keep Sakishima Gunto neutralized. The third major phase of the Japanese Kamikaze attacks occur on the 16th and 17th. The carrier *Intrepid* and battleship *Missouri* are among the ships hit.

On the 18th and 19th there are especially intense attacks on targets on Okinawa itself from two fleet carrier groups and two escort-carrier groups. The positions of the Japanese 62nd and 63rd Divisions on the Shuri Line are hard hit in support of the ground offensive which begins on the 19th.

On 20th April the British carriers return to Leyte for a brief refit.

16 April 1945

Eastern Front After receiving Eisenhower's 28 March message Stalin has become convinced that the British and Americans will not head for southern Germany but go for Berlin. He has, therefore, ordered preparations for the last great offensive to take the German capital to be hurried forward. Zhukov's First Belorussian Front and Konev's First Ukraine Front are to lead the attack with support from Rokossovsky in the north. Perhaps in an effort to divide the glory and retain credit for himself and not the army or any one of its leaders, Stalin has not made it clear whether Zhukov or Konev has to make the final assault on the city. Between them the two Soviet Marshals have well over 2,000,000 men, more than 6000 tanks and self-propelled guns, a similar number of aircraft and almost 16,000 guns – one gun for every 13 feet of the front on which the assault will take place. Although the Germans have about 1,000,000 men deployed in fairly strong and well-prepared positions overlooking the west bank of the Oder and Neisse, they are totally outmatched in the air and on the ground they have nothing to compare with the lavish scale of Soviet equipment. The German troops are organized in General Heinrici's Army Group Vistula and Field Marhal Schoerner's Army Group Center. After the massive artillery preparation Zhukov's attacks begin from the Soviet bridgehead already taken west of the Oder near Kustrin. Konev's attack begins a little later over the Neisse north and south of Triebel. By a well-timed short withdrawal the Germans have avoided the worst effects of the Soviet bombardment, but they have too little strength to do more than hold the Soviet attack temporarily.
Western Front US Seventh Army units reach the outskirts of Nuremberg. The special POW camp at Colditz is freed by other Allied units.
Okinawa The US 77th Infantry Division lands on the small island of Ie Shima. The island and its airfield are occupied by 21 April aftrer a fierce battle in which 5000 Japanese are killed. The 77th Division is then ferried over to join the main fighting on Okinawa.
Burma In the Arakan. Taungup falls to the British forces.

17 April 1945

Eastern Front The Soviet attacks east of Berlin continue. In the very fierce battles which have developed the Germans are fighting with skill and desperation but are slowly being forced to give ground.

In Austria and Czechoslovakia the Soviet attacks and German losses continue. Zisterdorf and Pölten are taken in Austria.
Italy All Eighth Army units are now making fine progress in the continuing Allied offensive. On the right Argenta falls to V Corps with help from an amphibious move across Lake Comachio. North and east of Argenta there are no more rivers before the Po and the British units are soon passing through this 'Argenta Gap.' West of Argenta XIII Corps has now come into the line between V Corps and the Poles who are themselves moving northwest toward Bologna. Fifth Army attacks are also continuing, but with slightly slower progress because of the more difficult terrain south and west of Bologna.
Western Front German units in the Ruhr are beginning to surrender on a large scale. There is also fighting near Bremen and Nuremberg.
Philippines There are US landings in Moro Gulf at Cotabatu. The assault units are from 24th Infantry Division from General Sibert's X Corps. Admiral Noble leads three cruisers and a destroyer force in support. The US forces which landed at Zamboanga early in March have already cleared a large part of the southwest of the island, but the majority of General Suzuki's Thirty-fifth Army remains in being. There is no opposition to the new landings at first.

18 April 1945

Western Front The German forces in the Ruhr pocket surrender. Field Marshal Model commits suicide. Altogether 325,000 prisoners have been taken in this area by the Allied forces. Patton's troops cross the Czechoslovakian border after a whirlwind advance. The US Ninth Army takes Magdeburg.
Eastern Front Except in a small area in Konev's sector the Soviet forces have made less than 10 miles in their advance toward Berlin, but the German opposition is gradually being worn down.

19 April 1945

Okinawa The XXIV Corps now has three divisions, 7th, 27th and 96th, in line and all three begin attacks after a heavy ground and air bombardment. The heaviest efforts are on either coastal flank.
Western Front The US First Army captures Leipzig. The British Second Army reaches the Elbe south of Namburg.
Burma In the Sittang Valley Pyinmana falls to the 5th Indian Division which now leads IV Corps' advance. Farther north between Meiktila and the Irrawaddy, XXXIII Corps completes the clearance of the Mount Popo area and takes Chauk also. Farther south along the Irrawaddy Magwe is taken by 20th Indian Division which has advanced southwest from Meiktila.
Philippines In the advance of US I Corps units on the northwest coast of Luzon Vigan is taken.

20 April 1945

Eastern Front Rokossovsky's troops join Zhukov's and Konev's in the advance from the Oder. Rokossovsky's Second Belorussian Front attacks on a 30-mile front southwest of Stettin. To the south the German resistance on the Oder and Neisse has been smashed and the Soviet forces on both fronts are beginning to move forward more rapidly. Many of Konev's units are over the Spree while Zhukov's troops have taken Prötzel.
Western Front Nuremberg and Stuttgart are taken in the Allied advance. In the Stuttgart area the French First Army is advancing rapidly.
Okinawa III Corps completes the capture of the Motobu Peninsula and the whole of the main northern part of the island. The US attacks on the Shuri Line continue, but the few gains made cannot be held against the Japanese counter-attacks.

21 April 1945

Eastern Front Some of Zhukov's leading tank units reach the eastern suburbs of Berlin.
Italy Bologna is captured by units of the Polish II Corps. Units of II US Corps also enter the town a few hours later. The main forces of Fifth Army have now fought their way down from the Apennines into the Lombard Plain and their advance to the Po, therefore, quickens. East of Bologna Eighth Army is also moving forward rapidly.
Burma The IV Corps advance in the Sittang Valley is beginning to pull ahead of the parallel

Below: A Russian M1935 152mm gun fires into the center of Berlin, early May 1945. The tracked carriage was unique to Soviet artillery.

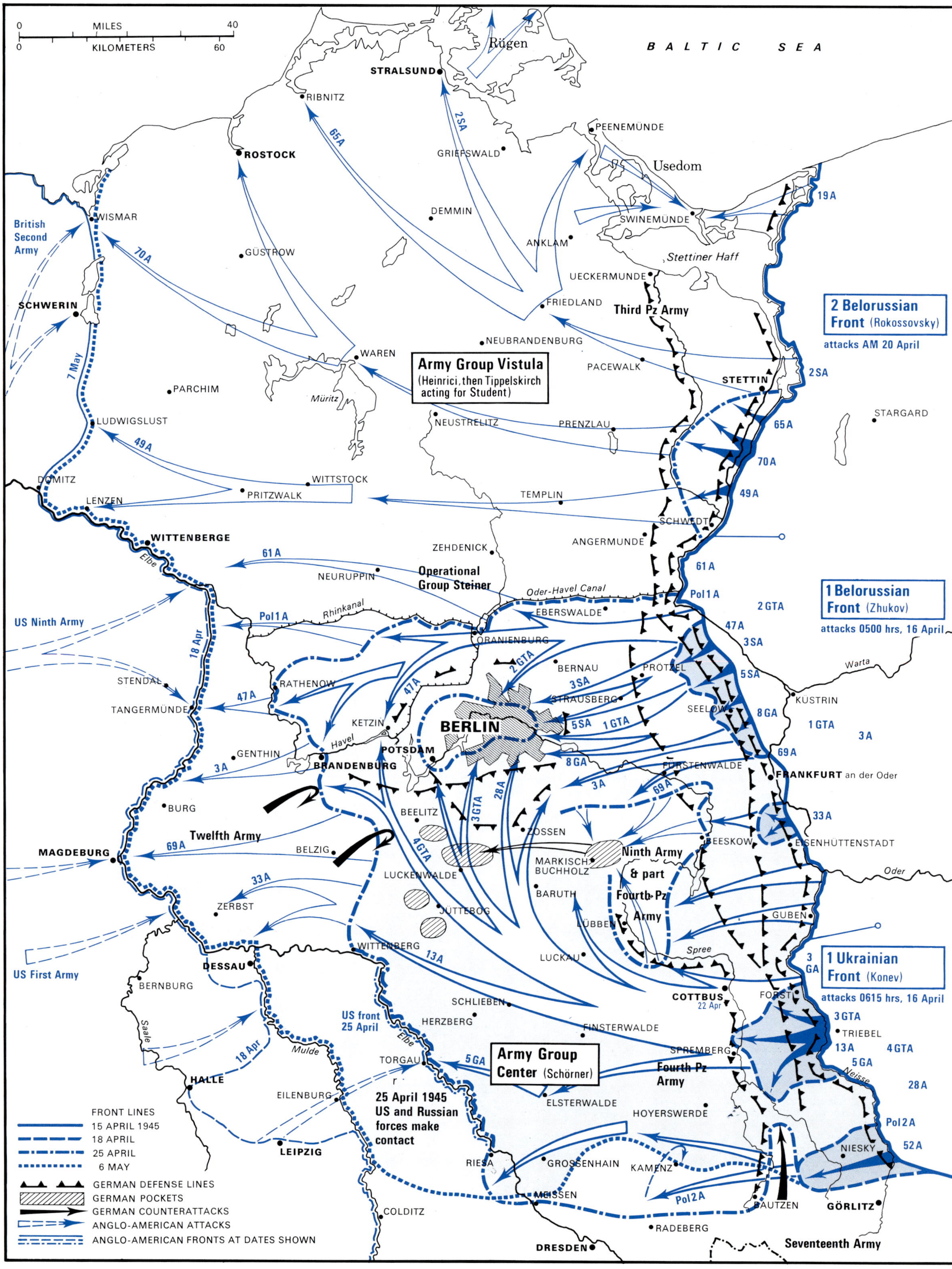

0 MILES 40
0 KILOMETERS 60
BALTIC SEA
Rügen
STRALSUND
RIBNITZ
ROSTOCK
PEENEMÜNDE
GRIEFSWALD
Usedom
SWINEMÜNDE
19A
DEMMIN
ANKLAM
Stettiner Haff
UECKERMUNDE
WISMAR
British Second Army
GÜSTROW
70A
65A
2SA
SCHWERIN
FRIEDLAND
Third Pz Army
2 Belorussian Front (Rokossovsky)
attacks AM 20 April
NEUBRANDENBURG
WAREN
Army Group Vistula
(Heinrici, then Tippelskirch acting for Student)
PACEWALK
STETTIN
2SA
7 May
PARCHIM
Müritz
STARGARD
LUDWIGSLUST
NEUSTRELITZ
PRENZLAU
65A
49A
70A
DÖMITZ
WITTSTOCK
PRITZWALK
LENZEN
TEMPLIN
49A
SCHWEDT
WITTENBERGE
ZEHDENICK
ANGERMUNDE
Elbe
61A
NEURUPPIN
Operational Group Steiner
61A
Oder-Havel Canal
Pol1A
1 Belorussian Front (Zhukov)
attacks 0500 hrs, 16 April
US Ninth Army
Pol1A
Rhinkanal
EBERSWALDE
2GTA
47A
3SA
ORANIENBURG
2GTA
BERNAU
PROTZEL
Warta
5SA
18 Apr
STENDAL
RATHENOW
3SA
STRAUSBERG
47A
KUSTRIN
47A
TANGERMÜNDE
KETZIN
BERLIN
5SA
1GTA
SEELOW
8GA
1GTA
3A
Havel
POTSDAM
GENTHIN
BRANDENBURG
8GA
FÜRSTENWALDE
69A
FRANKFURT an der Oder
3A
3A
69A
28A
3GTA
BURG
BEELITZ
33A
ZOSSEN
Twelfth Army
BEESKOW
MAGDEBURG
69A
BELZIG
4GTA
MARKISCH-BUCHHOLZ
Ninth Army
& part Fourth Pz Army
EISENHÜTTENSTADT
LUCKENWALDE
Oder
BARUTH
33A
ZERBST
JÜTTEBOG
LÜBBEN
GUBEN
WITTENBERG
Spree
13A
1 Ukrainian Front (Konev)
attacks 0615 hrs, 16 April
US First Army
LUCKAU
3 GA
DESSAU
BERNBURG
SCHLIEBEN
COTTBUS
22 Apr
FORST
US front 25 April
Saale
HERZBERG
Elbe
FINSTERWALDE
3GTA
TRIEBEL
13A
4GTA
18 Apr
Mulde
5GA
Army Group Center (Schörner)
SPREMBERG
5GA
Fourth Pz Army
Neisse
28A
TORGAU
HALLE
EILENBURG
25 April 1945
US and Russian forces make contact
ELSTERWALDE
HOYERSWERDE
Pol2A
FRONT LINES
15 APRIL 1945
18 APRIL
25 APRIL
6 MAY
GERMAN DEFENSE LINES
GERMAN POCKETS
GERMAN COUNTERATTACKS
ANGLO-AMERICAN ATTACKS
ANGLO-AMERICAN FRONTS AT DATES SHOWN
LEIPZIG
RIESA
GROSSENHAIN
KAMENZ
NIESKY
52A
MEISSEN
Pol2A
BAUTZEN
GÖRLITZ
COLDITZ
RADEBERG
DRESDEN
Seventeenth Army

efforts in the Irrawaddy Valley. Yedashe is taken by 5th Indian Division, while in the rear the airfields around Pyinmana are being cleared to be put into Allied service. In the Irrawaddy Valley Yenangyaung falls to XXXIII Corps units mopping up in the rear of the main advance.
Philippines The heavy fighting near Baguio is continuing, with the attacks of the US 37th Division making some gains near the River Irisan and the 33rd Division making ground to the west of the city.
Diplomatic Affairs A mutual assistance treaty is concluded between the Soviets and the Lublin Polish Government. This is a further indication that Stalin will not be scrupulous about his Yalta promises to arrange free elections and political processes in Eastern Europe.

22 April 1945

Diplomatic Affairs Himmler meets Count Bernadotte of the Swedish Red Cross and gives him a message to pass to the Western Allies, offering a German surrender to the British and Americans but not to the Soviets. The message is passed to the Allies on the 24th.
Western Front Seventh Army units cross the Danube at Dillingen and Baldingen.
Philippines The US 31st Infantry Division is landed at Moro Gulf. The 24th Division is already advancing inland and has nearly reached Kabakan.

On Jolo the last Japanese resistance comes to an end as their final strongpoints fall to the US forces. Some scattered individuals remain at large but they can achieve nothing.
Italy Units of II and IV US Corps reach the River Penaro in their advance to the Po. On the left flank Modena is taken.
Burma In the Sittang Valley Toungoo falls to the 5th Indian Division.

23 April 1945

Germany, Politics Goering sends a message to Hitler offering to take over the leadership of the Reich if Hitler is unable to continue with that task when he is besieged in Berlin. Hitler is furious at Goering's presumption and orders his arrest.
Eastern Front As both Zhukov's and Konev's troops continue to close in round Berlin in the rear of their advances Frankfurt (on Oder) and Cottbus are captured.
Italy Advance units of both Fifth and Eighth Armies reach the Po. Fifth Army units manage to cross the river south of Mantua.
Okinawa The attacks of XXIV Corps at last begin to make some ground.
Philippines Units of 37th Division reach the outskirts of Baguio.

24 April 1945

Eastern Front Konev's troops penetrate into Berlin from the south joining with Zhukov's attacks from the east. Other units are moving round the city to the north and south to complete the encirclement. Large parts of the German Ninth Panzer and Fourth Armies have been cut off by Konev's advance.
Western Front Dessau on the Elbe is taken by First Army. The British forces begin attacks near Bremen. To the south on the Danube Ulm is taken and in the Black Forest area the French First Army continues its advance.

Left: The final Russian advance to take Berlin and push westward to the Elbe.

Italy Both Fifth and Eighth Army units begin to pour across the Po at several points near Ferrara and to the west. Ferrara itself is taken. On the west coast La Spezia falls to the US 92nd Division. Now that the Allied forces have burst free into open ground there is almost nothing that the Germans can do to slow their advance.
Okinawa The Japanese forces begin to pull back to the second section of the Shuri Line.

25 April 1945

Eastern Front The encirclement of Berlin is completed near Ketzin. Zhukov's and Konev's units are still also driving into the city from south and east. South of the capital Konev's forces have also attacked east to the Elbe at Torgau where they link with American units.

In East Prussia Pillau is taken. There are still a few German troops holding out at the tip of the Samland Peninsula. Since early in the year 140,000 wounded and 40,000 refugees have been evacuated to the west from Pillau.
Italy Mantua, Parma and Verona are among the towns liberated by the Allies as the German resistance begins to collapse and large-scale surrenders begin. The extensive partisan operations are extended by risings in Milan and Genoa.
Western Front The US First Army meets up with the Soviet forces at Torgau on the Elbe. US Third Army crosses the Danube near Regensburg, which is attacked.
Burma In the Irrawaddy Valley mopping up operations continue. Salin is captured by the British forces. The main XXXIII Corps advance is closing in on Allanmyo. The spectacular progress of the 5th Indian Division in the Sittang Valley continues with the capture of Perwegen. The Japanese forces around Rangoon and in other parts of southern Burma are beginning to withdraw through Pegu to the east so as to be able to retreat into Thailand.

25 April-26 June 1945

World Affairs A conference is held at San Francisco to draw up the constitution of a United Nations Organization. It is decided that the UN should have a General Assembly of all nations and as a recognition of the difficulty and importance of unanimity among the major nations a Security Council in which the great powers would have permanent seats and the power of veto. The permanent members of the Security Council are to be the United States, the Soviet Union, Britain, France and China. The Soviets have been among the stronger advocates of the major powers having a veto because they expect that they will be consistently outvoted by the memberships of the organization as it will stand at first. As well as the main bodies for international debate and peace keeping, there are proposals for the creation of an International Court of Justice and specialized social and economic agencies.

The text of the Charter of the United Nations is completed on 23 June, formally approved on the 25th and signed on the 26th.

26 April 1945

Eastern Front As well as the continuing advances in the Berlin fighting, Soviet units take Stettin in the Baltic and Brno in Czechoslovakia.
Western Front The British complete the capture of Bremen. Third Army units take Regensburg while other parts of Patton's force enter Austria. French First Army reaches Lake Constance.
Italy Fifth Army units are now heading north from Verona toward the Brenner Pass and west toward Milan. Eighth Army has crossed the Adige and is moving northeast toward Venice and Trieste.
Philippines There is a further US landing on Negros, this time by units of the Americal Division in the southwest of the island. The troops advance well inland before meeting the first Japanese resistance.
France, Politics Marshal Pétain is arrested when he crosses into France from Switzerland. He will be tried and condemned to death for treason and collaboration. De Gaulle will commute the sentence to life imprisonment.

Below: US Marines on Okinawa flush out Japanese defenders from one of the myriad of bunkers and caves which littered the island.

Above: Josef Stalin heavy tanks of the Soviet Army enter Berlin, May 1945. Signs of the fighting may be seen all around.

27 April 1945

Diplomatic Affairs The Allies reply to Himmler's peace proposals with a total refusal and a reminder of the already established demands for unconditional surrender.
Eastern Front In Berlin the Soviet forces have taken the Templehof airfield and are making progress in the Spandau, Grunewald and other areas. To the north of the capital Rokossovsky's troops begin to advance more freely, taking Prenzlau and Angermünde.
Italy Genoa, already largely controlled by partisans, is completely liberated by US forces.
Philippines Baguio is taken by the US forces. Fighting in other areas of the island continues, especially in the Bicol Peninsula.

27-30 April 1945

Borneo Admiral Berkey leads a squadron of three cruisers and six destroyers in a preparatory bombardment of targets in the Tarakan area in the northeast of the island. On the 30th there is a small landing by a US force on the offshore island of Sadan.

27 April-2 May 1945

Okinawa, Sea and Air Operations From the 27th to the 30th there is a fourth phase of Kamikaze attacks. About 125 planes make attacks, hitting nine destroyers and other smaller ships. Not all of the US carrier force is present to support the operations on the island until 8 May when the absentees return from a brief visit to Ulithi.

28 April 1945

Italy Mussolini and his mistress Clara Petacci and other Fascist leaders have been caught by partisans near Lake Como as they attempt to escape to Switzerland. They are now shot and their bodies are mutilated and hung up by the heels in the main square at Milan.

Brescia, Bergamo and Allessandria are taken by Fifth Army units.
Eastern Front The siege of Berlin proceeds with the Soviets now having penetrated to within a mile of Hitler's Bunker in the east and south. Most of the Potsdamer Strasse has been cleared by Konev's troops.
Western Front The US Seventh Army takes Augsburg in its advance south toward Austria. Other Allied units are crossing the Elbe in the north and others are advancing on Munich in the south.
Okinawa The fighting along the Shuri Line continues with the US forces employing tanks, flame throwers and artillery of all calibers in an attempt to destroy the Japanese defensive positions.

29 April 1945

World Affairs Hitler marries Eva Braun and prepares his Political Testament, appointing Admiral Doenitz as his successor and describing how Germany has failed him in the struggle against Bolshevism.
Italy The surrender of the German forces in Italy is signed at Caserta in the south. The German representatives are present here because of a secret negotiation between the head of the OSS mission in Switzerland, Allan Dulles, and the SS General Wolff. These talks have been going on since much earlier in the year, but because of their clandestine nature the German representatives at Caserta cannot guarantee that the surrender will be ratified by Vietinghoff.

In the north the Allied armies continue to advance quickly. Venice is liberated by Eighth Army.
Eastern Front In Berlin the Soviets make gains in the Moabit district and in the Wilmersdorf area. North of the capital Red Army units continue their advance capturing Anklam and other towns. In the southern sectors of the front Soviet pressure in Austria and Czechoslovakia continues.
Western Front The concentration camp at Dachau is liberated along with 30,000 surviving inmates by troops from US Third Army. The advance then goes on toward Munich. South of the Danube US Third Army units reach the River Isar.
Burma In the Irrawaddy Valley Allanmyo falls to the advances of XXXIII Corps. The remaining Japanese forces in this area are becoming very disorganized by the British attacks. In the Sittang Valley the 17th Indian Division has now taken over the lead, and after capturing Nyaunglebim is attacking near Payagyi.
Philippines General Brush's 185th Regiment lands near Padan Point with support from a destroyer force led by Admiral Struble. There is little Japanese resistance.

29 April-2 May 1945

Arctic The last convoy battle of World War II is fought around the convoy RA-66. This has 24 ships with an escort of two escort carriers, one cruiser, nine destroyers and 13 other ships – a very lavish force when compared with any Arctic convoy in 1942, for example. There are 14 U-Boats involved in attacks. Not one merchant ship is sunk but one escort is hit and two U-Boats sunk.

30 April 1945

World Affairs Hitler and Eva Braun commit suicide in their rooms in Hitler's Bunker at 1530

Below: Bodies of victims of Nazi terror, discovered at Dachau concentration camp by advancing American troops, 1945.

hours. Their bodies are carried outside and cremated with gasoline.

Eastern Front The Soviet advance in Berlin reaches the Reichstag from the north. Other government buildings are also captured. In other sectors of the front Rokossovsky's troops advance toward Stralsund, Waren and Wittenberge. In Czechoslovakia Mor Ostrava is taken after a long fight. The Germans now hold only a part of Moravia and most of Bohemia. Slovakia has been completely overrun.

Western Front The advance in all sectors continues. The French forces enter Austria near Lake Constance and British units in the north push on toward the Baltic.

Okinawa Japanese counterattacks and infiltration attempts in the Shuri Line area are beaten off. There is particularly fierce fighting in the Maeda and Kochi Ridge positions. The 1st Marine and 77th Divisions take over at the front from the 27th and 96th Divisions.

May 1945

Far East, Air Operations The Superfortresses drop 24,000 tons of bombs on targets in Japan. Nagoya is the target for two very heavy raids on the 14th and 16th, both times by over 470 bombers. Tokyo is hit by 502 planes on the 25th. Otaka, Oshima and Tokuyama are also heavily attacked. The Pacific Fleet carriers also attack many targets in Japan.

In the SEAC area the operations are mostly restricted by the onset of the monsoon but there is some tactical support provided around Rangoon and against Japanese concentrations near Moulmein. In China Fourteenth Air Force strikes against tactical targets in many areas.

Europe, Air Operations The last operation by RAF Bomber Command is an attack by a Mosquito force on Kiel on the night of the 2/3 May. Many Allied aircraft are involved in food drops in Holland and in the evacuation of prisoners of war back to Britain.

1 May 1945

World Affairs Hamburg radio announces that Hitler is dead and that Doenitz is the second Führer of the Reich. Doenitz himself broadcasts, announcing rather pathetically that 'it is my duty to save the German people from destruction by the Bolshevists.'

In Berlin Goebbels and his wife commit suicide after poisoning their six children. Martin Bormann disappears, most probably killed trying to escape from the bunker.

Eastern Front General Krebs visits Zhukov to try to negotiate surrender terms for Berlin, but is told that only unconditional surrender is acceptable. In the city the Soviet advance continues and only a tiny area remains in German hands.

Western Front The US First and Ninth Armies are firmly established along the line of the Elbe and Mulde. They have been forbidden to advance farther, into the zone designated for Soviet occupation. To the north the British continue their moves toward Lübeck and Hamburg while in the south the US Seventh Army presses on into Austria.

Italy General Vietinghoff agrees to the surrender terms signed at Caserta. Tito's Partisans take Trieste. Possession of this city will become a point of dispute between Italy and Yugoslavia after the war. Italy will regain the city but Yugoslavia will take much of the disputed land nearby.

Burma The British attacks in the Sittang Valley have now reached nearly to Pegu. The monsoon begins in southern Burma. As an alternative in case the land attacks have not made sufficient progress before this break in the weather, an amphibious operation to take Rangoon has been prepared and now goes into action, with parachute landings at the mouth of the Irrawaddy on the east bank.

Borneo There are Allied landings at Tarakan. General Whitehead leads 18,000 men of the reinforced 26th Australian Brigade in the landings. There is little Japanese opposition.

Above: A Russian soldier, steadied by a colleague, attaches a flag to the roof of the *Reichstag* building in Berlin, 2 May 1945.

2 May 1945

Eastern Front The Soviet forces complete the capture of Berlin with the attacks from north and south linking up along the Charlottenburg Chaussee. North of Berlin Soviet units have taken Rostock and many other towns. The only large German forces which remain in contact with the Soviet armies are those isolated in Latvia and those in Austria and Czechoslovakia. These last are now under pressure from all sides, by forces from the Eastern and Western Fronts and from Italy.

Western Front The British Second Army takes Lübeck and Wismar on the Baltic coast. Canadian units take Oldenburg. US units continue their advances in Austria and Bavaria.

Italy At noon the German surrender becomes effective. The long, difficult and controversial campaign in Italy is over. Allied forces reach Trieste, Milan and Turin during the course of the day, while others are advancing north toward the Brenner Pass where they will link up with US Seventh Army forces from the north.

Burma The British carry out Operation Dracula, the amphibious attack on Rangoon. Admiral Martin leads the four escort carriers and other naval units involved and 26th Indian Division provides the landing force. There is no Japanese resistance. Admiral Walker leads TF 63 with the battleships *Queen Elizabeth* and *Richelieu* and two escort carriers as well as cruisers and destroyers in covering operations in which Port Blair and Car Nicobar are bombed and shelled.

The attacks of IV Corps against Pegu to the north of the landings finally complete the capture of the town.

Philippines The XIV Corps units advancing west along the Bicol Peninsula of Luzon link near Naga with units from the Legaspi area who have moved east. Only mopping up operations remain to be done in this part of the island.

3 May 1945

Eastern Front Soviet forces have now reached the Elbe west of Berlin and made contact with the US First and Ninth Armies and in the north with the British Second Army.

Western Front The British XII Corps occupies Hamburg. This virtually completes the British offensive operations. In Austria Innsbruck falls to the US Seventh Army while other units advance near Salzburg.

Burma Rangoon is taken by 26th Indian Division without any resistance from the Japanese. Farther north on the Irrawaddy, Prome is taken by XXXIII Corps.

Philippines Admiral Noble lands 1000 men near Santa Cruz in the Gulf of Davao. Davao City is taken by 24th Division units.

3-4 May 1945

Okinawa During the night the Japanese forces begin a large-scale counteroffensive from the south, but although the attacks are very fierce they do not break the American front. Much of the Japanese artillery, until now concealed from the overwhelming firepower of the American forces, gives its positions away by operating in support of the attacks.

3-29 May 1945

Okinawa, Air and Sea Operations TF 58 is now organized in three groups of 13 carriers altogether and two groups are present at all times in this period. The British TF 57 makes attacks on Sakashima Gunto on 11 days. Escort carrier groups continue this work when the British carriers are replenishing. Among the damage done in the Japanese attacks are hits on the *Bunker Hill*, *Enterprise*, *Victorious* and *Formidable*. The escort carrier *Sangamon Bay* has to be written off after Kamikaze damage incurred on the 3rd.

There are four main spells of Japanese attacks, 3-4 May, 10-13 May, 24-25 May and 27-28 May. Altogether the Japanese send 560 Kamikaze planes in these periods. As well as the carrier casualties the battleship *New Mexico* is hit on the 10th, several destroyers are sunk and many more small warships or transports badly damaged. On 24 May two groups of TF 58 attack the airfields used by the Kamikaze forces on Kyushu. On 28 May Admiral Halsey takes command of the US naval forces involved in the operations and they return to being known as Third Fleet and TF 58 becomes TF 38.

4 May 1945

Western Front Doenitz sends envoys to Montgomery's headquarters at Luneburg Heath and they agree on the surrender of German forces in Holland, Denmark and north Germany. The surender becomes effective at 0800 on 5 May.

In the fighting which continues on the 4th Salzburg is taken by US forces. Other units push into Czechoslovakia toward Pilsen.

5 May 1945

European War Zone In Prague resistance forces rise against the Germans and a very fierce battle begins with SS units in the city. The Soviets are closing in on Prague from the north and east but are not yet in striking distance. Other Soviet units take Swinemünde and Peenemünde on the Baltic coast. The German Army Group G surrenders to the US forces with the surrender being concluded at Haar in Bavaria. In Denmark fighting breaks out in Copenhagen but is brought to an end when British units arrive by air in the evening.

United States, Home Front The War Department announces that about 400,000 men will remain in Germany to form the US occupation force, that 2,000,000 men will be discharged from the armed services and that this will leave 6,000,000 serving in the war against Japan.

Above: General Eisenhower (center), accompanied by members of his staff, following the surrender of the Germans at Reims.

Okinawa The Japanese counterattacks continue with some minor successes.

United States A woman and five children are killed by a bomb falling from a Japanese balloon near Lakeview, Oregon. The Japanese have been releasing these balloons for some time, hoping that they will drift in the wind over the United States before releasing their explosive cargo. This is the only success they will achieve.

5-6 May 1945

Indian Ocean There are attacks by aircraft from four British escort carriers on Japanese bases between Mergui and Victoria Point in southern Burma and on the 6th the battleships and cruisers of TF 63 shell Port Blair in the Andaman Islands.

6 May 1945

European War Zone Units of the US Third Army take Pilsen in Czechoslovakia but Patton is ordered, much to his disgust to halt his advance there and allow the Soviets to occupy the rest of the country as has been arranged. The fighting in Prague between the resistance and the German forces goes on.

Below: British sailors aboard the carrier HMS *Formidable* clear up after a Japanese *kamikaze* attack, 1945.

Burma Troops from 26th Indian Division advancing north from Rangoon, link with units from IV Corps at Hlegu. Although many scattered Japanese forces remain in Burma west of the Sittang toward Thailand and in the southwest of the country, the campaign is virtually over. Mopping up operations will continue as far as the monsoon weather permits, but British attention will be directed more to preparations for the campaign in Malaya which is to be the next major move. This, of course, will never take place because of the Japanese surrender.

Okinawa The Japanese offensive peters out after taking very heavy losses of at least 5000 killed. Even while it has been going on US forces have made gains near Machinto airfield and Maeda Ridge. These gains are now confirmed.

7 May 1945

European War Zone Admiral Friedeburg and General Jodl sign the unconditional German surrender at General Eisenhower's HQ. British, French, Soviet and American representatives are all present. Operations are to end at 2301 on 8 May.

War at Sea Two merchant ships sunk by *U.2336* off the Firth of Forth are the last U-Boat victims of World War II.

8 May 1945

Europe The British and Americans celebrate VE (Victory in Europe) Day. Truman, Churchill and King George VI all make special broadcasts. In Prague the German forces surrender. The units of Army Group Kurland, long cut off in Latvia surrender also. Most of the German pockets which have been holding out in eastern Germany have also given in. Crown Prince Olaf and British and Norwegian troops land in Norway.

9 May 1945

Europe The German surrender is ratified in Berlin. For Germany Keitel, Friedeburg and Stumpf sign, and for the Allies Spaatz, Tedder, Zhukov and de Lattre. The Soviets celebrate VE-Day.

The last German forces holding out in East Prussia and Pomerania capitulate. Among the

Above: Soviet commander Marshal Zhukov puts his signature to the instrument of German surrender, Berlin, 9 May 1945.

prominent captives are Goering and Kesselring who surrender to the US Seventh Army.

10 May 1945

Philippines Part of the US 40th Division lands in the north of the island at Macalajar Bay. The landing is successful, but everywhere else on the island there is heavy fighting between the US and Japanese forces already present.
Europe Quisling and some of his supporters are arrested by the resistance in Norway. Reichs Commissioner Terboven and the German Chief of Police in Norway both commit suicide. Quisling will be put on trial for treason by the Norwegians, and will be found guilty and executed.

11 May 1945

Europe Schoerner's Army Group Center, now confined to a pocket east of Prague, surrenders to the Soviets. Some German units in Yugoslavia keep fighting for a few more days but gradually they too give in. The war in Europe is over.
Okinawa After making some minor advances in the past four days the US forces now go over to a more ambitious coordinated attack on the Shuri Line. The US forces are now deployed with the III Corps facing the right of the Line and the XXIV Corps to the left. In the attacks some of the III Corps units manage to make gains, but none of Hodge's force achieve any of their objectives.

13 May 1945

Philippines After more heavy fighting on Mindanao the Del Monte airfield is taken by units of the US 40th Division.

15 May 1945

Okinawa The pattern of heavy fighting, slow US advances and costly and only partially successful Japanese counterattacks is maintained. There are particularly fierce battles on Sugar Loaf and Conical Hills.

15-16 May 1945

Indian Ocean After an attempt to reach the Nicobars on the 10th and 11th the Japanese cruiser *Haguro* and a destroyer try once more to get through with supplies for the Japanese garrisons on the islands. British battleship and escort-carrier forces try to make an interception, but it is achieved by a destroyer force, five strong, commanded by Captain Power. They make their attacks on the Japanese ships in the Malacca Straits area during the night 15/16 May, and in a classically delivered attack from all directions *Haguro* is sunk by the destroyers' torpedoes. This is the last surface action of the war involving major warships.

17 May 1945

Marshall Islands The carrier *Ticonderoga* attacks targets on the Japanese held islands of Taroa and Maleolap in what is virtually a training exercise in view of the weakness of the defense.

18 May 1945

Okinawa The US 6th Marine Division takes most of the Sugar Loaf Hill after several days of bitter fighting.

19 May 1945

Philippines In the I Corps sector Japanese resistance ends in the Ipoh Dam area of Luzon.

21 May 1945

Okinawa There are American successes near the Horseshoe, Half Moon and Wana positions in the III Corps sector, while on the east side 7th and 96th Divisions attack near Yonabaru. Faced with these US gains, the Japanese begin to pull out of the Shuri Line.

22 May 1945

Okinawa The US forces occupy Yonabaru.
United States, Politics President Truman reports to Congress on the Lend-Lease program. He announces that up to March 1945 Britain had received supplies worth $12,775,000,000 and the Soviets $8,409,000,000. Reverse Lend-Lease, mostly from Britain has been worth almost $5,000,000,000 in the same period.

23 May 1945

Okinawa After advancing to take Naha very easily the 6th Marine Division tries to move on to the south but again meets very heavy resistance.
Britain, Politics The Labour Party has decided not to maintain the coalition government until after the end of the war and Churchill, therefore, resigns in order to prepare for the election. He forms a new caretaker government to hold office until the election.
War Criminals Himmler has been captured by the British forces, but he commits suicide before he can be searched or questioned by the British Authorities.

27 May 1945

Okinawa The slow and meticulous US advance continues to be met by very fierce resistance.
Philippines Units of the US I Corps take Santa Fe on Luzon. There is still heavy fighting in several areas of Mindanao.

29 May 1945

Japanese Command Admiral Ozawa replaces Admiral Toyoda as commander of the Combined Fleet.

Below: US M-18 tank destroyer fires into Japanese lines, Okinawa, May 1945.

30 May 1945

Okinawa The US advance reaches Shuri south of the former Japanese positions.

June 1945

Far East, Air Operations B-29 bombers fly 6500 missions over Japan and drop 42,000 tons of bombs. Osaka and Kobe are both attacked several times and other targets include Tokyo and Nagoya. Aircraft plants, naval bases and airfields are the favorite aiming points for precision attacks. In China Fourteenth Air Force attacks communications targets especially in the rail system. Planes based in the Philippines and on Okinawa join in these operations.

1-13 June 1945

Okinawa, Air and Sea Operations The carrier groups of TF 38 now under Admiral McCain's command, continue to give support to the Okinawa operation. There are also attacks on 3/4 June on airfields on Kyushu and again on the 8th. On the 9th and 10th there are attacks on Okino-Daito-Shima and Minami-o-Shima. Both these targets are bombarded by battleship and cruiser forces.

The ninth wave of Kamikaze attacks on the US forces around Okinawa occurs between 3 and 7 June when one battleship, one cruiser and one escort carrier are all hit. The fast-carrier groups suffer heavily from the effects of a typhoon on the 5th. The cruiser *Pittsburgh* loses 110 feet from its bows and all the ships of TG 38.1 are damaged in some degree. After completing the program of attacks TF 38 returns to Leyte on 13 June after three months of nearly continuous operations in which the carriers and their supports have almost constantly kept the sea and been supplied and rearmed by the well-organized work of the fleet train.

4 June 1945

Okinawa Two regiments of 6th Marine Division make landings on the Oruku Peninsula in an attempt to outflank some of the Japanese defense lines. Many of the Japanese troops formerly in the Shuri Line have in fact retired on to the Oruku Peninsula so it will be a hard fight.

Below: Incendiary bombs rain down from US Boeing B-29 Superfortress bombers onto the Japanese port of Kobe, 4 June 1945. Japanese opposition to the raids was now minimal.

5 June 1945

Germany The Allied Control Commission meets for the first time in Berlin and announces that it is assuming the government of Germany.

6 June 1945

Okinawa The 6th Marines have made good ground in the Oruku Peninsula following their landing. Other US units also push forward on the main front.

7 June 1945

Philippines On Luzon forces from US I Corps take Bambang and move on northeast toward the Cagayan Valley. Other units are moving round the coast from the northwest to the north of the island.

Above: Russian soldiers lower captured Nazi standards as a symbol of Germany's defeat, Red Square, Moscow, 1945.

8 June 1945

Java Sea The Japanese cruiser *Ashigara* is sunk by the British submarine *Trenchant* after evacuating 1200 men from Batavia.

10 June 1945

Okinawa Heavy fighting continues on the Oruku Peninsula and to the east and south, but it is becoming clear that the last stages of Japanese resistance on the island have been reached.

Borneo Almost 30,000 men of the 9th Australian Division land from a naval force commanded by Admiral Royal in Brunei Bay and on the islands of Labuan and Muara nearby. A preparatory bombardment has been fired by a force of cruisers and destroyers under the command of Admiral Berkey.

12 June 1945

Okinawa Many of the Japanese troops on the Oruku Peninsula commit suicide believing that further resistance can achieve nothing.

13 June 1945

Okinawa The Japanese resistance on the Oruku Peninsula ends. Almost 170 prisoners are taken – a large number when compared with previous totals of Japanese prisoners. The fighting continues to the southeast, especially in the Kunishi Ridge area.

Borneo US and Australian troops enter Borneo town.

14 June 1945

Okinawa XXIV Corps units take Mount Yagu.

14-15 June 1945

Caroline Islands Planes from the British fleet carrier *Implacable* and an escort-carrier attack the long isolated Japanese base at Truk on both days. There are also bombardments by some of the accompanying cruisers and destroyers of small islands nearby. US naval firepower dominates these amphibious operations.

16 June 1945

Okinawa Mount Yuza is taken by the US forces.

17 June 1945

Okinawa The American units begin to make gains in the Kunishi Ridge area which has been very stubbornly defended.

18 June 1945

Okinawa General Buckner is killed by Japanese artillery fire while he is on a visit to the front line. General Stilwell is appointed to command Tenth Army in succession to Buckner.

Britain, Home Front William Joyce, Lord Haw Haw, is put on trial for treason in London. He will be convicted and executed for broadcasting propaganda from Germany.

18-20 June 1945

Borneo In the north Australian troops take Tutong on the 18th and on the 19th there are Australian landings at Menpakul. On the 20th there are landings in Sarawak at Lutong.

19 June 1945

Philippines In the Cagayan Valley Ilagan falls to the advance of I Corps.

20 June 1945

Wake Island Admiral Jennings leads TG 12.4 with the carriers *Lexington*, *Hancock* and *Cowpens* in attacks on Wake. The carriers are en route to join TF 38 and are using this opportunity to work up their skills with a real target. There are similar attacks directed against Wake on 18 July by the carrier *Wasp*, on 1 August by the *Cabot* and on 6 August by the *Intrepid*.

21 June 1945

Okinawa The final Japanese HQ on Hill 69 is taken by the US forces. General Ushijima's body is found nearby.

22 June 1945

Okinawa The fighting on Okinawa comes to an end. It has been a very bitterly fought campaign. The US forces have lost 12,500 dead and 35,500 wounded. The navy has had 36 ships sunk and 368 damaged. In the air the American forces have lost 763 planes. The Japanese losses are horrific. There are 120,000 military and 42,000 civilian dead and, if US reports are to be believed, they have lost 7830 planes and among other vessels the battleship *Yamato*. For the first time there is a significant number of Japanese prisoners – 10,755.

23 June 1945

Philippines There is a US paratroop landing near Aparri on the north coast of Luzon at the mouth of the Cagayan River.

25 June 1945

Philippines Tuguegarag is captured by the US forces in the Cagayan Valley. The surviving Japanese units on the island, about 50,000 strong, are now mostly concentrated in the Sierra Madre area to the east of the Cagayan Valley.

Borneo In Sarawak the Australian forces complete the occupation of the Miri oilfield area.

26 June 1945

World Affairs The United Nations Charter is signed by representatives of 50 countries.

Above: Japanese naval troops surrender to the Americans on Okinawa, June 1945. Such surrenders were a sign that the end was near.

28 June 1945

Philippines MacArthur announces that the operations on Luzon are over. It is now five months and 19 days since the invasion. Although there are still many Japanese on the island who will go on fighting until the end of the war, much of the mopping up will be left to Filipino units aided by US Eighth Army troops, who will take over responsibility for Luzon in addition to their present tasks in the other Philippine Islands in order to free Sixth Army to prepare for the invasion of Japan. Apart from on Luzon the only other significant bodies of Japanese resisting are on Mindanao.

29 June 1945

United States, Planning The invasion plans for Japan are presented to President Truman and approved. They provide for landings in southern Kyushu on 1 November by forces already in the Pacific and on Honshu near Tokyo on 1 March 1946, when forces brought from Europe will participate. British and British Empire forces are to play a small part.

July 1945

Far East, Air Operations Among the targets for the US bomber forces are Akashi, Osaka, Kure and Kumamoto. A new tactic is tried starting on the 28th when 11 cities are told by leaflets that they are on the US target list and six of them are bombed on the 29th. Medium bombers join in the attack early in the month doing particular damage to shipping around the Japanese islands. There is much activity over China. In addition to the Fourteenth Air Force attacks there are two heavy attacks on Shanghai by planes based on Okinawa.

1 July 1945

Borneo After a preparatory bombardment beginning on 25 June by nine cruisers and 13 destroyers led by Admiral Barbey, 33,000 men of the reinforced 7th Australian Division land at Balikpapan. Three escort carriers give support to the landing for the first three days ashore. General Milford commands the troops.

3 July 1945

Borneo The troops landed at Balikpapan take Sepinggan airfield and by the 5th have cleared most of the oil producing area in the immediate vicinity.

5 July 1945

Philippines General MacArthur announces that the Philippines have been completely liberated.

United States, Command It is announced that General Spaatz will lead the US Strategic Air Force against Japan.

Britain, Politics The British election is held. The results are not available until 26 July because of the time taken to bring home and count the soldiers' votes.

Diplomatic Affairs Britain and the United States recognize a new Polish government of National Unity. Mikolajczyk, formerly leader of the London exile government, is one of the deputy Premiers.

10-18 July 1945

Japan The American and British carrier forces send attacks on targets in the Japanese Home Islands. Admirals Halsey and McCain lead 15 carriers, eight battleships, 15 cruisers and 55 destroyers in the carrier groups alone and many more ships are on supporting missions.

On 10 July Tokyo is attacked by 1022 planes and after a break until the 14th attacks continue with targets on north Honshu and south Hokkaido being hit. Shipping is also a target and 50,000 tons is sunk in the Tsugaru Strait area. These attacks are repeated on the 15th. On the

Above: Winston Churchill, dressed as Colonel of the Cinque Ports Battalion of the Royal Sussex Regiment, tours Berlin, July 1945.

14th three battleships lead a bombardment of steel works at Kamaishi and on the 15th another three head a bombardment of iron and steel works at Muroran. On 17 July the three carriers and one battleship of the British TF 37 join the American carriers in more attacks on the Tokyo-Yokohama area. The battleship *Nagato* is put out of action in these operations. During the night six battleships, two cruisers and 10 destroyers shell targets in the Hitachi area northeast of Tokyo, and on the night of the 18th there is a smaller bombardment of targets in the Cape Nojima area southeast of the Japanese capital. The Task Force then withdraws because a typhoon is forecasted.

11 July 1945

Germany There is the first meeting of the Inter-Allied Council for Berlin. The Soviets agree to turn over administration of the allocated areas to the British and Americans who have themselves made arrangements to allocate some of their sectors to the French.

12 July 1945

Borneo There is an Allied landing near Andus. Australian troops take Maradi in the north of the island.

14 July 1945

Europe General Eisenhower announces the closure of SHAEF (Supreme Headquarters Allied Expeditionary Force) and eases some of the restrictions on private contact between American soldiers and German civilians.

16 July 1945

Atomic Research The world's first atomic weapons test takes place at Alamagordo in New Mexico. The bomb used is based on the element plutonium and gives a yield of between 15 and 20 kilotons. It is mounted on top of a steel tower which is vaporized by the heat of the explosion which is greater than the temperature inside the sun. The explosion is visible and audible up to 180 miles away.

The type of bomb dropped on Hiroshima will not be identical to this but based on the isotope Uranium 235. The Nagasaki bomb will be a second plutonium weapon.

17 July-2 August 1945

World Affairs Truman, Stalin and Churchill meet at Potsdam. There are further clarifying discussions of plans for dealing with defeated Germany and all the former occupied countries of Europe. Stalin confirms his undertaking to join the war with Japan but also tells the other Allies of peace moves that the Japanese have made via the as yet neutral USSR. There are no definite proposals contained in these approaches and it is therefore decided to do nothing direct to follow them up. On 26 July a broadcast is made to Japan with what has become known as the Potsdam Declaration. This repeats the demand for unconditional surrender, but states that the Allies do not want to reduce Japan to poverty in the postwar world. It says nothing of allowing or preventing the Emperor to remain at the head of the Japanese government.

On the 24th Truman and Churchill mention to Stalin that they have a new and powerful weapon for use against Japan but do not explain what it is. It is possible that Stalin already knows of the bomb through his espionage organization in the United States.

There is a recess in the conference between 25 and 28 July when the British delegation leave for their election results. Attlee is the new prime minister and Bevin the foreign secretary.

19 July 1945

United States, Politics Congress ratifies the Bretton Woods monetary agreement.

24 July 1945

Pacific War Truman takes the decision to use the bomb on Japan if they do not very soon come to terms. Whatever the later doubts about the morality of using the weapon, at the time there is very little doubt. It is simply a question of quickly persuading the Japanese to surrender in order to save the many lives on both sides that would be lost if the Allies invaded the Home Islands. No real thought is given to the possible forms of a demonstration use of the bomb to frighten the Japanese without having to destroy a city.

24-30 July 1945

Japan The British and American carriers continue their operations. There are now 15 US ships and four British. There are entensive air operations on the 24th, 27th and 30th. Many targets in the Inland Sea area are hit including Kure and Kobe. Several of the remaining large ships in the Japanese navy are hit and badly damaged. Three battleships and four carriers head the list. There are two bombardment operations. One, on the night of the 24th, is aimed at Kushimoto and Shionomisaki, and on the 29th the targets for five battleships and several cruisers and destroyers are aircraft factories at Hamamutsu in southern Honshu.

26 July 1945

Britain, Politics The election results begin to be announced. It is a massive victory for the Labour Party and a terrible defeat for Churchill's Conservatives. Attlee becomes prime minister. The reason for the Conservative defeat, despite Churchill's war record, is that they have failed to convince the electorate that they would be active and original enough to prevent any return to the conditions of the 1930s when the Conservative governments did too little, it is felt, to mitigate the economic effects of the world depression and failed to stand up to Hitler. In the war years, too, it has mostly been the Labour politicians who have been responsible for the government departments charged with running the rationing system and organizing industry and it is felt that they have done this in a way that has benefitted the people in ways apart from helping the war effort.

28 July 1945

World Affairs The Japanese Premier Suzuki holds a press conference in which he says that the Japanese government will take no notice of the Potsdam Declaration. At least that is the interpretation that is put on his speech by the Allies, but it is possible that the word he used was intended to mean 'make no comment on for the moment' and that more might have been done to encourage a diplomatic response. It is upsetting to the Japanese that the declaration has not been delivered through the proper diplomatic channels via a neutral power and this contributes to their decision to take no immediate action on it.

29-30 July 1945

Pacific The US cruiser *Indianapolis*, returning to the United States after delivering the atom bomb to the Marianas air base, is torpedoed and sunk by the Japanese submarine *I.58*. It is not recognized that the *Indianapolis* is overdue for three days and many of the 316 survivors rescued are not found for several days after this.

31 July 1945

War Criminals Laval surrenders to the US forces in Austria. He is handed over to the

Below: Colonel Paul W Tibbets stands in front of the B-29 Superfortress 'Enola Gay' which he flew to Hiroshima on 6 August 1945.

French authorities and is later tried and executed.

August 1945

Far East, Air Operations The atomic attacks on Hiroshima and Nagasaki dominate the events of the month (*see* 6 and 9 August). There are also conventional strikes against many Japanese cities. Among the targets are Tokokawa, Yawata, Hikari, Nagoya and Toyama. The last strategic bombing raid is on the night of 14 August when Kumagaya and other targets northwest of Tokyo are bombed.

6 August 1945

Hiroshima The first atomic bomb is dropped on the city by a plane from the 509th Composite Group of the Twentieth Air Force piloted by Colonel Paul Tibbets. The plane is named by Tibbets after his mother, *Enola Gay*. The bomb is an uranium fission weapon and the yield is in the region of 20,000 tons of TNT.

Sixty percent of the city is destroyed in the blast or the firestorm that follows. There are about 80,000 dead, many of them being killed instantly. Many more will be horribly burned or will become ill in later years with the effects of the radiation. It is not the most devastating bombing attack of the war – the March fire raids on Tokyo have had a larger effect – but the economy of effort involved in sending only one plane on a mission to destroy a city shows only too well the complete change in military and political thinking which has been begun.

8 August 1945

World Affairs The Soviet Union declares war on Japan, citing as the reason Japan's failure to respond to the Potsdam Declaration.

Truman signs the UN Charter, making the US the first country to ratify its signature.

9 August 1945

Nagasaki The second atomic bomb is dropped on Nagasaki.

The attack is less devastating than at Hiroshima even although the bomb is of the technologically more advanced plutonium type. About 40,000 Japanese are killed.

Truman broadcasts threatening Japan with destruction by atomic bombs and the Japanese Supreme War Council agrees late that night that they should accept the Potsdam Declaration if the monarchy is to be allowed to be preserved. Some objections from the military are overruled by the Emperor himself.

Manchuria The Soviet forces begin a powerful offensive against the Japanese. The Soviets have assembled about 1,500,000 men in three fronts, First Far East Front, Second Far East Front and the Transbaikal Front. The 1,000,000 men of Yamada's Kwantung Army have no answer to the mechanized Soviet forces and are almost equally powerless in the air. The Japanese defense lines are almost immediately smashed.

9-15 August 1945

Japan The British and American carriers return to the attack after a replenishment period. The carrier *Wasp* and the battleship *Duke of York* have joined the force. Admiral Fraser is now present to command the British contingent. Airfields and shipping on Honshu and in the waters nearby are attacked with great effect on 9-10 August and there is a bombardment of Kamaishi. On the 13th there is a raid on Tokyo in which many Japanese aircraft are destroyed on the ground. On the 15th new attacks are under way when the order ending hostilities arrives and not all planes hear the recall. There is some air fighting also with Admiral Ugaki leading final Kamikaze attacks.

10 August 1945

World Affairs Japanese radio announces that a message has been sent accepting the terms of the Potsdam Declaration provided this 'does not compromise any demand that prejudices the prerogatives of the Emperor as sovereign ruler.'

On the 11th the Allies reply, saying that the Imperial authority would be subject to the de-

Below: The aftermath of the atomic raid on Hiroshima: the utter devastation of the city is apparent.

Above: General MacArthur signs the instrument of Japanese surrender, 2 September 1945.

cision of the Supreme Commander of Allied Powers in the occupation force. The Japanese are not yet ready to accept this demand which still seems close to unconditional surrender.

14 August 1945

Japan At a government meeting Emperor Hirohito decides to end the wranglings of his politicians and orders that the war should end. He records a radio message to the Japanese people saying that they should 'Bear the unbearable.' During the night there is an attack by a group of officers on the Imperial Palace in an attempt to steal the recording and prevent it being broadcast. This is foiled by the palace guards. The Japanese decision is transmitted to the Allies and it is announced by them that Japan accepts unconditional surrender. That Japan would have accepted such a position just six months before would have been impossible – such has been the speed of events.

Since the event it has often been debated what the final cause was that made the Japanese decide to surrender. Examination of Japanese records and of the people concerned seems to show that it was from a combination of the threat of atomic attack, but also and perhaps predominantly from the defeat by the Soviets of the Kwantung Army.

15 August 1945

Pacific War This is VJ Day. Emperor Hirohito's broadcast is made to the Japanese people, many of whom cannot at first accept what has happened because the tight control of the government has prevented civilians knowing the full extent of the weakness of Japan's position.

16 August 1945

Japan Prince Norukiko Higashi-Kuni forms a new government. The emperor issues a ceasefire order to all Japanese troops.

17 August 1945

Indonesia The Republic of Indonesia declares itself independent of Dutch colonial rule. No British forces will arrive to take over from the Japanese for six weeks.

In the postwar period there will be various spells of fighting between the Indonesian Nationalists and the Dutch before, in August 1950, the new republic is recognized as an independent state worldwide.

18 August 1945

Manchuria Virtually the whole province has been overrun by the Soviet forces. They have taken Harbin and are closing in on Mukden and Changchun.

20 August 1945

United States, Home Front The War Production Board removes most of its controls over manufacturing activity. On the 14th all restrictions on the production of automobiles were removed. These and many other measures help the US economy to convert very quickly to a peace basis. It is stronger and more productive than before the war and with the impetus given by wartime inventions is ready to move into new fields also. The American standard of living, unlike that of any of the other major participants in the war, has increased.

21 August 1945

United States Policy President Truman orders the supply of Lend-Lease aid to stop immediately. Truman has been scantily briefed on this issue, and in its effects it contrasts very considerably with American generosity in settling Britain's Lend-Lease bill or in the establishment of the Marshall Plan.

22 August 1945

Manchuria The Japanese Kwantung Army surrenders. Soviet forces reach Port Arthur and Dairen.

27 August 1945

Japan The Allied fleets anchor in Tokyo Bay within sight of Mount Fujiyama.

Below: Japanese soldiers and civilians stand shocked and weeping at the news of the surrender.

Above: Sailors of the Soviet Pacific Fleet hoist a flag over Port Arthur at the end of the swift and decisive Manchurian campaign, August 1945. *Left:* A US B-29 heavy bomber over Osaka, towards the end of the war.

2 September 1945

World Affairs The Japanese surrender is signed aboard the battleship *Missouri* in Tokyo Bay. Foreign Minister Shigemitsu leads the Japanese delegation. MacArthur accepts the surrender on behalf of all the Allies. Admiral Nimitz signs for the United States and Admiral Fraser for Britain. There are representatives of all the other Allied nations. Also present are Generals Percival and Wainright who have been Japanese prisoners since they surrendered at Corregidor and Singapore.
Vietnam Ho Chi Minh proclaims the existence of the Democratic Republic of Vietnam. As in the Dutch East Indies the colonial power will try to reimpose its control after the war and will eventually be forced to leave after much fighting. Even after the French have left, however, the history of Vietnam will continue to be troubled.

12 September 1945

Malaya The surrender of Japanese forces in Southeast Asia is concluded before Admiral Mountbatten in Singapore. The Japanese garrisons in the various islands of the Pacific and in the East Indies will also surrender one by one in the next few days.

THE POSTWAR WORLD

October 1945

Germany General Patton is relieved of his post as military governor of Bavaria for failing to remove former Nazi officials from the local government.

World Affairs On 24 October the United Nations Charter comes into force. There are 29 signatories at this stage.

November 1945

Europe There are elections in Austria, Hungary and Yugoslavia. In Yugoslavia Tito's National Front Party wins easily. In Austria all but five percent of the vote is roughly equally divided between the Catholic People's Party and the Socialists. The communists only win three seats out of 165. This effectively confirms Austria's place as a western nation, and although there will be no peace treaty or Soviet withdrawal until 1955 there is no real change in the situation. In Hungary the Small Landowners Party wins a majority of the votes with the communists receiving about 20 percent. A coalition government is established.

War Crimes The trial of the major German war criminals begins at Nuremberg. Twenty-one are put on trial including Goering, Hess, Ribbentrop, Rosenberg, Speer, Jodl, Keitel, Raeder and Doenitz.

The trials are important particularly because the evidence produced gives a full and public account of the horrors of the Nazi treatment of the Jews and many other crimes. The evidence of Hoess, former commandant of Auschwitz, is particularly harrowing with its calm recital of perhaps 2,000,000 murders.

As an exercise in International Law the trials have been much criticized because the offenses cited, preparing for aggressive war and crimes against humanity, had not been specifically recognized before. Equally there was some suggestion of 'victors' justice' in the way the evidence of Soviet aggression in the 1939 attack on Poland was carefully disregarded.

Previous page: A ship, loaded down with Jewish refugees from Europe, approaches the coast of Palestine. *Below:* American C-47 Skytrain transport aircraft fly in supplies to Berlin.

December 1945

War Crimes General Yamashita, former Japanese commander in the Philippines, is condemned to death by a US Military commission for maltreatment of prisoners by forces under his command especially during the famous Death March in 1942.

January 1946

World Affairs The first meetings of the General Assembly of the United Nations and of the Security Council are held in London. Immediately there are disagreements between the west and the Soviets. The Soviets are first to use the veto power.

March 1946

India The British offer full independence to the Congress and Muslim League leaders. Talks to settle details begin and last until June, but no agreement is reached.

World Affairs In a public speech delivered in Fulton, Missouri, in the presence of President Truman, Churchill describes how an 'Iron Curtain has descended across Europe.' This is not yet a universally held view in the West.

Greece Elections are won by the conservative parties after a boycott by the communists. Civil war begins in May 1946 and lasts until October 1949 when the Western backed government comes out on top. The communists receive aid from Tito and the government forces British and from May 1947 American help.

April 1946

China Full-scale civil war begins between the communists and the Nationalists. Also this month the Soviets withdraw from Manchuria, leaving a vacuum which the communists are quick to fill.

May 1946

Germany The British and Americans agree to end the taking of reparations payments from their zones of Germany and to unite their administrations and share costs. This is the first definite step toward the creation of a divided Germany. Western policy is beginning to move toward supporting German recovery.

War Crimes The trial of major criminals begins in Tokyo. Tojo and four others will be sentenced to death at the end of trials in November 1947.

June 1946

Italy In a referendum the Italian people confirm that they wish to live in a republic.

January 1947

Britain The coal industry is nationalized. This is only one of a series of socialist measures introduced by the Labour government which have a far reaching effect on British society. The welfare system is overhauled in line with the Beveridge Reports, the Bank of England, the gas and electricity industries are all nationalized. Perhaps the most ambitious scheme is the creation of a National Health Service providing for free treatment for all. This begins to operate in July 1948. All these changes arise out of wartime experience, which showed that the government could intervene in such affairs and run them in such a way that the worst miseries of the Depression could be avoided.

February 1947

Palestine Negotiations sponsored by the British between the Jewish and Arab leaders fail and under economic pressure Britain announces that the mandate will be returned to the United Nations. A United Nations Committee is appointed and reports in September that Palestine should be partitioned into a Jewish and an Arab state with Jerusalem staying international. Britain is to be in charge while this is created. The British are not altogether in favor of this plan and therefore announce that the mandate will end on 15 May 1948. Both Arabs and Jews step up their military efforts before this time ignoring UN calls for a truce. The British continue with their plans for withdrawal despite the fighting.

Greece Also as a consequence of economic difficulties Britain tells the United States that she can no longer afford to stay in Greece supporting the government economically and militarily. The US agrees to take over Britain's role. This is the first sign of what will become known as the Truman Doctrine (*see* March 1947).

Eastern Europe The final peace treaties between the Allies and Finland, Rumania, Bulgaria, Hungary and Italy are concluded. This means that Britain and the United States are not even loosely involved through the Allied Control Commissions in these countries. The Soviet presence in Eastern Europe remains.

March 1947

United States Policy In a major speech to Congress on the 11th President Truman says, 'It must be the policy of the United States to support free peoples who are resisting attempted subjugation by armed minorities or outside pressures.'

This policy becomes known as the Truman Doctrine.

China In the Chinese civil war the Nationalists take the communist capital at Yunnan. This success proves transitory and from this time on the communists begin to gain the upper hand.

May 1947

Hungary There is a communist-backed change of government in Hungary after Prime Minister Nagy is 'implicated' while on holiday in

the disappearance of Kovács, another prominent member of the Small Landowners Party.
France and Italy In both countries governments are formed which exclude the communist parties.

June 1947

Marshall Plan General Marshall, now Secretary of State, announces a plan to give economic aid to Europe and prepare a joint scheme for economic recovery. It is avowedly designed to encourage the formation of strong economies and free institutions. For the Soviets it holds a threat of German recovery as the dominant economic power in Eastern Europe and it is therefore unacceptable. The Soviets compel the other Eastern European nations to refuse Marshall aid.
Rumania The leader of the Peasant Party, Iuliu Maniu, is arrested, 'tried' and imprisoned at Soviet prompting.

August 1947

India and Pakistan Two new independent nations, India and Pakistan, are established on 15 August. The British government and the Viceroy in India, Lord Mountbatten, have decided that the timetable for granting independence should be speeded up from the original target of June 1948. This has avoided the period of tension being stretched out for so long, but inevitably in the haste not all arrangements have been made in the best way. Perhaps 250,000 die in the troubles between Muslim and Hindu which follow independence and about 12 million refugees cross the border to reach the appropriate state for people of their religion.

September 1947

Eastern Europe As a response to the Marshall Plan, Stalin establishes the Cominform as an economic organization for Eastern Europe. The Eastern European and French and Italian communist parties join the new organization.

October 1947

Poland The communist supremacy in Eastern Europe is confirmed when the former prime minister of the London exile government, Mikolajczyk, flees the country after striving unsuccessfully to protect the Peasant Party.

February 1948

Czechoslovakia The first postwar elections give the communists 38 percent of the vote, the largest single share. The Soviets withdraw and a coalition government is established led by the communist, Gottwald. Beneš becomes president and Jan Masaryk becomes foreign minister. Gottwald and Masaryk are in Moscow when Marshall aid is officially offered to Czechoslovakia, and they are told that they can choose between Soviet friendship and the Marshall aid. They refuse the American help. Nonetheless the West hopes that the communists will do less well in the elections due in May and that they will be removed from the government as in France and Italy. On 21 March, however, a government crisis is precipitated by the resignation of some members over communist monopolization of senior offices in the police. The social democrats, led by Beneš, do not respond decisively enough and a more predominantly communist government is appointed. Masaryk remains a member of the government but early in March he is found dead after having 'fallen' out of a window in a government building.

Above: Communist Chinese troops surrender to US Marines at Koto-ri during the Korean War, December 1950.

This sequence is particularly shocking to Western opinion because, even without violent tactics, the communists fairly won the elections but were not content with this.

March 1948

Marshall Plan Congress passes the Foreign Assistance Act on 31 March allocating $5,300,000,000 for aid to Europe.
Western Europe The Benelux countries and Britain and France conclude a mutual assistance agreement known as the Brussels Pact. Ostensibly it is aimed at preventing any future German aggression, but it is really as assertion of the principle of collective defense against the Soviets.

May 1948

Middle East As soon as the British mandate ends, the Jewish leader Ben Gurion proclaims the existence of the state of Israel. Israel is immediately recognized by both the United States and the Soviet Union. Fighting between Jews and Arabs continues intermittently until agreements with the Arab countries are concluded from February 1949 onward. The new state has been so successful in establishing itself that its frontiers are considerably wider than originally proposed by the United Nations.

June 1948

Germany The Berlin blockade begins. After disagreements over currency reform beginning in March and the unilateral implementation of the rival schemes in the various zones, the Soviets close the border between Berlin and their zone because the western currency grows in strength and threatens their control of their zone. The blockade begins on 24 June. The western powers decide to airlift supplies into Berlin as a temporary expedient while they decide what action to take. The airlift proves so successful that it continues until the blockade ends in September 1949.
Yugoslavia The idea that all communist parties are dominated by the Soviets takes a serious knock when Yugoslavia is expelled from the Cominform beause of Tito's independent policies over Trieste and Greece and manages to survive and after some difficulties to prosper without Soviet help or interference.

September 1948

West Germany A Parliamentary Council meets in Bonn to draw up a constitution for West Germany as a new independent country. It is completed in April 1949 and the first elections in August 1949 install Konrad Adenauer as Chancellor. In October 1949 East Germany is established under the leadership of Walter Ulbricht.

January 1949

China In the fighting Tientsin is taken by the communists. After many defeats Chiang Kaishek resigns his post as President in the Nationalist government.

February 1949

Britain Clothes rationing comes to an end.

April 1949

NATO The United States, Britain, Canada, France, the Benelux countries, Norway, Denmark, Italy and Portugal sign the North Atlantic Treaty agreeing on the principles of collective defense.

August 1949

Atomic Weapons The Soviet Union explodes its first atomic weapon. The American monopoly comes to an end.

October 1949

China The People's Republic of China is proclaimed on 1 October. By December the Nationalists have withdrawn to Taiwan.

June 1950

Korea Confirmation of the cold war hostility between the United States and the Soviet Union is made when the war in Korea begins. The United States reacts by mobilizing the United Nations to intervene and send forces to support the South Koreans. The Soviets happen to be boycotting the Security Council as a protest at the recognition of the Taiwan Government as the legal Chinese government and therefore miss their chance to use the veto. The United States regards Korea as a test case for the West's ability to resist communist pressure throughout the world and believes it is valid to fight in Korea because the actions of the North Koreans are controlled from Moscow. Later appraisals do not confirm this view entirely since, as Yugoslavia and China are to showm the USSR cannot control national communist parties all the time. Korea is also taken as a sign of communist intentions in Europe and this provokes rearmament programs throughout the west. Among the countries which will arm themselves is West Germany: a new nation emerges from the ashes of World War II.

INDEX

Page numbers in *italics* refer to illustrations

Picture credits

Archiv Gerstenberg: pages 164(Below).
Bison Picture Library: pages 6-7, 8, 9, 10, 11(Both), 13, 28, 34(Both), 35(Below), 38(Both), 45(Top), 46(Left), 49, 50(Top), 51(Left), 54(Both), 55(Top), 62-63, 67(Top), 81(Top Left), 84(Both), 89(All 3), 92(Both), 93(Top), 96(Both), 97, 100(Below), 102(Below), 104(Bottom 2), 106, 109(Both), 112, 113, 114-115, 117(Both), 118, 122(Top), 123, 129(Both), 131(Both), 134, 139, 143(Both), 149(Below), 150(Below), 151, 155(Below), 157(Below), 160(Top), 167(Top), 168, 169(Below), 170, 171, 176(Both), 183(Below), 185, 186, 193(Below), 201(Both), 209(Top), 212, 213, 225, 231, 232(Both), 233, 236, 238(Top), 243(Top), 247(Below), 259, 262(Below), 264(Below), 271, 273(Top), 275(Below), 278, 281(Below), 284(Below), 289(Top), 295, 296, 298(Below), 299, 302(Top), 303, 305(Top), 306(Top), 310(Both), 311, 314.
Bundesarchiv: pages 14, 16-17, 18(Below), 19, 29, 36(Top), 41(Top), 45(Below), 46(Both Right), 45, 57, 67(Below), 71, 72, 73, 74, 78(Below), 80(Below), 82(Below), 83, 86, 90(Both), 93(Below), 94(Both), 100(Top), 119, 124, 132(Below), 135, 140(Below), 141(Below), 146, 154, 160(Below), 164(Top), 180, 181(Top), 217(Below), 228, 238(Below), 248, 263, 270(Top), 297(Below), 302(Below).
Dwight D Eisenhower Library: page 181(Below).
Fleet Air Arm Museum: page 304(Below).
Fleet Photographic Unit: page 147.
Imperial War Museum: pages 15, 18(Top), 22(Both), 26-27, 31, 32, 33, 36(Below), 40, 41(Below), 43, 44, 50(Below), 52, 53, 56, 64, 65, 66, 70(Both), 75, 78(Top), 79, 81(Top Right & Below), 87, 91, 95, 99, 101(Both), 102(Top), 103, 104(Top), 108, 110, 120(Top), 121, 137, 142(Both), 149(Top), 150(Top), 155(Top), 156, 157(Top), 158, 162-163, 165, 167(Below), 169(Top), 173(Top), 174, 175(Top), 178, 179(Top), 187(Top), 190, 194(Both), 196(Top), 198, 202(Top), 206(Both), 207, 209(Below), 217(Top), 218(Top), 219, 220, 223(Both), 224, 227(Both), 229(Both), 234(Right), 237(Both), 239, 243(Below), 244, 246, 247(Top), 249, 250(Top), 252, 253(Both), 255, 256(Below), 258, 260, 261(Both), 268, 270(Below), 274, 275(Top), 279, 280, 287(Top), 289(Below), 290(Both), 291, 292, 294(Below), 306(Below), 308(Top), 312-313.
Keystone Collection: pages 138, 183(Top), 199(Top), 284(Top).
Library of Congress: page 191.
Museum of London: page 60.
Orbis Publishing Ltd: pages 55(Below), 184(Top).
Robert Hunt Library: pages 12, 21(Both), 23, 25(Both), 30, 35(Top), 51(Right Both), 58, 59, 61, 68, 77, 82(Top), 120(Below), 122(Below), 125(Both), 130, 136, 173(Below), 175(Below), 179(Below), 187(Below), 197, 226, 230, 245(Below), 273(Below), 283.
Spaarnestad Fotoarchief: page 269.
US Airforce: pages 184(Below), 188(Top), 189, 202(Below), 218(Below), 221(Both), 250(Below), 285, 308(Below), 309.
US Army: pages 153, 166, 188(Below), 199(Below), 200, 203, 222, 234(Left), 256(Top), 267, 281(Top), 286, 304(Top), 305(Below).
US Defense Dept: pages 144(Top), 159, 2045, 205(Both), 216, 241(Below), 242, 276-277, 287(Below), 288, 298(Top), 307, 315.
US National Archives: pages 107(Top), 128, 132(Top), 133, 140(Top), 141(Top), 144(Below), 152(Below), 161, 172, 182, 208, 193(Top), 196(Below), 210-211, 214, 215(Both), 241(Top), 245(Top), 262(Top), 264(Top), 266, 294(Top), 301.
US Naval Historical Center: pages 107(Below), 127, 240, 297(Top).
US Navy: page 152(Top).
US Signal Corps: page 116.
WZ Bilddienst: pages 69, 80(Top).